HOMILETICS

A Manual of the Theory and Practice of Preaching

M. REU, D.D.

ENGLISH TRANSLATION BY
ALBERT STEINHAEUSER, D. D.

Wipf & Stock
PUBLISHERS
Eugene, Oregon

Wipf and Stock Publishers
199 W 8th Ave, Suite 3
Eugene, OR 97401

Homiletics
A Manual of the Theory and Practice of Preaching
By Reu, M.
ISBN 13: 978-1-55635-585-1
ISBN 10: 1-55635-585-8
Publication date 7/1/2009
Previously published by Wartburg Publishing House, 1924

PREFACE

APART from an elementary sketch by the late Dr. J. Fry, the Lutheran Church in America has produced no Homiletics, either in the English, German or Scandinavian tongue. And yet preaching is, and will always remain, a fundamental function of the Church; moreover, the distinctive character of our Church must express itself also in her preaching, so that the many valuable contributions to the subject by scholars of other American Churches cannot satisfactorily supply our need.

This manifest and widely felt gap in our theological literature, the present volume seeks to fill. It is intended to serve as text-book in seminaries and as handbook in pastors' studies. The material printed in large type, at least, ought to be mastered by all candidates for the sacred office, while the material given in greater detail and printed in smaller type should be found of value even by the full-fledged preacher, provided he has not stopped growing. The sections in large type are so arranged that they form an independent and consistent whole, which may be read consecutively, and should indeed be so read, at least for the first time, in order to obtain a connected view of our treatment. To aid the reader, since these sections sometimes lie rather far apart, we have indicated at the close of each of them the page on which its continuation may be found.

It may occasion surprise that so much space has been devoted to the first part, on the nature and purpose of the sermon. In English and American text-books it is customary to pass lightly over these subjects. This cannot but lead to harm, for whatever is said in the later discussion concerning the subject-matter and structure of the sermon is necessarily determined by the underlying conception of its nature and purpose. Many homiletical aberrations might have been avoided if these fundamental matters had received at the outset the attention they deserve. For this reason, and also with the view of bringing out clearly the distinctive characteristics of the Lutheran sermon, we have gone fully into these questions.

In the second part, we were concerned particularly about two matters. We desired, first, to make it plain that, despite the inroads of modern criticism, which are by no means lacking in this country and which have wrought havoc in many quarters, the preacher may with a good conscience take as basis for his preaching the whole Scripture, the whole Gospel, Paul no less than Jesus, and the whole Jesus. This subject could not, naturally, receive adequate treatment in a volume on Homiletics. But we have indicated at least the principal lines along which the position of negative critics may be met from a scientific point of view, and we have referred the student to the literature in which these questions are fully discussed. The day is not far distant when the American Lutheran Church, also, will have to face this problem. Secondly, we wished to lay all possible emphasis upon the principle that all sound homiletical work must be based on thorough exegesis, and to show to some extent the nature of such exegesis and its relation to the sermon. It is unfortunately a notorious fact that many men enter the ministry with never an inkling of what exegesis really means. One has heard even of professors of exegetical theology who had no proper conception of the meaning of their department, who never advanced beyond the outworks of their science or else remained life-long slaves to the "annotation" method. Such exegetes will of course have little to offer the preacher. There can be, on the other hand, no sounder basis and no more efficient aid for preaching than an exegesis whose principal aim is to ascertain the main lines of thought in the sacred writings, as a whole or in part, and that makes all else tributary to this aim. A glance into current homiletical literature will reveal, alas! how broad a gulf yawns between homiletics and exegesis. The author of this text-book could wish for no finer reward than the consciousness of having helped in some degree to bring the two into closer relationship.

While we have everywhere quoted liberally—some may think, too liberally—from the whole range of homiletical literature, so far as it was accessible to us, we have given preference, in the last part, to works by American authors. We have done this of set purpose, in view especially of the discussion of the style and structure of the sermon. While style has its universal laws, valid in all languages, it is also largely conditioned by the individual peculiarities of each language. Here English and American works will naturally serve best as our authorities. With respect to the structure of the sermon, we had another consideration in mind. In the transition from an old world tongue to the language of our country, the mistaken view frequently prevails that, while the traditional conception as to the nature and purpose of the sermon should be retained, the conception as to its structure may be abandoned not only with impunity but even with profit. Our numerous quotations from American homiletical literature are intended to show those laboring under this misconception that the best and soundest American homileticians apply to the structure of the sermon the same principles that have always been regarded as essential by their German and Scandinavian fellow workers. For these principles are inherent in the subject itself and are of universal validity. They have always and everywhere been ignored by immature and one-sidedly subjective spirits, but they are accepted and followed by those who have attained to maturity and true objectivity.

The practical examples added at the close are intended to demonstrate in a concrete way how the theories advanced may be applied in practice, and to illustrate step by step the making of the sermon.

For its English dress the manual is indebted to the Rev. Albert T. W. Steinhaeuser of Allentown, Penn. I count myself fortunate to have found in this well-known translator of Luther's works so congenial a collaborator, and I am sure that my readers will share this feeling. Besides reproducing my work in English, Dr. Steinhaeuser has been of assistance in numerous other ways, adding many a valuable suggestion of his own—especially in the section on style—and calling to my attention many English and American works that had eluded me. I wish to assure him, in this place also, of my grateful appreciation.

The work as a whole I commit to the grace and goodness of my God, who has given me strength to prepare it in the midst of so many other duties.

M. REU.

Wartburg Seminary,
Dubuque, Iowa, March 15, 1922.

CONTENTS

INTRODUCTION
1. Definition of Homiletics 1
2. Justification of Homiletics 15
3. Division of Homiletics 29

I. THE NATURE AND PURPOSE OF THE SERMON
4. Synopsis 37

A. The Sermon as Organic Part of the Service of the Worshiping Congregation
5. The Nature of the Service of the Christian Congregation.. 39
6. The Nature of the Sermon as Organic Part of the Service... 43
   (1) The Sermon in Its Relation to the Word of God........ 44
   (2) The Sermon in Its Relation to the Congregation and the Church 65
   (3) The Sermon in Its Relation to the Preacher as Organ of the Congregation and the Church 74
7. The Purpose of the Service of the Congregation 94
8. The Purpose of the Sermon as Part of the Service of the Congregation 98

B. The Sermon as Oration
9. The Attributes of the Sermon as Oration in the Congregational Service 169
10. The Duties of the Preacher as Orator 233

II. THE SUBJECT-MATTER OF THE SERMON AND ITS DERIVATION
11. The Subject-Matter of the Sermon in General 247
12. The Subject-Matter of the Individual Sermon 289
13. The Derivation of the Subject-Matter from the Text 338

III. THE STRUCTURE OF THE SERMON
14. Fundamental Principles Governing the Structure of the Sermon 389
15. The Structure of the Individual Sermon 425

16. The Theme of the Sermon 437
17. The Divisions of the Sermon 456
18. The Introduction and the Conclusion 486
19. The Preparation of the Sermon for Delivery and the Delivery of the Sermon 508

PRACTICAL ILLUSTRATIONS

1. Illustrations of the Exegetical-Homiletical Treatment of the Text for the Gathering of Materials 527
2. Illustrations of the Arrangement of Materials in the Outline.. 605
3. Illustrations of the Expanding of the Outline Into the Completed Sermon 613

INDICES 623

INTRODUCTION

§ 1. THE DEFINITION OF HOMILETICS

F. Schleiermacher, *Predigten*, 1801, ²1843. R. Stier, *Grundriss einer biblischen Keryktik*, 1830, ²1842. A. Schweizer, *Schleiermachers Wirksamkeit als Prediger*, 1834. E. Porter, *Lectures on Homiletics and Preaching and on Prayer*, 1834. Chr. Palmer, *Evangelische Homiletik*, 1842, ⁶1887. A. Schweizer, *Homiletik der ev.-prot. Kirche*, 1848. D. P. Kidder, *A Treatise on Homiletics*, 1864, ²1868. W. G. T. Shedd, *Homiletics and Pastoral Theology*, 1867, ⁹1888. J. A. Broadus, *A Treatise on the Preparation and Delivery of Sermons*, 1870. Ph Brooks, *Lectures on Preaching*, 1877. A. Phelps, *The Theory of Preaching*, 1881. J. M. Hoppin, *Homiletics*, 1883. A. Krauss, *Lehrbuch der Homiletik*, 1883. G. von Zezschwitz, *Homiletik oder die Kunstlehre von der geistlichen Beredsamkeit* (in Zoeckler's *Handbuch der theol. Wissenschaften*, vol. iv), 1883, ³1890. E. Chr. Achelis, *Lehrbuch der praktischen Theologie*, vol. ii, 1890, ³1911. T. H. Pattison, *The Making of the Sermon*, 1898. W. Caspari, *Homiletik* (in *Prot. Realencykl.* ³, vol. viii), 1900. F. Steinmeyer, *Homiletik*, 1901. J. J. A. Proudfoot, *Systematic Homiletics*, 1904. H. Hering, *Die Lehre von der Predigt*, 1905. H. C. Graves, *Lectures on Preaching*, 1906. W. Rhodes, *Homiletics and Preaching*, 1906. P. Kleinert, *Homiletik*, 1907. J. Gottschick, *Homiletik und Katechetik*, 1908. D. J. Burrell, *The Sermon, Its Construction and Delivery*, 1913. E. Schuerer, *Geschichte des juedischen Volkes im Zeitalter Jesu Christi*, ³1898-1901, ⁴1901-09. Th. Zahn, *Skizzen aus dem Leben der alten Kirche*, 1893, ³1908. H. Achelis, *Das Christentum in den ersten drei Jahrhunderten*, 1912. A. Harnack, *Die Mission und Ausbreitung des Christentums in den ersten drei Jahrhunderten*, 1902, ³1915. W. Bauer, *Der Wortgottesdienst der aeltesten Christen*, 1930.

The Church is the congregation of true believers in Christ. Faith, though primarily an inner attitude of the heart, cannot remain hidden in the heart, but must express itself outwardly in word and action. This is true of the faith of the congregation no less than of that of the individual. The faith of the congregation expresses itself in a common confession, in common praise and thanksgiving for the wonderful works of God, in hymns and prayers, in a reciprocal setting forth and celebrating of all that its Lord and God means for the congregation, in mutual edification upon the basis of the one faith, in short, in a common worship or service. Without such common worship the congregation of believers, or the Church, cannot long exist.

From the moment of its founding the Church appears as a worshiping congregation. When the Holy Spirit descended upon the disciples of Jesus and constituted them the Church, they were assembled in the temple, according to the custom of the typical service of the Old Testament Church. This common worship remained henceforth the centre of the entire life of the early Christian community.[1] Like the worship of the synagogue, it consisted of common prayer[2], the calling upon the name of Jesus[3], both in free prayers and in fixed formulas; the singing of psalms and hymns and spiritual songs[4], the reading of Scripture[5], and the administration of the Lord's Supper with the love-feast, or *agape*.[6] To this liturgical part of the service, there was soon added another. The reading of Scripture would naturally be accompanied by a discussion of the portion read, and of all that God and faith in God meant to the congregation. One brother would address the rest of the brethren, with whom he felt himself united as disciple of one and the same Lord. These discussions bore the character of fraternal intercourse, of familiar conversation. Originally participated in by whoever felt an inner prompting or had anything of value to communicate to

---

[1] Acts 2:42.—[2] Acts 2:42.—[3] Acts 9:14; 4:24 ff.; 12:5.—[4] 1 Cor. 14:15; Col. 3:16; cf. also the recently discovered Odes and Psalms of Solomon. See J. Rendel Harris, *The Odes and Psalms of Solomon*, 1909, and A. Harnack, *Ein juedisch-christliches Psalmbuch aus dem I. Jahrhundert*, 1910.—[5] Rev. 1:3.—[6] 1 Cor. 11:17-34; 10:16.

the brethren,[7] these discussions became in the course of time the particular prerogative of the elders and deacons of the Christian congregations and formed an important part of their official duties. Justin Martyr tells us in his First Apology: "Then, when the reader has ceased, the president verbally instructs, and exhorts to the imitation of these good things."[8] As a result, this fraternal address and familiar instruction assumed more and more the form of a set oration, of a unified and well rounded discourse, complying more or less closely with the generally accepted rules for public speaking. The viewpoint remained, however, that of an address to Christian *brethren;* not to *catechumens,* who needed previously to be instructed and prepared for full participation in the service and fellowship of the congregation, nor to *those without,* in whose hearts the decision to join themselves to the congregation must first be awakened, but to *mature Christians,* who were already members of the congregation, and whose Christian consciousness did not need to be aroused, but was to be deepened and strengthened. It was an address before equals, who like the speaker himself were of the company of Christ's disciples. It became, in short, a congregational sermon. (P. 6.)

The outline of the public worship of the Jewish synagogue is sketched by Schuerer[9] as follows: According to the Mishna, the service consisted of five main parts: the Schema', prayer, the reading of the Law, the reading of the Prophets, and the priestly benediction. To these must be added the translation of the Scripture lessons, and their exposition in the form of an edifying address, which latter appears in Philo to constitute almost the principal part of the service.

The Shema' ("Hear"), so called from its opening words, "Hear, O Israel," consists of the passages, Deut. 6:4-9; 11:13-21; Num. 15:37-41, with introductory and closing benedictions for morning and

---

[7] 1 Cor. 14:1 ff.; 12:27 ff.; Jas. 3:1 ff.; Heb. 10:25.—[8] Section 67.—[9] 3. ed., ii, 451 ff.

evening. Its significance was that of a confession of faith. It is very probable that the Shema' was in use in the time of Christ; it is certain that at that time fixed formulas of prayer formed a part of the service. It has been recently rendered highly probable that the major portion of the Shemone' esre,[10] which is still prayed by Jews today, was in use in Jesus' day.[11] The prayers were said standing, with the face turned toward the holy of holies in Jerusalem. They were not spoken by the entire congregation, but recited by a leader chosen by the president of the synagogue. The congregation took part by means of several responses and the final Amen. The leader in prayer might be any adult member of the congregation, and the same person might also recite the Shema', read the lesson from the Prophets, and in case he was a priest, pronounce the benediction. The Scripture lessons, both from the Pentateuch and from the Prophets, might be read by any member present, with the exception of Esther even by a minor; priest or Levites who were present were given the preference. The reader was accustomed to stand.[12] The Pentateuch was read through continuously in a triennial cycle, and was divided for this purpose into 154 sections, called *parasha*. Various members of the congregation took part in the reading; on the Sabbath day the number of readers was seven. The reading of the Torah was followed by the reading of the Prophets (*nebiim,* including the historico-prophetical book of Joshua, Judges, Samuel and Kings).[13] Since the prophetic lesson concluded the Scripture reading, it was called *haphthara,* from *haphthar,* to dismiss, to adjourn a meeting. Unlike the fixed lessons from the Law (*lectio continua*), the prophetic lessons were selected according to the reader's choice (*lectio selecta*).[14] The reading of the Scripture lessons was followed by a translation or paraphrase (Targum) of the Hebrew text into the Aramaic vernacular (in Palestine and Babylonia); it is uncertain whether there were regularly appointed interpreters or targumists for this purpose. The translation was coupled with an expository and hortatory address, or sermon (*derasha*), in which the lesson read was explained and practically applied. That these expositions were the common rule is proved by the frequent references in the New Testament to "teaching in the synagogues,"[15] by the narrative in Luke 4:20 ff., and by the direct statement of Philo. The preacher sat, while

---

[10]The "eighteen", consisting of eighteen—now nineteen—petitions and benedictions.—[11]Cf. E. Schwaab, *Historische Einfuehrung in das Achtzehngebet,* 1913.—[12]Luke 4:16.—[13]Luke 4:17; Acts 13:15.—[14]Luke 4:16 f.—[15]Matt. 4:23; Mark 1:21; 6:2; Luke 4:15; 6:6; 13:10; John 6:50; 18:20.

speaking, upon a raised platform.[16] These expositions were not confined to a particular class, but might be delivered by any competent member of the congregation. The service closed with the Aaronic benediction,[17] pronounced by a priest and followed by the Amen of the congregation; in the absence of a priest, the benediction was offered as a prayer by any other member.

Still less than the Old Testament Church, could the Church of the New Testament remain without a common service. That Jesus willed a cultus for His followers is evident from John 4:23, as well as from His institution of the Lord's Supper with its injunction, "This do in remembrance of me."[18] The apostles agree that the planting of the Church by means of the Word must be followed by the watering of it by the same Word.[19] The numerous references scattered through the Corinthian letters and the various directions given in the Pastorals rest upon the assumption that addresses for the purpose of instruction and edification were held in connection with the assemblies of the congregation for worship.

In so far as the Church was composed of Jewish Christians, it retained the observance of the Sabbath as day of worship, but began very soon to observe alongside it also the first day of the week. The heathen Christian congregations, whose freedom from the yoke of Jewish holydays Paul had triumphantly established,[20] kept Sunday as the day of Christ's resurrection,[21] in much the same fashion as the synagogue observed its Sabbath, without however transferring the Sabbath idea to the Sunday. It was the day on which the congregation gathered for common worship, as well as to bring its offerings for the poor,[22] the day on which the Lord's Supper was received,[23] the day on which Paul preached.[24] When about the year 112, Pliny, the friend of the emperor Trajan, had before him a number of Bithynian Christians for trial, among them some who had up to that time been Christians but now denied their Master, these latter confessed that the principal item in their alleged offence against the state had been their custom of assembling on a certain day before dawn to sing praise to Christ as God, and to bind themselves by oath to lead a virtuous life, and of returning in the evening to partake of a simple and harmless meal.[25]

---

[16]Luke 4:20.—[17]Num. 6:22 ff.—[18]1 Cor. 11:23 ff.—[19]1 Cor. 15:1; 1 Pet. 2:2 ff.; 2 Pet. 1:12; Jas. 1:18; Col. 3:16; Acts 2:42.—[20]Gal. 4:8-11; Col. 2:16.—[21]Matt. 28:1; Rev. 1:10.—[22]1 Cor. 16:1, 2.—[23]*Didache*, xiv, 1.—[24]Acts 20:7.—[25]*Epist.* x. 97.

A specific reference to the sermon is found in the description of the Christian observance of Sunday given by Justin Martyr,[26] in his First Apology. "On the day called Sunday," he writes, "all who live in the cities or in the country gather together to one place, and the memoirs of the apostles or the writings of the prophets are read, as long as time permits; then, when the reader has ceased, the president verbally instructs, and exhorts to the imitation of these good things.[27] Then we all rise together and pray, and, 'as we before said, when our prayer is ended, bread and wine and water are brought, and the president in like manner offers prayers and thanksgivings, according to his ability, and the people assent, saying Amen; and there is a distribution to each, and a participation of that over which thanks have been given, and to those who are absent a portion is sent by the deacons. And they who are well to do, and willing, give what each thinks fit; and what is collected is deposited with the president, who succors the orphans and widows, and those who, through sickness or any other cause, are in want, and those who are in bonds, and the strangers sojourning among us, and in a word takes care of all who are in need."[28] Despite its distinctive features, the kinship of this Christian service with that of the synagogue is evident. And it is no less evident that the Christian sermon meets us here in the form of a congregational address. From the oldest extant Christian sermon, the so-called Second Epistle of Clement of Rome,[29] we gather further that this congregational sermon was a fraternal discourse, brother addressing brother, recalling to his mind the truths he already knew or had once upon a time learned, comforting him, and exhorting him to every good work.

In keeping with its character as congregational address, with its informality and fraternal intimacy, the sermon of the Christian Church was designated by the term ὁμιλία, derived from ὁμοῦ, together, and ἴλη, a crowd, and signifying a being or living together, an assembly, then intercourse, converse, *confabulatio, colloquium*. Both noun and verb occur in Attic Greek and in the New Testament Koine. The Attic poet Menander coined the maxim quoted by Paul in 1 Cor. 15:33, φθείρουσιν ἤθη χρῆσθ' ὁμιλίαι κακαί; the context of the Pauline

---

[26]About A. D. 150.—[27]ὁ προεστὼς διὰ λόγου τὴν νουθεσίαν καὶ πρόκλησιν τῆς τῶν καλῶν τούτων μιμήσεως ποιεῖται.—[28]i, 67.—[29]See von Gebhardt, Harnack and Zahn, *Patrum apostolicorum opera*.

passage shows that ὁμιλίαι denotes the influence exerted by their pagan fellow-countrymen upon the members of the Christian congregation. The Vulgate renders *mala colloquia;* Luther, *boese Geschwaetze;* A. V., evil communications; R. V., evil company. Luke uses ὁμιλεῖν of the conversation of the two disciples on the way to Emmaus,[30] and of Paul's "communing" with the proconsul Festus.[31] He also applies the term to the religious discourse or sermon delivered by Paul to the gathering of Christians at Troas.[32] Here the later churchly usage emerges, according to which ὁμιλία, as the specific designation of the sermon before a Christian congregation, is sharply distinguished from κήρυγμα, or the missionary preaching to non-Christians, as well as from κατήχησις, or the indoctrination of catechumens. In this sense ὁμιλία is used by the apologist Tatian,[33] and by the author of the *Acta Johannis*,[34] in the II Century, and forms the title of Origen's sermons in the III Century. As late as the IX Century, Photius, the patriarch of Constantinople, defended ὁμιλία as designation for the sermons of Chrysostom, because in them the great preacher addressed his hearers in a colloquial style, putting questions to them and answering them himself.[35] These sermons were all of them addresses before a Christian congregation, the company of those who had been instructed and baptized. Although the catechumens were required to attend the preaching service, and there might be others present who were in no sense connected with the congregation, nevertheless the baptized members formed the majority, and the true believers composed the nucleus of the audience.

Augustine introduced the term *homilia* into the language of the Latin Church, although he restricted its use to the analytical form of the sermon, and employed *sermo* for the

---

[30]Luke 24:14, 15.—[31]Acts 24:26.—[32]Acts 20:11.—[33]πρὸς "Ελληνας, ed. Schwartz, 26.—[34]Zahn, *Acta Johannis*, 1880, p. 241.—[35]*Photii Bibliotheca*, ed. Bekker, i, 171-174.

other forms and then for the congregational sermon as such. *Sermo* and *praedicatio* thus became the standing appellations for the congregational sermon as well as for the sermon in general. From these the English words "sermon" and "preaching" are derived, as well as the German *Sermon* (which, however, came to mean in the Reformation period a tract or treatise;[36] e. g., Luther's "Sermon vom Neuen Testament," a treatise on the Lord's Supper) and *Predigt,* both of which designate usually the sermon before the congregation. But the word *homilia* persisted, especially as appellation for the sermons of the Fathers.[37] In this sense it was current throughout the Middle Ages. Paulus Diaconus collected *homiliae patrum,* and this and similar compilations go by the name of *homiliarium.* Hence is derived the English "homily," found already in the Middle Ages. After the Reformation its vogue was established especially through Cranmer's original and selected homilies,[38] which were published in Elizabeth's reign, under the title, "The Two Books of Homilies Appointed to Be Read in Churches," and continued in common use for centuries. Here, too, the usage indicates a discourse in the worship of the Christian congregation.

In the XVII Century the scientific treatment of the sermon with practical directions for its construction was known in Germany as *Cursus homileticus,*[39] *Compendium theologiae homileticae, Methodologia homiletica.* It was Herder and Menken in the XIX Century, who revived the German word *Homilie,* though with a restricted application to a particular variety of the sermon. In the same century *Homiletik* be-

---

[36]Cf. a long chapter on the use of *tractatus* as designation of the sermon, in Bern. Ferrarii *De Ritu sacrarum ecclesiae veteris Concionum,* Veronae, 1731. "Ex quibus omnibus intelligitur facillime, vocem Tractatus apud Ecclesiasticos Scriptores illud potissimum Concionum genus significasse, quo certus aliquis Divinae Scripturae locus explanabatur" (Lib. I, cap. ii).—[37]The decrees of the Council of Vaux, 529, refer, e. g., to *homiliae sanctorum patrum.*—[38]1547.—[39]First used by W. Leyser in Wittenberg, † 1649.

comes in Germany, despite opposition at the beginning, the exclusive name for the science of the sermon as congregational discourse. The Frenchman Vinet also calls his presentation "Homiletique," and the first American text-book, published by E. Porter in 1834, bears the title "Lectures on Homiletics and Preaching." Porter's lead is followed by Kidder in 1864, J. M. Hoppin in 1883, J. J. A. Proudfoot in 1904, H. C. Graves and W. Rhodes in 1906.

The present discussion has in view the sermon preached before a Christian congregation, not the missionary sermon nor the catechetical lecture,—the congregational sermon as it takes its place in the framework of the Christian service and presupposes a Christian congregation. While not ignoring entirely the needs of "inquirers," it is oriented by the character of the service of which it forms an organic part, and by the fact that it appeals to baptized and instructed Christians, among whom there are those who are also subjectively united by genuine faith to Christ. We employ, therefore, the term "Homiletics" (ἡ ὁμιλητική, scil. τέχνη) to designate the science and art of the sermon in this sense, since none other, either as to history or linguistic usage, so exactly expresses the idea of the congregational sermon. (P. 15.)

The attempt has been made,[40] to deduce the biblical conception of the Christian sermon from a combination of the passages in which the verbs εὐαγγελίζεσθαι and κηρύσσειν, and even καταγγέλλειν, διαλέγεσθαι and λαλεῖν occur, and in which the proclamation of the good news concerning Christ is enjoined upon Christians.[41] But εὐαγγελίζεσθαι denotes primarily the missionary preaching, and in Paul's usage only the initial proclamation of the Gospel. The same is true of κηρύσσειν both as to etymology and usage, while καταγγέλλειν and especially λαλεῖν are very general terms, and διαλέγεσθαι receives its specific meaning only from the context. It is not our business to enquire here what the Scriptures say about the duty, nature and content of Christian

---

[40] E. g., by Kidder.—[41] Matt. 11:5; Rom. 1:15; 10:15; Matt. 10:7; Mark 16:15; Col. 1:28; Acts 17:17; 20:9; Mark 2:2.

preaching in general, but what they have to say concerning the sermon at the public service of a congregation already called and gathered. For we are not now concerned with the question as to how the foreign missionary or the evangelist at home is to present his message, the catechist his instruction in the fundamental truths of Christianity, or the apologist his defence of the Gospel before a company of skeptics; but how the pastor of a congregation already gathered is to break the bread of life, Sunday after Sunday, to his people, in order that they may become ever more truly that which they already are, namely, the people of God. To be sure, there cannot be a congregational sermon without a real εὐαγγελίζεσθαι and κηρύσσειν, without καταγγέλλειν and λαλεῖν; but we are discussing now the peculiar function and the specific form of the congregational sermon, not what it has in common with all other forms of the proclamation of Christian truth. For this reason we cannot make the term *praedicatio* our starting point, for etymologically this term[42] has the same significance as κήρυγμα (κῆρυξ = *praeco*), while in actual usage it covers the whole range of preaching without reference to the kind of hearer involved.

Hence we are unable to accept as adequate the definition of preaching given by Phillips Brooks, — "Preaching is the communication of truth by man to man."[43] This is much too general, as is also Kidder's definition, — "The proper idea of preaching embodies three important elements: (1) the announcement of joyful tidings; (2) the proclamation of truth by a herald, that is, urgently and authoritatively; (3) the conviction or persuasion of men to belief by means of arguments."[44] The same is true of the definition of Pattison, — "Preaching is the spoken communication of divine truth with a view to persuasion,"[45] and of that of Phelps, — "A sermon is an oral address to the popular mind upon religious truth as contained in the Christian Scriptures, and elaborately treated with a view to persuasion."[46] Burrell comes nearer the truth when he defines a sermon as "an address to a congregation on the subject of religion, from the standpoint of the Scriptures, with the purpose of persuading men."[47] But when he explains the important phrase, "to a congregation," as follows, —"that is, to a company of people assembled to hear religious truth. An assembly on Areopagus was not ordinarily a congregation, but it became one when it invited Paul to speak of 'The New Doctrine' and heard his sermon on 'The Unknown God,'"—he shows that he, too,

---

[42]First applied to the preaching of the Church by Lactantius, *Div. institut.*, iv, 21.—[43]P. 5.—[44]P. 30.—[45]P. 3.—[46]Pp. 1-27.—[47]Pp. 11-12.

has failed to grasp what is to us an essential. Hoppin's definition, on the other hand, marks a decided advance: "Homiletics is the science that teaches the fundamental principles of public discourse as applied to the proclamation and teaching of divine truth in regular assemblies gathered for the purpose of Christian worship."[48] When, however, he proceeds: "We would say that the true object and design of Christian preaching, in the largest and most stimulating view of it, is: So to set forth divine truth, the Gospel of the Lord Jesus, with such clearness, simplicity, power, fullness, love, and utter dependence upon and union with the Spirit of Christ, as to persuade men to receive it truly to the conversion of their souls, to the upbuilding of their whole life and character in the faith of Christ; or, in other words, to enlighten, renew, and sanctify them unto eternal life in the kingdom of God's dear Son," and when he understands "conversion" in its narrower sense, he, too, fails to do justice to an aspect of the sermon on which we are compelled to lay the greatest stress.

The sermon whose nature and construction we are here concerned with tracing presupposes, under normal conditions, baptized and instructed hearers, persons who have been objectively regenerated, and among whom there exists a larger or smaller proportion of genuine believers. Does the sermon have to do only with the unregenerate? Or is it true that it addresses itself, in the case of God's children, only to the old Adam remaining in them? In that case there would indeed be no difference between missionary preaching and the congregational sermon. That was the view held by Stier and is the view underlying the practice of many of the churches today. Stier wrote in 1830, in the second paragraph of his *Grundriss einer biblischen Keryktik*: "Those who preach in the service of the kingdom of God, and those to whom they preach, are men. But men to whom God's herald is sent in order to proclaim, teach and witness the divine counsel, must, so far as they still need this preaching, be conceived as fundamentally estranged and separated from God and as still outside His kingdom. The first and foremost purpose of preaching and the offer of divine truth concerns those who do not as yet know what is told them, and who do not as yet have what is offered to them. Even if true children of God were exhorted to act according to their will, or comforted and admonished to live by their faith, it would not be so much the child of God that was being exhorted or comforted,

---

[48] P. 9.

as rather the indolence or faintheartedness still remaining in him. Consequently the person preached to is always in the final analysis the natural man, in his blindness and sinfulness." For this reason Stier demanded that our discipline be called "Keryktik;"[49] Sickel[50] similarly proposed the name "Halieutik.[51] But does the sacrament of baptism no longer impart the new birth and make us children of God?[52] Or, if it does, do all the baptized lapse, in the course of their youth, from this high estate? Is not the Word, as employed in the Christian instruction of the young, a living seed of regeneration, and the power of God unto salvation?[53] Moreover, since the natural man is dead in trespasses and sins, and unable to receive the things of the Spirit of God,[54] of what avail would it be to admonish the old Adam in the Christian to spiritual and divine things? Above all, who would venture to comfort the old Adam? No; the old Adam in the Christian is overcome only by means of the heightened efficiency of the motives controlling the new man, and it is this new man who must be the object of all preaching of repentance, comfort and sanctification to the children of God.

Schleiermacher comes much nearer the heart of the matter when he writes in the preface to his collected sermons: "To others much will doubtless appear strange; for example, that I speak as though there still were congregations of believers and a Christian Church, and as though religion were still a bond uniting Christians in a peculiarly intimate manner. It does not indeed appear to be so; but I do not see how we can help assuming it. Even if it were true that our religious assemblies were missionary gatherings with the purpose of making men religious, we should have to set to work in a totally different fashion. . . . . Perhaps we can produce the condition by assuming to be true. Certain it is, that nothing can have a more harmful effect upon our religious discourses than a halting between these two opinions—whether we are to address men as Christians or as non-Christians."[55] Schleiermacher, indeed, did not realize the underlying reason for this conception of the sermon — the sacrament of baptism was for him merely a sign, and the creative power of the Word of God was not given its proper place in his system—but the conception itself was sound and true. Paul addressed his readers as Christian

---

[49]From κῆρυξ, a herald.—[50]1829.—[51]From ἁλιεύς, a fisherman. cf. Luke 5:10.—[52]Ti. 3:5; Gal. 3:26, 27; Rom. 6:1-11; 1 Cor. 6:11.—[53]1 Pet. 1:23; Jas. 1:18, 21; Rom. 1:16; 10:17; Isa. 55:10, 11; 2 Cor. 2:16.—[54]1 Cor. 2:14; Col. 2:13.—[55]i, 6 f.

congregations, as elect and saints of God, despite the many serious shortcomings he was compelled to rebuke in many of them. Luther ascribed to the sacrament of baptism and to the remnant of Gospel that lingered even in the darkest period of the Middle Ages, the fact that children were born unto the Lord and that the Church was preserved for the better time coming. Zinzendorf declared that the preacher could do no more foolish thing than regard his congregation as a mere Babel. The whole of our common service, of which the sermon forms an organic part, is built up on the assumption of the existence of a congregation of believers.

Nor does the practical carrying out of this idea, in the face of the sorry reality as it meets us in the actual condition of our churches, require a false and self-deceiving optimism. What it does require is, as Gottschick well puts it, the preacher's estimate of faith and love,— of faith in the life-producing power of the Gospel, that cannot remain permanently without fruit; of love, able to discern true Christian piety even in the midst of doctrinal error, immaturity and actual moral shortcomings, all of which it seeks faithfully to remove. Especially in a free Church, from which external compulsion has been removed, and in which even the compelling power of habit and custom is fast disappearing, it will be impossible for love to believe that the worshiping congregation may not be treated as a congregation of believers. no matter how evident its defects or how great the number of hypocrites and nominal Christians among its members. It does not follow from this that the congregational sermon should represent merely the average Christian consciousness of the hearers, or that it should, on the other hand, regard the hearers as having reached the highest stage of Christian development and merely recall to them their Christian convictions, emotions and ideals. "Since the believing congregation and the Word of God are correlatives," says Gottschick, "it is the function of the sermon to present the Christian faith in all its fulness and with all its seriousness. Such a presentation will impart, at every stage of Christian development, a forward impulse, leading from the presumed initial assent to Christianity onward to an ever completer apprehension, from an imperfect knowledge and attitude of will to clearness and decision, and to conflict with whatever impedes this forward movement. The assumption of an initial assent to Christianity does not therefore become meaningless, but points to the common positive basis underlying the various stages of the Christian life of the hearers, on which the sermon must build up its appeal. A sermon of this sort will, finally, minister indirectly also to the conscious needs of the seekers and to the unconscious needs of the conventional Christians; for the shortcomings in the believer's faith and life, which it rebukes, spring in most cases from the same soil as the indifferent unbelief of the conventional Christian and the painfully felt unbelief of the seeker." In addition to this it should be remembered that the mighty works of God need to be presented again and again even to the believing congregation, in order that by means of such preaching of the Gospel its faith may be renewed from day to day; for faith lives only so long as it is daily produced anew by God through the Gospel.[56] Now it is just this preaching of the Gospel that is the divinely appointed means by which alone saving faith can be produced in the heart of the unbeliever, while, on the other hand, the preaching of God's righteous judgment upon sin, by which alone the terrors of conscience are awakened, without which there can be no saving faith, and which must therefore be directed to those who are as yet without faith, is needed no less by the congregation of believers, so long and in so far as they are still in the flesh.

We fully acknowledge that not only the missionary sermon to the heathen, but the evangelistic sermon to the masses who have become estranged from the Church or were never in connection with it, though living under its very shadow, belong to the duties of the Church and fall under the generic concept of the sermon. But we just as emphatically insist that we have to treat here only of the sermon as a part of Christian worship, and that this sermon presupposes a Christian congregation, a congregation of believers. Therefore, we retain the term "Homiletics," as the most adequate designation for our discipline, for by it we certify at the very outset our conception of the sermon, in agreement with Schweizer,[57] Zezschwitz[58] and Achelis,[59] as a congregational sermon.

---

[56]Cf. Reu, *Heilsordnung* (Chicago, Wartburg Publishing House, 1914), P. 45.—[57]P. 125.—[58]P. 161.—[59]P. 82.

§ 2. THE JUSTIFICATION OF HOMILETICS

John Wilkins, *Ecclesiastes, or a Discourse Concerning the Gift of Preaching, as It Falls Under the Rules of Art*, 1646, [8]1704. E. Porter, *Lectures on Homiletics and Preaching*, 1834. A. Vinet, *Homiletics, or the Theory of Preaching*, Eng. tr. by Skinner, 1853, [2]1861. D. P. Kidder, *A Treatise on Homiletics*, 1864, [2]1868. J. A. Broadus, *A Treatise on the Preparation and Delivery of Sermons*, 1870. R. L. Dabney, *Sacred Rhetoric*, 1870, [3]1902. C. H. Spurgeon, *Lectures to My Students*, 1874. J. J. van Oosterzee, *Praktische Theologie*, 1878-79. M. Simpson, *Lectures on Preaching*, 1879. A. Krauss, *Lehrbuch der Homiletik*, 1883. H. Hering, *Die Lehre von der Predigt*, 1905. P. Kleinert, *Homiletik*, 1907. E. Sachse, *Evangelische Homiletik*, 1913. A. S. Hoyt, *Vital Elements of Preaching*, 1914.

While the right and the need of Christian preaching are universally acknowledged, there are those who raise objection to a science of preaching, to an art-theory laying down definite rules for the preparation and delivery of sermons. Such a science they regard as either dangerous or at best unnecessary. It is regarded as dangerous, because it applies to preaching the rules of rhetoric; but rhetoric, it is contended, is not justifiable from the ethical standpoint. It is regarded as unnecessary, some maintaining that the Spirit of God alone produces gifted preachers, others that Nature is the best teacher.

These objections have no weight. As to the first, it is true that rhetoric and oratory may be and have been put to base uses in the service of falsehood and evil, and that there have been schools of rhetoric, not only in ancient Greece, that were nurseries of sophistry and instilled the art of making an evil cause appear good. But the fault in this case lies not with rhetoric, but in the character of its teachers and practitioners. Plato already set himself sternly against such an abuse of oratory and the art of rhetoric, and was ably supported by Quintilian. The latter laid down the principle, *abusus non tollit usum,* and demanded that the orator be a *vir bonus.* He held it an injustice to call anything evil which could be put to a good use, and maintained that, since language marked the essential distinction between man and the brute creation, nothing was better worth one's labor and cultivation than the gift of speech. When oratory was later termed by Kant the art of deceiving by a fair outward show,[1] it must be borne in mind that this antipathy is to be traced ultimately to the great philosopher's erroneous opinion that there is no ethically permissible means of influencing man other than logical demonstration. This objection carries no weight even in the sphere of rhetoric, much less in that of Homiletics, which is indebted to rhetoric on its formal side alone.

So far as the second objection is concerned, namely, that Homiletics is unnecessary, since the Spirit of God alone makes a successful preacher, it is true that without the aid of the Holy Spirit there cannot be a successful preacher; but it does not follow that the Holy Spirit will put the words in the preacher's mouth without the latter's own diligent labor. The reference to Matt. 10:19 f. betrays a careless or capricious reading of this text. Jesus is speaking here not at all of the regular activity of the preacher, but of the plight of the disciple compelled to defend himself before a heathen tribunal. The reference to 1 Cor. 2:4 and 13 is no happier. Paul's declaration that his speech and preaching in Corinth was not ἐν πειθοῖς σοφίας λόγοις, and that his apostolic preaching in general was not couched ἐν διδακτοῖς ἀνθρωπίνης σοφίας λόγοις, ἀλλ' ἐν διδακτοῖς πνεύματος, cannot be understood as militating against careful training for the preparation of regular sermons. In the former passage the apostle sets his own

---

[1]*Kritik der Urteilskraft,* § 53.

method over against the sophistic arts of a decadent Greek rhetoric and over against the unfortunate fondness of the Corinthians for oratorical display; in the latter he emphasizes the ultimate source of the apostolic message. Nor is it possible to make capital of the fact that the apostles were unlettered fishermen and publicans,[2] who none the less achieved a blessed ministry. This would be to overlook the principle, that what is true of the period of the Church's founding, when Christianity entered the world as something absolutely new, cannot be applied without modification to all succeeding periods. It must not be forgotten that, although the apostles were plain, uncultured men, they were unquestionably men of rich native endowment, chosen by Christ Himself, and trained for three years in His school. Moreover, the apostle whose labors accomplished most in the cultured ancient world was the very one who had enjoyed the most thorough academic training.

The direct opposite of the preceding are the objectors who, instead of leaving all to the Holy Spirit, ascribe all to Nature and hold that Nature is an abler teacher than Homiletics. The former place the emphasis upon the Holy Spirit, these upon the spirit of man; yet both are at one in the futility of their argument. These nature-lovers operate with a mistaken view of both nature and art. Nature does not signify a purely aboriginal condition, but includes growth and development. Where nature meets us at its loveliest and best, it is generally as the result of a preceding development. True art, including a proper Homiletics, is never in conflict with nature. Art indeed exerts an influence upon nature, but in such a manner as to accommodate and adjust itself to its inner being, in order to lead nature to its completion and make it tributary to the ideal of the human spirit. Art presupposes nature with all its inherent possibilities, but it sets these pos-

---

[2]Luke 5:1-11; Matt. 9:9; Acts 4:13.

sibilities in their proper combination, strips them of impediments, assists them to attain to free expression, and thus brings what was originally latent in nature as a sort of raw material to complete and harmonious realization. Thus the native gift of speech is brought by Homiletics to fuller development and fitted to serve the definite purpose of the kingdom of God. Even if it were true that nature is the sole teacher, especially in the case of the genius, it would also be true that whoever mastered the laws according to which nature produces the gift of oratory in a genius would be in possession of her secret and in a position to duplicate her success. But history teaches us that geniuses are by no means mere children of nature, but consciously pursue their art and strive with infinite pains to master its underlying laws. And when their finished products appear before us in such perfection of form as to move us to confess that here art has again become nature, it is only because by dint of laborious studies and continual practice they made the rules and canons of art so completely a part of themselves that their native ability could not but express itself in complete conformity with these canons. To be sure, an art-theory of preaching cannot compensate for a lack of natural ability, but it can develop and improve such ability where it exists. It can even take one who is without native ability to preach and enable him to prepare and deliver a passable sermon, the more since a sermon cannot be judged solely from the viewpoint of rhetoric.

Alexander Vinet,[3] justly calls attention to two errors that commonly arise in connection with the discussion of the value of Homiletics. The one, he says, consists in expecting too little from Homiletics, the other in expecting too much. The former sets nature and grace over against art, the latter mistrusts grace and nature. The best result will un-

---

[3] Pp. 32 ff.

questionably be attained when the native ability of a man submits to the discipline of art, and when the natural is filled and transfigured by the Spirit of God. Van Oosterzee,[4] well likens the preacher of the Word to a vessel setting sail for a distant harbor. The science of Homiletics equips it with rudder and compass, but the wind that is to swell the sails must come from above. No human art or science can take the place of God's Spirit; nevertheless without the rudder and compass of art the ship will never reach port.

Homiletics, therefore, so far from being dangerous or superfluous, is both necessary and helpful. If we have realized the supreme value of preaching and know that no natural gift is so fine but art can ennoble and direct it, and that Homiletics can assist even the man who lacks a native gift to become at least a passable preacher, and if we reflect that geniuses are, alas! but few and far between, while congregations needing preachers abound, we shall not refuse to Homiletics an equal place alongside the other theological disciplines. What a sacred duty devolves upon the man who has chosen the office of preaching as his life-work, who expects a proper emolument from men for his labors, and who must render an account of his stewardship to God! He dare not obstruct the reception of the Word by his own incompetence or indolence. He will rather strive with all that is in him to apprehend ever more completely the laws that govern the sermon and make them the basis of his own preaching, until he is ruled and directed by them as though they were his second nature. He will endeavor to learn from the God-gifted preachers of the Church's past the secret of their power, the rules and directions that they followed. He will ponder the nature and purpose of the sermon, he will seek out whatever directions have been laid down concerning its subject-matter and its structure. In other words, he will give him-

---

[4] i, 79, 83.

self to a thorough and painstaking study of the science of Homiletics. (P. 29.)

In his first lecture, E. Porter writes: "The preaching of the Gospel is a great work. In the magnitude of its objects, it surpasses, beyond all comparison, every other employment in which men can engage. This might be illustrated, did my limits allow the detail, by an ample exhibition of facts, showing that the highest degrees of intellectual cultivation, of civil liberty, and of social order, which are found in the most favored communities, result not so much from all other causes combined, as from the sanctifying influence produced by the faithful preaching of the Gospel. But the consideration which attaches pre-eminent importance to this work is; that God has appointed it as the grand instrument of salvation to men. The scheme of salvation is an object to which all other objects and events in our world are subordinate. This is the radiant point, where all the attributes and works of God converge into a blaze of glory. In contemplating the 'great mystery of godliness, into which angels desire to look' we see how infinite wisdom, love, justice, and grace unite in the forgiveness of sin, and in suspending the immortal hopes of sinners on the cross of Christ. Now the principal means, which God has instituted to make known this scheme of mercy to a lost world, is the preaching of the Gospel. This consideration invests the preacher's work with a character of exalted and awful dignity, which very far transcends the most elevated employments of this world. Well did Paul say, and had he been an angel, well might he have said, 'Who is sufficient for these things?' Surely then, a pious, uninspired man should aim at the highest attainable degree of perfection, in his preparation for this work."[5]

Broadus has the following to say of the importance and the difficulty of the work of the preacher: "Preaching can be superseded by nothing. *Printing* has become a mighty agency for good and for evil; and Christians should employ it, with the utmost diligence and in every possible way, for the spread of truth. But printing can never take the place of the living word. When a man who is apt in teaching, whose soul is on fire with the truth which he trusts has saved him and hopes will save others, speaks to his fellowmen, face to face, eye to eye, and electric sympathies flash to and fro between him and his hearers, till they lift each other up, higher and higher, into the

---

[5] Pp. 4 f.

intensest thought, and the most impassioned emotion—higher and yet higher, till they are borne as on chariots of fire above the world,—there is a power to move men, to influence character, life, destiny, such as no printed page can ever possess. *Pastoral work* is of immense importance, and all preachers should be diligent in performing it. But it cannot take the place of preaching, nor fully compensate for lack of power in the pulpit. The two help each other, and neither of them is able, unless supported by the other, to achieve the largest and most blessed results. When he who preaches is the sympathizing pastor, the trusted counsellor, the kindly and honored friend of young and old, of rich and poor, then 'truths divine come mended from his lips,' and the door to men's hearts, by the magical power of sympathy, will fly open at his word. But on the other hand, when he who visits is the preacher, whose thorough knowledge of Scripture and elevated views of life, whose able and impassioned discourses have carried conviction and commanded admiration, and melted into one the hearts of the multitude, who is accustomed to stand before them as the ambassador of God, and is associated in their minds with the authority and the sacredness of God's Word,—when *he* comes to speak with the suffering, the sorrowing, the tempted, his visit has a meaning and a power of which otherwise it must be destitute. . . . *Religious ceremonies* may be instructive and impressive. The older dispensation made much of these, as we employ pictures in teaching children. Even Christianity, which has the minimum of ceremony, illustrates its fundamental facts, and often makes deep religious impressions, by its two simple but expressive ordinances. But these are merely pictures to illustrate, merely helps to that great work of teaching and convincing, of winning and holding men, which preaching, made mighty by God's Spirit, has to perform.[6] It follows that preaching must always be a necessity, and good preaching a mighty power. In every age of Christianity, since John the Baptist drew crowds into the desert, there has been no great religious movement, no restoration of Scripture truth, and re-animation of genuine piety, without new power in preaching, both as cause and as effect. But alas! how difficult we find it to preach *well*. How small a proportion of the sermons heard weekly throughout the world are really good. The dilettanti men of letters who every now and then

---

[6] This is the estimate of a Baptist, for whom Baptism and the Lord's Supper are not actual bearers of divine grace. But for us Lutherans, too, the Word, and particularly the Word as preached, is the primary means of grace.

fill the periodicals with sneers at preaching, no doubt judge most unkindly and unjustly, for they purposely compare ordinary examples of preaching with the finest specimens of literature, and they forget their own utter lack, in the one case, of that sympathetic appreciation without which all literary and artistic judgment is necessarily at fault; but we who love preaching and try to preach are better aware than they are, of the deficiencies which mar our efforts, and the difficulties which attend our work."[7]

Considerations such as these may well humble us and drive us to our knees in prayer for the Holy Spirit's aid. They also point out to us the importance of our work and the necessity of instruction as to how we may best perform it. Claus Harms, on once being told by a flattering friend that he surely had no need of preparation for his sermons but was inspired at all times by the Holy Spirit, replied that he could recall only a single instance when he had been compelled to mount his pulpit unprepared, on which occasion the Holy Spirit had indeed whispered something in his ear, but what He said was this,—*"Klaus, Klaus, du bist faul gewesen!"* And Spurgeon told his students: "The Holy Spirit has made no promise to supply spiritual food to the saints by an impromptu ministry. He will never do for us what we can do for ourselves. If we can study and do not, if we can have a studious ministry and will not, we have no right to call in a divine agent to make up the deficits of our idleness or eccentricity."[8] Alfred Krauss writes: "Reliance upon the immediate illumination of the Holy Spirit, whenever it is hostile to technical study, reveals itself as a mantle for an anti-churchly sectarian activity or for an indolent pride which, not content with posing before its own mirror, covets the compliments of others. But how soon the shallow stream of ideas dries up for these persons, and what torture it must be for their hearers to listen to sermons which aim at being inspired, only to end, in just punishment on idleness, in a sandstorm of empty phrases."[9]

Let no one imagine himself to be a genius, superior to all homiletical rules, which by virtue of his natural endowment he incorporates within himself. Here, too, Krauss has some pertinent words: "It is claimed by many, and they are probably right, that there are a great many more talented men and a great many less geniuses in the world than would appear at first glance. It is a disastrous mistake for a talented person to mistake himself for a genius. Many a talented man

---

[7] Pp. 2 ff.—[8] P. 152.—[9] P. 22.

might accomplish a brilliant and useful work, if he but remained within the bounds of his ability and contented himself with the gifts divinely conferred upon him. The geniuses do not kick against the pricks of discipline; but the talented person, in his effort to lift himself by his own boot-straps, cries out against academic constraint, the needless ballast of the schoolbag, and against all laws and rules. His achievements fall out accordingly. A large number of finely endowed persons, who might have accomplished excellent things, have proved failures simply because they attempted the super-excellent."[10] In a similar connection Porter cites the following from Dr. Samuel Johnson: "Men have sometimes appeared of such transcendent abilities, that their slightest and most cursory performances excel all that labor and study can enable meaner intellects to compose; as there are regions of which the spontaneous products cannot be equalled in other soils by care and culture. But in most cases it is the fruit of intense preceding labor; at least it is no less dangerous for any man to place *himself* in this rank of understanding, and fancy that *he* is born to be illustrious without labor, than to omit the cares of husbandry, and expect from his ground the blossoms of Arabia."[11]

It needs hard work to become an able preacher, careful study of the men who have achieved greatness in this sphere. "No process," says Porter again, "in which one is merely passive, can transform him into an able preacher, or a useful man in any respect. Important acquisitions of every kind must be the result of care and labor. There is no royal road to knowledge in our profession, more than in others. It would indeed be unwise at this day for a Christian student to adopt a course like that of the Athenian orator, who transcribed the history of Thucydides eight times with his own hand, that he might learn to imitate the conciseness, strength, and fire of the historian. But the same *industry,* though it may be better applied in this age of books, is as necessary as it was in the age of Demosthenes. . . . Johnson almost re-wrote his Rambler for subsequent editions, although as it was first published, competent judges had classed it among the finest specimens of English composition. Chalmers, in his biographical preface to the Rambler, has preserved one of its original papers, as a literary curiosity. Any student who will carefully compare this with the corrected copy, and see with what punctilious inspection this great man revised his own composition, will find himself amply repaid for his trouble."[12] Hoyt, in his book, *Vital Elements of Preaching,* de-

---

[10] P. 20.—[11] P. 27.—[12] Pp. 28 f.

votes an entire chapter to "The Cost of Preaching," in which he says among other things: "To train speech so that it will shadow forth our thoughts, so that it will pulse with the feeling of our heart, this is the longest and hardest art. Robert Louis Stevenson had the supreme gift of taking pains. 'I imagine nobody had ever such pains to learn a trade as I had; but I slogged at it day in and day out; and I frankly believe (thanks to my dire industry) I have done more with smaller gifts than almost any man of letters in the world.'[13] Mr. Jas. Chamberlain gained his leadership in the Commons by the rapier-like thrust of his speech, by his sentences that went to their mark like rifle-balls. And he said to a group of younger speakers: 'The trouble with you young fellows is that you don't take enough pains with your speeches.' Every one knows the clearness of Mr. Huxley's essays. Language never expressed thought more unmistakably. And they were written over and over until criticism had done its utmost. And that's the way Newman gained his style that has the revealing quality of the light: 'I have been obliged to take great pains with everything I have written.' And when our words try to express God's thought, to interpret the person and purpose and love of the Divine Father, we may well exclaim with the prophet, 'I cannot speak; I am a little child,' or with another: 'I am a man of unclean lips.' We ought to feel that nothing is good enough for the Gospel. It is a monstrous bit of irreverence to deal carelessly with the Word, in any way to fail to commend the Gospel by our speech and manner. . . . No man is worth much in the Kingdom of God who is not beaten out of all self-conceit, and made to see that in preaching also the way of the cross is the way of growth and of power."[14]

But by no means all depends upon the acquisition and employment of a good style; much more is required in preaching: the assistance of the Holy Spirit, one's own faithful labor, a thorough training are above all necessary. Dabney closes his discussion of 1 Cor. 2:4 with the sentence,—"Let us make our sacred rhetoric just Paul's, so far as it was primarily taught him by the Holy Spirit, and taught him next by his high culture and pure devotion."[15]

A special training in Homiletics is necessary even for one who is at home in all other branches of theology. This was so well stated by Wilkins, as far back as 1646, that his words, *mutatis mutandis,* are applicable to this day. He writes in his introduction: "It is the end of all sciences and arts to direct men by certain rules unto the

---

[13]Balfour's *Life of Stevenson,* ii, 169.—[14]Pp. 241-262.—[15]P. 17.

most compendious way in their knowledge and practice, those things of which we have in ourselves only some imperfect confused notions being herein fully and clearly represented to our view from the discoveries that other men have made after much study and long experience. And there is nothing of greater consequence for the advancement of learning than to find out those particular advantages which there are for the shortest way of knowing and teaching things in every profession. Now among all other callings this of Preaching being in many respects one of the most weighty and solemn, should therefore have its rules and canons, whereby we may be directed the easiest and readiest way for the practice of it. Besides all those Academical Preparations by the study of Languages, Sciences, Divinity, with which men should be qualified and predisposed for this calling, I say, besides all these, there is a particular art of preaching, to which, if ministers did more seriously apply themselves, it would extremely facilitate that service, making it more easy to them and more profitable to their hearers. There are two abilities requisite in every one that will teach and instruct another: σύνεσις and ἑρμηνεία, a right understanding of sound doctrine and an ability to propound, confirm, and apply it unto the edification of others. And the first may be without the other, as a man may be a good lawyer, and yet not a good pleader, so he may be a good divine, and yet not a good preacher. One chief reason, why divers men otherwise of eminent parts are herein so slow and unskilful, is because they have not been versed in this study, and are therefore unacquainted with those proper rules and directions, by which they should be guided in the attaining and exercise of this gift. It hath been the usual course at the University to venture upon this calling in an abrupt overhasty manner: When scholars have passed over their philosophical studies and made some little entrance upon Divinity, they presently think themselves fit for the pulpit without any farther enquiry, as if the gift of preaching and sacred oratory, were not a distinct art of itself. This would be counted a very preposterous course in other matters, if a man should presume of being an orator because he was a logician, or to practice physics, because he had learned philosophy; and certainly the pre-eminence of this profession above others must needs extremely aggravate such neglect and make it so much the more mischievous by how much the calling is more solemn."[16]

---

[16] Pp. 1 f.

We may assent to Hering's words: "When a knowledge of logic, grammar and of the general principles of rhetoric, as well as of exegetical, systematic and historical theology, combines to produce, so far as this is possible in the case of a youthful theologian, a certain integrity, symmetry, and independence of judgment, he is thereby so far equipped for the work of Christian preaching that he may become a true preacher even without the aid of an homiletical theory, provided always that he is a man of parts and a believer."[17] But we can assent to this statement only when we take it in connection with what follows: "This is, however, scarcely possible without the unconscious influence of examples such as are furnished by the actual praxis and literature of Homiletics. The attentive observation of such examples, the calling them to mind, the reflection upon that which constitutes the secret of their activity,—these, if they do not degenerate into slavish imitation, are always accompanied by a conscious act of abstracting rules and therefore, to a certain extent, of theorizing. In this way there arises in the mind an homiletical ideal, a sort of private and individual theory. The accidental character, however, the uncertainty and the haphazard and piecemeal nature of the maxims that compose such a theory can be overcome only when the individual observation, from which no one is absolved, is supplemented by a scientific treatment surveying the whole praxis." This scientific treatment does not propose to teach the preacher "how to influence the heart of man by means of definite artistic theories or man-made religious rules. Its purpose is neither to foster a superstitious belief in the supreme value of pedagogical or psychological methods, nor to stake off, according to a capricious methodistic theory, the way by which God enters into the soul of man. It has no concern, in view of the infinite variety of God's creative activity, in rounding out a completed system, a theory carried to the last detail. But even if it availed only to prevent the typical aberrations to which a praxis left to itself is so prone, such a critical antidote must be regarded as useful. It aspires, however, to something higher. If preaching is an art that must be learned and practiced, which no one denies, then there must be also a doctrine of the sermon consisting of theoretical instruction, in which the deductions from the premises, together with the results of present experience and the lessons of history, combine to form a *Weisheitslehre*. This may then be called a science of the sermon, provided we bear well in mind that the unique content, which forms the heart and soul of the

---

[17] P. 258.

sermon, must condition the whole at every point and exclude a mere technique."[18] The last sentence needs especially to be underscored. Homiletics can never become a merely technical study, for the simple reason that it must derive its distinctive character from the nature and content of the sermon and from the characteristics of the hearers to whom the sermon is addressed. Hence these must be its first and chief concern.

With the foregoing the relation of Homiletics to the other theological disciplines has already been indicated. We have seen that it is the function of Homiletics to investigate the peculiar nature and subject-matter of the sermon. The results of this investigation, constantly taking into consideration the specific character of the hearers, must exert a determining influence upon the theory of the form of the sermon. If that is true, then Homiletics cannot be merely a rhetorical appendage tacked on to the rest of theology, but is, despite its many points of contact with the other disciplines, an independent discipline within the complex of theology. Indeed, if properly understood, all scientific theology finds in Homiletics its practical culmination. This is the element of truth in Dabney's otherwise one-sided words to his students:[19] "In one respect, it may be said, sacred rhetoric bears an important relation to all other theological studies, not unlike that which Lord Bacon[20] describes as the *vindemiatio* of deductions. The observation, comparing, classifying of phenomena are preparatory; the final inference from the comparison, leading us to the true law of causation, extracts that precious juice for the sake of which solely the clusters have been collected with so much care. In like manner I may claim, that as you come here to be made preachers of the Gospel, and as its proclamation from the pulpit is to be your prominent task, all other studies are ancillary to this which we now undertake. It is sacred rhetoric which teaches you to apply to the lips of perishing man the expressed wine of all other acquisitions." R. Seeberg hits the truth when he says: "That dogmatic will survive, which helps us to preach the best sermons;"[21] and again: "The importance of a dogmatician for his period must be estimated, above all else, by the impetus he has given to preaching."[22]

---

[18]P. 259.—[19]P. 19.—[20]*Nov. Organum*, ii, 20.—[21]*Die Kirche Deutschlands im 19. Jahrh.*, [3]1910, p. 214.—[22]*Zur systematischen Theologie*, ii, 1909, P. 49.

Exegetical theology discovers to the preacher his treasure-trove, and assists him in finding therein the jewels his preaching is to flash before the eyes of his people, in their proper setting and radiating light and life.[23] *Systematic theology* introduces him to organic unity and totality of Christian doctrine, and shows the perspective in which he must view the individual truth of each text, in order to present it in its proper relation to the centre of all saving truth.[24] *Historical theology*, leading him into the past, helps the preacher to understand the present with its complex tendencies, to view the new in the light of the old, and to trace the resemblances and differences between the two, giving attention to the resultant demands and duties; to say nothing of the wealth of illustrative material which history supplies. The other branches of *practical theology*, especially the care of souls and the science of missions, fructify the preacher's life, the former by giving him an admirable course in practical psychology, and both together by furnishing ever fresh evidences of the life-giving power of the Word of God, without faith in which there never has been nor ever will be a blessed ministry.

---

[23]Cf. W. G. T. Shedd, *Homiletics and Pastoral Theology*, chap. i: "Relation of Sacred Eloquence to Biblical Exegesis."—[24]Cf. A. D. C. Twesten, *Vorlesungen ueber die Dogmatik*, ³1834, vol. i, pp. 87-92: "Verhaeltnis der Dogmatik zum Lehrvortrage des Geistlichen in der Gemeinde."

§ 3. THE DIVISION OF HOMILETICS

Augustine, *De doctrina christiana*, ed. Bruder, 397-426. Joh. Ulricus Surgant, *Manuale curatorum praedicandi praebens modum*, 1502, ²1507. Hier. Dungersheim, *Tractatus de modo discendi et docendi ad populum sacra seu de modo praedicandi*, 1514. Desid. Erasmus, *Ecclesiastae sive de ratione concionandi libri IV*, 1535. Andr. Hyperius, *De formandis concionibus sacris seu de interpretatione Scripturarum populari*, 1553 (German tr. by E. Chr. Achelis, 1901). Joh. Jak. Rambach, *Erlaeuterung ueber die praecepta homiletica* (edited by J. P. Fresenius), 1736. J. L. von Mosheim, *Anweisung, erbaulich zu predigen*, 1763. F. Schleiermacher, *Praktische Theologie* (1832-34), 1850. Chr. G. Ficker, *Grundlinien der ev. Homiletik*, 1847. C. Imm. Nitzsch, *Praktische Theologie*, vol. ii, 1848. G. Baur, *Grundzuege der Homiletik*, 1848. J. W. Alexander, *Thoughts on Preaching*, 1864. G. W. Hervey, *A System of Christian Rhetoric*, 1873. H. W. Beecher, *Yale Lectures on Preaching*, 1872-4. E. Henke, *Vorlesungen ueber Liturgik und Homiletik*, 1876. Phillips Brooks, *Lectures on Preaching*, 1877. Theod. Harnack, *Geschichte und Theorie der Predigt und Seelsorge* (*Praktische Theologie*, vol. ii), 1878. A. Cruel, *Geschichte der deutschen Predigt im Mittelalter*, 1879. R. W. Dale, *Nine Lectures on Preaching*, 1882. N. J. Burton, *Yale Lectures on Preaching*, 1888. R. F. Horton, *Verbum Dei. The Yale Lectures on Preaching*, 1893. W. B. Carpenter, *Lectures on Preaching*, 1895. John Watson (Ian Maclaren), *The Cure of Souls*, 1896. A. S. Hoyt, *The Work of Preaching. A Book for the Classroom and Study*, 1905.

The history of Homiletics shows that it is hardly possible to suggest a division of Homiletics that is universally accepted. In our judgment, however, the purpose will best be served by treating (1) of the Nature and Purpose of the Sermon, (2) of its Subject-Matter, and (3) of its Form or Structure. In choosing this division we consider the independent study of the History of Preaching as a necessary complement to Homiletics proper. (P. 37.)

Although the scientific character of a discipline does not depend solely on its disposition, the lack of an orderly division is usually fraught with harmful consequences. Especially ought Homiletics, which in one of its parts lays down rules for the proper division of sermons, to present its materials in a well ordered and logical manner. The older rhetoric presented its subject-matter in the four categories—*inventio, dispositio, elocutio, pronunciatio.* These may readily be reduced to two, since the first has to do with the contents the last three with the form. This was done by Cicero, who in *De oratore,* lib. ii, 27, 120, assigns to rhetoric the task of treating *primum quid, deinde quomodo dicamus.* Cicero is followed by Augustine, who in his *De doctrina christiana,* the first Christian Homiletics, treats, as he himself indicates, in the first three books principally of the content of the sermon and its invention (*de inventione*) and devotes the last book to its form (*de prolatione*). This division underlies, consciously or unconsciously, most of the mediaeval discussions of the subject, down to that of Surgant. In Surgant's work the formal side overshadows all else; in only a single *consideratio* does he discuss the question, *quid sit praedicandum,* while twenty-two are devoted to the form. It should be said, however, that the first *consideratio* treats, though very meagrely, the question, *quid sit praedicatio,* and the second the question, *quid sit praedicare.* In the original *Tractatus* of Hieronymus Dungersheim, the well known opponent of Luther, who discusses (1) the preacher, (2) the sermon, (3) the hearers, we find the entire second part given over to a discussion of the form of the sermon, after two opening chapters on its value and its contents. Erasmus treats in his first book of the virtues of the preacher, gives in the second rules governing the invention of material, and discusses in the third book *dispositio, pronunciatio* and *elocutio.* The older rhetoric with its fourfold (or, if we count *memoria* separately, its five-fold) division is followed also in the first Protestant treatment of Homiletics by A. Hyperius. Its distinctive reformatory element consisted rather in its return to Augustine, in the laying of all stress upon *inventio,* that is, on the *quid,* or subject-matter, and subordinating to this all questions concerning the *quomodo,* or form, thus permitting the peculiar content of the sermon to exhibit its divine power and achieve its definite purpose. The influence of the older rhetoric was, however, not yet broken, for the peculiarily reformatory features in Hyperius' treatise found but a slender following.

This liberation was achieved especially through the labors of J. J. Rambach and Joh. Lorenz von Mosheim. Rambach stressed the purpose of the sermon, which consisted for him in the edification of its hearers, and which he made the dominant principle of his treatment. Mosheim so arranged his *Anweisung, erbaulich zu predigen* that the entire first part is devoted to the purpose of the sermon, while the second deduces from this the rules for its preparation and delivery. This marks a decided step in advance, which is, however, not carried forward in the succeeding discussions of our subject. Thus Schleiermacher treats (1) of the unity of the religious discourse, (2) of the theory of the outline, (3) of the invention or production of the ideas composing the discourse, and (4) of the theory of expression. So, too, Palmer discusses (1) the Word of God, 2) the custom of the Church, (3) the congregation, (4) the personality of the preacher. A. Schweizer,[1] on the contrary, returned to the principles laid down by Mosheim and Rambach and established their predominance. His work opens with a discussion of principles, followed by a material and a formal section. "Even where Homiletics treats both material and form in their order," he writes, "it cannot accomplish all it should; in that case it is merely special Homiletics, partly material, partly formal. In the best text-books, however, there has always been room for the discussion of principles, in which the conception of 'Homiletics must be determined before a division of the subject is attempted. Such a discussion of principles can by no means be disposed of in a mere introduction; it demands a place within the discipline itself."[2] In his principial section Schweizer discusses therefore (1) the homiletical conception as a part of the cultus, (2) as distinguished from the liturgical, and (3) considered as oratory. Nitzsch's treatment, of the same year, has the same threefold division without its clearness. He discusses (1) the conception and purpose of the sermon, (2) the determination of its contents, then passing on to the formal side, (3) the outline, (4) the construction, (5) the homiletical style, (6) the delivery. Baur's work, published in the same year, is distinguished by an admirable clarity, although the discussion of the material of the sermon is not set in its proper light. He treats (1) the conception of the sermon as an expression of the churchly life growing necessarily out of the nature of the Christian congregation, (2) the laws for the construction of the sermon arising out of its conception, (3) the rules to be followed by the minister so far as he is a preacher.

It was a fruitful idea, and one not to be lightly given up, when Baur and especially Schweizer conceived and treated the sermon as an integral part of public worship. This thought had previously found expression, from the Lutheran viewpoint, in the work of Ficker. The Word of God is to be preached not only for the sake of the cultus, but

---

[1]1848.—[2]P. 113.

because the Church, created by the Word of God in Christ, must be preserved and extended by this Word. Hence Ficker conceives Homiletics as giving directions how the Word of God, which must be drawn from and controlled by the Scriptures, is to be preached to the salvation of the Church in general and of the souls entrusted to the local congregation in particular. Schweizer, moreover, contends that the sermon, if full justice is to be done to its nature, must be treated also as public discourse. Both of these viewpoints find a place in the third, or constructive, part of Harnack's work (part i is principial, part ii historical), not always in an unobjectionable manner. None of the subsequent German homiletes surpasses Ficker and Schweizer; several even fall below them by briefly disposing in their introductions of the discussion of principles, as, e. g., Steinmeyer and Sachsse. Krauss, on the other hand, deliberately joins himself to Schweizer. The French homilete Vinet returns to the divisions of the older rhetoric, treating (1) *inventio*, (2) *dispositio*, and (3) *elocutio*, which here, too, can be reduced to two, material and form. But this division is not strictly adhered to, the lack of systematic presentation forming a flaw in an otherwise admirable piece of work.

The English and American treatments are also rarely distinguished by a strict division and a systematic structure. Wilkins, indeed, discussed in his day, (1) method, (2) matter, (3) scheme of the chief heads in Divinity, (4) expression. But Porter, Shedd, Kidder, Alexander, *et al.*, set their chapters alongside each other with no very close connection between them, though all that they have to say may be roughly reduced to the two divisions, subject-matter and formal arrangement. Porter's book contains two lectures on the history of preaching, and Kidder's on the history of Homiletics. The formal side is generally over-emphasized. Broadus and Hervey show more interest in the architectonics of their science. The former divides: (1) materials of preaching, (2) arrangement of a sermon, (3) style, (4) delivery of sermons; the latter, whose work is termed a "system," treats (1) of inspiration in preaching, (2) of invention, (3) of style, (4) of elocution. The founding, in 1871 at Yale, of the Lyman Beecher Lectureship on Preaching, and of other similar lecture courses elsewhere, has not proved conducive to a systematic treatment of our discipline. It was found impossible to discuss the subject as a whole within the narrow limits of a lecture course; the lectures, moreover, delivered by men in the active ministry, were supplementary to the regular theological course; hence the lecturers chose some particular phase of the subject that most appealed to them. This may be seen by a glance into the published Yale lectures of Henry Ward Beecher, Phillips Brooks, R. F. Horton, M. Simpson, R. W. Dale, N. J. Burton, W. B. Carpenter, Ian Maclaren, *et al.* Of them all, Beecher goes farthest afield, discoursing, for instance, in his first lecture, on "Health as Related to Preaching," through twenty-five pages. The more recent homiletes, as Phelps, Pattison, Hoyt, Burrell, are likewise lacking in systematic structure, though Hoyt's volume professes to be a "text-book." All of them deal only briefly and by way of introduction with the nature and purpose of the sermon, as though clearness on these questions were to be taken for granted, and the answer to them did not exert a determining influence on all other parts of Homiletics.

The proper division of our subject we find to lie along the line marked out by the works of Ficker, Baur, Schweizer, Harnack, and Krauss. We are unable to conceive of an adequate and systematic treatment of Homiletics without a principial discussion, at the very outset, of the nature and purpose of the sermon. Only in proportion as the results of this discussion pervade and determine the treatment of the material and of the form, or structure, of the sermon, will our presentation become a rounded whole and appear as a truly independent discipline.

To this threefold division we should like to prefix a short history of preaching, because unless the student is afforded some insight into this history and made aware how important a factor of homiletical culture it forms, he is deprived of a valuable aid in the performance of his work as preacher. The course of study in our own seminary requires one term of study in the history of preaching. A brief historical outline, however, is of little value unless it is supplemented by a complete selection of sermon material drawn from the sermon literature of all centuries. Since it would make this volume too bulky to present all of this material, we have decided to dispense here with the treatment of the history of preaching and to offer it in a separate volume.

I
The Nature and Purpose of the Sermon

§4. SURVEY

We have to treat the nature and purpose, not of missionary preaching by which Christian congregations are called into existence, nor of catechetical indoctrination which lays the foundation of Christian thought and life, but of the congregational sermon presupposing a Christian congregation at some stage of its development.

The congregational sermon, however, is not an isolated or independent act, but a portion of a larger whole, the service of the worshiping congregation, of which it forms an integral part. Whatever is true, therefore, of the service as a whole must likewise be true somehow of the sermon. With all its peculiar characteristics, it must agree with the service at least in nature and purpose; otherwise it will form a disturbing element in the service. Hence we shall have to discuss the sermon, first of all, as a cultus act, as an organic part of the service of the worshiping congregation.

Now this service of the congregation falls into two well defined divisions—the liturgical and the homiletical. The former is fixed and constant, and is determined by the service-book, or *agenda*, used by the respective church body as the expression of its common faith. The homiletical part of the service, on the other hand, is variable, free and individual, and appears in the form of public discourse.[1] We shall therefore have to treat the sermon also as discourse or ora-

---

[1] The term ὁμιλία, though denoting according to etymology and usage, verbal intercourse or conversation, was not applied to the liturgical parts of the service but to the utterances of the Christian brethren which, at first entirely free and informal, developed very early into the formal discourse or sermon; comp. p. 6.

tion. This second feature, however, must be kept subordinate to the first; for the sermon, while a discourse, is a discourse having its place in the service of the worshiping congregation and deriving its peculiar character as to both form and contents from this service.

A. The Sermon as Organic Part of the Service of the Worshiping Congregation

§ 5. THE NATURE OF THE SERVICE OF THE CHRISTIAN CONGREGATION

Theod. Harnack, *Praktische Theologie*, i, 1877. H. Bassermann, *Handbuch der geistlichen Beredsamkeit*, 1885. J. Gottschick, *Luthers Anschauungen vom christl. Gottesdienst und seine tatsaechliche Reform desselben*, 1887. G. Rietschel, *Der evang. Gottesdienst unter dem Gesichtspunkt der Anbetung im Geist und in der Wahrheit*, 1894. Id., *Lehrbuch der Liturgik*, i, 1900. J. Smend, *Der evang. Gottesdienst. Eine Liturgik nach evang. Grundsaetzen in 14 Abhandlungen dargestellt*, 1904. E. C. Achelis, *Lehrbuch der praktischen Theologie*, ii, ³1911.

The cultus, or service, is the expression in outward acts of the religious life of the heart. The service of a congregation is the expression in definite outward acts of the common religious life of its members. A Christian service is, accordingly, the outward expression of the peculiar religious life common to the Christian Church. This common Christian life consists in the communion between God and man mediated by Jesus Christ.[1]

Whatever the chronological order of the acts expressing and mediating God's communion with man and man's communion with God, the former are in fact always primary and fundamental. God first offers and imparts Himself, in Word and sacrament, to man and is accepted by him; then only can the congregation offer itself to God in prayer, praise and thanksgiving. What is said in 1 John 4:19 of the Christian life in general is true of the service in particular. Thus

---

[1] 1 John 1:3, 6.

Luther: "In the service our blessed Lord Himself speaks to us through His holy Word, and we in turn speak to Him in prayers and hymns." The former is known as the sacramental, the latter as the sacrificial element in the service;[2] together, in their constant interaction, they constitute the two chief portions of the service.

It must also be borne in mind that many of the service parts cannot be performed, and are not intended to be performed, except through the divinely instituted office of the ministry. The minister acts, on the one hand, as the divinely appointed organ for the public administration of Word and sacrament by which God enters into communion with the congregation. On the other hand, he acts also, in the interest of good order, as *choragus*, when the congregation in its turn enters into and represents its communion with God by means of prayer, praise and adoration. The minister, though only the go-between, dare never descend to the level of a mere instrument, lifeless and without inner participation; his every act in the service must be the expression of the religious life which he shares with the worshiping congregation. (P. 43.)

The distinction which Luther makes in the Communion office he applies also to the service as a whole, dividing it into a sacramental and a sacrificial part. Of the Communion he says in *The Babylonian Captivity* (1520): "We must not confound these two—the mass and the prayers, the sacrament and the work, the testament and the sacrifice; for the one comes from God to us, through the ministration of the priest, and demands our faith; the other proceeds from our faith to God, through the priest, and demands His answer. The former descends, the latter ascends."[3] Of the service as a whole he writes in the *Ennaratio in Psalmos graduum* (1540) on Ps. 122:4,—"The first part of the right worship of God is to learn what is the most effective way of serving God and of offering Him that worship in which He

---

[2]Comp. *Apologia Confessionis*, xii, 18, 19, — Sacramentum est ceremonia vel opus, in quo *Deus nobis* exhibet hoc quod offert annexa ceremoniae promissio. . . . econtra sacrificium est ceremonia vel opus, quod *nos Deo* reddimus, ut eum honore afficiamus.—[3]*Works of Martin Luther* (Philadelphia), ii, 217.

most delights, viz., to teach the Word of God and to hear God speaking through His witnesses. The second part is to confess the name of the Lord. The latter is active, the former passive. For the first thing is to accept the Word, or to be taught by the Word. The next is, having heard the Word, to render God thanks." Likewise in his *Ennaratio in Genesin*, 28: 2-3,—"Through the benediction, the sermon and the administration of the sacraments, God descends and speaks to me; here I am the hearer. On the other hand I ascend and speak in God's ears, and He hears my prayer." But clearest of all is his consecration sermon at Torgau of the same year, which begins: "My dear friends,—We are about to bless this new house of God and consecrate it to our Lord Jesus Christ. This is not alone for me to do, but you, too, must seize the incense pot, in order that this may become a house wherein nothing else shall take place than that our blessed Lord Himself speak to us through His holy Word and we in turn speak to Him in prayer and praise." Farther on he continues: "Sundays and festival days are appointed in order that all may by common agreement prepare and come together to hear God's Word, and to pray to Him for all things needful and thank Him for His benefits.... This we know to be a right service, in which He is well pleased and really present with us."

When Gottschick defines the evangelical service according to Luther as the common thank-offering of the priestly congregation, he does not do justice to Luther's position, for whom, as we have seen, praise and thanksgiving invariably occupy the second place. To hold that the service consists solely in the common thank-offering of believers leads to dangerous consequences; for in that case, as Achelis well points out, "the stress would lie, not on man's receiving something from God, which is the fundamental characteristic of all religion, but on man's doing something, even though prompted by God; and the religious character of the service would be destroyed" (p. 28). How could Luther have departed, in his views on the service, from the conception he had already expressed so clearly in 1520, in his *Treatise on the New Testament?* "If a man is to deal with God," he says there, "and receive anything from Him, it must happen in this wise, not that man begin and lay the first stone, but that God, without any entreaty or desire of man, must first come and give him a promise. This word of God is the beginning, the foundation, the rock, upon which afterwards all works, words and thoughts of man must build.... Thus it is not possible that man of his own reason and strength should by works ascend to heaven and anticipate God, moving Him to be gracious; God must rather anticipate all works and thoughts, and make a promise clearly expressed in words, which man then takes and keeps with a good, firm faith."[4]

No: we do not go to service in order primarily to serve God with our praise and thanksgiving, nor even to "represent and express" the religious life present in us;[5] we go to service in order to let God serve and enrich us. It is necessary today, over against a one-sided emphasis on activity, to insist that the one thing needful is to sit with Mary at Jesus' feet and to hear His word. Receptivity is the essence of religion; it must also be the distinctive mark of the evangelical service. From this receptivity the acts of thanksgiving, praise, and service to others will naturally flow.

---

[4]*Works of Martin Luther* (Phila.), i, 297 f.—[5]So Schleiermacher and Bassermann.

§ 6. THE NATURE OF THE SERMON AS ORGANIC PART OF THE SERVICE

A. Tholuck, *Predigten ueber Hauptstuecke des christl. Glaubens und Lebens* (Vorwort zur zweiten Sammlung), 1836. Cl. Harms, *Mit Zungen reden* (Stud. und Kritiken), 1838. Chr. Palmer, *Evang. Homiletik*, 1842 (⁶1887). A. Schweizer, *Homiletik*, 1848. J. W. Alexander, *Thoughts on Preaching*, 1864. C. H. Spurgeon, *Lectures to My Students*, 1876. Theod. Harnack, *Praktische Theologie*, i, 1877. A. Krauss, *Lehrbuch der Homiletik*, 1883. H. Bassermann, *Handbuch der geistlichen Beredsamkeit*, 1885. H. Cremer, *Die Aufgabe und Bedeutung der Predigt* (1877), 1892. Th. Christlieb, *Homiletik*, ed. by Haarbeck, 1898. F. L. Steinmeyer, *Homiletik*, ed. by Reylaender, 1901. R. L. Dabney, *Sacred Rhetoric* (1870), ³1902. O. Baumgarten, *Predigtprobleme*, 1904. F. Niebergall, *Wie predigen wir dem modernen Menschen?* i, 1904 (³1909), ii, 1906. H. Hering, *Die Lehre von der Predigt*, 1905. P. Kleinert, *Homiletik*, 1907. P. T. Forsyth, *Positive Preaching and the Modern Mind*, 1907. H. Johnson, *The Ideal Ministry*, 1908. A. Hoyt, *The Preacher*, 1909. K. Roehrich, *Die Aufgabe der Predigt in unserer Zeit*, 1909. E. C. Achelis, *Praktische Theologie*, ii, ³1911. E. Sachsse, *Evang. Homiletik*, 1913. D. J. Burrell, *The Sermon: Its Construction and Delivery*, 1913. D. H. Bauslin, *The Socialization of the Church* (Lutheran Quarterly), 1914. K. Fezer, *Das Wort Gottes und die Predigt*, 1925.

If the nature of the sermon grows out of the nature of the service, the three factors mentioned above will be found also in the sermon: (1) In it God offers Himself through the Word to His Church and congregation; (2) the Church, as well as the individual congregation, having received the Word and constantly receiving it anew, bears witness to the Word, and (3) it does this by means of the divinely appointed office of the ministry. These three factors, however, are no more to be co-ordinated in the sermon than in the service as a whole. Here, too, the first mentioned must be the chief factor, on which the second will follow, while the third is but the individualizing of the second.

(1) THE SERMON IN ITS RELATION TO THE WORD OF GOD

Apart from the Word of God there can be no sermon. On the Word of God the sermon is based, from the Word it draws its contents. Indeed, the sermon is nothing else than the offer and proclamation of the Word. This must necessarily be the case if the sermon is really to have a religious character and to be, like the service as a whole, the expression of the religious life peculiar to the Christian Church, i. e., the expression of the communion between God and man mediated by Christ. For there can be no communion between God and man without the Word. It was so in the beginning: after the Fall God must approach man in revelations of word and deed if the broken communion between Himself and man was to be restored. It is so today: this communion can be realized only by His drawing near to man in His Word,—the permanent and living record of those revelations of word and deed,—only by His speaking to man and acting upon him. Without the Word written in the Scriptures, and read, preached and heard, God remains for us an unknown God.[1] We can indeed learn much from nature, history and conscience concerning His omnipotence, wisdom, holiness and righteousness; but His real nature, the thoughts of His heart, His final attitude toward us men and our salvation, remain hidden until He comes to us in the Word[2] and tells us who and what He is. In the Word in which He reveals Himself to us[3] He withdraws one veil after another from His face, and lets us see into His very heart glowing with holy love to lost sinners. Nor can we, on the other hand, come to God except through the Word.

---

[1]Acts 17:23.—[2]Rom. 10:5-15.—[3]1 Cor. 2:10-13.

There is no other way of approaching Him and making Him ours; for He is Spirit, while we are spiritual-physical beings and dependent on our sense perceptions.

Every sermon, therefore, that is not a proclamation of the Word of God destroys the one bridge between God and man, so that neither can approach the other. Such a sermon is not only a disturbing factor in the service of the evangelical congregation, but an actual hindrance to true religion. And since the Word of God is not a mere record of His thoughts toward us, but the actual medium and channel whereby His saving grace and life are imparted, the divine power unto salvation here and hereafter, a heavenly seed quick with eternal life,[4] the sermon that does not proclaim this Word relinquishes man to the guilt and weakness of his sin; it may indeed incite him to escape his doom by his own reason and strength, but only plunges him, when his efforts have inevitably failed, into despair and destruction.

It is a particularly vicious misconception of its nature when the evangelical sermon, instead of being as it should be the life-giving proclamation of the divine Word, is turned into a discussion of *political, social* or similar problems. When this is done, man usurps the place of God, human wisdom the place of revelation, Law the place of Gospel, human merit the place of grace, the temporal the place of the eternal, the body the place of the soul. What remains is but natural religion and natural morality, so that one might well inquire why Christ needed to come or to send out His apostles into the world.

The Reformation recalled to men's minds the truth that God's Word alone has place and power in the Church and bestows peace and comfort. Hence all fables and human wisdom were banished from the sermon as from the service,

---

[4] Rom. 1:16; Jas. 1:18, 21; 1 Pet. 1:23; 1 Cor. 1:18; 2 Cor. 2:14; Heb. 4:12; Isa. 55:10 f.

and men were reminded that the sermon can possess dignity, power and authority, impart grace, and make men certain of their salvation, only in proportion as it is the proclamation of the Word of God. (P. 57.)

In his little treatise, *Von Ordnung des Gottesdienstes in der Gemeine* (1523), Luther writes, "It is necessary to know first of all that a Christian congregation ought never to come together unless the Word of God be preached and prayers said." And at the close, "In short, everything should have this end in view, that the Word be kept before the people and the service be not turned again into empty noise as before. Everything else had better be omitted than the Word, and nothing better can be done than to proclaim the Word. For all the Scriptures show us that the Word should have free course among Christians, and Christ Himself tells us that one thing alone is needful, namely, that Mary sit daily at His feet and hear His word (Luke 10:42). This is that good part which is to be chosen and which shall never be taken away; for it is an eternal Word. All other things must pass away, how careful and troubled soever Martha may be about them." Elsewhere he writes in similar vein: "A preacher should not spin things out of his head nor teach human folly and traditions, but draw his message from Jacob's well, or the Word of God, the writings of the prophets and apostles." In his treatise *Against Jack Pudding* (1541) he says: "A preacher, after preaching his sermon, need not say the Lord's Prayer nor seek forgiveness (if he be a right preacher), but he should boast with Jeremiah, 'Lord, Thou knowest that what came out of my mouth was right and well pleasing to Thee;' nay, he should say boldly with Paul and all apostles and prophets, 'Thus saith the Lord,' and 'I have been in this sermon an apostle and prophet of Jesus Christ.' Here it is not necessary, indeed, it is not right, to ask forgiveness of sins, as if the teaching had been wrong; for it is God's Word and not my own, so that God neither need nor can forgive me, but must rather confirm, commend and crown my work, saying, 'Thou hast taught well, for it is I that spoke by thee and the Word is mine.' Whoever cannot boast thus of his sermons, let him leave his hands off preaching; he will of a certainty only lie and blaspheme God." This was Luther's position to the end. In his last sermon, preached February 14, 1546, at Eisleben, he said: "The right sort of preacher should faithfully and diligently preach nothing but the Word of God and seek His glory and honor alone. The hearer likewise should say, 'I do not believe in my pastor, but he tells me of another Lord whose name is Christ; Him he declares unto me, and I will listen to his words so far as he leads me to this true master and preceptor, God's own Son.' If this were done, the Church would prosper, be well ruled, and everywhere be at one; otherwise there will everywhere be confusion, as it is under the rule of the world. A city council will not tolerate a fool who continually sets the whole town by the ears, but will eject him to the great relief of all. So it ought to be in the Christian Church; no one should be preached or taught but the Son of God alone. Of Him alone it is said, 'This is my beloved Son; hear ye Him' and none other among the sons of men, neither emperor, king, pope nor cardinal."

But does this still hold today? May the sermon, in this our modern world, proclaim nothing but the old Word of God? Ought this Word not rather to be modified, supplemented, touched up, or even replaced by something new? Isaiah long ago gave the answer: "The grass withereth, the flower fadeth; because the Spirit of the Lord bloweth upon it: surely the people is grass. The grass withereth, the flower fadeth; but the Word of our God shall stand forever."[5] And Jesus said, "Heaven and earth shall pass away, but my words shall not pass away."[6]

In the midst of the complex intellectual life of modern times W. Laible wrote in 1914, out of the fulness of his personal experience: "Man changes, customs change, peoples change. And because everything changes, later centuries no longer understand what former centuries have spoken. Each new age has its new thoughts. Only the Word of God takes no part in this change. It is understood today by all, as it was of yore. If Jesus came today, He would speak precisely as He spoke then, of the prodigal son, the rich man, the unfruitful fig-tree, the fourfold soil; He would deliver the same Sermon on the Mount and pronounce the same Woes on those who heard Him and would not repent. Some have attempted to modernize His sayings—'How Jesus would speak today.' Their efforts proved vain. If Jesus were to speak as they propose, He would not be understood by the common people fifty years hence. The eternal cannot be imitated. It is the majestic right of God to speak words which are understood at all times and by all peoples. This right He resigns to no man. . . . The message of Jesus knows no time. 'Never man spake as this man.' So the people of Jerusalem judged almost two thousand years ago. It is even today the unanimous verdict. In the same form in

---

[5]Isa. 40: 7, 8.—[6]Matt. 24: 35.

which He spoke them to the fishermen of Galilee His words still produce their effect today, overwhelming men's hearts like a stream of fire, comforting the weary, giving life to the dying. Because Jesus' word is unchangeable as God Himself, it was able to gather a Church of the same faith and the same worship from among all peoples and nations and tongues, in all centuries and all periods. His Word overcame all differences of civilization and philosophy. How different the thinking of the Greeks and Romans, of the Germanic peoples, of the Middle Ages, of the modern man! The Word of Jesus had for them all 'words of eternal life.' All have found in Jesus the same Saviour and Redeemer." The Word of God fits every age because it belongs to eternity, far above all changes of time. It fits every man because it is not the word of a man standing as one among many, but the Word of God, who is the Creator and Saviour of all men.

It is folly, therefore, for the servants of the Word to cast about how to reach men's hearts, how to fill the pews, how to bring people to the fear of the Lord; it is folly to suppose they must discover new powers, find a new content for their sermons, or try this or that new method. The hammer that breaks the rock in pieces has not been cast aside, it needs only an arm to swing it; the Lord's fire is still burning, it needs only servants to carry it among men. Here is God's plenty, to win men and to hold them. Ahab puts on sackcloth when Elijah speaks; Josiah rends his garment when the words of the covenant are read; Saul, disconsolate in his darkness, rises and receives his sight when Ananias brings him the Word of the Lord. This was the "sword of the Spirit" which the great Apostle thereafter never let go out of his hand. With this Word he founded his congregations, repaired the breaches in the Corinthian Church, and preserved his Galatians from apostasy. "By the Word the world was made; by the Word the Church was preserved: by it she must also be reformed,"—so Luther writes to Spalatin. And in the second of his famous *Eight Wittenberg Sermons* (1522) he calls the Word his sole weapon, by which he overthrew Rome and now hopes to put down the fanatics. "In conclusion," he says, "I will preach it, teach it, write it, but I will constrain no man by force. I simply taught, preached, wrote God's Word; otherwise I did nothing. And then while I slept, or drank Wittenberg beer with my Philip and with Amsdorf, the Word so greatly weakened the papacy that never a prince or emperor inflicted such damage upon it. I did nothing, the Word did it all. Had I desired to foment trouble, I could have brought great bloodshed upon Germany. Yea, I could have started such a little game at Worms that even the emperor would not have been safe. But what would it have been? A fool's play. I did nothing, I left it all to the Word."[7] Whenever any great onward and upward movement arose in the kingdom of God, it was inaugurated by the Word of God. And this Word is given also to us. Our concern should be, not to seek after new ways of making our preaching effective, but to proclaim the Word of God in all its ancient power, unaltered and unabridged. Those who would oppose this in the name of reason and scientific progress have no substitute to match the old hammer that breaks the rock in pieces, the ancient fire tended by prophets and apostles. If the sermon would reach men's hearts it must march in the complete armor of the old Word of God. What those men must still attempt this Word has long since accomplished, namely, given proof that it is living and sharper than any two-edged sword, mighty to beat down all defenses, to raise up the faint-hearted, to save every one that believeth, and to create withal this faith itself in the soul.

"The preacher's task," says R. L. Dabney, for many years professor of systematic and practical theology at the Southern Presbyterian Seminary in Virginia, "may be correctly explained as that of (instrumentally) forming the image of Christ upon the souls of men. The plastic substance is the human heart. The die which is provided for the workman is the revealed Word; and the impression to be formed is the divine image of knowledge and true holiness. God, who made the soul, and therefore knows it, made the die. He obviously knew best how to shape it, in order to produce the imprint He desired. Now the workman's business is not to criticise, recarve, or erase anything in the die which was committed to him; but simply to press it down faithfully upon the substance to be impressed, observing the condition of the work assigned him in his instructions. In this view, how plain it is, that preaching should be simply representative of Bible truths, and in Bible proportions! The preacher's business is to take what is given to him, and to endeavor to imprint it on the souls of men. All else is God's work. The die is just such, so large, so sharp, so hard, and has just such an 'image and superscription' on it, as God would have. Thus He judged, in giving it to us. With this, 'the man of God is perfect, thoroughly furnished unto all good works' (2 Tim. 3:17). This is enough for us .... But there are many who shrink with fear from what they regard as so confined a walk of ministerial instruction. They think it necessary to take a more ample range in

---

[7] *Works of Martin Luther* (Phila.), ii, 399 f.

preaching than simply showing the people what the Bible means, and imprinting that meaning on their souls. The secret feeling is: 'This would not allow variety and interest enough. There would not be verge enough for the preacher to display his own powers. This is a business too simple and plodding for your profound theological philosopher. There is not mental *pabulum* enough for the intellects of enlightened hearers.' So, in some pulpits, we have grandiloquent expositions of the 'moral system of the universe.' In others the Sabbaths of the people are wholly occupied with those polemics by which the outworks of Christianity should be defended against the foreign assaults of infidel philosophy; as though one would feed the flock within the fold with the bristling missiles which should have been hurled against the wolves without. Others deal in scholastic discussions of the propositions of the church-symbols, cleaving the 'bare bones of their orthodoxy' into splinters as angular and dry as the gravel of the desert. Others again offer metaphysical discussions of the psychology of religion, as though they would feed the babes of Christ with a sort of chemical resolution of the sincere milk of the Word into its ultimate elements, instead of the living, concrete nourishment provided for them by their Saviour. Now what is this but the very spirit of unbelief and selfseeking? The selection of such forms of truth is evidently not guided by the lowly, self-devoted spirit of the 'servant' of the Church, but by a single eye to self-display. God puts the 'sword of the Spirit' into this man's hand, and tells him that with this he shall conquer. He distrusts it, he will add something more trenchant. God tells him that the 'Word is quick and powerful, and sharper than any two-edged sword, piercing even to the dividing asunder of the soul and spirit, and of the joints and marrow, and is a discerner of the thoughts and intents of the heart' (Hebr. 4:12). 'No,' says the unbelieving servant, 'I can devise truths more piercing.' These, my brethren, are not the men to do the work of that God who 'hath chosen the foolish things of the world to confound the wise.' Theirs is the spirit of infidelity, and their preaching breeds infidelity... The appropriate mission of the minister is to preach for the salvation of souls. The servant who by diverging into some other projects not especially enjoined on him, nor essential for him to perform, precludes himself from his allotted task, is clearly guilty of disobedience to his master, if not of treason to his charge."

The preacher who descends to the level of a *political* orator in the pulpit is in no position truly to serve his congregation, among whom there will always be persons who differ with his political views.

He deludes his hearers into the belief that temporal things are of more importance than heavenly things, by dragging the former into the brief hour set apart for divine worship, which should be sacred to the heavenly and eternal and devoted to the interest of immortal souls. Instead of setting men before God and leading them to a true knowledge of themselves, he sets them in the midst of the world with its discords and conflicts and arouses their baser instincts of self-righteousness, the censorious temper, and not seldom the passion of enmity and hatred. This is an especial danger in time of war, as we have, alas! experienced. Edmund Burke's words should ever be borne in mind: "Politics and the pulpit are terms that have little agreement. No sound ought to be heard in the Church but the healing voice of Christian charity. The cause of civil liberty and civil government gains as little as that of religion by this confusion of duties. Those who quit their proper character, to assume what does not belong to them, are, for the greater part, ignorant both of the character they leave, and of the character they assume. Wholly unacquainted with the world in which they are so fond of meddling, and inexperienced in all its affairs, on which they pronounce with so much confidence, they have nothing of politics but the passions they excite. Surely, the Church is a place where one day's truce ought to be allowed to the dissensions and animosities of mankind."[8]

A present day demand on the preacher is that he discuss *social problems* in the pulpit. "A danger to which Protestantism in America is exposed," says Professor Shailer Mathews of the University of Chicago, "is that its churches shall become mere agents of social service." And Gregory writes in his *Trumpet Call to the Ministry*: "There are two modes of preaching in the present age that are diametrically opposed. The one presses the Gospel upon men as a saving power, aims at regeneration, and encourages spontaneous conformity to gospel principles. The other dwells constantly upon social and political questions, and attempts to lay down rules that shall govern the entire range of human activity, and to say to men everywhere and on every occasion, 'Thus shalt thou do, and thus.' The former is the method of the Reformation, and the true method of Protestant Christendom; the latter the method of the new reformers and the old Romanism. The one, as Paul teaches, carries the Church back to the covenant from Mount Sinai, which gendereth to bondage (Gal. 4:24), to ritual observance and legal obedience; the other carries her forward

---

[8]*Reflections on the French Revolution.*

to the covenant that is from Mount Zion, from the 'Jerusalem above which is free, which is the mother of us all,' and tends to free spiritual activity by bringing her members more thoroughly under the influence of love, the higher law of the spirit of liberty (see Rom. 8 and 13:8-10)." This is an admirable description of the fundamental difference between these two types. The sermon that makes social reform its chief contents turns the Gospel into a new Law and aims at changing the environment instead of the man.

To be sure, social problems—such as the conflict between "classes" and "masses," the problem of labor and wages, housing conditions, prohibition, the Sunday question, etc.—stand in the closest relation to religion and morality, and every Christian is bound, so far as he can, to assist in their solution. It is therefore the duty also of the sermon to clarify the judgment and sharpen the conscience of its hearers with respect to these questions. But this can be done most effectually, not by making social reform the subject-matter of the sermon, but by leading the individual members of the congregation, through the power of the divine Word, to the faith that worketh by love. Thus they will become willing and able to recognize and assume their duties in the social order and induce others to do the same. Christianity brought about a new order of things also in the social sphere, but it did this only as the love of Christ conquered the hearts of men and only in proportion as men submitted themselves to the Word of God. "The soul of all improvement is the improvement of the soul,"—this word of Horace Bushnell applies here also. And Dr. C. E. Jefferson says: "The way to christianize the social order is to christianize the souls of men." But this can be done only through the Word of God. The Presbyterian Dr. Howerton agrees with the Congregationalist Dr. Jefferson, and says even more clearly: "The Church as an organization cannot and ought not to engage in secular reforms, political or economic. She always makes mischief when she does so. She turns aside from her own proper mission, and at the same time violates the freedom of conscience of her members. The only real good the Church has ever done, in advancing such reforms, is by her influence in forming the character, the principles, and the motives of the men and women whose real business in life it is to engage in such services to business, to society, and the State. She can reform law by reforming the lawyers and judges. She can reform politics by reforming the politicians. She can reform business by reforming the business men. She can reform society by reforming social leaders, and in no other way."

Dr. Cunningham of England writes in his volume *Christianity and Social Questions*: "The Church, indeed, consists of men, each of whom as a citizen of an earthly kingdom is called upon to do his political duties, as well as his other duties in the name of the Lord Jesus. For ordinary purposes in ordinary life, it may not be important, or even perhaps possible, for a man to distinguish that which is incumbent on him as a citizen of an earthly realm from that which is incumbent upon him as a child in the family of God. But the distinction is of vast importance in regard to those who are called to office and ministry in Christ's Church. The terms of their commission lay down the limits of what they are to do by Christ's authority; they have no commission to put the affairs of society right, or to eradicate the evils in this present naughty world. In the Gospel of the grace of God, they have committed to them the supreme means of touching men personally and inspiring them with high but practical ideals. This is the grandest work to which any man can give himself; and it is a miserable thing if he fails to put his best energies into this task, and prefers instead to compete with journalists and politicians in guiding some project for social reform. It is to forsake the fountain of life and to strain at accomplishing some apparent improvement by taking up implements that are less certain and less effective, even for securing human welfare, than the means of grace instituted by Christ Himself. . . Christ sent His apostles on evangelistic work and bade them administer the sacraments and exercise pastoral care; but He did not enjoin them to agitate for social reforms." Herrick Johnson, the veteran professor of Homiletics, first in Auburn Theological Seminary, then at McCormick Theological Seminary, is in accord with this. He says: "Call the roll of the men of God who have cut wide swaths, who have been conspicuous as winners and builders of souls—Luther, Knox, Edwards, Whitefield, Robertson, Spurgeon, Finney, Maclaren, Hall, Moody and a multitude more—and see whether the men who have preached Christian ethics and Christian socialism and Christian civics, and made these and like topics central in their ministry, have been any match, in spiritual power and spiritual victories, for the men whose central theme has ever and conspicuously been Christ crucified! Did a Gospel of Christian socialism, or a Gospel of Christian ethical precepts, or a Gospel of educational culture ever turn any community upside down, or bring any great multitude to Christ, or make any Church a harvesting-place for souls? Never. They are impotency itself, in the presence of the god of this world ruling in an unregenerate heart. Are then a sociological Christ and an ethical Christ and a civic righteousness Christ of no value in the Gospel ministry? Of absolutely no value whatever except as they are adjuncts to the crucifixion—fringes on the robe of Christ's righteousness woven in the loom of suffering, side-lights to that central sun that flung out from Calvary its beams of light and life upon a world of darkness and death. Nothing but 'Christ crucified' is 'the power of God and the wisdom of God'."[9]

David James Burrell of New York, in his Sprunt Lectures, says: "The Gospel in its relation to society is like the atmosphere, which rests with an equable pressure of fifteen pounds or thereabouts to the square inch on every part of the human body. It touches and regenerates not only the individual but domestic, communal and political life." It is the *Gospel* he is speaking of, and he adds: "It begins with one man as centre and, as in concentric circles, spreads outwardly, driving out, by what Chalmers calls 'the expulsive power of a new affection,' all hurtful and iniquitous things. It is apparent, therefore, that the preacher becomes a true social reformer as far forth as he holds himself to the strict duty and privilege of preaching the Word."

The well-known Dr. J. H. Jowett, speaking in his book, *The Preacher*, about the broadening conception of the preacher's mission, writes: "Men may become so absorbed in social wrongs as to miss the deeper malady of personal sin. They may lift the rod of oppression and leave the burden of guilt. They may seem to correct social dislocation and overlook the awful disorder of the soul. It seems to me that some preachers have made up their minds to live in the Old Testament rather than in the New, and to walk with the prophets rather than with the apostles and evangelists." Alexander Maclaren of Manchester shows how education and reform are unable to cope with sin, which only God's Word can overcome. "God forbid," says he, "that I should not give full weight to all other methods for the partial reformation and the bettering of humanity. I would wish them all God-speed. But, brethren, there is nothing else that will deal with my sin in its relation to God, or in its relation to my future, except the message of the Gospel. There are plenty of other things, very hopeful and very good in their places, but I do want to say in one word that there is nothing else that goes deep enough. Education? Yes, it will do a great deal, but it will do nothing in regard to sin. It will alter the type of the disease, because the cultured man's transgressions will be very different from those of the illiterate boor.

---

[9] P. 76.

But wise or foolish, professor or student, thinker or savage with narrow forehead and all but dead brain, are alike in this, that they are sinners in God's sight. I would that I could get through the fence that some of you have reared around you, on the ground of your superior enlightenment and education and refinement, and make you feel that there is something deeper than all that, and that you may be a very clever and a very well educated, a very highly cultured, an extremely thoughtful and philosophical sinner, but you are a sinner all the same."

R. L. Dabney dwells on the permanent attraction which just such preaching of the divine Word alone exerts upon its hearers: "The pomps of a liturgical drama may attract occasional crowds to the cathedral of the ritualist. Party rage may for a time cause the multitude to throng the steps of the clerical demagogue; yet the permanent hold upon the popular mind and heart is possessed by the evangelical preacher. Sooner or later, the mere moralist, the Socinian, the political preacher, the philosophizer, the choir of ghostly pantomimists, are all seen performing to empty benches, while from age to age the multitude of Christians surrounds those who preach 'Christ and Him crucified.' May not even we perceive a reason for this? The conceit and self-love of the natural mind persuade the would-be pulpit philosopher that his newly-coined ideas are wondrously attractive, because they are bantlings of his own invention. Perhaps he is not fully aware of his own motive, but it is his intellectual vanity which selects them as his clerical hobbies. Now he forgets a very simple fact, that his hearers have toward these favorite topics not a particle of his pride of paternity. They are thoroughly conscious that they did not beget them; that they are the preacher's only. Hence he is perpetually disappointed by finding that he cannot sustain the enthusiasm of the people for his favorite topics. He never wearies of them; his hearers do. But God's topics, the fall, the curse, sin, death, immortality, duty, redemption, faith, hope, judgment, hell, heaven, these transcendent subjects have an abiding, an overmastering common interest. All men share it, because they are men. These assert their power over the human soul under every condition, and in spite of man's natural carnality, with a force akin to their vastness. Honor God then by urging no other truths than those He has given you, urging them with disinterested fidelity, and He will honor your ministry."[10]

---

[10] Pp. 46 f.

It is well known that modern theology advocates a weakening rather than a strengthening of the relation between the sermon and the Scriptures; so in the deliverances, for example, of O. Baumgarten. But these men operate with totally different conceptions of God, revelation, and the nature of religion, indeed with a fundamentally different definition of Christianity. We regard the New Testament as something more than merely the *"Urform* and elementary stage of Christianity," to which must be added "the entire historical development up to the present time," in order properly to understand "the whole of Christianity as a spiritual force, a complex of ideas, the power over life and its moods." For us Christ is the definitive culmination of God's revelation, and the New Testament is the trustworthy, authoritative and sufficient record and medium of this revelation. We refuse, therefore, to twist the New Testament to suit our "experience of life," but place ourselves unreservedly under its authority, in order to be brought by its power to a constantly growing inner experience of its divine fulness. As Burrell well puts it: "The so-called 'New Evangelism' is a misnomer, inasmuch as it has no evangel. It minimizes sin and sin's penalty; it sterilizes faith; it denatures the influence of the Holy Spirit; it puts dishonor on the blood of Calvary without which there is no remission of sin. But there is an evangelism, a genuine evangelism, which will never be out of date until the last revival shall sweep the last sinner into the kingdom of God." This evangel, this Word of God, is what we have to preach—nothing less, nothing more.

Thus we are brought back to our starting point, that nothing but God's Word can be the proper contents of the sermon. Herrick Johnson's praise of the Word may therefore fitly sum this part of our discussion. He says: "What want is there it cannot meet? What burden is there it cannot lighten, or help to bear, or take away? What sin is there for which it has not expiation and atonement? What sorrow is there it cannot heal? How its doctrine of God's fatherhood has brought the wandering prodigal back to his Father's house! How its doctrine of forgiveness has hushed feuds! How its uplifted cross has drawn men! How its divine ὀργή, thundered from the pulpit, has arrested some persecuting Saul, breathing out threatenings and slaughter, and led him to cry for mercy! How this sword of the Spirit, which is the Word of God, has cut clear through many a pharisaic refuge of lies and shown the whited sepulchre to be full of dead men's bones and all uncleanness! There is not a kind of man, or a state of heart, or a twist of conscience, or a sophistry of reason, or a pride of intellect, or a lust of the flesh, or a hell of hate, or a rottenness of social condition, to which the subject-matter of Holy Scripture has not made successful appeal."[11]

The above discussion has made it plain that the relation of the sermon to the Word of God is not yet sufficiently defined by saying that it must proclaim this Word. The heart and centre of the Word, as well as of the whole saving revelation of God, is Jesus Christ. The Old Testament points to Him as the coming one; the New Testament testifies of Him as come. To preach the Old Testament alone would be a deplorable relapse to the stage of pre-Christian preparation. God the Father can be known only through the Son, in whom He has revealed Himself;[12] the Holy Spirit speaks not of Himself but takes the things of Christ and declares them unto us.[13] If God, in all the fulness of His grace and truth, is to be brought to the souls of men by means of preaching, and if men are thus to know and appropriate Him for an ever completer communion between God and man, it is necessary that the sermon be Christocentric, have no one and nothing else for its centre and content than Christ Jesus. This is true not only of the missionary sermon as Paul practiced it,[14] but also of the sermon before the established congregation, as is clear from the whole epistolary literature of the New Testament, and as John expressly states at the close of his gospel.[15] Indeed, this follows of itself from the fundamental truth that a genuine Christian faith and life can exist only so long as it remains a daily appropriation of Christ.[16] "Believe on the Lord Jesus Christ," must ever be the watchword, until we ascend from faith to sight. The sermon must, therefore, continually placard Christ before

---

[11]*The Ideal Ministry*, p. 48.—[12]John 14:9; Matt. 11:27; John 8:19; 12:44; 1 John 2:23.—[13]John 16:13, 14.—[14]Gal. 3:1; 1 Cor. 2:2. —[15]John 20:30 f.—[16]Gal. 2:20; Rom. 1:17. John 2:11 compared with John 1:41, 45, 50.—Comp. M. Reu, *Heilsordnung* (Chicago, 1914), pp. 44 f.

its hearers' eyes and glorify Him before men;[17] otherwise it ceases to be a Christian sermon.

But Christ cannot be the content of the sermon as mere revealer of God's will to men, as teacher, prophet or exemplar. These sides of Him will indeed never be absent. The sermon will need to present the holy will of God as revealed by Christ, if it is to inculcate New Testament and not merely Old Testament morality, an evangelical and not a mere natural or legalistic piety. No other embodiment of the divine will can exert so strong an attraction upon men as its embodiment in the person and life of Christ. But the sermon of which Christ is the heart and centre must come nearer than this to the heart and centre of Christ. No one can so completely and reliably reveal the riches of the Father's will to salvation as the Only-begotten Son who is in the bosom of the Father. Whoever undertakes, therefore, to declare the saving will of God must bring to men the message of Christ concerning the Father in heaven. He can not omit from his message, notwithstanding the objections of modern theology, the miracles of Jesus, nor will he treat them as a mere nimbus round His person, but rather as the inner expression of His personality and as His proper works and "signs." As little will he conceal from his hearers the mystery of the person of Christ, as it is confessed in the Small Catechism,—"True God, begotten of the Father from eternity, and also true Man, born of the Virgin Mary." This will rather form the constant undercurrent of all his preaching, breaking forth again and again in unmistakable clearness and spontaneous adoration.

But the preacher will need to rise higher and to delve deeper even than this, if his sermon is to be truly Christocentric in the sense of Jesus Himself and of His great Apostle. It must be a witness to the Son of God who loved me

---

[17] John 16:14.

and gave Himself for me, in His whole life from the manger to the cross, and who rose on the third day and lives and reigns forever as Saviour and Lord.[18] Such preaching alone can produce faith, justifying and saving faith, which can have no other object than Jesus the Son of God, who gave His life a ransom for all. Christ crucified must ever be the alpha and omega, the heart and centre, the life and soul of the sermon; for nowhere else has God so fully revealed Himself as on the cross of Calvary, where, in order to declare Himself as both just and a justifier, He set forth Jesus as propitiation for the sins of the whole world.[19] Here is the glory of God in the face of Jesus Christ. Here the veil is completely rent in twain, and God bares to us His inmost heart. The sermon, if it is to set forth God as He really is, so that He may draw men to Himself, must present Him as the God who was in Christ reconciling the world to Himself.[20] Only then will the sinner venture to draw near to Him and rejoice in His salvation.

The preacher should, however, by no means permit himself to divorce the cross of Christ from His life, teaching, and works, as preachers of the "old faith" were not without reason accused of doing. He will on the contrary find in the cross of Christ a "summary" of His whole life—not indeed in Ritschl's sense, but as the apex and culmination of the lifelong work and sacrifice whereby He obtained our redemption in accordance with the divine council, a culmination without which His life would remain incomplete and its purpose unattained.

If the foregoing is true, then the sermon becomes a testimony of sin and grace,—since the Fall and Protevangel, the two chief factors in the relation between God and man,—a testimony of the sin-forgiving grace of God in Christ. This

---

[18]Gal. 2:20; Matt. 20:28; John 10:11, 15, 17 f.; Matt. 26:28; Rom. 8:34; 4:23-25.—[19]Rom. 3:25 f.; 1 John 2:2.—[20]2 Cor. 5:19.

makes the sermon, on the one hand, a testimony of the holiness of God, which punishes and condemns the sinner; for the cross of Calvary is the supreme revelation of God's wrath upon sin. In this sense it must proclaim the law; for law is, in dogmatic usage, whatever commands, uncovers sin, punishes, or declares God's wrath and judgment. The sermon thus becomes a mighty incentive to a new and God-pleasing life, to sanctification and the imitation of Christ. For it was God's purpose in our redemption to produce a new humanity zealous of good works;[21] and gratitude for the forgiveness received forbids us to continue in the old life of sin. The centre of the sermon will, however, always be the Gospel, i. e., the testimony of the grace of God, forgiving sin and conferring righteousness; for "the law was given by Moses, but grace and truth came by Jesus Christ."[22]

This was clearly seen in the Reformation, after the Middle Ages had turned the New Testament into a *nova lex*, Christ into a second Moses, and the sermon into a preaching of law. It is its testimony of the forgiving and life-giving grace of God in Christ, that assigns to the sermon its place in the sacramental part of the service and gives it the character of a general absolution. In this sense Luther says of it: "It is a definition of the office of preaching to say that we are to proclaim the Gospel of Christ and forgive the sins of contrite and timid consciences, but to retain their sins unto the impenitent and secure and to bind them. If a sermon does not do this, it is not a right preaching of Christ, and such preachers are not sent by Him. . . . . The right priesthood is to preach the Gospel, that is nothing else than a public sermon of the grace and forgiveness of God, which Christ Himself commanded to be everywhere publicly proclaimed, and to be bestowed upon all who believe in Him." (P. 65.)

---

[21]Titus 2:14; 1 Pet. 2:24.—[22]John 1:17.

Emphasis was laid now and then, in the Middle Ages, upon the Scriptures as the proper source of the sermon. Hieronymus Dungersheim writes in his *Tractatus de modo dicendi et docendi ad populum sacra seu de modo praedicandi* (1514): "If preachers wish to be shepherds of Christ's flock, God's Word furnishes them the sole meadow and pasture; if they wish to be physicians of the soul, God's Word furnishes the one medicine; if laborers in the Lord's vineyard, God's Word is the well from which to draw water; if spiritual leaders, God's Word is the sword they must know how to wield, in order to repulse all enemies. How then can they perform their task without thorough understanding of the Word and diligent study and practice in the art of using it aright?" But even for the greatest theologians of that time the Word of God was merely directive, nothing but precept and law; they had not as yet grasped its living center, Jesus Christ, whereby alone the Word becomes Evangel, or glad tidings. Luther could justly say of the sermons he heard during his student years at Erfurt, that there was not a single "Christian" sermon among them. The new and reformatory feature of Luther's preaching was his discovery, in the Scriptures, of Christ and the Gospel, which he made henceforth the contents of his sermons. As early as in his *Lectures on Romans*, delivered in 1515-16, he treated the Word of God as *nuntius bonus* because it "brought Christ." In increasing measure Christ became the heart and soul of all his preaching, up to the end. "All our sermons," said he later, "have this purpose, that you and we may believe Christ is the only Saviour and hope of the world, the shepherd and bishop of our souls; for the whole Gospel points to Christ, as did the witness of St. John (John 1:8, 29). Hence we do not draw men to ourselves, but lead them to Christ, who is the way, the truth and the life. All those who preach and testify, not of Christ, but of themselves, are false teachers." What he meant by preaching Christ is clearly expressed in the dedication of the winter series of his *Church Postil* to Duke Albrecht of Mansfeld, where he says over against the preaching of the Middle Ages: "It is an evil custom to treat the gospels and epistles as books of law, from which we should teach what men ought to do and present the works of Christ as nothing more than so many examples or illustrations. . . . Beware of turning Christ into a Moses, as if He had nothing more for us than precept and example, like the other saints. . . . You should interpret the word, work and suffering of Christ in the following two ways: First, as examples proposed to you for your imitation, as St. Peter shows, 1 Peter 2:21; so that when you see Him praying, fasting, or helping and showing love to men, you should do the same with respect to yourself and your neighbor. But that is the least important side of the Gospel and does not yet stamp it as Gospel; for in such works Christ is of no more use to you than any of the saints. His life stays with Him and profits you nothing. In short, this mode of preaching makes never a Christian, but only hypocrites. You must rise much higher than that, although this best sort of preaching has been practiced but little these many years. The chief and fundamental thing in the Gospel is this, that before you take Christ as your example, you recognize and accept Him as God's gift to you; so that when you see or hear Him in any of His work or suffering, you do not doubt but believe that He, Christ Himself, with such work or suffering of His, is most truly your very own, whereon you may rely as confidently as if you had done that work or endured that suffering, nay, as if you were yourself that Christ. See, this is to understand aright the Gospel, that is, the infinite grace of God, which no prophet, apostle or angel could ever wholly express, nor any heart sufficiently admire or comprehend. This is the mighty fire of God's love toward us whereby He makes the conscience confident, joyful and content. This is to preach the Christian faith. This it is that makes our preaching a Gospel, viz., glad, good, comfortable tidings . . . When you open this book of the Gospel and read or hear that Christ comes to this or that place, or that someone is brought to Him, you are to understand this to mean the sermon or good news by which He comes to you or you are brought to Him. For the preaching of the Gospel is nothing else than Christ's coming to you or your being brought to Him." When Christ comes to a soul through the sermon, there rises *die allerliebste Sonne,* which "brings life, joy, activity, and every good thing" (On Romans 13:11-14.) Then the night is past and the bright day begins; for "to preach the Gospel means to point poor troubled consciences to Christ and comfort them, and to make glad fearful hearts sunk in gloom and woe." "Hence the Gospel is a gracious and blessed instruction and comforting message; as if a rich man promised a thousand *gulden* to a poor beggar. That would be for him a joyful piece of news, which he would greatly rejoice to hear. But what is money or property compared with this comfortable and gracious message, that Christ succors the needy and is a king willing to assist poor sinners, held captive under the law, to gain everlasting life and righteousness?" (On Matthew 11:2-10; A. D. 1531.) "What will the day [that dawns in our life when Jesus comes into it] manifest to us? It will teach us all things: concerning God, ourselves, the past, the future, concerning hell, earth, angels, devils. We shall see what is our duty in and toward all these, whence we come and whither we go." (On Romans 13: 11-14.) Macaulay's words are well known,—"Logicians may reason about abstractions, but the great mass of mankind never feel the least interest in them. They must have images. God, the uncreated, invisible, the uncomprehensible, attracted few worshipers. It was before Deity embodied in human form, walking among men, partaking of their infirmities, leaning on their bosoms, weeping over their graves, slumbering in the manger, bleeding on the cross, that the prejudices of the synagogue and the doubts of the academy and the pride of the portico and the fasces of the lictors and the swords of thirty legions were humbled in the dust." But Luther's words go to the mark straighter: "Only in Christ have we God for our God; outside of Christ He is a consuming fire," and, "I find God nowhere save in Christ alone."[23] That is why the sermon must be Christocentric, the preaching of Christ and Him crucified; so that men may not flee from God but hide themselves in Him. Much of the preaching in our day, even in evangelical pulpits, is struck to a lower key. It is Christ to be sure, but not Christ crucified. It deals much with the life of Christ, in its tender human sympathies— "the Christ whose face was sculptured benevolence, whose hand was friendship's symbol, whose eye was liquid sympathy for all human burdens and woes; much with the works of Christ as the pattern and inspiration of all helpful doing; much with the words of Christ as a divine philosophy, with heights to which no human imagination has ascended, depths which no human plummet has fathomed and breadths which no human mind has compassed." This is all very well as far as it goes. We may even add that the preaching of our day, and the research of our day, tracing as they do the life and ministry of the "historical Jesus," have emphasized many details in the portrait of Christ that were overlooked or kept in the background. But if that is the sole aim of preaching, it runs the danger of making central such features as "are incidental rather than essential, ephemeral rather than eternal, facts rather than truths, mere chippings, as it were, from the grand corner-stone on which is reared the everlasting and ever glorious superstructure of divine glory and human redemption."[24] More than that, these historical details, valuable as they are in themselves, lose their inner truth when they are treated as features in the life of a man self-deluded as to His true mission and future. Inseparable from

---

[23]Thomasius, *Dogmengeschichte*, ii, p. 573.—[24]Kerr Boyce Tupper.

the picture of Christ as portrayed in the New Testament, are His suffering, death and resurrection on our behalf. His life on earth began only to culminate in these acts. The truth of this is seen in the altogether disproportionate space assigned in the gospels to the story of the passion, John devoting well-nigh one half of his gospel to the events of the last two days. The passion and resurrection are the holy of holies into which the evangelists deliberately lead their readers. Here especially they are to learn how the Son of God obtained for them an eternal redemption. The same is true of all the Scriptures. "The cross," says Herrick Johnson, "the blood, the death, the propitiation, the sacrifice, the crucifixion—surely, it is upon this the Word of God throws the tremendous emphasis. Everywhere in the Scriptures the cross is lifted up; every page is splashed with the blood. Look where we may, we find a sign-board pointing to Calvary and the Crucifixion. The four great facts in the gospel record—the Incarnation, the Resurrection, the Ascension and the Intercession of Jesus Christ—that form what may well be called the gospel quadrangle—have at their center an uplifted cross. They face that cross, point to that cross, have no worth and no significance apart from that cross." Tupper observes how the whole Old Testament points to Christ the crucified, without whom it would remain unfulfilled:—"He reads this grand old Book amiss, who fails to see running, like a thread of gold, through all its warp and woof—through genealogy, type, prophecy, psalm, and history, both national and individual—the glorious doctrine of redemption through a future Messiah, slain from the foundation of the world."

It was not the preaching of Jesus as mere man, as transcendent personality, that conquered the world, but the preaching of the passion of Christ, with its blood, but also with its blessed peace. And the preaching that founded the Church must preserve and extend it. The Church cannot live without hearing constantly the word, "Behold the Lamb of God, that taketh away the sin of the world." She entreats her preachers to tell it to her again and again. She does not consist of saints who have passed beyond sin and the need of redemption. She is the poor flock of Christ and has in her midst so many erring souls who have lost sight of Christ because they turned away to sin. But they have not lost sight of the fact that their way is a way of darkness and that the flowers of their prayer lie withered on the ground. Their strength has failed and they cannot rise. But it would bring them to their feet, could they but hear in their hearts this cry, "Behold the Lamb of God", could they be assured that there is salvation for such as they. The message of the cross and the crucified would help where all else failed. And for the weak soul, realizing the challenge of the Christian life and desirous of responding but not knowing how, the one source of strength is the cross of Christ and the Christ of the cross. The preacher's model may well be that old Church father who said, "Were the highest heaven my pulpit and the whole host of the redeemed my audience and eternity my day, Jesus Christ would be my theme."—"Christ the God," Tupper reminds his brethren in the ministry, "Christ the man, Christ the God-man, the dying Christ, the risen Christ, the reigning Christ, Christ the end of the law to every one that believeth—of all the themes that inspire human hearts and fire human lips, this alone is sufficient to magnify the name of God, exalt the divine Son, convict and convert human souls and transform a Paradise Lost with all its blight and woe into a Paradise Regained with all its celestial songs and eternal triumphs."

Nor need anyone fear that such preaching of Christ and Him crucified can ever grow monotonous. "This will be," as Herrick Johnson well says, "the apprehension only of him who has failed of comprehending the cross of Christ in its relation to God, and eternity, and the divine law, and the human soul, and duty, and destiny. The maturest and ablest men in the Christian ministry will testify with tears of delight and thanksgiving that the gracious mystery of redemption by the cross has evermore grown before the vision of their reverence and love until it has filled all things with its mournful, holy and infinite glory. Preaching Christ monotonous? Then infinite variety is monotonous."[25]

(2) THE SERMON IN ITS RELATION TO THE CONGREGATION AND THE CHURCH

We have seen that the sermon is the proclamation of the Word of God in its essential content,—Jesus Christ and Him crucified. This proclamation is made by the properly appointed minister acting as instrument of the congregation. On the one hand, the mouthpiece and spokesman of God, he

[25] The student is referred to the sermon on "The Pre-eminence of the Atonement," delivered in 1859 by Edwards A. Park at the consecration of Broadway Tabernacle, New York (printed in F. Barton's *Pulpit Power and Eloquence*, 1901).

is on the other hand the mouthpiece and spokesman of the congregation. The congregation, invested as it is with the sacred office, speaks and preaches through the minister. In this aspect of the sermon, therefore, as in the former, we are dealing with an act of the congregation as such. Now this Word which the congregation administers is not something foreign to her and lying outside of her, but something she has appropriated as an intimate part of herself. In her public administration of the Word she praises God who gave her this precious treasure, and she proclaims it to men. She proclaims it as Word of God living in her life and experience. Thus her proclamation becomes a testimony or witness. It becomes a testimony to the grace and power of God experienced in her own life; a testimony setting forth the praise of His wonderful works, and of His holy and morally perfect nature, in accordance with which it is His will to make man holy. It becomes a sacrifice of praise and thanksgiving to the Lord, revealing Himself in His Word—in its essential content, Christ crucified—as gracious and merciful, as holy love. This is the sacrificial side of the sermon, emphasized already by Luther when he says: "The preaching of the Gospel is *sacrificium laudis*, that is, a giving of thanks, whereby we confess with gratitude to God that we have this treasure of the Word." Again: "When I preach I do it in praise of our Lord God, that I may perform this morning and this evening sacrifice. Preaching is the highest form of sacrifice, for whoever preaches aright must needs praise the Lord our God." The correctness of this position becomes the clearer when we bear in mind the one content of the sermon, as described above. How can the believing congregation bear witness of Christ without breaking forth in praise and thanksgiving for the revelation He has made to it? (P. 68.)

Luther regarded the sermon as *sacrificium laudis* not only on the part of the preacher but of the whole congregation or church, as we see from the following two quotations. The first is from a consecration sermon preached at Torgau in 1544, in which he said: "My preaching in the assembly of the congregation is not my own word and act, but is done in behalf of you all and of the entire Church. There must needs be one person to speak and utter the Word in the name and with the consent of the rest; but the rest by their attention to the Word consent to and take part in the preaching. The same thing is true when a child is baptized. It is not the pastor alone who performs the act, but no less the sponsors and witnesses and indeed the whole Church. For baptism, as well as the Word and Christ Himself, is the common possession of all Christians. So, too, all pray, sing and give thanks together, and none has or does any of these things for himself alone, but what each one has belongs to all the rest." The second quotation is from *Von der Winkelmesse und Pfaffenweihe* (1533). Here he is speaking of the Lord's Supper, but what he says applies necessarily also to preaching:—"God be praised, in our churches we can show to every Christian a right and Christian mass, according to the ordinance and institution of Christ, and according to the true intention of Christ and the Church. Our pastor, bishop, or minister,— properly and publicly called to his office, but previously consecrated, anointed and born as a priest of Christ in his baptism, without any *Winkelchresem*—goes to the altar, and intones audibly and distinctly the order of service as Christ appointed it in the Lord's Supper: he takes the bread and the wine, gives thanks, and distributes them by virtue of Christ's words, 'This is my body, this is my blood; this do ye, etc.' He distributes them to the rest of us who are present and desire to partake, and we, especially those of us who desire to commune, kneel beside, behind and about him—man and wife, young and old, master and servant, mistress and maid, as God brings us together—all of us true and holy fellow-priests, sanctified by Christ's blood and anointed by the Holy Spirit and consecrated in baptism. And we are there by virtue of this our innate and inherited priestly pomp and dignity, with our golden crowns upon our heads (as represented in Rev. 4), harps in our hands and golden censers. Nor do we let our pastor say the service of Christ alone and for his own person; but he is the mouthpiece of us all, and all of us say it with him in our hearts, our faith lifted up with his to the Lamb of God, who is for us and present with us and feeds us, according to His words, with His body and blood. That is our mass, and the right mass, which does not deceive us."

The life of the congregation, so far as it is lived in the Word, is reflected in the sermon, and not only the life of the individual congregation but of the Church of which the congregation forms a part. Sometimes it becomes necessary for the preacher to oppose to the majority in the local congregation the religious experience of the Church at large; in this way alone can he remain the representative of God and of the congregation of genuine believers. Thus the sermon, besides being the mirror of the faith and life of the Church in general and of the particular congregation, becomes a mirror of the hindrances to this life which the sermon must constantly encounter until they are overcome by the Word.

It is therefore a distinct advance that historians have begun to include in their portrayal of the religious-ecclesiastical life of a period the homiletical literature of that period. Victor Schultze (*Altchristliche Staedte und Landschaften*, i: *Constantinopel*, 1913), for example, could not have given so accurate an account of church, state and society in Constantinople between 324 and 450, without making as full use as he did of the rich sermonic literature of the period, especially the sermons of Chrysostom. The rapid decline of genuine Christianity in Asia Minor is readily understood after an examination of the bombastic orations and fulsome funeral eulogies of the great Cappadocians. And how can the condition of the Church at the close of the Middle Ages be adequately described without drawing upon the contemporary sermon? The historian of the future desiring to account for the sudden change that took place in the public opinion of America during the last years of the World War, will do well not to overlook the sermon of that period.

This gives the sermon its *confessional* character. For the spiritual life produced in the Church by the Word takes invariably a confessional tinge. The expression of this life in the sermon must therefore bear the marks of the respective confession. This is not an arbitrary requirement, but is on the contrary natural and self-evident, growing out of the relation between the sermon and the Word as apprehended by the Church. A sermon without confessional stamp is colorless, while a sermon that actually contradicts the confession of the

Church is a disturbing element in the service, denying what is elsewhere confessed in creed, hymn and formulated prayer. Far be it from us to advocate a self-assertive or condemnatory confessionalism in the sermon; what is needed is confessional clearness and definiteness as a fundamental attitude of the preacher. In this sense, the demand for the confessional character of the sermon conforms to the distinctive nature of the Lutheran Church, which is neither so narrowly biblical as to become unhistorical nor so historical and traditional as to sacrifice the authority of the Word of God. (P. 74.)

Confession is the correlative and necessary expression of living faith. Where there is genuine faith in the heart, it will spontaneously and of necessity utter itself in confession.[1] And since the Church is the communion of believers, founded by the Holy Spirit through Word and sacrament, it too will need to confess its faith and publicly express its unity by means of a common creed. Thus the Church has been from the beginning a believing and confessing Church.[2] It could not be otherwise. The same necessity exists today with respect to the various denominational groups into which in the course of time the Church has been divided. They must confess their faith, and they must do this in the particular forms which this faith has assumed as a result of their understanding of the Scriptures and their experience of the truth. If any group were to set aside and ignore these forms as unimportant, it would thereby deny its right to a separate existence. But if it is necessary to hold fast to these confessions, they will naturally find expression in the service, which is the utterance and representation of the congregation's life of faith. Kolde therefore holds that the cultus, or service, of the various churches is an important source for ascertaining the confessional position of the several groups. In this service, as we have seen, the sermon plays a chief role. If the whole service must bear a confessional character, this is certainly true also of the sermon.

The truth of this, so far as the distinction between *Protestantism* and *Romanism* is concerned, is conceded by all; the fundamental differences are too apparent. In practice, however, these differences are often overlooked. This is the case especially when, in preaching, morality is severed from its root in justification by faith, and when

---

[1] Rom. 10:10; 2 Cor. 4:13; Heb. 4:14.—[2] 1 Tim. 6:12.

the position is held (in whatever *nuance*) that man becomes good by doing good. This is the Romish way of salvation, and mediaeval morality Such preaching gives Rome no offence; it is rather welcomed as a preparation for its own position, as flesh of its flesh and bone of its bone. We saw above[3] how closely the "social sermon" approaches the Romish view. The Roman invasion of so-called Protestant pulpits of our land is becoming a growing menace.

Ought the differences between the *Lutheran Church and the Reformed* family of Churches to find expression in the sermon? This is sometimes denied, in view of the fundamental agreement of these two groups in their conception of faith and the way of salvation. A true Lutheran will, indeed, devoutly thank God for the many treasures of evangelical truth in the Reformed confessions, and will gladly acknowledge all who sincerely accept this truth and live according to it as his brethren in Christ and members of the true Church. But he would prove unfaithful to his convictions and deny his Church the right to exist, if he regarded the distinction between it and the Reformed group as negligible and too unimportant to find expression, negatively or positively, in the preaching of his Church.

It is certainly not a matter of indifference whether the Christian life is presented as controlled by an arbitrary decree of predestination, precluding an objectively founded assurance of salvation, or on the other hand as leading necessarily, in consequence of the stress laid upon the objective means of grace, to such assurance; whether God's omnipotent majesty or His fatherly grace is set in the foreground. It is not a matter of indifference whether the Word is preached as the mere revelation of the divine will, independently of which the Spirit works where and when He listeth, or on the contrary as actual means and bearer of this Spirit. Whether baptism is conceived as having placed the hearers of the sermon in communion with God and as forming the basis of their entire life in Christ, or as merely a ceremony, divinely instituted indeed, but without any fundamental relation to their Christian development. Whether the Lord's Supper is regarded as consisting in mere bread and wine, bringing home so forcibly to the believer the blessings of his salvation that he soars in spirit to heaven and there feeds on Christ, or on the contrary as "the real body and blood of Christ, under the bread and wine, given unto us Christians to eat and to drink, as it was instituted by Christ." It does make a difference whether the preaching of morality is con-

---

[3]Page 17.

trolled by the Old or by the New Testament, by legal or by evangelical principles; whether motivated by puritanic ideals or by the ideal of Paul in 1 Cor. 3:22; 1 Tim. 4:4; Col. 2:16 f., plus 1 Cor. 8 and 9. Whether the ethical sermon is bound by Paul's word in Rom. 10:4 (in nowise contradicting Gal. 3:24 or Rom. 7:7-13), and appreciates Luther's bold word concerning our liberty even from the Decalogue,[4] or on the contrary binds its hearers again under the Old Testament yoke. Whether the preacher takes seriously the saying of Jesus in Matt. 7:18 as fundamental to all Christian ethics, and follows Luther in making the application to everyday life,[5] or on the other hand imagines that the moral life can have value before God without flowing with inner necessity from a regenerate heart. It does matter whether the sermon is controlled by the thought of the founding of a theocracy upon earth, and thus meddles in political matters, or by the principle of the complete separation of Church and State. Whether it looks to legislation to maintain law and order, or to the Gospel with its miraculous power.

---

[4]"Images and the Sabbath, as well as all other precepts of Moses, which he put forth over and above the natural law, because he had not the natural law, are matters of freedom. They are abolished and put away, and pertain solely to the Jewish people. Just as an emperor or king sets up particular laws and statutes for his own land, such as the *Sachsenspiegel* in Saxony, while the natural and common laws remain in force throughout all lands,—e. g., to honor parents, not to kill, not to commit adultery, to serve God, etc. Even so we should regard Moses as the Jews' *Sachsenspiegel*, which has nothing to do with us Gentiles. France does not respect the *Sachsenspiegel*, and yet agrees with it on the basis of the natural law. Why then do we teach the Ten Commandments? Because nowhere else are the natural laws so finely and so logically summarized as in Moses."—*Wider die himmlischen Propheten.*

[5]"Believers are a new creation, a new tree. Hence none of the terms used in the law apply in their case, such as, e. g., that the believer shall do good works. We do not say the sun *shall* shine, a good tree *shall* produce good fruit, three and seven *shall* make ten. The sun *must* not shine, it does this unbidden and by nature, for it was created for this purpose. A good tree produces good fruit of its own accord; three and seven already make ten and do not need a command. The question is not, what *should* be or be done, but what already *is* and *is being* done. To be sure, you might make the distinction and say, if it be a sun it must shine; if you are a believer you must do good works. But that is the way we speak of a counterfeit faith or a counterfeit sun; to say it of actual faith or of the actual sun would be absurd."—*Weimar Ed.*, xxii, 71.

So far nothing at all has been said of the many differences among the various subdivisions in the Reformed family of Churches, all of which bear more or less directly on the sermon. So for instance, the emphasis on a particular method of conversion or a particular mode of baptism; the depreciation of baptism owing to a belief in the natural innocence of childhood; the dream of sinless perfection, in opposition to Paul's word and example in Phil. 3: 12 f., the neglect of Christian education, etc. Can the sermon really be an essential part of the cultus of any of these communions and remain silent concerning their differences? If it can, then the religious life of these communions and of their preachers must indeed be without definite color or character and completely cut off from all historical development—an artificial return to a condition of things which never existed in reality and never can exist. The question then arises, why such congregations and preachers should still retain their connection with this or that historical form of Christianity.[6]

Whither the unconfessional sermon leads may be plainly seen in modern unionistic tendencies, looking to the amalgamation of all Protestant forces and the consequent abolition of confessional distinctions and the reduction of the Gospel to a number of universal religious concepts and ethical rules. Thus the heart is torn from the Gospel of the grace of God in Jesus Christ, and we arrive at a purely natural religion and natural morality. *Principiis obsta, vestigia terrent.* Our faithfulness to the truth as committed to us will of itself affix to our religious life, and to its expression in the sermon, a confessional stamp. If I have become convinced of the truth of the Lutheran position, for example, does not this truth deserve to be openly and courageously expressed also in the pulpit? Can I live and move in this truth and yet suppress it in the very place where I stand as divinely authorized witness to the truth? Sound doctrine is just as important today as it was in Paul's day, who so strongly emphasized it in the pastoral epistles, and as it was in Luther's day, who dedicated his life to its service. Pure teaching is as necessary for the life and health of the soul as pure air for the life and health of the body.

This is one of the reasons why the Lutheran Church has set up the rule: Lutheran pulpits for Lutheran preachers, and why she dislikes to see her preachers in the pulpits of other denominations. The

---

[6]The formerly Unitarian Church of the Messiah, New York, the Rev. John Haynes Holmes, pastor, calls itself, in utter freedom, "The Church of All Nations."

sermon of non-Lutheran preacher cannot be expected to be a representation of the religious life of a Lutheran congregation, nor can a Lutheran sermon serve as expression of the religious life of a non-Lutheran congregation; when the attempt is made, the inner truth of the sermon as well as the truthfulness of the preacher cannot but suffer.

Nevertheless, the sermon, as expression of the confessionally determined religious life of the Church, dare never degenerate into the weapon of a bigoted and heretic-baiting *confessionalism.* In this way, too, it would become a disturbing factor in the service. The Church cannot live by negations, however great a necessity "sound doctrine" may be. Least of all dare she foster in her midst a censorious and judging temper. The clear and positive presentation of the truth must be the rule, and this will accomplish more than all polemics or apologetics. Where it becomes a duty to oppose an erroneous position, this should not be done with a view to condemning those who hold that position or of pillorying them as disobedient to God's Word and enemies of the truth,—in short, not with a view to diverting attention from the matter under discussion to the representatives of opposing views, —but in order, by way of contrast, to bring the congregation to a fuller apprehension of the truth itself.

On the other hand, the habit of constantly alluding to Luther and the fondness for boasting of the mighty past, the splendid present and the still more glorious future of the Lutheran Church, so prevalent in certain quarters, are by no means in themselves the hallmarks of a genuinely Lutheran sermon. They conduce to a smug superficiality, rather than to that true inwardness that must go hand in hand with a soundly confessional sermon and life.

Alfred Krauss, the admirable Reformed homilete, writes on this point as follows: "Religion as such, even Christianity as such, is, to employ a hackneyed simile, as much a pure abstraction as fruit as such, which can exist in reality only as apple, plum, pear, etc., but never as mere fruit. All cultus is determined by confessional peculiarities and is hence as unpalatable to some as it is satisfying to others. The value we attach to the sermon is in itself an evangelical-confessional position. It would be surprising if this confessional element were not to become evident in its tone and manner. The stronger not only the confessional but the religious consciousness is, the more spontaneous will be its confessional expression. Such naive, original and involuntary confessionalism, as a rule, refreshes and captivates the heart. Beyond these limits however, the confessional element in the sermon ought not to go. As soon as it attacks other confessions it forsakes the sphere of homiletics and enters that of missions. In the service, in which those of kindred mind are gathered, it is only by way of exception that occasions to oppose other confessions will arise. And even when this is the case,—as on the festival of the Reformation or anniversaries of prominent men of God,—anything that smacks of theological controversy is out of place. On such occasions the festival spirit should prevail, and this cannot be achieved by polemics. . . . The fanatically inclined will indeed never miss an opportunity to indulge in confessional polemics; but the preacher who is concerned about the things that make for peace and edification will be content to preach as no one of another confession could possibly preach, yet without constantly making prominent the sharp point or the cutting edge. But when it becomes necessary to give confessional differences a place in the sermon, the proper treatment will always be to take the positive truth as one's point of departure and pay only so much attention to the negative position as is inevitably demanded by the presentation of the positive. This follows from the cultus character of the sermon. It is for the present, not the absent, and the former are to be regarded, especially on festival occasions, as persons not to be converted but to be the more firmly grounded. Since their edification can be attained only by a heightening of their confessional consciousness, our Church would indeed possess an essentially negative character, if the confessional consciousness could be satisfied with no other nourishment than polemics. References to opposing positions will indeed be unavoidable, yet never for the purpose of vilifying the opponents, but rather of setting one's position in a clearer light."[7]

(3) THE SERMON IN ITS RELATION TO THE PREACHER AS ORGAN OF THE CONGREGATION AND OF THE CHURCH

The Church, as well as the individual congregation, bears witness in the sermon to the Word of God contained in the Scriptures, as apprehended and experienced by her in the course of her history and to be experienced anew in ever increasing measure. But she bears this witness through her organ or agent, the preacher. He dare not be a lifeless instru-

---

[7]*Homiletik*, 186 f.

ment, a wooden fingerpost, with no living relation to his message, a mere courier bearing a strange and unknown message. On the contrary, as the Word he preaches has become a living power in the congregation and entered into its experience, so it must be for him also the living and powerful Word of God. It must have been received by him in faith and have become wedded to his personality, producing in him a new life. His preaching, like the service of which it forms an integral part, must be the expression and presentment of the religious life within him. As the centre of the Word is Christ crucified and His saving grace, so to the preacher's soul Christ must be all in all and His saving grace have entered into his experience. What is the good of all his Bible knowledge and skill of interpretation, the correctness of his Christian ideas, the artistic structure and beauty of style of his sermons, if there be not felt through it all the throb of personal religious life?

Not that this personal life is to form the contents of his sermon or the source from which he draws his material. That would amount finally to a preaching of himself instead of Christ. But this personal life is the necessary prerequisite and constant accompaniment of every sermon. Nor is it the preacher's faith that gives to the Word of God its vital power. That would run counter to John 5:39,[1] as well as to the Lutheran conception of the objective efficacy of the means of grace. Nevertheless it is true that the Word of God unfolds its inherent power in a very different manner when it is united with a living personality whom it has gripped in his inmost heart and from whose lips it pours as living testimony.

It is the nature of the human mind, that it is most powerfully and permanently influenced by the immediate touch of person upon person. And it is the nature of the divine

---

[1] Referring to the life-giving power of the Scriptures as such, apart from their use by a preacher.

Word, that it seeks a human personality in which to embody itself and reveal to the full its inner vital force. When the Word finds and becomes embodied in a preacher, his personality becomes to his hearers a guaranty of the power of the Word to perform what it promises. The Word of God and the spirit of man belong together, in Harnack's fine saying, as seed and soil belong together. It is only when this seed of the Word falls into a man's heart and transforms and renews from within his whole life, that we discover its latent life-power. The Word proclaimed by such a personality awakens confidence in others and is the more readily received by them. Luther will have had this in mind when he said, "The devil cares not a whit for the written Word; but when we speak it and preach it he takes to his heels." Likewise the older dogmaticians, when they applied the *efficacia verbi* specially to the Word as preached.

The preacher must therefore experience what the psalmist and the apostle say of themselves,—"I believed, therefore have I spoken."[2] Otherwise he will become sounding brass and a tinkling cymbal; he will preach to others, and himself become a castaway. But when he surrenders his heart to the Word and becomes a living witness of the same, there will be an end of all reciting of memorized doctrines and the parrot-like repetition of scholastic formulas; almost imperceptibly a new vigor will steal into his discourse and a new virtue will go out from it. Speaking from the depths of his own heart, he will find the way to other hearts and become to them a fountain of living water.

This is nothing strange or peculiar to preaching. The same thing holds true in other spheres of life. Whoever undertakes to convince others must have a living conviction within himself. Horace's dictum is well known,—

---

[2] Ps. 116:10; 2 Cor. 4:13.

> *Si vis me flere, dolendum est*
> *Primum ipsi tibi.*

It finds a modern echo in Dante Gabriel Rossetti's "Song-Throe":

> By thine own tears thy song must tears beget,
> O Singer! Magic mirror hast thou none
> Except thy manifest heart; and save thine own
> Anguish or ardor, else no amulet.

Here lay the roots of the noble popularity of Wordsworth, as William Watson has so truly sung of his simple verse,—

> Right from the heart, right to the heart it sprang.

So, too, Erasmus writes in his *Ecclesiastes* (lib. i, 26): *Ardere prius est, lucere posterius. Ardor mentis est lux doctrinae.* And in lib. iii, 53, he applies this directly to the preacher: *Tantum repetam . . . . nihil esse efficacius ad concitandos pios affectus, quam si ipse fueris pie affectus, neque quidquam utilius ad sedandos improbos affectus, quam ipse fueris ab his alienus.* This it is that imparts to man's speech its captivating power,[3] as we see it in its perfection in the words of Him who spake as never man spake. (P. 83.)

The preparation under Charlemagne, and later in the Reformation period in England, of *homiliaria*, collections of sermons to be read to the congregations, though demanded by the condition of the times, was not an unmixed blessing for the development of preaching. It not only prevented originality of thought, but gave rise to a mechanical and external conception of the art of preaching with little need for the participation of the inward man. This was especially the case when the selfsame sermons were read year in and year out. The sermon, to be true to its real nature, must be a part of the inmost life of the preacher—the proclamation indeed of the Word of God, but of the Word of God as apprehended by and passed through the faith of the preacher.

The words of Jesus were the expression of His unique and intimate communion with the Father; hence He regarded Himself as witness.[4] The disciples were sent out to testify of what they had seen

---

[3] Cf. Acts 26:24.—[4] John 3:11 f.; Matth. 11:27; John 10:15; 14:10; 17:21, 25.

with their eyes and heard with their ears and experienced in their souls.⁵ The sermon of today must likewise be a testimony and witness of what the preacher, through the Spirit, has experienced. This is what Claus Harms meant when he demanded a "speaking with tongues." The same thing was emphasized by Tholuck out of his abundant experience. On this point Cremer, Braun, Christlieb, Harnack, and all modern homileticians of every tendency are agreed.

"The specific blessing," says Braun, "that attaches to the sermon, over and above the reading of the Scriptures, consists in this that the witness of the apostles is revived in a living fashion in a man of today. The congregation is deprived of this blessing if the preacher merely reproduces the words of the Bible by means of his natural powers, without making his mind a focus in which the truths of Scripture are gathered into a living unity, a kindling flame." "The congregation demands to hear what God has commanded the preacher to speak. To some God has given no message; then the preacher stands in the pulpit with empty hands, a poor man though he speak with the tongues of angels. But even he who holds faithfully to God's Word in the Scriptures does not always stand in God's employ. The congregation feels that God has committed no message to its preacher and the most precious promises sound in his mouth like a tinkling cymbal. Whoever would speak at God's command, to him God must have previously spoken, and he to God. He must lay aside whatever is his and let God fill the empty vessel with His Spirit. Then his preaching will no longer be an empty form and a deception, but he will speak as a man commissioned of God."⁶

Schleiermacher observes: "The religious orator can become such only by an extraordinary intensity and purity of the religious element in him. From this permanent state his several productions arise... The pastor must project himself into the state of the congregation in such a manner that this state becomes his own.... It is impossible to imagine a proper performance of the work of his office apart from the diligent study of the Bible,—not only a regular reading of it for certain periods of time; it must rather be the centre of all his thinking. Its contents must enter into his permanent consciousness, so that no high moment in life can occur without a return to the Scriptures."⁷ If this makes rather too much of the intellectual, Bassermann demands of the preacher: "He must have a certain

---

⁵John 15:27; 1 John 1:2.—⁶*Die Bekehrung der Pastoren,* ⁴1892, p. 23.—⁷*Praktische Theologie,* pp. 240 f.

knowledge and inner experience of the life hidden in God, as the constant fructifying accompaniment of all thoughts and actions of the religious life; of the blessed fellowship with God which Christ made possible for His redeemed who repose and find peace in Him, a refuge in all distress, a comfort in sorrow, a defence against temptation, strength for all their doing and clearness in all their thinking."[8]

Laible writes on John 1:41,—"'We have found the Messiah,' says Andrew to his brother Simon. He brings him not a doctrine but an experience which he has made, and his eyes shine as did the face of Moses when he came from God. For Andrew has come from Jesus. He has found Him—that is what he desires to tell his brother. For no man can keep it to himself when the great hour has dawned in his life. Simon's heart is pierced by the brief message. It was not the message concerning Jesus in and of itself, but the fact that this man before him had himself seen and spoken with the Messiah. No words carry stronger conviction than the words of a witness. It has always been so in the Kingdom of God. The prophets spoke with soul overwhelmed, for they came from God's immediate presence-chamber. The apostles preached, filled with the Holy Ghost. Pious phrases have never accomplished anything, still less can they do this today. They arouse conflict and contempt. A preacher may perfectly declare what the Scriptures declare, but if the best of all is lacking, if there does not go throbbing through his message the blessed certainty—'I have found Him'—if the hearers do not feel that his heart's blood is mingled with his message, there will be but little response. Can anyone seriously demand that others come to Jesus, while he holds himself aloof from Him? That others live to Christ so long as he himself cannot say, 'Jesus, I live to Thee; Jesus, I die to Thee'? Here was the secret of Andrew's power, that he could say, 'We have found the Messiah'."

Spurgeon says in his *Lectures to my Students*: 'How horrible to be a preacher of the Gospel and yet to be unconverted! Let each man here whisper to his own inmost soul, 'What a dreadful thing it will be for *me* if I should be ignorant of the power of the truth which I am preparing to proclaim!' Unconverted ministry involves the most unnatural relationships. A graceless pastor is a blind man elected to a professorship of optics, philosophising upon light and vision, discoursing upon and distinguishing to others the nice shades and delicate blendings of the prismatic colors, while he himself is absolutely in the

---

[8] Pp. 377 f.

dark! He is a dumb man elevated to the chair of music; a deaf man fluent upon symphonies and harmonies! He is a mole professing to educate eaglets; a limpet elected to preside over angels. To such a relationship one might apply the most absurd and grotesque metaphors, except that the subject is too solemn. It is a dreadful position for a man to stand in, for he has undertaken a work for which he is totally, wholly, and altogether unqualified, but from the responsibilities of which this unfitness will not screen him, because he wilfully incurred them. Whatever his natural gifts, whatever his mental powers may be, he is utterly out of court for spiritual work if he has no spiritual life."[9] It must constantly be borne in mind, however, that an initial conversion is of no value unless it be followed by daily conversion, and that the spiritual life of man, also of the preacher, can be preserved only by its daily renewal by the Spirit of God. If the preacher were to depend on his past conversion, his message would be based upon a memory instead of being a fresh immediate testimony of the actual life within. The teacher is required to be interested in his material, to love it and prefer it above all else, to stand in personal relation to it. Only then will he be able to awaken interest in his pupils. Dare less be required of the preacher? The sermon is indeed concerned not only with intellectual but vital truth, with materials to be not intellectually apprehended but taken up into the sphere of the emotions and the will, with materials which are foolishness to the natural man and must be spiritually discerned. All the more must the preacher have the mind of the Spirit, in order to present these spiritual realities to the hearts of his hearers.

This requirement that the sermon be a testimony of experienced reality has been driven to an erroneous extreme by Pietism and Methodism. The demand has been made and is still made,[10] that the fact of the preacher's regeneration and actual sanctification must first be established before he can preach to the edification of his hearers. It is held that the sermon of the unregenerate cannot possibly produce faith and sanctification. A similar claim, from a different point of view, is made by many representatives of modern theology. Baumgarten, for example, writes: *"Ichpredigten* are interesting sermons. The beginner, in particular, ought to preach himself. This is the surest way to win others."[11] In *Wie predigen wir der Gemeinde der Gegenwart?* W. Wolf says: "As Ulysses must needs let the shades drink of the blood before he could communicate with them, so the

---

[9]P. 4.—[10]See Munz, *Homiletik*, p. 64.—[11]Pp. 52 f.

biblical conceptions must drink our blood. In this sense we must actually preach ourselves." From our point of view such a position must be rejected. While rejecting such erroneous extremes, however, we insist that the sermon must be a personal testimony to the Word of God as experienced in the preacher's heart and life. This is demanded in the interest of truthfulness, the purpose of the sermon, and above all, the ethical position of the preacher himself.

It is demanded in the interest of truthfulness. For "to speak of sorrow over one's impurity and weakness, of the longing for freedom and life in fellowship with God and man, of the need of assistance to bring our will to actual attainment, of the purification and concentration of all one's powers, of prayer, etc.—to speak of these matters is altogether meaningless if one has no inner life of one's own and is unconscious of any inner progress or retrogression; it is mere empty sound unless one is habitually experiencing all this in one's own life with joy and sorrow, with fear and trembling. . . . . . Here especially we must demand an inner sincerity and truth, which will certainly embrace first the contents, then the presentation and even the delivery of the sermon. It is a falsehood if one, even without maintaining a false position, defends and commends a position which to him is a matter of indifference. Glowing epithets and all purple patches, unless they come from the preachers heart, are lies. The very modulation of the voice and gesticulation are untruths unless they arise naturally from the absorption of the mind in the subject and not from the mere desire to produce an effect."[12] Again, the true purpose of the sermon demands that it be conceived as personal testimony. "Power to move men proceeds only from a soul that has been moved; the unmoved soul moves none."[13] "From man to man, from heart to heart, from mood to mood—so the stream of discourse must roll on its liberating course. Then the words will grip and hearts will be kindled. If a preacher's whole heart is in his message, it will be true that out of the abundance of the heart the mouth speaketh. He is not uttering a truth strange to him, but a conviction that has become part of his very life. This makes his conviction pass over into the hearts of his hearers and move not only their intellect to assent, but their mind seriously to ponder and draw the consequences from his warning and comforting message."[14] The same demand grows out of the purpose to awaken confidence in the living power of the proclaimed Word. The hearer will distrust and shut himself up against the influence of a

---

[12]Henke, pp. 424 f.—[13]Kleinert, p. 14.—[14]Krauss, p. 191.

sermon when he discovers that what is proclaimed as the saving possession of the believing congregation is not at the same time the possession of the preacher. And finally, the moral status of the preacher himself demands this. For "here are the roots of the *ethos* of the sermon: a quiet courage declaring without fear or favor what has approved itself as the power of God unto salvation (Rom. 1:16); a simple humility, not strutting in vain splendor, but subduing the hearer by its own surrender to the majesty of the Most High; the sacred fervor of love which Baxter describes in his lines,

> I preach as though I ne'er should preach again,
> And as a dying man to dying men."[15]

Would that there might be an end in the Church of all stereotyped passing on of the merely traditional and acquired; an end of the speaking of phonographs and gramophones; and that their place might be taken by living human beings, personalities touched and renewed by the Spirit of God! Then the sermon would resume its rightful place, unfold afresh its power over the hearts of men, and bring in a new era.

A word of caution must be uttered here, which may be given in the words of Hering. "The sermon as testimony," he says, "does not involve the reference to unusually profound experiences of faith, of one's sin and conversion, of what one has become through Christ. God has implanted in the deepest and tenderest emotions of human love a reverence and chastity that shrinks from publishing its secrets. Even so the inner shrine of communion with God and the abyss of Godforsakenness, or the dark places in heart and life, are not to be disclosed to the congregation, simply because Christian brethren are present and might be edified thereby. Paul's self-revelations lie on a different plane. In letters one lets oneself go in a much more informal manner than in public discourse. Moreover, Paul's genius and his fervid temperament must be taken into account. And however profoundly his congregations were moved, and the Church today is moved, by his references to his past, his humble praise of God's undeserved mercy in his conversion, his testimony to the unique value of divine grace, his deeply personal description of his life in Christ, nevertheless these things do not constitute the essence of his sermon as testimony. Besides, the special circumstances must be borne in mind in which Paul so often found himself compelled to become personal and retrospective, as we see especially in Galatians, Romans and Corinthians. In

---

[15]Kleinert, p. 14.

Galatia his whole work was in jeopardy; in Rome it became necessary to create an understanding for the world-wide scope of his Gospel; in Corinth his opponents forced upon him the role of 'fool.' No preacher has a right to generalize this and apply it to his own case. There may be times when it is justifiable to lift the veil, but the preacher who habitually does this is in danger of losing the deepest blessing of his experience and of repelling those among his hearers who have no sensorium for such things. There is a chastity and reticence in these matters that cannot be violated with impunity. The fact that it may be done now and then in an intimate circle, sometimes even by inner necessity, gives no one the right to do it as a matter of course in his pulpit before the assembled congregation. Augustine tells in his *Confessions* the story of his sin and of his conversion, with traces of the deepest emotion, but makes no use of these reminiscences in his sermons. And Luther, who was so outspoken in his *Table Talk* and whose struggles and inner development have been most liberally drawn upon in many later sermons, very rarely dragged himself into his own preaching of repentance and faith. We have no occasion today to make any change in this respect."[16] If the sermon as a whole is not upborne by the spirit of witness bearing, such subjective references will add but little. This is further emphasized by the fact that the preacher does not only represent himself in the pulpit, but officiates primarily as mouthpiece of God and of the congregation.

The demand that the sermon be the expression of the spiritual life of the preacher should not be understood to mean that he must have attained, at the very outset of his ministry, to a notably high level of spiritual life. It is not necessary that he have measured the whole depth of sin and grace, nor have drawn and applied in his life of sanctification all the consequences of his faith. This would be to demand the impossible: a whole life-time is all too short for such a task. The necessary result of such a demand would be to cause sincere souls to shrink from entering upon the work of preaching, or else to encourage insincerity and hypocrisy in the holy office. The beginner would be tempted to project himself artificially into the mature believer's world of ideas

---

[16] Pp. 411 f.

and emotions, and to prate of the experience of sin and grace, of divine wrath and judgment, of the gracious leading of the Spirit, of world-weariness and heavenly homesickness as of self-evident truths, while his heart knew nothing of them. This insincerity and falsehood would soon be accompanied by a repulsive vanity, taking pride in its description of the above experiences and seeking to impress shortsighted hearers and to win the nimbus of a saint. No: what we demand of the preacher is, on the contrary, an unreserved truthfulness and a sincere selflessness. Where these are lacking, the confidence of the congregation—at first in the more mature members, then in all honest souls—is soon irrecoverably lost, and the preacher himself suffers injury to his soul.

Hence the demand that the sermon be the utterance of the religious life of the preacher must be accompanied, in the case of the beginner, with the qualification that spiritual life must be truly present in him at least in its beginnings. He must know that sin separates between him and his God and that he needs Christ for his Saviour, and he must have apprehended and been apprehended by Christ in a penitent faith and have taken up in His strength the struggle with sin. There must be in him a sincere longing to draw ever nearer to God and to enter ever more fully into His truth and life. Where this beginning, however rudimentary, exists, he will experience the truth of the word, "To him that hath shall be given." He should confine himself, for the time being, to an objective presentation of such matters as lie beyond the pale of his experience. This he can truthfully do since his assent to the confession of the congregation is taken for granted and is the precondition, certified in his ordination, of his whole ministry. He must above all guard against standing still or retrogressing (these two are one). Retrogression will surely follow as soon as he intermits his struggle against sin and rests content with the experience already gained, instead of striving continually to renew and deepen it. He will still be operating with Christian concepts and may imagine himself to be speaking from the depths of a Christian life; in reality he is but a tinkling cymbal. (P. 92.)

The question of *intellectual assent* to the confessions of the Church must be distinguished from the question as to the degree in which spiritual life, justifying faith and the striving after sanctification, should be present in the beginner. With respect to the question of confessional subscription, far reaching concessions are often made. Witness the repeated discussions as to the formula and meaning of the ordination vow in German churches,[17] and similar agitations in our own land.[18] The most that can be demanded, it is thought, is that the preacher do not directly oppose the confession. Even though the confession is treated as in the main untenable, it is held that "theology" and theological controversy have no place in the pulpit. In practice even these modest bounds are overstepped, so that Hering finds himself compelled to warn the immature preacher "not to shut himself up prematurely against the whole Gospel nor to oppose the great masters of Christendom, the apostles, with his sceptical, critical and contradictory judgment."[19] Experience should teach us that this way of "liberty of teaching" leads finally to the disruption of the Church—not indeed of the church as a free religious society in which every *nuance* of natural religion and morality has a right to exist, but of the Church as Christ willed it and as He founded it on the day of Pentecost.

As long ago as 1842 Palmer wrote in his *Homiletik*: "If there were no difference between the faith of the theologians and that of the evangelical Church no one would doubt that the Church had the right to bind her preachers to the *symbolum*. The formal right is obviously on her side. Whoever desires to be a teacher of the evangelical faith, by commission of the Church, must teach this faith and no other. Otherwise he puts himself outside the pale of the Church. It is absurd to complain of being deprived of liberty of conscience, as though the Church forced anyone to believe this or that. She conducts no inquisition, but simply says, 'I demand of whoever wants to be one of my teachers that he occupy in matters of faith the same

---

[17]Cf. H. Mulert, *Die Lehrverpflichtung in der evang. Kirche Deutschlands*, 1906, and *Wahrhaftigkeit und Lehrverpflichtung*, 1911.—[18]E. g., the controversy in the Presbyterian Church over the ordination of graduates of Union Seminary, New York.—[19]P. 410.

standpoint as I. If anyone is unable to do this I do not expect him to enter my house. But neither should he expect me to change my standpoint to accommodate him. He must not expect me to provide him with an office and a living, in order that, vested with the authority of the Church, he may immediately use his advantage to work injury to my cause. It is not for him nor for any theological faction to decide for me what is sound and what is injurious.' . . . But apart from the formal, judicial question, there is the material, the theological. It is said the symbol is indeed the faithful expression of the faith of the Reformers, but no longer of us who have advanced three hundred years farther. Whoever has kept pace with the times and learned to think in the schools of our wisdom can no longer regard the creeds as true. Evangelical truth has changed, and whoever expects us either to cease to consider ourselves members of the evangelical Church or else to submit to its creeds, violates our liberty of thought and of faith, and demands the impossible. We answer: In the first place, you are only saying over again that *you* can no longer hold the faith of the Church. But to wish to remain members of the evangelical Church, that you have no right to do, so long as there is still an actual evangelical Church which has preserved its unity with the historical evangelical Church in which the creeds were produced. In this Church you have no place. . . . Besides, this is no longer the question. . . . At present we are conscious of a radical opposition to the faith of the Reformers; men no longer hesitate to admit it openly; there are even many who find an irresistible fascination in calling themselves 'modern pagans.' With respect to such persons the question is no longer whether they ought to be admitted to the ministry of the Church, for the honest ones among them cannot desire this. But the question is, whether *we* can continue to exist if, as they say, Christianity and the Church are nothing more than a ruin hindering the building of a new world. Well, the decision as to that belongs neither to them nor to us, for neither party can be judge. But One is the Judge, who cares not for human decrees, predictions or threats, and He will decide. And as long as thousands and tens of thousands find salvation, peace, strength and wisdom on the basis of the evangelical *Glaubenslehre,* as long as it still possesses such power that the Church, after having for a time forgotten and despised her true self, can return to it and, kindled anew at its flame, manifest a fresh, joyous, active life, in liturgies and hymnbooks, in thousands of sermons every Lord's day, in missionary activity and Bible distribution, the Lord and, to speak humanly, the spirit of the time have not yet given judgment against us, and we shall hold fast,

THE PREACHER'S RELATION TO THE CONFESSIONS   87

whatever our outward fortune, to this position,—whoever wants to be a preacher in the actually existing and living evangelical Church must preach what she preaches and teaches."[20] These principles of Palmer's hold good today. The State Church, indeed, to which all citizens of the state equally belong, and in support of which they all pay taxes, whatever their relation to the Church, cannot carry these principles through. Their consistent application would be a moral injustice; for the persons who pay church taxes have a right to demand sermons suited to their religious point of view, and justly regard it as oppression if this be denied them by either state or church. The Free Church, on the contrary, can carry out these principles. Indeed, she must enforce them, for she knows no other bond of unity among her members and no other mark of distinction from non-members than the common confession. She would endanger her existence and eventually bring about her own dissolution, if she admitted to her pulpits men who were not even intellectually in accord with her faith and teaching.

From our own premises we are driven to the same position. For how can the sermon be an organic part of the service and in harmony with its other parts, if the preacher does not share the faith confessed in the service? Hence Kliefoth writes in his *Theorie des Kultus der evangelischen Kirche* (1844): "In order to be a preacher, or the witness-bearing mouth of the congregation, the first thing is that a man find in the creed of his Church the expression of his own faith. . . . If the subjective conviction of the preacher be at variance with the creed and thus with the type of faith found in the congregation, he has the choice of one of two things. Either he can oppose his own subjective opinion to the faith of the congregation; then he is no longer an organ of the congregation and his sermon no longer its testimony. Or else he can suppress his own opinion and place himself externally on the standpoint of the congregation's faith; then he is (to say nothing of the coldness and deadness of such preaching) the mouth indeed, but the lying mouth, of the congregation. For not only he is a liar who expresses his own false opinion, but he no less who utters the truth and does not believe it to be the truth."[21]

The question arises as to the duty of the preacher who in the course of his scientific studies—which should indeed never cease—comes to doubt some point in the creed of his Church. Should he ignore his doubts and lightly brush them aside? By no means. They would then, as Henke puts it,[22] only work the greater havoc in his

---

[20] Pp. 265 f.—[21] Pp. 91 f.—[22] P. 426.

soul, like a disease checked and driven inward. Above all, his sincerity and truthfulness would be seriously impaired. He ought rather to make such doubts the occasion for a renewed and more thorough study of the Scriptures and the history of the confessions, until he has mastered his doubts. In no case will he take them with him into the pulpit, especially since they may mark only a transition period in his development. He will "resist the temptation to drag, in the pose of writer or professor, his own novel views into the pulpit; for the sermon is neither a *brochure* nor a university lecture, but a part of the cultus of the congregation, whose purpose is nothing else than the upbuilding of the Christian life of the congregation." Should the transition period harden into a permanent condition, so that the preacher finds himself in irreconcilable conflict with the confession of the Church, he dare not shrink from drawing the final consequences and demitting the ministry, especially when the point at issue is one that dare not be avoided in a genuinely Lutheran sermon.

The question of intellectual assent to the confessions, which is open to investigation and must be present even in the case of the beginner, must be distinguished from the question as to the actual spiritual life of the beginner. Here we dare not set our standard too high, as is generally admitted. Hering writes, in opposition to Munz: "We dare not require of a young man who chooses the ministry as his life-work, the full definiteness of a conscious Christian, nor may the Church defer its call until such a one has proved himself in possession of the Spirit by influencing others.[23] Whenever, according to human judgment, there are in young theologians the beginnings of an inner development leading to Christ, they fall under the head of the apostolic word in Phil. 3:12-14."[24] More clearly Gottschick: "That man may preach with a good conscience, who understands the divine *lex* as the ideal that binds and judges him, the divine *promissio* as the highest good, and Christ as the *pignus promissionis* [He is, of course, infinitely more than this], and who strives in earnest self-discipline to let these control his actual personal life, even though desire be the fundamental characteristic of his personal experience."[25]

Our view that the young preacher lacking in spiritual experience had better confine his preaching to the objective statement of truth is shared by so modern a homilete as Niebergall, who stresses this point in view of the tendency of immature preachers to exaggerate their

---

[23]Munz demanded that "a man must have converted others before it is to be supposed that preaching is his vocation."—[24]P. 409.—[25]P. 12.

own inner experience. He writes: "In order to inculcate trust in God it is well to portray the experience of historical personages who lived their lives in God. This is a good rule for all conscientious beginners to whom the conventional exaggeration [*Plusmacherei*] of immature youths bubbling over with alleged experiences is so repellent that they are in danger of shrinking too timidly from any revelation of their own inner life."[26] Unless this be granted, it will be necessary to banish from the pulpit many matters required by the treatment of the text and which the congregation has a right to hear and needs to hear. This would mean a spiritual loss for the congregation, extending often over years, and in case a number of beginners succeed one another, over decades. If the young preacher cannot speak of the exceeding sinfulness of sin and of the dreadfulness of God's wrath as impressively as the older preacher who has matured in God's school, and if he must be chary in such discussions of the use of the personal pronoun "we" and especially "I," why should he not illustrate these scriptural truths by a portrayal of the life of Jacob or David, above all, of the atoning life and death of Christ? In this way the congregation will receive what God intends it to receive from the sermon, and the preacher will preserve his own integrity. Why should he not set forth the glory of forgiving grace, of which he has perhaps only a meagre experience, by portraying the life of St. Paul? or incite his people to trust in God under all trials, by picturing the life of Paul Gerhardt and interpreting his great hymn, *Befiehl du deine Wege?* or awaken love and longing for the Lord's appearance by combining the corresponding scripture passages and one of the Church's great hymns of eternity? To be sure, preaching on these themes will take a different tone when it is upborne by personal testimony and the congregation feels behind every word the religious experience and the whole personality of the preacher. Nevertheless, God will not withhold His blessing from the purely objective presentation of these subjects, and we must always bear in mind that the Word does not become the power of God through any experience of the preacher. Moreover, the congregation will learn to receive with the more confidence the sermons of its young preacher when it sees that he reverences God's Word, respects the spiritual experiences of great men of God, and takes seriously, according to his lights, the great facts of sin and grace. The young preacher who lacks these qualities and ceases to "press toward the mark" is either a frivolous or a super-spiritual

---

[26] *Wie predigen wir dem modernen Menschen?* ii, 81.

person[27] and is repudiated by his congregation. But the young preacher who, though he must still struggle with his sins, does really struggle, is tolerated by his people and will be able to influence them. For the inner strife and struggle of the soul must appear to every thinking Christian as something sacred and to be honored and respected. For this reason the sermons of theologically liberal but deeply religious and morally active preachers have for so many souls a profounder and more satisfying religious message than the theologically sound sermons of the "orthodox" preacher delivered without inner participation.

The beginner who takes seriously the proclamation of God's Word, so far as he has intellectually apprehended it, and is, besides this, concerned about his religious and moral growth, will find God leading him to ever greater depths of inner experience. He will also find the circle of materials upon which he can preach from the viewpoint of his own experience growing constantly larger. All depends on his being not only "one who speaks for God" but "one who listens to God," keeping always the inner ear wide open to the voice of the Spirit. F. W. Krummacher's experience, as he describes it in his autobiography, is that of many others. "Many things," he writes, "that I said in my sermons about the glory of the inward life of the Christian impressed me merely as ideals. Only through fuller self-knowledge and a growing illumination from above, and after many internal struggles, did they become the actual possession of my inner life."[28] While this should comfort the diffident beginner, he must be cautioned, on the other hand, against regarding his intellectual appreciation of the religious experience of others or his sympathetic understanding of their emotional moods as equivalent to his own personal experience. This would be confusing a purely psychological process, possible to every natural man of refined feelings, with that which is born of the Spirit alone. The honest beginner, on the other hand, perplexed with the question whether his longing for Christ can really be called faith, and fearing he may have no more than a mere intellectual apprehension of Him, should find cheer in a word used by Richard Baxter and by John Wesley,—"Preach Christ *until* you have Him; then you will preach Him *because* you have Him."

On the danger of spiritual retrogression Spurgeon has this to say: "If your zeal grows dull, you will not pray well in the pulpit, you will pray worse in the family, and worst in the study alone. When your soul becomes lean, your hearers, without knowing how or why,

---

[27]Baumgarten dubs him an *ekelhafter Bursche*, p. 53.—[28]P. 97.

will find that your prayers in public have little savour for them; they will feel your barrenness, perhaps before you perceive it yourself. Your discourses will next betray your declension. You may utter as well-chosen words, and as fitly-ordered sentences, as aforetime; but there will be a perceptible loss of spiritual force. You will shake yourselves as at other times, even as Samson did, but you will find that your strength has departed. In your daily communion with your people, they will not be slow to mark the all-pervading decline of your graces. Sharp eyes will see the grey hairs here and there long before you do. Let a man be afflicted with a disease of the heart, and all evils are wrapped up in that one—stomach, lungs, viscera, muscles, and nerves will all suffer; and so, let a man have his heart weakened in spiritual things, and very soon his entire life will feel the withering influence. Moreover, as a result of your own decline, every one of your hearers will suffer more or less; the vigorous amongst them will overcome the depressing tendency, but the weaker sort will be seriously damaged. It is with us and our hearers, as it is with watches and the public clock: if our watch be wrong, very few will be misled but ourselves; but if the Horse Guards or Greenwich Observatory should go amiss, half London would lose its reckoning. So it is with the minister; he is the parish-clock, many take their time from him, and if he be incorrect, then they all go wrongly, more or less, and he is in a great measure accountable for all the sin which he occasions. This we cannot endure to think of, my brethren. It will not bear a moment's comfortable consideration, and yet it must be looked at that we may guard against it."[29]

Of the necessary spiritual growth of the preacher A. S. Hoyt says: "The best work of the preacher is conditioned by his growth and gives incentive to it. He must be a wise householder that bringeth forth things new and old from his treasury. There are but few principles of religion and these need endless iteration; but only a growing soul can repeat them so as to form a literature of spiritual power. Truth is not a discovery made once for all, stored up to be used at demand. But truth is a life never fully attained, ever struggling and learning, ever seeing and doing more because of its growth. It is growth that sustains the ideal, the vision of what ought to be and what can be by the grace of God. It does not suffer the soul to rest in any comfortable and low content. A living message, the truth for today, and not the scribe's dull repetitions of yesterday, must be the word of a

---

[29] P. 99.

life that is ever learning."³⁰ "Many a tailor," Richard Baxter warns the preacher, "goes in rags that maketh costly clothes for others; and many a cook scarce licks his fingers when he hath dressed for others the most costly dishes. Believe it, brethren, God never saved any man for being a preacher, nor because he was an able preacher; but because he was a justified, sanctified man, and consequently faithful in his Master's work." And St. Paul's words should ever be kept in mind,—"Lest that by any means, when I have preached to others, I myself should be a castaway."³¹ A quotation from James W. Alexander may fitly close this section: "The question has been much discussed, whether a minister should ever preach beyond his own experience. In one sense, unquestionably, he should. He is commissioned to preach, not himself, or his experience, but Christ Jesus the Lord, and His salvation; he is a messenger, and his message is laid before him in the Scriptures; it is at his peril that he suppresses aught, whether he has experienced it or not. Yet every preacher of the Gospel should earnestly strive to attain the experience of the truths which he communicates, and to have every doctrine which he utters turned into vital exercises of his heart; so that when he stands up to speak in the name of God, there may be that indescribable freshness and penetrativeness, which arises from individual and present interest in what is declared."³²

When these requirements are met, they impart to the sermon a peculiar charm and a personal appeal. In it are gathered up the manifold rays of the light of God's Word, experienced in the life of the congregation, and passed through the individuality of the preacher. For every original preacher has his distinct individuality, which is not destroyed by the grace of God, but purified, hallowed and transfigured. Hence, with all the unity of faith and community of the spiritual life, there is a beautiful variety in the sermon, as we trace it through the history of preaching down to our own day. The one

---

³⁰*Vital Elements of Preaching*, 1914, pp. 186 f.—³¹1 Cor. 9:27.—Cf. R. Loeber, *Das innere Leben*, ³¹1900. Id., *Seelsorge an den Geistlichen*, 1906. D. Vorwerk, *Kann auch ein Pastor selig werden?* ⁵1912. J. H. Jowett, *The Preacher*, 1912. One or two books for the cultivation of the preacher's devotional life may be mentioned: Dieffenbach-Mueller, *Evangelisches Brevier*, 1869. Thomas Wilson, *Sacra Privata*. Bishop Andrews' *Devotions*.—³²*Thoughts on Preaching*, pp. 78 f.

melody recurs in infinite variations, even in the same communion.

To sum up our discussion of the nature of the sermon: The sermon of the Christian Church is the proclamation, in the form of testimony or witness, of the pure Word of God, in its essential contents—Jesus Christ the crucified and risen Saviour—passed through the individual personality of the preacher, and experienced by him as well as by the Church whose organ and mouthpiece he is.

§ 7. THE PURPOSE OF THE SERVICE OF THE CONGREGATION

F. Schleiermacher, *Praktische Theologie* (pub. 1850). F. Ehrenfeuchter, *Theorie des christlichen Kultus,* 1840. Th. Kliefoth, *Theorie des Kultus der evang. Kirche,* 1844. A. Schweizer, *Homiletik,* 1848. L. Schoeberlein, *Liturgischer Ausbau des Gemeindegottesdienstes,* 1859. H. Bassermann, *Entwurf eines Systems der evang. Liturgik,* 1888. Id., *Beitraege zur praktischen Theologie,* 1909. J. W. Richard and F. Painter, *Christian Worship: Its Principles and Forms,* ²1910.—Comp. also literature on p. 3.

The purpose of the Christian cultus is *edification,* οἰκοδομή, in both its active and passive sense. In order that we may be built up in ever increasing measure into His holy temple, God offers us His Word; and in order that we may in increasing measure build up ourselves in Him, we accept His Word with prayer, praise and thanksgiving. The purpose of the service has been defined in many different ways,—as the instruction of the youth and the common people: thus Luther in many places, especially in the preface to his "Deutsche Messe" and in the "Large Catechism"; or as indoctrination in the will of God in general: so, e. g., Zwingli; or as the self-representation of the faith and religious life of the congregation, from which the idea of worship is inseparable: so Schleiermacher, Ehrenfeuchter, Schweizer, Schoeberlein and Bassermann; or as the enjoyment of God, a resting in Him, a fore-Sabbath preliminary to the great Sabbath of eternity: so Loehe, Palmer, von Zezschwitz and others. But each of these definitions, so far as it is true, expresses but one element of the truth; they may all be summed up under the idea of edification, so long as this idea is taken both actively and passively. (P. 98.)

Luther emphasizes the pedagogical purpose of the service in the preface to his *Deutsche Messe* (1526) as follows: "We are not setting up this order of service for those who are already Christians; for they need none of these things. Nor does man exist for the sake of these things, but they exist for our sake, who are not yet Christians, that they may make Christians of us. Those who are already Christians worship God in spirit. But these services are necessary for the sake of those who are to be made Christians or to be made better Christians. In the same way, a Christian does not need baptism, the Word or the Sacrament (for he has all this) so far as he is a Christian, but only so far as he is a sinner. But most of all, the service is for the common people and the youth, who must daily be trained and brought up in the Scriptures and the Word of God, that they may become well versed in them and be able to give a reason for their faith, to instruct others in course of time, and to help extend the kingdom of Christ. For their sake we must read, sing, preach, write and compose. Yes, and if it would help, I should set all bells ringing, all organs playing, and everything sounding that can make a sound, into the bargain. . . . I am by no means willing to see the Latin language altogether banished from the service; because my one concern is for the youth. If it could be done, and if the Greek and Hebrew languages were as familiar to us and had as many fine chants and hymns as the Latin, they should hold mass, sing and read the lessons in all four languages in turn,—German, Latin, Greek, and Hebrew. . . . Secondly, there is the German mass or service, of which we are treating now, and which ought to be conducted for the simple laymen. . . . There are among them many who as yet neither believe nor are Christians; most of them simply stand gaping at the strange things they see. Here there is not yet a well ordered or organized congregation, in which it is possible to direct Christians according to the Word of God; what takes place is rather a public invitation to faith and Christianity. . . . Meanwhile I will be content with these two kinds [of service, viz., Latin and German] and do what I can to further such public services, together with preaching, for the purpose of instructing the youth and calling and inviting the rest to become believers. . . . Since the first and chief part of every service is the preaching and teaching of God's Word, let us arrange our sermons and scripture lessons as follows. . . . " And in the *Large Catechism* he says in his explanation of the third commandment: "Notice therefore that we do not keep the day of rest for the sake of the intelligent and instructed Christians, for these do not need it. But we keep it, in the first place, because of the needs of the body, as demanded by nature for the common people, man-servants and maid-servants, who labor all the week at their work or trade, so that they, too, may have one day of rest and recreation. But secondly and chiefly, in order that men may on this rest-day (for otherwise it could not be done) take time to attend public service, come together to hear and administer God's Word and thereupon praise Him with hymns and prayers. . . . This is therefore the simple meaning of this commandment: Since men in any case observe a day of rest, we should devote this day to the learning of God's Word; hence the proper work of this day is the work of preaching, for the benefit of the young and the common man."

While Luther here emphasizes exclusively the pedagogic purpose of the service, he treats it elsewhere as a testimony to the faith of the congregation, and therefore as a sacrifice of thanksgiving and praise. Thus he says in a Holy Thursday sermon: "Many ancient fathers termed the Lord's Supper the Eucharist, or thank-offering. Under the Papacy it was called a sacrifice and office [*Amt*], that is, rightly understood, a service. When I preach the Word of God I am offering a sacrifice; when you hear the Word with your heart, you are offering a sacrifice; when we pray, give or lend to our neighbor or otherwise help him, we offer a sacrifice. So, too, when I receive this sacrament, I offer a sacrifice, that is, I do God's will and serve Him, I confess and give thanks to God, who has given me this sacrament (as well as all other blessings of His heavenly kingdom), as He hath commanded me to do. Hence it may indeed be called a sacrifice: not that the sacrament in itself is a sacrifice, but its reception and use may so be termed; yet not a sacrifice for sin, but a sacrifice of praise and thanksgiving, by which I confess that Christ died for my sin. . . . The use of the sacrament, or the remembrance of Christ, as the Lord Himself calls it, is a sacrifice of thanksgiving by which we confess and thank God that we are redeemed, justified and saved by pure grace, through the passion, death and blood of Christ. In the same way the sermon is a *sacrificium laudis*, i. e., a sacrifice of thanksgiving, by which we confess and thank God that we have received from Him the treasure of His Word. Thus the reception of the sacrament is a sacrifice of thanksgiving by which whoever partakes expresses his gratitude to Christ for His suffering and grace."[1]

These two sides Luther combines when he says, in the Torgau sermon referred to above:[2] "In this new house of God nothing else is to take place but that our dear Lord Himself speak to us by His holy Word and we in turn speak to Him in prayer and praise." These

---

[1] *Erlangen Edition*, iv,[2] pp. 496 f.—[2] P. 41.

two sides of the service, however, aim at nothing else than our edification. Thus Harnack says: "The Christian service consists of rest [*Feier*] and action [*Tat*], that is, a representative and a communicating activity, with the view of building up the congregation in God. . . . It serves to magnify the grace of God and thus to edify [*Selbsterbauung*] the congregation (Eph. 2:20; 4:12 f.)."

§ 8. THE PURPOSE OF THE SERMON AS PART OF THE SERVICE OF THE CONGREGATION

A. Hyperius, *De formandis concionibus sacris*, 1553 (German translation by E. Chr. Achelis, 1901). F. Schleiermacher, *Praktische Theologie*, published 1850. Chr. Palmer, *Evang. Homiletik*, 1842. A. Schweizer, *Homiletik*, 1848. A. Vinet, *Homiletics*, translated by Skinner, 1853. J. Nitzsch, *Praktische Theologie*, 1859. H. Cremer, *Ueber den biblischen Begriff der Erbauung*, 1863. J. W. Alexander, *Thoughts on Preaching*, 1860, ²1864. D. P. Kidder, *Treatise on Homiletics*, 1864. F. M. Zahn, *Etwas ueber den biblischen Begriff der Erbauung*, 1864. Th. Weber, *Betrachtungen ueber die Predigtweise und geistliche Amtsfuehrung unsrer Zeit*, 1869. R. L. Dabney, *Sacred Rhetoric*, 1870. J. A. Broadus, *On the Preparation and Delivery of Sermons*, 1870. Chas. Spurgeon, *Lectures to My Students*, 1876. Ph. Brooks, *Lectures on Preaching*, 1877. R. L. Dale, *Nine Lectures on Preaching*, 1877. H. Bassermann, *Ueber Erbauung* (Zeitschrift fuer prakt. Theol., 1882; reprinted in his Beitraege zur prakt. Theologie, 1909). A. Krauss, *Lehrbuch der Homiletik*, 1883. H. Bassermann, *Handbuch der geistlichen Beredsamkeit*, 1885. G. v. Zezschwitz, *Homiletik* (Handbuch d. theol. Wissenschaften, iv), ³1890. W. B. Carpenter, *Lectures on Preaching*, 1895. F. Steinmeyer, *Homiletik*, 1901. F. Niebergall, *Wie predigen wir dem modernen Menschen?* 1904-1906. H. Hering, *Die Lehre von der Predigt*, 1905. A. Kleinert, *Homiletik*, 1907. P. T. Forsyth, *Positive Preaching and the Modern Mind*, 1907. F. Loofs, *Ueber die Aufgabe der Predigt in der Gegenwart* (Akademische Predigten), 1908. A. Uckeley, *Die moderne Dorfpredigt*, 1908. J. Gottschick, *Homiletik und Katechetik*, 1908. A. Uckeley, *Moderne Predigtideale*, 1910. F. Niebergall, *Erbauung* (Religion in Geschichte und Gegenwart, vol. i), 1910. E. Chr. Achelis, *Praktische Theologie*, i and iii, 1911. A. Pilger, *Was koennen wir von der modernen Predigt lernen?* (Kirchl. Zeitschrift), 1915. Chas. S. Gardner, *Psychology and Preaching*, 1918.

If edification is the purpose of the Christian service, the sermon must have the same purpose in view, since it is an organic part of the service and dare not disturb its unity.

In the Scriptures the term edification is not only used in a general sense—thus we read that God is able to build up His people (Acts 26:32); that the Christian should curtail his liberty rather than insist on doing things lawful in themselves but not ministering to edification (1 Cor. 10:23, comp. 1 Cor. 8:1); that the Apostles received of the Lord authority for edification (2 Cor. 10:8)—but the idea of edification is applied directly to the service and to the various forms of Word-administration in the service. We see this most clearly in 1 Cor. 14. Here in vv. 3-5 and 12, the charismatic gifts are to be employed in the service solely for the edification of the congregation; and in v. 26 this principle is laid down for the whole of the service,—"Let all things be done unto edifying," πάντα πρὸς οἰκοδομὴν γενέσθω. While there is indeed a difference between the sermon of today and those primitive utterances of Christian brethren, it is not a fundamental difference and does not imply a difference of purpose. We are therefore in complete accord with the New Testament when we assert that the purpose of the sermon is the edification of the congregation, both as a whole and with respect to its individual members.

But what meaning does the New Testament attach to the word *edification?* It is clearly a figure of speech, representing the Christian Church on earth as an edifice, as the house or temple of God. According to Eph. 2:19-22, Jesus Christ is the corner-stone, controlling and indicating the lines of the foundation, which consists of the apostles and New Testament prophets. Upon this foundation the individual Christians, as they are added to the Church, are built up (edified) as living stones (1 Peter 2:5). But these same Christians, built up once for all upon this foundation, are again described as being built up or edified, so that what took place once for all is to be constantly repeated, and they are to become more completely that which they already are. Thus Paul says of his readers in Ephesus, first, that they *have been built—*

ἐποικοδομηθέντες—and then, that they *are being built* together—συνοικοδομεῖσθε (Eph. 2:19-22). The meaning of this becomes clear when we recall Luther's saying that the individual Christians are in a state of becoming (*Werden*), not in the finished state (*Gewordensein*), and when we remember that the Church as sum-total of believing Christians is already God's temple and must at the same time grow ever more "unto an holy temple in the Lord" (Eph. 2:21). In the very passage in which the purpose of the various forms of Word-administration in the service is said to be "unto edification," the existence of the congregation is presupposed. This implies that the purpose of the sermon is not to gather a Christian congregation out of the mass of non-Christians, but to establish the congregation anew upon the old foundation, to build it up and lead it onward to perfection, to the high goal of its divine ideal. That is what is meant by edification. (P. 103.)

The English word "edification" is clearer and more expressive than the German "Erbauung." Luther does not use this word in its figurative sense. He renders the New Testament οἰκοδομή as *Besserung* or by a paraphrase; the verb οἰκοδομεῖν he translates *bessern*. Only when the comparison of the Church with a building is expressly brought out, does he translate *erbauen* (Acts 9:31; 1 Peter 2:5). The single exception is 1 Thess. 5:11, where he has "bauet einer den andern." In Spener, on the other hand, the use of the metaphorical sense is already established, especially in his *Theologische Bedenken*[1] and in his explanation of the Catechism, where question 1215: "Are not all Christians, by virtue of the priesthood, preachers of the Church?" receives the following answer: "No; a particular call is necessary in case one is to hold such office publicly in the whole congregation. Da hingegen der Christen Pflicht allein die absonderliche bruederliche *Erbauung* seines Hauses und anderer Naechsten, mit denen man Gelegenheit hat umzugehen, in sich fasset." Afterwards, apparently through the later pietism with its emotionalism, and through rationalism with its sentimentality, edification assumed a strongly emotional and sentimental cast. The objective element was indeed somehow retained:

---

[1] E. g., i, 631; ii, 157, 179, 708, 802; iv, 548.

the soul immature or retrogressive in its Christian development, was conceived as being advanced, or returned to its former position, by a power outside itself. Nevertheless, with this objective element there were combined the two subjective factors of rest and enjoyment, so that edification came to signify a pleasurable excitation of the emotions by which the soul, becoming aware of God and the presence of God, was carried out of itself with delight and enjoyed a measure of heavenly bliss. Frequently this edifying was identified with the pathetic, and an edifying sermon meant one that set the lachrymal glands in motion. But this is foreign to the biblical as well as to the English use of the word. The significance of οἰκοδομή as a mental or spiritual, as opposed to a material operation is peculiar to the New Testament. In classical Greek the noun is never used in a metaphorical sense, and the verb only in the sense of building up an argument. The Septuagint prepared the way for the New Testament usage, under the influence of the Hebrew *bana*, to build, in the sense of establishing or furthering some one's welfare (Mal. 3:15; Ps. 28:5, etc.).[2] In the strictly religious meaning it is especially a peculiarity of Paul's style. For him the primary meaning of οἰκοδομή is not the establishing of a thing as opposed to its destruction (as in 2 Cor. 10:8; 12:10), but the furtherance of the religious-ethical life. This we see from the contrast in 1 Cor. 8:1, where charity as an act of love is opposed to the selfish enjoyment fostered by knowledge that "puffeth up." Similarly in 1 Cor. 10:23 f.; while it is true that all things are lawful, the liberty of the Christian is limited by the further truth that all things do not edify, these two truths being parallel respectively to "seeking one's own" and "seeking every man his neighbor's good." As objects of this ethico-religious edifying we have: the other (1 Cor. 14:7), one another (1 Thess. 5:11), the Church (1 Cor. 14:4, 12), one's self (1 Cor. 14:4a). The edification of others is commended by Paul; the edification of one's self which is not at the same time the edification of one's neighbor or of the Church is deprecated.

The presentation of the Word in the service is to minister to the edification of each individual member and thereby to the edification of the congregation as a whole. In thinking of edification, Paul does not have in mind primarily the closer identification of the individual Christian with the congregation, after the analogy of a stone built into an edifice. When the context demands this or a similar thought, he

---

[2]Cf. Cremer-Koegel, *Bibl.-theol. Woerterbuch der neutest. Graezitaet*, 10. ed., 1915.

uses the compounds ἐπι- or συνοικοδομεῖν. To edify always means to him primarily the furthering of the religious and moral life of the individual. When this is done, the individual will naturally become more closely identified with and built into the Church. The religious-moral life which is to be edified is always conceived by Paul as already existing. This life is not to be implanted by means of edification, but existing as it does in whatever degree, it is to be strengthened, deepened, increased, advanced. Here we see the principal difference between the literal and the metaphorical sense of our term. In its literal use, a thing which is built comes into existence by that very process. In the metaphorical sense, it exists before its building up or edification, by which it is only intended to become the more truly what it already is. Not heathen are to be edified by the Word, in Paul's sense, but Christians, members of the Church. Hence Schweizer says correctly: "Edification is possible only on the basis of Christianity. It exists only for such as have already become Christians. It has no place in missionary or catechetical work, except in so far as Christianity, i. e., Christian piety and an inner relation to the service of the Church, is present. 'I have been edified,' can be said only by one who can regard himself as already a Christian. This is so essential to the idea of edification, that even the decided Christian will speak of being edified only when he feels the sound elements which are already present in him stirred up into fuller life, either by being set in a clearer light or vitalized for his feelings and will. He will be less likely to speak of being edified when unchristian elements in him are discovered or antichristian elements disturbed. It is only because the positive Christian elements are indirectly furthered by the removal of unchristian and antichristian elements in the soul, that this negative operation can be included under the head of edification."[3] And Achelis well says: "Underlying the Pauline conception of edification is the idea of the *perfectio christiana seu evangelica* as it is touched on in articles xvi and xxvii of the Augsburg Confession. That is to say, the Christian has entered upon the *status perfectionis* through faith in Christ, he has become a child of God, and more than this he can never become in all eternity; his task is now to be and become that which he is, that is, to work out his faith within the bounds of his calling."[4] Hence we may define the Pauline term "edification" as the furtherance of the existing spiritual life of the Christian, or the advancement of this life toward perfection.

---

[3] P. 161.—[4] i, 24.

We must guard, however, against reducing the conception of the religious-ethical, or spiritual life to certain emotional conditions or religious moods. That would lead back again to the sterile narrowness of the periods of pietism and rationalism. The religious life, like all soul-life, is threefold—intellectual, emotional and voluntative. Hence, when my religious and moral understanding is stimulated, broadened and deepened; my religious and moral feelings stirred, so that I take delight in good and divine things; and the religious and moral efforts of my will are given an impetus in the direction of God and His will, so that I turn more and more from sin and live to God—then I have been truly edified. It is not necessary that all these factors be present at the same time; now this, now that side will predominate. Such all-inclusive furthering of the religious-moral life, such advancement of it on the road to perfection—that is the purpose of the sermon. And especially of the congregational sermon, which is a part of the service, presupposing a Christian congregation and some degree, be it the very lowest, of Christian life.

Edification, thus understood, involves two things. In the *first* place, the Church must have constantly refreshed her consciousness of what God has done and is still doing for her and of what she has become by the grace of God, of what God and faith in Him and His Word mean to her, so that she may rejoice in her faith and Christian life and learn to cherish her communion with God as the chief of all her blessings. When the sermon awakens and deepens this consciousness and this joy, the Church, so far from falling into self-righteousness, self-complacency and moral lassitude, will be driven to a renewed examination of her status; the believers in her midst will be established, the faint-hearted encouraged, the sorrowing comforted, the weak strengthened, and the whole congregation truly edified. Her spiritual life will be deepened and enlarged: her spiritual understanding enlightened, her religious feeling satisfied, her regenerate will strengthened and stimulated. Even those standing aloof from the Church may be attracted and won by this sort of preaching.

This follows necessarily from the nature of preaching, as well as from the nature of Christian life. We have seen that preaching is the proclamation of the Gospel, the presentation of the wonderful works of God for us men and for our salvation, a bearing witness to the crucified and risen Lord. The sermon cannot be this without calling upon men to rejoice in their Lord and to thank Him for His salvation. And the Christian life is a life of faith;[5] we become Christians and we remain Christians through faith; when faith departs the Christian life ends and spiritual death sets in. How can the sermon edify, i. e., further this spiritual life, except by aiming at the continual renewal, growth and deepening of faith? But faith can be preserved and strengthened only by setting before the soul God as the God of salvation, so that it will stretch out eager hands to Him, meditate on His gracious works, and rejoice in the Lord. And as there can be no renewal of faith without this, so there can be no motive for moral living, and all exhortations to a holy life are in vain unless by the daily renewing of faith fresh springs of power to lead a godly life are set flowing in the soul.

With this is closely connected the *second* aspect of edification. The sermon must bring the congregation to the realization of that which, on the basis of what she is through the grace of God, she must now become. It must set before her the divine idea of the Church of God, awaken in the hearts of her members an earnest desire to reach this goal, and move them to a ceaseless struggle with sin and to the faithful imitation of Christ. It was the mistake of Schleiermacher and of many of his followers that they overlooked this second element. Yet what a prominent place it occupies in the New Testament epistles—those substitutes for the sermons of the absent apostles—and in the preaching of Jesus to His disciples. It is imperatively demanded by the actual condition of the Church on earth. Despite of all objective holiness, she is

---

[5]Gal. 2: 10; Rom. 1: 17.

not yet subjectively holy and blameless but full of spots and wrinkles,[6] and must confess with Paul[7] that, while she knows herself to be apprehended of Christ and set in the way of the Christian life, she knows, too, that she has not yet attained, but is only on the way to her goal, and that she will lose her way if she does not press toward the mark for the prize of her high calling. In the true Christian the knowledge of sin is found side by side with the knowledge of grace. If the latter is present without the former, he deceives himself.[8] He is indeed born again, but still bears in himself the old Adam, and is to that extent carnal and sold under sin.[9] In this dual capacity, with this twofold nature, he comes to church, and the sermon must take account of him, and deal with him, as he is. He is to be treated as a Christian, but as an imperfect Christian, who needs not only comfort, but doctrine, exhortation, reproof and correction. Indeed, despite their continual connection with the Church, the spiritual life of individual members may have completely died out, so that it must be implanted anew by the sermon.

This second feature of edification also grows out of the nature of the sermon, which, as witness to Christ crucified, is necessarily a testimony to God's wrath against sin and a witness to the life of the Christian as it ought to be. In either case the sermon is a proclamation of the law. In the former, it sets forth primarily the punitive, in the latter the imperative will of God. If this belongs to the nature of the sermon, how can it be realized unless the sermon bring this will of God to bear on the edification of the Christian—i. e., on the advancement of his spiritual life—by spurring him on to take up the struggle against all hindrances to Christian living, and to grow in the likeness of Christ's example? This second element in edification follows also from the essential nature of the

---

[6]Eph. 5:27.—[7]Phil. 3:12-14.—[8]1 John 1:8.—[9]Rom. 7:14.

sermon as preaching of the Gospel. For, as such, it implants in the heart vital forces which spontaneously prompt to action, renewing the whole of life and imparting strength for the struggle against sin and for the imitation of Christ. Unless these vital forces find a field of operation they will become atrophied. The sermon, by bringing them to bear practically on the preservation of the Christian life, truly edifies its hearers. This second element results, finally, from the relation of the sermon to its text, the latter dwelling often upon what the congregation, as well as the individual, should become and do, on the basis of what it is by the grace of God. (P. 119.)

Both sides of edification we find combined in Ps. 95 and applied directly to the service of the congregation. In verses 1-5 the individual worshipers, on their way to the temple, exhort one another to praise the works of Jehovah, the great God. On their arrival at the entrance, they are met by the choir of priests,—"O come, let us worship and bow down; let us kneel before the Lord our maker." For He is worthy to be praised, since "He is our God, and we are the people of His pasture, and the sheep of His hand" (6-7a). While the congregation enters, a solo voice is heard impressively warning them, in verses 7b-11,—"Remember that you are not only to rejoice in the fact that you are by His grace God's people, but that you must become ever more completely what you are by being converted to the Lord. Today, when you hear His voice, harden not your hearts!"

Schleiermacher conceived the entire service, and the sermon in particular, as a purely representative act expressing the faith of the congregation. In this he was followed by Schweizer, Baur, Palmer, Th. Harnack, and others. If this means the representation of the faith not only of the respective congregation but, as Schleiermacher held, of the ideal congregation as well as of the true Church, and if this faith is not divorced from the Scriptures but finds in them "the normal representation for all time," as Schleiermacher also held, though less clearly[10]—the position contains valuable elements of truth. We share this view, thus modified, only we should like to deepen it and emphasize more strongly the purpose underlying it. We deepen it by regarding the sermon as a living presentment of the words and acts

---

[10]Cf. *Vorlesungen ueber praktische Theologie,* 1850, 241 ff.; *Kurze Darstellung des theol. Studiums,* 2 ed., §§ 83, 103.

of God, as apprehended by the believing congregation, and thus of His saving person. We emphasize more sharply the purpose by regarding the edification of the congregation as not only the by-product (so Bassermann), but the deliberate and proper aim of the sermon. For us the sermon must aim at awakening faith and joy in our salvation divinely obtained in Christ. Without this there can be no edifying sermon. The Church, gathered by the Holy Spirit and assembled for worship, is to be strengthened in her faith and brought to a deeper realization of God's saving work for her; she is to grow in the knowledge of His infinite love, faithfulness, and truth, and her God is to become to her ever greater and more glorious, so that compared with Him all else grows ever dimmer and disappears. She is to learn more and more the length and breadth and depth and height of His saving thoughts, and thus grow more and more certain of her salvation here and hereafter. Thus Paul's paean of assurance in Romans 8 is so impressive because it is sung out of a life of increasing faith and constant absorption in the greatness of God his Saviour. With such assurance comes true joy. For all joy in God must be based on fellowship with Him, growing out of the forgiveness of sin, and is only a vivid consciousness of this fellowship and its resultant bliss. The sermon that never takes a man out of himself, out of his sin and guilt, his fear and anxiety, his doubt and uncertainty, and never sets him in the presence of God in whom he has found salvation and strength, a refuge for time and eternity, so that in the vision and experience of God's saving power his eyes and heart are enlarged, and he stands at first dumb with admiration, then breaks out in loud praise—such a sermon cannot edify. The measure of a man's growth in the knowledge of God is the measure of his realization of what God has done for him. The farther the naturalist or nature lover progresses, the greater and more marvelous do many things appear to him which he formerly overlooked. His eye is opened to beauties to which he was formerly blind. The sermon should assist the lover of God to make the same experience with respect to God's nature and works. Then it will edify, for then it will further and advance his inner life and increase its joy.

Already in the Old Testament the prevailing note is one of gratitude and joy over what God does for His people. Moses and Miriam sound this note after the passage through the Red Sea, that type of our salvation. And Moses has not forgotten it when at the close of his life he cries, "Yea, He loved the people," and, "Happy art thou, O Israel: who is like unto thee, O people! saved by the Lord, the shield of thy help, and who is the sword of thy excellency: and thine enemies shall be found liars unto thee, and thou shalt tread upon their high places."[11] This note is taken up by psalmists and prophets and swells to a mighty chorus of joy. "O taste and see that the Lord is good," cries one;[12] "Behold your God,"[13] another; and a third, "Who is a God like unto Thee, that pardoneth iniquity, and passeth by the transgressions of the remnant of His heritage?"[14] How eloquently Isaiah sings of the future works of God for His people and becomes thereby the evangelist of the Old Testament—setting in the foreground now the deliverance from Babylon by One who is greater than all gods, as in ch. 40-48; now the deliverance from sin and guilt, by the Servant of Yahveh κατ' ἐξοχήν, as in ch. 49-57; now the final deliverance and bringing of the saved into the new heaven and earth, as in ch. 58-66.[15] This was the sort of preaching that rendered "beautiful" to the congregation, "the feet of him that bringeth good tidings, that publisheth peace, that bringeth good tidings of salvation, that saith unto Zion, Thy God reigneth!"[16] This was the preaching that "built up" Zion, the Old Testament city of God, for it kept alive and renewed its faith in God the Saviour who was even then present with His people, and awakened and nourished the hope that He would reveal Himself in future in greater measure as Saviour.

In the New Testament the good news is heard in clearest strains, with the view of arousing faith in the Saviour who is now come to liberate men from sin and the sorrows of life and bring them to certainty of salvation and to joy. John the Baptist opens the chorus with his "Behold the Lamb of God, that taketh away the sin of the world." This prophet in the wilderness, to whom all Israel came confessing their sins, had an insight, equalled by few, into the sin of his people, and aimed to edify them by pointing them to the fulfilment of Old Testament prophecy in the incarnate Son of God. John the Divine closes the chorus when in Rev. 5 he lets us hear some strains of the heavenly song of the redeemed, concerning the Lamb that was slain and has redeemed us with His blood, and is now worthy to receive "power, and riches, and wisdom, and strength, and honor, and glory, and blessing." Between these two stand Jesus and His apostles, whose testimony reaches nowhere a higher note than when

---

[11]Deut. 33:3, 29.—[12]Ps. 34:8.—[13]Isa. 40:9.—[14]Micah 7:18.—[15]Cf. also, in the first part of the book, ch. 9, 11, 12, 25, 26, 35.—[16]Isa. 52:7.—[17]John 1:29.

they tell of the love and grace of God, who has become our **Father-in-Christ,** and when they endeavor thereby to awaken or strengthen faith and implant peace and joy in men's hearts, so that now a soft and low rejoicing, now a loud thanksgiving rises from the souls of those who have been thus edified.

W. Laible writes, on Matth. 9:36,—"Scattered, famished and utterly helpless—so Jesus found city-dwellers and country folk among whom He journeyed. They would not have been so forlorn, had they but had the right shepherds. But they were 'as sheep having no shepherd'. The Pharisees were keepers of the law, not keepers of the sheep. They did not succor the weak, but starved them. They did not seek the lost, but condemned them. They had no sympathy with the anxiety of heart and conscience round about them. Otherwise they could not have sat in Moses' seat with such hard hearts, nor scattered the sheep until they were exhausted. Nor were the Sadducees shepherds. They sought to quiet men's souls by supplying cushions for their heads and by making the gate wide and the way broad. But that could not satisfy the longing for God. This longing is not content with any substitute; it seeks God and all of God, in His love and grace, but also in His righteousness and truth. The poor deluded people soon awoke from their dream and found themselves in the midst of the wilderness. If only there had been one among them who was a true shepherd. He would have flung wide the door and cried, 'Behold your God.' He would have opened all the wells and fountains of the divine Word and bidden men drink. But there was none to do this. Among these scattered ones comes Jesus, and from every side they flock to Him. He did not diminish the wrath of God but rather increased it. 'Ye have heard that it was said by them of old time. . . . but I say unto you.' He made it not one whit easier for those who refused to believe the Scriptures. In all its strength the stream of divine revelation rolled from His lips, and they never tired of hearing Him. It was the voice of a shepherd and bishop of souls. He knew their sin and did not call it innocence, but He knew also their weakness and reached out His hand to the weak. And He knew their despondency, and said to them 'Be of good cheer.' He knew their silent weeping and crying after God, and He took them by the hand and brought them back to the Father." And here at the Father's heart they were made whole and found peace and joy and strength. If we wish to preach edifying sermons we must stand, like Jesus, as His heralds and divine evangelists in the midst of our people and cry, "Behold your God! Acknowledge Him and His salvation! Here is the way to certainty and joy." For "this is life eternal, that they might know Thee, the only true God, and Jesus Christ, whom Thou hast sent."[18] The sermons of Augustine were edifying because in them he showed men again the gracious countenance of God. Luther's sermons were edifying because he led souls wearied with laws of every sort back to Him who says, "Come unto me, all ye that labor and are heavy laden, and I will give you rest." Such sermons produced faith and prepared the way for joy.

Many accept the principle that the sermon must edify by recalling men to faith, and yet are ignorant of the means by which the soul is to be recalled to faith or strengthened in its faith. The Lutheran sermon, also, frequently errs here. It operates too often with faith as an intellectual act, as a rational assent to the truths of the Scriptures, and demands of its hearers that they *must* believe, as though faith were something a man could achieve, a condition he could fulfil, on his own initiative. The tripartite definition of faith given in the older dogmatic—*notitia, assensus, fiducia*—has helped to foster this error. Again, many who in their dogmatic reject every trace of Pelagianism, Semi-Pelagianism and synergism, do not carry the consequences of their dogmatic into their preaching. A recent volume of sermons by a pastor of the Lutheran Church has been not unfairly criticized as unorthodox in its teaching on faith. Certainly there can be no justifying and saving faith without knowledge of and assent to the facts of salvation, but this knowledge and assent do not in themselves constitute justifying faith. They may be found, and are often found, even in the natural and unregenerate man. Justifying faith is in its essence nothing else than *fiducia,* trust in the salvation which Christ has for me and which is offered to me in the Word,—a *fiducia* wrought by the Spirit through the Word, and not a *fiducia* resting upon *notitia* and *assensus* as acts of my natural intellect. This *fiducia* includes *notitia* and *assensus,* but these as well as *fiducia* itself are the result of the working of the Spirit of God. They are by no means to be identified with natural knowledge and assent, but differ from them *toto genere.* Justifying faith has for its object things that belong not to this visible world of cause and effect, but to an entirely different order, to an invisible and eternal world revealed in God's Word. Such faith therefore, both in its first beginning and in its constant renewal, is not the product of man's knowledge and assent, but comes solely through the operation of the Holy Spirit, utilizing indeed those faculties of the

---

[18] John 17: 3.

mind but creating in the soul, after His own miraculous fashion, both the ability to believe and faith itself.[19] The realization of this must become part of the very fibre of the preacher's mind, and must pass over into his entire theological and Christian thinking, before he can preach rightly about faith. Besides which, he must of course live in the daily experience of such faith. Then the phrase, "you *must* believe," will be not only distasteful but impossible to him, unless he uses it in the sense that whoever claims to be a Christian must believe, just as the sun must shine if it is indeed the sun.[20] He will know of no other way to bring men to this faith than by constantly presenting to them the saving works of God and in and with them the person of God Himself, the author of all salvation. If the glorified Lord, present in the Gospel, cannot reach men's hearts and produce faith, no one and nothing else can in heaven or earth.

An equally unsound preaching of faith proceeds on the supposition that the natural man can be brought to faith without having previously passed through the *terrores conscientiae,* and that faith can be renewed in the Christian without sorrow for sin and a lively hatred of sin. Both are impossibilities. Though the stings of conscience will vary according to the individual temperament, they must be present in some measure in all. Man must feel himself in the presence of the divine Judge, and must tremble under His sentence, before he can acknowledge Christ and accept Him in faith as his only Saviour. Faith is, moreover, incomplete as long as the desire to continue in sin and the love of sinning remain in the heart. The child clinging to the Father's knees and trusting in His forgiveness cannot at the same time cling to the old sin. In the shame of the penitent at having so deeply grieved and offended his gracious God all love of sin must be burned up and completely destroyed, at least in principle. Otherwise faith is, in Melanchthon's phrase, only a "painted," a counterfeit faith; it lacks life and reality. How can it be otherwise, when the God whom faith lays hold of is the Holy One who cannot abide sin, who in forgiving sin and justifying man does not deny His moral nature, and can therefore forgive only because He has first condemned and punished man's sin in Christ, his substitute. The preacher, therefore, who has learned how to preach faith aright has thereby also paved the way for the preaching of good works, the new obedience, the struggle against sin, and holiness of life. All carnal security, which says, "I

---

[19]Cf. M. Reu, *Die Heilsordnung,* 1914.—[20]Cf. Luther on the necessity of good works, above, page 44.

have obtained, now I can lack nothing"; the moral indolence so prevalent in our congregations, that will not exert nor deny itself nor give or sacrifice anything, and that forms so great a hindrance to all church work,—these have at their root this fatal mistake regarding faith. The cause does not lie, as is commonly contended, in the fact that the Lutheran Church teaches too much faith and not enough good works, but—apart from the hardening of men's hearts against God's Word—the cause lies in a wrong preaching of faith. God grant our Church a right preaching about faith, in which not only the *fides quae creditur* is taught purely and without abridgment, but in which the *fides qua creditur* is set forth earnestly and vigorously, and is implanted by God's grace in the hearts of men! Our whole church life would then be renewed—assurance of salvation, joy in the Lord, strength and motive-power for a new life would return. We should still have to give attention to the second element in true edification, but how different would be our treatment of it and how much greater the results.

Before turning to this second element, it will be well to correct another misunderstanding that attaches to the first. We said that the sermon should cause the congregation to rejoice in its God. By this we do not mean an hilarity of faith such as peals out of many "Gospel hymns," which flows from a one-sided emphasis upon the emotional or from a superficial experience, and which is soon silenced when it encounters the realities of life. We mean on the contrary that sound, pure joy which is not dependent on certain exalted moods and is still less made up of a series of such moods, but consists in a quiet and even elation of the heart, rising at times to exultation, yet persisting in the midst of tribulation, as we find it in Paul in Phil. 1:18b ff. It is born of the certainty of salvation in Christ and is its natural accompaniment. Thus our view differs from that of those who picture this joy in such exalted terms, likening it to that of Moses on Mount Nebo and of Christ in the Transfiguration, that they leave behind all reality and transcend the experience of most of their hearers. We know only too well that there are times when this joy is altogether absent, and the believer feels nothing but God's wrath and can struggle through such periods of depression only by clinging to the objective Word against all subjective emotions. At such times it is for him not to see and yet to believe.

"Ich glaube was Dein Wort verspricht,
Ich fuehl' es oder fuehl' es nicht."

The Second Element in Edification

The second element in the edification of the Christian congregation is its incitement to become ever more completely what it already is. This is especially emphasized by Kleinert. "It is contrary to the nature of Christian salvation," he says, "to regard it as a common possession, to be exposed on certain festival occasions as a sacred treasure for reverent contemplation. It is an essential characteristic of the word, and especially of the divine Word, to seek to enter as a dynamic force into the life of the individual. This force would come to a standstill and be converted into complacent rest if an ideal congregation of perfect members had realized all the energy latent in this force. All desires would then be satisfied by the service as festival [*Feier*], in which the Word was presented as message of a salvation experienced and lived through by all, and purely with a view to festal enjoyment and praise. In the worship of the blessed in heaven the Word as incentive has no place. But is this the case with the congregation as it now is? .... Only in its ideal state, and from the viewpoint of its consummation in eternity, can the congregation be regarded as made up of members all of whom participate equally and to their full ability in the life of Christ. In its temporal reality the congregation is always the sphere in which the results of this life in Christ are seen in operation. It contains so many members in whom the life of faith is present only potentially and must be brought to light or at least continually furthered. Indeed, no sincere member of the congregation will claim to be above the need of such furthering, and those most advanced will be the last to make such a claim. The Church of Christ is nowhere and never *in esse*, always *in posse*, in a continuous process of assimilating new and immature members who must be led onward to perfection, or backsliders who must be restored to conscious participation in the salvation the Church offers. To build up the true Church within the visible Church is the ultimate purpose of all church activity, and pre-eminently of its central activity, the work of preaching."[21] Certainly there can be no new life without the forgiveness of sins, still less can there be any joy; whoever, therefore, does not bring the tidings of forgiveness to the congregation cannot edify it. But when the forgiveness of sins is accepted in faith and, as a result, peace, joy and strength have entered the heart, then the new life can and must begin, a life of work upon ourselves and for others. When Jesus healed the sick it was not only in order to relieve them from their pain, but to restore them to a life of

---

[21] *Homiletik,* pp. 10 f.

activity. The same is true of spiritual healing by means of the forgiveness of sins. Its purpose is to enable men to take up their moral life-work; it is healing in order to be hallowing. The moral ideal is God's ultimate purpose. His intention is not only to restore men to a blessed fellowship with Himself, with which they are to rest content, but to lead them thereby to accept His will as the supreme norm of their life and to put themselves unreservedly at His service.[22] Only then are revealed in their fulness the vital forces that have come into the heart with faith in His purifying grace, and the entire life of the Church becomes one loud song of praise to her God who incites and enables her to willing surrender to Him. The more the congregation becomes what it can and should be, the more readily will it measure up to its missionary responsibility to the world. This makes it incumbent upon the preacher to make his sermons contribute to this end. "The supreme aim," says Herrick Johnson, "is perfect manhood in Christ Jesus. The preacher's finished work is not a finished sermon, but a Christlike soul. He constructs a sermon that he may reconstruct a man."[23]

The preacher must not, however, overlook the fact that this is a matter of gradual growth, an organic unfolding of the faith-life within the Christian, and not an external alteration or mechanical addition. That was the weakness of the ethical sermons of many early Fathers, even of Basil and Ambrose, and especially of the mediaeval sermon. It is likewise the weakness of much of the moral preaching of today. It is an attempt to sew a new piece of cloth on an old garment, as though that would make the garment new. It is forgotten that we cannot gather grapes from thorns or figs from thistles, and that only a good tree can bring forth good fruit and only a justified Christian perform good works, but that such a one must perform them by an inner necessity.

Hence the Scriptures sum the whole of sanctification with its multiplicity of works under the term "fruit" or "fruits."[24] If this is borne in mind we shall avoid all external pressure, and stress always the inner motive, faith. We shall show men that, if they lack the fruits of the Christian life, the fault lies here. And we shall point faith to its pattern in the life of Jesus, and indicate the channels along which it is to set its life-stream flowing, according to the various spheres of Christian duty. Whether calling its hearers to battle with

---

[22]Ex. 19:6; 1 Peter 2:9; Titus 2:14.—[23]P. 29.—[24]Gal. 5:22; Eph. 5:9; Matth. 3:8, 10; Jas. 3:18; Phil. 1:11; 2 Pet. 1:5 ff.

their besetting sins, or presenting to them the virtues they are to strive after, the sermon but summons the faith that is in them to self-expression. The power of the new life, given in faith, must drive out the old and rule in its stead. The Word of God, falling like a seed into the heart, will, in order to unfold, and by its very unfolding, force out of the heart whatever impurity and remnant of wickedness[25] may still linger there. The sermon that aims at helping the Christian to become more completely what he is, will follow the example of Luther in his explanation of the Decalogue, in which he demands and recognizes no other morality than that which is based upon fear and love of God—fear, which is nothing else than reverence of God's greatness and majesty; and love, which is produced by God Himself, who loved us first, and whose love has found lodging in the heart through faith.

A contributor to the *Evang.-Luth. Kirchenzeitung* (1910, No. 25), writing on "The psychological foundation of the sermon," says: "The sermon is in many respects too one-sidedly soteriological, too exclusively oriented by the idea of justification. Some appear to think they can preserve what is central, only by taking their stand firmly in the centre and carefully refraining from making any movement toward the circumference." This may truly characterize many a Lutheran preacher and points to one of our grave defects; but there is a still more serious defect. It consists in losing sight of the essential character of evangelical morality, as the organic unfolding of the potentialities inherent in justifying faith, and in fostering (often unconsciously but none the less harmfully) a morality which, instead of growing out of and revolving about the centre of justifying faith, has lost touch or is in danger of losing touch with this centre. Over against the mediaeval preaching on virtues and vices, which divided what is organically connected and came perilously near to the ethical sermons of pagan moral philosophy, it was the merit of Luther's preaching that he never warned against sin or exhorted to virtue without calling attention to justifying faith as the root of all morality. All preaching of ethics not thus rooted leads inevitably to the same result as the preaching of the scribes and Pharisees. The flock of God is goaded to exhaustion by the relentless rod of the driver, instead of being made to lie down in green pastures and led beside still waters. What wonder that sincere souls cry out in utter weariness! These may be silenced for the moment, but will later break out the more

---

[25] $\pi\epsilon\rho\iota\sigma\sigma\epsilon\iota\alpha$ $\kappa\alpha\kappa\iota\alpha\varsigma$, Jas. 1:21.

loudly, and, unless their needs are understood and met by the preacher, will seek relief elsewhere or despair of all help.

The sermon must certainly, from this centre, shed light into all departments of domestic, congregational, church, and civil life, so that the individual members, as well as the congregation as a whole, may know and perform their respective duties until the Church of Christ upon earth becomes ever more the salt of the earth and the light of the world, the preservative and renovating force of mankind, a leaven permeating all relationships of human life. Paul and the other apostles were continually doing this in their Epistles, and Luther, not content with laying down in the first part of his Catechism the true norm of a God-pleasing life, added at the close a "Table of Duties, or certain passages of the Scriptures, selected for various holy orders and conditions of men, wherein their respective duties are set forth." A right sermon will not be satisfied with setting forth in vague general terms ethical concepts and moral duties, but will be direct, concrete and specific.[26] This will make for variety, definiteness, and effectiveness. The ethical concepts will be filled with life, and religion, instead of hanging in the clouds, will be brought home to men's business and bosoms and set in the midst of the actual circumstances of everyday life, there to unfold its truth and transforming power. In this way, too, the sermon can make its most valuable contribution to the social and other problems of the day. But its method of procedure must in every case be from the centre to the circumference, from within outwards, by way of organic development and gradual growth. Otherwise it may endanger men's salvation and will certainly not lead to genuine morality. It will be more likely to tear down than to build up or edify.

In essaying to show by the example of Jesus what the congregation and the individual must become on the basis of justifying faith, the preacher should beware of giving a one-sided portrayal of Jesus. Jesus was not only meek, lowly, tender, non-resistant; He was also firm, decided, hard, ruthless. The energy of His holiness was no less relentless in casting out sin from His presence, than His seeking Saviour-love was patient in pursuing the sinner, if haply He might win him. He would not have been "true God, begotten of the Father from eternity," if both had not been combined in Him in inseparable unity. The modern sermon is fond of dwelling on this union of opposites in Jesus. This is true of its more positive exponents such as

---

[26]See below, pp. 134 ff.; 151 ff. for fuller discussion of this point.

Naumann, Aeschbacher, Benz, no less than of decidedly liberal representatives like Bitzius, Doerries, Rittelmeyer. Aeschbacher says: "Christ was not only calm, He was also storm. He was not only gentleness but also flame, an agitating, troublous, lightning-like figure, big with tempests. Probably He could not have lived among us for three years without being put out of the way."[27] Rittelmeyer writes in one of his sermons: "Whoever undertakes to describe Jesus will, almost as a matter of course, paint Him in sharply contrasting colors. An overwhelmingly serious outlook on life, and yet a sunny joyousness of soul; the most ardent enthusiasm underlying and ennobling the whole of life, and yet a serene clarity of spirit; the most matter-of-fact facing of reality, and yet a unique self-possession; a living completely in the moment, and yet an unshakably firm and constant holding to the loftiest goals; unreserved truthfulness, penetrating to the last recesses of the heart, and yet an extremely shrewd and courteous dealing with men; inexorable sternness of moral requirement, and yet an intimate sympathy and forgivingness; a profound and keen knowledge of mankind, and yet an inexhaustible love without the faintest shadow of contempt; an irresistible mastery over men, and yet utter willingness and ability to serve; absolute certitude in every word and act, and yet the finest delicacy and considerateness for all; a regal self-consciousness, and yet the tenderest restraint and sincere humility of heart—and all this blent in a harmony soaring high above all melodies ever heard upon earth: that was Jesus."[28] It is a thousand pities that the highly-gifted Rittelmeyer has not discovered the secret of this harmony in the mystery of the divine-human person of Jesus. For us who know and confess this mystery, Jesus does not cease on that account to be the pattern of our moral life. Not that we are to look in His life for an exact parallel to every detail of our lives today—an error exemplified in Charles M. Sheldon's *In His Steps*. But "the mind that was in Christ Jesus" is to govern His followers in every time and place, and to assist them to solve in His spirit the several problems of the ethical life as they arise. Thus Christ will "be formed" in His Church and she will become more and more completely what she already is.

When the sermon combines these two sides of edification, it will also supply the need of those who no longer belong to the congregation or have not yet become members, but attend its services. The

---

[27]*Wir sahen seine Herrlichkeit*, 41913.—[28]*Gott und die Seele*, Predigten von Geyer und Rittelmeyer (1906).

same message that serves to renew the faith of the believer is able to produce faith in the non-believer. That which uncovers and reproves the sin of believers can also bring the unconverted to a knowledge of his sinful condition. That which is held up before the congregation as the ethical ideal it should strive after is able also to move the unconverted to seek the strength which enables men to strive effectually after this ideal. Thus we re-affirm the position expressed in the Introduction[29] and cannot see the wisdom of adding to the two elements in edification, the missionary element as a third of equal value. Kleinert, writing in the midst of a state-church in which the missionary element might be expected to stand out as a separate factor, says: "That at present an increased importance is attached to the missionary element in the sermon scarcely needs proof. Our age is characterized by the inquiry and seeking of unsatisfied minds, and this is the soil that seems specially adapted to the mission of the Gospel. The wide diffusion and infinite variety of the results of civilization, moreover, have heightened, multiplied and refined the demands of the human mind to an extraordinary degree. Many are led to flit about from one transient excitement to another, but each unfulfilled promise of satisfaction leaves the mind empty and the personality unedified. Others are brought to a conscious realization of emptiness and unsatisfactoriness. Driven about by the meaninglessness of a life without higher contents and the torment of an existence without eternal foundations, they stray from one recommended substitute for Christianity to another, seeking peace and finding none. Hosts of other seekers, scarcely knowing themselves as such, groan under the needs and burdens of life. Doubtless the practical imitation of the love of Christ will find among these its appointed sphere of labor, but if this imitation be genuine it will also hear, amid the clamor of the day, through the misery and need, the voice of the weary and heavy laden crying out with the deathless cry after salvation, after rest for the soul. If the field is white unto the harvest, the congregational sermon dare not shut its ears to the missionary summons coming to it in this and similar forms. At the same time it remains true that it is a congregational sermon, and that the preacher must speak, not as a missionary among heathen, but with and in the congregation, although in such a way as not to send even these seeking ones empty away. 1 Corinthans 14:23 ff. For their search would not have brought them to the service of the congregation but left them con-

---

[29] Above, p. 14.

tent with personal or printed advisers, unless they expected, from that which gathers and moves the worshiping congregation, a power to enlighten and uplift. The proper procedure will be, therefore, not to take over this missionary (halieutic) element, as of equal value, into the conception of the sermon, but to include it under the head of *Gemeindeseelsorge.*"[30] A reference to Buechsel[31] is in place here. What lent to his preaching its power and led many to conversion, was the fact that it was pervaded by the peace of the children of God, and that it left a living impression of the rest found in God by all seeking souls. This attracted even those who were as yet far from the Lord and from His Church. This "synopsis of 'I am' [*Sein*] and 'I ought to be' [*Sollen*], of experienced grace and acknowledged duty," is a characteristic not only of Pauline[32] but of all Christian piety. And this must find expression in our preaching, if it is to edify in the right way.

In these two aspects the sermon must regard its hearer and from these two sides endeavor to lay hold upon his heart, so that he may be truly edified in this double sense. It must lay hold of him in his inmost nature, as to intellect, feeling, and will, and set these faculties in motion, so that he may really lay hold anew on what he is and advance on the way of sanctification. Unless it is the aim of the sermon thus to reach and move the heart, there can be no true edification; for then the Christian will neither rejoice in what he already is by the grace of God nor reach out after sanctification and perfection.

But what makes it possible for the sermon to touch, in so intimate a manner, the whole soul-life of man? The possibility of this is given, first of all, in the psychological law according to which the word is, above all else, the medium of intercourse between soul and soul, whereby knowledge is communicated to the intellect, and feeling and will are set in motion. This is true especially of the living spoken word of person to person, and of this word in the highest degree when

---

[30]*Homiletik,* p. 12.—[31]*Erinnerungen aus dem Leben eines Landgeistlichen,* i, 69 ff.—[32]Cf. E. von Dobschuetz, *Der gegenwaertige Stand der neutestamentlichen Exegese* (1906), p. 29.

it is the expression of an ardent feeling, a clear conviction, and a masterful will. This universal psychological law is fully applicable in the sphere of the sermon. When the preacher expresses Christian knowledge, feeling and effort, with the requisite clearness, warmth and power, the corresponding chords in the soul of his hearer will be set in motion; he will be moved to sympathy, assent, and action. When this is done repeatedly, the Christian knowledge of the hearer will be clarified, his emotions deepened, and the exertions of his will strengthened. This again is in accordance with a well known psychological law, the law of the association of ideas. Such repetition, however, dare not become spiritless and mechanical, blunting and stunting the mind, but must be a presentation of the same materials from ever new angles and in new combinations, and in such a manner that the preacher's interest in his materials is seen to be continually fresh and strong.

Again, the possibility of moving the soul and truly edifying it depends upon the nature of the Word of God proclaimed in the sermon. This Word is the power of God and is sharper than any two-edged sword. By virtue of the fact that God, in Christ, through the Spirit, approaches the hearer in and with the Word as used in the sermon,[33] this Word, in a much higher degree than any merely human word, gains admission to the heart and sets the faculties of the soul in motion. It creates new powers of cognition and volition, and strengthens those it has created. Hence it is the duty of the preacher who desires to preach "unto edification" to find, through diligent toil, those elements lying in his text, and not always lying on the surface, that will enlighten the intellect, kindle the emotions, and move the will, and after submitting to them himself, to bring them to bear upon his hearers. Wealth of

---

[33]*Immanentia spiritus sancti,* John 6:63; Titus 3:5; Jas. 1:18; *efficacia verbi,* Rom. 1:16; Heb. 4:12; 2 Cor. 2:16.

ideas, beauty of diction, clear delivery, however desirable in themselves, do not constitute the edifying character of the sermon, and may on occasion even prevent or diminish its edifying effect. This effect does not proceed from them, but from the above-mentioned elements in the Divine Word alone. To this Word the external features of thought, language and delivery stand in the relation of handmaids, serving but to unfold its inherent power and to adapt and apply it to the capacity of the hearers. (P. 128.)

If the sermon has a purpose the preacher must keep that purpose clearly before him and concentrate every effort upon its attainment. And if this purpose is to bring the members of the congregation to a realization of what God has done for them, so that they may apprehend it in faith and rejoice therein, and to lead them to become, on the basis of what they are by the grace of God, more completely what God wills them to be, then the preacher will need to touch and actually influence the thinking, feeling and willing of his congregation, those three sides of its soul-life. Hence there is no more important problem before him than this: How can I touch the inner life of my hearers, so as to awaken them out of their spiritual lassitude and cause them really to occupy themselves with my message, ponder it trembling with joy or fear, and be moved by it to choice and action? Unfortunately, so many sermons are preached which have apparently no other aim than to consume a certain portion of time or to serve as a decorative adjunct to the service. One would never dream that they were addressed to immortal souls redeemed by Christ and to be made actually His. There is no attempt on the part of the preacher to put himself *en rapport* with these souls, and he might just as well be preaching (as he often is) to empty pews. His sermons neither come from the soul nor go to the soul. Just as we say impersonally, "it rains," so we might say of such sermons, "it preaches." There is no living and original personality behind the words, which fall upon the hearer's ears with the monotony of a dripping rain-spout, and with the same lulling effect. We are not thinking now of the monotony of delivery, but the monotony of contents and structure. Such sermons bore, and boredom breeds indifference and, if it becomes the rule, disgust. This monotony is a powerful ally of unchurchliness and frequently the forerunner of permament estrangement from religion. Hering has this to say of it: "It enervates the service, drives away the members, has no attraction for the estranged, encourages the lame excuses of the indifferent, and drives to desperate attempts to revive and strengthen the moribund by extraordinary means apart from the sacred office."[84] "Liebe Brueder, nur nicht langweilig!"—so Emil Frommel admonished his brethren at a mass-meeting in Berlin to discuss ways and means for preserving to Church and nation the benefits of the war of 1870-71. Otto Baumgarten devotes a long chapter in his *Predigtprobleme*[85] to "Tiresome and interesting sermons." His warning against the former is most timely, for more complaints are heard now than formerly about the tiresomeness of the average sermon. Not that the preaching of today is more tiresome than formerly; for, apart from the self-satisfied and indolent preachers whom, like the poor, we have always with us, there have never been so many preachers who sincerely endeavor to preach interesting, pointed and carefully phrased sermons. But as a result of the changed conditions of our age and its culture, audiences are more quickly bored than before. Where in bygone days the Sunday sermon was the one outstanding event and mental stimulus of the week, the farmer of today has his daily or weekly newspaper. He has gathered some sort of library, however modest; he travels to the city, where he spends hours at the motion pictures; he attends political and social meetings and institutes in whose discussions he takes part. The country school has opened his mind to the great world about him, and the number of farmers' children whose education does not stop at the country school is constantly increasing. No wonder that church attendance is no longer so regular as before, and that those who do attend are no longer so receptive, are more quickly bored, and must be dealt with in a manner very different from that of former days, if the sermon is to leave a real and lasting impression. This is still more true of the city. Here the public school is supplemented by the high school, which, with its multiplicity of courses and the inadequacy of the average teaching force, turns out pupils equipped with a dangerous smattering of many things and with minds crammed and incapable of any deeper impression. The public libraries abounding in every city and village frequently cultivate a mania for omnivorous and indiscriminate reading; the numberless magazines and periodicals on sale at almost every street corner introduce, often in the most readable fashion, to every possible department of life; public lectures of every sort offer mental stimulus; sumptuous motion pictures with their vivid appeal and ques-

---

[84]P. 308.—[85]Pp. 30—60.

tionable motives blunt the power of discrimination in moral and religious matters; the screaming headlines in endless editions of great dailies of varying shades of yellow accustom the mind to the extraordinary and abnormal; the herding together in shop and factory, in train and trolley-car; the widely advertised Sunday amusements; the graphophone grinding out its noisy music in almost every home—all these and many similar features have produced a superficial, sensation-mad public to which the quiet church-hymn and the sermon, moving in a narrow circle of ideas apparently far removed from actual life, seem exceedingly tame and tiresome, so that it can hardly await the Amen and meanwhile has its thoughts elsewhere. It is no easy matter to preach to such hearers, if one undertakes to reach and move their soul, i. e., truly to edify them. An uninteresting sermon is altogether helpless here; it does not even attempt to hold the wandering mind or to leave on jaded souls an impress of the eternal and divine. Hence Baumgarten's demand for interesting sermons is so much needed. He gives the following twelve rules for making the sermon interesting: "(1) Reach down into the teeming life of man! (2) Interesting sermons must be timely; (3) they must take into account the actual condition of the congregation; (4) they must be social; (5) intensely individual; (6) as direct as possible; (7) they must be *Ichpredigten*;[36] (8) they must bring out the paradoxes of the Gospel in their full force; (9) they must be plain didactic sermons, solving the difficulties of the thinking man; (10) not affected, but natural and simple; (11) as pointed as possible; (12) based upon one assumption: freedom from bondage to the written Word."[37]

This is not the place to pass judgment on the merits or defects of this program, nor is it our intention to match these twelve rules with a fresh dozen of our own. What constitutes a truly interesting sermon can be determined only on the basis of a complete treatment of Homiletics. The point here is simply to emphasize the necessity of keeping the sermon interesting and avoiding everything tiresome, if it is to edify. At the same time it must not be forgotten that the demand for interesting sermons may come from two widely different sources. It may mean no more than that the sermon should win the casual attention of the hearer and make a transient appeal to his taste by turning itself into a series of anecdotes, historical incidents or clever epigrams, by descanting upon happenings of the day or the personal experiences of the preacher, or by a departure from the conventional and a revel-

---

[36]See above, p. 80.—[37]See above, p. 56.

ing in the sensational. Much indeed has been gained when the attention of the hearer is won. Attention or interest, as the opposite of indifference and *ennui*, is the essential precondition without which the soul cannot be influenced. Hence the awakening of interest is one of the primary duties of the preacher who wishes to edify. But on a higher plane than this, and leading directly to the solution of the problem of edification, is the awakening of interest in the sense of the Herbartian psychology and pedagogy. This, while forming no less a contrast to the mental state of indifference, denotes no merely casual and transient but a definite and permanent condition. When I am indifferent to a certain thing, it in no wise touches or moves my soul, and leaves neither joyous nor sorrowful impressions behind; its presence is as little a gain as its absence is a loss. But when I am interested in a thing, it begins to possess value for me and awakens pleasurable emotions in my soul, so that I delight in its possession and prefer it to other things. I am no longer indifferent or a stranger to it, but a living relation grows up between it and myself (*inter-esse*, to be between; *inter-est*, it matters). In short, the object of my interest has suddenly assumed importance for me, and I have become aware of this importance. If interest denotes my value-judgment with respect to a thing, it is closely related to my emotions, which are the mental organ by which values are measured. It presupposes also an activity of my intellectual life, for an object must enter into my world of perceptions before my emotions can weigh its value. And it also stimulates my will, so that I reach out toward the object to appropriate or reject it. To awaken such an interest on the part of his hearers in the subject-matter of his sermon, must be the aim of the preacher. He must set before them God's words and acts, the person and work of Christ, the blessings of faith, in so winning a manner, and in ever new aspects, that the soul will find itself quickened and attracted in its emotions, will delight to dwell in this new world of ideas, preferring it to all others, and will become willing to strive after these goods and make them its own. He must lay bare sin in all its hideousness, with the host of temporal and eternal disasters that follow in its wake, in its debasing power, poisoning the imagination, deceiving the emotions, crippling the will to good and deadening the conscience, and in its fundamental spirit of opposition to God and His will and of rebellion against 'His person; so that the soul will tremble, draw back, turn away from sin, and earnestly hate and forsake it. On the other hand, he must picture the bliss of communion with God, the inner beauty and lasting glory of the righteous, the delights of a good conscience, and the greatness and transcendent reality of the life eternal, in such living and glowing colors that their inherent power will be unfolded to the hearer and lift his soul toward the good, the perfect, and the eternal. If the hearer oppose no special hindrance, this goal may be attained even without the special co-operation of the Holy Spirit in the preacher or His creative operation in the hearer. In so far all may proceed from purely natural causes— the psychologically oriented discourse and the natural receptivity of the audience. But when the preacher is animated by the Spirit of God and each new aspect of the truth is as if it were born anew out of his constant communion with God, and when God's hour has struck for the individual hearer,[88] so that the Spirit, working through the preacher's word, begins His faith-producing operation in the heart, then we have, if man does not now wantonly and persistently resist, not only an awakened interest, but a penitent faith, an actual desire for the good on the part of the new will created by the Spirit, a real striving after moral perfection, the peace of forgiveness, joy in the Lord and His salvation, a zeal unto good works. The soul, the congregation, has been really edified.

Let the preacher who seeks to interest in this sense beware of cant phrases of religion, the use of words with no meaning behind them.[89] They have a pious sound but glide past the ears of the hearers, who have heard these phrases, Scripture passages or hymns a thousand times over and feel at once that they roll mechanically and without inner meaning from the preacher's lips. Such cant phrases, instead of rousing, lull to sleep; if they are met at first by a nod of approval, this soon turns into the first symptom of sound spiritual slumber. They leave the impression that the things treated in the sermon are not living, concrete realities, and so they lead finally to the death of all spiritual life. It has been said that "there is no poison that will so surely kill spiritual life at its very roots as the talking about sacred things which has degenerated into a mere phrase." And the aggressively sincere Carlyle says: "The beginning of all is to have done with falsity, to shun falsity as death eternal." And yet many a preacher mounts his pulpit and flings about pious platitudes, declaims familiar hymn stanzas, recites Bible verses like a man in his sleep, connecting the whole by a series of highly impersonal sentences,—and then won-

---

[88]*Augustana*, v; cf. Reu, *Christliche Ethik* (1915), p. 52.—[89]E. g., "With the help of God," "Our Lord and Saviour Jesus Christ," "For Christ's sake through faith," etc.

ders why his sermon produces no effect. How in all the world can mental and spiritual death produce mental and spiritual life?

Sermons truly interesting, that awakened interest and were perceptibly influenced by the Holy Spirit, were preached in the olden days by such men as Heinrich Mueller, Christian Scriver, Georg Conrad Rieger: Mueller, whose sermons bubbled forth out of the Scriptures, with their short sharp epigrammatic sentences, and mingled the divine truths with the everyday life of the people; Scriver, with his fine sense for things great and small in the world of nature, who found everywhere comparisons for the eternal; Rieger, driving straight at the individual with his persistent appeal and occasional bluntness. Among interesting preachers of the last century and the recent past we may mention the following: Tholuck, with his brilliant double talent for religious intuition and ingenious combination; F. W. Krummacher, with his modernization of biblical personages; Ahlfeldt, with his gift of poet-painter, truly popularized in his applications; H. Caspari, with his folk-style, teeming with proverbial sayings and his exemplary simplicity; Thomasius, with his pastoral method, putting his finger on the fundamental needs of the Christian life; E. Frommel, drawing nature, history and human life into the service of the sermon; F. W. Robertson, with his fine psychological tact, his wide culture, and his skill in conveying to his hearers, in imaginative language, his own experience of the Word; Spurgeon, with his vigorous search for souls, his impressive earnestness, apt illustrations, and poetic feeling; Phillips Brooks, with his intellectual riches, his fluency and religious fervor; Alexander Maclaren, with his noble popularity based on severe exegesis, his brilliant structure and perfection of impromptu style, for thirty years the chief literary influence in Manchester.

These brief characterizations of a few truly interesting preachers serve also to show how many and varied are the elements that go to make a sermon interesting. It is imposisble now to enumerate them all; what we are immediately concerned with is to emphasize the necessity of keeping in mind this approach to the soul, in every sermon, if the preacher is truly to edify his hearers. But the merely "interesting" is often confused with what awakens true interest. This confusion is found even in Augustine, Saurin is not free from it, Beecher frequently succumbs to it. Many others, especially younger preachers, but also not a few of riper experience, fall into this error, especially in the French and American pulpits. Since the endeavor to be interesting often leads to much that is far-fetched and mechanical, extravagant and undignified,[40] and goes hand in hand with flattery and vanity, we add the twofold warning of Hering. "The merely interesting," he says, "as well as the superficially brilliant, may lead to secularization, the corruption of taste, and confusion of sensational effect with the result that alone counts with God. For the 'interesting' may, as the highly colored and all too attractive covering of shallow and even erroneous ideas, mislead babes in Christ or the religiously immature into wrong paths or separatistic byways. At times the external form, product of the wit and fancy of a vain preacher, may outweigh the contents and make so strong an appeal to the intellectual whim of the hearer as to draw him away from the serious and divine contents, intended to reach his will, into weakly sentimental enjoyment. . . . If a preacher has acquired the beautiful and useful art of introducing the full contents of the Gospel in its original spiritual power, with the assistance of his own natural gifts, into the sphere of his hearer's will, he will be the more concerned, with earnest prayer, to put down every vain effort to shine, to resist a luxuriating aestheticism and the confusing of the divine with the human, and to keep the desire to achieve results subject to the discipline of the Spirit. This is the truth underlying Theremin's famous dictum, 'The orator should strive to please God alone.' "[41]

That which edifies is, in the last instance, not the mental ability of the preacher, but the divine Word alone. Wealth of ideas, psychological skill, beauty of language, charm of delivery, have their value in the awakening of interest, and should be sought after by the preacher, but they cannot produce nor strengthen justifying faith. This is done solely by the edifying power of the Word of God. These edifying elements are found in every text that is not chosen wholly at random. Hence one of the principal parts of the preparation of the sermon must be the preacher's endeavor to find and apply these elements. As the catechist teaching Bible History dare not, according to Doerpfeld confine himself to the external events in the story, nor content mself with the geographical, scientific or historical setting, but must penetrate to the mainspring of action, i. e., the thoughts, feelings, deliberations, motives, etc., of the actors and their religious and moral value :[42] so the preacher, especially when handling histori-

---

[40] As we see in Abraham a Santa Clara; more glaringly in many modern so-called evangelists and representatives of the supposedly new *genre* of "object-sermons"; most glaringly of all in William A. ("Billy") Sunday.—[41] Pp. 309f.—[42] Cf. Reu, *Catechetics*, p. 473f.

cal texts, dare not remain on the surface but must delve into the depths, until he has come upon the edifying elements in his text. He must find there that which is adapted to enlighten the intellect, stir the emotions, and move the will of the hearers; and not merely stimulate these natural faculties, but quicken the knowledge of sin and salvation, set the emotions atremble with horror at sin and joy in God and His forgiveness, and produce and strengthen the will to do the good. What is the use of describing, in a Christmas sermon, the condition of the Jewish people and of the Roman empire, unless as background for the fact of the Saviour's birth, and unless even the story of the birth itself be but the means of bringing Christ to the hearts of men today? What is gained when a sermon on the raising of the widow's son discusses at length the burial customs of the Jews, or portrays in minute detail the mournful procession passing through the gates of Nain, unless the hearers be put in a position to recognize the Lord as One whose heart is pierced by our sorrows and who is mighty to deliver? What is the good of picturing, in a passion sermon, every item of our Lord's physical and mental sufferings, in vivid colors, unless the whole presentation be controlled and illuminated by the testimony to the holy love of God our Saviour? What is the use of treating, with painstaking accuracy, in a Whitsuntide sermon, the Jewish harvest festival, the various countries from which the festival pilgrims came, or the speaking in other tongues, unless all this be made tributary to the central thought: the glorified Christ sends His Spirit to renew and unite men to Himself? To impart antiquarian, historical or other items of information is a thing wholly different from communicating spiritual knowledge and moving feelings and will toward the eternal verities.

Since it is the individual congregation that is to be edified, and each congregation has its individual peculiarities, the preacher must have an accurate *knowledge of his own congregation* in order to be in a position truly to edify it. This will involve a study of the social conditions, the circle of ideas, and the vocabulary of his congregation, of its cultural standards in general and its particular interests and tendencies. The preacher must stoop to the more restricted viewpoint of his uncultured members, in order, by understanding and sympathy, to lift them to his own level; he must maintain himself on the higher level of his cultured members, and seek to induce them to christianize all elements of their cultural life by bringing them under the guidance of God's Word.

This knowledge of the local congregation includes above all a thorough insight into the state of its spiritual life. The preacher must know whether his congregation possesses and is established in the knowledge of salvation, or whether he must begin by laying the foundation of such knowledge. Whether this knowledge, where it exists, has pervaded the congregation's life and is leading to sanctification, or whether the majority of its members are only nominally Christian. Whether self-righteousness and a Pharisaic temper prevail, or whether contrition, the consciousness of sin and the need of comfort are present. Whether there has been an experience of joy in the possession of Christ and His forgiveness, of Word and sacrament; whether the congregation is threatened with any special intellectual or moral dangers and its growth hindered by special defects in its spiritual life, or whether spiritual life has altogether departed, so that the congregation needs first of all to be awakened out of its deadness and brought back from its estrangement to God.

A preacher may preach well-founded textual sermons and ably apply the edifying elements in his text, but he will be preaching at random unless he knows exactly which of these edifying elements his congregation needs. Indeed, unless he has this knowledge, his preaching may do more harm than good, may tear down rather than build up. The Apostle's word about "rightly dividing the word of truth" applies here with particular force. Preaching is fundamentally a part of the care of souls, and the care of souls involves a thorough understanding of the congregation. The preacher, therefore, who would succeed must be a faithful pastor. To be sure, he will not go spying about among his people, still less lend an ear to the tittle-tattle of his members; but he will keep an open eye on his pastoral rounds, at the sickbed, in the school, in social visits and pastoral interviews, when children are entered in the catechetical class, or when members announce themselves for confession and communion, so that he may become intimately acquainted with the inner life of his people. And this in no inquisitorial manner, but in the spirit of a true pastor and shepherd of souls, who seeks to know his sheep and be known of them, in order the better to minister to them, in paternal, fraternal and friendly fashion. Such faithful pastoral work will always be the prerequisite of all truly edifying and therefore successful pulpit work.

Corresponding to the state of the congregation, the sermon will be either doctrinal, pastoral or awakening. The doctrinal sermon aims at clarifying and deepening the knowledge of salvation. The pastoral sermon addresses itself chiefly to the emotions and the will, prompting to renewed appropriation of forgiving grace and to progress in sanctification. The hortatory sermon arouses from the sleep of sin and calls to repentance or to some specific duty of the Christian life. The second of these, the *pastoral* sermon, is the purest type of the congregational sermon. Here we have, more truly than elsewhere, a ὁμιλεῖν, a speaking of Christian brother to Christian brother; here troubled souls are shown the way to joy in their Lord and in their divine sonship, while the lax are spurred on upon the road to Christian perfection. While it appeals primarily to the emotions and the will, it addresses itself also to the understanding and judgment. The pastoral sermon, however, dare not be cultivated at the expense of the *doctrinal* sermon, which has always been one of the distinctive features of our Church. The doctrinal sermon cannot allow its place to be taken—save under abnormal conditions—by catechetical instruction. Its function is rather to take the results of catechetical instruction as its point of departure and to carry farther, deepen and enrich the knowledge there gained. It must elaborate the great fundamentals of Christian dogmatics and ethics in their organic connection, and make them the living possession of the hearer, so that he may attain to a well rounded and Christian *Weltanschauung*. From this central position light will be shed also upon the more peripheral elements of Christian truth, as occasion arises, either because the text itself requires it or because of certain dangers or spiritual movements in the congregation. The preacher cannot be warned often enough against allowing his doctrinal sermon to degenerate into a dry dissertation that leaves the hearer unmoved. Against this danger, especially the beginner who has not yet clearly drawn the distinction between the sermon and the essay, must be constantly on his guard. Beside these two types the *awakening* sermon takes its legitimate place. This follows not only from what has been said of the need of the congregation, but also from the history of preaching, which records a large number of influential hortatory preachers. That this type of sermon must not apply external pressure nor make its chief appeal to the nerves of the hearers, is self-evident. Not to force results by extraordinary measures, but to content itself with the simple and impressive use of law and Gospel—this must be its aim. Nor should it seek to convert men by means of the law alone; for necessary as the law is to rouse the sinner out of sleep and bring him to a consciousness of his sin and the wrath of God, it is nevertheless the Gospel that awakens life and thus regenerates and converts.[48] Only grace attracts and wins, only the Gospel creates faith. The preaching of Christ crucified, which is at one and the same time the most crushing revelation of God's

---

[48] 2 Cor. 3:6 ff.; Gal. 3:21.

wrath and the most attractive revelation of His saving love, is after all the only true preaching of repentance. And where it is a matter of awakening men to specific acts and duties of the Christian life, it ill accords with the genius of the Gospel merely to hold up God's law before the soul and to urge and threaten men therewith. This may be justifiable and necessary in so far as there is a side of the Christian on which he is still under the law; but more will be gained and a more truly evangelical sermon preached, if the stress is placed upon the love of God experienced in the heart, and warming and rendering it willing to love Him in return and freely to undertake the duties which He sets before His Church on earth.

But it is not only the study of the spiritual condition of the congregation that determines whether the sermon is to be doctrinal, pastoral or awakening. This will depend upon the *individuality of the preacher* himself—whether intellect, feeling or will predominates in him—as well as upon the divine leading in his life. Nevertheless, while the rights of personality as a divinely bestowed gift must be guarded, the preacher's individuality must be subordinated to the actual needs of the congregation. Hence the preacher should here, too, practice the necessary self-discipline. It is evident that none of these three sermon types dare monopolize his preaching to the exclusion of the other two, if he is to edify truly and thoroughly. It can only be a question of one of them predominating over the others and giving to the sermon its distinctive character. (P. 167.)

The preacher must *know the age in which he lives,*—its ruling ideas and underlying tendencies, its problems and needs, its attainments and shortcomings, and how they react upon the inner life of his contemporaries. This is his duty as man and as Christian; for God has not called him to the life of a recluse, but placed him in the midst of the world and set him a task which he cannot perform without knowing the time. It is his duty also as a preacher. Not only because as a preacher he is, in a higher degree than the individual layman, the representative of God's cause and kingdom on earth, but because the congregation he serves forms part of the present generation of mankind and part of one or other of the nations of the world, and cannot escape this double influence of time and place.

The necessity of this was not so apparent, in the past, to the American Lutheran preacher of foreign tongue. German, Danish, Swedish and Norwegian settlements were scattered over our land, like lonely islands, isolated by language, custom and creed from the remainder of the population, and cut off more or less from the intellectual and spiritual life-currents of the nation. This is no longer the case. These communities now find themselves out in the midst of the stream of national life with all its favorable and unfavorable trends. The preacher who holds himself aloof from this life and remains ignorant of these trends is not able to fulfil the duties of his calling. He will not know his people and they will not understand his message. The preacher's duty is rather to make a thorough study of his people, in their industrial and educational conditions, their political and social tendencies, their spiritual attainments and aspirations, their literature and life, so that he may exert upon them, in the course of his ministry, a directing and correcting influence. This was one of the redeeming features of the compulsory attendance of divinity students at the great universities, in the Lutheran church of Germany. Here they were in the midstream of the intellectual life of the nation and familiarized with its currents and eddies by continuous living contact. We are well aware of the evils inevitably bound up with this system and are by no means advocating its imitation. What we have in mind is the sound principle underlying it—that the preacher needs to have a thorough and firsthand knowledge of and contact with the whole cultural life of his nation and people. "All that I have learned shall serve Thee alone"—so Augustine, in his Confessions, vows to his Lord. And is it not one of the secrets of his greatness, that he was equipped with an intimate knowledge of the life of his time?

But more important for the preacher than a knowledge of his age and nation, is *the knowledge of his congregation,* which he is especially called to edify. His knowledge of the time will assist him in gaining this knowledge, but he would make a serious mistake and jeopardize the success of his labors, if he neglected to make the life of his own congregation the subject of systematic observation and painstaking study. In former years, the "general city, court, house and country sermon" was in high favor, "which could be understood as well by the illiterate housemaid as by the most cultured city-dweller." This was, even at that time, an absurd and extravagant claim, and ought in our day to require no lengthy refutation. The multiplicity and variety of intellectual interests and the diversity of modern culture at once rule out of court such "general" sermons, even though it remains true that the Gospel is the same for all classes and that the heart of man is today fundamentally the same as it has always been.

The *social life of the congregation* must be familiar to the preacher if his sermons are to fit his particular congregation. The divine truth is to be applied to the actual life and to the peculiar conditions of the members. The conditions of life in a rural parish are entirely different from those in a city congregation. A wealthy congregation in central Illinois or Iowa, with its regular and plentiful harvests, has a totally different complexion and a different mode of life and thought from a poor congregation, say in Oklahoma, that must content itself with a harvest once every five years. A suburban congregation composed of business men and retired farmers requires very different treatment from a congregation in a large city. Again, how great is the contrast between a congregation whose members move in the world of business, and one made up of laboring people of more or less limited outlook. The pastor must share in the life of his people, must know their troubles and wants, their tasks and dangers, their pleasures and all that goes to make up their life. For it is these very thoughts and fears and hopes of theirs, with which he is to mix and mingle the leaven of the Word of law and Gospel, till the whole be leavened. Otherwise he will never be able to bridge the gulf between Sunday and weekday Christianity, and to make the synthesis of folk-religion and biblical religion. The latter will hover like a bright ideal in the clouds, painted and retouched, Sunday after Sunday, by the sermon; the former will rule upon earth and will take good care not to be too greatly disturbed by the latter. Hesselbacher tells of a peasant who said to his pastor, "What you're saying there is all very fine, and once we all get to heaven it'll be just like that; but here in this world it won't go." A true social sermon, for example, on neighborly or brotherly love, will point the congregation of wealthy businessmen to those sections of the city where poverty dwells, with their problems of housing and food, of labor and vice, and will drive home to the consciousness of the hearers their responsibility to provide sufficient, systematic and permanent relief. It will set before the employers in the congregation their duty to pay their workmen a decent living wage, to treat them not as "hands" but as souls, as brothers, and it will set before the members in general their duty to take a public stand, according to their ability, for the general amelioration of industrial conditions. On the other hand, the social sermon in a congregation composed of the poor, while fully acknowledging their right to an existence worthy of human beings created and redeemed by God, will counsel contentedness, the faithful discharge of duty, and especially faith as the way to inner freedom and joy. Though social reform as such cannot be the subject-matter of the sermon, as we have seen,[44] the social factor dare not be omitted, whenever the application of the text to the actual life of the congregation demands its emphasis. In this way, too, we avoid and oppose the error that social problems can be solved by social legislation, or that there can be real freedom without freedom from sinful desires.

To the social differences, and often out of them, come the differences of *intellectual life in the congregation.* The preacher will fail if these remain to him a sealed book. Foremost among these we mention one that is frequently overlooked, with harmful results—the difference of vocabulary. The working vocabulary of a simple rural community includes scarcely two hundred fifty words, while in cities a familarity with from three to five times this number may often be presupposed, and in individual instances a command of practically all the ordinary resources of language. How absurd, then, for the preacher in a rural congregation to shoot over his people's heads with words a foot and a half long![45] His simple hearers will at first gape at him in amazement, and then either stay away or resign themselves stolidly to their fate. In either case they will receive the perhaps lifelong impression that it belongs to the nature of the sermon, and of religion, to be incomprehensible and therefore out of touch with life. It would be a mistake, however, to think that the preacher dare never rise above the linguistic level of his hearers. Here, too, he is to exert a cultural influence and strive to lead his people to higher standards. But before he can do this, he must descend to the plane of their limited vocabulary, familiarize himself with it, find in it points of contact and so lead gradually from the known to the unknown. W. Loehe would hardly have been understood by his peasants in Neuendettelsau if he had preached to them at the outset in the cadenced and classically beautiful prose so familiar to us from his published sermons, and

---

[44]Above, pp. 51 ff.—[45]If instead of this we said "sesquipedalian words" we should be doing exactly what we are here counseling him not to do.

characterizing still more, according to von Zezschwitz, his sermons of the '60's. The "new minister" may gain an insight into the linguistic ability of his congregation by an examinaton of the schoolbooks in use, the home newspapers, and the idioms and provincialisms of local speech. If this is a necessary duty in all rural or village communities, it becomes an absolute essential where the transition is taking place from an old-world language to English, and where the majority of the people received their religious training in German, Scandinavian, etc. Here the use of the vocabulary of Church hymn, Catechism and Bible, otherwise so helpful, is of no avail. In general, let the preacher avoid all abstract expressions, and bear in mind that verbs possess greater carrying power than nouns, that polysyllabic vocables should be translated whenever possible into shorter words and Latinisms into plain Anglo-Saxon, and that technical terms, especially those of dogmatics,[46] should be used as the physician uses his hypodermic needle, as a last resort, and then accompanied by precautionary explanations.

Akin to the social status and the vocabulary, is the whole *realm of sensations, perceptions and concepts.* How narrow and confined mostly to rural conditions is the farmer's circle of sense-impressions. His farm, with all that relates to it, makes up his world. This he knows, this determines his vocabulary and his world of ideas. And here, where he is at home, the preacher must meet him on common ground, and seek every possible point of contact to lead him, by the method of apperception,[47] from the known to the unknown. Otherwise he will be speaking a language unintelligible to his hearers, since its concepts, images and comparisons will belong to a strange world. What is true of the farmer is true, *mutatis mutandis,* of the workingman, the merchant, and all the rest. I have no eye, no receptivity, no understanding for a thing with which I have no thoughts in common, no point of contact, no common concept material. It would be well worth while for someone to undertake an analysis of the circle of ideas and interests of the American farmer of the Middle West, the factory-worker in our large cities, our miners, our fishermen and the sailors in our ports, based on careful observation and similar to the studies we have in the pedagogic field.[48] More valuable, however, than

---

[46] E. g., justification, which glares by its absence in the Small Catechism; regeneration, reconciliation, etc.—[47] Comp. Reu, *Catechetics* (1918), pp. 23 f.—[48] E. g., Hartmann, *Die Analyse des kindlichen Gedankenkreises,* and essays by Barnes, Wissler, Dawson, and others in the *Pedagogical Seminary.*

such scientific studies, is the acquaintance with the congregation's world of ideas gained by long residence and personal observation. When Jesus desired to bring His truth home to His hearers, He spoke in parables taken from the daily life of the people, who consequently heard him gladly. So pronounced is the Palestinian coloring of many of His sayings that they are comprehensible to the occidental mind only after careful research in the topography and botany, the industrial and domestic life, the ethics and customs of His time and country. Paul, in his epistles, draws his imagery from the Greek athletic contests (1 Cor. 9), the triumphal return of the victorious general (2 Cor. 2:14, θριαμβεύοντι), the παιδαγωγός (Gal. 3:24), or from incidents in Old Testament history (1 Cor. 10, Gal. 4, etc.), with all of which his readers were familiar; James employs the figure of the sirocco (1:11), well and unfavorably known to everyone in Palestine; John, that of a book with seven seals (Rev. 5 ff.) which every member of the churches in Asia Minor would recognize as a last will and testament.[49] Later, Caesarius of Arles, preaching on his visitations to country-folk, drew his comparisons from agriculture and cattle-raising and from the vineyards of Southern France. Much of the success of Berthold of Regensburg and Geiler of Kaisersberg was due to the local color pervading their preaching. Luther, Mathesius, Simon Musaeus, H. Mueller, Scriver, B. Schuppius—how the sermons of them all draw upon the world of perceptions in which their congregations lived and moved. It was not only for his translations of the Bible that Luther took his words and images from the lips of the common folk, and wrote as late as 1536 to Linck at Nuernberg to send him what he could find of "German pictures, rhymes, songs, books and mastersongs." The same attempt to enter into the popular world of perceptions is seen in his preaching. Mathesius adapted his language and his presentation to his Joachimthal miners, without descending to the vulgar or common. Reading Schuppius one looks into the mental world of his Hamburg congregation and almost seems to be living and moving among them. In later years, Ludwig Harms' sermons are notable for this trait, and especially Caspari's admirable sermons on the Decalogue. Among recent preachers, Hesselbacher[50] is pre-eminent for his ability to enter into the intellectual life of his Baden peasants; E. Gros[51] and G. Frenssen, the novelist,[52] are less successful in capturing the

---

[49]Cf. Zahn, *Einleitung in das N. T.*³ (1917), ii, 600.—[50]*Aus der Dorfkirche. Predigten.* 3 vols.—[51]*Auf der Dorfkanzel.* 4 vols.—[52]*Dorfpredigten.*

earth savor of their locality. In proportion as the American Lutheran sermon succeeds in accommodating itself to its hearers' world of impressions, it will meet one of the most important conditions of an edifying sermon. Obviously, a frequent change of pastorates will not help to bring about such a consummation.

The preacher who is to edify his congregation needs further a knowledge of its *cultural standards,* and in particular of the intellectual tendencies found in it or seeking entrance. With respect to the former, little need be added to what has already been said. Luther once made the statement: "All your sermons should be exceedingly simple; do not regard the prince, but rather the simple, foolish, rude and illiterate people." Again he said: "We must play the wetnurse to our people, and treat them after the manner of a mother nursing her child. She prattles and plays with it, and feeds it out of her heart; for this she needs no wine nor malmsey." Again: "In preaching here [at Wittenberg] I stoop to the lowest level; I take no account of the two score doctors and magisters who are present, but rather of the throng of young people, children and servants, of whom there are some hundreds or thousands. To them I address myself, to their needs I adapt my sermon. If the others do not care to listen, the door is open." This principle holds good today, but rightly interpreted. Luther did not mean that nothing but peasant sermons are to be preached, but that the preacher is to be governed not by the cultural standards of the few but of the majority. Chrysostom's preaching was suited to a Constantinople audience, but Caesarius of Arles would have shot over the heads of his hearers if he had adopted this style of preaching on his journey through Gaul. Loofs could take a good deal more for granted in preaching before his academic congregation than could Stoecker in his "penny sermons" which circulated among the masses of Berlin and beyond. Bezzel could preach to his deaconesses as Hesselbacher would not have dared to his peasants. F. W. Robertson was more in his element in Cheltenham and Brighton than he would have been in Spurgeon's Tabernacle. Pfatteicher in his Philadelphia congregation including students from the University, could adopt a tone very different from that of Wessel before his congregation of farmers. There is indeed a noble simplicity of language which at the same time is intelligible to the uncultured and appeals to the cultured hearer; but the method of approach and the structure, the choice of illustrations and the intellectual interests to be appealed to will vary greatly according to the cultural standard of the congregation, and demand a different sort of sermon for either class of hearers. Not a different Gospel, but different vehicles or channels by which the Gospel can be conveyed to the soul and there unfold its power.

In order to gain an acquaintance with the particular tendencies prevalent in a congregation, the preacher will need to *know what his members read*. "Reading," says Lord Bacon, "maketh a full man;" but not everything that fills a man improves him. Along with the good and uplifting thoughts that enter the mind by way of the printed page, there goes much that is dangerous and harmful, much that not only awakens doubts and questionings—often a good thing—but that undermines the very foundations of Christian faith. In order to counteract such influences the preacher must be conversant with this literature. He will be induced thereby to place a new emphasis on many a biblical truth and give particular attention to many an ethical question, in his preaching, which he might otherwise pass over. While this will ordinarily suffice, he may have at times to give to his sermon a directly *apologetic* or even *polemical* character. The insidious influence of materialism, godless evolutionism, and monism has filtered down through schoolbooks and periodical literature into our congregations and affected especially the younger members. A false but proudly strutting moral evolutionism, modeled on Spencer and attractively represented by Woodrow Wilson, has confused the minds of many. Utilitarianism, for which the useful alone is the morally good, is not confined to Bentham and his school nor to its English homeland, but has found a home in our own land and is seen here in its grossest form as heartless selfishness, finding its natural ally in every breast. The fundamental principles of many secret and other organizations, with their substitution of natural for revealed religion and the morality of the natural man for the ethics of the Gospel, make their appeal to wide circles. The World War, with its catch-words about humanity, democracy, freedom and brotherliness, has cast a fresh halo round this natural man and his natural morality. Must not the sermon, therefore, finding its hearers a prey to these tendencies and realizing their danger, sound a clearer note and adopt a more definite tone? There would be a clearer and deeper Christian consciousness, a sounder moral judgment, and less flabby and spineless conduct among our members, if our preaching had more generally taken account of this situation and more earnestly striven to meet it.

Where the intellectual level of the congregation is equal to that of the preacher, he is of course relieved of the necessity of raising it to his own level. It becomes his duty, instead, to bring the light of God's Word to bear upon all sides of its culture, to judge art and literature in no puritanic temper indeed, yet according to their relation to the truly religious and moral, and to prove himself in a real sense the leader of his flock, including its most highly cultured members. While the preacher should be conversant with the general culture of his day, to affect a specialty and to pose as connoisseur will not win him any great confidence. As Dabney well says: "You need not pretend to talk agriculture, physics, politics, belles-lettres, fine art, with the experts in these various branches of knowledge; but you may honestly avow, when they are the subjects of conversation, that you have not judged it your business to master them, and may keep your mouth closed. Such an attitude is always respectable. But when the votaries of those arts and sciences approach the theology of redemption, show them that there you are the master of them all."[53] In the domain of the eternal and religious the preacher should be so much at home and take so authoritative a stand as to be able to throw many a helpful sidelight on the knowledge of his time, so that the congregation will not be confused but kept always in sight of the way to its heavenly goal.

It is self-evident that the preacher must know the *spiritual life of the congregation*. Only so can he rightly divide the Word of truth and truly edify. If he should undertake to minister comfort to the secure, to threaten the troubled, or to encourage the lax, he would do vastly more harm than good. The right dividing of the Word means the right application of law and Gospel, as indicated by the inner life of the hearer. The importance as well as the difficulty of this is well brought out by Luther in his *Sermon on the Distinction between Law and Gospel* (1532). Here he says among other things: "It is therefore highly necessary to distinguish properly between these two words. Where this is not done, neither law nor Gospel can be understood and the conscience is lost in blindness and error. The law has its goal, beyond which it cannot go—i. e., Christ. The Gospel likewise has its own office and work—i. e., to proclaim forgiveness of sins to the troubled conscience. These two, therefore, cannot be confused or one substituted for the other without corruption of doctrine. For though law and Gospel are both God's Word, they do not teach the same thing... Hence, if one understands the art of rightly dividing law from Gospel, give him the chief place and make him a Doctor of Sacred Scripture. For it is impossible to achieve this division without the Holy Spirit. I have experienced it for myself, and observe it every

---

[53] P. 265.

day in others, how difficult it is to distinguish between the teaching of the law and that of the Gospel. The Holy Spirit must here become the master and teacher, otherwise no man on earth will be able to understand or teach it. Therefore no papist, false Christian nor fanatic can divide these two. . . . It is easy to say that the law is a different word and teaching from the Gospel; anyone can do this; but to apply this distinction in actual practice is labor and sorrow." Among recent writers on this subject, C. F. W. Walther has fully discussed this distinction. Compare his writings,—*Gesetz und Evangelium*, and *Die rechte Anschauung von Gesetz und Evangelium*. We append a paragraph from his *Pastorale* (St. Louis,[3] 1885): "Whoever uses the Gospel to deprive the law of its rigor, or the law to deprive the Gospel of its sweetness; whoever teaches in such a way as to console the secure and to trouble still more those already troubled by their sins; whoever directs those whom the law has convicted simply to pray for grace, instead of pointing them to the means of grace; whoever, in his exposition of the law, so presents its demands and threats as to make God appear to be content when the Christian does what he can and to be willing to overlook his weakness, and so presents the Gospel as to make it seem a comfort for none but such as are already righteous; whoever seeks, by means of the demands, threats and promises of the law, to move the unregenerate to the performance of good works, and requires love to God and their neighbors of such as have not yet come to faith; whoever demands a special degree of contrition, and will comfort only those who have already become new creatures; whoever confuses not being able to believe with not being permitted to believe, and the like,—such a one does not rightly divide the Word of truth, but confuses law and Gospel. His teaching is false, even though he may preach the law and the Gospel and even properly define the peculiarities of each."[54] The preacher will do well to study these writings of Walther's as well as his sermons. Besides Walther the following have given helpful discussions of the subject: Harless, *Christl. Ethik*, [7]1875 (Christian Ethics, 1880); Frank, *System der christl. Sittlichkeit*, 1884-87, i, 360-443; W. Walther, *Die christl. Sittlichkeit nach Luther* (1909); O. Dittrich, *Luthers Ethik* (1930). Valuable for the guidance of the pastor in and out of his pulpit, is a writing by F. Bente, *Gesetz und Evangelium: Busse und Gute Werke* (St. Louis, 1917). See also M. Reu, *Christl. Ethik* (1914), 43-47, 55, 58-59, 118-122.

---

[54]P. 79.

A few fundamental principles may here be recalled to the preacher. Law, in the dogmatic sense in which we employ it here, is whatever declares the mandatory or punitive will of God; whatever commands or prohibits, uncovers sin, judges, punishes, condemns—whether it proceed from Sinai or Golgotha, from Moses or Christ, from the prophets or from the Sermon on the Mount, from natural or revealed law. Gospel, on the other hand, is whatever declares the gracious and saving will of God; whatever promises, proclaims, communicates God's grace, justifies and saves—whether it come from the Old or the New Testament, etc. When I preach, therefore, on the basis of John 3:16 of the perdition of man apart from Christ, my sermon is in so far purely a preaching of law. But when, from the same passage, I preach the love of God saving the lost sinner through Christ, my sermon is purely a preaching of Gospel. Or when, taking for my text Jesus' saying, "I am the Light of the world," I show my hearers that outside of Christ all is darkness, I am preaching law. When I show them, from the same text, that Jesus alone leads from darkness to light, my sermon is a Gospel sermon. If, in preaching on the Old Testament ceremonial law, specifically the sacrificial system, I draw out the truth inherent in this system, that sin demands punishment, death, and thus satisfaction, I am a preacher of the law; but if I set forth that in the sacrifices of the Old Testament God Himself provided a means of such satisfaction and prefigured thereby the perfect satisfaction of Christ, I am a preacher of the Gospel. When I treat the Passion of Christ as revelation of God's punitive righteousness, I am performing "the office of Moses;" but when I portray the Passion as revelation of the saving righteousness of God, I am performing "the office of Christ" (John 1:17). When I picture the life of Christ as a pattern for Christian conduct, I am dealing with law; when I preach this same Jesus as calling to all who groan under the yoke and burden of the law, "Come unto me, all ye that labor and are heavy laden, and I will give you rest"—I am to them a herald of the most sweet Gospel. The unregenerate needs the law, to awaken him and bring him face to face with his offended God. When he has sunk in despair before Him, he needs the Gospel, to set Christ before him, who will work in his heart faith in His forgiving grace, raise him up out of his despair, and convert his contrition into filial sorrow for having so deeply grieved his loving God and Father. Having been brought to faith and sonship, through the Gospel, he is no longer to be driven by the law, but is free from its curse and from its bondage, and possesses in his new, divinely created will the motive and strength to do God's will.

This new will must be established and strengthened by means of the Gospel, so that it may spontaneously and actually accomplish that which it is potentially able and willing to do. Only in so far as the knowledge of the regenerate and justified man concerning God's will is still incomplete, the will of God and the perfect man in Christ must be presented to him, in order that he may in every respect find the right expression for his new life. Only in so far as he is still in the flesh and sins much every day, does he need the preaching of the law, in order to recognize his sins as in a mirror and be filled with fear on account of them. But if he is not to remain in this fear, he again needs the Gospel, to confirm his faith, so that he may turn anew to Christ and find peace in Him. I should be depriving the Gospel of its sweet comfort and confusing it with law, if I gave my hearers to understand that faith was something they had to produce by their own natural strength. I should be depriving the law of its sternness, if I brought them this comfort of the Gospel before making it clear that God cannot tolerate sin and must exclude whoever loves sin from fellowship with Him. The genuineness of repentance, the comfort of faith, the reality of the Christian life, the salvation of the soul, depend on a right dividing of law and Gospel. This should impel every preacher to exercise the utmost care in his preaching and to be most diligent in his endeavor to understand his congregation in its spiritual life and needs. Many a pastor has spoiled the work of his predecessor by an insufficient knowledge of the actual state of Christian life among his members: by preaching nothing but Gospel where the greater part of the congregation required to be stirred by the hammer blows of the law; or by preaching nothing but law, in blissful ignorance that he was keeping souls already troubled from coming to faith and finding peace and power.

A special difficulty meets the preacher in *a congregation* almost exclusively *of young people,* as is often the case in the transition from German or Scandinavian to English. To handle such a congregation precisely as one would a congregation of older members, would be a great mistake. Its special make-up brings with it special requirements. In our *Catechetics*[55] we have treated at length the physical and mental development of the youth from the thirteenth or fourteenth to the eighteenth or twenty-first year; it must suffice here to refer the reader to that discussion. The moral and religious leader of such young people as we have there described them must be willing to take

---

[55]Pp. 294-301.

them unreservedly as they are. To treat them as weak and ignorant, in a word, as children, is to estrange them at once. To bring external authority to bear, is to court rebellion. To remain ignorant of their problems and difficulties, or to ignore them, is to lose their confidence. To attempt to train them in an ascetic direction, is to lose all contact with them. To prohibit as sin what is not sin, is to find oneself without authority when it comes to reproving what is really sin. The preacher whose religion has become an empty form will find them turning from him; for they are hungry for life and reality, and all insincerity repels them. But whoever acknowledges their right to the development of their powers, and in times of weakness and discouragement walks by their side as understanding friend, wins their confidence and may become to them a pillar of strength. The man who does not despise the knowledge they have but sets it further tasks and aims, and is not afraid to learn with them and from them, frankly acknowledging any gaps in his own knowledge and not concealing them under rhetoric or pious cant; the man who enters sympathetically into their doubts and objections, without feeling or expressing the holy horror of the Pharisee, and gradually helps them to overcome them; the man who is seen to be truly religious with and despite his thorough knowledge of the world, its intellectual heroes, its literature, its perplexing problems—he is their man, him they will gladly hear and devotedly follow. Only a truly Christian character, radiating life and strength, liberal and yet bondslave of Jesus Christ, is able to lead the youth in their storm and stress, their diffidence and despondency. He allows them their freedom and yet remains their guide.

To come from these general to some more particular considerations. In such **youthful congregations** the doctrinal sermon is especially in place, to strengthen and enlarge their religious and moral knowledge. But the doctrinal sermon, which should never be dry and lifeless, must here beware of this as death eternal. It should abound in instances and illustrations, and be concerned not only to relate the particular truth treated to the sum-total of evangelical religion and ethics, but to point out **its practical bearing** on everyday life. When current objections to the Christian religion—here the preacher may well study Ingersoll—are taken up, they should always be approached from the centre of Christian truth and the Christian conscience. Since young people, despite their strongly asserted individualism, set great store by authorities, let the preacher make a collection of quotations from the world's greatest thinkers, especially in the domain of science, philosophy, history and art, concerning Christ, the Scriptures, the

Christian religion and ethics, for use in his preaching. History and especially biography should find much room in his sermons, the stress falling naturally not so much on the outward as on the inner life. Much is gained when the youthful congregation leaves the service convinced that reverence for God's Word, prayer, faith, humility, unselfishness, purity, self-control, are realities and make life noble and fine. So central a truth as justification becomes real and will take a proper hold on young people when it is illustrated from the life of Paul or Luther or John Gossner, or by incidents from the history of missions. To awaken consciousness of sin and the need of salvation, let the preacher not operate with the scriptural teaching of the total depravity of mankind, but take his point of departure in actual life, in the individual instance, and use it to awaken the consciousness that this particular instance involves an offense against God and requires His forgiveness. Christ must indeed be proclaimed as Saviour from sin, but it will be advisable here to portray him rather as pattern of the ethical life and the source of strength, without whom we can do nothing. Above all, the preacher must beware of employing external pressure. Let him rather trust the quiet growing-power of the heavenly seed in the hearts of his hearers. Let the objective stand in the foreground. It will unfold its power in secret, whereas an undue emphasis on the subjective leads easily to insincerity and untruth, so repellent to youth.

Preachers in such congregations of young people will do well to consult the works of three Danish authors: Olfert Ricard (*Ungdoms liv*, 1905, [12]1910; *Jugendkraft* [Stuttgart, Gundert, 1909]; *Om at foere andre Mennesker til Kristus*, 1899; *Kristus som Exempel i kristeligt Arbeide*, 1906; *Christus und seine Getreuen*, 1910), Skovgaard-Petersen (*Troens Betydning for den, der vil frem i Verden*, 1899; *Des Glaubens Bedeutung im Kampf ums Dasein*, 1908; *Hvorlades findes Guds Vilje*, 1900; *Troens Hemmelighed*, 1904; *Das Geheimnis des Glaubens*, 1906; *Et Blik i Guds Kjaerligheds Dyb*, 1907; *Ein Blick in die Tiefe der Liebe Gottes*, 1908; *Das Buch der Jugend*, 1911), H. Martensen-Larsen (*Tvivel og Tro*, 1909; *Zweifel und Glaube*, 1911), especially the first two. Helpful are also the following publications: Weitbrecht, *Heilig ist die Jugendzeit*, [18]1912, *Maria und Martha*, [11]1912; Siedel, *Der Weg zur ewigen Schoenheit*, [21]1911, *Der Weg zur ewigen Jugend*, [22]1909; Weniger, *Ratschlaege fuer den Lebensweg*, 1906; H. v. Holst, *Glueckliche Leute*, 1914; the collection *Lehr und Wehr* (Hamburg, Agentur des Rauhen Hauses); Hennig, *Welch eine Wendung, Bilder von Gottes Walten in der Geschichte der Voelker*, 1908; *Aus Gottes Werkstatt, Skizzen und Bilder aus Natur- und Geisteswelt,* 1909; *Christuszeugnisse,* 1911; *Taten Jesu in unsern Tagen,* 1906; *Unserer Kirche Herrlichkeit,* 1913; Hilty, *Glueck,* 1891-98 (Engl. tr. by F. G. Peabody, 1903); *Das Geheimnis der Kraft,* 1912 (Hilty's books to be used with caution; the Lutheran counterpart to his *Happiness* is H. Ebeling, *Glueck und Christentum,* 1905); C. Wagner, *Le courage,* 1894; Henry Drummond, *The Greatest Thing in the World,* 1890.—Besides the pericopes the preacher may frequently select free texts. It goes without saying that, however highly individualized his congregation may be, he will not forget that his preaching must conform to the principles set forth in chapter six.

Answering to the need of the congregation, the sermon will have to be doctrinal, pastoral, or hortatory. The older homiletics, basing on 2 Tim. 3:16, 17 and Rom. 15:4, posited a five-fold use of every text and presented for every sermon an *usus didascalicus, elenchticus, paedeuticus, epanorthoticus* and *paracleticus.* This was not only a wrong use of these two texts and introduced an intolerable monotony into the art of preaching, but failed completely to take into account the actual make-up of the various congregations. It was a step in advance when J. J. Rambach wrote in his *Erlaeuterung ueber die praecepta homiletica:*[56] "Some preachers have become such slaves to the familiar five *usus* that they deem it a mortal sin to omit a single one of them, because they imagine there can be no complete sermon unless there is in it (1) a little doctrine, (2) a little polemics against heretics, (3) a bit of reproof, (4) a bit of exhortation, (5) a bit of consolation, even if the *usus elenchticus* must be lugged in by the ears and long mouldered heretics roused out of their graves. Moreover, the hearers are so accustomed to this sort of thing that they no longer pay any attention to it, knowing their pastor to be harping constantly on a harp of five strings. His teaching, reproof, correction, exhortation and comfort have no effect upon them, especially since it all takes place in a sleepy, cold and lifeless fashion. Now and then these five *usus* do flow naturally and without force from the same text, but the preacher must always examine what the materials of the text, the state of his congregation and other conditions will demand or endure. Prudence must decide whether more than one *usus* is to be employed and which one is to be stressed, which omitted or only briefly touched on."

Of only one of these *usus,* to employ this unedifying term, is it true that it should find room in every sermon. Every sermon, to be

---

[56] Ed. by J. P. Fresenius, 1736.

The Doctrinal Element in All Sermons 147

truly edifying, must have in it a *doctrinal element*. I cannot really comfort anyone unless my comfort rests on what the Scriptures teach about God's saving work and His self-revelation. I cannot admonish and exhort to good works without first teaching what God wills us to be and to become. I cannot awaken anyone out of his sinful state without portraying the nature and wretchedness of sin, contrasting it with God's holiness and righteousness, and characterizing it as black ingratitude toward God for His work of grace. In this sense we agree fully with Walther when he says: "Let a sermon be never so rich in exhortation, rebuke and comfort, if it is devoid of doctrine, it is a lean and empty sermon, whose exhortation, rebuke, and comfort float in the air. It is almost beyond belief how many preachers sin in this respect. Hardly has the preacher touched his text and the doctrine to be taught, before he starts exhorting or reproving or comforting. His sermon consists of scarcely anything but questions and exclamations, blessings and woes, admonitions to self-examination and a belaboring of the emotions and the conscience, until the feeling and conscience of the hearer are so continuously harried he cannot possibly find an opportunity for quiet reflection. So far from actually reaching the heart and kindling life, such sermons are more likely to preach people to death, to destroy any hunger they may have for the bread of life, and systematically to produce disgust and loathing for God's Word. It cannot but repel every hearer, to be admonished or reproved, again and again, without being shown the reason why, just as it must repel him to be comforted in soft and savorless fashion. It is of course much easier to shake this sort of thing out of one's sleeve and thus give the sermon the appearance of vivacity and effectiveness, than it would be lucidly and thoroughly to present a doctrine. This is probably the main reason why so few preachers preach doctrinal sermons, and why so many choose subjects that are already well known to their hearers and that readily lend themselves to a purely practical treatment. But another reason is, undoubtedly, that many preachers have themselves no thorough knowledge of the revealed doctrines, and hence are unable properly to present them to others. Still another reason is found in the foolish notion that the extended treatment of doctrine is dry, leaves the hearers cold, and does not minister to the awakening of conscience, to conversion and a living, active heart-Christianity. This is an utter mistake. It is just these eternal thoughts of God's heart, revealed in the Scriptures for our salvation, these divine truths, counsels and mysteries of faith, hidden from the foundation of the world, but now revealed in the writings of prophets and apostles, that are the divine seed which must be planted in the hearers' hearts, if there are to spring up in them the fruits of true repentance, unfeigned faith, and a sincere working love. Actual growth in Christianity is not possible in a congregation without sermons rich in doctrine. The preacher who neglects this is not true to his calling, even though by zealous exhortation, earnest reproof, or consolation claiming to be particularly evangelical, he appears to be consuming himself in faithful care for the souls committed to him."[57]

While the doctrinal element must be present in all sermons, circumstances will arise that call for sermons of a more pronounced doctrinal character, whose purpose is not so much to soothe the conscience or spur on the will as rather to enlighten the religious and moral understanding. This is the case particularly in congregations in which many of the members never received a thorough religious training in their youth or else have forgotten what they learned or lost their hold upon it from one cause or another. But even the Christian living in daily communion with his Lord still lives in the "flesh" and must suffer its darkening effect upon his mind. The thoughts of God which the doctrinal sermon presents are needed to counteract this influence and must continually supply fresh oil to the lamp of his understanding. By constant meditation on these truths the new man in him will be strengthened as with heavenly food; he will penetrate more deeply into the unity of the divine plan, and not only will God grow greater and more adorable to him, but he himself will grow to a larger and nobler stature.

How could Luther and the other Reformation preachers have renewed the life of the Church without the diligent preaching of doctrinal sermons? How could state and Church have been rebuilt after the ravages of the Thirty Years' War without the doctrinal sermon with its positive teaching of Christian truth? What dammed the flood of rationalism in the Church but the preaching of doctrine? And what else will lead us today, out of our doubt and religious uncertainty, to clearness and certainty in religion and morals? This is no new demand. Finney, the great revivalist, said long ago: "There has never been a revival that was not brought about by doctrine, set forth with power and clearness." And his contemporary, J. W. Alexander, was a sturdy advocate of the doctrinal sermon, as is seen in his posthumous work, *Thoughts on Preaching* (1860).[58] Broadus writes: "Doctrine, i. e., teaching, is the preacher's chief business. Truth is the

---

[57]*Pastorale*, p. 81.—[58]See pp. 10-12, 42-43, 51, 234-36, 249-52.

life-blood of piety, without which we cannot maintain its vitality or support its activity, and to teach men truth, or to quicken what they already know with freshness and power, is the preacher's great means of doing good."[59] Dabney emphasizes the truth that the feeling and will of the Christian can be set in motion only by means of the presentation of doctrine to his intellect. He says: "Man is a reasoning creature, and the word and Spirit of God deal with him in conformity with this rational nature. All those emotions and volitions, which have right moral character, are prompted in man by intelligent motives. To say that one has no reason for his volitions, is to describe them as either criminal or merely animal. In the things of God man only feels as he sees, and because he sees with his mind. A moment's consideration of these obvious facts will convince you that there cannot be, in the nature of the case, any other instrumentality to be used by creatures for inculcating religion and procuring right feeling and action than that which begins by informing the understanding."[60] Elsewhere in the same work he writes: "To move we must instruct. No Christian can be stable and consistent, save as he is intelligent. Instruction alone can prevent revivals from becoming mischievous excitements, and Christian zeal from degenerating into fanatical heat. Let it be considered, in addition, that the desire to know, or rational curiosity, is the natural appetite of the mind and that knowledge is its proper food. Knowledge is the light of the soul, and as sweet as the light is to the eye so pleasant is truth to the mind. It is true that the understanding is conscious of a species of *vis inertiae*, and that an effort is often necessary to rouse it to the labor of apprehension. But that effort is wholesome and cheerful. The desire to know is one of the most vivid sentiments of the soul, and its gratification is one of the purest and most uncloying pleasures of our nature. The apostle (1 Cor. 13:12) enumerates it among the elements which compose the immortal bliss of heaven. Hence, you may securely rely upon instructiveness as an unfailing power to attract the people permanently to your ministry. If you would not wear out after you have ceased to be a novelty, give the minds of your people food. Young pastors yield not seldom to a timidity, lest the multitude should be repelled by the homeliness of the truth; and they imagine that they are catering better for the popular tastes, by relieving them of the labor of attention and amusing them with rhetorical pyrotechnics. I do not here remark upon the wickedness of such an expedient. Pastoral experience proves that it is not adapted to

---

[59] P. 76.—[60] Pp. 50 ff.

its end, low as the end is. The men who draw the multitude are (if we except those who have more successfully satisfied the depravity of our race by positive error) the instructive pastors. The crowd flocks a few times to behold the empty show. But when it feels the necessity of being fed, it resorts to the place where solid food for the mind is provided, even if it be with plainer equipage. Make your people feel that they are gaining permanent acquisitions of knowledge from you, and they will not desert you." To which Dabney appends the following note: "I once asked a sensible plain man, who was familiar with the popular oratory of Randolph, what was its charm with the common people. He did not mention, as I expected he would, his magic voice, his classic grace, the purity of his English, his intense passion, the energy of his will, his pungent wit, his sarcasm, or the inimitable aptitude of his illustration. But he answered: 'It was because Mr. Randolph was so instructive, he taught the people so much which they had not known before'."[61] Phillips Brooks said in 1876, in his *Yale Lectures on Preaching*: "No preaching ever had any strong power that was not the preaching of doctrine. The preachers that have moved and held men have always preached doctrine. No exhortation to a good life that does not put behind it some truth as deep as eternity can seize and hold the conscience. Preach doctrine, preach all the doctrine that you know, and learn forever more and more; but preach it always, not that men may believe it, but that men may be saved by believing it. So it shall be live, not dead. So men shall rejoice in it and not decry it. So they shall feed on it at your hands as on the bread of life, solid and sweet, and claiming for itself the appetite which God made for it."[62] R. W. Dale, in 1877 at the same place, reiterated the same truth: "I believe that there is no congregation whose taste is so hopelessly corrupt, and whose intellectual life is so completely demoralized, that it may not be trained to value sermons which are full of instruction."[63] Boyd Carpenter said in 1895, in his *Lectures on Preaching*: "I find many saying, I wish that our clergyman would really teach us. We do not so much want vehement or earnest exhortation as clear and methodical teaching." He then goes on to show what is not wanted.[64] As recently as 1913 D. J. Burrell wrote: "In these days every tyro must have his whack at creed and 'dogma' and orthodoxy. One who lends an ear to philippics of this sort would think that doctrinal preaching no longer gets a hearing: but a canvass of congregations leads to a different con-

---

[61] P. 119.—[62] P. 129.—[63] *Nine Lectures on Preaching*, pp. 225 f.—
[64] P. 221; comp. below, p. 152.

clusion. The average man is as hungry for plain statement of positive truth as he ever was. Wind is poor diet, though it be filtered through the sweetest hautboy; milk is little better, even when sterilized, except for babes; men want meat; and though they may be deceived for a while, they are likely, in the long run, to insist on having it."[65]

It is objected that the doctrinal sermon is dry and dull, and many avoid it for this reason. It cannot be denied that many doctrinal sermons *are* dry, but this is the fault not of the sermon but of the preacher. "Doctrinal preaching," says Broadus, "is not necessarily dry. In fact, properly presented doctrine, didactic instruction, may be the most interesting kind of preaching. Men wish to know, delight in knowing. All depends on the way in which it is done. The dry preacher will make all subjects dry."[66] There are especially three ways to make the doctrinal sermon dry. It will become dry whenever it enters into the subtle distinctions of dogmatics and forgets the difference between the technical knowledge of the specialist in theology and the saving knowledge of the Christian congregation. This was the mistake, e. g., of Aegidius Hunnius, who dragged into his catechism sermons on the Lord's Supper the whole apparatus of scholastic theology;[67] of M. Loy, who in a sermon on Phil. 2: 5-11, develops the dogmatic theory of the *communicatio idiomatum* with its three *genera;* of Kessler's sermon on the subject, "Does the ethical teaching of Jesus fit our time?" which in contents and form made demands on its hearers which the most highly cultured congregation could not be expected to meet.[68] Such dogmatizing sermons are particularly out of place on festival days. The religious needs of the congregation are scarcely met in L. S. Keyser's Good Friday sermon on "The Divine Reason of the Cross" (text, John 18: 1-19, 42), in which he discusses, under the lengthy first division, the various theories of the atonement—the placating, moral influence, governmental and penitential theories—and then, in the brief second part, presents the correct theory. The sermon, even the doctrinal sermon, is not a dogmatic lecture, the church not a lecture-room, the congregation not a class of theological students! Unless our preachers zealously guard against this confusion, our Church will suffer great harm.

The second cause of dryness in the doctrinal sermon is its failure to bring the truth it treats to bear on practical life. The doctrine of

[65]Pp. 81 f.—[66]P. 77.—[67]See M. Reu, *Quellen zur Geschichte des kirchlichen Unterrichts,* i, 2, 161 ff.—[68]Cf. R. Falke, *Warum zweifelst du? Ein Jahrgang apologetischer Predigten* (1914), pp. 416-24.

the divinity of Christ may be developed fully and faultlessly, but the presentation will not grip the hearer unless he is made to see that this doctrine alone satisfies the desire of his inner life for the reality of salvation. I may set forth the doctrine of the Trinity scripturally and convincingly, but I shall fail to enlist the genuine interest of my hearer unless I can show him that the certainty of our communion with God depends upon this great truth. A doctrinal sermon on sin will move no one unless it paints sin in colors taken from actual life and sets it as a concrete reality before the hearer, so that he begins to recognize its features in himself. Boyd Carpenter has well illustrated this point. He says: "What is this dogmatism of which people are impatient? It is not teaching itself which is objected to; nor is it teaching which is clear and definite, and which sets forth distinct principles of faith and conduct. It is rather that form of teaching in which truth is treated as a thing apart from life. It is that dogmatic insistence on the acceptance of a series of theological propositions, but which fails to bring them into line with the facts and needs of human life and experience. It is the preaching of theological theories instead of living truths. Theological theories may enshrine living truths, but they may be set forth in such a fashion that they sound only as arbitrary propositions. Truth to be true to men must touch man and man's life. An anatomical museum is no doubt a useful place for studying the structure of the human frame, but it does not interest everybody. It is a display of dead truth. The sight of a little child building castles on the shore has more life in it. The bones of men are not men. The scientific parade of theology is not religious teaching. 'As art for art's sake ends in depraved taste, so mere theology ends in depraved religion'—so wrote Julius Hare. It is a true saying, and one which we do well to lay to heart. The resentment of people is not against religious teaching, but against the arid dogmatism which is offered to them as a substitute for fact. This is the danger which besets us. We shall therefore be under the necessity of considering our teaching in the light of human need. We shall not be satisfied with setting dry bones before our people. We shall seek to feed them with food convenient for them. We shall be earnest in maintaining principles, but we shall seek to make them principles of life. We shall strive to show that the things of God are things of man, because we believe that whatsoever things were written aforetime were written for our learning, and that the message of God, must have a fitness for man."[69]

---

[69] Pp. 222 ff.

Similarly Alexander says: "We do not think sermons should be theological lectures, didactic or polemic. We think doctrine, being clearly defined and established, should always be developed in its practical and experimental bearings."[70]

Finally, the doctrinal sermon becomes dry and uninteresting when the preacher forgets that he is to *preach,* that he has living hearers before him with whom he is to enter into personal and living contact, whom he is to address, to interest, and by entering into their thoughts, objections and doubts to win to participation in the development of the subject. When this is forgotten, the sermon becomes an essay, whose author is concerned only with his material and its development. For the essay as such is devoid of oratorical character. But without the element of allocution the doctrinal sermon cannot but become lifeless and fail. Yet the three faults just mentioned may be overcome and the doctrinal sermon remain none the less dry and impersonal; whenever, namely, the hearer does not feel throbbing through it the whole personality of the preacher, to whom the truth he is presenting is of supreme importance and of whose intellectual and spiritual life it has become a part.

The doctrinal sermon must treat especially the great fundamental truths of Holy Scripture, such as sin, grace, redemption, repentance, faith, conversion and regeneration, justification, adoption, sanctification, good works, the means of grace, the assurance of salvation, death, resurrection, judgment, everlasting life, everlasting condemnation. "The great questions," says Alexander, "which have agitated the world, which agitate our own bosoms, which we should like to have settled before we die, which we should ask an apostle about if he were here. . . . . these are to general Scripture truth what great mountains are in geography. Some, anxious to avoid hackneyed topics, omit the greatest, just as if we should describe Switzerland and omit the Alps!"[71] And Broadus notes: "True, they are familiar, but sermons upon them need not be commonplace. The sunlight is as fresh every morning as when it shone upon our first parents in their Paradise; young love is still as sweet, and parental grief as heart-rending, as was theirs. And so the great doctrines of the Gospel, to him who has eyes to see and a heart to feel them, are forever new. Our task is, loving these truths ourselves, to make others love them."[72]

Not only are these truths capable of treatment from various points of view, but each text from which they are drawn presents them

---

[70] P. 250.—[71] P. 11.—[72] P. 78.

from a new angle. Frequently the text itself will point the way in which the difficult doctrinal material can be brought to bear directly upon life. Thus 2 Cor. 5: 17-21 requires a doctrinal sermon on reconciliation, but suggests the point of view—"How can old things pass away for us and all things become new?" If the answer is found to be—"Not by our own strength, but because all things are of God, who reconciled us once for all to Himself through Christ," the text is properly interpreted, the congregation is shown the meaning of reconciliation, and yet, from first to last, all has been kept constantly related to practical life. Or the text Heb. 8: 7-13 suggests a doctrinal sermon on the specifically new features of the new covenant as over against the old. Especially three items are mentioned as new —forgiveness of sins, a true knowledge of God, and complete obedience to His will. Suppose we choose this text for a Whitsunday sermon and take as our theme, "The Church of Christ is established: do you belong to it?" and treat this theme under the following three heads: (1) The Church alone possesses the treasure of forgiveness: have you made this treasure your own? (2) The Church alone possesses the true knowledge of God: have you this knowledge to your soul's salvation? (3) In the Church alone there is complete obedience to God's will: are you rendering God this obedience? We shall be preaching a doctrinal sermon, yet everything in it is applied to the individual and set in relation to his personal life. No one can justly accuse it of being tedious or lifeless; its effect will rather be profound and to some salutary. Or let us base an ethical doctrinal sermon[73] on James 1: 13-18, and propose as our theme: "Whose is the fault when we succumb to temptation?" answering, (1) Not God's, who suffers us to be tempted, (2) but man's, who lets himself be drawn away by his own lust and enticed. Here again we have a doctrinal sermon leading straight to life. Siedel[74] has a doctrinal sermon on Rom. 5: 1-6, with this outline: "The righteousness of faith, a tree bearing precious fruit— (1) Peace with God, (2) access to His grace, (3) glorying in tribulation, (4) hope in the glory to come."—G. C. Rieger[75] has an Easter sermon on Mark 16: 1-8 on "The Justification of Christ in His resurrection," and divides: (1) How Christ was justified in His own person, through the resurrection, (2) how all men have been justified to-

---

[73]This looks and sounds strange only because we have so largely forgotten that dogmatics and ethics belong inseparably together.—[74]*Lebenswasser aus dem Heilsbrunnen, Epistelpredigten*, 1897.—[75]*Herzpostille*, 1742 (1853).

gether with Christ, (3) how each individual man should appropriate this justification to himself and live and triumph in the same. Again, on the Sunday after Christmas (Luke 2: 33-40) he treats the spiritual priesthood of Christians, and shows (1) what this priesthood means, (2) to whom it belongs, (3) what its duties are, (4) what its high dignity and solemn obligations, and (5) how it in no wise conflicts with the office of the ministry, but on the contrary forms its foundation and support, and may under its direction prove a blessing and a means of improvement in the Church. Neither of these sermons betrays any trace of dogmatism or dryness.—W. Walther of Rostock[76] discusses on the basis of 1 John 4: 19, God's love to us and our love to God, yet all is intensely practical as he shows how God first loved us, and how we, therefore, must and can love Him in return. Again he treats of "Doubts" (on John 1: 45-50), (1) their danger, (2) their justification, (3) their defeat. Here is a doctrinal sermon so practically conceived and worked out that there is no trace of the doctrinaire about it. Again, Walther presents from the text John 20: 24-29, the relation between "Believing and seeing; (1) not seeing and yet believing,—that is the goal; (2) seeing and then believing,—that is the way to this goal." Once more a doctrinal sermon, but interesting from beginning to end, and interesting not only by reason of the original formulation of the thought, but because a vital question is answered with constant reference to actual life. A final illustration from Walther: Preaching on Paul's word, "When I am weak, then am I strong" (2 Cor. 12: 7-10), he divides: Let us try (1) to understand this wonderful saying, and (2) to learn from it the wonderful leading of God. Again a purely doctrinal sermon, yet pulsating in every word with life.—Lenski[77] offers the following outline on Eph. 2: 4-10: "What does it mean to be saved by grace? It means (1) deliverance from sin, death and perdition; (2) quickening, resuscitation, sitting in the heavenly places; (3) humility, gratitude, good works." This may, despite its unwieldy phraseology, be made the basis of a doctrinal sermon that will be interesting and practical.—Uhlhorn's doctrinal sermons[78] are admirable. For example, his Christmas sermon on Heb. 1: 1-14, in which he describes the sending of God's Son as (1) the culmination of divine revelation, (2) the completion of salvation for all men, (3) the final and decisive act of God. Or an Epiphany sermon on Titus 3: 3-8 develop-

---

[76]*Der Wandel im Licht* (1907); *Gottes Liebe* (1901). —[77]*The Eisenach Gospel Selections*, i, 561.—[78]*Gnade und Wahrheit. Epistelpredigten* (1877)

ing the thought that regeneration and renewal in Christ are universal and all-inclusive; or his Laetare sermon on Heb. 9:11-15 with the theme, "An eternal redemption," and the three divisions: (1) No redemption without sacrifice; (2) Christ's suffering and death, the perfect sacrifice, (3) by which He obtained eternal redemption for us. Or his Whitsunday sermon on Acts 10:42-48, discussing the relation between Pentecost and baptism under the two heads, "(1) Pentecost the baptismal day of mankind, (2) our baptismal day our Pentecost." Or a sermon on John 3:3-8, propounding and answering the questions, (1) What are we? (2) What ought we to be? (3) How may we become what we ought to be?—Among Lutheran preachers in America Walther of St. Louis was pre-eminently a doctrinal preacher. We quote the following outlines from his volume of Gospel sermons entitled *Licht des Lebens* (1885). On Matt. 8:1-13: "Why is faith praised so highly in the Bible? (1) Because salvation is a gift of grace which faith alone can lay hold on; (2) because this faith transforms the heart of man so that he performs truly good works."—Luke 2:23-40: "How the thoughts of men's hearts are made manifest by the preaching of Christ. (1) These thoughts are not manifest without the preaching of Christ; (2) the preaching of Christ makes them manifest."—Matt. 20:1-16: "The last shall be first and the first last. (1) Who are meant by the first and by the last? (2) What is it that makes the first last and the last first?"—John 16:11-23: "Godly sorrow leads to true joy, (1) to joy in the kingdom of grace here, (2) to joy in the kingdom of glory hereafter."—John 16:5-15: "Unbelief, the chief sin; because (1) from it all other sins flow, (2) on account of it alone man will be damned."—Mark 7:31-37: "The great importance of the sacraments for Christian faith and life; (1) of Baptism, (2) of the Holy Supper."—Luke 14:1-11: "The true Sabbath observance, of which the Old Testament observance was a mere shadow and type. (1) It consists in resting from all sinful works; (2) this inward Sabbath, however, impels us to a voluntary outward Sabbath observance." —Sometimes there is in Walther a surprisingly loose connection between sermon and text, and some of the sermons must be pronounced too dogmatical, but they always take their stand in the midst of the Scriptures and not infrequently enter with impressive seriousness into the midst of life (see especially the sermon on Matt. 20:1-16).[79]

---

[79]Two recent volumes of doctrinal sermons, much too doctrinaire and abstract, are L. Wessel's *Sermons and Addresses on Things Fundamental* (St. Louis, 1918), and *Vesper Sermons. Forty-two Even-*

The more strongly we insist that the doctrinal sermon relate itself to life, to feeling, will and action, the fainter will become the line of demarcation between it and the *pastoral sermon*. This is all the more true when we demand also that the pastoral sermon bear a doctrinal character, that it do not exhort or reprove without presenting the positive truth on which its exhortation or reproof is built up. Yet there remains a difference between these two types of sermon, a difference determined by their respective aim and purpose. In the doctrinal sermon my purpose is to teach, to reach the understanding, to produce clear religious and ethical convictions. I refer to the practical significance of the doctrine for man's life, only in order to bring out its value and importance and to make it the more acceptable to my hearers. In the pastoral sermon I also teach, but here my teaching is subordinate and contributory to my purpose to reach the feeling and the will of my hearers, to move them to actual acceptance of the proffered grace, to joy and gratitude, and thereby to right conduct. It would, however, be a mistake to suppose that the doctrinal element in the pastoral sermon must on this account be reduced to a minimum or confined to merely calling to the hearer's mind that which he already knows. It would be a mistake, because it is always dangerous to take too much for granted, but especially because such a sermon would, with its exhortation, demand and reproof, degenerate into a mere preaching of law. It must be the aim of the pastoral sermon to produce penitent faith in the hearts of its hearers; how can it accomplish this without constantly setting the holy love of God before them? It must seek, on the basis of its faith, to proclaim to the congregation the assurance and the joy of its salvation; how can it do this unless it holds before the soul the rich treasure God has laid up for it and offers to its faith? It must bring men to a knowledge of their sin and an examination of their faith and life; how can it do this without declaring to them the true nature of sin, faith and the Christian life? It must inspire them to become more and more changed into the image of Christ, from glory to glory; how can it accomplish this but by constantly setting the image of Christ before the congregation? And what is all this but teaching, didactic instruction? There is thus no inconsistency in saying, as we did above, that every sermon must contain a doctrinal element and in holding at the same time that

---

ing Sermons (St. Louis, 1919). The doctrinal series in Golladay's *Lenten Outlines and Sermons* (viii. The Atonement series) can scarcely be considered as outlines for *sermons*.

not the doctrinal but the pastoral sermon best expresses the real nature of the congregational sermon.

The spirit underlying and animating the pastoral sermon is preeminently the spirit of the shepherd of souls; for its purpose is to preserve, improve, and protect against all foes the spiritual life existing in the congregation. It is the spirit of the educator; for it calls attention to the sins that hinder its healthy development, sets up the ideal to be striven for, and points to the one source of strength. It is the spirit of the friend; for it seeks to comfort the sorrowful, encourage the faint, counsel the erring, spur on the indifferent, warn the careless, raise up the fallen. It finds its specific type in the ministry of Jesus to His disciples, which He Himself characterized as παρακαλεῖν (comp. ἄλλος παράκλητος John 14: 16), a calling to them, an encouraging them, a comforting, uplifting, challenging them, an influence at once upon the understanding, the emotions and the will. So the pastoral sermon takes its place alongside the member in the church pew, and seeks by a faithful and untiring appeal, adapted to his particular need, to show him the joy of the Christian life and lead him nearer the mark of his high calling. While the pastoral sermon is compelled to rebuke sin and urge men to the new life of holiness, nevertheless at its centre must always stand the glad tidings of the justification of the sinner through grace for Christ's sake by faith. F. W. Walther well says: "The preacher whose sermons are predominantly moralizing or who, because he has not experienced the power of the Gospel and is still under the bondage of the law, fears to pour out before his hearers, again and again, the whole riches of the Gospel with its fulness of comfort, lest by so doing he might render their souls secure and lead them to hell; and who, whenever he speaks of faith is quick to add all sorts of warnings against self-deception and against premature faith, but is not concerned to preach faith into men's hearts—this preacher may imagine himself to be employing the best safeguard against mutilating the Word of God and neglecting souls, but is in reality guilty, above all others, of mutilating God's Word and neglecting the souls purchased by Christ at so great a cost. It is not true that he who sparingly dispenses the comfort of the Gospel and lets the law predominate, will foster living faith and a truly Christian life; he will, on the contrary, hinder such faith and life. A true Christin preacher must be able to repeat Luther's vow after him, —'In my heart (and in my preaching) this article alone rules and shall rule, namely faith in my dear Lord Christ, from whom, through whom, and to whom all my theological ideas proceed and return, day and night, in continual ebb and flow'."[80]

In its treatment of sin, the pastoral sermon will do well to avoid harping on the universal sinfulness of mankind; else it will lull rather than rouse. Let it rather deal with sins in the concrete and lay bare the glaring contrast to the divine ideal. Let it describe the terrible power of sin by tracing its continual recurrence even in the life of sincere believers, as well as the guilt of sin by tracing the continual forgiveness of God and the strength of God striving in our weakness. By so doing, the pastoral sermon will constantly send its hearers back to Christ and thus enable them to understand aright the doctrine of original sin and the universality of sin. A merely intellectual knowledge of these truths can have no saving value.

In calling men to holiness of life, let the pastoral sermon beware of driving them by means of the law. Whatever may be accomplished in this way is external, dead, and does not please God. Whatever does not grow out of grateful love to God, freely and by an inner impulse, cannot have God's approval, however it shine before men. If only our preachers seriously applied this truth in practice! We should then have less self-righteousness and self-deception in our congregations, Christians would be brought to a realization of their sins and to an ever more eager and constantly renewed desire for their Saviour, both as the remover of guilt and the giver of strength, and would learn to distinguish between evangelical and natural morality. That the Christian needs to be constantly admonished to holy living because of the flesh still clinging to him, is emphasized by Luther in a sermon on the epistle for the XIX. Sunday after Trinity. "The churchly office of preaching," he says, "is necessary not only for the ignorant who must be taught, for the simple and stupid populace and the youth, but also for those who well know what they ought to believe and how they ought to live, in order to awaken and admonish them to be daily on their guard, not to grow weary and listless, nor to lose heart in the battle they must wage upon earth against the devil, their own flesh and all vices. Hence St. Paul so diligently admonishes all Christians that he almost seems to be overdoing the thing, by continually dinning it in their ears, as though they were so ignorant as not to know it of themselves or so careless and forgetful as not to perform it without his telling and urging them. But he knows full well that, although they have begun to believe and are in that state in which fruits of faith

---

[80]*Pastorale,* 93 f.—Comp. above, pp. 147 f.

must appear, the thing is nevertheless not so easily carried out and brought to completion. It will not do to think: 'It is enough to have given them the truth; when the spirit and faith are present the fruits of good works will follow of themselves' For while it is true that the spirit is present and is willing, as Christ says, and works in them that believe, it is likewise true that the flesh also is present, and the flesh is weak and indolent. The devil, moreover, is not keeping holiday, but seeks by temptation and incitement to cause the weak to fall. Here you dare by no means be negligent or indolent; as it is, the flesh is too indolent to obey the Spirit, nay it is strong to resist it, as Paul says in Gal. 5:17. God, therefore, must deal here as a good householder or faithful regent, who has a lazy man-servant or maid-servant or indifferent officials. (They need not be actually wicked or disloyal.) He must not think it enough to tell them once or twice what to do, but must be constantly at their heels and personally urge them on. So, too, we have not reached the point where our flesh and blood go leaping in pure joy and eagerness to do good works and obey God, as the Spirit would gladly have us do and directs us to do. On the contrary, even though faith unceasingly urge and buffet the flesh, it scarce succeeds in accomplishing very much. What would be the result if this admonition and urging were omitted and one were to think, as many Christians think, 'Well, I know of myself what I ought to do; I have heard it so many years and so often, and have even taught it to others, etc.' I verily believe that if we were to cease our preaching and admonishing for a single year, we should become worse than heathen."—"The pastor, therefore," as F. Pieper says, "who does not exalt the glory of Christian works and thereby make Christians eager to perform good works, deprives his congregation of a precious gift and commits a grievous sin."

Elsewhere, indeed, Luther makes it abundantly clear that such admonitions to Christians to perform good works must not degenerate into legal compulsion. In his *Church Postil* he writes on Rom. 12, in the sermon for the I. Sunday after Epiphany,—"Paul does not say, 'I command you,' for he is preaching to persons who are already Christians and pious through faith, new men, and who are not to be driven by commands, but admonished to do willingly the works they have to do through the sinful old man. For whoever does not do these works willingly, as a result of friendly admonition alone, is no Christian. And whoever exacts them from the unwilling, by means of law, is no Christian preacher or ruler, but a worldly slave-driver. A legal taskmaster employs force, with threats and punishments; a preacher of grace beseeches and invites, by showing God's goodness and mercy. The latter desires no unwilling words or grudging service, but an eager and glad service of God. Whoever will not let himself be besought and invited, by such sweet and pleasant words of God's mercy so abundantly bestowed upon us in Christ, to do willingly and gladly what he is told, to the glory of God and the good of his neighbor, he is nothing and nothing can be done with him. How can he be softened and made eager by laws and threats, when the fire of heavenly love and grace does not melt him?"

Particular care must be taken when the pastoral sermon operates with the fear of punishment and the hope of future reward as motives of moral conduct. Where this care was lacking, the sermon frequently encouraged ideas contrary to the doctrine of justification by faith and leading directly to Romish and natural morality. The Scriptures speak of the fear of punishment and of the reward of the righteous,[81] but never as a primary, still less as the only motive of moral living. The primary motive is everywhere in Scripture the inner impulse of grateful love to God, given immediately with faith, impelling the regenerate to an ever completer surrender of himself to the fulfilment of his Lord's will, by the constant unfolding of his inner powers. But because this inner impulse is hindered and held back by the flesh, it is spurred on by the promise of temporal and especially eternal reward,—the temporal (James 1:25) or eternal bliss which accompanies the doing of the divine will. Similarly, the resisting and hindering flesh is reminded of the temporal or eternal punishment which accompanies disobedience of God's will, in order that it may be deterred and compelled to leave the spirit more freedom for its unfolding. Luther indicates this secondary character of the motive of reward and punishment in the very arrangement of the first part of his Catechism, where while he introduces fear (reverence)[82] and love ten times as ethical motives, he has but one reference (in the conclusion) to the fear of punishment and the expectation of reward. When, on a low plane of Christianity, the reverent fear and love in a Christian prove insufficient to lead to true Christian living, the reminder of the inevitable punishment of sin or the inevitable bliss of righteousness may induce him to turn from evil and do the good.[83]

---

[81] E. g., Matt. 6:1, 2; Luke 6:23; Rom. 8:15; 1 John 4:18; 1 Peter 1:17; Heb. 12:28; Phil. 2:12.—[82] See *Catechetics*, pp. 367 ff.—[83] Comp. L. Ihmels, *Der Lohngedanke und die Ethik Jesu* (1908); F. Mahling, *Lohn und Strafe in ihrem Verhaeltnis zu Religion und Sittlichkeit nach neutestamentlicher Anschauung* (1912).

Examples of the pastoral sermon are found in Macarius (?), Chrysostom, Augustine, Bernard of Clairvaux, Luther, Veit Dietrich, Simon Musaeus, J. J. Rambach, *et al.* This type of sermon is most numerously represented in the sermon literature of the Church. Among more recent preachers, it formed the peculiar *charisma* of men like Muenkel, Petri, Loehe, Ahlfeld, Thomasius, H. Hoffmann, Max and Emil Frommel, W. Walther, H. Bezzel, L. Ihmels. F. W. Robertson has a number of fine specimens. H. W. Beecher's gift lay largely along this line, although in the absence of biblical content his sermons frequently fall below the high level that might have been expected. Alexander Maclaren's sermons belong to this class, though their predominating intellectual cast would seem to stamp him rather as a doctrinal preacher. It is owing to the German *Gemuet* and to Lutheran inwardness that the pastoral sermon found its foremost exponents in Germany and the Scandinavian countries. It should also not be forgotten that the Lutheran sermon is more deliberately congregational than the Reformed sermon of England and America.

There follow a number of examples, taken from the collected sermons of W. Walther of Rostock[84] whom we regard as the foremost Lutheran preacher of the present day, equally admirable in the pastoral as in the doctrinal sermon. His sermon on Matt. 11:28, perhaps the bright particular jewel in the copious homiletic literature on this passage, has this structure: "Jesus calls all men to Him! (1) What lowliness—that all men are to come to Him! (2) What greatness—that He promises rest to all!" His conclusion is: "So Jesus passes through the world: lowliness and greatness are His marks. Divine greatness stooping down to those whom it would raise on high. Oh, do not stumble at His greatness, do not stumble at His lowliness! If it were not for His greatness—how could a man like ourselves help us to find eternal rest? If it were not for His lowliness—how could we sinners be helped by a king who jealously and selfishly hedged round his highness? Oh, that you might experience them in yourself—this greatness that makes you feel: 'Without Him I am lost!' and this lowliness that tells you: 'He calls me, too, even me!'"—Mark 6:45-51 is treated under the theme: "*In Gottes Namen fahren wir.* (1) We say this with firm determination, for it is no easy thing; (2) we say it with proud joy, for it is a precious thing."—At Christmastide he preaches on Ps. 144:3 and outlines: "Im Lichte der Weihnachtstat Gottes erkennen wir den Menschen, (1) sein Elend, daraus dass Gott

---

[84] See above, p. 155, note 76.

sich seiner so annimmt, (2) seine Hoheit, daraus dass Gott ihn also achtet."[85]—On Good Friday he selects 2 Cor. 5: 19-21 and takes as his theme the words, "Be ye reconciled to God!" Let us consider (1) those who say this to us, and give ear to their call, (2) those to whom they say it, and attend to our reply.—On John 14: 2-6 he bases an Easter sermon with the theme: "The true Christian can say, Ich fahre, und weiss wohl, wohin! For I know the Father's house at the end of the way and I know the way."—A Whitsuntide sermon on Eph. 1: 13-14: "Blessed are they that have the Spirit of God! He is (1) a mirror of what they now have, (2) an earnest of what they shall have hereafter."—John 18: 37-38 is impressively treated by representing Jesus as saying: "(1) I alone give the truth, (2) and with it an infinite good, (3) but I cannot give it to all."—On 2 Cor. 3: 3 he shows (1) how we are to be epistles of Christ, and (2) how we are able to be this.—"In the Father's house, and yet lost" is the impressive theme drawn from Luke 15: 25-32, portraying (1) the sin, and (2) the misery of the elder brother, and of all kindred souls. Over Luke 19: 1-9 he sets Jesus' word, "I must abide at thy house," (1) with my all-conquering love, (2) with my all-conquering might.—On Mark 6: 17-29: "How heaven and hell contend for the soul of man."—The preacher who desires to learn the art of the pastoral sermon may well study these sermons, of whose wealth of thought and fine psychological tact the above outlines give but the faintest hint.

Beside the doctrinal and the pastoral sermon the *awakening sermon* has its place. It is true that a hortatory element inheres in all true preaching. Menken says, as truly as quaintly, "Whoever speaks of righteousness, of chastity, of the last judgment, without making the *felices* tremble and giving them a sleepless night, has not preached properly, truthfully, apostolically." That there is room, however, for the specific type of awakening sermon follows from the fact that there are in every Christian congregation souls who must be awakened for the first time to faith, because they are still living in indifference and sin and have only an external connection with the Church, or who must be exhorted to give expression to their faith in one direction or another. There are many Christians living in faith who have never realized that foreign missions are a necessary expression of their faith; it is necessary to bring them to this knowledge and to the determination to undertake this work of faith. Little needs to be added here to what

---

[85]This outline is completely dependent on the rendering of the text in the German Bible and cannot be reproduced in English.

has been already said. Only this must be emphasized over and over again, that no one was ever awakened to the new life in Christ by means of the law. The law does not make the natural man a better or more pious man; it only uncovers his wickedness and increases his sin, his anger and hostility to God. It cannot even awaken a secret longing for grace. Its function is only to disclose sin, to judge, punish and condemn. It rather drives men away from God and into despair and damnation. Hence it is so necessary that the Gospel enter in and creatively produce in those fleeing from their judge, confidence in His grace, i. e., faith, the beginning of the new life. Bente well says: "We often hear it said, 'True repentance always grows into faith; faith springs from a penitent heart.' But faith, while it is born in repentance, does not spring from repentance, but from the Gospel." Indeed, the second element in repentance—hearty sorrow at having grieved and offended so gracious a God—is possible only on the basis of the faith wrought by the Gospel, and is the constant accompaniment of this faith.[86] The preacher who imagines himself able to awaken a dead congregation by preaching nothing but law, by reproving, chiding, threatening, judging and condemning, or by setting up a moral ideal, will not only fail but will sin against the souls entrusted to him and plunge them into either despair or self-righteousness. The preacher who, on the other hand, preaches nothing but Gospel, will likewise fail; for there can be no faith without repentance, or more precisely, without the first element in repentance, namely, contrition and the fear of the soul before a holy God.

The target to be aimed at by the awakening sermon is not the nervous system but the conscience. It is easy to play on people's nerves. Rag-time hymns (?), sensational preaching, vivid description of the torments of hell or a realistic portrayal of the pangs of Christ upon the cross will readily excite the nerves and lachrymal glands of the hearers. It needs more than this to reach the conscience. This was reached by Peter in his sermon on Pentecost. How his words went to the hearts of his hearers! They were "pricked in their hearts"; they were "convicted,"[87] so that they had not a word of self-defence, but stood like criminals who have heard the witnesses, one by one, give their damning testimony and who now have nothing to look forward to but the verdict of guilty and the inexorable sentence.

The most effective awakening preacher of the ancient Church

---

[86]See Reu, *Heilsordnung,* 1914, pp. 14ff.—[87]Comp. John 16:8,— ἐλέγχειν.

was Ephraem the Syrian. His sermons would have been still more effective had he made more frequent use of the Gospel than of the law, especially in his graphic descriptions of the judgment day and the torments of the damned. In the Middle Ages Berthold of Regensburg stands out. Luther's sermons contain many hortatory elements in the best sense. To a later period belong Balthasar Schuppius in Hamburg, G. C. Rieger in Stuttgart, Richard Baxter, John Bunyan, John Wesley and George Whitefield in England, and Jonathan Edwards in America. In the last century Hofacker in Wuerttemberg, Tholuck in Halle, and Spurgeon in London, shone as awakening preachers.

There follow several illustrations from the sermons of George Cunrad Rieger,[88] whom we regard as the standard preacher of this type. For I. Advent he has the elaborate outline (text, Matt. 21:1-9), "The first day of this new church year should be a day of solemn, sacred and general homage to Jesus Christ, the King of glory, on which (1) we on our part swear allegiance to Him and vow: 'O Jesus, we are Thine, and stand upon Thy side, O King of glory; peace be with Thee and grace with Thy helpers, for Thy God is Thy help.' (2) We devoutly hear what the Lord royally declares concerning this, as He on His part graciously accepts our homage and replies: 'If you truly mean this, my heart shall be with yours, I will accept you and love you, mightily defend you, take you under my blessed rule and keep you forever; but if you do this lightly, deceitfully and in hypocrisy, may God my Father see to it and punish you, for there is no violence in me'." Rieger's purpose in this sermon is seen in the prayer which he adds to this division: "Gird then, Thy sword upon Thy loins, the Sword of Thy Gospel, which goeth forth out of Thy mouth, O doubly descended heir of David's line! Gird on, I again pray Thee, Thy beauty, O Thou fairest among the sons of men! Prosper Thou in Thy royal beauty, and let the honorable glory of Thy Kingdom be manifested in our hearts. Ride on in Thy truth and righteousness, as in a chariot, into our hearts. Be pleased Thyself to open them and make wide the door. Let Thy right hand teach Thee terrible things, and through Thy knowledge awaken in us all, love, reverence, fear and obedience. Make sharp Thine arrows, for our hearts are very hard. Let the people, let the people here present, fall down before Thee; let all hearts and names and all knees bow down before Thee. O almighty King, let Thine arrows fly straight to the mark, into the hearts of

---

[88]*Herzenspostille, oder zur Fortpflanzung des wahren Christentums im Glauben und Leben* (1742, reprinted 1853).

all present, that we may vow allegiance and come under Thy sceptre and righteous rule: Amen."—On II. Advent (Luke 21:25-36) he pricks his hearers' hearts by showing "How the solemn contemplation of the Last Day binds us (1) to holiness and a godly life in general, and (2) to watchfulness and prayer in particular."—On Ascension Day (Mark 16:14-20) he tells his congregation, "All depends on Faith," and proves his thesis in a manner not surpassed even by Luther, using every resource at his command to win his hearers to this faith.—His sermon on Luke 14:16-24 takes the form of an "Invitation to a willing embrace of Christianity." Such an invitation is necessary (1) "because we spend so much of our time in things not nearly so important, (2) because it is easier and pleasanter to be saved than to be lost, (3) because if we lightly esteem and neglect this gracious invitation to communion with God, it will one day be an inexpressible sorrow to us in hell, (4) because it will ere long rejoice us unutterably to have followed this invitation and taken our place at the supper of our God."—Here again these brief outlines give scarcely a suggestion of the pleading love and the profound seriousness of these sermons; they should be read and studied as a whole.

Although, as we have said, the specific needs of the congregation and, to a certain extent, the individuality of the preacher must determine which of these three types of sermon is to be followed, this does not mean that every other consideration is to be excluded. That the particular character of the text must be taken into account, is self-evident. It may be so pronounced as to demand peremptorily one of these three types and no other. In such a case the preacher has no choice. If the congregation needs something else, he must find another text. No one should be such a slave to the system of pericopes as to make this impossible or difficult. There are, however, a great many passages which, without wresting or forcing their original meaning, may be used as texts for any of the three species of sermons. For example, on Hebrews 11:6-7 Menken[89] has a doctrinal sermon, Tholuck[90] a pastoral sermon, and Gerok[91] (on vv. 1-10) a hortatory sermon. Romans 1:16-17 may be used as text for a doctrinal sermon, explaining what it is that makes the Gospel a divine power to salvation; for a pastoral sermon, in which the congregation is cheered by being shown what a priceless treasure it has in the Gospel; or for a

---

[89]*Das II. Kapitel des Hebraeerbriefs in 14 Homilien* (1821).—[90]*Gewissens-, Glaubens- und Gelegenheitspredigten* (1860).—[91]*Predigten fuer alle Fest-, Sonn- und Feiertage. Epistelpredigten* (1857).

hortatory sermon, aiming at awakening the hearers to interest and activity in the cause of missions.

If the preacher succeeds in applying, out of the fulness of his conviction, those elements of God's Word which lay hold on man's inner nature, and in applying them in a manner answering to the nature and need of his congregation, he may rest assured that his preaching will minister to edification in the twofold sense described above. He may rest assured of this, even though there be at times no improvement perceptible in the souls committed to his charge. While his preaching may prove to some, because of their obstinacy, a means of hardening instead of renewing their hearts, there will always be others in whom the Word, after lying for a long time dormant in their subconsciousness, will yet unfold its life-giving power and work in their souls the beginnings of eternal life. The work of the preacher is the work of a sower of seed. Hence it is true, not only that "one soweth, and another reapeth,"[92] but also that "the husbandman waiteth for the precious fruit of the earth, and hath long patience for it, until he receive the early and latter rain."[93] Times of depression caused by the apparent failure of his work,[94] the preacher will overcome by recalling our Lord's parable in Mark 4: 26-29 and by his faith in the life-power of the Word he preaches.[95] His constant urging and "compelling"[96] is, therefore, not a sign of human impatience but of patient reliance upon the Word, whose life-giving power is many a time revealed to him when he least expects it. God has His times and seasons for nations and for the individual as well. We cannot, with all our impatience, set His clock forward. "All my times are in Thy hand." And if there should actually be no fruit unto eternal life to show for all our labor, it has still not been in vain; God needs also His ministers of judgment, as He needed Elijah of

---

[92]John 4: 37.—[93]James 5: 7.—[94]1 Kings 19: 4; Isa. 49: 4.—[95]Isa. 55: 10-11.—[96]Luke 14: 23 (R. V., "constrain").

old.[97] In how far our labor must serve this doleful purpose, He alone knows. It is not for us to pry into these mysteries, but rather to examine ourselves anew, in order to find whether we are faithfully using and applying the edifying elements of His Word, or whether we are not perhaps ourselves obstructing their fullest operation. It is for us to labor on unwearied, with a patience patterned after the patience of God toward us, and with the sure confidence expressed by Paul at 2 Corinthians 2: 16 f. (p. 170.)

---

[97] 1 Kings 19: 11-18.

B. THE SERMON AS ORATION

§9. THE ATTRIBUTES OF THE SERMON AS ORATION IN THE CONGREGATIONAL SERVICE

Aristotle, *Rhetoric*, ed. by Becker and Brandeis, tr. by Theo. Buckley (1914). Cicero, *De Oratore; Brutus de claris oratoribus; Orator*, ed. by C. F. W. Mueller, tr. by J. S. Watson (1897). Horace, *Epistles* (Liber ii, ep. 3, Ad Pisonas, De Arte Poetica), ed. by G. T. A. Krueger, tr. by Conington (1895). Quintilian, *Institutio Oratoria*, ed. by Meister, tr. by J. S. Watson (1856). Longinus, *On the Sublime*, ed. by R. Roberts, ^{2}1907, text and tr. by A. O. Prickard, 1907-8. Augustine, *De Doctrina Christiana*, ed. by Bruder, tr. in NPNF. Fr. Fenelon, *Dialogues on Eloquence*, 1700 (we use the tr. published in Porter's "The Young Preacher's Manual," ^{2}1829). Edm. Burke, *A Philosophical Inquiry into the Origin of our Ideas of the Sublime and Beautiful*, 1756. Geo. Campbell, *The Philosophy of Rhetoric*, 2 vols., 1776. Geo. Campbell, *Lectures on Pulpit Eloquence*, 1775 (reprinted in "The Preacher and Pastor," New York, 1849). J. G. von Herder, *Vom Geist der hebraeischen Poesie*, 1782. Franz Theremin, *Die Beredsamkeit eine Tugend*, 1814, tr. by Shedd. Rich. Whately, *The Elements of Rhetoric*, 1828 (^{7}1840; reprinted Louisville, Morton & Co.). Rich. Whately, *Elements of Logic*, 1826 (^{9}1850). E. Porter, *Lectures on Homiletics and Preaching and on Public Prayer*, 1834. W. Gresley, *Ecclesiasticus Anglicanus, a Treatise on Preaching*, 1840. A. Vinet, *Homiletics, or The Theory of Preaching*, 1840, tr. by Skinner, 1853 (^{2}1861). H. J. Ripley, *Sacred Rhetoric, or Composition and Delivery of Sermons*, 1489. Wm. Taylor, *The Model Preacher, a Series of Letters on the best mode of Preaching*, 1859. D. P. Kidder, *Treatise on Homiletics*, 1864 (^{2}1868). Wm. G. T. Shedd, *Homiletics and Pastoral Theology*, 1867. R. L. Dabney, *Sacred Rhetoric*, 1870 (^{3}1902). John A. Broadus, *Treatise on the Preparation and Delivery of Sermons*, 1870 (^{30}1902). G. W. Hervey, *A System of Christian Rhetoric*, 1873. H. W. Beecher, *Lectures on Preaching*, 1872-4. Ph. Brooks, *Lectures on Preaching*, 1876. Th. Harnack, *Praktische Theologie*, 1878. A. Krauss, *Lehrbuch der Homiletik*, 1883. A. Phelps, *English Style in Public Discourse*, 1883. F. W. Fiske, *A Manual of Preaching*, 1893

J. Genung, *Outlines of Rhetoric*, 1893. A. S. Hill, *Principles of Rhetoric*, 1895. H. Hering, *Die Lehre von der Predigt*, 1905. A. S. Hoyt, *The Preacher*, 1909 (²1912). C. L. Slattery, *Present-Day Preaching*, 1909 (²1912). W. A. Quayle, *The Pastor-Preacher*, 1910. A. S. Hoyt, *Vital Elements of Preaching*, 1914. C. S. Gardner, *Psychology and Preaching*, 1918. Theo. Graebner, *Inductive Homiletics*, 1919.

In distinction from all other parts of the service, the sermon appears in the form of oration, or public discourse. As such it falls under the rules which rhetoric imposes upon every oration. The oration differs from the soliloquy, in which one utters one's thoughts to one's self alone, as well as from the audible meditation, in which one pursues one's reflections without regard to a listener. It invariably includes the element of address to others; it does not exist for itself but altogether in the interest of its auditors, to whom it addresses itself and in whom it aims to produce a definite mental reaction. Its purpose is to influence their understanding, their emotions, and their will. It must therefore possess the qualities of convincing clearness, pleasing elegance, and moving force. (P. 173.)

If the prevailing conception of works of "pure" art is correct—that they "are for the world simply phenomena, and it is no concern of the artist to take account of the effect they produce, whether that effect be one of pleasure, of discomfort, or of demoralization," since his object is to express himself and not to influence others—though this view is not without its opponents,[1]—then the oration in general and the sermon in particular cannot claim to be works of art in this sense, although they contain a distinctive artistic element, as we shall show later in Part III. For both the oration and the sermon emphatically purpose to influence others and to produce a distinct effect. The orator as well as the preacher is not only concerned with his own intuitions nor content to externalize his impressions for his own pleasure, but has constantly before him an audience, concerning whom he is asking himself at every step of his preparation and delivery, How can I bring what fills my heart to bear upon their hearts? How can I best achieve the desired *docere, delectare,* and *movere?*

---

[1] Compare, e. g., Henry Newbolt, *A New Study of Poetry* (1910), chap. xii, "The Poet and his Audience."

Hence Cicero says, in his *De Oratore*: "All the emotions of the mind, which nature has given to man, must be intimately known; for all the force and art of speaking must be employed in allaying or exciting the feelings of those who listen."[2] . . . "The greatest part of a speech is to be devoted to the excitement of the feelings, either by exhortation, or the commemoration of some illustrious action, or by moving the people to hope, or to fear, or to ambition, or desire of glory; and often also to dissuade them from temerity, from rage, from ardent expectation, from injustice, from envy, from cruelty."[3] And Fenelon writes, in his second Dialogue: "To make a complete orator, we must find a philosopher, who knows both how to demonstrate any truth and at the same time to give his accurate reasoning all the natural beauty and vehemence of an agreeable, moving discourse, to render it entirely eloquent. And herein lies the difference between the clear, convincing method of philosophy, and the affecting, persuasive art of eloquence." "A philosopher's aim is merely to demonstrate truth and gain your assent, while the orator not only convinces your judgment, but commands your passions." "When a hearer is fully convinced, what is there more to be done? There is still wanting what an orator would do more than a metaphysician, in proving the existence of God. The metaphysician would give you a plain demonstration of it, and stop at the speculative view of that important truth. But the orator would further add whatever is proper to excite the most affecting sentiments in your mind, and make you love that glorious Being whose existence he had proved. And this is what we call persuasion." "You see then what reason Cicero had to say, that we must never separate philosophy from eloquence. For the art of persuading without wisdom and previous instruction must be pernicious, and wisdom alone, without the art of persuasion, can never have a sufficient influence on the minds of men, nor allure them to the love and practice of virtue." "Persuasion has this advantage beyond mere conviction or demonstration that it not only sets truth in the fullest light, but represents it as amiable, and engages men to love and pursue it. The whole art of eloquence, therefore, consists in enforcing the clearest proofs of any truth, with such powerful motives as may affect the hearers, and employ their passions to just and worthy ends; to raise their indignation at ingratitude, their horror against cruelty, their compassion for the miserable, their love of virtue, and to direct every other passion to

---

[2]Lib. i, 5.—[3]Lib. ii, 82.

its proper object. This is what Plato calls affecting the minds of an audience and moving their bowels."

Vinet says: "We must distinguish oratorical discourse from didactic discourse, which concludes with an idea, and poetry, which has no conclusion and of which the purpose is not out of itself but in itself. Oratorical discourse is ultimately an appeal to the will." "An oratorical discourse is a discourse delivered to an assembly with the view of inculcating on it certain ideas, impressing it with certain sentiments or inducing certain resolves, or of doing these three things at once. The last, however, is the final purpose, that in relation to which the other two are means, instruments. The orator should address the heart as well as the understanding, since his desire is to reach the will, and our will is under the control of our affections."[4] And in another connection: "The pursuit of an actual and practical purpose, which injures other arts, is the strength of eloquence, particularly of the eloquence of the pulpit; it is its very principle; and every art, like every institution, is corrupted by separating it from its principle."[5] Phillips Brooks also emphasizes this peculiarity of the sermon: "A sermon exists in and for its purpose. That purpose is the persuading and moving of men's souls. That purpose must never be lost sight of. If it ever is, the sermon flags. It is not always on the surface, not always impetuous and eager in the discourses of the settled pastor as it is in the appeals of the Evangelist who speaks this once and this once only to the man he sees before him. The sermon of the habitual preacher grows more sober, but it never can lose out of it this consciousness of a purpose; it never can justify itself in any self-indulgence that will hinder or delay that purpose. It is always aimed at men. It is always looking in their faces to see how they are moved. It knows no essential and eternal type, but its law for what it ought to be comes from the needs and fickle changes of the men for whom it lives. Now this is thoroughly inartistic. Art contemplates and serves the absolute beauty. The simple work of art is the pure utterance of beautiful thought in beautiful form without further purpose than simply that it should be uttered. The poem or statue may instruct, inspire, and rebuke men, but that design, if it were present in the making of the poem or the statue, vitiated the purity of its artistic quality. Art knows nothing of the tumultuous eagerness of earnest purpose. She is supremely calm and independent of the whims of men.

---

[4]English edition, pp. 27, 26.—[5]P. 349.

The Appeal to the Intellect—Clearness

Phidias cast among a barbarous race must carve not some hideous idol which shall stir their coarse blood by its frantic extravagance, but the same serene and lofty beauty of Athene which he would carve at Athens. If it wholly fails to reach their gross and blunted senses, that is no disgrace to it as a work of art, for the artistic and the didactic are separate from one another."[6] And David J. Burrell says: "There are preachers who read beautiful essays on themes more or less closely related to theology and ethics; but that is not preaching. Talking about a thing is not preaching. The essayist takes his hearer by the hand and leads him round and round a centre; the preacher takes his hearer by the hand and escorts him to the next town. It is thus that preaching helps men on."[7]

The sermon as oration aiming to influence the *understanding* of its hearers and to bring the intellect of the preacher to bear upon that of the congregation, must possess *convincing clearness*. An unclear discourse cannot produce a clear impression. The thinking man turns from it unsatisfied, his doubts and difficulties have not been met, the views presented have proved unable to compel acceptance. But (a) when the subject-matter is presented in *perspicuous language,* (b) when it is arranged in *logical order,* and (c) when by a frequent use of *allocution* the actual or possible objections and the divergent viewpoint of the hearer are fairly met and overcome, then the sermon awakens interest, convinces the hearer of the value of its ideas, and wins him over to its own position. Far from becoming monotonous, it stimulates, invites to mental co-operation, holds the attention, draws the hearer away from his erroneous position and wins him for the truth. This is the *dialectic* element in the sermon, finding its analogy in the development of the subject-matter in catechetical instruction and employing, like it, both the synthetic and the analytic method. The former method is followed when the sum of ideas and observations contained in a term or a statement is logically deduced; the latter, when by examining

---

[6]*Lectures on Preaching*, p. 110 f.—[7]*The Sermon*, p. 11.

its particular aspects we advance to the higher unity of a term or a statement. A sound and interesting doctrinal sermon is hardly conceivable without this dialectic element; in specifically apologetic sermons it will naturally predominate. (P. 182.)

(a) *Perspicuity* must characterize the oration and hence also the sermon, if it is to convince the hearer of the truth to be imparted. Perspicuity, or clearness, has always been ranked among the primary rhetorical requirements. Already in Quintilian we find this rule laid down, "Nobis prima sit virtus perspicuitas."[8]

Broadus says: "The most important property of style is perspicuity. Style is excellent when, like the atmosphere, it shows the thought, but itself is not seen. Yet this comparison, and the term 'perspicuity' which was derived from it, are both inadequate, for good style is like stereoscopic glasses, which, transparent themselves, give form and body and distinct outline to that which they exhibit. A certain grand-looking obscurity is often pleasing to some hearers and readers, who suppose that it shows vast learning, or great originality, or immense profundity. To treat subjects in this fashion is no new thing. Quintilian says it was not new in his day (viii, 2:18), for that he found mention in Livy of a teacher who used to direct his pupils to *darken* the idea. He adds a witticism of some one whose hearers complained that they did not understand, and who replied, 'So much the better; I did not even understand it myself,' and elsewhere speaks of men who think themselves talented because it requires talent to understand them. M. Huc says that in the Lama convents, where the Buddhist professors lecture to their pupils, the more obscure and unintelligible their sayings, the more sublime they are reckoned. Alas! that preachers of the Gospel are not always proof against this pitiful temptation. A preacher is more solemnly bound than any other person to make his language perspicuous. This is very important in wording a law, in writing a title-deed or a physician's prescription, but still more important in proclaiming the Word of God, words of eternal life." Vinet writes: "On subjects as to which our design is not only to instruct but to persuade and determine the will, we have no power if we are not perspicuous; we are powerful sometimes merely by being perspicuous. There hence results a particular necessity of perspicuity

---

[8]Lib. viii, 2.—The student should consult works like Campbell's *Philosophy of Rhetoric*, Whately's *Rhetoric*, Bain's *Composition and Rhetoric*.

in the pulpit; but this necessity results also from the nature of public discourse, from the character of the auditories to which preaching is addressed. The labor of understanding what is spoken prevents the soul from yielding itself to its power. The precept of Quintilian may here be applied: Oratio debet negligenter quoque audientibus esse aperta."[9]

Broadus well says that "a preacher has greater difficulty than any other class of speakers in making his style perspicuous to *all* his hearers, for no others speak to so heterogeneous an audience, including persons of both sexes, of every age from early childhood, and of every grade of intellect and culture. But this difficulty, when most deeply felt, should but stimulate to diligent and painstaking effort. For what is the use of preaching, unless we may hope to do good? And what good can be done, save in proportion as we are understood? Pretentious obscurity may excite a poor admiration, unmeaning prettiness may give a certain pleasure, mere vociferation—like Bottom's part, 'nothing but roaring,'—may affect some people's nerves, but only truth, and truth that is understood, can bring real benefit. Moreover, something worse may happen than the failure to do good; we may do harm. Some hearers are repelled and disgusted by obscurity. Others are misled. It is a mournful thing to think of, but one of not infrequent occurrence, that men should so misunderstand us, as to take what we meant for medicine and convert it into poison. As we love men's souls we must strive to prevent so dreadful a result. One cannot expect, as Quintilian already remarks, 'that the hearer will be so intent upon understanding as to cast upon the darkness of the speech a light from his own intelligence. What we say must be made so clear that it will pour into his mind as the sun pours into the eyes, even when they are not directed toward it. We must take care, not that it shall be possible for him to understand, but that it shall be utterly impossible for him not to understand' (viii, 2:23). The German philosopher Fichte wrote a treatise with this title: 'An account clear as the sun, of the real nature of my philosophy; an attempt to compel the reader to understand.' None but a very self-confident man would put forth such a title; but it indicates what every teacher of men ought to aim at, not arrogantly but resolutely,—to compel the reader or hearer to understand."[10]

(b) But perspicuity of style alone will not lend convincing clearness to the sermon. To it must come perspicuity of thought, or *logical succession of ideas*. The individual sentences may be ever so

---

[9] P. 370.—[10] Pp. 362 ff.

distinguished by clearness of style, they will nevertheless fail to convince, unless they are ranged in the proper order, one following the other in the most natural succession, i. e., in logical sequence. Without this sequence there may be a welter of words, but there is no oration. Hence movement and order have from ancient times been counted among the fundamental requirements of an oration. The oration cannot remain static, fixed at any one point or thought; it must take the hearer by the hand and lead him from one point, from one thought to another, until it has brought him whither it intended, that is, until it has convinced him of the truth under discussion, so that he gives his assent and abandons his opposition to it. "Movement is the royal virtue of style," says Vinet.[11] And since this movement of style is accompanied by a corresponding movement in the mind of the orator, which he desires to communicate to the mind of his hearer, Cicero says: "Eloquentia nihil est nisi motus animae continuus." This demand that movement be continuous and uninterrupted, true as it is, is purely negative, forbidding the oration to rest idly at any given point and ruling out all interruptions and digressions. The continuous movement needs to have therefore a positive goal set before it and to be directed toward this goal. As Paul demands of his διώκειν τὸ βραβεῖον that it be κατὰ σκοπόν, directed toward a goal, so each member in the thought sequence of an oration must be chosen with a view to the final goal: excluded if it lies off the direct line, included if it is adapted to advance the thought a step nearer the goal. This is true of the oration as a whole, as we shall show, as well as of its individual parts. If this all-controlling movement toward a definite goal is lacking, the orator will not only fail to move the minds of his hearers in the direction desired, but will have himself to blame if they lose interest in or even doubt the truths already presented.

The movement of ideas will lead to the goal, only if the succession of thoughts and sentences is determined by logical order. "Every mind," says Vinet, "instinctively requires order. Every mind delights in order and is pained by its opposite. It suffers for the want of it, without knowing why, and perhaps without being apprised that it does suffer; we have an uneasiness like that which one feels in a tainted atmosphere, or, not to leave the intellectual sphere, like suffering which we experience from sophistry, when the fault in the reasoning is not detected. If it is man's destiny to err, still his natural element, his essence, so to speak, is truth. However unjust a mind may be, and

---

[11] P. 288.

what errors it may allow in itself, it does not allow errors in others. The same mind which does not lead others aright would itself be so led, and every deviation from the true route which perhaps it is itself unable to indicate, disconcerts and wearies it. The mere interposition of a thought which the progress of the ideas does not yet call for, or calls for no longer, destroys rising interest. A mind hesitating, uncertain, no longer lends itself to the orator's intention; for we see him assailed by several ideas at once, without knowing to which he is to attend, and in the perplexity, breaking his thought at every stroke, retracing his steps, mistaking gradations and confounding relations. The fact may be inexplicable; it is nevertheless real, and the certainty is, that where there is less of order, there is equally less of power. If order, or the connection of ideas, is always necessary, it is especially so in the eloquence of the pulpit, in which we should spare the hearer every useless and unwelcome trouble. We should even leave something to be supplied, by a hearer as well as a reader; but it is by no means allowed to us to require him to do a work which properly belongs to us."[12]

When to the thought already expressed I join immediately, of all the thoughts I have still to express, that one which is most closely akin to it, I have succeeded in bringing logical order into my discourse. It then marches forward step by step. The fewer gaps there are in the development of the thought, the more convincing my discourse becomes and the more complete my conquest of my hearers. Vinet illustrates this by the following two examples. Note the gain in clearness by reason of the more closely knit logical order of (2).

(1) "Those who accuse Christianity of foolishness should at least admit that it foresaw and braved this reproach. It was in haste to charge itself with it. It has avowed the bold design of saving men by foolishness. It was not under an illusion; it knew that its doctrine would be regarded as madness; it knew this before experience, before anyone had said it, and with this foolishness in its mouth, with this foolishness as its standard, it went forth to the conquest of the world. Christianity then has not left to infidelity the satisfaction of taxing it with foolishness, and if it is mad, it is in good earnest and willing to be so."

(2) "Christianity has not left to infidelity the satisfaction of being the first to tax it with foolishness. It has been in haste to bring this accusation against itself. It has avowed the bold design of saving men

---

[12] Pp. 382 ff.

by foolishness. It has not been under an illusion; it has known that its doctrine would be regarded as madness; it knew this before experience, it knew it before anyone had said it, and with this foolishness in its mouth, with this foolishness as its standard, it went forth to the conquest of the world. If then it is mad, it is in good earnest, and is willing to be so; and those who reproach it with foolishness are at least constrained to confess that it has foreseen their reproach and braved it."[13]

(c) The goal will be the more readily attained if the oration or the sermon is characterized further by the *dialectic element*. "We claim the dialectic for the sermon," says Krauss,[14] "with respect not to the contents but to the form in which the contents are expressed. It is especially when viewed as oration that the sermon may be described as dialectic or not dialectic. Many imagine this attribute to be necessarily connected with a philosophic or speculative discussion; but that is wrong. The dialectic, wherever it occurs, in preaching or philosophy, in narrative or in descriptive science, is nothing else than the conversational method of presentation. The orator or the writer imagines a give and take, a dialogue, as taking place between himself and his hearer or reader. He sets forth a statement and anticipates the objections it is possible to make to it, by making them himself and then refuting them. In this way, by finding the balance of thesis and antithesis in a synthesis, he reaches a new thesis which calls forth new doubts and explanations, until finally a synthesis is found that is capable of serving as point of departure for the direct application or that may bring, as final result, the oration to a close. . . . The specifically homiletic-dialectic differs from the scientific-dialectic on the one hand and from the conversational-dialectic on the other. The sermon avoids these two extremes by never losing sight of its purpose, which is edification. Not truth as such, but saving truth; not theology, but religion; not doctrine, but the relation of doctrine to life—this is the object of homiletical dialectic."[15] The homiletic-dialectic is distinguished from the conversational-dialectic by the fact that the oration is a public act, and the sermon a part of the congregational service, which as such can not descend to the level of the merely entertaining with its freedom and unconstraint.

Psychologically, the value of the dialectic method is derived from the fact that every investigation becomes interesting in proportion as it

---

[13]Pp. 391 f.—[14]P. 159.—[15]Comp. what was said about the dangers of the doctrinal sermon, above, pp. 152 ff.

is conducted by ourselves; for one's own work always interests one more than the work of some one else. Whoever desires, therefore, to interest others in his thought must let them take part in his mental processes. This is not only true of the cultured congregation. The day laborer as well as the farmer is able and eager to think for himself; he has his own ideas, his own doubts and difficulties. Unless we dispel these doubts by carefully taking them into account and showing him their untenableness and inconsistency, their harmfulness and danger, he will not be inwardly convinced of the Christian truth nor really won over to its side. The fundamental religious and ethical principles, in particular, cannot be properly presented without careful use of the dialectic element. The sermon must pursue the objections of the natural mind to their final hiding places, if it is to succeed in convincing men of their responsibility, of sin and judgment. How can a sermon treat satisfactorily and effectively of the answer to prayer, the uses of adversity, the blessing of temptation, the certainty of divine providence, or even of Jesus' struggle in Gethsemane, of the final judgment, etc., without entering carefully into the questions and objections arising in the minds of the hearers? Only in this way will these truths become to them living and self-evident realities, which they will not lightly let go.

Vinet, again, gives a good characterization of the oration and, *mutatis mutandis,* of the sermon, from this point of view. He says: "Oratorical discourse thus appears as a contest, a combat; this idea is essential to it. At one time, the orator combats an error by a truth; at another, he opposes one sentiment to another sentiment. In its just use, oratory is a combat, waged against errors of the mind and heart, with the weapon of speech. The orator seeks to make himself master of our will [first of all, however, of our intellect]. His attempt is a bold aggression; he lays siege to the soul as though it were a fort; a fort, however, which he can never take unless he keeps himself informed of the interior of the place; for eloquence is but an appeal to sympathy. Its secret consists in disengaging and arresting properties in others which correspond to what is in us, and in every one; its object is to lay hold of a hand which, unknown to ourselves, we are ever extending to it. It arms itself against us from ourselves; fortifies itself by our admissions; it supplies itself from our gifts; with our confessions it overwhelms us. In other words, the orator invokes intellectual and moral principles, which we hold in common with him, and causes us to feel and like this agreement. In a word, as has been said, in a bold form of speech, we are only convinced of what we believed before."[16]

What a prominent place this dialectic element holds in Paul's epistles, especially in Galatians, Romans and II Corinthians. Romans 2: 11-3: 20, for example, is one long contest with an imaginary opponent who refuses to admit that the Jews also are under the wrath of God and will be judged finally according to the criterion laid down in 2: 6-10. The apostle returns again and again to the charge, takes up each new objection in turn, and does not give over until he has forced his opponent to the wall. In this way he brings him to the point where his objections fail him and he is compelled to assent to the apostle's thesis. This element appears freely in Augustine's writings, and not only in his sermons against the Pelagians and other opponents. The expository preacher simply cannot do without the dialectic element; he must admit his hearers into the inner working of his mind and invite them to weigh the various interpretations of the text, to assist in rejecting the erroneous ones and in choosing the correct one. It is therefore not by accident that we find the dialectic element in preachers like Saurin, Menken, and Steinmeyer, whose sermons are pre-eminently contributions to the understanding of Scripture, as those of the last named are entitled.[17] Whoever would counsel and capture doubting and seeking souls will use the dialectic method; compare Beyschlag's sermons, *Erkenntnispfade zu Christo,* i, ³1902, ii, 1889. The preacher whose duty it is to strengthen and stablish those who would fain, amid the problems of modern thought, retain their childhood's faith, cannot dispense with this element; compare Ihmels, *Eins ist not,* 1906; *Siehe, ich mache alles neu,* 1913. The apologetic sermon offers a specially fruitful field; compare *Warum zweifelst du?* ed. by R. Falke, 1914. That the pastoral sermon may often employ this method to good advantage, may be observed in the sermon outlines given above.[18] An example of how the dialectic element is sometimes employed, in the doctrinal sermon, in a manner grazing the bounds of the permissible may be seen in Edwards A. Park's sermon on "The Prominence of the Atonement."[19]

---

[16] Pp. 26 ff.—[17]*Beitraege zum Schriftverstaendnis in Predigten,* ²1859-66; *Predigten fuer das ganze Kirchenjahr,* 1902.—[18]See pp. 157 ff. —[19]A paragraph of this sermon follows: "Did we hold a personal interview with the author of our text, we should be prompted to put three additional queries before him. Our first inquiry would be: 'Is not your theme too contracted? It is well to know Christ, but in all the varying scenes of life is it well not to know anything else? Will

Charles S. Finney illustrates its use in the hortatory sermon; his evangelistic *Sermons on Gospel Themes* (1876) and *Revival Lectures* (1875) are chains of irresistible reasoning, coils in which the hearer is folded, and from which, when once the first premise is granted, there seems no logical escape. Hence his marked success with persons given to exact thinking.

Sometimes entire sermons have been devoted to weighty objections made to one or another religious or moral truth. Bourdaloue, Massillon and Saurin have left us such discourses; compare, besides the above mentioned sermon of E. A. Park, also R. Watson's sermon on Acts 17:28, with the theme: "God with us," Vinet's sermon on "The Mysteries of Christianity" (1 Cor. 2:9), or Chalmers's on "The Golden Rule" (Matt. 7:12). Hervey concludes his discussion of this point with the warning,—"Follow not the example of those Jesuits and other reasoners who very seldom or never take any notice of objections. Even Jonathan Edwards, we are sorry to say, was not always careful enough to pause at real obstacles that might be thrown in his way. 'His preaching,' said Charles Simeon, 'reminds me of a man holding another's nose to the grindstone, and turning with all his might, in spite of all objections and expostulations.' Thomas Watson of Walbrook, on the contrary, is so attentive to the doubts and difficulties of his hearers, that some of his sermons read like dialogues."

---

not the pulpit become wearisome if, spring and autumn, summer and winter, it confine itself to a single topic? We have known men preach themselves out by incessant repetitions of the scene of Calvary,—a scene thrilling in itself, and on that very account not bearing to be presented in its details, every Sabbath day. How much less will the varying sensibilities of the soul endure the reiteration of this tragic tale every day and at every interview? Such extreme familiarity induces irreverence. The Bible is not confined to this theme. It is rich in ecclesiastical history, political history, ethical rules, metaphysical discussion, comprehensive theology. It contains one book of ten chapters which has not a single allusion to God, and several books which do not mention Christ; why then do you shut us up to a doctrine which will circumscribe the mind of good men, and result in making their conversation insipid?'

Contracted—this is the reply—and do you consider this topic a limited one, whose height, depth, length, breadth, no finite mind can measure? Of what would you speak?

'We would speak of the divine existence.'
But Christ is the 'I am.'
'We would speak of the divine attributes.'
But Christ is the Alpha and Omega; He searcheth the reins and trieth the hearts of men; He is the same yesterday, today, and forever;

Even if the sermon does not employ the dialectic element in the above sense, it must always be distinguished by perspicuity of style and by orderliness of thought, if it is to influence decisively the understanding of its hearers.

Not only the understanding of the hearer but his *emotions* are influenced by the sermon when to its convincing clearness is added *pleasing elegance*. For this there is needed (a) care in the choice of words, excluding everything vulgar from its language as offending the sense for the beautiful. Also (b) a constant observance of the laws of variety, euphony, and rhythm: variety, guarding against monotony in vocabulary and construction; euphony, giving attention to the choice and alternation of vowel and consonant sounds;

---

full of grace and truth; to Him belong wisdom and power and glory and honor; of His dominion is no end. Of what, then, would you speak?

'We would speak of the divine sovereignty.'

But Christ taught us to say: Even so, Father, for so it seemed good in Thy sight—and He and His Father are one.

'We would converse on the divine decrees.'

But all things are planned for His praise who was in Christ, and in whom Christ was at the beginning.

'We would discourse on electing love.'

But the saints are elect in Christ Jesus.

'We would utter many words on the creation of men and angels.'

Now by our Redeemer were all things created that are in heaven and that are in the earth, visible and invisible.

'We would converse on the preservation of what has been created.'

Now Christ upholdeth all things by the word of His power. What would you have, then, for your theme?

'We would take the flowers of the field for our theme.'

But they are the delight, as well as the contrivance, of the Redeemer.

'We would take for our theme the globes in space.'

But they are the work of His fingers.

'Then we would take the very winds of heaven for our theme, lawless and erratic as they are.'

But Jesus taught us to comment upon these as an illustration of His truth.

And is this the doctrine which men call a contracted one? Narrow? The very suspicion of its being narrow has now suggested the first reason why you should place it and keep it as the crown of all your words and deeds:—it is so large, so rich, so boundless, that you need nothing which excludes it."

rhythm, looking to the rise and fall, the cadence, of sentence and paragraph. But especially (c) the avoidance of everything abstract and the cultivation of a concrete, vivid and graphic presentation.[20] Here is where the imagination comes into play, and the orator or preacher is akin to the poet. Like him he creates

"Forms more real than living man,"

in order to unfold through them the treasury of Christian truths and to kindle a love for those truths in the hearts of his hearers. Thus he will portray the great figures of antiquity with a plastic energy that sets them before his hearers' eyes in life-like form, with all their spots and faults, producing horror and loathing, and with all their beauty and greatness, moving to desire and imitation. He reaches into the broad field of nature and the whole life of man, and finds everywhere similitudes of the eternal, in order to awaken in the soul intimations of its own glory. He paints in living colors the true image and ideal of the Christian congregation, in order to call forth an inner pleasure in the same. He is inexhaustible in finding apt figures and images to present most vividly the truth and grace, the omnipotence and holiness of God. Well did Cicero say of the oration, and Augustine of the sermon, that it must not only instruct but also please and delight (*delectare*). In proportion as the preacher sets the imagination at work in his preaching, the emotions of his hearers will be charmed. There is here the danger, however, of making the poetic element an end in itself, instead of pressing it into the service of the edifying purpose of the sermon; and also of

---

[20]Henry James wrote to his friend, Robert Louis Stevenson, criticizing the latter's *Catriona*: "The one thing I miss in the book is the note of *visibility*—it subjects my visual sense, my *seeing* imagination, to an almost painful underfeeding." (*Letters of Henry James*, 1920, vol. i, 208.) The *novelist* may perhaps retort with R. L. S., "Death to the optic nerve!" but the *preacher* never.

attempting to atone for the lack of natural endowment by a mechanical and affected use of the poetic element, which can not but produce in the hearer the reverse of a proper *delectatio*. (P. 203.)

While convincing clearness is the first requirement of the oration or sermon, its purpose will be attained more readily and more permanently if this clearness goes hand in hand with *pleasing elegance*. In the intellectual contest of speech it is necessary that the weapons be keen and able to pierce the opponent's defense; but, as Cicero says, "the fencer and the gladiator discipline themselves not only to give and parry blows with dexterity, but to move with grace, *cum venustate*."[21] The preacher who fails to introduce into his sermons, or who even bars from them, this element of grace and beauty should heed what Broadus says,—"There are thoughts which naturally incline to blossom into beauty; why sternly repress them? There are grand conceptions which spontaneously clothe themselves in robes of majesty, and march forth in a stately but native dignity. And besides subjects that naturally shine and blaze, there are very many commonplace topics which the preacher must be constantly bringing to view, and which will gain a much more interested attention, from even the most devout hearers, if delicately touched with some hues of fancy. It is a noble thing thus to take important truths which have grown dull by use, and give them new brightness."[22] But the cultivation of the beautiful in preaching rests upon an even deeper foundation. The beautiful appeals to the emotions in man, which are the faculty by which he measures values. When therefore religious or moral truth is presented not only with convincing clearness but with captivating beauty, it is received by the mind not only as true but also as valuable. And if it is seen as valuable, it at once gains attention and interest.[23] The mind reaches out toward it to appropriate it and rejoice in its possession. Moreover, through this arousing of feeling and interest lies the way to the will. Hence if I wish to set the will in motion and induce it to occupy itself, positively or negatively, with certain objects of knowledge, I must first lay hold on the feelings. This I accomplish by the cultivation of the beautiful, by such a presentation of truth as may justly be termed beautiful. There is no reason why beauty of presentation need detract from the clearness or the force of such presentation;

---

[21]*De Orat*, iii, 52.—[22]P. 408.—[23]Comp. above, pp. 171 f.

for in nature the beautiful and the useful commonly appear in closest union. "Are the blossoms of the apple-tree, and the silks of the corn, not remarkable for their rich and varied, but delicate beauty, and may a family mansion not be thoroughly suited to convenience and comfort, and yet have a pleasing form and even a certain moderate ornamentation? Impassioned feeling often cannot express itself otherwise than by bold images, and these, though chosen for their strength, may also have an unstudied beauty. A painted cheek is an abomination; but let there be high health, and animated feeling, and without an effort or a thought the cheek takes to itself a color most bright and fair. The Creator meant that it should be so; are you wiser than the Creator?"[24] A discourse, clear and transparent, but bare of beauty, is likely to leave the hearer cold; just as a discourse, full of energy and force, but offending the sense for the beautiful, will probably repel. Nietzsche knew what he was about when he advised counsel in a criminal case to dwell in his defense solely upon the terrifyingly beautiful in his client's deed. De Quincey's *Murder considered as one of the Fine Arts* may profitably be studied from this point of view. How much more should the preacher, dealing as he does with eternal and divine truth and life, enlist in his service these uses of the beautiful!

(a) That elegance in a discourse depends upon the *careful choice of words,* relentlessly barring from its language everything unseemly, gross or vulgar, including all slipshod and slang expressions, needs no elaborate proof. This is not to say that the weakly and effeminate, the neutral and colorless, are to be the preacher's aim. Far from it. The use of a forcible expression may on occasion have a refreshing effect and mark the sermon as massive and manly, without transgressing the laws of beauty. A colloquial or even slang phrase may in exceptional cases be directly called for, especially before an uncultured audience, or when it alone will express the thought with the desired clearness. Thus the fastidious Alexander Maclaren could say and write: "There is an infinite depth of despondency, of 'throwing up the sponge,' of giving up the whole thing, in that word, 'we *trusted* that it had been He which should have redeemed Israel'."[25]

(b) While monotony is the death of beauty, a right *variety* always pleases. "The one rule," says Stevenson, "is to be infinitely various." How can the sermon be beautiful and delight the emotions of the hearer without movement and variety? When sentence follows sentence, and paragraph paragraph, each one fashioned exactly like

---

[24]Broadus, p. 409.—[25]*After the Resurrection,* p. 31.

the other, what wearisome iteration, what deadly monotony! It is beauty's funeral. Four or five successive sentences all beginning with "whereas" or "forasmuch" may be in place in a resolution of respect for the minister who has departed this life, but while he remains in life he ought to make a resolution to keep such forms out of his pulpit. Comparisons (just as—so) may possess beauty to a high degree, but their too frequent use puts beauty and the hearer to sleep. An unbroken succession of long sentences wearies, but if interrupted by an occasional short sentence, will come safely through. No less monotonous and still more exasperating is a long series of short sentences with its staccato effect. Declarative sentences should be varied with occasional interrogatory and exclamatory sentences. Why not? The frequent comparison of discourse to a stream should be taken to heart by every orator. There is nothing in the least monotonous about a stream: now it rages and roars, now it lies quietly between its banks, now it rushes foaming over a dam, now it flows in leisurely expanse across the plain; and this very variety lends to it its beauty and its charm. Hervey borrows from Lucian the figure of horse and rider; he says: "The bold and skilful horseman, whose steed is well trained and obedient to the rein and the spur, may sometimes venture to leap the highest fences and clear the widest ditches, but when the chase is over, he will slacken his pace and be content to walk slowly along the well-beaten bridlepath. The orator ought to know how to distribute, to vary, and to govern his movements in order to attain not only beauty but 'grace' of style at the same time. The laws of *chiaroscuro* in painting and of *forte-piano* in music are not without their applications to eloquence. In the fine arts, as in nature, the best effects are produced by contrasts. There we must reconcile oppositions and agreements, discords and accords, and so many contraries that out of unity and diversity may spring one harmonious whole."[26]

Broadus says of Gibbon that "he wearies by his uniform stateliness," and of Prescott that "his style would be improved by the occasional introduction of sentences quite different in pattern." If this is true of the written word, how much more of the spoken! Alliteration is no foe to beauty, if its "artful aid" be not invariably invoked and usually used. Antithesis may contribute much to beautiful movement, but if too freely employed produces stiffness; as witness the Latin Augustine, the German Koegel, and the English Jeremy Taylor. Adjectives belie their Latin name. *epitheta ornantia,* when they become

---

[26] Pp. 448 ff.

the foes of their nouns. An old hearer of Gerok's sermons commended the brilliant preacher-poet for his discriminating use of the adjective. Chosen as well as rejected with care, they are real ornaments of speech; as Hervey says: "Take any beautiful composition, such, for example, as Gray's 'Elegy' or Cowper's 'Prophetic Anticipations,' and draw your pencil over every adjective; what have you left? Pictures without color, without light and shade, without life and activity. Repeat the same act upon any eloquent passage of Jeremy Taylor's or of Edmund Burke's and you produce a similar effect."[27] But when adjectives are so profusely used that never a noun can appear unless escorted by two or three of them, or when the same adjective insists upon pairing off continually with the same noun, they become a nuisance. Indeed, repetition and redundancy of every sort are to be sedulously avoided. Generally, to use two words where one will do the work is poor economy. The student may be advised to study from this viewpoint such "beautiful bare narratives" (as Charles Lamb calls them) as *Robinson Crusoe* or *The Vicar of Wakefield*. Sometimes, it is true, repetition is permissible and valuable, and serves to impress a certain phase of the subject upon the memory; compare this use of repetition in Matthew Arnold's essays. Sometimes it may greatly enhance the beauty of the discourse, as the refrain does in poetry. But apart from this, it should be studiously avoided. Broadus calls attention to a minor but important detail:—"There is in English special danger that certain pronouns, particularly *it, that*, and *which*, and the preposition *of*, will be too often repeated in quick succession."

Euphony must be cultivated by every orator who would have his discourse please. This term is here employed to mean such a choice and collocation of letters, syllables and words as will secure their smooth and melodious enunciation. It has principally to do with the qualities of articulate sounds in their relation to speaking and hearing. Hervey, who pays particular attention to this part of our subject,[28] says with respect to the single word: "The English language has for hundreds of years been corrupting its native beauty." He illustrates this by the gradual change from "eth" to the simple "s" in the third person singular of the present indicative, as well as by the change of such verbs as "drowned," "walked," etc., from dissyllables to monosyllables. With Addison he laments that "this has very much disfigured the tongue and turned a tenth part of our smoothest words into as many clusters of consonants," which is the more to be deplored since "the

---

[27] P. 460.—[28] Pp. 501-7.

want of vowels in our language has been the general complaint of our politest authors." We mention this in order to show a fundamental difficulty that euphony has to contend with and to emphasize the necessity for the very greatest care. The hissing sound of "s" is to be avoided wherever possible, especially in close succession, and words that glide are to be preferred to those that hiss, as often as this can be done; although we realize that this must seem very like a counsel of perfection in view of "Jesus Christ, Son of God, Saviour." Dionysius of Halicarnassus wrote of the Greek sigma: "It is disagreeable and harassing, and when it recurs frequently it is very distressing; this hissing sound seems more proper for wild beasts than for rational creatures."[29] And Broadus recalls that because of its hissing sound English has been termed a "snake-language." One horrible example may be set down here in warning; it is from Richard Crashaw's otherwise beautiful communion hymn (Common Service Hymnal, No. 185)— "When glory's sun faith's shade shall chase." This example likewise illustrates the necessity of avoiding ugly "clusters of consonants" (compare: fledged and hedged, damaged and adjudged) and the importance of choosing words in which vowels and consonants, especially the liquids, alternate. "Avoid," says Hervey, "if possible, the use of compound words, the several parts of which are not closely united, and consequently are not enunciated as one word, as unsuccessfulness, barefacedness, wrongheadedness. Shun such words as have the syllables which follow the accented syllable, crowded with consonants that do not readily coalesce, as questionless, chroniclers, conventiclers. Employ, if possible, no such words as have too many syllables following the accented syllable, as primarily, cursorily, circumstances; nor such words as have a short or unaccented syllable followed by another short or unaccented syllable very much resembling it, as holily, sillily, lowlily, farriery."—Coming from the single word to the phrase and clause, we must warn the student against a singsong repetition of the same or similar vowel or consonant sounds. Cicero's *O fortunatam natam me consule Romam* is certainly not euphonious. No more is the English sentence, "Peter was needy, feeble and peevish," or the German, "Ein schreiender Reiher bleibt bei der Beize im Weiher." Only a person with a trained ear, sensitive to musical sounds, will be able to achieve euphony and avoid cacophony. He who possesses such an ear will need few rules; he will instinctively find the word,

---

[29]*De Comp. Verb.*, 14.—Note the intentional hissing of the words, well reproduced in the English translation.

phrase and sentence that "shall be musical in the mouth." He who does not possess it must be doubly on his guard lest his anxious pursuit of euphony render his style artificial and unreal. Finally, Hervey's closing words should be borne in mind. "We should remember," he says, "that euphony may be cultivated to excess, and harsh combinations of sounds are sometimes admissible for the sake of preventing a satiety of mellifluous words. Besides, the sense to be conveyed not infrequently demands what are in themselves very disagreeable sounds. When Milton is describing the gate of hell turning on its hinges, the words have a jarring, harsh, and grating sound; when representing the opening of the gate of heaven, the words, like the golden hinges themselves, emit celestial melodies. In some measure applicable to the orator is Pope's well known advice to the poet:

"Soft is the strain when Zephyr gently blows,
And the smooth stream in smoother numbers flows;
But when loud surges lash the sounding shore,
The hoarse, rough verse should like the torrent roar."

Special attention should be given to the *rhythmical arrangement* of phrases and sentences. Prose rhythm is something different from rhymed prose, as we find it in Apuleius, Gregory of Nazianzus, Augustine, and others.[30] It is also something very different from metre which is distinctive of poetry. Aristotle already drew the clear distinction when he described prose as "neither possessing metre nor destitute of rhythm."[31] Rhythm, as we use the term, while not destroying the nature of prose, imparts to it a recurrent and balanced flow, so that the discourse, while never overstepping the limits of prose, answers fully to the elevated emotion of the orator: now soaring aloft, now lightly running or leaping, now marching solemn and slow, now boldly charging, now yielding with "a dying fall." Such rhythmic prose passages are, no less than poetry, susceptible of scansion; but while in poetry rhythm, by the regularity of foot and verse, becomes metre, it is the absence of this regularity that constitutes the very nature of prose. Thus Cicero, recognizing the propriety of "number" in the prose-speaker, advised that two or three of the same feet should follow each other and that then some other foot should be introduced, in order that the speaker might not fall into a disagreeable mimicry of metre.[32] "This always," says Dabney correctly, "offends the ear, because it

---

[30]The student will find an interesting modern analogy to this in Amy Lowell's "polyphonic prose." Comp., e. g., her *Can Grande's Castle.*—[31]*Rhetoric,* iii, 8: μήτε ἔμμετρον μήτε ἄρρυθμον.—[32]*De Orat.,* iii, 47, 182.

suggests the appearance of inappropriate and abortive effort. The occurrence of the modern rhyme in prose discourse is a positive sin against euphony. But when the oration flows in short but frequently varied chains of equal or equivalent feet, this adds great expressiveness and beauty to the style. Nature recognizes it: all primitive languages, like the Hebrew, tend toward a regular arsis and thesis. Many critics have supposed that the first continuous recitation of every people was in metre, and that their first composers were always poets and bards. All music has its rhythm, which is essential to melody. There is something naturally pleasing and impressive to the human ear in the reverberations of a regularly occurring emphasis. It seems to make the strain palpitate with sensibility, like the voice of a living heart. The different feet are, moreover, expressive of their different sentiments. The 'fortis iambus' (ᴜ -) breathes vigor, haste, excitement; the spondee (- -) suggests pensive and meditative ideas; the paeon (ᴜ ᴜ ᴜ -) and choriambus (- ᴜ ᴜ -), by their roll, express some advancing majesty. By clothing your prose with number, you add therefore to its expressiveness as well as to its euphony."[33] When the feet at the beginning and the end are clumsily managed, the oration lacks harmony. Aristotle recommended for the beginning the "paeon anterior" (- ᴜ ᴜ ᴜ), for the close the "paeon posterior" (ᴜ ᴜ ᴜ -). Cicero and Quintilian preferred for the close the double trochee (- ᴜ - ᴜ); e. g.: *Patris dictum sapiens temeritas filii comprobavit.* Other rules are given by others; compare the whole section in Hervey.[34] The classical work on prose rhythm is E. Norden's *Die antike Kunstprosa* (Leipzig, 1898). Norden's companion in modern English is Prof. George Saintsbury's *History of English Prose Rhythm* (London, 1912), which the student should consult; it will give him, if nothing else, a treasury of great English prose.

But here, too, more is gained by training the ear for music and rhythm of speech than by a slavish observance of rules. The preacher whose ear has been sharpened for the rhythms of prose by the study of the great masters will intuitively add here a syllable and there elide one in his own productions, without thinking of any specific rules. He will naturally avoid ending a sentence with a number of unemphasized words or unaccented syllables (occupancy, profitableness, comparable, exquisitely). His ear will teach him to conclude with a word accented on the last or at least on the syllable next to the last. And he will give thanks, with the elder Beaumont, that

---

[33] P. 227.—[34] Pp. 489-98.

"Our Saxon shortness hath peculiar grace
In choice of words fit for the ending place."[35]

Chrysostom, who kept himself unspotted from the rhymed prose of his time, had nevertheless a fine ear for prose rhythm. What made Luther's German so musical was his marked sense of rhythm. Read aloud his explanation of the second article of the Creed, and you will meet there every quality that can lend vigor, grace and melody to a sentence: parallelism of members, the use of the triad, a full rich harmony, a wealth of expression corresponding to the wealth of thought, lovely cadences achieved by a cunning choice of words and phrases, and all carried along on a musical stream of rhythm. Attempt to change but one syllable and the whole is spoiled. No less felicitous are the prose rhythms of his German Bible, especially in the psalms. Whoever goes to school here will soon acquire a sure sense of rhythm. Of recent German preachers Caspari was a diligent pupil in the school of Luther's prose.[36]

The English Authorized Version of the Bible is if anything still more distinguished for its rhythmic movement, particularly in the Old Testament. The one thing the Revisers could find no fault with and which they strove to retain in its entirety was "the music of its cadences, and the felicities of its rhythm." Read for example, Ex. 15, Deut. 6:4 ff., 2 Sam. 18:33, 1 Chron. 29:10 ff., 2 Chron. 6:14-18, Ps. 103, 107, Matt. 7:24-29, 11:25-30, 2 Cor. 6:1-10, Rev. 5, 7:4-17; but especially Isa. 60 and 1 Cor. 13, which Saintsbury sets in the forefront of English prose rhythm. A careful examination will show that the most impressive passages of the greatest English prose writers are distinguished by rhythm, having its basis in an actual sequence of metrical feet with frequent variations. The last phrase needs underscoring, for where these variations of metrical feet are not found, we get the abominable embedded blank verse in the prose of not a few great English writers such as Bacon and Ruskin; Dickens is a particularly grave offender. The words of Jasques to Orlando in *As You Like It* apply here,—"Nay, then, God buy you [God be with you], an you talk in blank verse."

[35]Comp. below, p. 192, the third last sentence in the quotation from Robert Hall, at the close of which he changed the original "penetrate" to "pierce," for said he, "Penetrate is too long a word."—The prose of John Donne, Sir Thomas Browne and Thomas De Quincey is particularly worth studying for these happy endings.—[36]Comp. K. H. Caspari, *Das erste Hauptstueck des kleinen Katechismus Luthers ausgelegt in Predigten fuer das christliche Volk* (1852); *Von Jenseits des Grabes. Predigten* herausgegeben von Harless (1861).

Robert Hall's famous discourse on "Modern Infidelity" abounds in rhythmic passages such as the following:—"If the question at issue is to be decided by argument, nothing can be added to the triumph of Christianity; if by an appeal to authority, what have our adversaries to oppose to these great names? Where are the infidels of such pure uncontaminated morals, unshaken probity, and extended benevolence, that we should be in danger of being seduced into impiety by their example? Into what obscure recesses of misery, into what dungeons have their philanthropists penetrated, to lighten the fetters and relieve the sorrows of the helpless captive? What barbarous tribes have their apostles visited; what distant climes have they explored, encompassed with cold, nakedness and want, to diffuse principles of virtue, and the blessings of civilization? Or will they rather choose to waive their pretensions to this extraordinary and, in their eyes, eccentric species of benevolence (for infidels, we know, are sworn enemies to enthusiasm of every sort), and rest their character on their political exploits—on their efforts to re-animate the virtue of a sinking state, to restrain licentiousness, to calm the tumult of popular fury, and by inculcating the spirit of justice, moderation, and pity for fallen greatness, to mitigate the inevitable horrors of revolution? Our adversaries will at least have the discretion, if not the modesty, to recede from the test. More than all, their infatuated eagerness, their parricidal zeal to extinguish a sense of Deity must excite astonishment and horror. Is the idea of an Almighty and perfect Ruler unfriendly to any passion which is consistent with innocence, or an obstruction to any design which it is not shameful to avow? Eternal God, on what are thine enemies intent? What are those enterprises of guilt and horror, that, for the safety of their performers, require to be enveloped in a darkness which the eye of Heaven must not pierce! Miserable men! Proud of being the offspring of chance; in love with universal disorder; whose happiness is involved in the belief of there being no witness of their designs, and who are at ease only because they suppose themselves inhabitants of a forsaken and fatherless world." Theo Graebner quotes a fine passage by Newman Hall on the word "now":— "A short word; a shorter thing. Soon uttered, sooner gone. Now! A grain of sand on a boundless plain! A tiny ripple on a measureless ocean! Over that ocean we are sailing; but the only part of it we possess is that on which our vessel at this moment floats. From the stern we look backwards and watch the ship's wake in the waters; but how short a distance it reaches, and how soon every trace disappears! We see also some landmarks farther off, and then the horizon closes the view; but beyond that the ocean still rolls far, far away. Memory contemplates the few years of our individual life; history shows us a dim outline of mountains, but all that we possess of it is represented by this small word—now! The past, for action, is ours no longer. The future may never become present; it is not ours until it does. The only part of time we can use is this very moment—now! O listen to the voice of warning now. 'Awake, thou that sleepest!' Awake now! 'Seek the Lord while He may be found!' Seek Him now! 'Believe in the Lord Jesus Christ, and thou shalt be saved.' Believe now! Confess to Him your sins, ask pardon through His blood, rely on His atonement, implore the help of His Spirit, devote yourself entirely to His service! Do it now!"

That rhythm is not incompatible with the utmost simplicity of thought and language is illustrated by Graebner's brief quotation from John Henry Newman:—"May He support us all the day long till the shades lengthen, and the evening comes, and the busy world is hushed, and the fever of life is over, and our work is done. Then in His mercy may He give us a safe lodging, and a holy rest, and peace at the last."[86a] The same combination of rhythm and simplicity may be profitably studied in the Vailima prayers of Robert Louis Stevenson.

(c) But an orator may select his words with the utmost care, and observe scrupulously all the laws of variety, euphony and rhythm; nevertheless, his oration will be beautiful only if at the same time *imagination* plays in it the role which belongs to it. Imagination rejoices in tropes and figures. She trails the ornamental epithet round the bare substantive as the gardener trails the ivy round the pillar. She loves to speed home her thought by climax and antithesis. She cultivates the figures of simile and metaphor in order to shed new light upon old truths, comparing spiritual with natural and natural with spiritual things. Not content with these, she goes on from metaphor to allegory, expanding the chosen figure in more intimate and loving detail (compare the Song of the Vineyard in Isa. 5 or the Good Shepherd in John 10). Or she apostrophizes and personifies, breathing life into the inanimate and a personal soul into the inorganic (compare the personification of Wisdom in Proverbs). She sits down and spins a parable to illustrate religious or moral truths by the happenings of every day. For she is the sworn foe of the abstract and must present everything in forms of concrete reality. She desires to catch the eye of the hearer as well as his ear; the one is to assist the other, so that the discourse may be doubly sure to attain its

[86a]Comp. also Newman's *Meditations and Devotions* (1893).

goal. Thus the spoken word becomes in her hand, as it were, a painter's brush with which she imparts outline and color to the inmost thoughts and feelings of the heart. This gives to the oration its true beauty and causes it to produce impressions in the soul deeper and more decisive for the will than convincing clearness alone could possibly attain. Quintilian was well aware of this when he wrote: "Distinctiveness, or, as some call it, representation, is something more than perspicuity; for while perspicuity merely lets itself be seen, ἐνέργεια forces itself upon the reader's notice. It is a great merit to set forth the objects of which we speak in lively colors, and so that they may as it were be seen; for our language is not sufficiently effective, and has not that absolute power which it ought to have, if it impresses only the ears, and if the judge feels that the particulars, on which he has to give a decision, are merely stated to him and not described graphically or displayed to the eyes of the mind. . . To the attainment of this excellence (an excellence, in my opinion, of the highest order) the way is very easy: We must look to nature, and follow her." (Lib. viii, cap. 3.) With him agrees Longinus, who says in his *On the Sublime*: "In a general way the name of image or imagination (φαντασία) is applied to every idea of the mind, in whatever form it presents itself, which gives birth to speech. But at the present day the word is pre-eminently used in cases where, carried away by enthusiasm and passion, you think you see what you describe, and you place it before the eyes of your hearers. What, then, can oratorical imagery effect? Well, it is able in many ways to infuse vehemence and passion into spoken words, while more particularly when it is combined with the argumentative passages it not only persuades the hearer but actually makes him its slave" (Περὶ ὕψους, c. 15)."

Fenelon expresses most forcefully this idea. He says in his second Dialogue: "We have seen that eloquence consists not only in giving clear convincing proofs, but likewise in the art of moving the passions. Now, in order to move them, we must be able to paint them well, with their various objects and effects. So that I think the whole art of oratory may be reduced to proving, painting, and raising the passions. . . . . . To paint is not only to describe things, but to represent the circumstances of them in such a lively, sensible manner, that the hearer shall fancy he almost sees them with his eyes. For instance, if a dry historian were to give an account of Dido's death, he would only say, she was overwhelmed with sorrow after the departure of Aeneas; and that she grew weary of her life, so went up to the top of her palace, and, lying down on her funeral pile, she stabbed herself.

Now these words would inform you of the fact; but you do not see it when you read the story in Virgil, he sets it before your eyes. When he represents all the circumstances of Dido's despair; describes her wild rage; and death already staring in her aspect; when he makes her speak at the sight of the picture and sword that Aeneas left, your imagination transports you to Carthage, where you see the Trojan fleet leaving the shore, and the queen quite inconsolable. You enter into all her passions, and into the sentiments of the supposed spectators. It is not Virgil you then hear, you are too attentive to the last words of the unhappy Dido to think of him. The poet disappears, and we see only what he describes, and hear those only whom he makes to speak. Such is the force of a natural imitation, and of painting in language. Hence it comes that the painters and the poets are so nearly related; the one paints for the eyes, and the other for the ears, but both of them ought to convey the liveliest pictures to people's imagination. I have taken an example from a poet, to give you a livelier image of what I mean by painting in eloquence, for poets paint in a stronger manner than orators. Indeed, the main thing in which poetry differs from eloquence is, that the poet paints with enthusiasm, and gives bolder touches than the orator. But prose allows of painting in a moderate degree, for without lively descriptions it is impossible to warm the hearer's fancy or to stir his passions. A plain narrative does not move people; we must not only inform them of facts, but strike their senses, by a lively, moving representation of the manner and the circumstances of the facts we relate. 'But seeing what you call painting is essential to oratory, does it not follow that there can be no true eloquence, without a due mixture of poetry?' You are right, we only must exclude versification, that is, a strict regard to the quantity of syllables, and the order of words, in which the poet is obliged to express his thoughts, according to the measure or verse he writes in. Versification indeed, if it be in rhyme, is what injudicious people reckon to be the whole of poetry. Some fancy themselves to be poets, because they have spoken or written measured words; but there are many who make verses without poetry, and others are very poetical without making verses. If, therefore, we set versifying aside, poetry in other respects is only a lively fiction that paints nature. And if one has not this genius for painting, he will never be able to imprint things on the hearer's mind; but his discourse will be flat, languid, and wearisome. Ever since the fall of Adam, man's thoughts have been so low and grovelling, that they are inattentive to moral truths, and can scarce conceive but what affects their senses. In this consists the degeneracy of human nature. People soon grow weary of contemplation; intellectual ideas do not strike their imagination; so that we must use sensible and familiar images, to support their attention, and convey abstracted truths to their minds."

If then it is the duty of the orator to take imagination into his service, this holds especially of the preacher. Hervey's words may seem somewhat extravagant when he says: "However well abstract and unimaginative style may become the lawyer, the judge, the statesman, or the man of science, let it ever be remembered and deeply considered that the preacher has to deal with matters of divine revelation, and, consequently, with themes that, from the intense secularity and atheism of the diction of the cultivated and refined cannot be touched, much less handled, without the assistance of figures. Not more essential is the atmosphere as a medium of solar light than figurative diction as a medium of divine communication. God's unfathomable truths and feelings towards us can by no other language be conveyed; and even this, when applied by its best masters, strives in vain to embrace and carry their golden gleams. Revealed religion is fraught with subjects too vast for any human vehicles however seemingly extravagant. The broadest hyperbole refuses to encompass their immensity, and the highest climax does not begin to scale their secret summits."[37] Nevertheless the Scriptures with their wealth of imagery and similes, parables and allegories, with their description, often verging on the crass, of the messianic age or the glories of everlasting life and the terrors of everlasting death, furnish the very strongest proof that the preacher in his portrayal of supersensual realities has a perfect right to go to the world of the senses for figures that will illustrate and drive home his meaning.

If anyone has begun to fear that with our stressing of imagination and the poetic element, the simplicity of the sermon may suffer, we admit, indeed, that the inexperienced and especially the vain might misconceive our meaning and imagine themselves called to cultivate the artificial, the affected and the superlative, to riot in a welter of figures and fancies, and to let their imagination carry them to the clouds, far from the common haunts and the common speech of men. But this would be the sheerest caricature of our position. It must ever remain true, as William Taylor says in his *Model Preacher*: "Solemnity, moral grandeur, and stirring effect do not consist in a display of magnificent words, but in the truth with all its native simplicity and

---

[37] P. 387.

variety. A mere display of sublime words, solemn forms, and ministerial dignity is, whatever the design may be, a burlesque on the solemn grandeur and dignified simplicity of Gospel truth, and the natural Gospel mode of proclaiming it." And Bacon, quoted in Kidder,[38] says: "This lisping poetry, this mincing elegance of diction, this trumpery and moonshine of superficial rhetoric, this would-be eloquence, which is uttered only to be admired, how impious the impertinence!" Nothing is so well calculated to correct this foolish error as the study of the language of the Bible. Its authors betray a pronounced fondness for the figurative and the concrete, yet what models of simplicity their writings are! Certainly, one who is out merely to please, not to convince and move, whose chief concern is to set himself and his ability in the foreground, instead of the materials he has been called to proclaim, such a one will glory in mincing elegance of diction and would-be eloquence! It is again Fenelon who well distinguishes what is permissible here from what is prohibited. He says: "We must distinguish between such ornaments as only please and those that both please and persuade. That which serves to please in order to persuade, is good and solid: thus we are pleased with strong and clear arguments. The just and natural emotions of an orator have much grace and beauty in them, and his exact and lively painting charms us. Thus all the necessary parts of eloquence are apt to please, but yet pleasing is not their true aim. The question is, whether we shall approve such thoughts and expressions as may perhaps give an amusing delight, but in other respects, are altogether useless: and these I call quaint turns, and points of wit. You must remember now that I allow all those graces of style and delicate thoughts that tend to persuasion. I only reject those vain, affected ornaments that the self-conceited author uses, to paint his own character, and amuse others with his wit, instead of filling their minds entirely with his subject. In fine: I think we ought to condemn not only all jingle and playing with words, as a thing extremely mean and boyish, but even all witty conceits, and fanciful turns: I mean such thoughts as only flash, and glitter upon the fancy, but contain nothing that is solid, and conducive to persuasion." To the objection that such severity would exclude the chief beauties of discourse, he replies: "Do you not reckon Homer and Virgil very agreeable authors? are they not the most delicate you ever read? and yet in them you do not find what we call points of wit. Their poems are full of a noble simplicity, their art is entirely concealed, nature itself appears in all that they say. We do not find a single

---

[38] P. 294.

word that seems purposely designed to show the poet's wit. They thought it their greatest glory never to appear, but to employ our attention on the objects they describe as a painter endeavors to set before your eyes wide forests, mountains, rivers, distant views, and buildings, or the adventures, actions, and different passions of men, in such a lively manner, that you cannot trace the masterly strokes of his pencil, for art looks mean and coarse when it is perceived. Plato (who had examined this matter more thoroughly than any other orator or critic) assures us that in composing the poet should always keep out of sight, make himself be quite forgotten by his readers, and represent only those things and persons, which he would set before their eyes."

Among the homileticians of the last century, Vinet, Brooks and Dabney in particular point out the pitfalls awaiting those who make the poetic element an end in itself. Vinet says: "The orator who supremely speaks to please, will not please; even as virtue which proposes happiness as its end, does not find happiness. Without insisting too much, I affirm that the desire of speaking well, the literary point of view, just in proportion as it has ascendency over a minister, degrades his ministry. I affirm that the preacher is not, in the highest view, a man of literature. I affirm that there is a seductive intoxication in the use of speech, which should be feared. I affirm that we should fear being insensibly carried away from action into the imitation of action, from reality into poetry. This deviation is but too easy; such is the mysterious conjunction between moral beauty and literary beauty. . . . . . It is between the idolatry of art and the contempt of art that God has required us to walk."[39] Phillips Brooks says in his *Lectures on Preaching*: "We find a constant tendency in the history of preaching to treat the sermon as a work of art. [He understands this word in its absolute sense. See above, p. 170]. It is spoken of as if it were something which had a value in itself. We hear of beautiful sermons, as if they existed solely on the ground that 'beauty is its own excuse for being.' The age of the great French preachers, the age of Louis XIV. with its sermons preached in the salons of critical and sceptical noblemen, and of ladies who offered to their friends the entertainment of the last discovered preacher, was full of this false idea of the sermon as a work of art. And the soberer Englishman, whether he be the Puritan praising the painful exposition to which he has just listened, or the Churchman delighting in the polished periods of Tillotson or South, has his own way of falling into

---

[39] P. 349.

the same heresy...... The sermons of the apostles were tools, and not works of art. To turn a tool into a work of art, to elaborate the shape and chase the surface of the axe with which you are to hew your wood, is bad taste; and to give any impression in a sermon that it has forgotten its purpose and been shaped for anything else than what in the largest extent of those great words might be described as *saving souls,* makes it offensive to a truly good taste and dull to the average man, who feels an incongruity which he cannot define. The power of the sermons of the Paulist fathers in the Romish church and of Mr. Moody in Protestantism lies simply here: in the clear and undisturbed presence of their purpose; and many ministers who never dream of such a thing, who think that they are preaching purely for the good of souls, are losing the power out of their sermons because they are trying, even without knowing it, to make them not only sermons, but works of art."[40] Dabney's discussion of this matter is worth printing in full, despite its length, because it illustrates the dangers the beginner is especially exposed to, not least in the matter of the funeral sermon. "We are told," says Dabney, "that 'it is appointed unto men once to die, and after that the judgment.' What imaginative painting could more fascinate and harrow the fancy, than that which describes the accessories of a death bed! The shuddering listener may be made to thrill at the thought of the pangs by which the silver cord is loosed, unimagined by living man and indescribable by mortal tongue; the irrevocable sundering of ties of love from which the worldly heart has drawn its very life; the spirit's plunge into the dread mystery of the nether world; the aspect of the living man frozen into a ghastly corpse; the gloom, the chill, and the corruption of the grave with its loathsome worm and dust. But what have you done when you have spellbound your hearer's fancy with these terrors? You have but stimulated the instinctive love of life—a passion at best only social or selfish, in its prevalent element nearly animal, and common to him with the beast that writhes and shrieks under the hunter's steel. All this is naught unless you make it the introduction to the truth that 'the sting of death is sin, and the strength of sin is the law,' and to that victory over the grave given through our Lord Jesus Christ; for it is the latter which teaches us the whole significance of death to the rational soul. 'But after death is the judgment.' To depict the grandeur of this final consummation, the Scriptures array material images whose terror and majesty infinitely transcend all the phenomena of nature

---

[40] Pp. 111 f.

and the uninspired imaginings of man. The preacher may suppose that he finds here a precedent, which authorizes him to stimulate the natural fear and fancy to their utmost tension. He, therefore, exerts all his pictorial powers, and brings forth his most pompous stores of language to represent the vast and astounding events which will usher in that great day. He so paints the opening graves and gathering hosts of quickened dead, the paling sun, the blushing moon and decadent stars, the ocean of fire which floods the continents and exhales the seas, and so makes them hear the echo of the archangel's trump, that their blood runs chill with delicious horror. They are the entranced spectators of the catastrophe of this world's drama. But, I ask, is this the whole intent of God in this apocalypse of the final consummation? If these material images are all destined to be literally fulfilled, what are they but symbols of solemn moral facts? of the quickening of the slumbering conscience, of the voice of the accusing Law, of the unveiling of that **divine holiness and glory** before which the world with its vanities will shrivel into an atom, and sin will stand unmasked in its hideous blackness? Such a material portraiture has not even poetic truth; for it leaves out the chief elements of the dread transaction, and misrepresents its true impression on the real actors. When the justice of God, like a spirit of burning, shall have taken hold upon the awakened conscience of the sinner, and when eternity with all its issues shall be set before the eyes of his resurrection body, it will be the great conceptions of sin and of righteousness, of a broken law and a divine satisfaction and of the just awards of infinite rectitude, which will occupy and overpower his mind. In that day it will be *Sin,* and not a flaming world, which shall appal the soul. The ulterior aim of the sacred orator must be at the *conscience* alone. Unless these natural affections which his rhetoric awakens are speedily superseded and eclipsed by the spiritual, to which he makes them subservient, they are only mischievous counterfeits. Not only the ambition and vanity of preachers, but the temper of the hearers seduce them into this error; for man naturally loves excitement for its own sake, and there is nothing which he so much hates as to be challenged to forsake his sin. He is grateful, therefore, to the orator who at once provides for him the sentimental luxury, and who suggests this substitute for the abhorred duty of *repentance.* You will ever, I trust, resist this temptation, and keep these appeals to the natural but unregenerated affections in their proper place. Of all this art of persuasion he is the greatest master who seems to have none. Let your aim be to persuade men in Christ's name, and not to be praised for skill in persuading. These two distinct ends many preachers confound. You saw that the power over others' hearts depends upon your own disinterested and genuine emotion. You must so hunger for the salvation of the souls before you that you shall desire to make the effect of sacred truth fill them to the exclusion of yourself. You must be willing to be nothing in their eyes and to let the effect be everything. He is not the true preacher who sends his hearers home exclaiming, 'How eloquent the minister was today; how beautiful his imagery; how artful his arrangement; how skillful his argument and his persuasion!' But he is the true sacred orator who dismisses them so possessed and overpowered by God, that they have forgotten the creature who was the channel of truth. The message should hide the messenger. To make you masters of the emotions of others, then self-seeking must be annihilated, and self-renunciation must have its perfect work. It is divine grace which makes the effective minister."[41]

The warning of James, cited by Kidder (page 294), is well worth noting:—"An elaboration that is betrayed in every part of the discourse, and which makes it but too evident to any serious or observant mind that it was the preacher's aim not to convert souls, but to catch applause; which in the view of the fashionable, the giddy, and the frivolous, entitles the sermonizer to the highest rank among pulpit orators; which fills the discourse with flowery diction and gaudy metaphors, with elegant declamation and fanciful descriptions, with tasteful addresses and beautiful pictures; which, though it takes the cross for its subjects, almost instantly leaves it and runs out into the fields of poesy, or the labyrinths of metaphysics, for its subtle arguments or its sparkling and splendid illustrations; which, to sum up all, engages the judgment or amuses the imagination, but never moves the heart, or calls the conscience to discharge its severe and awful functions, such preaching may render a minister popular, secure him large congregations, and procure for him the plaudits of the multitude; but where are the sinners converted from the error of their way, and the souls saved from death? Verily, I say unto you, if such a preacher has his reward only in the applause of the multitude, whose object and aim were as low as his own, it was what he sought and all he sought, and let him not complain if he have this and nothing else. From such preachers may God Almighty preserve our churches, and may He give us men who better know their business in the pulpit and better do it."

---

[41] Pp. 257 ff.

Before passing on to the third quality of the sermon, we must mention several preachers who were pre-eminent in the cultivation of the beautiful, especially the poetic element, in their sermons. Chrysostom is a conspicuous exponent of the beautiful in preaching. The preacher who is prone to extravagance and excess in the use of the imagination can learn much of him. In poetical imagination Ephraim the Syrian was easily first; a sermon such as his on the woman who was a great sinner could have been conceived only by a true artist. It is a pity that in his sermon on death and the last judgment he becomes crude and loses himself in details. In the Middle Ages Berthold of Regensburg stands out; his powerful imagination is shown not only in the whole structure of his sermons (Of the Seven Planets, Of the Three Walls, Of the Four Cords, etc.) but in his detail pictures, which are a distinguishing characteristic of his sermons. All the devices of poetic elaboration are constantly at his command, from the descriptive epithet and apt simile to the expanded parable and allegory, climax, antithesis, apostrophe and personification. For an estimate of Luther's sermons from this point of view we must refer the reader to our forthcoming *History of Preaching*. Luther's successor in the Reformation period, in this respect, was Simon Musaeus, while even a man who inclined so strongly to the abstract as Jacob Andreae showed occasionally a fine poetic gift. In the XVII century Scriver surpassed all other Lutheran preachers in poetic imagination, though Heinrich Mueller's sermons are rich in the same gold. In later times we have among Germans, Ahlfeld, Gerok, E. Frommel, Fr. Naumann and K. Hesselbacher. Among English preachers none has surpassed John Donne and Jeremy Taylor in the use of the poetic element in preaching; and both these men are exemplary in this respect. Taylor was called by Emerson "the Shakespeare of divines"; Donne was said by Walton to be able to carry some to heaven in holy raptures, and to entice others "by a sacred art and courtship to amend their lives: here picturing a vice so as to make it ugly to those that practiced it: and a virtue so as to make it beloved, even by those that loved it not; and all this with a most particular grace and an unexpressible addition of comeliness." Of Donne, a good collection of brief extracts from whose sermons, with an admirable introduction, has been published by Logan Pearsall Smith,[42] so competent a literary critic as Sir Arthur Quiller-Couch has said: "There is where you shall look for the great Donne,

---

[42]*Donne's Sermons* Selected Passages with an Essay (Clarendon Press, 1919).

the real Donne: not in his verse, with which posterity is constantly betrayed, but in his Sermons, which contain (as I hold) the most magnificent prose ever uttered from an English pulpit, if not the most magnificent prose ever spoken in our tongue."[48] While both these men frequently overstep the bounds of restraint and must be used, especially by the beginner, with due caution, this is much less the case with the Americans, Henry Ward Beecher and Phillips Brooks, although Spurgeon claimed for the former the richest imagination since Shakespeare, and the latter possessed an almost unique gift of illustration. If Brooks had let his imagination play upon the supernatural and religious as freely as on the natural and moral, he would doubtless have been the finest embodiment of the imaginative preacher in the English tongue. Old John Leland (1691-1766) in his sermon on "The Jarrings of Heaven Reconciled by the Blood of the Cross," probably following mediaeval models, carried the figure of personification to the extreme of dramatic elaboration. In our own time Adolf Schmitthenner produced in an Easter sermon on Ps. 89:20 and a discourse on the Tares among the Wheat, two sermons which could have been composed only by one who was both poet and preacher, although the poet rather pushes the preacher into the background.

So far as its effect on the *will* is concerned, the sermon as well as the oration must possess *force* and *energy* that will move to action; for it is an essential characteristic of public discourse that it shall summon the hearers to a decision and inspire them to the performance of certain definite acts.

The preacher, however, must not forget that his primary purpose is not, like that of the political orator, to move his hearers to perform certain outward acts. Nor must he imagine that it is his duty and within his power to produce such outward acts through the individual sermon and with the employment of the means at his disposal. This would lead to an unsound and legalistic use of force. It would be to forget that all God-pleasing activity must proceed by an inner necessity out of the regenerate heart; that God has put in His, not our power the times and seasons of His working; that the Word,

---

[48]Quiller-Couch, *Studies in Literature* (1918), pp. 107 ff.—For Izaak Walton's fine estimate see his charming *Life of Dr. John Donne.*

even though sown as living seed in the heart, overcomes only gradually the old life of sin; and that in the realm of the spiritual the law of organic development and gradual growth obtains. A sound evangelical sermon will aim rather to renew the inner attitude of the will and direct it toward God and all godly things, so that, when occasion offers, it may remind the hearer that this inner godward trend of the will must prove its existence by blossoming out in definite fruits and good works.

Such an action upon the will involves a continuous struggle with the old will that still remains in the Christian and is so prone to turn back to its forsaken possessions, its old habits, and its former sins. For this the force and energy of the sermon is needed, by which the preacher lays hold on the will of the hearer, brings to bear upon it all the power the human proclamation of the divine Word is capable of, and will not let it go until he has turned it in the right direction. Just as a true sermon is often a contest with the objections of the intellect, so it must become also a contest with the reluctant and refractory will of the hearer. This need not always be so marked as to form the distinctive feature of the sermon. It will appear now with greater, now with less prominence, according to the nature of the congregation, the contents of the text, and the individuality of the preacher. Nevertheless its presence in every sermon is essential.

The rhetorical means by which the sermon gains force are: (a) The choice of a concrete rather than abstract presentation of the subject; (b) an intelligent use of the figures of speech (economy in the use of the adjective; simile, but more often metaphor, asyndeton and polysyndeton, repetition, climax, antithesis, interrogation, exclamation, personification, apostrophe, dramatization, illustration by analogies, examples and parables); (c) the strategic selection and arrangement of paragraphs, sentences and words. (P. 224.)

To touch the will is the desire of the orator, the duty of the preacher. Perspicuity is needed in order that the subject may be plainly and unmistakably set before the intellect, and perspicuity should be combined with grace to charm and stir the emotions and awaken pleasure in the truth presented, but both these are in reality only means to an end. Through knowledge and feeling, the orator and preacher sets out to find his way to the will, in order to move it to action. Religion does not consist only in pure ideals and firm convictions nor in pleasurable emotional excitements; it is a life, in the broadest sense of this term, and includes, therefore, also the will and the activities of man and reaches in these its completion. The will must be laid hold of with energy and power, and this is done by means of the spoken word. By it, as by an unseen hand, the orator reaches into the soul life of his hearer and grasps with masterful touch his will.

Now what are the methods of presentation most adapted to this purpose? They are practically the same as those we pointed out above as conferring beauty and grace. (a) Thus the sermon will have the desired force when the *concrete* is preferred to the abstract, the *specific* to the general. Campbell says in his *Philosophy of Rhetoric*: "The more general the terms are, the picture is the fainter; the more special they are, it is the brighter. The same sentiments may be expressed with equal justness and even perspicuity, in the former way as in the latter; but as the coloring will in that case be more languid, it cannot give equal pleasure to the fancy, and by consequence will not contribute so much either to fix the attention or to impress the memory." He might have added, "to impress and move the will." Campbell thus illustrates by biblical examples the difference between concrete and abstract, specific and general: "In the Song of Moses, the inspired poet, speaking of the Egyptians, says, 'They sank as lead in the mighty waters.' Make but a small alteration in the expression, and say, 'They fell as metal in the mighty waters,' and the difference in the effect will be quite astonishing, yet the sentiment will be equally just, and in either way the meaning of the author can hardly be mistaken. The Lord says: 'Consider the lilies how they grow; they toil not, they spin not; and yet I say unto you that Solomon in all his glory was not arrayed as one of these. If then, God so clothe the grass which to-day is in the field and to-morrow is cast into the oven, how much more will He clothe you.' Let us here adopt a little of the tasteless manner of modern paraphrasts, by the substitution of more general terms, and observe the effect produced by this change. 'Consider the flowers how they gradually increase in their size; they do no manner of work, and yet I declare to you that no king whatever, in his most splendid habit, is dressed up like them. If, then, God in His providence doth so adorn the vegetable productions which continue but a little time on the land, and are afterward put into fire, how much more will He provide clothing for you.' How spiritless is the same sentiment rendered by these small variations!" Whately agrees with this and goes a step farther when he says: "Many, especially unpracticed writers, fall into a feeble style of resorting unnecessarily to the substitution of the general for the specific, or the specific for the singular, either because they imagine there is more appearance of refinement or profundity in the employment of such terms as are in less common use among the vulgar, or, in some cases, with a view to give greater comprehensiveness to their reasonings and to increase the utility of what they say, by enlarging the field of its application. Inexperienced preachers frequently err in this way, by dwelling on virtue and vice, piety and irreligion, in the abstract, without particularizing; forgetting that while they *include* much, they *impress* little or nothing." Consequently Dabney advises:—"Applaud not abstract magnanimity, but the living, magnanimous man. Speak not of the *genus homo* as depraved or as guilty, but of the men before you. Speak not of them, but to them, and that in the second person and in the singular. Say, 'Thou art the man'."[44]

Here, too, belong individualization and particularization. Hervey cites a good example from Vieyra's Advent sermon on "The Resurrection of the Righteous and the Wicked": "The separation of the wicked from the righteous will take place among all classes and conditions of men. But the separation of those who are allied by the strongest bonds of blood and affection will be the most painful. Indeed, all other circumstances will be deeply affecting, but this will be heart-rending. Parents will then be separated from their children; on the one side will Abraham stand, on the other Ishmael; brothers will be separated from brothers; there will be Jacob, and yonder Esau; wives will be separated from husbands; Esther will be on this side and Ahasuerus on the other; Jonathan will be here and Saul there. Thus will these be separated to see each other never more! Those who loved each other in this life— those who had so many reasons for loving each other in the life to come. Never more! Oh! what a saddening word. If for those who love one another it is even now a great grief when they are in traveling compelled to part, yet with the hope of seeing one another again; if it al-

---

[44] Pp. 221 f.

ready causes deep sorrow to separate in death, with the expectation of meeting one another in another world, oh, what a grief it must be for those whom nature and affection have transformed into one being to be separated then and there, with the felt certainty of never seeing each other's faces again as long as God lives! Surely, he must have a hard heart who does not desire to escape such a danger."[45]

(b) The use of *rhetorical figures* contributes to the force of the sermon no less than to its beauty, yet with a difference. The descriptive *adjective* tends to diminish rather than increase the energy of a passage. The preacher should bear in mind what Broadus says,— "If you cut a bough from an apple tree in spring to please your friends with its beauty, you would retain the twig and leaves and blossoms; but if you wish to knock a man down with it, all these must be trimmed away."[46] Still there are occassions when adjectives will heighten the force of a passage. "They may be," says Whately, "so many abridged arguments, the force of which is sufficiently conveyed by a mere hint; for example, if one says, 'we ought to take warning from the *bloody* revolution of France,' the epithet suggests one of the reasons for our being warned; and not less clearly and forcibly than if the argument had been stated at length."[47]

The *simile* usually possesses less force than the *metaphor*. "King David, when he would describe the virulence of the slander of his enemies, says, 'Their teeth are spears and arrows, and their tongue a sharp sword.' How would this be enfeebled were it expanded into a regular simile, which would describe the words of malice issuing from their mouths as lacerating his good name and comfort as spears, arrows and swords lacerate, gall and wound the body of an adversary!" Attention has repeatedly been called to Demosthenes' great oration *De Corona* in which this master of eloquence employs only a single simile, consisting of but two words. At the same time the language of the Bible reveals not a few instances of forceful similes. Broadus enumerates the following: "His eyes were as a flame of fire, and His voice as the sound of many waters"—"As the lightning cometh out of the East and shineth even unto the West, so shall the coming of the Son of Man be"—"The ungodly are like the chaff which the wind driveth away." A heaping of similes would, of course, deprive the oration of much of its force.

Onomatopoeia is seldom practicable in the pulpit except in rare

---

[45] P. 446.—Antonio Vieyra (1608-97), one of the few great preachers of Portugal.—[46] P. 385.—[47] Pp. 331 f.

cases where it spontaneously appears. *Asyndeton,* however, and *polysyndeton* contribute, especially when combined, much to energy of speech. The former may be illustrated by Psalm 104:6-13, the latter by Matthew 7:27. Dionysius of Halicarnassus[48] cites a good example from Aeschinus,—"Your argument is against yourself; it is against the laws; it is against the commonwealth." Change this to read, "Your argument is against yourself, the laws, and the commonwealth," and note the loss of force. *Repetition* as lending energy is well illustrated by the following examples cited by Graebner.[49] "Often is Christ *grieved* for His children, *grieved* at their coldness in His service, *grieved* at their wavering faith, *grieved* at their besetting infirmities." And: "Sitting still is no *proof* of election, but grappling with evil is a *proof,* and studying God's Word is a *proof,* and praying for assistance is a *proof.*"

Repetition is most effective when combined with *climax,* as in the following: "But at what expense was God put to secure this gift for the world? Let the Bethlehem manger answer. Let answer the Nazareth carpenter shop. Let answer the Galilean fishing boat. Let Gethsemane answer. Let Calvary answer. The humiliation of Christ, the poverty of Christ, the agony of Christ, the death of Christ, were the figures that entered into the sum of the cost of this gift." *Hyperbole* is an aid to energy and is much used by secular orators, but had better be avoided in the pulpit. When Baxter says in his sermon on "The Absolute Sovereignty of Christ": "Oh! that I did know what arguments would persuade you, and what words would work thy heart hereto. If I were sure it would prevail, I would come down from the pulpit and go from man to man upon my knees, with the request and advice in my text: 'Oh! kiss the Son, lest He be angry, and you perish'."[50] This sounds like an hyperbole, but came certainly from Baxter's heart.

Antithesis occurs frequently in the Scriptures and belongs doubtless to the most forceful figures of speech. Compare: "The Sabbath was made for man, not man for the Sabbath"—"The memory of the just is blessed, but the memory of the wicked shall rot"—"I do not live to eat, I eat to live" (Quintilian). And yet there is truth in what Pascal says,—"Those who make antithesis by forcing words, are like men who make false windows for the sake of symmetry." A forced

---

[48]*De Comp. Verb.,* 5-9.—[49]Pp. 358.—Compare also Donne's great passage on the death of James I, with its repetition of the word "dead" like a great bell tolling (*Donne's Sermons* Selected Passages with an Essay, by L. P. Smith, 1919, pp. 57 f.).—[50]*Works.* Vol. 17, p. 406.

antithesis loses all effect. Many of Augustine's antitheses are of this sort. In the history of Greek eloquence, the abuse of antithesis marks the period of decline. Vinet well says: "Far-fetched antithesis is always bad; it is admissible, if ever, only when it escapes involuntarily and proceeds from the soul. When there is an opposition in things, we must not fear to mark it in words; but opposition in ideas sometimes gains by not marking it in words."[51] It is different with antithesis not of clauses, but of whole paragraphs, or even of the two main divisions of a sermon. Such antithesis is always effective, not only adding to the force of the sermon but often bringing out the full scope of the subject on its positive side.[52] The antithetic paragraph structure may be illustrated from Bossuet's second sermon on the First Sunday in Advent: "Hear how the author of the Book of Maccabees speaks of the great King of Macedonia, whose name seemed to breathe nothing but victory and triumph. 'It happened that Alexander, son of Philip, reigned over Greece, and made many wars, and won many strongholds, and slew the kings of the earth, and went to the ends of the world, and took spoils of many nations, in so much that the earth was quiet before him.' What a grand and magnificent beginning!— But hear the conclusion: 'After these things he fell sick, and perceived that he must die; wherefore he called his servants, and parted his kingdom among them. So Alexander reigned twelve years, and he died.' To this fate is suddenly reduced all his glory; in this manner the history of Alexander the Great terminates. How different the history of Jesus Christ! It does not indeed commence in a manner so pompous, neither does it end in a manner so ruinous. It begins by showing Him to us in a sordid manger, then leads Him through various stages of humiliation, then conducts Him to the infamy of the cross, and at length envelops Him in the darkness of the tomb, confessedly the very lowest degree of depression. But this, instead of being the period of His final abasement, is that from which He recovers, and is exalted. He rises, ascends, takes possession of His throne, is extending His glory to the utmost bounds of the universe, and will one day come with great power to judge the quick and the dead."[53]

Interrogation and exclamation add to the energy of a discourse. Paul knew the value of them; compare, e. g., Gal. 3:1-5. Naturally, when unduly multiplied, they lose their strength. On this subject Robert Hall delivers himself, in a review of a volume of sermons, as

---

[51]P. 440.—[52]On this subject see Part III, below.—[53]Quoted by Graebner, p. 89.

follows: "Another blemish which strikes us in this work, is the frequent use of interrogations, not only in the warm and impassioned parts, where they are graceful, but in the midst of argumentative discussions. We have been struck with the prevalence of this practice in the most recent works of clergymen, beyond those of any other order of men. With Demosthenes, we know interrogation was a very frequent figure; but we recollect, at the same time, it was chiefly confined to the more vehement parts of his speeches, in which, like the eruptions of a furnace, he broke out upon, and consumed his opponents. In him it was the natural expression of triumphant indignation; after he had subdued and laid them prostrate by the force of his arguments, by his abrupt and terrible interrogations he trampled them in the mire. In calm and dispassionate discussion, the frequent use of questions appears to us unnatural; it discomposes the attention by a sort of startling and irregular motion, and is a violation of dignity, by affecting to be lively, where it is sufficient praise to be cogent and convincing. In a word, when, instead of being used to give additional vehemence to a discourse, they are interspersed in a series of arguments, as an expedient for enlivening the attention and varying the style, they have an air of undignified flippancy."[54] Of exclamation Vinet says it is in place only "when it is artless and flows from the heart, like that which the remembrance of a recent affliction drew from the soul of Bossuet: 'O disastrous night, O dreadful night, in which, like the peal of thunder, suddenly resounded the surprising news: Madame is dying, Madame is dead!' "[55]

The *dramatic* portrayal of a scene may add energy to the sermon, especially when it is concerned with calling out and vanquishing the old sinful will of the hearers. Chrysostom's and Augustine's sermons abound in illustrations of this.[56] There follows one from Spurgeon.— "I turn to another character. He says, 'Well, I don't trust in my morality nor in anything else; I say, "Begone, dull care, I pray thee, begone from me." I have nothing to do with talking about eternity, as you would have me. But, sir, I am not a bad fellow, after all. It is very little that I ever do amiss; now and then a peccadillo, just a little folly, but neither my country, nor my friends, nor my own conscience can say anything against me. True, I am none of your saints; I don't profess to be too strict; I may go a little too far sometimes, but it is only a little; and I dare say we shall be able to set

---

[54]*Works*, vol. 4, p. 141.—[55]P. 460.—[56]See our *History of Preaching*.

all matters straight before the end comes.' Well, friend, but I wish you had asked yourself the question, 'What have I done?' It strikes me that, if each of you would just take off that film that films your heart and your life over, you might see a grievous leprosy lurking behind what you have done. 'Well, for the matter of that,' says one, 'perhaps I may have taken a glass or two too much sometimes.' Stop a bit! What is the name of that? Stutter as much as you like! Out with it! What is the name of it? 'Why, it is just a little mirth, sir.' Stop, let us have the right name of it. What do you call it in any one else? 'Drunkenness, I suppose.' Says another, 'I have been a little loose in my talk sometimes.' What is that? 'It has been just a merry spree.' Yes, but please do call it what it ought to be called—lascivious conversation. Write that down. 'Oh, no, sir; things are looking serious.' Yes, they are indeed; but they do not look more serious than they really are. Sometimes you have been out on the Sabbath-day, haven't you? 'Oh, yes; but that has only been now and then—just sometimes.' Yes, but let us put it down what it is, and we will see what the list comes to. Sabbath-breaking! 'Stop,' you say. 'I have gone no further.' I suppose in your conversation sometimes during your life, you have quoted texts of Scriptures to make jokes of them, haven't you? And sometimes you have cried out when you have been a little surprised, 'Lord, have mercy upon me,' and such things. I don't venture to say you swear; though there is a Christian way of swearing that some people get into, and they think it is not quite swearing, but what it is besides nobody knows, and so we will put it down as swearing—cursing and swearing. 'Oh, sir, it was only when somebody trod on my toes, or I was angry.' Never mind, put it down by its right name; we shall get a pretty good list against you by and by. I suppose that in trade you never adulterate your articles? 'Well, that is a matter of business in which you ought not to interfere.' Well, it so happens I am going to interfere—and if you please we call it by its right name—stealing. We will put that down. I suppose you have never been hard with a debtor, have you? You have never at any time wished that you were richer, and sometimes have wished that your opposite neighbor would lose part of his custom, so that you might have it? Well, we will call it by its right name: that is 'covetousness, which is idolatry.' Now the list seems to be getting black, indeed. Besides that, how have you spent all this year? And though you have pretended sometimes to say prayers, have you ever really prayed? No, you have not. Well, then there is prayerlessness to put down. You have sometimes read the Bible, you have sometimes listened to the ministry, but have you not, after all, let all these things pass away? Then I want to know whether that is not despising God, and whether we must not put that down under that name. Truly, we need go but very little farther; for the list already, when summed up, is most fearful, and few of us can escape from sins so great as these if our conscience be but a little awake."

The value of *apostrophe* and *personification* in imparting not only beauty but power is illustrated especially by Berthold of Regensburg.[57] There follows an example of apostrophe from Massillon's passion sermons,—"An angel must descend from Heaven to comfort Him, to strengthen Him, to assist Him to bear this invisible cross, as Simon, the Cyrenian, the cross of Calvary. Angels of Heaven! This heretofore has not been your ministry; you have heretofore approached Him to serve and to worship; now He is debased below you." And an example of personification from a sermon of Saurin's,—"Give place, give place to our calamity, ye catastrophes of former ages, ye mothers whose tragical stories astonish posterity, who, forced by the horrors of famine, had to eat the flesh of your sons, and to preserve your own life by taking that of those who had received life from you. However dreadful your condition, you took from them only a transient life, and by a single stroke you saved them and yourselves from the rigors of famine. Here all follow one another into the same abyss, and by an unheard of prodigy, the mother, the mother feeds, if we must so speak, on the very soul of her son, and the son in turn devours the very soul of his mother." Exclamation, interrogation, and especially dramatization, the last almost overdone, are seen in Spurgeon's above quoted sermon, "What have I done?" (Jeremiah 8:6), which in its dramatic structure is a model of forceful oratory. Two illustrations of this dramatic method may be given, both from Saurin's great sermon at the beginning of the campaign of 1706. The first is a dramatic address to the congregation in the form of an address to the preacher's own soul:—"When the dove out of the ark found the winds unchained, the overflowing waters, the flood-gates of heaven open, the world buried beneath the waves, she sought refuge in the ark. But when she found plains and fields, she stayed in them. My soul, see the image of thyself When the world presents to thee prosperity, honor, wealth, thou hearest the voice of the enchanter, and sufferest thyself to be taken into its charm. But when thou findest in the world only poverty, contempt, misery, thou turnest thine eyes upward to seek happiness in thy centre.

---

[57]Compare our *History of Preaching.*

Now, notwithstanding the disappointment with which our life is accompanied, it is exceedingly painful to us to tear ourselves away from it. What would it be, then, if everything prospered here according to our wishes?" The second is in the form of dialogue:—"But regarding this whole text as applicable to you, my brethren, you are permitted to-day to pour out your complaints freely, and to declare before the face of heaven and of earth, the evils God has done you. My people, what have I done? Ah, Lord, what things hast Thou done to us! Ways of Zion covered with mourning, desolate gates of Jerusalem, lamenting priests, wailing virgins, prostrate sanctuaries, deserts peopled with fugitives, members of Christ wandering over the face of the world, children torn from their fathers, prisons filled with confessors, galleys crowded with martyrs, the blood of our countrymen poured out like water, dead bodies venerable as having witnessed for religion, but now cast out as refuse, and given for food to the beasts of the field and the fowls of heaven, ruins of our temples, dust, ashes, sad remains of houses consecrated to God, fire, wheels, gibbets, punishment till our day unheard of, answer and witness here against the Lord."

Finally, *illustrations* from history and contemporary life, in examples, instances and analogies, if well chosen and truly illustrating their point, serve both the beauty and the force of the sermon. The parables of the Good Samaritan and of the Ten Virgins must have gone straight home to men's business and bosoms. The warning against unduly multiplying these figures must here, too, be repeated. If examples are given in plenty, this must be justified by the mixed character of the audience; moreover, they must confine themselves to the central thought and should be presented in a climax. It was said of Edmund Burke: "His favorite argument is the example, instances real and fictitious being crowded upon each other, as if the speaker were resolutely determined to appropriate one to every individual who listened to him." In Tholuck we find the following illustration:—"'It is too late!' Oh! word of terror, which has often fallen like the thunder of God upon the heart of many a man. See that father, as he hastens from the burning house and thinks that he has taken all the children with him. He counts—one dear head is missing; he hastens back—'It is too late!' is the hollow sound that strikes his ear. The stone wall tumbles under the roaring torrent of flame. He swoons and sinks to the ground. Who is that hastening through the darkness of the night on the winged courser? It is the son who has been wandering in the ways of sin, and now at last longs to hear from the lips of the dying father the words, 'I have forgiven you.' Soon he is at his journey's end; in the twinkling of an eye he is at the door—'It is too late!' shrieks forth the mother's voice; 'that mouth is closed for ever!' and he sinks fainting into her arms. See that victim on the scaffold, and the executioner whetting the steel of death. The multitude stand shivering and dumb. Who is just heaving into sight on yonder distant hill, beckoning with signs of joy? It is the king's express; he brings a pardon! Nearer and nearer comes the step. Pardon! resounds through the crowd—softly at first and then louder and yet louder. 'It is too late!' The guilty head has fallen! Yea, since the world began, the heart of many a man has been fearfully pierced through with the cutting words, 'It is too late!' But oh! who will describe to me the lamentation that will rise when at the boundary line of eternity and time the voice of the righteous Judge will say, 'It is too late!' Long have the wide gates of heaven and its messengers cried at one time and another, 'To-day if ye will hear his voice!' Man, man, how then will it be with you when once those gates, with appalling sound, shall be shut for ever!"

This last quotation shows us that the orator employing these examples and illustrations must confine them to the main line of thought. "He must be suggestive," says Dabney, "rather than exhaustive in the development of ideas."[58] And Kidder says: "When a speaker shows a disposition to linger upon a figure and dress it out in too much detail, he wastes his strength and excites the impatience of his hearers."[59] Aristotle refers to the "agonistic style," which he chides for being inaccurate in detail, disjointed, rapid, representing images as the outline picture does.[60] Henry Ward Beecher, himself a master in the use of illustrations, says of them in his *Lectures on Preaching*: "Illustrations ought always to be clear, accurate and quick. Do not let them dawdle on your hands. There is nothing that tires an audience so much as when they have to think faster than you do. You have got to keep ahead of them. Do you know what it is to walk behind slow people and tread on their heels? How it tires and vexes one! You know how people are vexed with a preacher who is slow and dilatory and does not get along. He tires people out, for though he may have only six or seven words of his sentence completed, they know the whole of it; and what is the use, then, of his uttering the rest? With illustrations, there should be energy and vigor in their delivery. Let them come with a crack, as when a driver would stir up his team. The horse does not know anything about it until the crack of the whip comes. So with an illustration. Make it sharp. Throw it out. Let it

---

[58]P. 275.—[59]P. 275.—[60]*Rhet.*, iii, 13.

come better and better, and the best at the last, and then be done with it."[61]

Few things weaken a discourse more than unnecessary words. Franklin W. Fisk says, therefore, in his *Manual of Preaching*: "Use no more words than are needed. It is with thought as with gunpowder. Powder which, scattered over a surface, burns without force, might, if confined within a rifle, do fearful execution. So it is with ideas. The more briefly they are expressed, the more forcible they are. It is this which largely gives aphorisms their power." And Campbell writes in his *Philosophy of Rhetoric*, one of the older textbooks on this subject: "It may be established as a maxim that admits no exception, that the fewer the words are, provided neither propriety nor perspicuity be violated, the expression is always the more vivid. 'Brevity,' says Shakespeare, 'is the soul of wit.' Thus much is certain, that of whatever kind the sentiment be, witty, humorous, grave, animated, sublime, the more briefly it is expressed, the energy is the greater or the sentiment is the more enlivened. . . . As when the rays of the sun are collected into the focus of a burning-glass, the smaller the spot is which receives them, compared with the surface of the glass, the greater is the splendor. . . . so in exhibiting our sentiments by speech, the narrower the compass of words is wherein the thought is expressed, the more energetic is the expression."[62]

While conciseness is necessary for an energetic style, nevertheless Campbell's qualification is not to be overlooked—"provided neither propriety nor perspicuity be violated." This must especially be kept in mind when the hearers have slow-moving, undeveloped minds or are not thoroughly conversant with the language in which the sermon is held. In such cases greater diffuseness in expression, or, more correctly, a more extended variation of the thought is altogether in place. "A brief sentence structure flashes truth like lightning"; but it must be led up to in order to be understood. Occassionally even the broad stream of discourse, if it flows deep and strong, may be full of power; as is seen in the sentences of Ephraim the Syrian[63] or in the following extract from Saurin's above-mentioned sermon on the opening of the campaign of 1706: "When a people has been blessed of God with particular gifts of grace, it ought to exhibit particular expressions of gratitude. Every one of you feels the justice of this principle: none opposes it. Now was there ever in all the world a people so blessed of Heaven as the people of these provinces? A people—permit me to

---

[61]Vol. i, p. 174.—[62]P. 353.—[63]See our *History of Preaching*.

go back to your origin—a people born amid the most terrible anguish, under the most dreadful punishment; a people under the yoke of tyrants more cruel than the Pharaohs; a people not ashamed to take the name of *guises* (or beggars) as its title nor to set the beggar's scrip in their coat of arms; a people furnishing within six months six thousand victims for the wheel and the gallows; a people emerging from these conditions and reaching the stage of greatness and glory which you occupy to-day; a people which, though living in a small corner of the earth and possessing but a few acres of land, yet moved the whole world; a people throwing down the gauntlet to two mighty kings at once; a people for whose sake the sea withheld its floods on a day that was to decide for all times the fate of these provinces; a people, with the enemy in possession of its mightiest strongholds and with no other ally than the weak loyalty of a few citizens, which has just witnessed the enemy fleeing by seven ways, after having come by but one; a people inhabiting—if I may say so—a country constituted against the laws of nature, but which nature's God preserves as by a miracle; a people, mistress of her taxes, her laws, her rulers; a people beholding the Lord's candlestick beaming in all its splendor, and having the Reformation in its full purity. This is but an incomplete catalogue of the gracious gifts with which God has distinguished you. Do you distinguish yourselves by gratitude? Do men see among you more piety and devotion than among other nations of the earth? Do they see more attention paid to the Word of God and more consecration to His commands? Do they see more good examples among the heads of families and better training among children? Do they see more zeal for the restoration of the altars? Do they see more love of the truth and more work undertaken for the spread of the faith? Do they see more sympathy with the sufferings of Zion? I give no verdict, I decide nothing, I allow you to be the judges of your own conduct." Broadus says truly: "It must not be forgotten, that while diffuseness is unfavorable to energy, there may be a profuseness, as in Cicero, Barrow, Chalmers, De Quincey, Gladstone, which is highly energetic. The former spreads sluggishly over a wide expanse, the latter pours onward in a rushing torrent. Longinus compares the impassioned style of Demosthenes to a storm or a thunderbolt, that of Cicero to a conflagration, wide-spreading, all-devouring, long-continuing."[64]

(c) The energy of an oration is dependent also upon the

---

[64] P. 396.

sentence structure. The preacher must bear in mind the difference between the written composition and the spoken discourse. The long period, with the weight of thought falling at the end of the sentence, is better adapted to the former than to the latter. The reader has the composition before him and can easily survey the whole and refer at will to this or that portion, but the hearer must retain both beginning and end in his memory if he is to follow understandingly. This was one of the reasons why the exact Steinmeyer carefully re-wrote for publication in book form the sermons he had written out for pulpit delivery. In discourse, a looser arrangement of clauses and phrases, even if there be no long sentences, will be preferred to a strictly periodic construction. Campbell gives an instructive illustration of a sentence in four different constructions: "(1) At last, with no small difficulty, after much fatigue, through deep roads and bad weather, we came to our journey's end. (2) At last, after much fatigue, through deep roads and bad weather, we came, with no small difficulty, to our journey's end. (3) We came to our journey's end at last, with no small difficulty, after much fatigue, through deep roads and bad weather. (4) At last, with no small difficulty, and after much fatigue, we came, through deep roads and bad weather, to our journey's end." That it is permissible, under great stress of emotion, to break the construction of a sentence, is shown by Paul's style in many places. But this should not become a habit.

The position of individual words and phrases in the sentence will naturally affect the energy of the discourse. In compound sentences energy will be promoted by placing the shorter member last. Thus the sentence: "Inasmuch as you have not continued in all things that are written in the Law, you are transgressors of the Law," possesses greater energy than if its members were reversed, thus,—"You are transgressors of the Law, inasmuch as you have not continued in all things that are written in the Law." The words carrying the chief stress should have the most prominent place in the sentence. The student is referred to what is said above[65] on the beginning and end of sentences, especially on the importance of avoiding trivial and unaccented words at the end. He should note the "strong words" closing the sentences in the following passage from Spurgeon:—"Remember, thy sins are like sowing for a harvest. What a harvest is that which thou hast sown for thy poor soul? Thou hast sown the wind, thou shalt reap the whirlwind; thou hast sown iniquity, thou shalt reap damna-

---

[65]See pp. 188 f.

tion. But what hast thou done against the Gospel? Remember, how many times this year hast thou heard it preached? Why, since thy birth there have been wagon-loads of sermons wasted on thee. Thy parents prayed for thee in thy youth; thy friends instructed thee till thou didst come to manhood. Since then, how many a tear has been wept by the minister for thee! How many an earnest appeal has been shot into thine heart! But thou hast rent out the arrow. Ministers have been concerned to save thee, and thou hast never been concerned about thyself. What hast thou done against Christ? Remember, Christ has been a good Christ to sinners here; but as there is nothing that burns so well as that soft substance, oil, so there is nothing that will be so furious as that gentle-hearted Saviour when He comes to be your judge. Fiercer than a lion on his prey is rejected love. Despise Christ on the cross, and it will be a terrible thing to be judged by Christ on His throne." With Graebner, we refer you to the following passage from H. Douglas Spaeth, a masterpiece both as to the beginning and ending of sentences: "'I, if I be lifted up from the earth, will draw all men unto Me.' With supreme confidence Jesus, about to be betrayed, deserted, denied, bound, mocked, tortured, crucified, predicts His coming triumph. And at once the prophecy begins to be fulfilled. Ere yet that mighty, loving heart had ceased to beat, and those dear eyes were broken, behold the marvel of the drawing power of. the Cross! 'And he said to Jesus, Lord, remember me, when Thou comest in Thy Kingdom.' That was a thief, and in his very dying-hour he is drawn by the cross of Jesus and snatched as a brand from the fire. It threw into the dust on the highway to Damascus the proud Pharisee, Saul of Tarsus, and drew him to the side of the man he had so persistently persecuted. A sinful, God-estranged world felt and responds to the drawing power of the Cross. The votary of pleasure quits his lusts and runs to the Holy Sufferer. The philosopher in his eternal search for truth finds it here at last, the Cross of Jesus, the wisdom of God and the power of God. An emperor sees the sign in the skies and bows before the Cross which has conquered him and in which he now conquers. It draws the miser from his hoards, the sensualist from his pleasures, the self-righteous from his efforts, the abandoned from his vices, the proud from his arrogance, the stupid from his insensibility—I will draw all men unto Me. And who are these that fly as a cloud, and as the doves to their windows? He has drawn Jews, Romans, Greeks, and distant lands and isles have heard, and, hearing, faded out of the strong places, before the power of the Crucified. The Cross is to-day the only redemptive power in the world. It is the energy which vitalizes all missionary operations. It is the sign by which we shall yet overcome the world and bring it to the feet of our King, and what the poet has predicted of one false religion will be true of all:

> The Moon of Mahomet
> Arose, and it shall set;
> While blazoned as on heaven's immortal noon
> The Cross leads generations on."

The orator will further add to the energy of his discourse by avoiding all stilted and affected diction and employing language that is commonly used and commonly understood. Specifically theological or other scientific language is devoid of energy; technical terms should never be used, even in doctrinal lectures, without explanation. No great harm is done if the speaker be accused of using "vulgar" language on account of the prevalence of familiar, colloquial and common words in his style. John Leland, whose sermons were most effective among all classes of hearers, defended himself against this charge as follows: "It has generally happened that the most effective public speakers, whether secular or sacred, have by a fastidious class been accused of vulgarisms. So with Cicero, Burke and Chatham; so with Patrick Henry and Daniel Webster; and to turn to eminent preachers, so with Luther, Latimer, and Whitefield The reason was that, intent on the greatest good to the greatest number, they used what Dr. Johnson, after Daniel Burgess, called 'market language.' Dr. William Bates, an accomplished and courtly Non-conformist minister in the seventeenth century, once complained in the presence of his faithful and unpolished friend, Daniel Burgess, that he found very little success in his work as a minister; when his aged brother smartly replied, 'Thank your velvet mouth for that—too fine to speak market language.' Whitefield, very happily for thousands, had no squeamishness of this sort. Indeed it has been abundantly proved that our Divine Master and His apostles employed the market language of the Greeks, and that this very circumstance and its benevolent purpose furnish their best defense against the purists of all subsequent ages." No less a preacher than Theremin says the same thing, and gives besides the reason why the language of daily life is the most effective in preaching:—"In the throng of active life, amid heartrending misfortunes, during the silent hours of contemplation, does the hearer make known his thoughts and feelings to himself and to others in a highly flowery style, and in strange unusual phraseology? Certainly not. The style of expression which spontaneously associates itself with the silent emotions of our heart when they come forth into consciousness, is always as noble as it is simple. If, therefore, the orator would penetrate into our inner life, and renew again the traces of forgotten thoughts and feelings; if he would actually *address* you, he must employ the very same well known and customary language in which we are wont to communicate with ourselves. Every strange expression, nay, every unusual phrase, tears us away from ourselves, instead of leading us back into ourselves; and the stream of inward harmonies, which perhaps was on the point of flowing forth, suddenly breaks upon such unexpected obstacles and is dissipated. Moreover, with the disturbance of this flow is connected displeasure toward a man who decks himself out in a showy costume of sounding phrases, which, after all, are not so very difficult to collect together, instead of employing my common, every-day language along with me, to his own true advantage as well as mine. Those very rare instances when the speaker selects an unusual expression for an unusual thought are, of course, excepted here; but to allow one's self even the slightest departure from ordinary language, unless there is some particular reason to justify it, seems to me to be unadapted to the oration, and contrary to its aim; and is therefore morally blameworthy." If anyone conclude from this that the more vulgar his language the greater will be his effectiveness, or that common language means the same as slang, he should note what Ward says in his *System of Oratory*:—"It is not true that rough and hard language is more strong and nervous than when the composition is smooth and harmonious. A stream which runs among stones and rocks makes more noise, from the opposition it meets within its course; but that which has not these impediments flows with greater force and strength."[66] On the question of sustaining energy throughout a longer passage, Kidder says: "Energy should increase with the progress of a discourse. Its rise should be natural, and its movement calm and regular, culminating, if possible, in unanswerable demonstrations and resistless appeals."[67]

But with all his care to impart energy to his discourse by the employment of all the resources of style, the preacher must never imagine himself able to force his message upon his hearers. This is true even of the purely human effect of the Word: there are always persons who manage to shut their minds, either for a time or permanently, to the most forceful appeal. It is especially true of its converting, saving and sanctifying effect upon the soul. This effect can never be produced

---

[66] Vol. i, p. 337 —[67] P. 301.

by the power of human eloquence, but only by the power of God working in and through the sermon, and able to manifest itself through the most inadequate medium. But not even the fact that I am preaching the Word of God gives me the assurance that I shall permanently change the will of my hearer, or that I can change it whenever I choose, by this or that sermon. I have no assurance that I can permanently change his will; for though, under my preaching, the Law may batter down his inborn resistance to everything good and divine, still this resistance may immediately rise again to its feet and say defiantly, "I will not!" And even if it should not do so at the time, if a true conversion is effected through the Gospel, this resistance may yet assert itself later and thus hinder the saving effect of the Word. Still less can I change my hearer's will when I choose; for the day and the hour in which God will work faith in the hearts of those who hear His Gospel is in His own power and not in the preacher's.[68] To conclude from this, however, that it does not matter whether or not my sermon possesses force and energy, would be to prove unfaithful to my trust. For though I can never force my hearer's will by any art of mine, and have no right to presume to do this, I am none the less bound to use the means by which, according to the laws of psychology, which come from God, entrance is gained to the hearts and souls of men. These laws include, as we have seen, the convincing clearness, the pleasing beauty, and the moving energy of the spoken word. The preacher can never shirk with impunity the requirements which every other orator is bound to obey.

It would also be a mistake for the preacher to suppose himself obliged to effect by his sermons definite outward acts on the part of his hearers. This has been made sufficiently clear above in the text.[69] But an instructive passage from Hering may be quoted to emphasize the point. He says: "Both Scripture and life agree that a separation of the inner personal effect from its outward influence upon the community runs counter to Christian truthfulness (Matt. 7:17 ff.; Rom. 6:3 ff.; 12:1 ff.; 1 Pet. 1:22 ff.; 2:9; Jas. 2:14 ff.; 1 John 3:3 ff.). It was one of the primary concerns of the evangelical sermon in the Reformation period to show that good works proceed from faith. But on the basis of observation of the average effect of actual preaching it may be doubted whether the tangible results, the actual deeds, are not out of all proportion to the impulses given by the preaching. This apprehension was felt, e. g., by so conscientious a preacher as F. W.

---

[68]Comp. *Augsburg Conf.*, v.—[69]P. 203.

Robertson. It originated in his noble zeal to prevent the inspiration received from the sermon from fading away unused, from drying up in the lack of practical expression. But while some may be helped by the advice: Give immediate expression, wherever possible, to what you have inwardly appropriated, by the performance of some work or the carrying out of some resolve; it would nevertheless lead to a legalistic externalization if one were to make haste, immediately after the seedtime of the Word, to bring the harvest blessing of the sermon under cover. The most important sequel to sowing is growth. This growth, if it be genuine and. sound, because produced by the Holy Spirit, will issue in fruit. Such fruits, ripening under the patience of God and of His servants, may mature so long afterwards that there will be no conscious connection between the work and the Word that produced it. Our preaching would indeed stand in higher repute if the connection between it and the practice of Christian virtues were more evident than it is; if men could see how our preaching gave wings to the spirit of heroic sacrifice and the impulses of mercy and charity. But it remains true that the sermon is a life-power that works slowly by way of gradual development and secretly by hidden growth. This points the preacher who is a faithful servant of God to faith and prayer and hope. Such a spirit will foster self-discipline over against his own impatience and provide an inner defense against presumptuous demands and criticisms of others. But this inner, often hidden, gradual effect of the sermon dare not be used as a cloak for a lifeless, listless presentation, by which no growth is fostered and no life either engendered or nourished. After a period of faithful, vital preaching, a maturer life will manifest itself in the congregation by unmistakable signs and results. This stage of elevated objective life with its manifestations is a part of the edification of the congregation, even if it exist only in a small group, it may be only several persons. But with this true and deeper edifying activity there is commonly combined, by the attractive power of the Gospel preached in a living way, another result of a preparatory kind: a larger attendance upon the Word and an increased interest on the part of those regularly attending, reverence for faith and Christianity, and on the other hand, a deliberate and conscious enmity, a passionate opposition, and a hardened denial of the faith."[70]

The history of preaching reveals a conspicuous number of preachers pre-eminent for the energy of their sermons. We mention among

---

[70] P. 311.—Compare above, pp. 167 f.

preachers of the ancient church, Ephraim the Syrian, Basil, Chrysostom and Augustine; in the Middle Ages, Berthold of Regensburg and Geiler of Kaisersberg; in the Reformation period, Luther (compare especially the Eight Wittenberg Sermons preached after his return from the Wartburg) and Knox; in the following centuries, Balthasar Schuppius and Rieger, Bourdaloue and Massillon (occasionally). Baxter and Whitefield, Jonathan Edwards, Spurgeon, Beecher, Moody, Hofacker, Tholuck, Souchon, Harms, Bezzel[71]

In demanding that the sermon possess these three qualities—convincing clearness, pleasing beauty, and moving force—we of course do not mean that all parts of the sermon must possess them in equal measure. This can be the case as little as all parts can be addressed equally to the knowledge, the feeling and the will of the hearers. Every part of the sermon must indeed be clear, and neither its beauty nor its energy must be allowed to impair in any way its clearness. But the preacher will above all strive to make his sermon clear and convincing when he is concerned with the impartation, development and defense of divine truth. Convincing clearness may go hand in hand with pleasing beauty so long as the latter does not become an end in itself.[72] Beauty should be especially cultivated whenever the preacher wishes to commend and magnify God and the blessings of His Kingdom, in order to warm the souls of his hearers and awaken in them a longing for these goods. Cicero emphasized the close connection between the beautiful and the useful and illustrated this connection from nature.[73] And Vinet wrote: "Eloquence admits of only useful beauties, and nothing in it is mere ornament. And we use the term *useful* here with no vagueness of meaning. Utility with the orator lies in proving, convincing, determining. Eloquence in this view, has its type in nature, where everything beautiful is useful or springs from what is useful. Nature so admirably combines the useful and the beautiful, that according to the aspect in which we regard it, it appears alternately to have intended only the beautiful, and to have no thought except of the useful. Nature hastens to its result, but when we consider the beauties it develops in its course towards its end, can we say that it ever declines being at leisure? Under another view, nature is like a harp with a thousand vibrating chords, or an immense mirror of ideas; but all is activity, all is life, all is production in the sounds of this harp, and in the images of this mirror; nature is not

---

[71] On the individual preachers, comp. our *History of Preaching.*—
[72] Comp. above, pp. 183. 196 f.—[73] *De Orat.*, iii, 45. 46.

only a poet, nature is an orator; it acts, it produces, it argues, whatever it does is beautiful, but whatever it does is useful, that is to say, suited to produce, apart from itself, the sense of happiness."[74] But neither is energy in conflict with clearness or with beauty. On the contrary, it directly demands clearness and is glad of the aid of beauty. It is especially in place in those sermons or parts of sermons which have as their purpose the breaking down of the resistance of the old will in man, or the moving of the new will to a decision or to the carrying out of a decision.

Finally, every public discourse, to achieve its purpose, must be *popular*. It may be ever so clear, beautiful and vigorous, but unless it possesses also true popularity, it will fail of its purpose. To define this quality is not altogether easy. Generally speaking, a thing is popular when it expresses and corresponds to the true nature of a sound people. By this popularity of a discourse, therefore, we do not mean its agreement with the *Zeitgeist*, the prevalent ideas, passions and prejudices of a certain period. This is rather popularity in the unworthy sense of the term, flattering the spirit of the time and swayed by the instincts of the *populus*. Nor does the popularity of a discourse consist in an abundance of anecdotes and a multiplicity of illustrations and examples, however proper these, especially the latter, may be in the discourse and even the sermon; nor, as is often supposed, in a descent to a lower level, for the demand for popularity holds even in respect to the most cultivated audience. On the contrary, true popularity is present when the discourse or sermon corresponds to the inmost being, as it were the soul, of the people. The sermon is an oration having its place in the service of the congregation, and its audience is the people of God. That sermon possesses popularity, which answers in both contents and form to the peculiar nature of the congregation as the people of God.

---

[74] Pp. 426 f.

The common characteristics of all congregations as parts of the people of God are expressed in the Scriptures, the confessions, and the hymns of the Church. In these their common nature and needs find satisfaction. The Bible, not only in its original form, but no less in translation, especially into English and German, is a book truly of the people, by the people, and for the people. And in the confessions and hymns the soul of the people of God has found classic expression. The sermon will, therefore, most surely find the Christian folk-soul, and thus become truly popular, by keeping, not only as to contents but also as to form, close to the thought and language of the Bible, the confessions (especially the Small Catechism), and the Church hymn.

By this we do not mean a slavish copying of the individual formulations there given. This would frequently defeat the very end in view, by leading to a dreary antiquarianism and a complete ignoring of the difference between oriental-Semitic and occidental-Japhetic thought and speech. But it will always remain true that the sermon will be most easily understood by high and low and will most certainly reach and move the soul of the people of God, if it draws its contents from the centre of the Scriptures and presents it in a form modeled on the Bible, the Catechism, and the hymns of the Church. (P. 233.)

We have already insisted above that the sermon cannot possess convincing clearness, pleasing beauty and moving power unless it employ simple and in the best sense popular language. In dwelling separately on this element of popularity, our intention is to emphasize its importance from a fresh angle.

That popularity should not be sought after by lowering the standard of the sermon and reducing it to the level of the vulgar and low, nor by adapting it to the passing likes and dislikes of the audience, needs no long discussion, although it is unfortunately true that too many preachers cater to the itching ears of their hearers. Because people enjoy anecdotes and stories, others have crammed their sermons full of them and supposed that made them popular preachers. This was done not only in the Middle Ages, when Gottschalk Hollen († 1481), for example, strung together anecdote after anecdote and thus robbed the sermon of all dignity and seriousness. After the Reformation we find the same thing, and by no means only in the case of the Catholic Abraham a Santa Clara († 1709). I may indeed now and then introduce a fable or an anecdote into my sermon—Luther occasionally did with good effect—nor need the effect of a sermon be impaired if once in a while a smile should play about the lips of the hearer; but it is wrong to lug in anecdotes by the armful and it is wrong to imagine that they make the sermon truly popular. More than anecdotes, illustrations have a rightful place in the sermon. Ahlfeld, E. Frommel and Siedel used them with good effect. Beecher has in his *Lectures on Preaching*[75] a lengthy commendation of them, although he there takes a broader view and discusses the art of illustration in general. He says, among other things: "They assist argument, they help hearers to remember, they stimulate imagination, they allow certain faculties of the hearer to rest, they provide for various hearers, they change the mode of presenting argument, they bridge difficult places." Spurgeon wrote, as is well known, an entire book on *The Art of Illustrating*.

A few passages from Beecher follow here:—"The purpose that we have in view in employing an illustration is to help people to understand more easily the things that we are teaching them. You ought to drive an audience as a good horseman drives a horse on a journey, not with a supreme regard for himself, but in a way that will enable the horse to achieve his work in the easiest way. An audience has a long and sometimes an arduous journey when you are preaching. Occasionally the way is pretty steep and rough; and it is the minister's business, not so much to take care of himself, as, by all the means in his power, to ease the way for his audience and facilitate their understanding. An illustration is one of the means by which the truth that you teach to men is made so facile that they receive it without effort... Illustrations, while they make it easier for all, are absolutely the only means by which a large part of your audience will be able to understand at all the abstruse processes of reasoning. For a good, compact argument, without illustrations, is very much like the old-fashioned towers that used to be built before artillery was invented; they were built strong, of stone, all the way up above a ladder's reach without a door or a window-slit. The first apartment was so high

---

[75] i, 154-180.

that it was safe from scaling, and then came a few windows, and very narrow ones at that. Such were good places for beleaguered men, but they were very poor places to bring up a family in, where there were no windows to let in the light. Now an illustration is a window in an argument, and lets in light. You may reason without an illustration; but where you are employing a process of pure reasoning and have arrived at a conclusion, if you can then by an illustration flash back light upon what you have said, you will bring into the minds of your audience a realization of your argument that they cannot get in any other way. I have seen an audience, time and again, follow an argument, doubtfully, laboriously, almost suspiciously, and look at one another, as much as to say, 'Is he going right?'—until the place is arrived at, where the speaker says, 'It is like—', and then they listen eagerly for what it is like; and when some apt illustration is thrown out before them, there is a sense of relief, as though they said, 'Yes, he is right'. . . . Preaching a long sermon, the preacher cannot possibly hold his people unwearied, when they have become accustomed to his voice, his manner, and his thought, unless he moves through a very considerable scale, up and down, resting them; in other words, changing the faculties that he is addressing. For instance, you are at one time, by statements of fact, engaging the perceptive reason, as a phrenologist would say. You soon pass, by a natural transition, to the relations that exist between facts and statements, and you are then addressing another audience, namely, the reflective faculties of your people. And when you have concluded an argument upon that, and have flashed an illustration that touches and wakes up their fancy and imagination, you are bringing in still another audience,—the ideal or imaginative one. And now, if out of these you express a sweet wine that goes to the emotions and arouses their feelings, so that one and another in the congregation wipes his eyes, and the proud man, that does not want to cry, blows his nose,—what have you done? You have relieved the weariness of your congregation by enabling them to listen with different parts of their minds to what you have been saying. . . . You have got a little fine flour in your congregation, and more poor flour; then you have the graham flour, which is the wheat ground up husk and all; and then you have all the unground wheat, and all the straw, and all the stubble. You are just as much bound to take care of the bottom as you are of the top. True, it is easier, after you have fallen into the habit of doing it, to preach to those people who appreciate your better efforts. It is easier for you to preach so that the household of cultured and refined people will love to sit down and talk with you on this subtle feeling, and about that wonderful idea you got from the 'German' poet, and so on. But that is self-indulgence, half the time, on the part of a pastor. He follows the path that he likes, the one in which he excels, and he is not thinking of providing for the great masses that are under his care. You are bound to see that everybody gets something every time. There ought not to be a five-year-old child that shall go home without something that pleases and instructs him. How are you going to do that? I know of no other way than by illustration."

However true and worth noting this is, so long as illustrations are kept within bounds and the preacher does not degenerate into the mere story teller, nevertheless truly popular preaching is something more than this. It is the merit of Vinet to have expressed the truth that true popularity involves a certain familiarity by virtue of which the preacher gathers his hearers round him and unites them to himself as his own family, taking his stand on that which is common to all alike, and speaking to them with a warmth of heart, an open frankness, and an intimacy such as are possible only in a circle of like-minded friends. "When two friends meet," he says, "they give one another the hand; if it is covered they first make it bare; man must touch man; the contact and pressure of two naked hands make each one sensible to the life of the other. A preacher who is not familiar, and who carries into the pulpit the formalities of worldly politeness, who holds himself in reserve, who is not free, is a friend who extends a hand to his friend, but a hand in a glove, through which no warmth of life can be felt. What then of him, who, before he gives his hand, is careful to cover it,—of the preacher, I mean, who allows himself less freedom, less flow of heart in the pulpit than he does in the ordinary greetings and the superficial intercourse of social life? If we understand well the preacher's position, who, for a few moments at least, is invested with the liberty of a father and a brother, his language should be familiar, inasmuch as it ought to be open, and to consist entirely of terms, of movements and forms of expression taken from the relations of the family and of friendship. This language will indicate, in a lively manner, the relation which should consciously exist between his auditory and himself; it will make the impression that it is not a mere idea, but a common, present, urgent interest that is at stake between him and his hearers; it will bring them nearer to him. It is necessary to distinguish the familiarity we have in view, from another familiarity which is indecent and irreverent; it is in and before everything animated by Christian sentiment; this sentiment at the same time creates and limits it; as it is Christian familiarity, it is accompanied, necessarily, with those holy restraints which are not wanting in the freest intercourse of two Christians with one another."[76]

Vinet might have emphasized more strongly the distinctive character of the family to which the sermon is addressed. This has been done by Theod. Harnack[77] and A. Krauss.[78] It is the people of God, that has come together to hear the congregational sermon. Out of its life, out of its common treasury of ideas, the preacher's words must come, if he is to speak popularly, in accordance with the proper nature of the people of God. Then the congregation will recognize in his sermon the speech of their common homeland, will catch idioms and echoes of their mother-tongue.

The purest expression of the peculiar nature of the people of God will, therefore, be the best model for the truly popular sermon. That this is found nowhere else than in the Bible and in the classical hymns of the Church, but also in such a confession as the Small Catechism, born as it was out of the inmost religious life of the believing people, and, therefore, always regarded by them as their particular treasure,— needs, especially for Lutherans, no elaborate proof. The authoritative and reliable presentation of divine revelation in the Scriptures not only enshrines a unique content transcending all human thought, but has poured this content into a form thoroughly homogeneous to it. In this circle of ideas and impressions, in this world of words and images, the congregation lives; these it knows and understands; they are the common meeting ground for high and low, cultured and uncultured, so far as they have received a religious training and have not lost touch with the Bible, the creed and the Church hymn. This meeting ground holds them together in an inner oneness, despite all external differences. The true popularity of the sermon, therefore, cannot be thought of apart from its sound biblicity—it finds in this rather its proper realization and completion.

Theremin wrote, over against those who thought the best guarantee of biblicity was to make sermon consist of nothing but Scripture passages: "Each preacher should use his own language; Christian thought should individualize itself in him; the Word of God should become his word; the truth becomes his own, only when he is able to give it a form which is from himself; in short, a sermon composed only of quotations would not be a discourse, it would want oratorical unity and force, because there would not be perceived in it the con-

---

[76] P. 403.—[77] P. 384.—[78] Pp. 164 f.

tinuous presence and progressive action of a soul in which all the truths contained in the discourse are, in a sense, personified." But he said also, on the other hand: "I would recommend to all sacred orators the frequent employment of the expressions and images of the sacred Scriptures as a highly adapted and effectual means of exciting affection, provided only they be not brought in merely to fill up empty space, but are fused into the discourse, retaining their whole dignity and force. They are highly adapted, for the language of the Bible can never become antiquated, because it affords so many highly significant expressions for the manifold conditions of human life and states of the human heart, many of which appear as proverbial phrases in the language of common intercourse; and however much religious education and the reading of the Bible may have been neglected, the orator may yet, in the case of the generality of hearers, reckon with certainty upon a thought being understood sooner in a biblical than in a philosophical dress. But the great power of Bible language in awakening affection consists principally in this, that in it the expression for the understanding and the expression for the feelings are not so different as in merely human representations, but are always one and the same. The figures so frequent in the Bible, while they have all the precision of an abstract terminology, at the same time transfer the idea into the web of human relationships, and clothe it with all that can exert influence upon the mind; they are a ray which unites in one both light and heat, and passes over from the mind into the heart, thus kindling the whole man. If, now, as is often the case, a sentence from the Bible, on our first meeting with it, or upon after occasions, has awakened a whole series of pious emotions, the orator, by citing it as he passes on, can evoke anew the affection which already has become connected with it and can apply it to the purposes of his oration." Vinet, in particular, emphasizes the biblicity, or as he calls it, "the scriptural tone" of the sermon. He has in mind not so much the occasional use of Scripture quotations or references to biblical persons and facts for the purpose of illustration, as rather a close dependence upon the whole world of biblical ideas and language. "None of these extraordinary, unheard-of thoughts," he says, speaking of Scripture truths, "could have received a more complete and pure form than that which they have received from the Spirit who conceived them. This form is sacred, fundamental; the thought which it invests can never be perfectly separated from it; we may express it, develop it, in our own language; but we can never be justified in omitting the very terms in which it has been expressed by those who first revealed it to us.

It seems to me that we cannot suitably treat of what is most ineffable in our religion, unfold the unsearchable mercy of God, repeat His terrible threatenings, without at least starting with the very words of Scripture. Are we not happy to have the forms already prepared for truths which man would hardly have dared to pronounce, so greatly do they transcend and overwhelm him? Read, for instance, Gen. 6:5; Jer. 17:9; Rom. 3:22; Ps. 109:18; 1 Cor. 1:21; Is. 49:15; Ex. 33:11; Is. 62:9... I will not attempt to speak of the eloquence and the poetry of the Bible. I will only remark, that what distinguishes it and sets it above all literary performances, is, that its beauties are not literary, that the thought always gives the form, so that the union of the thought and form was never so intimate. The beauty then of biblical language has everywhere something substantial, which connects the mind immediately with the essence of things, without permitting it to take pleasure in the exterior covering. We are impressed before we have had time to be delighted or scarcely to admire. It is remarkable, too, that oriental language, at first view so strange to western imaginations, should be at the same time so human, and on this account so universal, that it assimilates itself to all people, all forms of civilization, all languages, much more readily, than the language and literature of any age or people, though much less remote from us, would do. Whatever, in the holy book, relates to man, whatever portrays man, has a depth and simplicity to which there is no parallel; the Bible here speaks a universal language, displays a universal poetry; the Bible in this respect as in all others, was intended as a book for the human race. Setting aside authoritative claims, we can draw from no other source images, descriptions, more suitable to the subjects we have to treat in the pulpit, or adorn religious discourse with beauty more becoming or more grave. All the forms of beauty which are proper in religious discourse abound in Holy Scripture, and our position in relation to it gives us the privilege, imposes on us the duty, of appropriating them all... The Bible is more than a source or a document; the Bible, we may almost say, is our subject; we have to speak from it, our voice is as its echo; it is as a forest which we subdue, as a field which we reap; the labor is less an addition to our task, than our task itself; boldly and freely then may we draw from this treasury. And what a treasury! This book has in everything reached the sublime. The most perfect models of the grand and the pathetic, of the human and the religious, of the strong and the tender, are here as in their depository. Among all the books which have expressed ideas of the same class, if we were free to choose, if the authority was equal, we should always recur to this. It has given names to all divine and human things, which are definite and irrevocable. Its manner of expressing things could not without loss of strength be exchanged for any other manner. Whole nations have appropriated this language and interfused it with their own: the Bible has given to human speech a multitude of expressions, as it has also given to human thoughts some of the most sacred of its terms. *We would remind men of their family traditions when we repeat to them the words of the Bible.* . . . All the congruities which I think should be found in the style of preaching, simplicity, popularity, familiarity, nobleness, I think I see them all united in the scriptural style, and that this is its compendium and its measure. The Bible I regard as the true *diapason* of the preacher, who assuredly should take from it the general tone of his discourse; his imagination should be steeped in the Bible; he should come forth in the spirit of this book, if he would have true power, dignified simplicity, noble and grave familiarity. It is the Bible, let me say with emphasis, that imparts and preserves to pulpit discourse the just measure of popularity, which from the existing state of civilization we are constantly liable either to fall short of or to exceed."[79]

---

[79] Pp. 413 f.

§ 10. THE DUTIES OF THE PREACHER AS ORATOR

For literature see the preceding section, also the note at the end of this section.

If the sermon as oration in the service of the congregation is to possess convincing clearness, pleasing beauty and moving energy, and all these combined with a noble popularity, there follow from this important duties for the minister. He must possess, first of all, *linguistic ability*. No one who is not master of the resources of language should imagine himself equipped to stand in the place where the work to be done is done by means of the word. How can he speak convincingly, pleasingly, movingly, who lacks the ability to express his thoughts, who confuses by his unclearness, offends by his clumsiness, or awakens pity by his helplessness? The degree of linguistic skill will naturally vary, but where this skill is entirely lacking, an essential prerequisite of pulpit work is lacking. Hence every preacher should give himself to the constant and careful study of language. The best method is to study the recognized masters of a simple prose style, both in sacred and profane literature. Hence he will also hold himself to the rule to prepare his sermons with a meticulous care extending to individual words, and to write them out in full, for years and years.

Besides linguistic ability, a *logical mind* is an indispensable requirement. For how can the preacher convince, dispose of objections, and in the conflict of ideas conquer his opponent, if his discourse is without logical order, and his arguments are poorly put together and fly in the face of correct thinking? The clearer the development, the more logical the progression of ideas, the more directly the whole discourse makes for its goal, the deeper and more lasting will be the effect upon the hearer. If one is by nature inclined to undisciplined, disorderly, or "loose" thinking, he should spend much time studying the laws of logic; he should inexorably drill and train his thought until it has been brought under the yoke of discipline and order, and the habit is formed of thinking and speaking logically. Such studies in language and logic will not indeed make one a homilete, but they are an unescapable duty of the homilete. The preacher who is not concerned to meet ever more and more adequately the duties of his calling as herald of the divine Word, will soon find the majority of his congregation passing him by and will never deeply impress the thoughtful hearer.

A *sense of the beautiful* is the third requirement. The ugly and the tasteless repel, the beautiful and the elegant attract. And it is the duty of the preacher to attract. How beautiful was Jesus' speech, what words of grace[80] proceeded from His mouth, especially in the parables, which form the poetic element in His message. One scarcely knows whether to admire more the force or the beauty of His sayings. There is no other subject that has so good a claim to be treated beautifully as that dealt with in the sermon. No office or profession takes so great harm to itself by neglect or undervaluation of the beautiful as the office of preaching. Hence the preacher's taste must be cultivated, his sense for the beautiful must be trained, and every native gift looking in this direction must be developed, ennobled and hallowed. The transfiguration of the aesthetic life by the Spirit of God and a constant and loving communion with the noblest works of art—these point the way to the cultivation of the sense of beauty. The chief marks of beauty are simplicity and harmony. Pomp is not beauty,

---

[80]Luke 4:22.

nor display elegance. We become masters of an art only when our art has again become nature.

Finally—and here beginning and end of our paragraph meet—since the sermon is, as to contents, the presentation, in the form of oration in the service of the congregation, of the Word of God contained in Holy Scripture, and since the true popularity of the sermon depends upon the degree in which it has modeled itself, in both form and contents, on the Bible, the confessions and the hymns of the Church, it follows as last and most important requirement for the preacher that he must continually immerse his mind, must constantly live and move and have his being, in the Word of God as well as in the thought-world of the confessions and hymns. If the preacher is at home in these and strives to become ever more at home, the congregation will hear in his sermons the voice of their common country; kindred chords in their hearts will be touched, and the way will be opened for the message the sermon has to bring and the purpose it has to achieve—the true edification of God's people on the foundation He Himself has laid. (P. 247.)

That the preacher should spare no pains to perfect his *style*, is made plain by the following words of President John Quincy Adams: —"The pulpit is especially the throne of modern eloquence. There it is that speech is summoned to realize the fabled wonders of the Orphean lyre. The preacher has no control over the will of his audience other than the influence of his discourse. Yet, as the ambassador of Christ, it is his great and awful duty to call sinners to repentance. His only weapon is the voice; and with this he is to appal the guilty, and to reclaim the infidel; to rouse the indifferent, and to shame the scorner. He is to inflame the luke-warm, to encourage the timid, and to cheer the desponding believer. He is to pour the healing balm of consolation into the bleeding heart of sorrow, and to soothe, with celestial hope, the very agonies of death. Now tell me, who is it that will best possess and most effectually exercise this more than magic power? Who is it that will most effectually stem the torrent of human passions, and calm the raging waves of human vice and folly? Who is it that with the voice of a Joshua shall control the course of nature herself in the perverted heart and arrest the luminaries of wisdom and virtue in their rapid revolutions round this little world of man? Is it the cold and languid speaker, whose words fall in such sluggish and drowsy motion from his lips that they can promote nothing but the slumbers of his auditory, and administer opiates to the body rather than stimulants to the soul? Is it the unlettered fanatic, without method, without reason; with incoherent raving and vociferous ignorance, calculated to fit his hearers, not for the kingdom of heaven, but for a hospital of lunatics? Is it even the learned, ingenious, and pious minister of Christ, who, by neglect or contempt of the oratorical art, has contracted a whining, monotonous sing-song of delivery, to exercise the patience of his flock, at the expense of their other Christian graces? Or is it the genuine orator of heaven, with a heart sincere, upright, and fervent; a mind stored with that universal knowledge, required as the foundation of his art; with a genius for the invention, a skill for the disposition, and a voice for the elocution of every argument to convince, and of every sentiment to persuade? If, then, we admit that the art of oratory qualifies the minister of the Gospel to perform in higher perfection the duties of his station, we can no longer question whether it be proper for his cultivation. It is more than proper; it is one of his most solemn and indispensable duties."

Broadus writes: "The speakers and writers who have been widely and permanently influential, have usually accomplished it by good thoughts well expressed. Often, indeed, excellence of style has given a wide and lasting popularity to works which have little other merit. Goldsmith's Histories long held their place in many schools, because so charmingly written, though they were inaccurate and very poorly represented the historical attainments of their own age. The widespread, though short-lived popularity gained by Renan's fanciful 'Life of Jesus,' was due not merely to the sensational character of its contents, but very largely also to the extreme beauty of the style, particularly in the original French. When a student at a Jesuit College, Renan paid great attention to the cultivation of his style, and afterwards devoted himself mainly to the study of language and literature. In like manner science has in many cases gained a just appreciation only when recommended by a pleasing style. This was what Buffon did for Natural History. The popularity of Geology was immensely increased among the English-speaking peoples by Hugh Miller, through his marvelous power of description and the general freshness and animation of his style. And so it was later with Agassiz, and Huxley, and Tyndall. Such facts go to show that style is not a thing of mere ornament. Style is the glitter and polish of the warrior's sword, but it is also its keen edge. It can render mediocrity acceptable and even attractive, and power more powerful still. It can make error seductive, while truth may lie unnoticed for want of its aid. Shall religious teachers neglect so powerful a means of usefulness? True, Paul says, 'My speech and my preaching were not with persuasive words of man's wisdom' (1 Cor. 2:4). He refused to deal in the would-be philosophy and the sensational and meretricious rhetoric which were so popular in that rapidly growing commercial city; but his style is a model of passionate energy, and rises upon occasion into an inartificial and exquisite beauty."[81]

Under the heading, "Means of improving style," Broadus gives a number of suggestions born of his long experience as teacher, which we regard as so valuable that we reproduce the most important of them. He demands first a real study of *language,* both of foreign languages and of one's own. Among living foreign languages he prefers French and German, but promises the student a still greater gain from the study of Latin and especially Greek. "This careful study of other languages is not only useful as a part of the speaker's early training, but ought, so far as possible, to be kept up through life. It has been thus kept up by a very large proportion of those who attained great excellence of style." With respect to our own language he recommends a careful working through some good Grammar. "Grammars show us our faults and warn us where there is danger; they set us to observing language, and reflecting upon it." "It is true," he says, "that the rules of grammar have most effectually done their work, when conformity to them has become habitual, and we need the rules no longer,—yea, when we have so fully entered into the principles involved, that upon occasion we may even violate a rule." But he also says: "Men who have been to college are apt to think that they have no need to study their own language at all, and especially no need of consulting books on the subject,—the latter part of this opinion being a mistake, and the former a very great mistake. On the other hand, men who have had fewer educational advantages are in danger of supposing that without systematic instruction they can do nothing to improve their style, or else that after studying a book or two on English Grammar, they have nothing more to do." But in-

---

[81] Pp. 341 f.

dispensable as is this study of grammar and of foreign languages, more important is the reading and study of the best *literature*. "From reading we gain much in the knowledge of language, especially as to richness of vocabulary, fulness of expression. But more. It is chiefly by reading that we form our literary *taste*,—a matter of unspeakable importance. Cicero makes one of his characters say, referring to Greek literature: 'As, when I walk in the sun, even though I walk for another reason, my complexion is yet colored,—so when I read these books, I feel that my style of speaking is as it were colored by their influence' (*De Orat.*, ii, 15. 16.). . . . To bathe our minds in choice literature till they become imbued with correct principles of style, to nourish them with good learning till our taste grows healthy, so as to discern quickly and surely between good and bad, is a process surpassingly profitable in its results, and in itself delightful." "And not only do we need to cultivate good literature for its positive benefits, but also to counteract certain evil influences of great power. Few among us have learned from childhood to speak graceful and forcible, or even correct, English. And as men grow up and go on in life, so large a part of what they read in newspapers, and of what they hear in conversation and even in public speaking, is in a vicious style, that they inevitably feel the effect. Besides the more obvious errors as to pronunciation and syntax, which are too often committed by cultivated speakers, there results from these influences a more subtle and more serious injury to taste, which only a continued application to the best literature can remedy and prevent."

But what should one read to improve one's style? So far as homiletic literature is concerned, enough has been said in the preceding chapter, and the student will find in our *History of Preaching* a full collection of the best sermons from all periods of the Church's history. Nevertheless, Broadus' suggestions on this point are well worth adding. W. C. Wilkinson calls him, in his *Modern Masters of Pulpit Discourse*, "a man with every natural endowment, except perhaps plenitude of physical power, to have become, had he been only a preacher, a preacher hardly second to any in the world."[82] While this sounds like extravagant praise, he was undoubtedly a master of his subject, whose advice is well worth listening to. He says: "The great French preachers from Bossuet to Monod, with such Americans as J. M. Mason and R. Fuller, form admirable examples of passion combined with elegance. Baxter is remarkable for directness and

---

[82] P. 344.

pungency, Bunyan for homely and charming simplicity. If one's style is dry and barren, he may read Chrysostom, Jeremy Taylor, Chalmers, or Melvill. For a grand model of style, which, like some young Grecian athlete, stands glorious in disciplined strength and manly beauty, we must go to Robert Hall, his writings as well as his sermons. And if the influence of Hall should tend to produce monotonous elevation, never coming down to common phrases, nor coming close with personal applications, the exact remedy is to be found in familiarity with Spurgeon." Of German preachers we mention as exemplary: Luther (not only in his homiletic writings), Loehe, Caspari, Naumann, Schmitthenner, Bezzel. Among secular writers in German (they should be read in the original!) Goethe's prose will well reward careful study, especially his *Aus meinem Leben.* Broadus declares that "Goethe's prose style is scarcely surpassed in any language."[83] Also Grimm's Fairy Tales, a linguistic treasure; Matthias Claudius; and among moderns Wilhelm Raabe, for the true folk-style; and some things of Nietzsche's, to whom much must be forgiven for teaching his countrymen the forgotten splendors of German prose. Broadus mentions the following in English: Bacon, Milton, Barrow and Burke. To which we add: Bunyan, Goldsmith, Ruskin, Matthew Arnold, R. L. Stevenson, J. R. Lowell, and W. H. Hudson; among preachers: Newman, Trench, A. Maclaren, W. L. Clow. Broadus recommends, besides an acquaintance with the above masters, "a familiarity with some of the finest letters," if one "would see the English language in all its most prodigal strength and splendor, and in all its most flexible grace and delicate beauty." The letters of Charles Lamb, R. L. Stevenson, Thomas Carlyle, Edward FitzGerald, George Meredith, and Henry James will repay careful study. A good convenient collection is Prof. B. J. Rees's *Nineteenth Century Letters* (in Scribner's Modern Student's Library, 1919). The English essay affords one of the best vantage points for the study of flexible and intimate prose style. The essays of Bacon, Sir Thomas Browne, Addison, Hazlitt, Lamb, De Quincey, Ruskin, Carlyle, Emerson, Pater, Arnold and Stevenson, cannot be passed over by the student of English prose. Naturally, in the course of time, every living language undergoes a change and standards of taste and usage vary. To-day the short sentence is preferred to the long period, and a direct straight-forward English to the diffuse or stately style. C. P. Slattery illustrates this by the following incident. "Not many years ago the pastoral letter of the House of

---

[83] P. 343.

Bishops was written by a prelate who thirty years ago was counted one of the most effective preachers of the country. His position and fine Christian character gave weight to the short addresses he was wont to make in later life, but this pastoral letter he felt to be worthy of his best efforts: it must be a great sermon. The result was that he brought into it the cumbersome and stilted style of his past; and because of this atrocious style, many clergyman evaded their duty and did not read it from their pulpits. Nearly all, I suppose, took liberties with its pompous sentences. I remember meeting that fall a young clergyman, for whose ability I had respect. I asked if he had read the bishop's pastoral letter to his congregation. 'O yes,' he answered, 'I read it. But I rewrote it first.' "Nothing," he adds, "could show more plainly the necessity of molding the sermon of to-day in the form of the most straight-forward English."[84] The "cumbersome and stilted style" has at no time been regarded as classical. The truly classical stands above its particular time and is, therefore, exemplary for all times. Let the student, therefore, be sure that his models are truly classical, it matters not in what language they are composed.

The third and most effective means for improving one's style is for Broadus a continued and careful *practice* in writing and speaking, paying scrupulous attention to the minutest details of spelling and punctuation, and sedulously cultivating the grammatically correct and the stylistically elegant until they are mastered. Bacon's aphorism in his essay, "Of Studies," is well known: "Reading maketh a full man; conference a ready man; and writing an exact man." It is self-evident that for this purpose one need not have constantly his Grammar at his right elbow, his Rhetoric at his left, and classical models before his eyes. Indeed, it will be better for the beginner to confine himself to working through a good simple text-book on composition, going carefully over the examples and working out the exercises. Afterward, this practice should have a definite object in view, so that the writing will not be a mere essay, but will assume the character of the oration with its definite purpose. One should first of all become absorbed in the subject, set a definite goal before one, arrange one's material with a view to this goal, and then proceed to write out one's thoughts, if possible at a single sitting. Then should follow a painstaking revision, profitable in proportion to its mercilessness. Sometimes simple changes will suffice, sometimes whole paragraphs may need to be recast, sometimes the whole composition must be rewritten. Let no one

---

[84]*Present-Day Preaching* (1912), p. 34.

become discouraged at this; it leads slowly but surely to the goal. Greater ones than we have taken this way and not been led astray. "Think of John Foster, toiling over a sentence for two hours, determined to have it right. Virgil wrote his Georgics sometimes at the rate of one line a day. He would dictate some verses, then spend the day in revising, reducing, and correcting them. He compared himself to a she-bear, licking her offspring into shape. Tennyson wrote 'Come Into the Garden, Maud,' nearly fifty times before it suited him, spending nearly a month over it. He wrote 'Locksley Hall' in two days, and then spent six weeks in altering and polishing it. Macaulay and George Eliot were diligent and careful in rewriting their works; and there are numerous other instances among the great masters in literature, ancient and modern, who spent hours, sometimes days, in revising and altering their writings." Besides this practice of original composition, the practice of translating has approved itself as a means of improving style. Here ideas are given one ready-made, one has no trouble with seeking ideas or with arranging them. All we have to do is to render the ideas into English. One must find the exact equivalent of the ideas in one's own language, weighing one word against another; one must give attention to idioms. Most German orators of the last century obtained their mastery over language by being trained in this method in their youth. W. T. Brewster says of it: "In any event the student busies himself with style. Enthusiasts for this method maintain that this is the only way to learn to write, and evidently such arguments crystallize into the common saying that the only way to learn to write English is through the classics. Then when a young man is sufficiently trained in rewording foreign ideas he may be turned loose on ideas of his own. This is, on the whole, the alleged traditional British type of practice."[85] This formative value of Greek and Latin for the student of English may well give those pause who favor the curtailment or abandonment of the classics in education.

The importance of a careful study of the Bible from this point of view ought, after all that has been said, to be self-evident. And yet it needs to be specially stressed, because like most self-evident things, it is generally overlooked. Despite the praise of the beauty of the

---

[85] *Writing English Prose* (1913), pp. 239 f.—Nothing could be more valuable in this connection than to work through some of the classics in the Loeb Classical Library with the Latin or Greek text and the English translation on opposite pages: e. g., Cicero, *Letters to Atticus*, with Winstedt's fine idiomatic English translation.

biblical language in general and the classical style of the Authorized Version in particular,[86] this side of the Bible is still too much neglected. We close, therefore, with the admonition of Vinet:—"Feed upon the Bible, live in the Bible, unite yourself to it; let it abound in your memory and heart; let a frequent personal study of it reveal to you its force, give you the secret of a multitude of passages, which, without such study, would remain to you as mere commonplaces, and take no root in your memory; mix the recollection with your most tender affections, with your prayers, your gravest occupations; let the words of Scripture gradually become the natural and involuntary form of your most inward thoughts; then meditate on a subject for the pulpit; write; preach; your word will come filled with the richness, interblended with the colors of the Word of inspiration. The prophetic Word will be interfused in yours; it will not be distinguishable from it; it will not appear to be applied to it from without; it will not impair the individuality of your expression; you will never fall into intimidation, and thus it will come to pass, as the nature of the evangelical ministry demands, that the man will be heard by men.[87]

NOTE.—The student will find the following works serviceable in cultivating the above-mentioned qualities of style:—

Quintilian, *Institutio Oratoria* (this work was specially in Fenelon's mind when he said that our best thoughts come from the ancients); Campbell's *Philosophy of Rhetoric* and Whately's *Elements of Rhetoric* (older works); A. S. Hill, *Principles of Rhetoric;* Genung, *Practical Rhetoric;* B. Wendell, *English Composition;* Brewster, *Writing English Prose;* Creighton, *Introductory Logic;* J. W. Baldwin, *Thought and Things;* Theremin, *Beredsamkeit eine Tugend* (English translation by Shedd); Phelps, *English Style in Public Discourse with Special Reference to the Usages of the Pulpit;* Trench, *The Study of Words;* Greenough and Kittredge, *Words and Their Ways in English Speech;* Weekley, *The Romance of Words;* L. P. Smith, *The English Language;* Marsh, *Lectures on the English Language;* Quiller-Couch, *On the Art of Writing;* Kittredge and Farley, *Advanced English Grammar;* Maetzner's or Koch's *Englische Grammatik;* essays on Style by De Quincey, Herbert Spencer, Walter Pater and Rob-

---

[86]Comp. Saintsbury, *History of English Prose Rhythm,* pp. 141—158; C. B. McAfee, *The Greatest English Classic;* A. S. Cook, *The Authorized Version of the Bible and Its Influence;* J. S. Auerbach, *The Bible and Modern Life and Bible Words and Phrases.* The student should read especially Ruskin's tribute to the English Bible in *Praeterita,* vol. i, ch. 2.—[87]P. 420.

ert L. Stevenson (collected with others in *Representative Essays on the Theory of Style,* edited by W. T. Brewster); Stevenson's suggestions and counsel on writing have been gathered into a convenient hand-book entitled *Learning to Write;* W. C. Brownell, *Victorian Prose Masters* and *American Prose Masters;* L. P. Smith, *Treasury of English Prose* (to make up for the amazing omission here of John Bunyan, the student should read the whole of "Pilgrim's Progress" and "Grace Abounding"); Lounsbury, *Standard Pronunciation in English;* B. Matthews, *Americanisms and Briticisms;* R. P. Utter, *A Guide to Good English,* and *Every-Day Words and Their Usage;* Webster's *International,* the *Century,* or the *Concise Oxford Dictionary;* Skeat's *Concise Etymological Dictionary of the English Language;* Crabb's *English Synonyms;* Roget's *Thesaurus of English Words and Phrases;* Brewster's *Dictionary of Phrase and Fable;* W. Aldis Wright, *The Bible Word-Book* (indispensable for the correct understanding of the archaic words and phrases in the Authorized Version); H. L. Mencken, *The American Language* (2. ed., 1921), and Ernest Weekley, *An Etymological Dictionary of Modern English* (1921). R. Roberts, *The Preacher as a Man of Letters* (1931).

II

The Subject-Matter of the Sermon and Its Derivation

§ 11. THE SUBJECT-MATTER OF THE SERMON IN GENERAL

G. Menken, *Saemtliche Werke*, 1858. F. Schleiermacher, *Der christliche Glaube*, ³1835-36. A. Schweizer, *Lehrbuch der Homiletik*, 1848. L. Heubner, *Christliche Topik oder Darstellung der christl. Glaubenslehre fuer den homiletischen Gebrauch*, 1863. Lord Hatherly, *The Continuity of Scripture*, ³1869. F. L. Steinmeyer, *Die Topik im Dienst der Predigt*, 1874. P. Kleinert, *Zur praktischen Theologie. Probleme zur Kultuslehre* (Stud. u. Krit.), 1882. A. Krauss, *Lehrbuch der Homiletik*, 1883. H. Bassermann, *Handbuch der geistl. Beredsamkeit*, 1885. E. Bindemann, *Die Bedeutung des Alten Testaments fuer die christl. Predigt*, 1886. F. Hering, *Die homiletische Behandlung des Alten Testaments*, 1901. F. L. Steinmeyer, *Homiletik*, 1901. G. A. Smith, *Modern Criticism and the Preaching of the Old Testament*, 1901. E. Kautzsch, *Die bleibende Bedeutung des Alten Testaments*, ²1903. H. Hering, *Die Lehre von der Predigt*, 1905. James Orr, *The Problem of the Old Testament*, 1906. S. Oettli, *Die Autoritaet des Alten Testaments fuer den Christen*, 1906. C. F. Kent, *The Origin ana Permanent Value of the Old Testament*, 1906. E. C. Achelis, *Lehrbuch der praktischen Theologie*, ii, ³1911.

Our definition of the sermon as the presentation of the Word of God in the form of public discourse having its place in the service of the congregation, already implies what must be its subject-matter or contents. This cannot be anything drawn from *the preacher's own consciousness.* For that would lead to a reprehensible preaching of one's self, condemned already by St. Paul;[1] it would give to the preacher "lordship over the faith" of his hearers,[2] and make his experience the measure of all truth. Nor can the contents of the sermon be drawn from *the consciousness of the Church* as expressed in her creed. For the creed itself points backward

---
[1] 2 Cor. 4:5.—[2] 2 Cor. 1:24.

to the original Word of God in the Scripture, and professes to be nothing more than the deposit of this Word and a witness to its true meaning, so far as God has revealed this to His Church. Still less can the contents of the sermon be derived from *theological science,* dogmatics or ethics. For theological science is itself but a derived source and, on its formal side, a varying quantity; its place, moreover, is the professor's chair and not the pulpit. It is true that the preacher should have some experience of the truth he is to proclaim,[3] and that he must be in agreement with the creed of the congregation.[4] It is likewise true that, unless the materials he presents have been systematically worked through, the sermon cannot possess clearness and consistency. But these materials themselves must be drawn from the Holy Scriptures alone, as the witness-bearing and authoritative presentation of the divine revelation in act and word. This is the one and only source of the subject-matter of the sermon. Whatever else may be contained in the sermon—and indeed nothing human is foreign to it—serves but to illustrate and develop the subject-matter drawn from the Scriptures. (P. 253.)

The contents of the sermon cannot be drawn from the *consciousness of the preacher.* Steinmeyer well says: "There is particularly one sentence which St. Paul opposed to this error— οὐχ ἑαυτοὺς κηρύσσομεν (2 Cor. 4:5)—to which he adds in verse 7 this explanatory clause, ἵνα ἡ ὑπεροχὴ τῆς δυνάμεως ᾖ ἐκ θεοῦ, μὴ ἐξ ἡμῶν. Just as he repeatedly distinguishes between his own personal opinion and the ῥῆμα or ἐντολὴ κυρίου, so he is concerned in his preaching to bring out the fact that he does not expect the congregation to accept his own conviction as such, but requires them to accept that ἀλήθεια to which he himself bows, and by which both he and they must be saved. So he says· 'Not that we have lordship over your faith, but are helpers of your joy' (2 Cor. 1:24). In this sense he desires that ἡ πίστις ὑμῶν μὴ ᾖ ἐν σοφίᾳ ἀνθρώπων, ἀλλὰ ἐν δυνάμει θεοῦ (1 Cor. 2:5). The preacher should propose a truth to his congregation, not because it

---
[3]Comp. pp. 68 ff.—[4]Comp. pp. 73 ff.

has approved itself to his inner life nor in the form in which it has approved itself, but because it has proceeded out of the mouth of God and in the form in which it has proceeded out of His mouth. It is a mistake to bring forward passages in which the apostles appear as exponents of their individual conceptions of Christianity or of their own personal experiences. When John says: 'That which we have seen and heard declare we unto you' (1 John 1:1, 3), he is referring to nothing individual, but is expressing an objective truth. And though Paul speaks of his personal experiences, in 2 Cor. 11 and 12, and uses them indirectly as the basis of doctrinal communications, he states explicity that he regrets ἀπὸ μέρους doing this: he is speaking as a fool, they are to bear with him in his folly, he has not adopted this tone of his own accord but is speaking partially under compulsion. Still less apropos is the fact that Paul narrates repeatedly his experience on the road to Damascus; for he draws from this no inference valid for others, but uses it to account for his change of heart and to vindicate his apostolic position. As the apostles themselves, with incomparable chasteness, made this Word of God received by them the contents of their preaching, so they guard no less carefully against the over-emphasis of the purely individual on the part of any Christian arising to teach in public. They desire indeed that whatever is said be said as the Word of God; but they do not on that account regard every outpouring of the Christian heart as the Word of God, nor permit it to be given out as such. The remarkable demand of Paul in Rom. 12:6, that even the προφητεία uttered by one moved by the Spirit must be κατ' ἀναλογίαν πίστεως, and the existence of a separate charisma διακρίσεως πνευμάτων prove conclusively that, in the apostolic period, even that which was generally acknowledged as the expression of an enthusiasm produced by the Spirit was not unconditionally accepted. Let no one be misled by the fact that a fresher breath of life passed through the congregations in those periods in which such preaching predominated in the Church. This condition was so far from being founded on such an unjustifiable practice that the latter was responsible rather for the unsound and deplorable features of these periods. In the history of Christian preaching this subjectivism arose especially in the age of pietism. It was a natural and necessary result of the theory of a *theologia regenitorum et irregenitorum,* that in the public proclamation of the Word of God the subjective, individual Christianity of the preacher asserted itself as the dominating and fundamental influence of the sermon, and that preachers derived the substance of their sermons from their store of personal experience. It was not, indeed, the intention of Spener to foster such a practice. He stated repeatedly that he drew his sermon material solely from the Word of God, and that he never expected his hearers to accept or believe anything he taught them on his own authority or to please him. His later followers, however, abandoned this principle. The dangers of such self-production of sermon material are apparent. The preacher's Christianity is and remains imperfect and incomplete, pervaded by sin and mingled with error. Hence it can never be the criterion or the norm and corrective for others. Moreover, even in the most favorable case the preacher's Christianity is always a merely individual matter which cannot, in the great variety of the organization of individual life, be normative for all other individuals. Christ does not reflect Himself alike in every mind. There are in a great house many different vessels, and their variety is determinative of the greatness of the house. Special experiences vouchsafed to one person may be entirely strange and even impossible to another. One man may be firmly convinced, and it may be an objective fact, that he was tempted in a certain instance by Satan; but that gives him no right to judge another to be exposed in a similar situation to the assaults of the evil one. A man may experience certain emotions while partaking of the Lord's Supper, and these emotions may recur as often as he receives the sacrament; but he has on that account no right to demand that others experience the same emotions, and he is guilty of an improper, subjective exaggeration when he sees in them something normal and universally valid. One may correctly interpret the divine leading pursued by grace in his own life, but he dare not assume that God will take the same way with everyone else, nor put forth this opinion as a certain and definitely established theory. Such a procedure would be open to serious objection even in the pastoral care of souls; but in the case of the sermon, which is addressed not to individuals but to the worshiping congregation, it is in a still higher degree reprehensible, and should be inexorably rejected. Certainly a sermon that derives its materials in this way may under certain conditions produce a deep impression; but it is another question whether this impression will be a wholesome and truly edifying one. Such a sermon not only may, but in the nature of the case must, arouse opposition from various sides, and it must put up with this opposition because it has behind it no authority that is acknowledged by the whole congregation."[5] The history of preaching shows that the sermon

---

[5] Pp. 34 ff.

never flourished for long when it drew upon personal experience as the source of its materials. It attracted, indeed, at first, especially after a period of dry doctrinal preaching; but it soon lost its power to attract, became monotonous, thin and colorless, and ended in rationalism or fanaticism.

If we decline, further, to derive the contents of the sermon from the *consciousness of the Church* as expressed in its creed, it is clear from chapter VI that we do not do this because we share Schweizer's view that "the demand that the preacher be in agreement with the symbols of his Church in respect to their doctrinal statements cannot be carried out, and overlooks the continuous development of the Church, emphasizing solely what it has become and is." We demand, on the contrary, that he preach nothing contrary to the creed of his Church. Nor do we reject the creed as source of the sermon because we agree with Steinmeyer that the preacher would otherwise be "restricted to exceedingly short rations." For the Apology of the Augsburg Confession, the Small and Large Catechisms in particular, and even the maligned Formula of Concord abound in rich and truly edifying materials. But why go to the drawn water when the fountain is accessible in all its freshness and fulness? Nothing is so rich, so fresh, so inexhaustible as God's own Word. In the confessions, moreover, the polemical point of view necessarily predominates, while as a rule the sermon, though it must be confessional, ought not to be polemical.

Theological Science, especially dogmatics and ethics, cannot serve as a source of sermon material. Melanchthon, indeed, termed his *Loci* a source of homiletical material, and later on, Gerhard's *Loci* became, especially in the Lutheran Church, a mine of sermonic material, developing as it does the *usus practicus* of each locus. With a great show of learning the preacher would present one of these loci thetically, polemically and apologetically, and conclude with a simple exhortation to abide by the truth thus stated. In the nineteenth century, Leonard Heubner of Wittenberg wrote a "Topik" for preachers from this point of view. Rationalism forsook the field of dogmatics for that of ethics, selected this or that virtue, defined it in detail, and indicated the motives leading to its practice, now from the eudaemonistic viewpoint, again pointing to the example of Christ. The Middle Ages, and in a certain respect even the early Church, had taken the same way, following often the lead of heathen rhetoric and moral philosophy. Now, it is doubtless true that only the preacher who has systematically worked through the biblical truths can present his subject-matter in a clear and logical manner, and distinguish between what is fundamental and non-fundamental, central and peripheral. It is also true, as R. Seeberg has said, that that is the best dogmatic which best teaches how to preach. But it by no means follows that the sermon material itself is to be drawn from dogmatics or ethics. Over against this stands Spalding's word: "Not theology but religion is to be preached,"[6]—although we have to operate with a deeper conception of religion than Spalding's, and dare exclude neither the historic facts of our salvation nor the saving truths to be apprehended by the divinely illumined intellect. Where they are what they should be, dogmatics and ethics do indeed draw their contents from the Scriptures. But to go to them for the subject-matter of the sermon would again be to pass by the living fountain and resort to the drawn water. It would also be to resort to a source that draws its contents from the Scriptures in a totally different manner and for a totally different purpose. As Steinmeyer says, "The science of dogmatics pursues entirely different interests from those of the sermon. Whereas the purpose of the sermon is to lead its hearers to accept immediately the truth presented, in order that it may become their truth, an element in their lives and a factor of new life, the purpose of dogmatics is to give a survey of the whole complex of revealed truths in an organic system."[7] Hence in dogmatics the contents of Scripture are presented in a conceptual, almost stereotyped form, and not in the concrete and immediately practical form which is the proper requirement of the sermon. Moreover, which dogmatic or ethic has succeeded until now in incorporating in itself the whole truth of Scripture without exception?

Thus everything forces us back to the *Scriptures* themselves. They alone can be the source of the contents of the sermon. Where this is the case, the sermon need never suffer for lack of subject-matter. Its riches are on the contrary conditioned by the draughts it makes upon the riches of the Scriptures. As Kleinert well says: "The Scriptures in their entirety are able, as no other book in the world and as no doctrinal system, not even the richest, to bring home to one's consciousness the inexhaustibleness of the religious motives, needs and remedies, and their adaptability to all times, places, and spheres of duty. Any normative determination of the contents of the sermon that assigns to it any other limits, putting in place of the ocean a puddle or a mirage deceiving by its apparent illimitableness,

---

[6] *Ueber die Nutzbarkeit des Predigtamts* (Berlin, 1791).—[7] P. 48.

will only bring about an impoverishment of the sermon. The most meagre endowment, on the contrary,—and the Church cannot count on only gifted preachers,—will not succumb to the danger of emptiness or poverty, either for itself or for the congregation, if it takes seriously the principle that the sacred Scriptures in their totality are the source of the sermon, as Christ is its essence."[8]

The statement that the Scriptures form the sole source from which the subject-matter of the sermon is to be drawn must be qualified in a double direction. With respect, first, to the external compass of the Scriptures, we maintain that the *canonical books* alone, and not the *apocryphal*, form the source of the sermon. However high one's private judgment of the comparative merits of certain of the apocrypha, as homilete he must confine himself to what the Protestant Church regards as the normative source of Christian truth and life. The more, since there is not found in the apocryphal books any actual addition to the truth contained in the canonical Scriptures. (P. 254.)

The Apocrypha of the Old Testament are: I and II Esdras, Tobit, Judith, The Rest of Esther, Wisdom, Ecclesiasticus (Sirach), Baruch with the Epistle of Jeremiah, The Song of the Three Children, The Story of Susanna, The Idol Bel and the Dragon, The Prayer of Manasseh, and I and II Maccabees. Since the Greek translators of the Hebrew Old Testament added these books to the original Hebrew Bible, even giving them a place among the "Writings," and since this Greek translation was used by all Christians who were unable to understand Hebrew, these books came also to be used in the Christian Church. But when it was learned later that these writings were not a part of the Hebrew Bible, the Church in the East removed them from use in divine worship (hence apocryphal, i. e. hidden). The Western Church retained them in the Latin version which was used throughout the Middle Ages. Yet the fact was never lost sight of, that there is a difference between them and the canonical books. Attention was called to this especially during the times preceding the Reformation. Luther also took this position. He, indeed, translated them, but separated them from the other books, put them in a class by

---

[8] *Zur praktischen Theologie*, p. 41.

themselves and gave them this heading—"Apocrypha, i. e., books which must not be put on the same level as the Holy Scripture, but which are nevertheless wholesome and good to read." The Reformed churches also printed them at first, likewise separating them carefully from the other books. But, owing to a movement which began in Scotland in 1825, they were no longer reprinted in the editions of the British Bible Society after 1827, so that our English Bibles as a rule do not contain them. The apocrypha belong to the period of quiescent revelation, of oppression and decline in Israel, of the rise of Scribism and tradition, and of the development and supremacy of Judaism with its admixture of heathen ideas. Compare the Stoic judgment on suicide (II Macc. 14: 37 f.), the Platonic speculations concerning the pre-existence of the soul (Wis. 8: 19f.), the idea of the sinlessness of the patriarchs (Prayer of Man. 8), of the meritoriousness of almsgiving (Tob. 4: 11), etc. Their principal value consists in the evidence they afford of the religious development of Judaism in the centuries immediately preceding the coming of Christ. Krauss says correctly: "Because there are many good sentiments expressed in Sirach, it yet does not deserve the place of a separate witness of divine revelation; and because the books of the Maccabees contain various fine histories they can not lay claim to a higher rank than other excellent historical works."[9]

Again, *within the canonical books* themselves, we must distinguish between those portions which are and those which are not adapted to serve as source of materials for the sermon. Not, indeed, that we distinguish between what is and what is not inspired, for no such distinction exists even on the theory of grades of inspiration, as worked out, e. g., by Philippi in his "Glaubenslehre." Nor do we except the many passages which "do not proceed out of an authoritative mouth,"[10]— passages such as John 9: 31; 11: 16; 11: 50; Luke 5: 2; Acts 5: 38, 39, etc. For it must not be forgotten that even such utterances out of non-authoritative mouths may express true fundamental principles of the Kingdom of God which are still valid, or may reveal tendencies of the soul well adapted to serve even today as examples or warnings. The consistent

---

[9] P. 228.—[10] Steinmeyer, p. 60.

application of this canon of Steinmeyer's would rule out at the very outset no small portion of truly edifying material. Our distinction can best be made from the viewpoint of the nature and purpose of the sermon. The sermon, in its nature, is the presentation of the divine Word in its essential content, which is Christ crucified, His forgiving and sanctifying grace; and its purpose is edification, that is, a growth in grace, upon this foundation. Hence, whatever does not in some degree present Christ nor lead to the true edification of the congregation cannot serve as material for the sermon.

According to this principle, the *Gospels* are a pre-eminent source of sermon-material. And the Gospels in the sum of their contents, though certain portions naturally stand out as groundwork of the whole, to which Holy Scripture points both forward and backward and which it stamps unmistakably as of central importance. These portions are the narratives of Christ's birth, the fulfilling of the divine will to salvation in His life and work, His suffering, death, resurrection, ascension, and sending of the Holy Ghost. To these come, in the second place, the doctrinal discourses of our Lord concerning the Kingdom of God and the conditions of entrance into it, concerning God the Father, His own person, the Holy Spirit, concerning sin and redemption, the way of salvation and the completion of salvation by His coming again. Thirdly, there are the accounts of Jesus' intercourse with His disciples and with the people, and of His relations with His enemies.

In addition to these acts and words of Jesus we have, as further indispensable sources of sermon-material, the series of apostolic *Epistles*, which on the one hand give an authoritative interpretation of and introduction to the divine will to salvation in its accomplishment in the person and work of Christ and by the operation of the Holy Spirit, to sin and grace, faith and justification, setting forth the saving value of the works of God and pointing the way to their blessed fruition, and which on the other hand draw the ethical consequences from all this for the whole complex of human life, urge their thorough-going application, and waken a hearty longing for the final consummation.

Lastly, there are the *Acts* and *Revelation*,—the former bearing witness to the gracious presence of the glorified Christ with His Church, holding before her the duty of world-evangelization, and exemplifying the ideal of congregational life and activity; the latter keeping alive and strong the Church's faith in the ultimate victory of the Kingdom of God over the kingdoms of the world. (P. 271.)

In the *evangelic* accounts of the works of Jesus, by which above all else our salvation was achieved, and which rise like Alpine summits above the remaining contents of the Gospel—the narratives of the birth, suffering, death, resurrection and ascension—the emphasis should fall in the sermon, not upon this or that detail but upon the saving character of these acts for us. In this Jesus Himself[11] and the apostles found their value to consist. It is because of his constant insistence upon this that Luther's festival sermons rise so incomparably superior to most of the festival sermons of the ancient and especially the mediaeval Church. But the sermon dare not declare these saving facts of the past in such a way as to lose sight of the living Christ of the present. It must rather assert constantly that it is the ever present, exalted Christ who is the ἱλασμός, *expiator, reconciliator, redemptor* by virtue of what He accomplished for us once for all in the past. Paul, who so strongly stresses the saving work of Christ in the past, asserts just as strongly that it is the exalted Christ "who of God is made unto us wisdom, and righteousness, and sanctification, and redemption,"[12] and declares not only that He purchased and preached peace in the past but that He *is*, on the basis of this, now and forever "our peace."[13] The same thought is dwelt on repeatedly in the epistle to the Hebrews. This aspect is essential to the pure evangelical conception of faith. For faith, though it is a relation to

---

[11]Matt. 20:28; 26:28; John 10:12, 16.—[12]1 Cor. 1:30.—[13]Eph. 2:14.

the Word and to the saving works of the past witnessed in the Word, is yet much more than this, namely a personal relation to a person. By means of the Word and the past works of Christ, it comes to know and lay hold on the person who is witnessed to in the Word and who performed those works, the divine-human person of Christ, in whom, by virtue of the everlasting redemption obtained by Him in the past, all my salvation is bound up both now and forever.[14] Hence, whenever the narratives of these saving works of Christ contain details throwing light on His divine-human person, the preacher will do well to seize upon them, since all the saving value of the works comes from the person who performs them. Where these narratives demand a discussion of Jesus' relations to His friends or to the Jewish people, the treatment dare never be such as to force into the background the heart and centre of all—the saving value of Jesus' person and work. Even in preaching on the passion of Christ, this has not always been sufficiently borne in mind and much eloquence has been expended on details of minor importance. The modern English and German pulpits frequently betray this error by their choice of texts, showing a tendency to pass by in silence the great central passages of the Gospels.

Among the narratives of the works of Jesus, the *miracle stories* require special discussion. Not because the miracles were His chief work, but because in our scientific age, which views all events as happening under the inflexible reign of law, the tendency is to rule out the miracles as homiletic material. The results of the study of comparative religion, moreover, which show that the lives of all founders of religions were embellished with miracles, seem to support the view that the miracle stories in the Gospels are nothing but myths, in which the Christian imagination has been at work weaving a similar aureole round the person and life of Jesus. Yet faith cannot dispense with miracles. Not because the miracle is, as Goethe put it, "des Glaubens liebstes Kind;" for the reverse of this is the case and faith is the dearest child of the miracle. Faith owes its very existence to a miracle performed by God, the miracle of the second birth, and thus experiences God, in its own life, as a God that doeth wonders. But if my admission to fellowship with God has not come about by my own reason and strength, but by factors and forces belonging to an invisible, supernatural world, why should not this unseen world, at least in matters belonging to the same order and affecting my

---

[14]Acts 4: 12.

fellowship with God, be capable of reaching down into the natural world and producing the thing we call a miracle? Not only is faith assured, by its own experience, of the reality of miracles, but its idea of God demands at least the assertion of the possibility of the miracle. Faith could never say with Huxley, "Miracles simply do not happen." For its God is neither subordinate to the natural world, so that He is shut up in it and subject to its laws, able, indeed, to perform great and astounding works transcending the ordinary course of nature, yet bound to the operation of natural causes, nor is He merely on an equality with the natural order; but faith sets Him far above this world and thus posits an activity on His part which passes all understanding and cannot be explained now or at any future time by the laws of nature, because its origin lies elsewhere. For faith, God is both creator and governor of the universe and giver of all its laws. He is absolute freedom and knows, with respect to the whole order of nature and its laws, no limit or fetter to His working, least of all when it comes to the carrying out of His plan for the salvation of man, for whom He created the natural world. The miracle is but another name for the omnipotence, freedom and unsearchable wisdom of the divine working. He that would retain these must hold fast to the possibility of miracles. It is significant that in the newest new theology of Germany the rejection on principle of miracles has begun to wane. If a pure idea of God demands the possibility of the miracle as such, it appears only natural to us, holding as we do to the divinity of Jesus, that miracles should occur in the story of His life, especially when these miracles take place in the sphere of the restoration of communion between God and man, in which faith itself has experienced the reality of the miracle. And this is the only sort of miracle in the life of Jesus narrated in the New Testament. The miracles of the Incarnation and the Resurrection have for their purpose the carrying out of the divine counsel of salvation; all other miracles between these two are manifestations of Jesus' prophetic ministry and stand, like this ministry itself, in the service of His saving work, the restoring of men to fellowship with God. They are thus the indispensable accompaniments of His work as Saviour. He was to manifest Himself before all people as the divinely sent deliverer not only from sin, but from all the consequences of sin, from the whole δουλεία τῆς φθορᾶς,[15] caused by sin, whose most conspicuous symptoms were want, disease, death, and exposure to

---

[15] Rom. 8:21.

demonic powers. How else could He achieve this self-manifestation to a carnal-minded and miracle-seeking generation than by just such miraculous works as the Gospels record? They formed the best possible object-lesson of the divine love and power that dwelt within Him. It was wrong of the Jews to cling to the external visible signs, instead of being brought by them to Jesus' person, to faith in His message, and to trust in Him as all-sufficient Saviour. But this perversity of theirs does not alter the fact that the miracles of Jesus were a most expressive sign-language revealing the mystery of His person and purpose, as well as an indispensable pedagogical means to faith in Him. It is in this sense that they are to be employed in the sermon. They are intended to show to men of today how our Lord validated in those days His claim to be the Saviour in the fullest sense of that word. Their purpose is to strengthen our faith, and to help us to believe ever more firmly that His power today has no bounds, that He can interfere in the order of the natural world and in the course of our little lives, when and where and as He will, and that no one can gainsay Him and nothing in the whole causal nexus of nature prevent Him; nay, that He will interfere whenever it becomes necessary in the carrying out of His saving plan with us. "Let us imagine," we add with Hunzinger, "a Jesus unable to deliver from their physical needs any sick, blind, deaf, lepers, lame, palsied and dead; a Jesus who did not free them from their physical distress, but only comforted and pointed them to the forgiveness of sins. Suppose Him to have stood helpless at sickbeds and before the dead. Suppose His own life to have ended with His death on the cross, without the greatest of miracles, His resurrection. Suppose the apostles had gone out into the world with this miracle-less portrait of Jesus, with this message of a non-miraculous Gospel. Imagine their missionary preaching without the fact of the resurrection. Do we believe that they would have conquered the world with this Jesus-picture? I do not. I am certain that in that case none of us would be Christians."[16] We will thus, in order not to make Christ less than nor different from the Christ the Gospels portray, include the miracle narratives among the sources of materials for the sermon.[17]

[16]*Religion als persoenliches Leben und Erleben*, p. 39.—[17]Comp. R. Kuebel, *Ueber den christlichen Wunderglauben* (1883); K. Beth, *Das Wunder, prinzipielle Eroerterung des Gegenstands* (1908); W. Herrmann, *Offenbarung und Wunder* (1908); A. B. Bruce, *The Miraculous Element in the Gospels* (1886); J. Wendland, *Miracles and Christianity* (1914); J. A. Faulkner, *Miracle and the Modern Man* (Methodist Review, Sept.-Oct., 1919).

How these are to be homiletically treated will be discussed in chapter 13.

As we read attentively *the words of Jesus,* we receive from them the same impression as their first hearers—"never man spake as this man." In their simple majesty and majestic simplicity, they surpass the mightiest prophetic and apostolic testimonies. At the very outset of the sermon on the mount we see this in the beatitudes, which combine in winsome form the profoundest demands with the loftiest promises. Behind the historical allusions to the Old Testament and to the spiritual state of His pious contemporaries, there opens an infinite background. Their application to men of every age, station and temperament will present no difficulty to the preacher who has submitted himself to these demands and experienced something of these promises. Wherever there exists a sense for moral purity and inner truthfulness, men will find themselves drawn to these sayings, even when they make demands and picture ideals that appear impossible. For many this description by Jesus of the life of a true disciple has been a school of experience in which they became aware of their own moral infirmity and filled with a desire for strength, and were thus driven to Jesus as to the One able not only to furnish the power of a new life, but also by His forgiveness to blot out the old life.

We know that serious doubts have been raised as to whether Jesus' *ethical teaching* has any value for our day. It is said that His ethics are too fragmentary, passing by unanswered many of the questions that occupy the modern mind. But it is forgotten that, if Jesus had given specific directions concerning industrial and political problems or concerning science and art, they must perforce have become obsolete with changing conditions and would then indeed be valueless for us today. Also, that if He had given His disciples a detailed rule of life, He would only have succeeded in binding burdens upon them, limiting their freedom and preventing their independent ethical thinking. Jesus did not want to be a lawgiver, a second Moses. He was not concerned with individual precepts, but with a change of spirit. He knew that where this new spirit was formed, it would of itself find a way into the various spheres of life. Or it is said that Jesus' ethical demands are based on a view of nature and the universe which we no longer hold. But, supposing this to be true, is ethical insight derived from scientific knowledge, and from natural science at that? Does it not flow from *conscience* rather than from *science?* Again, it has been claimed that Jesus' ethic is an ethic for a world doomed to speedy destruction, and that it therefore betrays so little understanding of the goods of this life, of the preservation, domination and perfecting of this world, of the life of the family, and of the whole field of culture and civilization. We men of today no longer share this expectation of impending world-doom and cannot, therefore, consider ourselves bound by Jesus' moral teachings. But it would be difficult, and in the case of His most important ethical precepts impossible, to prove that Jesus based His ethic on the expectation of the near end of the world. Read Matt. 16:26; 6:19; 6:24; 6:25, 28; 5:48, etc., and examine whether Jesus does not rather base His ethical precepts on the idea of a holy and merciful God. Yet again, it is claimed that Jesus' ethical demands are too high, and that it is utterly impossible to comply with them in the actual world in which we live. It is true, demands such as those in Matt. 5:39-41 and 5:44 are severe, and only gain in severity the more spiritually and less literally they are understood. When He says, "Resist not evil," Jesus demands a meekness that would rather suffer wrong than do wrong. When He bids us turn the other cheek, or let him that would take away our coat have our cloak also, He pictures a spirit that will tolerate in itself not a spark of vengefulness or retaliation, and would rather forego its rights than let itself be drawn into hatred. When He says, "Give to him that asketh thee, and from him that would borrow of thee turn not thou aside," Jesus points to the spirit of love that knows no bounds and recognizes no exception, that feels itself with all it is and has a debtor to the brother. In His fundamental requirement, "Be ye therefore perfect, even as your Father which is in heaven is perfect," He sets God before us as our pattern, not in this or that aspect, but on all sides and in all phases of His ethically perfect being. The fulfilment of these demands is indeed impossible and a cause of offence to the natural man. But Jesus does not address them to the natural man, but to His disciples who believe in Him and possess His Spirit as the power and motive of a good life. They are high and difficult for them too; but not unreasonably and not impossibly difficult, because they know and have at least begun to experience that "all things are possible to him that believeth." We are bound therefore to include the ethical injunctions of Jesus among His sayings as a source of sermon-material.[18]

---

[18]Comp. W. Herrmann, *Die sittlichen Weisungen Jesu* (1904); Ph. Bachmann, *Die Sittenlehre Jesu und ihre Bedeutung fuer die Gegenwart* (1904); Hastings Rashdall, *Conscience and Christ* (1916).

Among the words of Jesus the *parables* have always been regarded as a specially valuable source of sermon-material. Nowhere else are the laws, the principal duties and the precious privileges of Christ's Kingdom, as well as His relations with men set forth more plastically than here. Unfortunately, nowhere else has the sermon sinned more grievously against the laws of interpretation than in the parables. We shall later on discuss more fully the rules governing sermons on the parables.[19]

Particular attention should be given by the preacher to *the self-witness of Jesus* concerning His person and work. For this forms the very heart of the Gospels, whose pulsebeat must be felt in every sermon. In proportion as modern theology denies the divinity of His person and the saving value of His death, and seeks to dig a gulf between Jesus and Paul, and as these ideas filter down into our congregations, the preacher needs to focus his thoughts upon these portions of Jesus' self-witness and make them the living soul and centre of his sermons on the Gospels. This is by no means to be confined to the Fourth Gospel, which specially abounds in such self-witness, but must be applied also to the Synoptic Gospels, which are richer in these materials than is commonly recognized. The synoptists set Jesus on a level with Yahveh of the Old Testament, in the passages in which He calls Himself the shepherd of His people (Matt. 15:24; Mark 14:27 comp. with Ps. 23:1; Ezek. 34:9 ff.), the physician (Matt. 9:12; Mark 2:17; Luke 5:31 comp. with Ex. 15:26), the bridegroom (Mark 2:19, 20 comp. with the central idea of Hosea, esp. 2:19, 20), the one who alone forgives sins (Matt. 26:28 comp. with the ascription in the Old Testament of forgiveness to Yahveh alone), the only Saviour (Matt. 11:28 comp. with Hosea 13:9), the judge of all the world (Matt. 25:31ff. comp. with the ascription in the Old Testament of world-judgment to Yahveh alone). And even if the expression "son" in Matt. 16:16, 26, 63. 64 could be taken in an Old Testament sense (Ps. 2:7, 12) and identified with "Messiah," which is exegetically hardly possible, there would still remain the great passage in Matt. 11:27, in which He co-ordinates Himself with the Father as equal divine mystery incomprehensible to men. Unequivocal is the witness of the synoptists to the saving value of Jesus' life and especially of His death, in Matt. 20:28; 26:28, and in the passages in which He declares the fulfilment in Himself of the Old Testament prophecies concerning the "Servant of Yahveh" (Luke 4:18-21) and

---

[19] See below, chap. 13.

even of Isa. 53 (Luke 22:37). To this will come, with all the greater force, the self-witness of Jesus in almost every chapter of John's Gospel, as when He calls Himself the light of the world, the good shepherd giving his life for the sheep, the Son who was with the Father from eternity (John 8 and 17) and who is one with the Father (John 10:30).[20] Only from this vantage-point—the divine-human person of Christ—is it possible to present properly the sayings of Jesus concerning the Kingdom, the Church and its missionary duty, the second coming, judgment, and the completion of salvation. With respect to the future development of the world and the kingdom of God, it is necessary to bring home with greater clearness and force to the Christian consciousness, on the basis of His self-witness, the second coming of Jesus to judgment. For under the influence of Spencerian evolutionism men are dreaming of a gradual advance of mankind toward perfection, and losing the right estimate of the present dominated by sin; they have forgotten that the present development can be brought to final completion only by a catastrophic intervention of divine judgment, and they have lost that love and longing for Christ's appearance which has always characterized the periods of intensest Christian life. To interpret Jesus' sayings concerning His return of the coming of the Spirit at Pentecost, or to oppose to them the fact that αἰών is a term of various meanings and that παρουσία signifies also "presence," is to carry an element of truth to an unwarranted extreme, and to indulge in arbitrary exegesis.[21] Finally, to assert that the eschatology of Jesus belongs to the human and fallible in His person and to that part of His teaching which is dependent on Jewish apocalyptic, is to put the human wish in the place of divine revelation, to destroy the unity of Scripture specially evident in this article, and to introduce into the portrait of Jesus features at variance with the portrait of Him drawn in the Scriptures. An illustration of the destructiveness of this tendency may be seen in the discussion of the other world published in 1913 in the *Christliche Welt,* in connection with Zastrow's article "Geheimreligion der Gebildeten," and adopting in general the watchword, "We seek eternal life not there, but

---

[20]Comp. Grau, *Das Selbstbewusstsein Jesu* (1887); J. Kunze, *Die ewige Gottheit Jesu Christi* (1904); W. Walther, *Das Ichbewusstsein Jesu dem Menschengeschlecht gegenueber* (1914); parts of J. Denney, *The Death of Christ* (1911), and J. Moffatt, *The Theology of the Gospels* (1913).—[21]Comp. Zahn's *Kommentar* on the respective passages, und Cremer-Koegel, *Woerterbuch der Neutestamentl. Graezitaet* (10. ed., 1915), for the terminology.

here."²² It is true, the sermon must insist, as Jesus did, that eternal life is a present possession of the Christian, but it must also train its hearers to live in constant expectation of Him who will come again to judge the quick and the dead. This "other-worldliness," so far from idly folding its hands, has always manifested the most faithful activity in the world that now is, both in the struggle for personal holiness and in the extension of the kingdom of God.

The third place in the Gospels we have assigned to the accounts of Jesus' *intercourse with His disciples* and with the people, and His relations with His opponents and enemies. 'Here are seen, for our comfort, admonition and example, His holy love, His grace and compassion, His pastoral wisdom, and the energy of the good shepherd seeking His own, as well as His divine anger, zeal and rebuke. The latter no less than the former, though the former carries the stronger appeal. Gustav Benz says: "How customary it is, not only in Christian art but also in and under the pulpit, in hours of devotion and in devotional literature, in our own thinking, feeling and speaking, to represent Jesus as a pathetic, tender, compassionate man with soft hands and sweet lips. O surely there was never a man of finer and tenderer feeling than He, never one with a soul so full of deep compassion for all that sickened and sighed. But in this soul dwelt also a flaming holy wrath against all wrong and insincerity. That gracious mouth could break out in overwhelming woes upon hypocrites who glorified God with their lips and in their hearts resisted His Spirit. Those tender hands that were laid so lovingly and helpfully upon the sick and afflicted could also wield the scourge and drive the mammon-seeking tribe of merchants from His Father's sanctuary.—Or men make of Jesus an eternal dispenser of consolation and gather out of His Gospel all the sweet words of comfort and promise, just as children with a sweet tooth pick the raisins out of a cake. Such persons, naturally, Jesus will no longer offend. It is true that He has balm for broken hearts and wondrous cheer for timid souls, that He has hope and love where man no longer dares or is able to hope and love. But this same Jesus has demands that fall upon the soul like iron weights, and makes claims against which flesh and blood rebel. This same Jesus speaks of repentance and conversion, of judgment and rejection, of the mammon of unrighteousness, the deceitfulness of riches, the strait gate, the cross awaiting His disciples, the account to be given of every idle word. It is en-

---

²²Comp. *Kirchliche Zeitschrift,* 1913, p. 450; 1914, pp. 390-396.

tirely right to have a beautiful picture of Jesus in our room and to adorn our walls with His sayings. But if Jesus appears to us always as so supremely sweet and dear and good, if we are continually in the mood to speak of Him in petwords, I fear we do not yet truly know Him, not to say that we have not really begun to place our life and being under His influence. For Jesus is, as someone has said, 'an agitating and disquieting figure, big with lightning and tempest.' He is come, as He said, to bring a fire and to kindle a conflict. On His account the strongest human ties may have to be severed. When one desires to follow Him, it becomes necessary to break with men and things, to surrender old customs and habits of mind,—for which Jesus Himself chose the figure of plucking out the eye and cutting off the foot and the hand."[23] How else could Jesus deal with men, seeing He is the revelation of the divine essence and Himself God? For God is both holiness and love. But let no one, while emphasizing, as he is bound to do, these features of a demanding, wrathful and punishing holiness which meet us in Jesus' intercourse with men, fall into the opposite error and neglect His Saviour love, forgiving and covering sin! For the very heart of God as of Christ is, after all, love; *holy love* indeed, but no less holy *love*. Luke 2:10 and 29-32 find their complement in Luke 2:34, 35, and by the side of Matt. 16:21-28 stands Luke 15. Moreover, the same warning we referred to above is in place here: The preacher must not make the mistake of confining himself to the past in treating these passages, and of forgetting that the exalted Christ possesses and manifests even now the same saving grace, long-suffering, patience, and the same holiness, judging sin and excluding it from His fellowship. A fuller discussion of this point will follow in chapter 13.

The importance of the *Epistles* as a source of sermon-material is obvious from the fact that they were originally addressed to established Christian congregations and intended to be read in their public assemblies, to furnish instruction, comfort, defence and exhortation in their various necessities, dangers and duties, and thus to help them to become what they should be, that is, to edify them. They were thus addressed to the same sort of persons and pursued the same purpose, despite the difference in form, as the sermon of today. Just as the latter must do today, so the epistles point back to Jesus' saving work, especially to His death and resurrection, which they regard as the basis of the whole Christian life; they exhort to a constantly

---

[23]From a sermon on Matt. 11:6 in *In der Gewalt Jesu*, pp. 20 f.

renewed appropriation of Christ and the salvation obtained by Him; they summon men to unfold the divine life-powers inherent in faith throughout a life of true morality, and they fix their eyes on the final consummation. This is done, indeed, especially in Paul's epistles, with a copious use of Old Testament and Jewish conceptions and imagery; so that the preacher of today for whose congregation these conceptions and images have lost their meaning faces the not always simple task of introducing his hearers to this whole circle of ideas, in order to convey to them the truths revealed under these forms. If it seems an unreasonable demand to make of the modern Christian, that he live himself into this strange world,[24] it must not be forgotten that Paul unhesitatingly made this demand of his heathen-Christian congregations, to whom many of these Old Testament conceptions must have been unfamiliar, and that he did not in the least endanger nor diminish thereby the success of his missionary labors. Moreover, it is a general rule to seek for points of contact in the hearers' world of ideas, but these ideas are never allowed to become the criterion of the truth to be communicated. Yet this is just what, in the last analysis, the demand to eliminate Paul's theology would amount to.[25] It must further be borne in mind that in these passages it is not a question merely of this or that formal expression of a certain truth, but in most cases

---

[24]Comp., e. g., Rom. 3:21-30, esp. 25-27; 4:1-25; 5:12 ff.; 6:1-11; 1 Cor. 15; 2 Cor. 5; Gal. 3:1-14, 15-20; 4:1 ff.; Eph. 1:3-14; Phil. 3:1-11; Col. 1:9-23; 1 Thess. 4:13 ff.; 2 Thess. 2:1-12; Tit. 3:5-7; 1 Pet. 1:18-20; 2:9-10; 2:22-24; 3:18-22; 1 John 2:1-2, and whole chapters in Hebrews.—[25]Comp. O. Baumgarten, *Predigtprobleme*, pp. 61 ff.—"Attention is called today," says Kleinert, "often very emphatically, to the fact that our age lacks the terrified consciences that gave such glad welcome to the Pauline and the Reformation preaching. This is entirely true, and it would certainly be wrong for us to preach as though such consciences were to be found, and as though the spiritual agonies of a Paul or Luther were familiar experiences to our hearers. But it is none the less certain that the preaching of the Gospel can never assume that this lack of a consciousness of sin and guilt must be regarded as a normal condition to which the sermon should accommodate itself. If Jesus had so regarded it, He would have been spared, humanly speaking, the great conflict of His life. But He regarded it in a different light (Matt. 9:12 f.). Not without significance does He base His works of healing upon the word, 'Thy sins be forgiven thee.' This shows the sermon its duty. It must awaken the sense of need, it must re-establish, in a generation that insists on its rights but takes its duties lightly, the sense of duty and responsibility, and sharpen men's consciences thereby, if the Gospel is not to become, through the sermon's own fault, a loathsome food" (*Homiletik*, p. 64).

a question of that truth itself; as for example in the case of the Old Testament sacrificial idea and its relation to redemption through the blood of Christ. Nor do we admit in the epistles so marked a difference between the types of doctrine in Paul, Peter, John, Hebrews and James as to destroy the unity of the sermon-material derived from these writings. If one will only do justice to the whole Paul, the whole John or Peter, one will find indeed a refreshing diversity of presentation and emphasis, due to the differences in personality which the Holy Spirit never suppresses, and to the requirements of the respective situations, but by no means a different way of salvation. The epistolary literature of the New Testament is not, and does not profess to be, a text-book of dogmatics with fixed and stereotyped terminology, but a living testimony, abounding in a great variety of images, conceptions and representations of one and the same truth. This is what the sermon also should be. Where there is a will and a modicum of pedagogical aptness, these differences will form a welcome enrichment of the sermon rather than a danger to its unity. One further observation needs to be noticed in this connection. It is thought by some to escape the difficulties we have mentioned by distinguishing between the ethical and the doctrinal portions of the epistles and by making use of the former while discarding the latter. As a result, we seldom find such passages as the following treated in sermonic literature: Rom. 3:21-30; Gal. 3:1-14; Rom. 4:1-25; 5:12 ff.; Eph. 1:3-14; Col. 1:9-23; Heb. 2:14-15, etc. This was a defect of the sermon in the ancient Church, for which it had to pay dear. It is a defect of the modern sermon as well, and we too shall pay dear unless we overcome it. Its penalties have invariably been a tendency toward the relegation of doctrine to the background, an indifference to clear religious conceptions, and the reduction of Christianity to morality. An examination of *The Sermon Bible,* for illustration, on Hasting's *Great Texts of the Bible,* will furnish the proof of this. Even Alexander Maclaren, in his admirable *Expositions of Holy Scripture,* passes by in silence many of these fundamental doctrinal passages; as witness his treatment of Galatians, and the omission of Rom. 6:1-11 while a whole sermon is devoted to one of Paul's salutations in Rom. 16. Surely this is a dangerous suppression of important sources of sermon-material and does not conform to Paul's example of declaring to the church πᾶσα ἡ βουλὴ τοῦ θεοῦ (Acts 20:27).[26]

---

[26]In wrestling with this by no means simple problem the preacher

The *Book of Acts* was, curiously enough, little used homiletically in the early Christian centuries. Origen is said to have left seventeen homilies upon it. From Chrysostom we have fifty-five homilies, beginning with the complaint, "Many do not even know that such a book exists." A change came with the Reformation, and especially since Schleiermacher. Several of the new systems of pericopes take many lessons for the Trinity season from the Acts. This is proper. For must not the account of the founding of the Church and its earliest history prove exemplary for the life of the Church today? Will not the story of missions in the Acts supply incentive and encouragement to the modern mission worker? And what edifying value does there not lie in the life of Paul for the believer of today![27]

Does the *Revelation* also contain sermonic material? With respect to certain portions of the book, this has never been disputed. The seven letters of Jesus to the churches in Asia Minor furnish admirable material for the preacher. But he must not forget that the conditions that prevailed in the seven churches, while they are reflected in certain periods of the Church's past as well as in certain churches of the present, have no analogy in the individual congregation except in this or that member or group of members. This should be borne in mind especially by the preacher taking up each of the seven letters in turn before one and the same congregation. Rev. 5:1-14 forms an excellent Easter text. Chap. 7:13-17, a witness of Christian hope, is often used toward the close of the Church Year or at burials; so, too, chaps. 14:13 and 21:1-5. Or why should there not be a treatment, in connection with 5:1-14; 11:15-18; 12:10-12; 19:7-9, of the whole comforting argument of the book—the certainty of the final victory of Christ and His saints? In general it may be said that any

---

will find much to learn from Luther; Heubner, *Praktische Erklaerung des N. T.;* Besser, *Bibelstunden zum N. T.;* Thomasius, *Erklaerung des Kolosserbriefs* (admirable); Koegel, *Der Roemerbrief in Predigten. Der 1. Petribrief in Predigten;* Dryander, *Der 1. Johannisbrief in Predigten;* Schlatter, *Erlaeuterungen zum N. T.* (3 vols., excellent); F. W. Robertson, *Sermons on St. Paul's Epistles to the Corinthians;* R. Leighton's *Commentary on First Peter;* Gess, *Bibelstunden ueber den Roemerbrief;* Moule, *Ephesian Studies, Philippian Studies, Colossian Studies* (to be highly commended); several volumes in Mayer's *Das N. T. in religioesen Betrachtungen;* K. Barth, *Der Roemerbrief* (1919; especially for the points discussed above).

[27]Comp. besides Besser's *Bibelstunden,* Gerok's *Von Jerusalem nach Rom* and Maclaren's *Expositions,* especially Roemheld, *Durch Kampf zum Sieg* (1900) and Dryander, *Das Leben des Apostels Paulus in Predigten* (1905).

portion of Revelation expressing a truth which has already been expressed by Jesus may unhesitatingly be regarded as a proper source of sermon-material. Many such passages serve by the grandeur of their imagery to make more vivid and clear the abstract truths elsewhere stated. To all other parts of the book Palmer's words may be applied,—"We know very well that by doing this [interpreting the various details] with a certain degree of skill we could gain the admiring respect of the multitude and attract throngs of hearers. Many for whom the simple preaching of the Gospel has lost its charm, would much rather hear the latest fad concerning the millennium, the first and second resurrection, etc. But what is gained by this? Spiritual curiosity alone is satisfied, or not so much satisfied as the more excited."[28] No one should undertake to treat the entire book in a series of sermons unless he possesses the sobriety of a Klaus Harms.[29] The treatment of Revelation before a smaller group of hearers is a different matter; but this should have for its purpose the refutation or forestalling of erroneous interpretations rather than the presentation of one's own view as the only correct one.[30] The nearer the world draws to its end, the more will the book as a whole minister to the comfort and instruction of the Church of God.

What is to be said of the results of modern research in the *history of religions?* Has it not been proved that all of the more important acts and sayings of Jesus and of the apostles, as reported in the New Testament, have parallels in the myths and legends of heathen religions, and that they therefore belong to the domain of the mythical or, if they contain historical elements, these cannot be regarded as distinctive of the New Testament nor assigned the importance in the history of salvation which the Church assigns them? Has it not been shown that there lingered in the religion of the apostolic Church and even of the apostles themselves numerous relics of heathen superstition, such as sorcery, the worship and fear of spirits, a belief in series of aeons and heavenly intermediary beings? So that the religion of primitive Christianity stood upon a much lower level than that of the Church of today, and consequently cannot be considered normative, as the preaching on New Testament and especially apos-

---

[28]*Homiletik* (2. ed., 1845), p. 207.—[29]*Die Offenbarung Johannis, gepredigt nach einzelnen Abschnitten aus derselbigen* (1844).—[30]Comp. Goesswein, *Die Offenbarung Joh.;* Busch, *Die Offenbarung Joh.* (valuable); I. T. Beckwith, *The Apocalypse of John* (1919), by far the best thing we have in English; A. S. Peake, *The Revelation of John* (1919); Bezzel, *Die Offenbarung Joh.* (1920).

tolic texts presupposes. It is not proved that the Apocalypse in particular, with its visions of heaven and revelations of the abyss, God and Christ taking the word, angels ascending and descending, blowing on trumpets and crying aloud, a pregnant woman in heaven, mysterious riders trampling the world, dragons emerging and cast out, the measurement of the earthly and the description of the heavenly Jerusalem, the river and the tree of life, utilizes apocalyptic materials current in contemporary Jewish and heathen circles? It is impossible to enter into a detailed discussion of the principles and methods of the study of comparative religion.[81] It must suffice to set down briefly the following considerations, for the sake of preachers who have allowed their relation to the Scriptures to be affected by the results of this school of research. How does it happen that the miracles and faith in the miraculous found in the non-Christian world, coincident with the rise of Christianity, exerted no religious or moral influence upon their votaries, while faith in the supernatural birth of Christ, in the authenticity of His prophetic ministry, and in the saving value of His death and resurrection, equipped its confessors with an unwavering assurance of peace with God, with an impregnable and soul-satisfying power and truth liberating their lives from superstition and the fear of men, and with gratitude to their heavenly Father whom they strove to honor and glorify by faithfulness in their calling and by love of their fellowmen?[82] Even if it were true that the doctrine of angels and demons, as we meet it in Matt. 18:10; Rom. 8:33, in Colossians and elsewhere, is mere superstition and a remnant of an only partially defeated heathenism, would these passages be thereby excluded from pulpit use? Will not the conviction underlying them, —that nothing can harm us, but that all things must serve our heavenly Father in His saving work for His children,—prove of the highest value even to the most advanced congregation of the present day?[83] Even if Paul's doctrine of the sacraments should be shown to reveal points of contact with the mystery religions, does it follow that it is

---

[81]Comp. C. Clemen, *Die religionsgeschichtliche Methode in der Theologie* (1904); L. Lemme, *Religionsgeschichtl. Entwicklung oder goettliche Offenbarung* (1904); P. Feine, *Das Christentum Jesu und das Christentum der Apostel in ihrer Abgrenzung gegen die Religionsgeschichte* (1904); A. W. Hunzinger, *Probleme und Aufgaben der gegenwaertigen systematischen Theologie* (1909); H. E. Weber, *Historisch-kritische Schriftforschung und Bibelglaube* (2. ed., 1914).—
[82]Comp. C. F. G. Heinrici, *Die Eigenart des Christentums* (1911).
[83]Comp. E. von Dobschuetz, *Der gegenwaertige Stand der neutestamentl. Exegese in seiner Bedeutung fuer die praktische Auslegung*

actually derived from them?[84] Does the fact that Revelation makes such ample use of apocalyptic imagery current among the Jewish and heathen contemporaries of its author prove that the ideas clothed in this imagery—the divine counsel and will of Him who sits above the turmoil of mankind, Christ the master of history, and His Church's final victory over all hostile powers—are purely imaginary, and that this book carries no message for the Christianity of today?[85] There is therefore no reason for altering or modifying our estimate of the New Testament as source of homiletic material.

We come to the *Old Testament*, which has been on the one hand excluded altogether, and on the other greatly overestimated as a source of sermon-material. Here again it is necessary to distinguish, according to the principle stated above, between those parts that lend themselves and those that do not lend themselves to homiletic treatment. To exclude the Old Testament entirely would be to deprive the Church of a rich treasure of truly edifying material, and to run counter to the attitude of Jesus as well as to the use of the Old Testament by the apostles and to specific New Testament references to its value for the Christian.[86]

We think of the *Psalms,* among the poetical books of the Old Testament, with their lofty descriptions of the omnipotence, omniscience, omnipresence and eternity of God, with their emphasis upon His mercy and grace, His faithfulness and truth, with their wealth of religious experience in penitent humility, jubilant faith and fervent prayer and waiting on the Lord. How seldom it becomes necessary here to translate Old

---

(Zeitschrift f. Theol. u. Kirche, 1906); H. von Soden, *Ist die historisch-kritische Behandlung des Neuen Testaments berufen, seine Bedeutung fuer das religioese Leben zu mindern oder zu steigern?* (1910).

[84] Comp. Heinrici, *Ist das Urchristentum eine Mysterienreligion?* (Internationale Wochenschrift fuer Wissenschaft, Kunst und Technik, 1911); Henry C. Sheldon, *The Mystery Religions and the N. T.* (1918); W. H. P. Hatch, *The Pauline Idea of Faith in Its Relation to Jewish and Hellenistic Religion* (Harvard Theol. Studies, ii, 1917.)—[85] Comp. H. E. Weber, *Die Vollendung des neutestamentl. Glaubenszeugnisses durch Johannes* (1912).—[86] Rom. 15:4; 2 Tim. 3:16.

Testament conceptions into those of the New Testament, and how irresistible is the *argumentatio a minore ad majus,* that is, the train of thought: If Old Testament believers could manifest such trust in God and obtain such benefits from Him, how much more can and should this be true of us, who have received so much greater and better things under the New Testament dispensation! In the *prophetic* books law and Gospel are presented in a truly New Testament sense. The predictions of good things to come may be used with profit especially in preparation for the great Christian festivals, when the Christian Church resembles that of the Old Testament in its expectancy and longing for complete redemption. In these predictions, moreover, the salvation of the world is set forth as the perfect fulfilment of the age-long yearning and striving of mankind, so that all that Christ is and means is thus seen in its true grandeur and inexhaustible riches.[87] The *historical* portions of the Old Testament likewise contain a wealth of permanently valid truths, whose place can be taken by nothing else, in their depiction of the leading of people and individuals, which repeats itself, in modified and heightened form, on the plane of the New Testament. The preacher who wishes to illustrate the nature of faith by living biblical examples must go to the narratives of the Old Testament. If he wishes to emphasize the principle that "righteousness exalteth a nation, but sin is a reproach to any people,"[38] he will find its finest exemplification in the history of Israel. Here is seen the practical application of true religion in the various social relationships, whereas in the New Testament the underlying principles are fully stated, but seldom developed and applied. Provided only that the preacher takes his stand under the cross of Calvary, it is scarcely possible to overestimate the edifying value of the entire course of Old

---

[87]Comp. Luke 10:23 f.—[88]Prov. 14:34.

Testament history, with its constantly recurring factors of human sin and divine grace, and with its continual forward trend toward Christ as its end and goal. It both magnifies Christ and makes it clear to the Christian congregation that all communion between God and man has depended from the very beginning upon grace and faith. Even the Old Testament law may become, in certain aspects of it, a legitimate source of evangelical sermon-material, if it is regarded from the viewpoint of Christ. What a wealth of material is contained in Deuteronomy, of value to the Christian so far as he lives in this imperfect state, to point out to him his sin and moral weakness and drive him again and again into the arms of his Saviour, and so far as he is regenerated, to teach him the unchangeable will of a holy God and thereby the true nature of good works.

But our principle also distinguishes for us those parts of the Old Testament that are not adapted as sermon-material. It excludes long stretches in Exodus and Deuteronomy, and still longer ones in Leviticus and Numbers. For though even the so-called civil and ceremonial law was a παιδαγωγὸς εἰς Χριστόν,[39] it was this for Israel alone; and though it is true that, despite its abrogation, it contains unchanging thoughts of God which still have value for the Christian, these are scarcely adapted to form the basis of Christian sermons. Our principle excludes also portions of the other historical books, such as the list of nations in Gen. 10, the genealogies, and the accounts of the partition of Canaan among the twelve tribes, as well as narratives lying on the outer rim of the history of salvation or by their minute detail precluding homiletic treatment, as the accounts of the building of the temple. And who would preach on the imprecatory psalms, unless for the purpose of bringing out the sharp contrast between Old and New Testa-

---

[39] Gal. 3:23.

ment morality? Or who would wish to preach through the whole of Job, despite the religious value and literary merit of this extraordinary book? Many a page even in the prophets, especially the numerous threats and woes upon Israel's neighbors, must either be excluded or treated in weekday lectures rather than in the sermon proper.

In order to preach wisely and well upon Old Testament texts, the preacher should always bear in mind two facts. On the one hand, that it is the same God of our salvation who has revealed Himself in the Old Testament, in deed and word, and who meets us in the New Testament as the Father of our Lord Jesus Christ. And on the other hand, that His revelation in the Old Testament, while leading up to Christ, is of merely preparatory character; so that it must be determined from the standpoint of Christ—both on the mount of beatitudes and on Mount Calvary—what in it is of value and what is not.[40] The former of these two principles was axiomatic for Jesus and for Paul; hence they regarded the Old Testament as Holy Scripture which could not be broken,[41] and the faith of Abraham as a type of New Testament faith.[42] And they were no less firmly convinced of the second; hence, while the life and works of Jesus are presented, even in minute particulars, under the aspect of prophecy and fulfilment, the "But I say unto you" of the sermon on the mount is given its full prominence, and Paul can on the one hand declare that the Christian life is the Spirit-wrought righteousness demanded by the Old Testament law,[43] and write on the other a word like Col. 2: 16, 17. The preacher who cannot draw clearly this distinction will only mislead, and not edify, his congregation. (P. 289.)

---

[40]Comp. J. Koeberle, *Heilsgeschichtliche und religionsgeschichtliche Betrachtungsweise des Alten Testaments* (Neue kirchliche Zeitschrift, 1906).—[41]John 10:35.—[42]Rom. 4; Gal. 3; comp. Heb. 11.—[43]Rom. 8:2-4.

THE OLD TESTAMENT IN THE ANCIENT CHURCH   275

In the Ancient Church the Old Testament was from a variety of causes a favorite source of the sermon. As long as the *lectio continua* was in vogue and furnished the text for the sermon,[44] it was only natural, because of the greater extent of the Old Testament, that sermons on Old Testament greatly outnumbered those on New Testament texts. In addition to this, the allegorical method of interpretation permitted the preacher to read the entire contents of the New Testament into the Old; there was no real sense of the difference between the two Testaments, and the centre of gravity in the Christian life was soon shifted from an evangelical to a legal basis. All this contributed to a disproportionate use of the Old Testament. Origen, in whom all of these tendencies meet, seems indeed to have preached upon every book of the Bible; but of his two hundred extant sermons, all but the thirty-nine homilies on Luke's gospel are on Old Testament texts. In the case of Augustine these tendencies do not enter in, and the Old Testament occupies a less disproportionate place in his preaching. And since, notwithstanding his habit of allegorizing, he regarded, much more decidedly than Origen, the Old Testament events as actual historical happenings, and usually examined their historical meaning before resorting to allegorical interpretation, and especially because he had a clear understanding of the place of the Old Testament in the history of salvation, his Old Testament sermons are much sounder than those of Origen and of all other preachers up to his time. The following quotations, chosen from various writings of his, indicate what he conceived to be the requirements of a sound treatment of the Old Testament. "Novum Testamentum in Vetere latet, Vetus in Novo patet." "Tales ergo illos viros vel homines habebat Deus et illo tempore tales fecerat praecones Filio venturo, ut non solum in his quae dicebant, sed etiam in his quae faciebant vel in his quae illis accidebant, Christus quaeratur, Christus inveniatur. Quidquid Scriptura dicit de Abrahamo et factum est et prophetia est."[45] "Omnia quae in Vetere Testamento scripta sunt, nos et vera esse dicimus et divinitus mandata et congruis temporibus distributa."[46] "Distingue tempora et concordabit Scriptura." "Whatever is written in Scripture prior to the coming of the Lord has no other purpose than to bring home to men's hearts His coming, and to designate the Church in her future appearance as the people of God, which is His body, scattered abroad among the nations. In this are included

---

[44]Comp. our *History of Preaching.*—[45]*Sermo* ii, tom. v: "De tentatione Abr. et de Deo."—[46]*Contra Faustum, lib.* x, 3.

also all the saints who lived before His advent into the world, these believing in His future appearance, even as we believe in His past appearance. Before he was born, Jacob stretched forth his hand out of his mother's womb and took hold of the heel of his brother born before him; then only did the head follow, and of necessity the remaining members. And yet the head surpasses in dignity and power not only the members that followed, but also the hand that preceded it, and is their leader, if not in the order of appearance, yet in the order of importance. Even so our Lord Jesus Christ, before He appeared in the flesh, and as it were emerged from the womb of the mystery of His being, a man before men, the mediator between God and men, God blessed over all for ever, sent before Him a part of His being in the blessed patriarchs and prophets, whereby as with His hand He announced aforetime His birth; nay, with the fetters of the law, as with the five fingers of His hand, He cast down to the ground the people that proudly preceded Him. . . . Now, although our Lord Christ sent before a part of His being in the person of the saints who preceded Him with respect to the time of birth, nevertheless He Himself is the head of the Church, which is His body; and to this same body all those saints belonged, by virtue of their faith in Him whose coming they foretold."[47]

In the Middle Ages, the Old Testament was seldom treated, principally because the system of pericopes, which had by this time arisen and which was largely followed in preaching, contained no texts from this Testament. What Old Testament preaching there was, was more nearly related to Origen than to Augustine.

Luther was deeply interested in the Old Testament and concerned that it should be homiletically utilized. In his *Von Ordnung Gottesdienstes in der Gemeinde* he writes: "This was the practice of Christians in the days of the apostles. And it should still be our practice today, to meet together for an hour every morning at four or five o'clock, and to have a scripture lesson read by the schoolboys, priests or whoever it may be, as is done in the present matin service. . . . Thereupon the preacher. . . . should arise and expound a portion of this lesson, so that all the rest may understand, learn and lay the same to heart. This lesson should be taken from the Old Testament, reading one book after another, chapter by chapter, until the whole Bible has been read through. . . . A similar service should be held in the evening, at five or six. And here again the lesson should be from the Old Testament, one book after another; the evening lesson from

---

[47] *De catech. rudibus*, 3, 4-10. Comp. M. Reu, *Catechetics*, pp. 31 f.

the prophets, as the morning lesson was from Moses and the historical books. But, since the New Testament is also a book, I assign the Old Testament to the morning and the New to the evening, or vice versa."[48] According to this, he would have the Old Testament read and expounded at least in the early service on week-days. In his *Deutsche Messe* of 1526, he goes a step farther. Though on weekdays he would substitute catechism sermons and the New Testament for the reading and exposition of the Old Testament, yet "on Sunday afternoon" he says, "at vespers, before the Magnificat, we preach the Old Testament in regular order."[49]—We possess a considerable number of Luther's Old Testament sermons, especially on Moses, a number of psalms, and portions of Isaiah. Besides Luther, Brenz, among the Lutheran reformers, was specially fond of Old Testament texts; most of his commentaries on the Old Testament grew out of his preparation for the pulpit. Thus, from 1534 to 1540, he preached on Genesis, Deuteronomy and Joshua, later on Isaiah, again on Genesis, and on Exodus. That there was no change in this attitude of the Lutheran Church in the years following, may be seen by consulting Aquila's Trostpredigt from Zephaniah (1530); the sermons on the psalms, in whole or in part, of Rhegius (1537), Coelius, Moerlin (1580), Menzel (1594), Jacob Andreae (1561) and Nic. Selneccer (1570); on the prophets by V. Dietrich (1548), Joh. Mathesius (1588), Saccus (1567), Cyr. Spangenberg (1560), Selneccer (1569), Mirus (1603), Strigenitz (1593) and A. Hunnius (1590, 1611), and on parts of Genesis by Andreae (1566) and S. Musaeus (1594). In the seventeenth century, too, Lutheran preachers frequently treated Old Testament texts. We mention Philip Nicolai's sermons on Hosea 14 (1609), Herberger's *Magnalia* (1601 ff.) and their continuation in *Psalterparadies* (1627 ff.), Samson's eleven sermons on Gen. 3:15 (1620) and on Ezek. 38, Ph. Han's *Postilla prophetica* (1610), J. Arnd's exposition of the Psalter in 451 sermons (1617), J. Luetkemann's *Harfe von zehn Saiten* (1658), W. Alardus' penitential sermons from Genesis (1635 f.)). With Spener's sermons on Daniel's penitential prayer (1706) and J. B. Carpzov's *Des Evangelisten Alten Testaments Jesajae Sonn- und Festtagsevangelien* (1719) we have already crossed over into the eighteenth century. These names by no means exhaust the list.

Luther's Old Testament sermons are not free from the defects that appear in his predecessors. We especially meet almost constantly the allegorical method of interpretation, which he had overcome in

---

[48] *Weimar ed.*, xii, p. 35.—[49] *Weimar ed.*, xix, p. 79. .

theory and employed with less and less frequency in his New Testament sermons. But even in his use of allegory a decided difference is to be noted. It is no longer so arbitrary as before; he never bases a doctrine upon it, but reads into his text only such truths as are already established as biblical in other texts; and he insists, more even than Augustine, not only that the historicity of the allegorized passages must be maintained, but that the literal and historical sense is "the principal thing," upon which more depends than upon anything else. Thus he writes in a sermon on Ex. 1: "We must take out of the Scriptures the true treasure, den Kern, Kraft, Macht, Saft und Schmuck, which is the example of faith and love; to this we must look. Where God has written it plain, you have no need to dig deep. Afterwards, when you have got the principal thing, you may introduce a secret interpretation alongside the plain text, and adorn the latter and hang beautiful spangles about it, as St. Paul also does." This explains why his commentary on Genesis, despite its allegorical eccentricities, is still a valuable treasure-house for those who wish to penetrate into the historical meaning of these chapters. Luther's fullest discussion of the homiletic use of the Old Testament is found in his introduction to Genesis, the "Unterweisung, wie sich die Christen in Moses schicken sollen." In Moses, he says, there are three kinds of material. There is, first, the divine preaching of the law, which preaching, however, is binding upon Christians only in so far as it agrees with the natural law. Secondly, there is "that which I have not by nature, viz., the predictions and promises of God concerning Christ; and this is by far the best thing in the whole book." "In the third place, we read Moses for the sake of the fine examples of faith, love and the cross in the good holy fathers Adam, Abel, Noah, Abraham, Isaac, Jacob, Moses, and so on to the end, by which examples we are to learn to trust and love God. We see also, on the other hand, examples of the unbelief of ungodly men and of the wrath of God, and are shown how God does not overlook the unbelief of unbelievers, but punishes Cain, Ishmael, Esau, and the whole world in the deluge. . . . And these examples are needed; for though I am not Cain, yet if I do as Cain did, I shall be punished as Cain was punished. Nowhere else outside of Moses do we find such fine examples of faith and of unbelief. Therefore Moses should not be hidden under the bench. And this is the right understanding of the whole Old Testament,—to keep in mind the fine sayings in the prophets concerning Christ, to comprehend and mark the fine examples, and to use the laws according to our good pleasure and turn them to our profit."

Here Luther draws the right distinction between the permanent and the temporary elements in the Old Testament, without which distinction there can be no sermons on Old Testament texts edifying for the Christian. The first of these three distinctions in particular lays down a principle of evangelical faith that had been hidden for many centuries. He sees clearly, moreover, that the prophets cannot be understood or expounded without an accurate knowledge of their times. Thus he writes in his "Preface to the Prophets" (1532): "Reason regards the prophets as very insignificant, as though there were little of value in them. This is specially true when Master Wiseacre comes upon them, who knows the whole Bible by heart and to a T; he considers them, in his wealth of intellect, nothing but empty and dead wish-wash. This comes from the fact that the happenings and works are no longer kept before men's eyes, and only the words or histories are heard." He accordingly made it his concern, in his own exposition of the prophets, to give more room than was customary to depicting the condition of the times, in order to interpret the prophetic message in its historical framework. The limitations of his attitude to the Old Testament do not lie in this direction, but rather in his failure to grasp fully and apply consistently the law of development and gradual progress of divine revelation. If he had known and applied this law, not only would he have been no less convinced that the Old Testament histories were "figures of Christ," and able to hold even more firmly than he did to the position that the whole old Testament history formed a type and prefiguration of Christ and His Church, but he would have found it impossible to read New Testament revelations and conceptions into the Old Testament, as though they were contained there in their full development and definiteness instead of being present only in germ. This continued to be the limitation of the later Lutheran sermon on Old Testament subjects; it remained for the nineteenth century to bring about a change.

Zwingli and Calvin diligently fostered the Old Testament sermon. Both of them rejected the system of pericopes and were fond of preaching through book after book of the Bible; both of them, though each in his own way, regarded the New Testament as law rather than as Gospel of the grace of God in Christ Jesus, and thus blurred the distinction between the two Testaments. Hence their sermons on the Old Testament greatly outnumbered those on the New. We have sermons by Zwingli on the psalms and the prophets; by Calvin on 1 Sam., Job, the minor prophets, the story of Melchizedek, the justification of Abraham, the sacrifice of Isaac, 134 sermons on

Deuteronomy, etc. This predominance of the Old Testament remained a characteristic of the Reformed Church, and from the same causes as in the case of Zwingli and Calvin. We mention, e. g., Bullinger's 190 homilies on Isaiah (1565), also on Jeremiah and Daniel, L. Lavater's 141 sermons on Job, R. Gualther's (Walter's) 327 *Archetypi homiliarum in Esaiam* (1590), A. Scultetus's *Psalmenpostille* (1620), J. Mueller's seventy-eight sermons on Joel (1667), and in the next century, the Old Testament sermons delivered at The Hague by the French preacher Jacques Saurin († 1730), which we shall more fully discuss, with honorable mention, in our "History of Preaching."

Zwingli's and especially Calvin's sermons on the Old Testament have the following features in common with those of Luther. They present the Old Testament saints as patterns and warning examples; they manifest—this is specially true of Calvin—pre-eminent skill in tracing analogies between Old Testament times and their own day, and they make much of the types of Christ. They surpass Luther's sermons in their almost complete freedom from the allegorical method; this is again specially true of Calvin. But they suffer, even more than Luther's Old Testament sermons, from the limitation mentioned above; they seem to know nothing of the gradual development of divine revelation and consequently of the merely preparatory character of the Old Testament. The unity and continuity of the Old and the New Testament people of God are so strongly stressed that there is no room for such development. Old Testament directions are taken over bodily into the life of the New Testament people of God, and the expositor unhesitatingly seeks and finds the whole New Testament revelation in the Old. Moreover, the conception so clearly and emphatically insisted on by Luther, of the temporary significance of the Old Testament law, is here applied to the ceremonial law alone, while the direct opposite is constantly claimed for the other portions of the law. Not only is Paul's fundamental principle of the law as an "interpolation"[50] forgotten, but the law is set in the very centre of the Old Testament, while for Calvin even the New Testament is nothing other than a *nova lex*. This fundamental defect has unfortunately characterized the Reformed sermon, not only on Old Testament texts, up to the present, as we may see and hear all about us.

It was characteristically enough, a Reformed preacher whose homiletic treatment of the Old Testament, at the beginning of the nineteenth century, marked an epoch. This was Gottfried Menken of

---

[50]Gal. 3: 19 ff.; comp. Moffatt's fine rendering.

Bremen († 1831). His preference was pronounced for Old Testament texts, or at least Old Testament persons, as in his fourteen homilies on Heb. 11. He tells us why, in the preface to his published sermons. "But why so many sermons on Old Testament texts? Among other reasons, in order that you, dear reader who ask this question, may not complain and ask: Why so many sermons on New Testament texts? Nothing but sermons on the New Testament. Does not the Old Testament manifestly need more elucidation and exposition than the New? Is the Old Testament to be treated thoroughly and scientifically only in the lecture rooms of our universities? And is not this the purpose of that thorough and scientific study, that the future ministers of the divine Word may one day be able to lead their congregations to an understanding and appreciation of the Old Testament? Why is there not more labor put, in the circle of Christian congregations, on the book that served the Son of God during His days upon earth as the light and rule of His whole life? Indeed, the New Testament without the Old is like a building without foundation; like the fragmentary second half of a tale whose first half has been lost and whose full meaning can now no longer be understood. It is like the beautiful and sonorous conclusion of a discourse torn from its beginning, which fills the soul, but cannot still it, leaving behind a sadness and burning desire to discover the beginning from which alone this more divine than human discourse could be built up, and which now, alas! does not quite convince, not quite satisfy, because it is broken off, and incomplete, and in its present form without meaning." Menken was admirably equipped for a fruitful homiletic treatment of the Old Testament. He possessed in a pre-eminent degree the ability to enter psychologically into the state of mind of the Old Testament personages, and can therefore depict exemplary features and situations with such clearness that but a few strokes suffice to drive the application home; in fact he usually leaves the hearers to make their own application. He was a pronounced opponent of allegory, yet had a keen eye for the prefigurative significance of Old Testament history and law. He regarded the Scriptures, like Hofmann after him, as a homogeneous, organic whole from which, despite its gradual growth, no single member can be separated without injury to the whole; and in this understanding of the whole he found the key to the interpretation of the several parts. Thus he says: "Many stand as if blinded before the glory of the Bible. They would fain behold it, yet cannot find the angle whence it must burst upon their sight. They gaze at the several parts, and these become to them so many stones of stumbling and rocks of offence. If they would find the place whence they could view the whole, they would find in this view of the whole the foundation and cornerstone of truth, and the rock of certainty from which they could see the billows and floods of doubt and quibbling, of opinions and misinterpretations dissolve in empty spray at their feet." He himself had found in Christ the point in which the whole is gathered up, and from which each part is seen in its true light. And he seldom interpreted the Old Testament in such a way as to obscure Rom. 10:4, or to impress a legal character upon the Christian life. But one particular Menken, too, failed to appreciate sufficiently,—the fact of the progressiveness of divine revelation, which once for all forbids the importing of New Testament conceptions into the Old Testament, and the portrayal of the lives of Old Testament saints as direct patterns of Christian faith and life.

That Menken's ardent championship of the Old Testament as a homiletic source, and the example of his own sermons did not bring about a more general use of the Old Testament in the pulpit, was due, apart from his rather isolated position, chiefly to the sharp antagonism of Schleiermacher to the Old Testament. In his *Der christliche Glaube* the latter writes: "With respect to the inspiration of the Old Testament writings, we must first distinguish between the law and the prophets. If the apostle is right in describing the law, though a divine ordinance, as something interpolated between the promise of Abraham's seed and the fulfilment of this promise (Gal. 3: 19), and in maintaining, moreover, that it lacks the power of the Spirit from which the Christian life must proceed (Rom. 7:6 ff.; 8:3), then it cannot be claimed that the law was inspired by this Spirit, of whom the same apostle says that He is not received by the law nor the works of the law (Gal. 3:3), but that God sends Him into the hearts of men by virtue of our connection with Christ. Similarly Christ never describes the sending of the Spirit, whose witness He co-ordinates with the witness of the disciples, in any other way than as the return of one who had already been present and had departed for a season. But on the law hang also all the historical books since the giving of the law. For if we set messianic prophecy, as most nearly related to Christianity, over against the law, as most foreign to it, no one will dare to claim that the Jewish historical books contain the history of messianic prophecy rather than the history of the law. Indeed, the greater part of the contents of even the prophetic books refers to the legal organization and the circumstances of the Jewish people as such; and the spirit out of which they arise is none other than that of the community of the people, and therefore is not the Christian Spirit which, as one, is to break down the wall of partition between this people and the rest. Thus there is left only messianic prophecy as having part in inspiration as we understand it. But if we reflect that the prophets rise to this prophecy only in isolated moments, and that the Spirit moving and animating them is called "holy" with respect to these moments alone (2 Pet. 1:21), we must conclude that here, too, inspiration can be spoken of only in a figurative sense, in so far as this community spirit, joined to the consciousness of the need of salvation, and expressing itself as the presentiment (Ahnung) of a more inward and spiritual rule of God, possessed in itself, and was able to kindle and preserve outside itself, the highest form of receptivity for the Holy Spirit. If we enquire, in the second place, as to the normal dignity, and first as to the productive normal dignity, it cannot on the whole be denied that the pious mind of the evangelical Christian recognizes generally a great difference between these two kinds of sacred writings. Even the noblest psalms contain some things that Christian piety cannot appropriate as its purest expression. So that one is compelled, by unconscious additions and omissions, to delude oneself, if one imagines it possible to construct the Christian doctrine of God from the prophets and psalms. On the other hand, a decided preference for the use of Old Testament passages as the expression of the pious self-consciousness is almost always accompanied by a legalistic trend of mind or an unfree worship of the letter. As to the critical side, finally, of the normal dignity of Scripture, there are indeed few Christian doctrines which men have not at various periods attempted to establish by Old Testament proof texts. But how can it be possible that anything pertaining to the doctrine of redemption through Christ should have been so plainly stated in the period of mere presentiment that it can still be profitably used alongside what has been said by Christ Himself and by His disciples after His completed work of redemption?"[50a] That Christ and His apostles found a point of contact in the Old Testament, is for Schleiermacher of merely historical value. So far from its being a proof of the permanent value of the Old Testament, it is on the contrary only natural that the later Church should no longer need this point of contact. For the New Testament Church the New Testament is all-sufficient. "It belongs indeed to historical truth and completeness, that that to

---

[50a] § 132; 3rd ed. (1835), vol. ii, pp. 347-51.

which Christ and His first heralds appealed should be preserved. This, however, applies almost exclusively to the prophetic writings and the psalms; and this fact justifies the practice of adding them as an appendix to the New Testament. But since these writings did not exist separately in the days of Christ, but only as parts of the sacred collection, and are frequently quoted in this way, and since, moreover, individual quotations from other books occur, no one can raise any objection to combining the Old Testament as a whole with the New, even though it cannot possibly be an indivisible whole for us in the same sense as for the Jewish people. Only, it would correspond more closely to the actual facts if the Old Testament followed the New as an appendix; for its present location clearly sets up the demand that one must first work one's way through the Old Testament, in order to find the right approach to the New."[51]—Among Schleiermacher's numerous published sermons there are only fifteen on Old Testament texts, and it is notable that fourteen of these are sermons on special occasions, mostly concerning the country and nation. In one of them he explain his choice of text: "From the bearing of this festival upon the society which we form as a nation it becomes clear that the books of the Old Testament contain richer material and are more appropriate for such a day, because these older writings refer exclusively to the common life of that nation which God chose for a peculiar destiny." These Old Testament sermons of Schleiermacher are well worth careful study.

It is not at all surprising that Schleiermacher's attitude to the Old Testament, considering the mighty influence he wielded upon the widest circles, completely discredited preaching on Old Testament texts. The more since his criticism, despite its one-sidedness, was based on premises containing important elements of truth, which it will be well for us to keep in mind. It required the life-long labors of Hengstenberg on the one hand, and of Hofmann and Delitzsch on the other, to bring about a return to the Old Testament and to lay a sound foundation for its homiletical use. Hengstenberg restored confidence in the Old Testament, but did not carry the work farther. This remained for Hofmann and Delitzsch. With others, they recognized the trend of the Old Testament toward Christ, the divine-human Saviour; but, more than any others, they applied this not only to individual events and words, but to the whole course of Old Testament history, and at the same time emphasized the progressiveness of revelation.

---

[51] *Ibid.*

Thus they made possible an appreciation of the Old Testament which did full justice to the historical character of the individual texts and also brought out clearly their relation to the New Testament and their meaning for the New Testament Church. Here there is no reading of New Testament conceptions into the Old Testament, but a careful examination of the respective stage of revelation and of the religious-moral life of the Old Testament saints, with all the imperfections that attach to both. And when all this is presented from the viewpoint of its preparatory significance for the New Testament and the New Testament Church, we get a clear view of the precise message of the Old Testament for the Christian of today. Under the sway of these principles there arose in Germany and beyond it a sound type of Old Testament sermon. We mention in particular the sermons of Koegel, Taube, Deichert, Witte, Stoecker, Stoeckhardt, Cremer, Matthes and Stoewesand. Not all do justice to the historical element, and some, like Ziethe and Muehe, return to the old paths. The above mentioned principles are carried consistently through in M. Reu, *Die Alttestamentlichen Perikopen nach der Auswahl von Professor Dr. Thomasius* (1901 and 1905).[52] Valuable material is found in W. Langsdorff, *Alttestamentliche Perikopen* (1897) and A. Pfeiffer, *Die neuen Eisenacher alttestamentlichen Perikopen* (1901). Among English preachers on the Old Testament, some of whom however still allegorize too much, we name Liddon, Robertson, Maclaren, Spurgeon (see also his *Sermon Notes* and *Treasury of David*), F. B. Meyer, G. Campbell Morgan and George Adam Smith.

The attitude of present-day homileticians toward the Old Testament may be seen from the following testimony of Kleinert, who devoted the half of his life-work to the Old Testament. "If Christ," he says, "is the principle of the divine Word, it follows that the Old Testament can only furnish materials for the preaching of this Word in so far as it forms a part of the revelation of Christ. It can become material for the Christian congregation, not by reason of its importance as document, basis and witness of the religion of Israel, but only in virtue of its relation to Christian salvation. And this relation actually exists. That is witnessed by Christ Himself in John 5:39 The appearance of Jesus cannot be separated from the Bible of Jesus and the Bible of Jesus was the Old Testament. As He called the temple of Yahveh in Jerusalem His Father's house; as the God o

---

[52]Comp. also the English sermon sketches published in *Kirchlich, Zeitschrift* during 1919 and 1920.

Abraham, Isaac and Jacob is for Him the same God He knows as His Father, as He addresses Him with His dying breath in the words of the psalmist: so there can exist no doubt for a serious historical view that He developed His consciousness as Messiah with the aid of the Old Testament, and was certain of carrying on His activity as Saviour upon this foundation, nor that it is impossible, apart from this foundation of His consciousness and activity, fully to understand or correctly to present the meaning of His person or His work. The New Testament does not posit the salvation it brings to the nations as something new that came into the world without roots and that hangs in the air, but as the crown and completion of the same revelation made aforetime to the fathers (Heb. 1:1 f.; Luke 2:29 ff.). Consequently, a great number of the most important fundamental religious conceptions and ideas of the Old Testament have been taken over into the New without material change of form. And the Christian preacher who would properly treat the oneness, personality, life, spirituality, omnipresence of God, His holiness, faithfulness and truth, or the chief factors of trust and obedience, in the idea of faith, will be led naturally to Old Testament materials. For the direct expression of the religious spirit in its communion with God, for prayer, the Church has not only from the beginning recognized the psalter as an exemplary formal type, but has adopted it outright as its own prayerbook. But it is especially the whole wide field of the world-relations of the religious subject, to nature, the family and civil society, concerning which the New Testament, with its central trend toward the inner regeneration of the individual and the race, is content to accept the Old Testament foundations and premises, as the fixed framework into which the leaven-nature of the new life pours its forces and within which it unfolds them. The order and beauty of creation, the glory of the Father in His preservation and government of the cosmos, in His control of the destiny of nations and His fatherly care for the individual; the civic virtues of thrift and discipline, of contentment, honesty and righteousness; the social goods of national justice, reverence for personality, brotherliness and mercy toward the poor—all these the preacher, stationed in a national church, will be glad to set before his congregation in the sententious luminosity of Old Testament utterances, in proportion as his concern is for illuminating simplicity in establishing his point of contact and in the presentation of his material. To this there comes, finally, the great main trend of the history of Old Testament revelation—the mighty impulse toward the future, felt so powerfully nowhere else in the history of religions. Everything moves on this forward striving road. Amid lamentations over the passing of the present, prophecy strengthens its expectation of the coming salvation, which, intended as it is also for the Gentiles, will burst the narrow bounds of nationality. How essential this is for Christ's salvation is taught by the obvious reflection that, without this seedtime of Old Testament hope, Jesus would not have found even the twelve plain people who forsook all and followed Him, and whom He called to be His apostles.—In short, the Marcionite attitude toward the Old Testament, which in the elaborate form in which Schleiermacher bequeathed it to theology and the Church denotes a perceptible defect, cannot be adopted by evangelical homiletics: it marks the breaking of an indissoluble historical continuity."[53]

But has not the use of the Old Testament become impossible today by reason of the results of *literary criticism* and the *historical study of religion?* The former represents the entire course of history narrated in the Old Testament as a perversion of the actual facts, reduces Genesis to a tissue of myths, puts the prophets before the law, places the origin of the latter in the exile, and explains the prophets' faith in Yahveh as the resultant of a century-long development from totemism, animism and polytheism. And the latter adduces so many parallels from the religious history of the Babylonians, Assyrians, Egyptians, etc., that the independence of Israelitish religion seems entirely destroyed, and it appears but as a bough on the great tree of the natural religion of man. With respect to the destructive school of literary critics, the preacher who finds his relation to the Old Testament as the preparatory revelation of God affected by its labors should bear in mind that it is premature to speak here of "assured results of science," because these negative critics are being opposed by a large and growing group of at least equally able scholars, who are attacking with good success their results as an untenable artificial construction, and establishing the historical character of the three grades of patriarchal, Mosaic and prophetic religion. In Germany this group is represented by W. Lotz, E. Sellin, W. Rothstein, F. Buhl, W. Caspari, J. Herrmann, O. Procksch, and especially J. Koeberle and E. Koenig; in America, by the scholars associated with the "Bibliotheca Sacra." So far as the comparative study of religion is concerned, we call the preacher's attention to the same circumstance, and ask him the following question: Whence come the noble simplicity and invariably monotheistic sobriety of the biblical accounts, as over against the

---

[53]*Homiletik* (1907), pp. 67-70.

luxuriant, fantastic, mythological and polytheistic ideas that meet us in the religious traditions of the nations surrounding Israel? How can the biblical tradition be a natural branch of the same tree? How can a blind groping, the ψηλαφᾶν[54] of the natural man, develop of itself into a seeing and knowing, the characteristic of Old Testament religion? "As surely as God is the God of the world," says Kleinert, "and a living God, so surely has He not left Himself without witnesses among the Gentiles; but over against their blind religions which, seeking and groping, pass by His face (or at least do not know His heart), stands the religion that sees, that has experienced His revelation."[55] Over against both schools, the preacher will do well to ask himself whether he really believes himself better able to estimate the Old Testament than Jesus and the apostles, for whom it was historically true and a harmonious, homogeneous whole that can not be broken.[56]

---

[54] Acts 17:27.—[55] *Hom.*, p. 71.—Comp. J. Koeberle, *Heilsgeschichtliche u. religionsgeschichtliche Betrachtungsweise des Alten Testaments* (Neue kirchl. Zeitschrift, 1906) and *Orientalische Mythologie u. biblische Religion* (ibid.).—[56] Comp. M. Kaehler, *Jesus u. das Alte Testament* (1906); C. F. Noesgen, *Die Aussagen des N. T. ueber den Pentateuch* (1898; Eng. tr. with the title, "The New Testament and the Pentateuch"). In general: F. Wilke, *Das A. T. u. der christl. Glaube* (1911); James Orr, *The Problem of the O. T.;* F. Niebergall, *Praktische Auslegung des A. T.* (the companion to his *Praktische Auslegung des N. T.*, vol. 5 in Lietzmann's Handbuch zum N. T.; both from an advanced modern-critical viewpoint, but exceedingly useful and bright); G. Mayer, editor, *Das A. T. in rel. Betrachtungen fuer das moderne Beduerfnis* (1911—13; from the conservative side; reveals a fine appreciation of the permanent elements in the Old Testament and their significance for the present day; among the collaborators, Rump shows how a New Testament congregation may be soundly edified even on the basis of Exodus to Numbers, Dunkmann treats Job in a practically helpful way, Busch finds homiletically valuable material even in Ezra, Nehemiah and Esther, and Rump and Hackenschmidt prove from Isaiah and Jeremiah what rich treasures are hid in the prophets).

§ 12. THE SUBJECT-MATTER OF THE INDIVIDUAL SERMON

Klaus Harms, *Pastoraltheologie*, 1830. Chr. Palmer, *Evangelische Homiletik*, 1842. E. Ranke, *Das kirchliche Perikopensystem*, 1847. K. I. Nitzsch, *Praktische Theologie*, ii, 1848. F. Schleiermacher, *Praktische Theologie*, 1850. M. Baumgarten, *Nachtgesichte Sacharjas*, 1854. J. W. Alexander, *Thoughts on Preaching*, 1864. J. A. Broadus, *On the Preparation and Delivery of Sermons*, 1870. Ph. Brooks, *Lectures on Preaching*, 1877. R. W. Dale, *Nine Lectures on Preaching*, 1877. Th. Harnack, *Praktische Theologie*, 1878. Hanne, *Ueber textgemaesses Predigen* (Zeitschrift f. prakt. Theologie), 1881. H. Weiss, *Wert und Bedeutung des Textes fuer die Predigt* (ibidem), 1881. A. Phelps, *The Theory and Practice of Preaching*, 1881. A. Krauss, *Homiletik*, 1883. G. v. Zezschwitz, *Homiletik* (Zoeckler's Handbuch), 1883. H. Bassermann, *Handbuch der geistlichen Beredsamkeit*, 1885. E. Chr. Achelis, *Praktische Theologie*, 1889. Wrede, *Der Prediger und seine Zuhoerer* (Zeitschrift fuer prakt. Theologie), 1892. Wohlfahrt, *Allgemeines Deutsches Perikopenbuch*, 1892. F. Steinmeyer, *Homiletik*, 1901. G. Rietschel, *Lehrbuch der Liturgik*, 1900, 1910. F. Uhlhorn, *Die Casualrede*, 1896. T. H. Pattison, *The Making of the Sermon*, 1898. *Perikopenbuch*, herausgegeben von der Deutschen Kirchen-Konferenz, ³1902. F. Niebergall, *Wie predigen wir dem modernen Menschen?* 1902. W. Caspari, *Perikopen* (Hauck's Realencyklopaedie), 1904. J. Gottschick, *Die Textgemaessheit und verwandte homiletische Fragen* (Monatsschrift fuer kirchliche Praxis), 1905. O. Baumgarten, *Predigtprobleme*, 1905. M. Schian, *Die Predigt*, 1906. C. Clemen, *Predigt und biblischer Text*, 1906. P. Kleinert, *Homiletik*, 1907.

If the Scriptures, within the bounds we have indicated, are the only source for the contents of the sermon in general, they must be the source also for each sermon in particular. Now this might be the case even if the sermon were based in a general way upon the Scriptures, without having a specific scripture passage as its text. Such sermons without texts have at various times been preached, and were rather frequent in the ancient Church. This, however, never became a general custom, and since the Reformation the use of sermon-texts was considered self-evident. It was only in the last century that the demand arose to dispense with a scriptural text and to draw instead upon the Scriptures as a whole. The attempt was made to justify such a procedure by pointing out that few preachers stuck to their texts or drew from them the contents of their sermons, as well as that, because of the critical attitude it was necessary to take toward so many portions of the Bible, including the New Testament, little or nothing was left on one's text for sermon use. Unsatisfactory as these and similar arguments are, it must be conceded that prefixing a specific text to the sermon is as little a guaranty of its scriptural, as the absence of a text is of its unscriptural character.

Although there exists, therefore, no absolute necessity for binding the sermon to a specific text, it is nevertheless clear that the dependence of the sermon upon Scripture is best expressed if the sermon is based on a specific and definitely stated text. This commends itself as the normal practice for the following reasons. (1) It is in the interest of a concrete apprehension of scriptural truth. I apprehend the whole only by mastering its several parts; and the contents of the Scriptures are accurately apprehended and concretely presented to the congregation only when definite passages of Scripture are preached on and explained. Provided the preacher does not forget that he is dealing in his texts with parts of an organic whole, this will prove to be the safest and pedagogically most correct method of gaining and imparting a profitable understanding of the whole truth of Scripture. (2) It is also in the interest of the preacher. For he has in his text a safe starting-point and a rich source of material for his sermon preparation, whereas he would otherwise find himself often in doubt just what to present to his congregation and exposed to the danger of frequently repeating himself. Having a fixed text, he is less likely to preach his own wisdom instead of the divine truth; he is constantly compelled to make a detailed study of the Bible, and finds occasion to correct his views by its teaching. His conviction, moreover, of standing in every sermon he preaches, upon a definite word of God is strengthened, and he is enabled, in case a hearer takes offence at his preaching, to declare confidently that he has said nothing but what his text contains. (3) It is further in the interest of the congregation. For the text, lying at the basis of the sermon and announced at its beginning, establishes a common meeting-ground for preacher and congregation. The latter feels itself less exposed to the whim of its preacher, and has a right to expect that he will keep his discourse within the lines laid down in his text, by the reading of which the hearers have been prepared and put in a receptive mood for the sermon. The congregation is the better able to judge the agreement of the sermon with the Word of God and the more inclined to submit to its message, when it is made clear that it is the exposition and application of a definite passage of Holy Scripture. (P. 299.)

In the Ancient Church we meet already all the possible relations between sermon and text. We find not a few sermons that not only prefix a text but expound it verse by verse, so that they come near to losing the character of orations; as for example, the homilies of Origen and Chrysostom. We find other sermons that attach themselves to a certain passage of Scripture, but without confining themselves to it and without basing their whole discussion upon it or developing it from this passage; so especially the artistic orations or λόγοι of Basil, Gregory of Nyssa, Chrysostom and Ambrose. Others again follow the lesson for the day, but so remotely that it is impossible to tell from them what the lesson was; so the oldest extant homily the so-called Second Epistle of Clement to the Corinthians. Still others are deliberately without any text and take their point of departure in the respective occasion (e. g., the festival idea) and their subject-matter from the Christian consciousness or the field of dogmatics or ethics; this is true of most of the sermons of Gregory Nazianzus. But we find also sermons that follow the chief thoughts of a text and achieve an oratorically finished and organic whole; as the logos on the Holy Theophany ascribed to Hippolytus.[1]

The sermon of the Middle Ages, from the beginning of the seventh to the close of the twelfth century, was largely nothing more than a mosaic of excerpts from sermons of the ancient Church adapted to the times, so that we need not look to it for any innovation with respect to the relation of sermon and text. All of the mediaeval sermons may be reduced to two types—*homiliae* and *sermones*. The former type was never without its text, for by its very nature it was the exposition of a Scripture passage as a whole or in its several parts. The sermo, on the other hand, whose distinctive feature was its topical treatment, while normally based on a text, was not seldom without one. Thus, the fifteen sermons ascribed to Boniface are all without texts and do not refer in any way to the lesson for the day. But the *Speculum ecclesiae* of Honorius Scholasticus (12. century) not only fits a text to each sermon but chooses besides this, for discussion in the exordium or introduction, a special *thema*, i. e., a Scripture verse differing from the sermon text proper.[2] In the second half of the Middle Ages sermons without texts grow more and more infrequent. The sermons of Berthold of Regensburg, Eckhart, Tauler, Geiler of Kaisersberg, all have texts. In Surgant's *Manuale curatorum* (1503) the sermon-text is treated as self-evident. It is not surprising, therefore, that Luther and the other reformers knew of no other usage. Indeed, this usage becomes for them a fixed principle as the inevitable result of their conviction of the dependence of the sermon upon the divine Word. Sermons without texts are the exception; even the numerous catechism sermons and sermons on hymns, if they had

---

[1]Comp. our *History of Preaching*.—[2]From this may have developed the later custom of not contenting oneself with the liturgical reading of the text but repeating it immediately before the sermon. The liturgical lesson was read in Latin, and a translation into the vernacular, if it did not occur in the course of the sermon, had to precede it. (Comp. for the close of the Middle Ages Ulrich Surgant's *Manuale, lib.* ii, *consideratio* 1.) In the "verse-sermons," moreover (so called because not the entire pericope but only a verse of it served them as text), the text was identical with the "thema" recited at the beginning of the sermon. Whether or not Alanus ab Insulis († 1202 or 1203) was the first to demand this usage, as Achelis (ii, pp. 98 f.) claims, will depend upon the interpretation of the respective passage in his *Ars praedicatoria*.

often no specific biblical text, were based on parts of the Catechism or stanzas of hymns and treated these as their text. That a specific scriptural text was not regarded as absolutely necessary may be seen in no less a preacher than Luther, whose eight Wittenberg sermons (1522) are without texts.

Voices were raised now and then against the use of sermon-texts. Roger Bacon (13. century) does not belong among them, despite Phelps;[3] for his prayer to God "to banish this conceited and artificial way of preaching from his church," has reference not to the choice of texts as such, but to the whole method of the scholastic sermon with its endless divisions and subdivisions and its lifeless presentation. Voltaire objected to the use of texts, although his opinion, too, was formed on a type of preaching which is by no means the result of the use of texts, namely, the wretched custom of almost invariably choosing short texts. "It were to be wished," he wrote, "that Bourdaloue in banishing from the pulpit the bad taste which disgraced it, had also banished the custom of preaching on a text. Indeed, to speak long on a quotation of a line or two, to exhaust oneself in subjecting a whole discourse to the control of this line, seems a trifling labor, little worthy of the dignity of the ministry, which the discourse develops."[4] Klaus Harms approached the question more seriously and wrote in his *Pastoraltheologie* (1830): "Might we be permitted to ask whether the demand that we must preach on texts is as well founded as it is customary? Might we further express the opinion that when text and theme stand together, the one cancels the other? Might we also venture the assertion that preaching upon texts has been a hindrance, not only to the art of preaching, but also to Christian knowledge and, what is much more important, to Christian life?" And he points out that "a sermon may be unbiblical despite its biblical text," just as on the other hand a sermon without a text may be biblical.[5] In his *Sommerpostille* Harms includes a number of sermons without texts, but also remarks that this is permissible only by way of exception, since the congregation would otherwise be deprived of the evidence for the scripturalness of the sermon. The first to oppose Harms's view was Nitzsch in "Studien und Kritiken" (1832, p. 454); he was followed by Tholuck in the "Theologische Anzeiger" (1838, nos. 63 and 64), and by Palmer in his *Homiletik* ([2]1845), who wrote: "If a preacher preach an unbiblical sermon on a biblical text his

---

[3] *Theory of Preaching* (1881), p. 47.—[4] Quoted in Vinet, p. 99.—
[5] Vol. i, p. 65; comp. vol. ii, p. 153.

text will judge him, and thus the inferiority of his discourse is revealed by its very juxtaposition with a text. The congregation is not edified, but it also suffers less harm, because it can tell by the text what the preacher ought really to have said. We know from experience that there are in every congregation persons competent to judge of these matters. But the preacher who preaches a biblical sermon without a text either has after all a text, for his sermon is based upon some particular Bible passage, only he does not announce it as such by reading it word for word—but why should he not do this?—or else, not finding enough material for his purpose in a single text, he takes a series of passages, proceeds from one to the other and constructs a whole out of them, somewhat as a composer constructs a fugue out of two themes. One cannot say, however, that in this case the sermon has no text; only the formal text is missing. Yet the question remains, whether by this procedure the inner unity is not destroyed, or whether, if the Scripture passages really represent a unity, one of them does not contain the whole, so that it is actually the text, while the others belong rather to the development. Or, in the third place, the sermon actually has no text at all. If it is an occasional sermon [*Kasvalrede*] this must be permitted; for in this kind of sermon the occasional and personal receive greater prominence and the occasion or fact, as an act of God, forms as it were the specific text, which is to be discussed in the light of God's Word as such. Still we must express our decided preference, even on these occasions, for an actual text whereby the address is consecrated. . . . With respect to sermons not occasional, the only remaining possibility is that a preacher might have suggested to him, by some happening or something he has read, a theme for which he can find no biblical text whatever. What should he do in that case? For our part, we have never been in such a predicament, since it is our custom to select first a text, and then our theme from that text. But we admit it to be possible that in the course of his ministerial life a preacher may come upon a thought worth preaching on, for which no special text expressing that thought can be found.[6] But that there can be anything essentially evangelical

---

[6]Stier here hits the point when he says in his *Kerytik* (2. ed., 1830, p. 88): "I may start out in my preparation, in many different ways, from anything that is possible here or that belongs here; but in any case I must soon arrive at a text, and only from the moment I have got my text does the actual preparation of the sermon, properly speaking, begin." This agrees fully with what E. Porter of Andover wrote at about the same time,—"Every wise preacher often fixes on some

that no prophet or apostle has expressed or that is not contained in a biblical book, either as corollary, presupposition or application—this we will not believe until we see it. Hence we demand, in common with the custom of the Church, a sermon-text; for the sermon it is the authorization and seal that it is the Word of God."——The Frenchman Vinet opened anew the whole question in his *Homiletic* of 1853. There are especially two considerations that cause him to hesitate before accepting the common usage. In the first place, there is the frequent abuse of the text by the preacher. "The use of a text," he says, "is not essential to pulpit discourse. What gives a Christian character to a sermon is not the use of a text, but the spirit of the preacher. A sermon may be Christian, edifying, instructive, without containing even one passage of Holy Scripture. It may be very biblical without a text, and with a text not biblical at all. A passage of Scripture has a thousand times served as a passport for ideas which were not in it; and we have seen preachers amusing themselves, as it were, by prefixing to their compositions very strong biblical texts, for the sake of the pleasure of emasculating them. We have witnessed

prominent doctrine or duty, which he wishes to discuss, and then goes to the Bible to ascertain what it teaches on this subject, selecting some single passage as a text that is especially pertinent to his purpose" (*Lectures on Homiletics and Preaching*, 1834, p. 60). Palmer calls attention to this concrete case: "C. I. Nitzsch published a sermon on 'The Hallowing of the Imagination.' This theme was clearly not suggested by the text, but existed before it; and a text had to be sought for it. Yet how finely, in 2 Tim. 2:8, everything was found that the preacher needed." In this connection Porter's words are worth bearing in mind,—"Here is a danger to be guarded against. Suppose you fix on your subject, and arrange your matter, and even write your sermon, as has often been done, and then go to the Bible in search of a text. Probably your text will either not contain your subject, or contain it only by inference or remote analogy, or combine with it other subjects, which must entirely be neglected. I do not say that there can be no case in which it is admissible to arrange the plan of a sermon, and even execute it, without having determined on a text. But from the specimens of motto-preaching which have fallen under my observation, I cannot doubt that the tendency of the above process is to sink the reverence due to the Bible, and hence it too often happens in point of fact, that, in what are called polite sermons, there is nothing but the text, to remind the hearers that there is a Bible. The text is obviously chosen with respect, rather to the usage of the pulpit, than to the authority of the Divine Word; and it would better accord with the end of the preacher, in such a case, to choose no text, or, like him whom Melanchthon heard preach in Paris, to choose one from the Ethics of Aristotle."

a formal immolation of the Divine Word. When the text is only a deceptive signal, when a steeple surmounts a playhouse, it would doubtless be better to remove the signal and throw down the steeple." Secondly, in his view, the text only fetters the preacher. "A proposition which has its precise expression in no passage of the Bible, is suggested altogether by the preacher's own mind, under the influence of circumstances or meditation. In compliance with a usage which has the force of a law, he would now obtain a text for this pre-conceived subject, and he probably finds a text which has some perceptible relation to his subject; but does he always find a text which expresses his subject? We cannot think so. And now he will do one of two things; either he will take from the Bible only what exactly suits his subject, and leave the rest, or he will make the text the mould of his discourse. Is it probable now that his plan will be a truly natural one, which, having been first formed in his mind according to the nature of things and from a particular point of view, has to be afterwards formed anew according to the sinuosities of the text which has not the form of his thesis or of any thesis? If you tell him to abandon the form of his thesis, or rather his thesis itself, in favor of the text, with what chains would you load the minister of the Word?" Vinet admits that both of his objections refer only to the thematic form of the sermon, and that even there they are not always in point. So that his discussion amounts finally to nothing more than a denial of the absolute necessity of the sermon-text. And he altogether gives away his case when he says of the use of texts: "Taking this method in general, without regard to the application which it may have received, and the abuse which may have been made of it, I make the following observations: In the first place, this method has received from time and universal consent a sacredness which gives it such force that only time, which introduced, can abolish it. . . . In the second place, this method, externally and formally at least, well represents the idea that the preacher is the minister of the Word of God. It recalls this to others and to himself. Thirdly, it has real advantages. The first is, the moral advantage to the preacher of having his discourse connected with a passage of the Bible. The second is, the impressions of respect which the enunciation of the Sacred Word makes on the auditors, at the beginning of the sermon. The third is, that generally a text well comprehended and closely followed will produce a discourse more special, striking, spirited than one founded on an abstract conception—a discourse thoroughly original. Finally, to the majority of preachers this method is better suited than the other, to multiply subjects."

Thus from an opponent, Vinet becomes a defender of the use of texts, so long as this usage does not become an absolute law and so long as important interests of the sermon are not neglected thereby.—M. Baumgarten's opposition to the churchly usage, in his *Nachtgesichte des Sacharja* (1854),[7] was founded in his enthusiasm and in his pronounced subjectivism and individualism. Against this Phelps' words may be called to mind,—"Yield this, and you revolutionize the pulpit in less than one generation."[8]—From the viewpoint of literary criticism, J. R. Hanne wrote an article in the "Zeitschrift fuer praktische Theologie" (1881), opposing the use of sermon-texts, but was answered in the same place by H. Weiss. We have set forth our position on this point in the previous chapter, and need add here only that such passages as are of uncertain authenticity or are certainly unauthentic, from the textual-critical viewpoint, ought not to be used as texts for sermons; comp. passages like Matt. 20:16b (the case is different in 22:14); John 7:53-8:11; 1 John 5:7, etc.

It has been objected, finally, that by the prefixing of a text the sermon is made to be different from every other kind of public discourse. There is some truth in T. H. Pattison's reply,—"The old philosophers detaching sentences from the writings of their famous sages, used them as texts; the orator who speaks to a toast and the statesman who previous to his address in the legislature calls for the reading of certain resolutions, both of them use texts; the musician varying the air, but at the same time preserving harmony by observing unity, finds in the motif of his composition his text; to the painter some familiar strain of song or some stirring scene in history furnishes a text; and when Milton opens 'Paradise Lost' with the words,

> Of man's first disobedience, and the fruit
> Of that forbidden tree whose mortal taste
> Brought death into the world, and all our woe,

or when Tennyson, in the first lines of 'In Memoriam,' holds it true with another singer that 'men may rise on stepping-stones of their dead selves to higher things,' they only illustrate the use of the text by the greatest of our poets." If these analogies leave us cold, let us ask: Why should not the sermon be different from all other discourses? seeing that, despite all resemblances, it differs in its inner nature, as the exposition and application of the Word of God, from every other discourse.—Among American homileticians, Phelps has discussed this

---

[7] Vol. ii, pp. 172 ff.—[8] P. 52.

question most fully. We conclude with what Gottschick wrote in 1908: "If it is used aright, viz., organically and not mechanically, the text denotes, for the particular task of producing homiletic ideas, a fructifying power rather than a cramping fetter. Holy Scripture, consisting mostly of occasional writings, is a many-sided monument of the history of the relations between God and man, and of historical revelation itself with its manifold personal operations of the Spirit. For this very reason it is favorable to the work of a personally living and concretely individualizing proclamation of the Word of God. By virtue of its wealth of individual types, its constant relation to the life of the world, especially in the Old Testament, and the typical character, in the New Testament, of the Christian spirit's statement of its case against its opposites of Jewish and heathen origin, of the self-development of this spirit in various directions, there will be found many fitting concrete texts for the actual themes that are thrust upon one by the present day. And where the life of the modern Church has grown too far beyond the scope of primitive Christianity, the Scriptures supply an abundance of guiding principles in general passages. The sermon as personal witness can only gain if the preacher, by taking a text, sinks himself into the inner life of the biblical personages and allows himself to be stimulated by their classic religious power and originality. In addition to this, the Scriptures offer him a completion and enrichment of his world of religious ideas, which is indispensable in view of his unavoidable one-sidedness due to his training, the trend of the time, his individuality, and the wear and tear of his official labors. The often classic, always venerable form of the scriptural word summarizes in a unified and impressive fashion the thoughts developed from it."[9]

The necessity of treating a subject more fully than the text provides for—by adding to the negative the positive side, to the fact the admonition, to the prophecy the fulfilment—has led to the taking of two or even three texts instead of one; e. g., Heb. 9:22 and 1 John 1:7, or Isa. 6:3 and Ps. 72:19, or Gal. 6:2a; Gal. 6:5 and Ps. 55:22a. Spurgeon has a sermon on the words, "I have sinned," as occurring seven times in the Bible, and gives interesting views of the different circumstances and states of mind in which they were uttered. In his collection of Old Testament sermons, *Aus dem Vorhof in das Heiligtum*, Koegel has a number of sermons with double texts. Epistle and gospel lesson have often been combined into a single text. In

---

[9] P. 43.

most cases, however, this practice leads to unspiritual trifling. If the single text is not torn from its connection, but treated as it should be, as part of an organic whole, these artifices will not become necessary.

The necessity of the sermon-text established, the question arises as to how the text is to be chosen. This question will not arise where entire books of the Bible are preached on consecutively. It is then a question not of selecting but of properly bounding one's text. The thinking man, particularly the preacher, working through his text in the original, will hardly require any rules for this; it will be self-evident that the text cannot end before it has expressed a complete thought. This need not be the whole thought presented by the biblical writer; it may be a smaller unity within the larger unity of the writer's thought, but it must be a unity, a thought complete in itself. Thus, Gal. 3:1-14 forms a complete thought-unity held together by the idea of "the reception of the Spirit," with its Old Testament analogy in the idea of "blessing." From the manner in which the Galatians have received the Spirit, the apostle undertakes to prove the truth of his gospel with its freedom from the law. To this end he reminds them first of all of their own experience (vv. 1-5). By this they are to know that they received the Holy Spirit, who sums up in Himself all the New Testament gifts and graces, not by virtue of the works of the law which they had performed, but solely by the hearing of faith. He then points them, in vv. 6-14, to the history of salvation, its beginning (vv. 6-10), and its goal (vv. 11-14). From its beginning, which lays the foundation and forms the norm for the whole subsequent development, there follows the truth of Paul's gospel; for justification with its sequel, the reception of the blessing—the Old Testament parallel to the New Testament reception of the Spirit—is from the very beginning connected with faith. The same truth follows from the goal to which the whole history of salvation tends; for Christ had to redeem us from the curse of the law before we could receive the "blessing of Abraham," i. e., the Holy Spirit. How then can a doctrine be true that leads back again to the law as to a necessary supplement of faith? I may, therefore, choose for my text the passage as a whole (vv. 1-14); or if I find it too comprehensive, I may take vv. 1-5 and 6-14, or 6-10 and 11-14 as shorter texts complete in themselves. It will not be advisable to break up the passage into still smaller portions, if I wish to bring out the closely knit structure of Paul's thought so characteristic of this epistle. Otherwise, I could subdivide the second section (vv. 6-10) and preach on 6-7 (despite its abrupt beginning with καθώς) or on 8-9; for these are two items in the beginning of the history of salvation which Paul found of value for his argument and which are still of value for a Christian congregation. It might be difficult, however, to differentiate sufficiently between these two historical items, both of which express the same thought from different angles, and to prevent the second sermon from becoming a mere replica of the first. It would be simpler to separate v. 10 from 6-9, to which it adds the argument of the impossibility of its contrary. In the third section (vv. 11-14), if the rendering of the Authorized and Revised versions is followed, one could take vv. 11-12 as a text complete in itself, although if one is preaching straight through Galatians, this had better be avoided; not that it is not right in itself, but because it would again lead to repetition. If the preacher, following Hofmann and Zahn, takes the first ὅτι in v. 11 as causative, makes v. 11a the protasis and vv. 13-14 the apodosis, and regards vv. 11b-12 as a parenthesis, he cannot possibly subdivide further this thought-unity, but must choose the whole of 11-14 as his text.

It is, however, a serious question whether it is well to preach consecutively for a whole year, not to say year after year, on entire biblical books. If one were to begin with the

Old Testament, even omitting all those chapters that are not adapted to homiletic use, one would come only after many years, perhaps never, to the New Testament; the congregation would thus be deprived of that which is intended specifically for it. Moreover, not all the biblical books are of equal value, not even those of the New Testament. Is the New Testament congregation to listen for a full year—especially where there is only one service a week—to nothing but James? Even if the preacher confined himself to the so-called primary books, and if there existed a consensus of opinion as to which these are, the various needs of the congregation would not be met. For most of these books—in the case of the epistles, all of them—are occasional writings, and do not present the divine truth as a whole, but only emphasize those portions that come in question in their respective situation. To preach for a whole year on Romans would lead to one-sidedness. And will the congregation obtain a complete picture of the work of Jesus if the sermon confines itself for years to the first gospel? Sermon series and the consecutive treatment of entire books are quite in order, provided that they do not extend over too long a period of time and have their place in secondary services, while a different choice of texts—an actual choice—is followed in the main service. This follows from the very nature of the Scriptures: God has given them to His Church, not in separate parts, but in their totality and organic unity. It follows also from the needs of the Christian congregation, which are so varied that they can be supplied only by the Scriptures in their entirety.

Shall it be left then to the individual preacher to make his own selections of texts? This would not be impossible. He could so choose his texts that the great passages of faith and life would recur in proper proportion year after year, and that there would be room besides for other texts taking into account the varying needs of the congregation, so that he would .treat in the course of time the various books of the Bible according to their relation to the centre of New Testament faith and life. Some preachers have done this, with full justice both to the Scriptures and to their congregations. And yet it is easy for such selections to become too individual and colored by the preacher's idiosyncrasy, and a glance into sermonic literature shows that few preachers have been so happy in their choice of texts as to do justice to the demands of Scripture and the needs of the congregation. Not a few, indeed, take their congregation, year after year, on labyrinthine excursions whose going out and whose coming in are hid from their own eyes. Here the idea of the *Church Year* naturally presents itself as a guide in the choice of texts. By following its guidance the choice of texts will best meet the above requirement, that the central truths of Scripture should regularly recur. The festival half of the Church Year passes before our eyes the great facts of sacred history which together form the foundation of our salvation, and summons us to a believing appropriation of the blessings inherent in those facts and present in the exalted Christ. And the second half calls attention to the development, preservation and completion, through the exalted Christ, of the life of faith in the Church as in the individual believer. The use of the Church Year does not yet involve fixed texts for the various Sundays nor determine the definite character of each Sunday. Nevertheless, it furnishes, at least in its festival half, important viewpoints and leading principles which make it easy to choose from the wealth of scriptural material such texts as will correspond to the nature of the seasons and the Sundays.

The *Festival Half* of the Church Year is opened by the *Christmas cycle,* the centre of which is Christmas, the festival of the Nativity, preceded by the Advent season and followed by the Epiphany season. *Christmas* is the festival of the birth of Christ bringing salvation; hence, beside the festival fact itself, which must always stand in the foreground, such other texts are appropriate as bring out the saving worth of this fact, showing the love of the Father for lost mankind revealed in the sending of His Son (John 3:16; 1 John 4:9, comp. 1 John 3:1 and Mark 12:6), the fulness of the time and the culmination of divine revelation in Christ and His birth (Gal. 4:4-5; Heb. 1:1-3), the world-historical significance of the birth in its dividing Israel and the nations into two camps (Luke 2:28-38), the adorable mystery of the Incarnation (John 1:1-14; 1 Tim. 3:16; Heb. 2:14), or in particular the humiliation of the eternal Son in His incarnation (Phil. 2:6-7; 2 Cor. 8:9), the saving benefits that come to man from Christ's appearing (Ti. 2:11-14; 3:3-8; Gal. 4:4-5; Isa. 9:6-7; Luke 2:29-32; 1:31-33; Matt. 1:21), or how the grace of God manifested in Christ enables us to walk in newness of life (Ti. 2:11-14; 3:3-8). The purpose of *Advent* is to prepare for Christmas; hence it demands texts that deal with Christ's coming—His coming in the past (Luke 1:67-79; Isa. 61:1-7), His coming in the future (Rev. 1:4-8; Luke 21:25-36; 17:20-30; 12:35-48; Rom. 13:11-14; 15:4-13), His coming in the present, especially at the beginning of a new Church Year (Isa. 40:1-11; Matt. 3:1-12; John 1:19-34); or texts which by setting forth the example of Old Testament saints awaken a true longing and waiting for the Lord (Gen. 3:15; 49:18; Ps. 25:1-7; 62:1-8) or describe the good things we may expect from Him (Deut. 18:15; Isa. 9:1-7; 42:1-8; 49:1-13; Jer. 23:5-6; Ezek. 34:11-16). Through the *Epiphany* season runs the thought, "We beheld His glory," and this calls for texts that give out rays of the glory of the Only-begotten of the Father, in His words as in His works (the prophetic office of Christ) (Isa. 60:1-6; 49:1-13; 42:1-8; Luke 2:41-52; Matt. 3:13-17; John 2:1-11; 1:43-52; Luke 4:14-22; Matt. 4:1-11; John 4:5-26; Matt. 8:1-13; 11:25-30;

8:23-27; John 4:47-54; 5:1-16; 8:12-16; Matt. 17:1 -8), or texts that show how this glory of Christ must shine also through the members of His kingdom, so that men may see their good works and glorify their Father in heaven (Deut. 6:1-9; Isa. 8:20-22; parts of the sermon on the mount; Luke 11:27-28; 8:4-15; Rom. 12:1-6, 7-16, 17-21; 10:1-12; 5:1-5; 2 Pet. 1:16-21; Col. 3:12-17; Matt. 16:21-27).

In the centre of the festival half stands the *Easter cycle,* with *Easter* as its centre. The feast of the resurrection of Christ requires texts which exhibit the festival fact itself and its saving value, by presenting the resurrection as proof of Christ's divinity (John 14:19-20), the reward of His obedience (Phil. 2:9-11), the divine seal upon His redemptive work (Matt. 28:1-10, comp. ἠγέρθη, v. 6; Acts 2:36; Rom. 4:25), the victory of the Prince of life over death, His own and ours (John 11:25; Acts 3:15), or as the foundation of a lively hope and joy that sorrow's night cannot quench nor the shadows of death destroy (1 Pet. 1:3-9; Job. 19:25-27; 1 Cor. 15:17-20) and of zest for our work and boldness in the hour of death (1 Cor. 15:55-58); or texts which treat of the risen Lord's intercourse with His disciples (Luke 24:13 -35), and summon us to a serious renewal of life in the power of Christ's resurrection (Rom. 6:1-11). The resurrection can be understood only in the light of the passion. Hence, before the days of Easter joy the Church has set the season of the *Passion.* The texts for this time should deal with the sufferings of Christ, not only the *passio magna,* though this must occupy the foreground. While the special passion services (held on Wednesday or Friday evening) are devoted to the devotional study of the various portions of the passio magna, for the Sundays in this season it will be well to choose texts that present Jesus wrestling for the souls of men, as well as the opposition and contradiction of sinners against

Him, and thus trace the climax of His sufferings to the passio magna (the highpriestly office) (Luke 4:16-30; John 5:15-30; 6:60-71; 8:48-59; 9:39-41; 10:22-30; 11:47-57; Luke 18:31-43; John 12:20-36; Matt. 22:31-46), or that contain Old Testament types and prophecies of the passion (Gen. 3:15; 22:1-18; Ex. 14:13-31; Ps. 22; Zech. 9:8-12); likewise texts that bring out the saving value of Christ's suffering and thus inculcate a profound knowledge of sin, a grateful appropriation of the blessed fruit of Christ's work, a more earnest denial of self, and a consecrated surrender to our Lord (Matt. 20:20-28; John 10:12-18; Heb. 2:10-15; 5:7-10; 7:24-27; 10:1-14; 9:11-15; 1 Pet. 1:13-21; 2:18-25; 1 John 2:1-2; Gal. 3:11-14; Rom. 3:21-28; 2 Cor. 5:17-21; Rom. 4:25; 5:1-11; Phil. 2:5-10; Matt. 16:21-27). For *Holy Thursday* the most appropriate texts are the words of institution of the Lord's Supper, in the synoptists and in Paul; also Ex. 12:1-14; John 13:1-17; 1 Cor. 10:16-17. For *Good Friday,* over and above the passion history, such texts offer themselves as Isa. 53; John 1:29; John 19:30; 2 Cor. 5:12-21; Heb. 10:19-23; 1 Pet. 1:18-21. The *post-Easter season,* running to Ascension Day, is characterized by Easter joy and Easter peace. With this mood the texts chosen for this season must be in accord. They must have as their centre the glorified Christ and treat of the peace with God, the lifepower and the triumphant strength against all hostile worldforces found in Him; but no less of the intimate communion between Him and His own that are in the world, and of how He is far above the heavens and yet constantly present (the royal office of Christ) (the accounts of the appearances of the risen Lord; John 10:27-30; 14:25-31; 15:1-11; 1 John 5:4; Isa. 61:10-12; Rev. 5:1-14; Gen. 32:22-31; Isa. 54:7-14; Ezek. 34:11-16; John 16:23-30; Luke 11:5-13; 18:1-8; Heb. 12:1-3; Rev. 2:1-7; 3:1-6; 3:14-

22). *Ascension Day* is the day of Christ's coronation (Ps. 110) on which there is given Him all authority in heaven and earth (Matt. 28:18-20) and He ascends in order to prepare a place for us in the Father's house (John 14:1-3), whither He will draw all men after Him (John 12:32), where He intercedes with the Father for us in all our sins and sorrows (1 John 2:1; Rom. 8:34; Heb. 7:25; 4:14-16), whence He establishes and extends His kingdom upon earth, and where our affections are to be set (Col. 3:1-4).

The third cycle, that of *Whitsuntide*, has its centre in *Whitsunday*, the feast of the outpouring of the Holy Spirit. Of His coming, person and work, of His relation to Christ who sends Him, and of the relation of men to Him, the texts chosen for this festival should treat. Also, secondarily, of the New Testament church which He, as Spirit of the glorified Christ, has founded upon earth. Besides Acts 2, Christ's promises to send Him as "an other paraclete," found in John 14-16, are adapted as texts; also passages like Isa. 44:1-6; Ezek. 36:1-6; Joel 3:1-5; John 7:37-39; Acts 2:37-38; Rom. 8:1-4, 26; Eph. 4:30; 1:13-14; Gal. 3:11-15; Rom. 8:15; Ti. 3:5-6; 2 Tim. 1:7; Eph. 2.19-22; Heb. 8:8-11; Acts 10:42-48. *The Sunday before Whitsunday* (Exaudi calls by its very name, which stamps it as day of prayer for the Spirit, for texts such as Ps. 42; Isa. 64:1; Luke 11:9-13. *The Sunday after Whitsunday*—originally simply the octave of Whitsunday, whence also the old gospel lesson from John 3—presents a resumé of the wonderful works of God the Triune; here the following passages will form appropriate texts: 2 Cor. 13:13; Eph. 1:3-14; Num. 6:22 -27; Rom. 11:33-36, also Matt. 28:16-20; 1 Cor. 12:4-13, and 1 Pet. 1:1-2. It is absolutely necessary, on festival days, to set the festival fact in the foreground, and to bring home to the hearers something of the wealth of the divine gifts contained in that fact, so that they may rejoice in their salvation and praise God for His wonderful works. Hence texts are to be chosen in which the stress lies not on what we are to do, but altogether on what God has done and is still doing for us and in us; texts in which above all things Gospel and not chiefly, still less exclusively, law is presented.

For the *non-festival half* of the Church Year there are no generally accepted principles governing the choice of texts. It will be most appropriate to select texts which bear on the order of salvation and treat of the origin, preservation, development and completion of the Christian life, and of the means of grace through which these are produced by the Spirit of the exalted Christ. To such texts might be added a series of texts, especially from the Acts and from the epistles, setting forth the progress of life in the Christian Church with its dangers, duties and struggles. In this part of the year it is permissible to take up in a cursory way, for a number of Sundays, longer portions of Scripture, such as the sermon on the mount, the decalogue, the seven petitions of the Lord's Prayer, or several of the letters to the seven churches. With respect to the last Sundays of the year, however, it has become customary in wide circles, since Luther's day, to preach on eschatological texts, viz., such as present the completion of the Christian life by a blessed death and the consummation of the Church by the coming again of Christ. The festivals falling in this half-year, such as the Harvest, the Reformation, and in many sections the Mission festival (the latter chiefly but not exclusively from external reasons appointed for this time), are also based upon works of God, either in the sphere of creation or of redemption. For the festival of *Harvest* the texts should chime with the note struck in Ps. 95 (Gen. 8:20-22; Ps. 34:1-9; 67:1-8; 2 Cor. 9:6-11; Ps. 104; John 6:24-29). *Reformation* texts should set forth the re-discovered Gospel and awaken love to the Church and faithfulness to the divine treasure committed to her (Matt. 11:25-30; Rom. 1:

16; Matt. 11:12; Rom. 3:28; 5:1-11; Gal. 2:15-21; John 2:14-17; Ps. 46; Hab. 2:4; Gal. 5:1; Rev. 3:11). For the *Mission festival* preachers ought not to choose invariably the missionary commission, but also such other texts as set the results on the mission field in the light of the great works of God, and reveal to the hearers the blessings they enjoy as members of the Church of Christ, so that their hearts will be warmed and they will be driven by an inner urgency to participate in mission work (Matt. 28:18-20; 5:13-16; 25: 14-30; Acts 15:12; John 12:24; 1 John 5:4; Isa. 42:1 ff.; 49:1-13; Ps. 95:1-7; Matt. 13:31-33; 13:44-45; Isa. 2:1-5; 60:1-6; Luke 15:1-10; 12:40; Rom. 1:14-15; 1:16-17).

If the preacher is convinced of the wisdom of following, in his choice of texts, the various seasons of the Church Year, he will examine also the system of *pericopes* which has been in use for centuries in the Church, in order to see whether it is not adapted to serve as textual basis for his sermons, the more since it is determined throughout by the idea of the Church Year. It must, however, be clear at the outset that a system of pericopes existing in the Church and offering itself to the preacher can never claim to be absolutely binding. It cannot be this because, among other reasons, the homiletical part of the service is not a fixed quantity in the same sense as the liturgical part. In the days when little was known about the origin of these old churchly pericopes and about the changes they had undergone in the course of time, and when men had lost the freedom which Luther maintained over against such matters, and thought themselves obliged to hold fast to this system in the interest of popular education, it was customary to regard the pericopes as an inviolable heritage from the earliest Christian times. Praise was lavished upon the wisdom and skill of their arrangement, and the use of other Scripture passages was prohibited in the main service of the Church (the secondary services were left free). But since the middle of the last century, historical research has shown beyond a doubt that the system of pericopes taken over by the Reformation contained only fragments of the pericope-collection of the ancient Church, and that a considerable number of its lessons was appointed with a view to days and services which have long since passed out of use and even out of memory. As a consequence of this, men turned away from this old system and became more and more inclined to abandon it altogether. But a sober judgment, while not blind to its defects and perhaps excluding certain pericopes from use in the pulpit (e. g., Gal. 4: 21-31), will nevertheless admit that it comprises fundamental and indispensable portions of Scripture concerning the person, life and work of Christ. Still it remains true that where these old pericopes form, year after year, the texts for the sermon of the main service, the congregation comes to know only a comparatively small part of the Bible, and that these pericopes, especially the epistles, do not bring out with sufficient clearness the fundamental teaching of the Reformation, as Luther already felt. Hence, in addition to them, the preacher will either make his own selection of texts or, which is preferable, use one of the modern systems of pericopes, such as the Eisenach system or that of Thomasius or Nitzsch. He will not omit the Old Testament, but take up an Old Testament series in his main service, say once every five years, especially if he has no evening service in which such texts might be treated. Not only will he be able, under this arrangement, to make his congregation better acquainted with the riches of the Bible, but he will run less danger of maltreating his text in the effort to avoid preaching every year the same sermon from it.

Formerly the Lutheran Church was rich, over and above the main Sunday service, in early, afternoon and week-day services. In these *secondary services,* when they fell on Sunday, the choice of text was determined by the season of the Church Year, unless the service was a catechism service with or without a sermon on a part of the Catechism. On weekdays—again excepting the catechism services—entire biblical books were taken up more or less continuously, the Old Testament being largely used. In America the week-day services have been continued in many sections, and besides a Sunday evening service is commonly held. These offer excellent opportunities for preaching on Old Testament texts, or on whole books of the New Testament, as well as on the Catechism, including the Table of Duties, on the order of salvation, subjects from Church history or parts of the Augustana in popular vein.

The choice of texts for *occasional sermons* or addresses is necessarily determined by their relation to the respective liturgical service in which they have their place, as well as by the particular occasion that calls them forth. For a *Baptismal* address, texts should be chosen which show that only through baptism does birth into this life become a true good, and which illustrate the nature, effect and obligation of baptism (Matt. 28:18-20; Mark 16:16; 10:13-16; John 3:5-6; Acts 2:38; Rom. 6:1-11; 1 Cor. 6:11; Gal. 3:26-27; Ti. 3:5-6; Heb. 10:22; 1 Pet. 3:19-22). For the *Confirmation* address, words of encouragement and admonition to faithfulness or forceful reminders of God's truth and grace should be selected, that will sink unforgettably into the heart; the more brief and striking, the better (John 15:5; 15:10; 1 John 4:19; Rev. 2:10; 3:11; 2 Tim. 2:5; 1 Thess. 5:24; 2 Thess. 3:3; 1 Cor. 16:13; Luke 17:32; Matt. 16:41). The *Confessional* and the *Communion* address demand as texts words of exhortation to self-examination and of admonition to sincere repentance, but no less words of God's forgiving grace and soul-winning love, awakening faith, a longing for union with Christ and humble joy in His feast of love (Ps.

51:4, 7, 10; Ps. 32:5; Isa. 1:18; 43:24-25; 53:3, 4-6; Matt. 5:6; Luke 22:15; Ps. 23:5; 1 Sam. 16:7; 1 Cor. 11:28; 1 John 1:8-9; 2:1-2; Isa. 6:1-7; Mic. 6:8; Hos. 2:19-20; Matt. 26:26-30; Rev. 3:20). In the development of these texts it must never be forgotten that the purpose of the sermon is to fit the soul to receive its Lord; hence the deepest tones should be struck and all should be pervaded by pastoral love; it should not be too long. For the *Marriage* address, texts are proper which set forth the estate of matrimony as ordained of God, admonish to a Christian life in it, and exhort to renewed consecration to God and a lively confidence in His constant aid (Gen. 1:27; 2:18; 2:24; Matt. 19:6; Mark 10:11; 1 Cor. 7:10; Josh. 24:15; Prov. 24:3 -4; Luke 1:6; Eph. 4:2; 1 Cor. 13:4-7, R. V.; Col. 3:18-19; Eph. 5:22-28; Gal. 6:2; Ps. 112:1-2; 127:1; Prov. 12:4; 18:22; Ruth 1:16-17; John 2:1-11; Ps. 37:4-5). *Funeral* addresses, which when they must be held should always be held for the sake of the living, should contain a public witness to the hope in the resurrection, a last tribute of love, and a solemn reminder of the inexorable hour of death. They require texts testifying to the life-power that comes from Christ to all believers and overcomes death; the faithfulness of God, who will be a father of the fatherless and a judge of the widows, and who never forsakes them that trust in Him; the seriousness and reality of death, showing the worthlessness of everything external and derived; the importance of life as preparation for a blessed death. The personal has its place in the funeral address and may determine the choice of text, especially where the departed was not only a well-known member of the congregation but made a marked impression upon it in his life. But in such cases the choice of text no less than the development of the sermon must be characterized by an inflexible truthfulness, without exaggeration, without suppression, speaking the truth, yet always in love. Nowhere is lying cant or loveless judgment more frequently found than at funerals; many a funeral sermon helps to dig a grave for the Church itself. Appropriate funeral texts are passages such as these,—Gen. 3:19; 2 Kings 20:1; Job 14:1-2; Ps. 39:4-7; 90:1-12; 103:15-18; Luke 12:20; Matt. 22:32; John 5:24; 10:28; 11:25-26; 14:2-3; 17:24; 1 Cor. 15:20; 15:42-44; 15:55-57; Phil. 1:21, 23; 3:20; 1 Thess. 4:13-14; 2 Tim. 1:10; 1 Pet. 1:3-4; 1 John 3:2; Matt. 24:42; 25:11-12; 7:21; Luke 19:42; 2 Cor. 5:10; Rom. 6:23; Gal. 6:7-9; Ps. 23:4; Heb. 13:14; Jas. 1:12; Heb. 9:27; Rom. 14:8; Gen. 49:18; 48:21; Luke 2:25-32; 7:11-17; Mark 5:22-43; for children: Mark 10:13-16; Gal. 3:26-27; 1 Cor. 13:5 ("love seeketh not its own"); Ps. 16:6.—*Ordination* and *installation* addresses (2 Cor. 5:19-20; 6:1-9; 1 Cor. 1:17-18; 3:9; 4:1-5; 2 Cor. 2:14-16; 3:4-12), the various *consecration* addresses (consecration of a church: Gen. 28:10-22; 1 Kings 8:10-11, 22-30; John 4:24; Rev. 21:1-5; of a school: Deut. 6:4-9; Mark 10:13-16; Luke 2:49; Matt. 5:13-16; Eph. 6:4b; of a parsonage: Josh. 24:15c; of a cemetery: Gen. 23; John 19:38-42; 1 Cor. 15:51-57), and addresses at the *installation of a church council* (Acts 6:1-7; Rom. 12:1-8; 1 Pet. 4:7-11) call for texts appropriate to the several occasions; while *introductory* and *farewell* sermons require texts in which, instead of the personal element, the simple presentation of fundamental truths of God's Word is central (Rom. 1:16-17; 1 Cor. 1:30; 2:1-2, etc.).

When the preacher makes his own selection of texts, whether for the regular or for the occasional sermon, there are certain considerations that should be kept in mind. (1) The text selected must in every case contain a complete thought, even though it be a subordinate item in the larger whole. Thus Rom. 3:28, while not forming a main thought in the argument of Rom. 3:21-30, is none the less adapted to serve as text of a sermon, because it represents a thought complete in itself. (2) The passage chosen must contain a thought of actual value for Christian faith and life; otherwise the congregation cannot be edified upon its basis. G. D. Krummacher's series of sermons on the encampments of the children of Israel in the wilderness (Num. 33) fulfils the first, but transgresses the second requirement: his texts form thoughts complete in themselves, but thoughts entirely indifferent so far as Christian faith and life are concerned; and Krummacher was able to apply them to his congregation only by attempting to interpret the names of the various encampments and then allegorizing his interpretations. Again, the words, "It is a little one," in Gen. 19:20, form a complete sentence, but it occurred to no one but Spurgeon to use them as text for a sermon on little sins; the sermon is valuable in itself, but to attach it to this particular text is a violation of Scripture. The notice in John 2:12 is a thought complete in itself and important for the historical study of our Lord's ministry, but it possesses no edifying quality and is therefore valueless for the sermon. Even a passage such as John 4:1-4 is scarcely adapted to homiletic use, unless we take Jesus' withdrawal from Judea as an illustration of His selflessness, or as an act of wisdom preferring to depart rather than by remaining to create a wrong impression and thus injure the cause of the Kingdom. Again, who would undertake to preach on Gal. 1:18-24? Important as these verses are as a part of Paul's argument in chaps. 1:11-2:14, the preacher can do nothing with them. (3) The text ought not to be a passage burdened with so much archaeological material that valuable time will be lost in its elucidation and the preacher experience difficulty in bringing out the edifying value of the main thought for the congregation of today. This applies, for instance, to many portions of Hebrews, such as the elaborate proof, in chaps. 7:1-9:12, that Jesus as a priest after the order of Melchizedek is superior to the Levitical highpriest. Surely a valuable truth, but so argued and so bound up with Old Testament matters foreign to a congregation of modern Christians that its value as text in the main service is more than doubtful. In a week-day Bible hour, before a smaller circle of hearers, it might be possible profitably to treat it; perhaps by showing, on the basis of chap. 7:11 ff., Christ's superiority to the Levitical priesthood, because (a) He is not of priestly but of royal lineage. (b) He is priest not by carnal descent, but in the endless life of His personality, (c) He is made a priest with an oath sworn by God. In order to preach such a sermon in the regular Sunday service, one would need to have before one a congregation like that of Menken, homogeneous in make-up and eager and able to penetrate into the Scripture in all its parts. (4) Short texts ought never to become the rule. For it is the function of the sermon to bring its hearers to a more thorough knowledge of the Bible, so that their ability to read and understand it for themselves may be constantly increased. Many English preachers have driven the choice of brief texts to an evil extreme, and not a few of the "modern" preachers of Germany are doing the same. Even American Lutheran preachers are aping this practice. Now it would be absurd to demand that no short texts should ever be chosen. Who would seriously call it wrong to preach on the several beatitudes, the petitions of the Lord's Prayer, the seven words of Jesus on the cross, the commandments of the decalogue, or on words such as Luke 2: 10-11; 2:14; 2:49; John 8:12; 14:6; Acts 4:12; Rom. 3:28; 5:1; 8:28; Phil. 1:20; Gal. 4:4-5; 1 John 1:7b; 2:2; 3:1; 4:19; 5:4; John 3:16; 1:14; Matt. 11:28; Ps. 37:5; 50:15; 51:10; 23:4, etc., in many of which the whole fulness of divine grace and truth is focussed? No: these golden texts of Scripture, printed in the old German Bibles in "hair spaced" type and in modern English editions in red letters, not only may but must be preached on again and again. But it dare not become the rule to choose such brief texts, if our congregations are really to be made acquainted with the Bible and trained to read and study it for themselves. Preaching on the great verses of Scripture, provided that they really are this, is a most valuable aid in impressing indelibly upon the memory the fundamental Scripture truths in quintessential form. But to confine oneself to such passages or to give them the preference would be to reduce the congregation's spiritual fare to very scant rations, and is not in keeping with the reverence due to Holy Scripture, which has not been given to us in the form of a book of maxims, but as a many sided organic whole comprising history, poetry, prophecy and doctrine, and which has a right to be treated as such in the pulpit. It was not by chance that in the ancient Church the development was from the longer portions of the *lectio continua,* covering often several chapters, to the selection, not of separate verses, but of whole sections (περικοπή), which became gradually the basis of the sermon; although separate verses were occasionally preached on. We must guard here against a one-sided attitude. The defenders of the short sermon-text ought to give heed to what the defenders of sermons on longer passages have to say, and the latter ought to ponder the method of the former, properly qualified, and to ask themselves whether it would not be possible to make whole chapters the basis of sermons, especially if the texts were announced beforehand to the congregation or, better still, if the hearers brought their Bibles with them to service. Saurin has an admirable Whitsuntide sermon on Acts 2:14-41 and a passion sermon on John 17. (5) Short or long, the text must represent a unity; this is as important here as it was above in the discussion of preaching on entire biblical books. Here is the defect of many of the epistle lessons in the old system of pericopes, and the preacher should simply take the liberty of changing them. If we are convinced, with Hofmann *et al.*, that the words, ἐν ταῖς καρδίαις ὑμῶν, in 2 Pet. 1:19, belong to the following verse, we cannot include them in the pericope. Or, if Jas. 1:13-27 falls for us into these two divisions: vv. 13-18, in which the writer is still speaking of temptation, and vv. 19-27, in which he takes up the relation of the hearer to the Word, we shall make the epistle for Cantate not Jas. 1:16-21, but 1:13-18 or 16-18. (6) It is a mistake to seek out *cruces interpretum* and drag them into the pulpit. It may become necessary to preach on one or the other of these passages, in response to requests for such a discussion or in order to oppose a wrong use of them in the congregation or outside it. But then it is no longer a question of seeking out these cruces. If they occur in an otherwise valuable passage, the preacher ought not to shrink back from treating them. Thus it may become necessary to preach on 1 Pet. 3:18-20 or on important passages in Revelation. The beginner had better keep his fingers off Gal. 3:15-25, because he will not be able to do much with vv. 15-18 and will not understand v. 20; the experienced exegete and preacher may attack them with better hope of success. (7) Is it necessary to say that texts that will strike the hearer as queer or that arouse only his curiosity or even a smile should be avoided? Broadus tells of a good sermon by William Jay on Hos. 7:8,—"Ephraim is a cake not turned."[10] The thought underlying the passage is this: As a cake that is not turned at the proper time will burn and be spoiled, so Israel, not having turned betimes from its evil way, can no longer be saved and faces imminent destruction. But the preacher who tears these words from their connection, not only obscures their meaning, but risks a descent into the comic,—a thing to be scrupulously avoided. (8) The following more general considerations,

---

[10] P. 26.

finally, are in place here. The preacher ought always to take into account the needs of his congregation, and first of all those that are fundamental. To avoid repetition and monotony, he will do well to vary his sermon-text for longer periods. Texts that have not yet awakened the preacher's interest had better be passed by for the present, but should nevertheless be chosen if best adapted to meet the needs of the congregation; the preacher should censure himself for his lack of interest in such texts, for the things his congregation needs ought properly to lie next his heart.

Whatever the text that has been chosen, it must come to its full rights in the sermon. The sermon dare not deal with matters that have nothing to do with the text; that would be to turn a word of God into a lying signboard, to use it as a mere stopgap or superficial adornment. Nor dare the text become merely a motto or title of the sermon, or serve as point of departure from which the preacher advances to the elaboration of his own ideas, the springboard for a plunge into the depths or shallows of his own thought. This might lead, under the most favorable conditions, to a scriptural but not to a textual sermon, and is out of keeping with the purpose the text is intended to serve. Instead of this, the text must rather be the source of the contents of the sermon, from which all its thoughts flow, so that the preacher draws from nothing else, is guided by nothing else, imparts to his congregation nothing else. His text must be for him beginning, middle and end, and whatever does not grow out of his text, be it ever so fine and true, biblical and edifying, must be ruthlessly excluded. This does not mean that the text may not be related to, or illustrated by, other parts of the Bible. This, on the contrary, is highly necessary; for the individual text is an integral part of the whole of Scripture. But it must be insisted that whatever is gathered from the rest of Scripture, to explain and illustrate the individual text, can only serve as aid to the exposition and application of the latter, and can have no other purpose than to magnify and impress upon the congregation the text itself. Nor does this mean that the life of the congregation may not be referred to in the sermon. On the contrary, it is an important and eminently proper requirement, that the preacher take into consideration the circle of ideas, the judgments, emotions, experiences, and all the various needs of his people,[11] in order that his sermon may come home to their business and bosoms and influence them for good. But the individual text must decide as to the manner in which this is to be done. It is only when the text, owing to a faulty fixing of its limits, does not form a unity—in that case its limits ought to be changed—or when it contains, despite its unity, so great a mass of edifying materials that they cannot be managed in one sermon, or is so general in character that it can be applied without violence to various spheres of Christian life—it is only then that the actual needs of the congregation may decide which elements in the text are to be treated or set in the foreground. If a certain text is of such a nature that the needs of the congregation which must be met at the time cannot be treated as they deserve, a different text should be chosen. For, true as it is that the needs of the congregation must be satisfied, it is just as true that the text is the normative source of the contents of the sermon, and that nothing may be presented in the sermon that has not grown organically out of its text. (P. 338.)

The importance of the choice of texts will at once be apparent to all. "A felicitous choice of text," says Broadus, "will animate the preacher throughout the preparation and the delivery of the sermon, and will help him to gain at once the attention of his hearers."[12] But how many preachers err gravely in this respect! To escape this difficulty, it seems better to preach continuously through entire books of the Bible. Few, indeed, if any preachers have undertaken to preach

---

[11]See above, chap. 8.—[12]P. 23.

through the whole Bible from beginning to end; the treatment of single books or larger portions of books has been more frequently attempted. George D. Boardman delivered before his congregation, the First Baptist church of Philadelphia, Pa., on successive Wednesday evenings from October, 1864 to April, 1882, six hundred forty lectures, going through every word of the New Testament, and then began a similar series on the Old Testament. Alexander Maclaren in his *Expositions of Holy Scripture,* and Joseph Parker in his *Family Bible,* treat selected passages from the various books. In the evangelical church of Germany, especially since the impetus given by Menken[13] at the beginning of the nineteenth century, such preaching on entire books of the Bible has been practiced more generally than in England and America.[14] "The First Book of Discipline" of the Scottish church laid down the rule: "We think it most expedient that the Scripture be read in order, that is, that some one book of the Old and the New Testament be begun, and orderly read to the end. And the same we judge of preaching, where the minister for the most part remaineth in one place, for this skipping and divagation from place to place, be it in reading or be it in preaching, we judge not so profitable to edify the church." Nevertheless this rule was forgotten later on in the

---

[13]Comp. his homilies on the story of Elijah (1822), on Matt. 1-14 (1822), on Heb. 9-11 (1821, 1831), etc.—[14]Comp. Schleiermacher on Acts, Philippians and Colossians and on Mark (all before 1834); F. W. Krummacher on Elijah (1828), Elishah (1835), David (1867); Fr. Arndt on the sermon on the mount (1838), the parables (1847), the life of Christ (1835); R. Rothe on the pastoral epistles and 1 John (delivered ca. 1830-37, published 1876 and 1878); Caspari on the Psalms (1863). Later we have Koegel on Romans, 1 Peter, and James; Luger on James; Dryander on 1 John; Simon on 1 Peter; H. Hoffmann and Kaiser on the sermon on the mount; Kegel on the lives of the patriarchs. To this incomplete list should be added the numerous "Bibelstunden" held in town and country, on week-days and sometimes on Sundays, many of which bear the character of expository preaching of the finest type. Of those published we mention Heim on Genesis; Gerok on Acts and the Psalms; Loehe on the lives of David and Solomon; Schlier on the life of Saul and David and on Romans; J. Mueller on Galatians; Polstorff on the Gospels; Pauli on the lives of the patriarchs; H. Beck on the life of Abraham; Muenchmeyer on Revelation; Behrmann on the parables, the sermon on the mount, the sayings of Jesus in John's Gospel; Gess on John 13-17 and Romans; Taube on the Psalms; Weber on Isaiah; Borrmann on Philippians; Ernst on Ephesians; Wenger on Mark; Pank, Dryander, E. Frommel and Koegel on the Four Gospels; Besser on almost the whole N. T.; Hoffmann on Acts and the epistles; Grashoff on the historical books of the N. T.

English and American churches, and preference was given to short texts, which served often as mere mottoes, so that the hearers learned less and less about the Scriptures as a whole. F. W. Robertson's lectures on Corinthians and, long before him, Archbishop Leighton's commentary on First Peter were some of the brilliant exceptions to this practice. But a return to truly expository preaching on whole books or on longer portions did not take place until the energetic sponsorship of this type of preaching by men like James W. Alexander in his *Thoughts on Preaching* (1860; the chapter in question was published earlier), R. L. Dabney in his *Sacred Rhetoric* (1870) and John A. Broadus in his widely used *On the Preparation and Delivery of Sermons* (1870). C. J. Vaughan, G. D. Boardman, Joseph Parker, and especially W. M. Taylor, F. B. Meyer and J. Campbell Morgan showed in a practical way how the exposition of biblical books in whole or in part could be made profitable for the congregation.[15] The following reasons for the cultivation of this sort of expository preaching are given by Alexander: "(1) It is the most obvious and natural way of conveying to the hearers the import of the sacred volume and, therefore, corresponds better with the very idea and design of preaching; (2) it has the sanction of primitive and ancient usage; (3) it is adapted to secure the greatest amount of scriptural knowledge to both preacher and hearers; (4) it is best fitted to communicate the knowledge of scriptural truth in its connection; (5) it affords inducement and occasion to the preacher to declare the whole counsel of God; giving occasion for remarking on many passages of the Bible which otherwise might never enter into one's sermons; and for giving important hints and admonitions which might seem to some hearers

---

[15] Comp. C. J. Vaughan, *Lectures on Romans* (1859), *Philippians* (1862), *the Revelation of St. John* (1863); Joseph Parker, *The Gospel by Matthew* (1869), *Adam, Noah and Abraham* (1880), *The Inner Life of Christ as Revealed in the Gospel of Matthew* (1881-2); Geo. D. Boardman, *Studies in the Creative Week* (1876), *The Mountain Instruction* (1880); W. M. Taylor, *David, the King of Israel* (1875), *Elijah, the Prophet* (1876), *Peter, the Apostle* (1877), *Daniel, the Beloved* (1878), *Moses, the Law-giver* (1879), *The Parables of Our Saviour* (1886); F. B. Meyer, *Jeremiah: Priest and Prophet; Zechariah: Prophet of Hope; Joseph: Beloved, Hated, Exalted; David: Shepherd, Psalmist, King; Peter: Fisherman, Disciple, Apostle;* G. Campbell Morgan, *The Parables of the Kingdom, The Ten Commandments, Wherein Have We Robbed God?* (Malachi.—*The Expositor's Bible* (Doran) and *The Shorter Course* (Scribner) contain admirable homiletic material for expository preaching on whole books or connected passages.

offensively personal if introduced into a topical discussion, but which are here naturally suggested by the passage in hand; (6) it admits of being made generally interesting to Christian assemblies; (7) it has a direct tendency to correct, if not to preclude, the evils incident to the common textual mode of preaching, for instance, to misinterpret texts by excessive allegorizing, by 'accommodation,' etc.; for men are often driven into such misinterpretation by the difficulty of finding for every sermon a short passage which will legitimately afford the requisite amount of material. We know that to compose a sermon upon a text of Scripture, with very little reference to its position in the Word of God, and a very little inquiry as to the intent of the Spirit in the words, is a thing not only possible but common. The evil grows apace, wherever the rhetorical aspect of preaching attracts undue attention; and the desire to be original, striking, ingenious, and elegant, supersedes the earnest endeavor to be scriptural. This abuse is in a good degree precluded by the method of exposition. The minister who from week to week is laboring to elucidate some important book of Scripture has this kept forcibly before his mind. It will necessarily be the chief subject of his studies. Whatever else he may neglect, he will, if he is a conscientious man, sedulously peruse and ponder those portions which he is to explain; using every auxiliary, and especially comparing Scripture with Scripture. Suppose him to pursue this regular investigation of any one book, for several successive months, and we perceive that he must be acquiring a knowledge of the very word of truth, vastly more extensive, distinct, and profound, than can fall to the lot of one who perhaps for no two discourses together, finds himself in the same part of the canon. Two men practicing upon the two methods, each in an exclusive manner may severally gain an equal measure of intellectual discipline and real knowledge, but their attainments will differ in kind. The one is driven from the variety of his topics to a fitful and fragmentary study of the Bible; the other is bound down to a systematic and unbroken investigation of consecutive truths. The knowledge of the Bible is something more than the knowledge of its isolated sentences. It includes a full acquaintance with the relation which every proposition sustains to the narrative or argument of which it is a part. This is particularly true of trains of reasoning where everything depends on a cognizance of the links which connect the several truths, and the order in which those truths are presented. Large portions of holy writ are closely argumentative and can be understood in their true intention only when the whole scope and sequence of the terms are considered. This logical connection is not less the result of inspiration than is any individual statement. In some books of Scripture the argument runs from beginning to end, and the clew to the whole is to be sought in the analysis of the reasoning. As instances of this we may cite the epistles to the Romans and to the Hebrews, of which no man can have any adequate conception who has not been familiar with all their parts as constituting a logical whole. This, however, is so universally conceded as a first principle of hermeneutics, that it is needless to press it further. But it is not so generally perceived that in the other methods of preaching this great advantage is sacrificed. It is true that a man may announce as his text a single verse or clause of a verse, and then offer a full and satisfactory elucidation of the whole context; but, so far as this is done, the sermon is expository. But this species of discourse is becoming more and more rare. In the sermons of the nonconformists this was usually the plan of proceeding. In modern sermons, there is, for the most part, nothing which resembles it. A text is taken usually with a view to some preconceived subject; a proposition is deduced from the text; and this confirmed or illustrated by a series of statements which would have been precisely the same if any similar verse, in any other part of the record, had been chosen. Here there is no interpretation, for there is no pretence of it. There may be able theological discussion, and we by no means would exclude this, but where a method merely textual or topical prevails, there is an absolute forsaking of that which we have maintained to be the true notion of preaching. We can conceive of a hearer listening during a course of years to every verse of the epistle to the Hebrews, laid open in connection with as many sermons of the popular sort, without obtaining thereby an insight into the grand scope and intricate contexture of that wonderful production. Now we say that the method which makes such an omission possible is unfit to be the exclusive method."

Shall we then be swayed by these considerations and demand successive sermons on biblical books? Hardly so emphatically as this. For one reason, because the contrast takes on for us a different form. Many of the products that Alexander allows to pass as sermons scarcely deserve in our opinion the name.[16] We demand that *every* sermon

---

[16]Comp. p. 290: "William Jay is justly celebrated as one of the most fascinating and instructive preachers of Great Britain. In his sermons we find many valuable scriptural truths, many original and touching illustrations, much sound argument, pungent exhortation, and great unction. In themselves considered and viewed as pulpit orations, they seem open to scarcely a single objection; yet as expositions of

with a text prefixed shall expound that text in its connection and apply it to the congregation. So that every sermon must bear the character of expository preaching, and a sermon that does not has no right to exist. Hence, only the fourth and fifth of Alexander's reasons really hold, and the fourth more than the fifth, because what the fifth requires can be met as well in other ways. It is certainly possible for an individual or a Church to prepare a series of texts in which the whole counsel of God is set forth. And if such a series is adopted by an entire church body, surely the preacher using it will not fall under the reproach of being too personal, if this be a reproach. Moreover, what becomes of the whole counsel of God when the preacher chooses only texts to which his personal preference inclines him? But Alexander's fourth reason is valid. It is without doubt the duty of the preacher to communicate to his hearers the knowledge of Scripture in such a way that they will become familiar with at least some of the books in their connection. Where there has been a thorough grounding in biblical history, this duty still exists with respect to the non-historical books, especially the epistles. It is a deplorable situation when intelligent members of the Church are unfamiliar with the contents of Romans or Galatians, James or 1 Peter as a whole; and the sermon cannot be held guiltless, even though it is not the only medium whereby such biblical knowledge may be gained. We are convinced, therefore, that the sermon should deal consecutively with the more important biblical books as a whole. For the best method of accomplishing this, we refer to the following chapter.

But two things must be kept in mind. First, there have always been and always will be members in the congregation who cannot comprehend Romans or Isaiah as a connected whole; and secondly, saving knowledge does not consist in detailed information as to the

---

the Scripture, they are literally nothing. They clear up no difficulties in the argument of the inspired writers; they give no wide prospects of the field in which their matter lies; they might be repeated for a life-time without tending in the slightest degree to educate a congregation in habits of sound interpretation. The same remark applies to the majority of American discourses, and most of all to those which conform to the prevailing taste of New England. In occasional sermons, and monthly collections, we are often forcibly struck with the absence of all logical concatenation. The text is a sign or motto, after announcing which the preacher glides into a gentle train of commonplaces, or a series of thoughts which, however ingenious and interesting and true, have no necessary connection, 'continuous in their discontinuity, like the sand-thread of the hour-glass'."

structure and argument of the various biblical books. Indeed, the latter may be present to a conspicuous degree, while the former is entirely absent, and vice versa. But the imparting of saving knowledge is the chief function of the sermon. From this it follows not only that the treatment of entire biblical books cannot be the exclusive method,—so far Alexander, Dabney *et al.* go with us,—but also that it cannot be regarded as of primary but only of secondary value. The choice of texts must primarily be such that the whole congregation, and not only an advanced circle in it, is served Thus we are led to prefer sermons on selected passages for the main Sunday service, in which we take for granted the presence of all types of church members, and to relegate the homiletic treatment of entire books to those services in which smaller groups are present, who are or may become interested in studying the Bible by books, i. e., to the Sunday evening or the week-day service, to which hearers may bring their Bibles and follow in them the exposition. Moreover, despite the fact that the Bible is an organic whole,—though the origin of its several books extends over a period of fifteen hundred years, and each of its books reveals a definite unity in its development,—it must not be forgotten that it abounds also in single passages, and even single verses, in which the great truths most vital to Christian faith and life are summarized, or which even if they contain only portions of these truths, form none the less a unity and, when interpreted in the light of the whole Scripture, are seen to be integral parts of the divine plan of salvation. It is these central passages by which the Holy Spirit, not exclusively but primarily, produces saving faith in the hearts of men. The importance of these central passages is recognized by the same Alexander whom we have found so vigorous an advocate of the homiletic use of entire books. Says he: "The great questions which have agitated the world, which agitate our own bosoms, which we should like to have settled before we die, which we should ask an apostle about if he were here,—these are to general Scripture truth what great mountains are in geography. Some anxious to omit hackneyed topics, omit the greatest. Just as if we should describe Switzerland and omit the Alps. . . Some ministers preach twenty years, and yet never preach on Judgment, Hell, the Crucifixion, the essence of Saving Faith—nor on those great themes which in all ages affect children, and affect the common mind, such as the Deluge, the sacrifice intended of Abraham, the death of Absalom, the parable of Lazarus. The Methodists constantly pick out these striking themes, and herein they gain a just advantage over us."[17] Dr. Burrell, of the Dutch Reformed Church, writes in the same strain: "There are many passages which are as familiar to Christians as the beaten paths leading to the doorways of their earthly homes; passages which are especially hallowed by association, perhaps as the means of their conversion, or by some experience of deep joy or sorrow. Not a few of these are like the scone stone in Westminster Abbey, on which sovereigns have been crowned from time immemorial."[18] And the Baptist Broadus emphasizes the same truth: "What has made some texts familiar to all, but the fact that they are so manifestly good texts? It is a very mistaken desire for novelty which leads a man to shrink from such fruitful passages as 'God so loved the world,' etc.; 'This is a faithful saying,' etc., which Luther used to call 'little Bibles,' as if including in their narrow compass the whole Bible... In point of fact, the great preachers, all the best preachers, do preach much upon the great texts and the great subjects. How is a feebler man ever to develop his own strength, unless he grapples with great themes? One may show skill, and add somewhat to the harvest, by cultivating out-of-the-way corners and unpromising ledges of rock; but the bulk of the crop, by which the family are fed, must come from the broad, open field."[19] No one need fear that the congregation will not be stimulated by means of these central texts, because they are already so familiar with them. Burrell's experience was the reverse of this. "He who will turn away," he says, "from the tradition of the pulpit as to the meaning and application of such passages, and make personal and earnest study of them, will often find much that is new to him and his hearers, as the skilful gold-hunter in California will sometimes follow in the very track of many searchers, and gain there his richest harvest. Besides, what we need is not absolute novelty, but simply freshness. If we can manage by prayerful reflection to obtain such views and provide such illustrations of a familiar text as will give it a fresh

---

[17] P. 11.—[18] *The Sermon, Its Construction and Delivery*, p. 39.— [19] P. 27.—Comp. Spurgeon: "I know a minister whose shoe-latchet I am unworthy to unloose, whose preaching is often no better than sacred miniature painting—I might almost say holy trifling. He is great upon the ten toes of the beast, the four faces of the cherubim, the mystical meaning of badgers' skins, and the typical bearings of the staves of the ark and the windows of Solomon's temple: but the sins of business men, the temptations of the times, and the needs of the age, he scarcely ever touches upon. Such preaching reminds me of a lion engaged in mouse-hunting, or a man-of-war cruising after a lost waterbutt" (*Lectures to My Students*).

interest to ourselves and the hearers, then all the riches of the passage are made available for good. . . Such texts, when treated in a novel way, are invested with a double interest; and those who know them best are most impressed; as when one returning to the home of his childhood sees new beauty in familar scenes." Austin Phelps, whose *Theory of Preaching* is distinguished among homiletical works for the attention it gives to the qualifications of a good text, sums up as follows: "Old biblical truths can be handled without conceits and without straining; and thus handled, they are the elementary forces of the pulpit. A preacher needs to believe this. Trust the common stock of biblical thought, and use it courageously. That very courage lifts a preacher's mind to a loftier level of working. Faithful manipulation of such materials is the thing needed. Do not use them, in the bulk, at second-hand. Work them over. Reconstruct them. Polish them. Put them through the laboratory of your own thinking. Get fresh robes for them from your own emotions. Do something, or the other thing, or all things, which shall make them your own. Quicken thus your own interest in them; and the result will be that, when they go from you, they will uplift hearers to the heavens."

As to which are the central passages of Scripture, the judgment of the liberal theologian will naturally differ from that of the preacher whose thinking is dominated by Scripture. For the latter these passages can be none other than those that treat of the birth, life and works, the suffering, death, resurrection and ascension of Christ, and of the Holy Spirit and His saving work. This being true, the Lutheran Church makes no mistake when she accommodates herself in her choice of texts to the Church Year, especially in its festival half, and uses the old churchly pericopes which are controlled by the idea of the Church Year and furnish valuable texts for the treatment of these central truths; provided this does not bar the use of other pericopes chosen according to the same principles, nor consecutive sermons on entire biblical books in secondary services or even in the main Sunday service during the non-festival half of the year.

The gradual development of the Christian Year, from the observance of Sunday (first century) to Easter and Lent (middle of the second century), Pentecost (third century), Epiphany (on January 6 since the end of the third century; feast of the baptism as well as the birth of Christ), Ascension (fourth century) and Christmas (on December 25, first in 354 at Rome; 379 in Constantinople; known in 380, but not celebrated until 388, in Antioch; 382 in Cappadocia; 432 in Egypt; since 451 in Palestine), cannot be traced here; the student is referred to a work like G. Rietschel, *Lehrbuch der Liturgik*, vol. i (1900). But in view of the prejudice against the Church Year still current in wide circles in our land, the following words of a liberal German theologian who is certainly not prejudiced in its favor may be set down here. "One is moved to think first of all of the religious value of this whole arrangement, not only in view of an individualistic and sentimental religion which is prone to regard with disapproval the fellowship of the festival celebration and its fixed order, but also when one looks beyond the individual and asks oneself whether the idea of the Church Year can take root in this day among a whole people. [This last does not concern us, living as we do in a free church and knowing from the example of the Roman-Catholic, Episcopal and Lutheran churches that the idea and use of the Church Year can maintain themselves in surroundings, even churchly surroundings, ignorant of and often ridiculing them.] The practical expression of the striving for religious fellowship, for a common service, must suffer impoverishment under the influence of a monotonous uniformity. The alternation of festival day and every day corresponds to the ebb and flood in the spiritual life, and is more natural and therefore truer than a uniformly high level, maintained on principle and often achieved with great pains. This alternation also takes into account the needs of the imagination, which is after all present in all but comparatively small, matter-of-fact circles. Besides this, the annual festival order furnishes a helpful opportunity for presenting in their unity and diversity, their ground tone and its variations, the wealth of religious perceptions and ideas which an historical religion such as Christianity comprises by its very origin, and which it has enlarged through a long development [sic]. Christmas preaches Christ in a different way from Easter and Good Friday, and the alternation of seasons in the Church Year sets before the celebrating congregation, on an historical foundation, the religious seeking and its fulfilment, the mood of solemn self-examination and soaring joy, the Christ of Paul and John and the Jesus of the synoptists, each in its turn. How naturally the great wealth of the Gospel fits into this frame and is illustrated in it, item by item, may be best seen, even by one who stands aloof, by a glance into a service-book prepared with care and affection, such as Smend's *Kirchenbuch*. But the churchly festivals do us this great service unaware,—they keep the present expression of Christian faith in vital touch with the history whence this faith has sprung. Thus they form a corrective to a 'Christianity without Christ,' a dilution of Christianity to an unhistorical natural religion, whether mystic or moralistic.

With this there enters into the celebration the element of devotion: to the stimulus to self-endeavor comes the objective, that which has become, that which operates upon us. Religion makes itself felt as a gift and brings the feeling of rest, of receiving, of giving thanks, and the congregation is in this way assured again and again of the great common possession that it has in its history. Religious art has therefore an inexhaustible opportunity to take its place in the service; we need think only of the Christmas mysteries and Passion music. Indeed, it is the highest churchly festivals that furnish a strong incentive to dispense with the preaching service and to permit the festival devotion alone to express itself in a purely liturgical service."[20] The Christian year runs like a thread of gold through the natural or calendar year and stamps upon it the character of the sacred. The days of the Christian's life are not to be passed in monotonous uniformity. His pilgrimage through time is not like a journey across a flat and dreary desert, where no alternation of hill and vale, no diversity of scenery refreshes the weary wanderer; where no vistas beckon, no friendly oasis invites to rest; where no sites hallowed by noble memories uplift his heart and call forth his reverence. He will pass rather, each twelve-month, guided by the Church Year, through the whole history of salvation and wander past all the mighty works of God enshrined therein, and live them over again one by one in his soul. The Church Year is a miniature, as it were, of the whole course of salvation compressed into the frame of a single year. It cannot but be of decided educational value for the congregation to have presented to it, year after year, the wonderful works of God in lesson and sermon, echoed in the hymns and prayers in which it praises and adores the love of God revealed in them and calling perennially to the soul. If we in the Lutheran Church did not have the Church Year with its festivals and its proper texts, we should be immeasurably less certain that we as Christians rest absolutely with all that we are and have upon the gracious doing of our God; while the thought of judgment and eternity, the return of Christ and the coming of life everlasting would mean still less to us than it does, if each Church Year did not testify, on its last Sundays, of the last things in the life of the individual and of the Church, and call upon us again and yet again to live our whole life *sub specie aeternitatis.*

The origin of the so-called old-churchly pericopes, which are the

---

[20]Wolff in *Die Religion in Geschichte und Gegenwart,* vol. ii (1910), p. 878.

chief bearers of the idea of the Church Year, is bound up with the history of the liturgical lesson. We must confine ourselves here to the salient features and cannot trace the development in detail. As already stated in the introduction, the whole structure of the Christian service with its lessons followed that of the service of the Jewish synagogue, with this difference that to the Old Testament lesson of the latter the former added its New Testament lesson. Already at the time of the so-called Second Epistle of Clement, and of Justin Martyr, there is evidence that the address or sermon was attached to this lesson. In its most fully developed form the lesson was fourfold, taken from the Law, the Prophets, the Apostle, and the Gospel. Since the prophetic lesson, at least, in the synagogue service was a *lectio selecta*, it is probable that the lesson in the early days of the Church was not exclusively a *lectio continua*. Even if it should have been, it was soon interrupted by the lessons of the various festivals, as they arose, on which days passages bearing upon the festival idea were usually read. Moreover, it was customary, especially in the weeks preceding Easter and Pentecost, to read particular books of the Bible; thus in various places Genesis was read during Lent, Job in Holy Week, Jonah on Good Friday, and Acts or Revelation between Easter and Pentecost. Chrysostom, in the year in which he preached on Genesis, found himself interrupted by Easter and continued the lessons from Genesis after Easter. It may be said in general, that during the first four centuries the *lectio continua* prevailed on the ordinary Sundays and on weekdays, but with the gradual development of the festivals the *lectio selecta* found a place on these latter days; but even the *lectio continua* on week-days and ordinary Sundays was interrupted by the martyrs' days as well as by other special occasions. Thus the soil was prepared for the predominance of the *lectio selecta* and for the preparation of a lectionary or system of pericopes. It was supposed formerly that Jerome, at the close of the fourth century, prepared such a system, or re-arranged and completed an earlier one and that this was approved by Bishop Damasus of Rome about the year 384. And, indeed, there is extant a *Comes Hieronymi*,[21] i. e., a series of pericopes bearing the name of Jerome. This is said to have formed the foundation of the system of pericopes that was completed by Gregory the Great and

---

[21]The name *comes* comes probably from the fact that the book of pericopes had to be used in the service alongside the *missale*, which did not contain the lessons, so that the comes was the constant "companion" of the missal.

officially introduced in Rome, as well as of that which Charlemagne later introduced. And, since Charlemagne's system agrees in substance with that taken over by Luther, it was thought possible to trace the pedigree of our pericopes back to Jerome, if not to a still earlier date. But it is a question whether Jerome had anything at all to do with the *Comes*, which was named after him only in the eleventh century. It is certain that an attempt was made between 450 and 500, in the Gallican Church,[22] to appoint fixed lessons in at least certain dioceses and for a part of the year; that in the course of the sixth century there came into use in Toledo, Spain, the still extant *Liber Comicus*, containing Old Testament, epistle and gospel lessons, as well as other pericope-series in other places; and that there arose in the Roman church a series of lessons that goes back at least to the days of Gregory the Great, who expounded forty of its gospels in homilies. Akin to this Roman series existing at Rome in the days of Gregory the Great, if not identical with it, was the Roman system of pericopes which displaced in the course of time those in use in other sections of the church[23] and strove for supremacy. It was especially Pepin the Short and Charlemagne who contributed to its spread; displacing in their empire the existing liturgies by the Roman liturgy, they introduced with the latter also the Roman system of pericopes. The Roman system differed from most of its competitors by including epistle and gospel lessons, but excluding all Old Testament lessons. Milan retained its own independent system and Spain the Mozarabic series; separate series remained in use for a time in parts of the Franco-German empire and England, but gradually disappeared before the Roman system. The so-called *Homiliarium* of Charlemagne greatly hastened this process. It was customary for the clerics to read a regular lesson at the "nocturnal hours," followed on Sundays and festival days by a selection from a sermon or from some commentary. Observing that these sermons bristled with errors and that their selection left much to be desired, Charlemagne entrusted Paulus Diaconus with the preparation of a usable collection of homilies; this was completed between 786 and 797 and was introduced in the entire empire. It was divided into a "winter part" (Advent—five weeks before Christmas—to Easter Eve) with 40 pericopes and 110 homilies, and

---

[22] We leave out of account the Oriental Church, because its lectionaries have no bearing upon the pericopes in use among us.—[23] Bede's *Homiliarium* followed the Neapolitan series in the so-called *Evangeliarium* of Cuthbert, which had early found its way to England.

a "summer part" (Easter to the close of the Church Year) with 78 pericopes and 134 homilies; the homilies being all of them on gospel texts. This book of homilies, following as it does the Roman system of pericopes introduced by Charlemagne, is our source for the gospel lessons of this system. Wiegand, in his *Das Homiliarium Karls des Grossen* (1897), has traced with absolute certainty Charlemagne's system of pericopes, which furnished the texts for all subsequent sermons. While Migne prints in his "seria latina" the Homiliarium in the form in which it circulated at the close of the Middle Ages, Wiegand goes back to the original form. From a "Comes" of the ninth century, of Gallican origin, we learn what were the epistle lessons of this system. In these two documents we have the pericopes which were in use with slight modifications during the entire Middle Ages, and were taken over without much change by Luther, so far as the lessons for the Sundays and the chief festivals are concerned.

This brief historical sketch will make clear with what right we may call these pericopes "old-churchly." Considered as a whole, they do not go back beyond the close of the sixth or the beginning of the seventh century. Many individual lessons may, indeed, be traced with certainty much farther back, some as far as the third or even the second century; thus the Easter and Pentecost lessons, and later those for Christmas, the Temptation of Christ for the beginning of Lent, the lessons for the first and second Sundays after Easter. Ambrose is familiar with Matt. 21 as text for Palm Sunday. In the Eastern Church, the Miracle at Cana, the Baptism of Jesus, and the Visit of the Magi were connected with Epiphany in the fourth century, the second of these probably earlier. The same will be true of the lessons for many apostles' and martyrs' days. But if the Homiliarium of Charlemagne contained no less than 138 gospel pericopes, it is evident that it could not have included only texts for the Sundays and festival days, and that the latter made up only a fraction of the entire number. This too can be studied in detail in Wiegand's book. To illustrate we shall set down here the pericopes prescribed in the Homiliarium up to Epiphany. (1) Hebdomada V ante natale Domini: John 6:5 ff.; (2) Hebdomada IV ante natale Domini: Matt. 21:1ff.; (3) Hebdomada III ante natale Domini: Luke 21:25 ff; (4) Hebdomada II ante natale Domini: Matt 11:2ff.; (5) Hebdomada I ante natale Domini: John 1:19ff.; (6) Feria IV ante natale Domini in mense decimo: Luke 1:26ff.; (7) Feria VI ante natale Domini in mense decimo: Luke 1: 39 ff.; (8) Die sabbati ante natale Domini in mense decimo: Luke 3: 1ff.; (9) In vigilia natalis Domini ad nonam: Matt. 1:18ff.; (10) In natale Domini. Nocte: Isa. 9:1-8 (11) Isa. 40:1-17; (12) Isa. 52:1-10; (13) Isa. 61:10-62:12; (14-15) In natale Domini: Luke 2:1ff.; Luke 2:15ff.; (16) In natale Domini ad missas: John 1:1ff.; (17) In natale sancti Stephani protomartyris Christi: Matt. 23:34ff.; (18) In natale sancti Johannis evangelistae: John 21:19ff.; (19) In natale innocentum: Matt. 1:13 ff.; (20) In octavas Domini, id est, in calendas Januarias: Luke 2:21ff.; (21) Dominica post natalem Domini: Luke 2:33ff.; (22) In Epiphania: Matt. 2:1ff.; (23) Infra hebdomadam, feria IV: John 1:29ff.; (24) In octava Epiphaniae: Matt. 3:13ff.; (25) Dominica I post Epiphaniam: Luke 2:42ff.— Since the greater part of this copious lectionary was dropped out in the Reformation period, and only the lessons for Sundays and festival days were retained, it is clear that what we possess is only a fragment of the original structure, and we need not be surprised if we are frequently unable to discover the connecting links between the several pericopes or if this or that pericope appears as a manifest intrusion. The pericopes for the Trinity season defy all explanation, so long as they are regarded as a consecutive series from the first to the twenty-fifth Sunday after Trinity. Their selection seems to have been determined originally by the apostles' and martyrs' days falling in this season. The Homiliarium of Charlemagne divides them into these four groups: post pentecosten, post natale apostolorum (Peter and Paul, 29 June), post Laurentii (10 August), post S. Angeli (St. Michael and All Angels, 29 September). This would explain perhaps the gospels for V to XV post Trin., but not the others. And where among us is there still to be found a consciousness of these apostles' and martyrs' days? So far as the epistle lessons for this season are concerned, the order of Paul's epistles seems to have been followed almost throughout, beginning with IV or VI post Trin. Even in the more orderly arrangement of the festival half, the order not infrequently offends. To say nothing of the lesson for St. Stephen (26 December) which is not appointed for Second Christmas, one wonders why the gospel lessons from Christmas to Epiphany were not arranged chronologically: why Matt. 2:13 ff. should precede Matt. 2:1 ff. Where Holy Innocents was observed this was not so strange, but we who no longer know this day (the Episcopal Church still holds fast to it), and yet would like to retain this lesson as a part of the infancy narrative, are confused by the order. A uniform thought runs through the Advent lessons, most of the Epiphany lessons, and the Passiontide lessons, though the selection of the last of these was determined as much by the churchly practice of fasting as by the sufferings of Christ.[24] For us who do not practice fasting these references are meaningless.

A knowledge of these historical facts will on the one hand prevent us from idolizing the old-churchly pericopes as a marvelous product of the wisdom of the Church, as possessing unity and organic completeness, as having been chosen with regard to the four seasons of the natural year,[25] or as even inspired by the Holy Ghost.[26] But this knowledge need not, on the other hand, cause us to look upon these old pericopes as devoid of all value nor to reject them altogether as sermon texts. This will be the attitude of those alone who confuse the needs of the congregation with the desires of the theologians. The latter would doubtless prefer a system complete in itself, in which the lessons of the year were linked together in an unbroken logical chain; but for this the simple layman cares little. For him it is enough that the leading ideas of Christian faith and life are presented to his view during the course of a year. And it cannot be denied that

---

[24] Comp. the gospel for Invocavit ("When he had fasted forty days and forty nights"); the epistle for the same Sunday ("in watchings, in fastings") and for Reminiscere ("abstineatis vos a fornicatione"); the epistle and gospel for Laetare, pointing in mid-lent to the joyous Eastertide with its freedom from the law.—[25] Simon Saccus fancied, in the introduction to the second part of his *Postil* (1590), that the gospel lessons of the sower, the laborers in the vineyard, and the miraculous draught of fishes were appointed for the spring of the year, when work was resumed in field and vineyard and the fishing season opened; and many gospels of the healing of the sick, for the autumn when there is commonly the most sickness!—[26] So John Habermann in his *Postil* of 1575, in connection with the gospel for IV Advent:—"The ancient teachers of the Christian Church who appointed the Sunday gospels and distributed them through the year were led by the Holy Ghost, so that they did not accidentally or unadvisedly appoint this lesson for this Sunday, but did it for strong and sufficient reasons, to wit: because it forms an evident and clear explanation of the gospel of last Sunday, in which we heard how John the Baptist sent to Jesus and asked, Art Thou he that should come or do we look for another? Now, in order that the plain man may not become suspicious and imagine that John was in doubt and did not know certainly and thoroughly that Christ was the true Saviour and promised Messiah, this gospel is appointed to be read; so that the one gospel is the interpretation and explanation of the other."—Comp. Lisko, *Das christl. Kirchenjahr* (1840); Wirth, *Die kirchl. Perikopen, ein Versuch, Geschichte, Plan und Zusammenstellung derselben zu entwickeln* (1842); Strauss, *Das evang. Kirchenjahr* (1850); F. Bauernfeind, *Das altkirchl. Perikopensystem d. abendlaendischen Kirche* (1892)—all of them interesting but untenable theories of the structure of the Church Year and its pericopes.

this can be done, without violence to the text, upon the basis of the old series of pericopes, especially as amplified and altered by Luther.

Luther was well aware of the defects of the old system of pericopes. For him the chief defect did not consist in its failure to form a harmonious whole; otherwise he would not have added to the lack of harmony and advised passing by the week-day and other texts and preaching upon the Catechism on Sunday afternoons and upon entire biblical books on week-days.[27] Its chief defect lay for him in its contents and particularly in its lack of a fitting close. His position may be gathered from the following quotations. In his *Von Ordnung Gottesdiensts in der Gemeine* (1523) he says: "Over and above the daily services for the smaller groups, there should be services for the whole congregation on Sundays, when mass and vespers should be sung, as we have been accustomed to do. At each of these services a sermon should be preached to the whole congregation; in the morning on the regular gospel for the day, in the evening on the epistle lesson. Or the preacher may also preach on continuous portions of biblical books, as he deems it most profitable."[28] In his *Formula Missae* of the same year he writes: "Post hanc [i. e., collectam] lectio Epistolae. Verum nondum tempus est et hic novandi, quando nulla impia legitur. Alioqui, cum raro eae partes ex Epistolis Pauli legantur, in quibus fides docetur, sed potissimum morales et exhortatoriae, ut ordinator ille Epistolarum videatur fuisse insigniter indoctus et superstitiosus operum ponderator, officium requirebat eas potius pro maiore parte ordinare, quibus fides in Christum docetur. Idem certe in Evangeliis spectavit saepius, quisquis fuerit lectionum istarum autor. Sed interim supplebit hoc vernacula concio. Alioqui, si futurum est, ut vernacula missa habeatur (quod Christus faveat), danda est opera, ut Epistolae et Evangelia suis optimis et potioribus locis legantur in missa."[29] In *Deutsche Messe* (1526): "Since the chief and most important part of every service is the preaching and teaching of God's Word, we order the sermon and the lesson as follows: On saints' days and Sundays we let the usual epistle and gospel lessons stand, and have three sermons. At five or six in the morning we sing several psalms, as at matins; then we preach on the epistle for the day, principally for the benefit of the servants, that they may also be provided for and hear God's Word, in case they cannot attend the other services. After the sermon, an antiphon and the Te Deum. . . . At mass, about eight or nine o'clock, we preach on the gospel for the

---

[27]See above, p. 277.—[28]*Weimar ed.*, xii, 36.—[29]*Weimar ed.*, xii, 209 f.

day, throughout the year. In the afternoon, at vespers, after the Magnificat, we preach on the Old Testament, book after book. We retain the epistle and gospel lessons arranged according to the seasons of the year, as we have been hitherto accustomed, for the following reasons: We have no particular fault to find with them. Moreover, there are at present in Wittenberg many who are to learn to preach in places where this selection of epistles and gospels is still in use and will probably remain in use. As long as we can aid and serve them in this way, without injury to ourselves, we leave it as it is. By doing this, however, we do not wish to censure those who take up whole books of the evangelists. In this way we judge the layman will have sufficient preaching and instruction. Whoever desires more, will find enough on the other days."[30] To Monday and Tuesday he assigns the Catechism; to Wednesday, Matthew; Saturday, John; Thursday and Friday, the apostolic letters and other New Testament materials. "Another reason why we retain the epistles and gospels as they are appointed in the postils is, because there are few intellectually endowed preachers, able to treat forcibly and profitably a whole evangelist or other book."[31] Hence Luther himself did not think too highly of the traditional pericopes; nevertheless, beside his numerous sermons on entire books, he took these old pericopes as texts for the sermons in his *Kirchenpostille,* that model sermon-book for preachers. Not, however, without correcting them in several places. Though he did not directly reject the epistle lessons for Jubilate, Cantate and Rogate, he nevertheless wished them displaced by 1 Cor. 15: 20-28; 35-50; 51 -57, and for the following reason: The passages from James are taken from a writing which is not apostolic and is not to be put upon the same level with the other New Testament writings; moreover, the season between Easter and Pentecost calls for instruction and comfort drawn from Christ's resurrection and our own.[32] Another change concerns the close of the year. The mediaeval lectionary concluded with Jer. 23: 1-8 and John 6: 1-14 and made thereby the transition to Advent (Jer. 23: 5, 6; John 6: 14), as in the Homiliarium of Charlemagne John 6 is appointed for the Fifth Sunday before Christmas and thus introduces the Church Year. But Luther says, in the *Hauspostille,* on the XXVI after Trinity: "In our churches here we are accustomed, on the Sunday before Advent, when there are two or three following the XXIV after Trinity (which seldom happens), to read and

---

[30]*Weimar ed.,* xix, 78 f.—[31]*Weimar ed.,* xix, 95.—[32]Comp. *Kirchenpostille,* Eine andere Epistel am Sonntag nach Ostern.

preach upon the epistle and gospel lessons concerning the second coming of our Lord at the last day, as they are appointed in the 'Kirchenpostille.'" We find there 1 Thess. 4:13-18; Matt. 25:15-28, and 2 Thess. 1:3-10; Matt. 25:31-42 assigned to the XXV and XXVI after Trinity respectively; and 2 Pet. 3:3-7; Matt. 24:37-51 suggested for a possible XXVII. In this way the yearly round of pericopes is brought to a fitting conclusion. Elsewhere in his sermons he criticizes the traditional series (thus the lessons for the Sunday after Christmas, the epistle for II p. Epiph., the epistle for VII p. Trin.) but he made no further changes. As a result, the pericope-system as accepted and revised by Luther became current in the Lutheran Church, a number of territorial churches making slight additional changes. The relation to the system became, later on, a decidedly closer one than Luther's had been, owing partly to the attitude of the clergy, partly to the needs of the common man,[33] partly also to confessional considerations. In Switzerland the pericopes were abandoned, Zwingli in Zurich preaching consecutively on Matthew, then on Acts, 1 Tim., Gal., 2 Tim., 1 and 2 Peter, Heb., Genesis. Similarly Bullinger and Calvin. When, during the sacramentarian controversy in 1555, Westphal attacked the latter for not using the old pericopes, Calvin replied, in his *Defensio secunda contra Westphalum*, that the use of pericopes as such did not conform to the practice of the ancient Church, and that even if their use were to be conceded, the traditional pericopes were inadequate; he maintained that the real cause of their retention was the convenience of the preachers. In England, the Book of Common Prayer included a copious lectionary for every day, the old pericopes being retained for the Sundays and festival days, but as lessons to be read rather than as texts for the sermon; the latter was to be read from the "Two Books of Homilies" of 1547 and 1574. The attitude of the church of Scotland has been referred to above.[34] In Germany, after the isolated attack of Dannhauer († 1666), strong opposition arose in the days of pietism, especially to the rule forbidding the use of any other texts in the main service. Later, rationalism desired the whole system abolished. Revisions of the old series appeared at various times, as well as entirely new series, to be

---

[33]This aspect is emphasized by Loehe, in his *Drei Buecher von der Kirche*: "He that changes texts every year is not fit to be a preacher to the common people. The constantly new and changing, without a point of contact with the familiar texts, presents difficulties at all times and to all. Everyone, on the other hand, will readily and gladly accept new thoughts if they appear as the newly apprehended contents of old truth."—[34]P. 319.

used alongside the old. Of these we mention the second Saxon series (1810), the Wuerttemberg (1830), Rhineland (by Nitzsch) and Bavarian (by Thomasius, 1867) series, besides those proposed by Ranke (1851) and the series of the Eisenach Conference (1896). The Eisenach series, like those of Ranke, Nitzsch and Thomasius, contains also Old Testament lessons. In America, the Old Testament series of Thomasius has been treated by M. Reu, the Eisenach New Testament series by R. C. H. Lenski.

§ 13. THE DERIVATION OF THE SERMON-MATERIAL FROM THE TEXT

M. Flacius, *Clavis Scripturae Sacrae*, 1567. J. L. von Mosheim, *Anweisung, erbaulich zu predigen*, ed. by C. E. v. Windheim, 1763. Geo. Campbell, *Lectures on Pulpit Eloquence*, 1775. Ebenezer Porter, *Lectures on Homiletics and Preaching*, 1834. Chr. Palmer, *Evang. Homiletik*, 1842. F. Schleiermacher, *Praktische Theologie*, 1850. G. Thomasius, *Kolosserbrief praktisch erklaert*, 1869. J. A. Broadus, *On the Preparation and Delivery of Sermons*, 1870. S. Goebel, *Die Parabeln Jesu*, 1879-80. J. C. K. von Hofmann, *Biblische Hermeneutik*, ed. by Volck, 1880. A. Phelps, *The Theory of Preaching*, 1881. A. B. Bruce, *The Parabolic Teaching of Christ*, 1882. E. Bindemann, *Die Bedeutung des A. T. fuer die christl. Predigt*, 1886. H. J. Holtzmann, *Der erste Thessalonicherbrief praktisch erklaert* (Zeitschrift f. praktische Theologie), 1880-86. G. A. Juelicher, *Gleichnisreden Jesu*, 1888-89, 2. ed., 1910. E. C. Achelis, *Lehrbuch d. praktischen Theologie*, 1890 (ii³, 1911). H. J. Holtzmann, *Zur praktischen Erklaerung d. Hebraeerbriefs* (Zeitschrift f. prakt. Theol.), 1891. J. Stockmeyer, *Exegetische u. praktische Erklaerung ausgewaehlter Gleichnisse*, 1897. T. H. Pattison, *The Making of the Sermon*, 1898. G. Heinrici, *Hermeneutik* (Prot. Realencyk.³), 1899. Idem, *Gleichnisse* (ibidem), 1899. F. Steinmeyer, *Homiletik*, 1901. G. A. Smith, *Modern Criticism and the Preaching of the O. T.*, 1901. Franz Hering, *Die homiletische Behandlung d. A. T.*, 1901. P. Drews, *Die Predigt im 19. Jahrhundert*, 1903. E. von Dobschuetz, *Der gegenwaertige Stand d. neutestl. Exegese in seiner Bedeutung fuer die prakt. Auslegung* (Zeitschrift f. Theologie u. Kirche), 1906. C. Clemen, *Predigt u. biblischer Text*, 1906. P. Kleinert, *Homiletik*, 1907. J. Gottschick, *Homiletik u. Katechetik*, 1908. F. Niebergall, *Praktische Auslegung des N. T.* (Lietzmann's Handbuch zum N. T., vol. 5), 1909. P. Wurster, *Gibt es eine Methodenlehre der praktischen Exegese?* (Monatschrift f. Pastoraltheologie), 1909. Idem, *Die Bibelstunde*, 1911 (³1920). Geo. H. Schodde, *Outlines of Biblical Hermeneutics*, 1917. A. E. Garvie, *The Christian Preacher* (International Theological Library), 1921. K. Holl, *Luther* (pp. 544-582), ²1923.

If the text is the sole source for the material of the sermon, the all-important question arises: How is the preacher

Exposition: The Literal Meaning of the Text

to derive this material from the text? Before answering this question it will be well to call attention to two fundamental requirements. First, the preacher must approach his text in the conviction that it really contains sermon material,—i. e., a truth ministering to the edification of the congregation,—and that his business is simply to discover and set forth this material. Without this conviction the preacher's relation to his text is from the outset a false one; he will find in it nothing conducive to edification, because he does not seek aright. But when this conviction controls his seeking, he will find—unless the text itself be ineptly chosen and unadapted to homiletic treatment. In the second place, the preacher must approach his task with inner concentration and a fervent prayer for enlightenment, firmly resolved to subject himself wholly to the truth contained in the text, its doctrine, reproof, correction, comfort and instruction.

The sermon is the presentation of God's Word in its meaning for the Christian congregation of the present. But before the preacher can know what his text means for the present he must understand it in its meaning for the past, in which it was originally set forth as a word of God. Only on the basis of what a passage originally meant can he show what meaning it has for today. Hence the first duty of the homilete is the *exposition* of the text, that is, the interpretation of a given passage according to the rules of scientific exegesis. The steps in such exposition need here to be merely summarized and reviewed.

First of all, the homilete will need, with the aid of grammar and lexicon, to ascertain the *literal meaning* of his text. "Sensus literalis," says Luther, "the literal sense, that's the thing!" This cannot be found, however, without giving careful attention to the *biblical usage* of words, and to the *context* in which a particular passage is set. We mention as examples such important biblical terms as ἱλασμός, καταλλαγή, ἀπολύτρωσις, παλιγγενεσία, etc., and such passages as Jas. 2: 14-26; Luke 11: 23 compared with 9: 50. This implies that the homilete must operate, as a general rule, with the original text of the Bible and cannot content himself with a translation. However great the interpretative and linguistic value of the King James Version and of Luther's German Bible, and however much the preacher must strive to attain the fullest familiarity with these masterpieces of translation,[1] he must take as the foundation of his homiletic work the original Bible text, whose freshness and finer shades of meaning cannot be reproduced by the best translation. If the preacher, owing to defective preparation, has no Hebrew, he may find not a substitute, but a stopgap in "The Cross-Reference Bible" with its valuable variorum readings and renderings. As for the preacher incapable of using the Greek New Testament, he will have difficulty to prove his right to exist.

In the second place, it is necessary to gain an accurate picture of the *situation* which the text sets forth or in which it was originally spoken or written. The more complete this picture is, and the more it abounds in minute and even apparently unimportant details, the better; for in this way alone the literal sense receives its individual coloring and its precise shade of meaning. If the finding of the literal sense is the function of reason guided by the rules of grammar and logic, here is the place where the historical imagination comes into play. Not fancy, which evolves pictures out of touch with reality and reads its own whims into the text, and is therefore an enemy to exegesis; but imagination, which fuses the materials of the text into a living and concrete whole. It projects itself into the past and enters into the mind of the speaker or actor. It is a foe to the abstract and a lover of the concrete, never content until it has visualized a

---

[1] See pp. 229 ff.; 241 ff.

person or a scene and made itself contemporary with it, yet without introducing anything foreign into the picture. Take for example Hab. 2:4. How the true meaning of the passage opens before us as soon as we visualize the historical situation in which this word was first spoken. We hear the tramp of the terrible army of the Chaldean, drawing irresistibly nearer and nearer. Judah, in despair, musters her man-power. reckons up her resources, looks to this and that neighbor nation for aid and alliance,—does everything but turn to her God. Then we see the prophet on his watch-tower, crying to his people words of warning and of comfort: "To what avail your desperate running to and fro? One thing alone can bring help, and that is faith, trust in the strong arm of Yahveh. The mighty Chaldean, raised up in judgment upon God's faithless people, will not be able to harm the righteous. The just shall live by faith. The just, and only he, and he only by virtue of his faith, his trust in Yahveh, will live in the midst of judgment; even though he seem to perish, he will yet have life and salvation." Or take Romans 1:16. How Paul's words gain in force when we imagine ourselves in spirit in the Rome of his day—Rome the centre of the world's culture, the seat of art and science, Rome where the wandering philosophers preached their εὐαγγέλιον as panacea for the ills of mankind. How will Paul fare here with his simple gospel, his word of the Cross? In the provinces he has met with a measure of success, but how will it be in the metropolis? Such thoughts must have come to Paul's mind, but he does not for a moment entertain them; he thinks more highly than that of his gospel. He is not only not ashamed, but "proud" of the gospel, as Moffatt so finely renders the word, proud to bring it even to Rome. Let the traveling philosophers puff their εὐαγγέλιον; it is but empty sound, signifying nothing, while Paul's εὐαγγέλιον carries the fulness of the power of God. Theirs can lead at best to mental and moral improvement; Paul's is "unto salvation," that is, it puts one in possession of the righteousness that God gives and makes one holy and happy in time and eternity. Their message is but for a select group of men; Paul's is for everyone. Theirs points men to their own doing and striving; Paul's offers salvation to everyone that believes, and confers the faith it demands. How can Paul hesitate for a single moment to carry such a Gospel to Rome?—No one, again, can grasp the full force of 2 Cor. 12:9 without imagining himself in the position of Paul, that man of fiery zeal, of restless activity, hindered in his world mission by a mysterious malady (12:7). Only as we enter sympathetically into Paul's feelings can we be sure that his Lord's words (ἡ γὰρ δύναμις ἐν ἀσθενείᾳ τελεῖται) cannot possibly refer to spiritual weakness, but that the ἀσθένεια must be a bodily infirmity. And we can make the proper application, valid even today, that it is in the midst of spent physical powers that God's grace rises to its fullest height and wins its finest triumphs. If you were well and strong, men might ascribe your missionary successes to your own strength; but since you have no strength of your own and are nevertheless successful, it is clear whose doing it is. Against the foil of your physical weakness there shines in fullest splendor the grace of God that is with you.

Thirdly, having found the literal meaning of the text and reconstructed imaginatively the situation portrayed therein, the homilete will now approach the *scope or purport* of the passage; that is to say, he will determine what is the main thought and what are the subordinate or auxiliary thoughts—or in case several main thoughts are co-ordinated in the same passage, he will trace the proper sphere of each—and what are the explanatory or illustrative elements of the text. In this way alone can he comprehend the actual trend and intention of his text and read its physiognomy and its characteristic features. This operation cannot be neglected, if in-

EXPOSITION: THE PURPORT OF THE TEXT 343

deed the function of the preacher is, not to preach whatever enters his mind, but to present to his people the particular truth set forth in the text. Thus, preaching on the Christmas epistle, Titus 2:11-14, he must be clear in his mind that the chief emphasis falls upon the clause, "the grace of God hath appeared, instructing us that we should live soberly, righteously, and godly." The whole context, both what precedes and what follows, demands the stressing of παιδεύουσα. To be sure, the Christmas sermon will give its full value to σωτήριος, to πᾶσιν ἀνθρώποις, and especially to the essential gospel in the passage, ἐπεφάνη ἡ χάρις; but this must be done in such a way that παιδεύουσα ἵνα κτλ. is kept in its central position. A careful comparison of parallel passages will often aid in determining the precise scope of a passage. The blood of Jesus as ransom price for our redemption is dwelt on in 1 John 1:7; 1 Cor. 7:23; 1 Pet. 1:17 ff., and Matt. 20:28. In the first of these passages it is employed as a means of comfort, since this blood cleanses us from our daily sins. In the remaining passages it is employed as the motive of the life of sanctification; yet each time from a different angle: in 1 Cor. 7:23, as warning against exchanging our dearly bought freedom for the bondage of men; in 1 Pet. 1:17 ff., as exhortation to a life of godly fear as children of a holy Father; in Matt. 20:28, as incentive to lowly service, instead of lording it over the brethren. The description of New Testament times in Rom. 13:11, 12 is more clearly understood by comparing this passage with 2 Cor. 6:2. In the latter passage these times are described as the bright day, while in the former they are compared to the break of dawn, when men rise from sleep, put on their clothes and go to work. Unless we are willing to make the attempt to understand our text in its specific scope, as distinguished from other similar passages, we shall not only fail to appreciate the manifold riches of the Scriptures, but run danger of repeating ourselves in our sermons, which will come to be recognized less and less by our congregations as the exposition and application of the text.

Finally, the homilete must bear in mind that his text, though only a part, is yet an *integral part of the sum total of the Scriptures,* and is to be interpreted from the viewpoint of its connection with the whole of God's saving revelation. Without in any way depriving the particular text of its characteristic features, this view of its larger relationship will indicate its comparative position in the organism of saving truth. It will determine whether or not the text forms one of the cardinal truths of revelation, and if not, what is its relation to them, and it will indicate how it is to be treated, so that these truths may not be contradicted but more firmly established. Thus the preacher will find that Hab. 2:4 contains a cardinal truth of the first order, pointing back to Gen. 15:6 and forward to Romans 1:17 and 3:28, absolutely fundamental to the whole relation between God and man, and therefore of central importance also for the congregation of today.[2] He will present the importance of good works as the expression of faith, so strongly emphasized in James 2:14 -26, but will always view them in their relation to justifying faith. The several precepts concerning obedience to the secular authorities, the duty of intercession for all men, the practice of hospitality, he will reduce to their common denominator of fear and love of God, and will thus emphasize the organic unity of the Christian life, as against a mere external addition of good works. At the same time, many an apparently difficult and unprofitable locution will take on flesh and blood and be found to possess definite practical value, as

---

[2]This was recognized even by the ancient rabbins, for the Talmud contains the statement that the 613 commandments of Sinai were reduced by David to eleven (Ps. 15), by Isaiah to six (33:15), by Micah to three (6:8), and by Habakkuk to one (2:4)—although their inclusion of this passage among the commandments is incorrect.

he traces its varying usage in a good concordance or Bible dictionary. (P. 361.)

It ought not to be necessary, in the Lutheran Church, to say that the work of the homilete should begin as a rule with the *original text* of the Bible. This is self-evident, but like so many self-evident things, it is often forgotten and neglected. Luther insisted upon the study of the ancient languages in order to the understanding of the Scriptures. In his tract, *To the Councilmen of all German Cities, that they establish and support Christian schools* (1524), which every Lutheran pastor should read at least once a year in order to quicken his conscience, he says, "There is a very great difference between a simple preacher of faith and an expounder of Scripture, or as Paul puts it, a prophet." He admits that the simple preacher has, indeed, so many clear texts and sayings in translation that he is able to understand Christ and to lead a holy life, as well as to preach this to others. "But," he continues, "to interpret and treat the Scriptures for himself, and to oppose false teachers, this is a task beyond his powers. It cannot be done without a knowledge of languages. Now we certainly need such prophets in the Christian Church who are able to treat and expound the Scriptures, as well as to defend them; it is not sufficient to lead a holy life and to teach aright." Later on in the same treatise he admits again that "faith and the Gospel may be preached by simple preachers without languages," but he adds, "It is a poor and languid thing, men soon weary of it and make no progress. But where there is a knowledge of the languages, the preaching is fresh and strong, the Scriptures are thoroughly understood, and faith is constantly renewed by a variety of words and works." In the same connection he says, "It was a foolish undertaking to attempt to learn what the Scriptures teach by reading the expositions of the Fathers and many books and glosses. Men should rather have studied the languages; for by reason of their ignorance of language the Fathers often belabored a passage with many words and hardly grasped its sense; it was guess-work and half error. And you run after them with much toil and labor, when by a knowledge of the languages you could in the same length of time make a much better guess yourself than the men you follow. For as the sun is, compared with the shade, so is language compared with all the glosses of the Fathers. Since, then, Christians are bound to use the Sacred Scriptures as their own and only book, and it is a sin and a shame not to understand our God's speech and language, it is a still greater sin and shame not to study the languages, the more that God is now offering and giving us men and books and many other aids and inducements to this study, and is eager to have His book become the property of all. How glad would the dear Fathers have been to be able to approach the Scriptures and learn the languages as we are able to do! What labor and pains they were at in order to gather up the mere crumbs, while we may have the whole loaf with only half their labor, nay, with scarcely any labor at all. How their diligence puts to shame our sloth, and what a rigorous account God will require of us for our indolence and ingratitude!" And farther back he has this passage: "In proportion as we love the Gospel, let us watch over the languages. . . . . . We shall not long preserve the Gospel without the languages. For they are the sheath in which this sword of the Spirit is contained; they are the casket in which one carries this jewel; they are the vessel in which one holds this wine; they are the larder in which this food is stored." Dr. Machen of Princeton Seminary applied this same principle, in 1918, to the preachers of the twentieth century, and even said that "there was never a time when a knowledge of the Greek New Testament was quite so important as it is today. Is the Bible to be abandoned altogether to its enemies? They will study it scientifically, we may rest assured, if the Church does not."[3]

But is it still necessary to go back to the original text when we have such excellent, even "authorized" translations? It is and will always remain necessary. Theological conscientiousness and evangelical truthfulness demand a return to the original sources. Moreover, the above question can be asked only by one who does not know how far even the best translation falls below the original work. And an "authorized" translation of the Bible may suffice for the Roman Catholic priest, not for the Protestant preacher. Kleinert reminds us that in Catholicism "the biblical sermon material is not the norm of the ecclesiastical, but vice versa; the interpretation of Scripture is subject to the will of the church, hence the original text of the Scripture is subject to the norm of the ecclesiastically sanctioned Vulgate. From the evangelical viewpoint, no ecclesiastical sanction, not even the recognized excellence of a translation, can obscure the fact that the original text must determine the content of Scripture and that consequently the biblical content of the sermon can be derived from the original text alone." He continues: "Only by carefully and faithfully investigating the original text will the preacher find the whole

---

[3] *Kirchliche Zeitschrift*, 1918, pp. 142 ff.

riches of the original content and the peculiar characteristics of the particular text opening unreservedly before him, and be on sure ground in making its application. Only in this way can he avoid the danger of drawing from his text statements or inferences which can be associated only with the translation or with a misunderstanding to which the translation gives rise."[4]

It is an ungracious task to pick flaws in our translations of the Bible: but every one knows that despite their many excellences they are far from perfect. No translation can do full justice to the fine change in John 21:15-17, when after Jesus had twice asked Simon Peter, ἀγαπᾶς με; and Peter had answered both times, φιλῶ σε, He suddenly alters the verb in His third question to φιλεῖς με. Only by going back to the original can one understand why "Peter was grieved because He said unto him the third time, Lovest thou me?"—Luther renders παιδαγωγός in Gal. 3:24 as "Zuchtmeister;" the A. V., "schoolmaster;" the R. V., "tutor;" none of which is satisfactory. Only to one familiar with Greek usage, is it clear that, before the word παιδαγωγός assumed the more general meaning of schoolmaster or tutor, and even afterwards, it denoted specifically the slave whose duty it was to accompany the children and youths of the house to the gymnasium and to see that they reached their destination. This is the precise meaning of the word in Gal. 3:24, as required by the context. The law was given to lead the Jewish people to Christ. Verse 24, accordingly, expresses the same thought as v. 23, but under a familiar figure taken from Greek life.—Luther translates θριαμβεύοντι in II Cor. 2:14 as "Sieg verleihen." The A V. "causeth us to triumph" is no happier; the R. V. finally found the correct rendering, "leadeth us in triumph"—which is supported by ὀσμῇ and εὐωδία, referring as they do to the burning of incense accompanying the triumphal processions.—So too, the book with seven seals in Rev. 5 will assume new meaning to one familiar with Greek legal terminology, who recognizes in a βιβλίον thus sealed the technical term for a last will and testament.[5] The majestic scene in heaven turns, therefore, upon the opening of a will. The divine bequest has long since been made and sealed, but has not yet been opened and put in force. No one but the Lamb is able to open this testament and carry out its terms. The events accompanying the successive loosing of the seals are the events leading up to the opening of the will and the distribution of the inheritance (cf. 1 Pet. 1:4). Terrible as they are, they only usher in this glorious consummation (cf.

---

[4] P. 90.—[5] Cf. Zahn, *Einleitung zum N. T.*, 3. ed., ii, 600, 608 f.

Luke 21:31).—How much, finally, is gained when one can go back of the translation, "be clothed with humility," in 1 Pet. 5:5, and see in ἐγκομβώσασθε the picture of the slave in his white apron, which instantly calls up the scene in John 13:4, so indelibly impressed upon Peter's mind.

It is another question, whether the preacher is justified in referring in his sermon to inaccuracies and defects of the translation in use among his people, when his study of the original has led him to a better rendering. This will be the practice of homiletes who have attained a mere smattering of Greek or Hebrew and whose "discoveries" have gone to their head, or of popinjays who delight in parading their scholarship before long-suffering congregations. The mature homilete, however, while always operating with the sense of his text acquired by first-hand study of the original, will refer to any deviations from the version in use only when this is required by the edifying purpose of his sermon, that is to say, when the translation sanctioned by the Church prevents the setting forth of the true intent of the text and the making of the application demanded thereby.[6] But even then he will proceed in the most sparing fashion, in order not to shake the confidence of his hearers in their version and consequently in the Bible itself, which they know only in that version. The remarks of Ebenezer Porter, the first American homiletician, in his *Lectures on Homiletics and Preaching* (1834), are worth noting today. "No translation," he says, "or commentary is to be regarded as exempt from the scrutiny of criticism; nor need we scruple to say, on any proper occasion, that the received English version of the Bible has many inaccuracies and defects. Yet to assail this version from the pulpit on all occasions, and thus to invalidate its authority with common minds, while we admit its correctness as to the great outlines of divine truth, is a mistake, which no preacher of good sense will commit. Besides in this case it is oftener pedantry, than learning, that is displayed. One of those venerable men, who assisted in forming this version, being afterwards on a journey, heard its defects pointed out, to an illiterate congregation, by a very young preacher, who, in one instance, assigned three reasons why a word should have been differently translated. In the evening, the learned divine said to the young man, 'You might have preached a more useful sermon to these poor hearers. The king's translators considered well the *three* reasons which you have suggested for another rendering of that word; but

---

[6] This was the procedure, e. g., of John Gerhard in his *Postil.*

they were induced by *thirteen* weightier reasons, to prefer the rendering that was adopted' . . . On the literary vanity, which employs an excess of criticism, in the pulpit, I add one more remark, that it has no countenance from the highest of all examples, that of our Lord and His Apostles. The great body of primitive Christians had access to the Hebrew scriptures chiefly through a translation, and one less perfect than the common version in our language. Yet the first preachers of Christianity, qualified as they certainly were to correct all mistakes, by gifts more adequate than those of scholarship, never perplexed their hearers with various readings and various renderings."[7] Paul, it is true, in his quotations from the Old Testament occasionally went back of the Septuagint to the Hebrew original, but he did this quietly and without any show of learning.

The necessity of arriving at the *literal meaning* of the text should require no elaborate argument. Well-known are Luther's struggles to free himself from the tyranny of the allegorical method of interpretation, first in theory, then with increasing success in practice. Already in 1520 he wrote: Scripture sacra ipsa per se sui ipsius interpres.[8] Especially in his book of 1521 against Emser, he defends the "grammatical" or "historical" meaning as the only correct sense of Scripture. "The Holy Spirit," he says there, "is the simplest of writers in heaven and on earth; hence His words cannot have any other than a simple meaning, which we call the written or the spoken sense. The Scriptures cannot have a double sense, but only the single sense expressed in the words."[9] This achievement dare never be surrendered; it must be applied even more consistently than it was done in the Reformation-period and than it is done in modern homiletic literature. But of this more below.

That the literal sense cannot be found without a careful study of the *context*, is a principle generally recognized, but not so generally practiced. The exegetical conscience of the homilete cannot be clear until this requirement is fully met. If the context of James 1:8 or 1:19-20, e. g., is overlooked, these passages will appear as general truths, correct enough in themselves, but scarcely needing an apostle as spokesman. The homilete will then agree with those commentators who complain of a lack of coherence among the various sections of the epistle and find the author leaping grasshopper-like from point to point. But if he keeps his eye on the context he will find in Jas.

---

[7]Pp. 101 f.—[8]*Erlangen ed.*, v. a., v, 160.—[9]*Erlangen ed.*, xxvii, 259-262.

1:8 a fine connecting link between 1:2-7 and 1:9-12; the idea of "doublemindedness" (ἀνὴρ δίψυχος) in v. 8 is prepared for by the "doubter" (διακρινόμενος) in v. 6, and is expanded in the lowly and the rich brother whose respective lot brings them into temptation in vv. 9-12. Again, the apparently so general statements in James 1: 19-20, when connected with the preceding reference to "the word of truth" in v. 18 and with the injunction in v. 21 to "receive the engrafted word," are seen to be concerned specifically with this Word of God. This is what the readers of the epistle are to be quick to hear, slow to speak—not over-zealous to proclaim the Word before it has done its work quietly in their own heart and life; and concerning it they are to be slow to wrath—not breaking out in angry denunciation when the Word as preached by them does not at once bear fruit, as though such human wrath could promote the righteousness of God. Again, if we begin a new section with James 1:16 or 1:17, the connection with v. 18 cannot but be a forced one; but if we read 16-18 in close connection with 13-15 and understand πᾶσα δόσις ἀγαθή as "only good giving," we remain within the line of thought begun in v. 13, and obtain in vv. 17 and 18 two admirable reasons for the injunction in v. 13 which v. 16 repeats. —The σῶσαι in James 2:14 and with it the whole passage 14-26 appear in a clear and distinct light when we remember that in the preceding verses 12-13 the reference was to the final judgment, in which only he who showed mercy will be able to stand. Hence it is in this judgment, according to v. 14, that no man's faith can save him if it consists merely in saying that he has faith; just as little as the other saying in vv. 15-16 can clothe and feed the needy brother. Thus it becomes evident that the reference here is not to the justification of the sinner before God in the Pauline sense, but to the justification of the Christian at the final judgment. The Christian whose faith does not lead to sanctification is warned that at the judgment he will be condemned to hell, if he has depended on a faith which merely professes to believe but does not produce good works. The agreement of James with Jesus (Matt. 7:21-25; 3:1 ff.) and with Paul (2 Cor. 5:10) becomes at once clear.—The figure of the rock in Matt. 7:24-27 is frequently connected with the "foundation" in 1 Cor. 3:11 to the utter confusion of the Matthew passage. The very tenor of this passage ("every one that heareth these words of mine, and doeth them"..... "and doeth them not"), but especially the context, should have prevented such a comparison; for Matt. 7:24-27 is simply a repetition in figurative form of vv. 21-23.—A careful consideration of the context will save one from many a slip, if one bears in mind that παρακαλοῦμεν in 2 Cor. 6:1 introduces the second aspect of the service which the ministers of the New Testament are to perform on behalf of Christ. Their first duty is (2 Cor. 5:20-21) to entreat all who are still without, to enter into the state of reconciliation obtained by Christ (δεόμεθα . . . . . καταλλάγητε τῷ θεῷ). Secondly, they are to entreat those who have entered, not to receive this grace in vain. To this παρακαλοῦμεν belong all the participles that follow in vv. 3-10; they characterize Paul and his fellow workers, showing their right to admonish the Corinthians not to receive the grace of God in vain and their right to expect a proper response.

The study of the *biblical use* of the words and phrases of the text is an absolute necessity in the work of the homilete. And yet, how often this is completely neglected and how easily unscriptural and antiscriptural statements may creep into our sermon in consequence of this omission, may be observed even with respect to fundamental Christian doctrines. How seldom do we hear preachers do justice to the biblical conception of "reconciliation;" they seldom advance beyond the idea of reconciliation current in human intercourse and they represent God and man as two hostile parties laying aside their enmity, gradually approaching each other, and becoming friends. Thus Dr. J. Ruehling of Leipzig undertook to illustrate the meaning of reconciliation by the following analogy from family life; his error is the more surprising because he gives, earlier in the same sermon, the correct interpretation of 2 Cor. 5:21. This is his illustration: A son has mortally offended his father, who in anger has forbidden him the house. The son has departed, vowing never to return. But the mother cannot forget her child. Her grief and longing are slowly killing her. As her end approaches she has only one wish—to see her son once more. For her sake the father sends word to his son to return. Silently both of them, father and son, stand beside the death bed, neither granting the other a look or a word. Finally the dying woman gathers all her strength together and grasping with one hand the hand of her husband, with the other that of her son, she joins both their hands together. Then she falls back and dies. But a strange warmth has stolen into the hearts of the two. They fall into each others' arms, and above the dead there takes place a festival of reconciliation [sic]. Now God and man were estranged in this very manner. For centuries and millenniums the separation lasted. Then Jesus came and took the hand of God and the hand of man and laid them both together, dying in the act, and under His cross God and man became reconciled."[10] This is all wrong. To say nothing of the sickly sentimentality of the scene portrayed, every item of the comparison is incorrect,—the description of God and man, the subjective conception of reconciliation; in short, the whole point of departure in the relation of man to man, especially since not 2 Cor. 5:20, but 5:19 is the passage intended to be explained. In the interest of a better understanding, and a correct use in preaching, of the biblical term reconciliation, it will not be amiss if we enter here into a somewhat detailed discussion of this term. Reconciliation is a translation of καταλλαγή. This, according to its root, means a change or exchange. So far Ruehling is entirely correct. But what is the nature of this change, who is the person in whom it takes place or from whom it proceeds, and who is the person to whom it extends—this must be decided by the particular usage and context. Applied to the relation between God and man, it is possible, in the abstract, to think of either God or man as the person in whom this change takes place or who causes this change to take place in the other. It might be conceived as a change taking place in the heart of both God and man, so that each of these two abandoned his former opposition to the other, and both approached each other and thus became reconciled to each other. This is Ruehling's conception. But in this sense we do not find the word used anywhere in Scripture when it refers to the relation between God and man. This is the human interpretation of reconciliation, but not the biblical conception. On God's side no change of this sort was necessary, for there was never in Him any opposition to man which He needed to lay aside. Though His wrath against man's sin prevented any communion with man, love to man dwelt uninterruptedly in His heart (John 3:16). On man's side there was indeed enmity against God (Rom. 8:7; 5:10), but this he could never end of his own accord. The heathen mind imagined man to be able to reconcile himself to the gods (θεοῖσιν ὡς καταλλαχθῇ χόλον, Soph., Ajax, 744), but of this the Scriptures know nothing, not even in 2 Cor. 5:20. The same objection holds against the other possibility, that reconciliation refers to a change taking place not in both parties, but in only one, either God or man, as though God's heart could change toward man or man's heart toward God. Here too it is true: God does not need, man cannot bring about, such a change. But the change might, from the viewpoint of abstract logic, be one produced by either of the two in the heart of the other. Man

---

[10] *In der Nachfolge Jesu* (1911, p. 133.

might conceivably exert an influence upon God by prayers, sacrifices, merits, or by repentance, so as to produce in Him an inner change of feeling toward man. But this is a heathen idea, assuming powers in man which he does not possess and operating with a conception of God unknown to Scripture. Above all things, the Scripture in II Cor. 5:18 f. unmistakably indicates God as the subject of καταλλάσσειν, and man, or the world, as the object (cf. Col. 1:19-20; Rom; 5:20). This is emphasized by many modern theologians, but in the sense that while reconciliation is a change produced by God, it takes place in the heart of man. To be sure, God works upon man in order to effect in him an inner change (μετάνοια); yet this is nowhere in Scripture called reconciliation, but repentance or conversion. Even when Paul calls upon men, καταλλάγητε τῷ θεῷ (2 Cor. 5:2), that is, enter by means of repentance and faith into the new relationship with God, he presupposes the existence and the completion by God Himself of this καταλλαγή. But the above notion is excluded especially by the fact that the Scriptures connect the καταλλαγή, brought about by God, with the work of Christ, particularly with His death (cf. 2 Cor. 5:19, 21; Rom 5:10; Col. 1:20). No one will seriously maintain that when Christ died upon the cross a change was produced in the heart of mankind, still less of the world (κόσμος, τὰ πάντα) (cf. also Rom. 5:10). If therefore God is designated in Scripture as the subject, the death of Christ as the means and as the point in time, and the world as the object, of reconciliation, and if reconciliation cannot be a change taking place in the heart of man, there is left only one other alternative: καταλλαγή must be a change in the relation between God and man; not a change in God nor in man, but in the relationship existing between them. The relation of wrath and enmity, which, despite the love dwelling in His heart, existed because of sin between God and man, and made impossible a communion between sinful man and holy God, was ended through God's own intervention by the gift of His own Son, and changed into a relation of good pleasure and peace. Hence Paul can interpret ἀποκαταλλάξαι by εἰρηνοποιήσας in Col. 1:17-21 (cf. Eph. 2:13-18: in so far as this change from a wrath-relation to a peace-relation was accomplished by Christ, and is present once and for all in His person, He Himself is "our peace;" see also Micah 5:4; Eph. 2:14; Luke 2:14). And just as the wrath-relation between God and man did not exist only in the imagination and erroneous conception of man (so Ritschl), but was an objective and actual fact, so reconciliation is not merely imaginary but an actual change of the actual wrath-relation into an actual peace-relation. "Reconciliation" is then closely related to "propitiation" (ἱλασμός, 1 John 2:2; Rom. 3:25), that is, the covering of sin by God by means of the work of Christ, especially the shedding of His blood; but is not identical with it. Reconciliation is the logical and actual result of propitiation. For if Christ, by His blood, has covered our sin before God, so that He no longer regards it, then the cause of God's wrath, on account of which He was our enemy, is also covered. Then the wrath-relation has come to an end, and the relation of peace has taken its place, that is, the change denoted by καταλλαγή has taken place.[11]

So far as the portrayal of the *situation* described in the text is concerned, it is much more important to understand the psychological than the external situation. In order to understand correctly, for example, the peculiar beginning of Genesis 15:1, we must make clear to ourselves the thought passing at that time through the mind of Abraham. In the preceding chapter he was described as full of confidence and joy. We saw him as man of faith and obedience, sacrificing without hesitation the present in order to gain the future, jeopardizing his welfare and his very existence, because his Lord and God demanded it. Now—for the development of the inner life seldom proceeds in an unbroken line, but has many obstacles to meet; the experience of a hero of faith like Abraham must pass through moments of despondency and distress—now we find Abraham in "fear." How do we account for this? Through his valiant act of faith in pursuing with his 318 trained servants and defeating Chedor-laomer, this former Beduin chief, living till now in retirement far from the world and its strife, found himself suddenly plunged into the midst of the powers of this world, with four mighty kings his mortal foes. Returned to the former tenor of his way and reflecting upon the possible consequences of his act, he was seized with wonder at himself and his act, and fear of Chedor-laomer's revenge. The course he had pursued on the impulse of faith in the assistance of his God now came to seem a piece of rash folly which might put a sudden end to his peaceful mode of life. If he had allowed these considerations to have their way with him, he would doubtless have lost the blessing God meant this experience to bring him in his inner life. Therefore God himself

---

[11] See M. Reu, *Die Wiederherstellung der Gottesgemeinschaft durch das Werk Christi* (Chicago, 1918), pp. 9 ff. For an illustration of the way in which this meaning of καταλλαγή can be used in preaching and be made clear and edifying to simple reason, see the author's sermon on 2 Cor. 5:17-21 in his forthcoming collection of sermons.

comes to his rescue and deals with him as the One who will not break the bruised reed nor quench the smoking flax. "Fear not," He tells Him, "I am thy shield." As a shield stops the arrows and covers the fighter's body, so Yahveh Himself,—the same God whom Abraham had learned to know on his pilgrimage, in Egypt, in his recent conflict, as the Almighty—will stop all arrows and cover Abraham's person against every hostile attack, in remembrance of the word (Gen. 12:3) almost forgotten by Abraham, "I will curse him that curseth thee." If we keep in mind this situation we shall cease to wonder at the abrupt beginning of Genesis 15:1. Or who can understand and make his hearers understand the account in Matt. 11 of John the Baptist's doubt, without entering into his world of thought and noting the clash between his expectation of what the Christ would do and his experience of what the Christ actually did?—The homilete cannot explain the apparently unmotivated θάρσει, τέκνον, ἀφίενταί σου αἱ ἁμαρτίαι in Matt. 9:2, unless he has peered as it were into the heart of the sick of the palsy, and seen how, before the pure radiance of the holy and just Saviour, all his sinful thoughts and desires rose up and accused him. These illustrations might easily be multiplied; the thoughtful homilete will need no more to make him regard as self-evident, if he would understand his text aright, the task of thinking and living himself into the situation described therein or often suggested by some apparently trivial detail.

The principal function of all exegetical labor, is the setting out, carefully and clearly, of the *argument* of the particular text which is to be expounded. This refers especially to the speeches and the letters in the Bible. Naturally, this cannot be done without the most painstaking detail work of exegesis. But as soon as this detail work is pushed so prominently into the foreground that the principal function of exposition is obscured, exegesis ceases to be what it should be. That was the defect of the so-called glossarial method in vogue, e. g., in the earlier editions of the well known New Testament commentary of H. A. W. Meyer, and followed even today in certain English expository works. The supplanting of this method by that of textual reproduction was the specific methodological advance made and carried through in a masterly way by J. Chr. K. von Hofmann. This method is more successful than any other in setting forth clearly the argument of the various passages and of each book as a whole. The *Kommentar zum Neuen Testament,* edited by Theodor von Zahn, and now nearing completion, while entering more particularly than Hofmann into the details of the text, has succeeded, in most of its volumes, in laying, with Hofmann, all stress upon introducing the reader to the development of the sacred writer's thought. This is one of the many reasons why this commentary should be made accessible in a good translation to the American theologian. In narrow compass and without scholarly apparatus, Schlatter follows a similar method in his *Erlaeuterungen zum Neuen Testament,* and especially Kuehl in his *Erlaeuterungen der paulinischen Briefe.*[12] If the above is true with respect to the exposition of entire biblical books, it applies also to the individual passages with which the homilete has to do. All his exegesis will avail him little or nothing unless it helps him to trace the main lines of thought, and therewith the original trend and purport of his text. Here is the chief defect of so many sermons; the preacher does not set before his hearers with unmistakable clearness the central thought of his text, and does not build upon it his application. And he does not do this, as a rule, because in his exegetical preparation he confined himself to individual details and did not grasp the central thought of the passage, which combines all these details into a unity and which forms the distinctive character, what we have called the peculiar physiognomy, of the particular text. The comparison, noted above, of the text with its *parallels*[13] may be of great value, if proper allowance be made for the distinctive characteristics of such parallels. The homilete should strive in this matter to attain the gift which Paul prayed God to bestow on his dear Philippians (of course in a different connection), δοκιμάζειν τὰ διαφέροντα, to distinguish the things that differ (Phil. 1:10).

The last step in the expository work of the homilete—the treatment of the particular text as an *organic part of the sum total of revealed truth,* and especially in its relation to the central teaching of Scripture—is especially necessary in the case of difficult and obscure texts and of texts dealing with less fundamental matters or with

---

[12]The English translation of Meyer is well known. The other titles mentioned above are: J. Chr. K. von Hofmann, *Die Heil. Schrift Neuen Testaments zusammenhaengend untersucht* (1862-86), 11 parts, incomplete. Theo. Zahn, *Kommentar zum N. T.* unter Mitwirkung von Bachmann, Behm, Ewald, Hauck, Riggenbach und Wohlenberg (1903-1934). A. Schlatter, *Erlaeuterungen zum N. T.,* new edition in 3 vols. (1908-10). E. Kuehl, *Erlaeuterung der paulinischen Briefe unter Beibehaltung der Briefform* (1907-09), 2 vols.—Comp. also *The International Critical Commentary* (1895 ff.); Althaus und Behm, *Das Neue Testament Deutsch* (1932 ff.), and *Theologischer Handkommentar z. N. T.* (1928 ff.).—[13]The parallel passages in the margin of Nestle's Greek New Testament are especially complete and helpful.

separate details of the ethical life. If the preachers of the ancient and the mediaeval church had followed this rule, many of them would not have preached on the Christian virtues in a manner almost indistinguishable from that of the heathen rhetoricians. The same is true of many modern ethical sermons. Their authors do not live and move in the article of justification by grace for Christ's sake through faith; they have no appreciation of the radical importance of such faith for each several item of the Christian life, which must be an organic outgrowth and fruit of this faith; hence they cannot but preach what is at the bottom pagan and not Christian ethics. Such aberrations will be prevented by a view of the particular text in its relations as an integral part of the whole organism of revealed truth. Again, a truth or a passage lying on the extreme periphery is sometimes given a position of central importance and made a criterion of Christian truth or Christian life. This can be easily corrected by a knowledge of systematic theology, which may become a valuable aid to the preacher by its systematic presentation of the individual parts of Christian truth and life in their relation to one another. Here, too, the Scripture is its own best interpreter. We are not thinking here of the demand of our older homileticians that the preacher should know to which particular locus of dogmatics or ethics his text and its contents belong. That demand resulted in destroying the individuality of the text, as well as in a dry dogmatic sermon method. Both of these evils are closely related and can best be avoided by giving to each text its proper place in the sum total of revealed truth, and letting it deliver from thence its peculiar message.

What is to be done when the preacher reaches in his exegetical studies results differing from the traditional interpretation? Has he a right to lay them before his congregation in his sermons? Some have denied this. Even Kleinert—he is discussing the advisability of correcting a received Bible translation in the sermon—says: "The preacher will always base these corrections on the certain and universally accepted results of exegesis and keep them free from personal caprice."[14] We must differ from this position. Certainly, the homilete should not approach his exegetical studies with the intention of bringing to light novel and startling things, else he will almost certainly go astray. "Whatever danger results," says Ebenezer Porter, "from a tame submission to authority on this subject, the attractions of novelty are still more dangerous, to a man of sprightly genius, not

---

[14] P. 91.

matured by experience and judgment."[15] It is taken for granted, further, that he will compare the result of his exegetical investigation of a passage with the fundamental teachings of Scripture, in order to discover any possible deviation from them. But if no deviation is found, and if after repeated examination of his work he can conscientiously claim to have hit upon the right interpretation, there can be no doubt but that he not only may but should utilize in his sermonic work the truth thus gained. It would not be the first time that the exposition of Scripture as presented in the sermon exerted a salutary influence upon scientific exegesis, recalling it from error and pointing the way to a better understanding of the truth. If, for example, the homilete is convinced after careful investigation that κοπιῶντες καὶ πεφορτισμένοι in Matt. 11:28 denotes not those who labor under the burden of sin or of sorrow, but those who bear the yoke and burden of Pharisaic precepts, he should make this and nothing else his point of departure in preaching on this passage. If the *tertium comparationis* in the parables of the lost in Luke 15 has been seen to be the self-evident necessity of seeking what is lost, the preacher should present this motif to his congregation and let it work. If he has become convinced with Hofmann, Zahn and Ewald that in Phil. 1:3-11, ἐπὶ πάσῃ τῇ μνείᾳ ὑμῶν (v. 3) does not mean Paul's remembrance of the Philippians, but their remembrance of him as expressed in their contributions toward the spread of the Gospel by Paul, that this thought underlies v. 6 and is expressed in v. 7, and that accordingly Paul's purpose in vv. 3-11 is to remove from the minds of his readers the wrong impression that he is dissatisfied with the smallness and the tardiness of their gift, then, even though the whole passage takes on a different meaning, the homilete cannot be justly criticized for taking this as the basis of his sermon. Nor is there anything to prevent his preaching, on the basis of Romans 15:4-13, on the hope that there will be a congregation in the last time consisting of Jews and Gentiles, if he is certain, from the use of the article in v. 4 (τὴν ἐλπίδα), that this is the main thought of the text. Similarly, if he is persuaded that Ewald's position is correct in Phil. 3:17-21, and the reference is not to Christian libertines, but to Jewish-Christian opponents of the Gospel; even though this throws a totally different light on the contents of v. 19 and in some measure also on v. 20 and changes the whole tenor of the passage. Within the limits mentioned above—agreement with the clearly revealed fundamentals

---

[15] P. 101.

of Scripture—which is also our best safeguard against a liberal theology, there must be the fullest freedom of interpretation. Otherwise the truthfulness of the preacher is imperiled; for he has also, or should have, an exegetical conscience.

A sermon, then, can be built up only upon the foundation of sound and careful exegetical labor. It is another question, how much of this labor should appear in the finished sermon. Here the beginner —but also the older preacher who is the victim of vanity—often commits a serious blunder. He undertakes to conduct his hearers along the entire route by which he has arrived at his result, with or without mentioning the names of his guides, and to refute all and sundry whose views differ from his own. This is under the best conditions a total misconception of the function of the sermon, and a woeful confusion of the pulpit with the professor's chair. Usually it is something a great deal worse. As Ebenezer Porter says: "To exhibit the points of difference between his opinions and those of others, gives opportunity to display at once the extent of his reading and the superiority of his discernment. But how does such puerile ostentation accord with the dignity of his office, 'who is a servant of the most high God, to show unto men the way of salvation'?"[16] It is well known what fearful and wonderful specimens of this sort of preaching were produced by the German preachers of the seventeenth century, though this art was by no means confined to Germany. Campbell, in his *Lectures on Pulpit Eloquence,* censured this method in 1775: "Particular care ought to be taken, in expounding the Scriptures, not to appear over-learned, and over-critical. There is no occasion to obtrude on an audience, as some do, all the jarring interpretations given by different commentators, for this knowledge can serve no other purpose than to distract their thoughts. Before you begin to build, it is necessary to remove such impediments as lie directly in your way; but you could not account him other than a very foolish builder who should first collect a deal of rubbish, which was not in his way, and could not have obstructed his work, that he might have the pleasure and merit of removing it. And do the fantastic, absurd, and contradictory glosses of commentators deserve a better name than rubbish? No, surely. Where a false gloss cannot be reasonably supposed to be either known or thought of by the audience, it is in the preacher worse than being idly ostentatious of his learning to introduce such erroneous gloss or comment." If the text is a passage mis-

---

[16] P. 101.

used by errorists known to the congregation, the preacher may profitably expose the error and oppose to it the correct interpretation. Or if the text is an important and commonly misunderstood passage, he may well take occasion to review before the congregation the various untenable interpretations, in order, after thus clearing the way, to bring home to his hearers the true meaning of the passage. Thus in view of the many perversions of the parable of the ten virgins (Matt. 25: 1-13), it would not be amiss to take an outline such as the following: What will be the principal reason why we shall finally not be excluded from the marriage feast of heaven? (1) It will not be because we have gone out from the world to meet the Bridegroom, necessary as this is; (2) nor because we have held to the communion of saints, salutary as this is; (3) not because we have let the light of true faith and of good works shine before men, important as this is; (4) nor because we have led for a time a life filled with the Spirit, though no one can appear at the marriage feast whose heart has remained closed to the Spirit; (5) but it will be because we have kept faith unto the end, so that it did not fail us when we needed it most. Such a treatment serves throughout an edifying purpose, the elements of truth in the wrong interpretations are fully recognized, and by the rejection of their one-sidedness the true meaning of the parable becomes the more clear and impressive. In general the rule must be: Only the positive results of exegetical investigation have a place in the pulpit, and even these should not carry with them the smell of the lamp. The manner in which they are presented should not be that of the commentary, but of the service before the worshiping congregation, and their form should be adapted to the intellectual level of the hearers. If anything beside the actual results of exegetical study may be given a place in the sermon it is the description of the historical situation in which the words of the text were originally spoken or written. But someone might raise the question: If only the results, and not the processes, of exegetical study should appear in the sermon, what is the use of our exegesis, our consulting of different commentaries, our examination of variant readings, and all our other, archaeological, linguistic and historical studies? We let Porter reply. "I answer," he says, "of the same value with any other knowledge, if you have no discretion to use it aright, that is, of no value at all. You may have a knowledge of *grammar*, and make it subservient to the greatest business of the pulpit, without giving your hearers in every sermon a disquisition upon etymology and syntax. Your *logic* may be made the instrument of instruction and conviction to sinners, without acquainting them with the ten categories of Aristotle, or the difference between abstract and concrete terms. Your *eloquence* may melt your hearers, while they know not that you have read Quinctilian or Longinus, and care not whether the figure that thrilled their bosoms, has been called metonymy or apostrophe, in technical rhetoric. Just so you may use your knowledge of sacred criticism, without abusing it. From its stores humility and good sense may draw the richest instruction for your hearers, without ostentation on your part, or perplexity on theirs."

Everything that has been said thus far has reference only to the meaning of the text for the original hearers or readers. The next step will be, to develop from this its meaning for the Christian congregation of today. In other words, the *exposition* of the text must be followed by its *application*.

That the word spoken or written in the past has a meaning for today, follows from the fact that it has become under divine guidance a part of Holy Scripture and is thus perpetuated for all time. That God's word in Scripture is capable of application to the present, follows from the identity of God and of man. Because God is in His nature and works the same now as He was in the past, His Word is still valid today; and because the heart of man has remained fundamentally the same as it was in the past, both the commands and the consolations of the past may be brought to bear upon it, now as then. Despite the many differences conditioned by time, mode of life and national peculiarities, man's heart continues the same, with its needs, its joys and sorrows, its follies and sins, but also with its inextinguishable longing after God. Therefore divine truth can find in it a constant point of contact and remains for it the one saving and life-giving power.

The application dare not, however, be anything alien imported into the text, as though the preacher needed to add to the contents of the text something of his own. He must, on the contrary, take the Word of God, whose meaning in the past he has ascertained, set it unaltered and un-

abridged, with all its winsomeness and all its severity, in the midst of the present, and let it say to the men of today what it said to the men of the past.

It is but a sorry fame when a preacher is ignorantly praised for his skill in twisting and turning his text and making it say things never dreamed of by the writer. Here nothing is to be twisted and distorted, nothing to be tortured and forced. The truth contained in the text is to be set forth in its value for the present, and laid in all naturalness, without violence, upon men's hearts, so that the application will grow by an inner necessity out of the text and will be nothing else than the organic unfolding of the text. The main thought in the text must be the main thought also in the application; what is subordinate in the text must be subordinate in the application; what is not found in the text has no place in the application; what gives the text its distinctive character dare not be absent from the application. In short, the whole application of the Word of God to the present day must follow the lines and reproduce the characteristic features of the text, so that the text may without difficulty be recognized from the application. This is demanded by the dignity of the text as well as by the homiletic conscience of the preacher. The homilete must so completely assimilate this principle that it will become his second nature, and that he will be unable to act contrary to it because his conscience will not permit. The author confesses that he has frequently rewritten his sermons twice and three times, because he found in the course of his preparation that he had deviated in his application from the text. The preacher who follows this practice will have the satisfaction of finding his hearers receive gladly the Word as applied by him, because they feel that the application, instead of being imposed upon the text, is its logical and organic outgrowth. (P. 366.)

Paul Drews, in his interesting and informing *Die Predigt im 19. Jahrhundert*, shows that in contrast to the period of rationalism, the sermon after 1840 or 1850 was much too general as to theme and subject-matter; there was a sameness in the contents of most sermons, which produced monotony and loss of interest. He contrasts the admirable manner in which Schleiermacher gave to his sermons an individual, specific coloring. In a New Year's sermon on Eccl. 1:8-9 Schleiermacher takes for his theme, "That the mood which finds nothing new under the sun is wholly in the spirit of religion;" in a sermon on Matt. 26:36-46, he chooses as theme, "The value and efficacy of petitionary prayer with respect to temporal events;" on Mark 15:34-37, "Emotions of the dying Jesus that we should covet for our last hour;" on 1 Cor. 12:31-13:1, "Let us remember that all spiritual pre-eminence divorced from a moral and adequate motivation is valueless;" on 1 Peter 3:15, "Our duty, in view of the attention with which men watch our conduct;" on John 15:9, 14-15, "How much more glorious it is to belong to the friends than to the servants of God." Drews quotes also from the sermon collections of F. A. Wolf (died 1841 in Leipzig), who preaching on James 4:13-16, took as his theme, "That man can destroy but not build up his fortune;" and on Psalm 119:66-67, "That under affliction we inevitably grow either better or worse." He cites a theme of K. W. Schultz's in a sermon on John 4:30-36, "To noble hearts God grants delights of which others know nothing." Over against these specific themes, Drews instances the following by Ahlfeld: Nicodemus' night visit to Jesus; The great supper of the Lord; The unjust steward; The examination of a soul by Jesus; My son, thy sins are forgiven; and the following by Gerok: The great day of the Lord; The Lord's farewell to Jerusalem; The bells of New Year's eve; Jesus at Jacob's well; The call of the Good Shepherd to His sheep.[17] It is obvious

---

[17] W. Wrede, in his article, "Der Prediger und seine Zuhoerer" (Zeitschrift f. prakt. Theol., xix, 1892, pp. 16-50) says: "Less than one-half perhaps of all sermons deal with the Christian life. If we examine the treatment of this field in the sermon, we find that invariably the great central truths are discussed. Conversion and repentance, regeneration and renewal, walking in the light, the life in Christ, faith, love, hope, sin, temptation, prayer—these and similar matters are the staple subjects. But who has ever heard sermons on truthfulness, envy, vanity, vain-glory, respect of persons, fear of men, the force of example, friendship, sociability in the spirit of Jesus, devotion and edification in public worship, the blessedness of the quiet hour, etc.—sermons in which these subjects were treated as explicitly

that the latter method, with its abstract and general themes, is inferior to the former, which abounds in the specific and concrete. Many causes have contributed to bring about this weakness. The preachers held too slavishly to the traditional pericopes, instead of supplementing them with other texts. While correctly recognizing the necessity of keeping the cardinal facts of Christian truth and life in the centre of their preaching, they forgot that the individual expression and exemplification of this truth and life also has its rightful place. Doctrine was frequently preached almost to the exclusion of life. Attention was fastened upon the Scriptures as such without regard to the needs of the congregation. Drews errs, however, when he finds the principal reason for this weakness in the too close attachment of the sermon to the text. We maintain, on the contrary, that one of the principal reasons for the defect of these sermons is that they are not sufficiently controlled by the text, that they are indeed scriptural but not sufficiently textual. The main thought of the text does not stand out clearly in them, nor determine the whole application; the preacher either does not grasp at all the peculiar and characteristic features of his text, or if he does, he cannot quickly enough pass from them to his application. What shall we say of an outline like this of Ziethe's on Rom. 13:11-14: "The epistle shows us the message of Advent as (1) a faithful cry to awake, (2) a solemn call to repentance, (3) a serious word of faith and life"? Or this on 2 Cor. 6:1-10: "This season of the Passion of our Lord Jesus Christ is for us (1) a solemn challenge, (2) a salutary example, (3) a glorious promise." Whoever has worked carefully through these passages must feel each of these outlines as a blow in the face. How can one justify a treatment like this of Muellensiefen's on 1 Kings 19:10-18: "The significance of God's revelations; (1) The reign of the law with its terrors, and the limitation of its functions; (2) the dispensation of God's love in the work of redemption, and the world-historical significance of this work; (3) the hidden congregation, our hope in dark times"? Or a Christmas sermon like Tholuck's with the theme, "The Lord is not in the wind nor the earthquake, but in the still small voice." It is a lack of thought on Koegel's part when, in a sermon on Num. 21:4-9, he depicts at great length the serpent as a type of sin, which we should flee because of its glittering color, its stealthy ap-

---

as their importance for Christian personalities warrants?"—While Wrede exaggerates somewhat, he has put his finger on an undeniable and common weakness of a homiletic method that is profoundly influencing modern preachers.

proach, and its repeated attacks. But the text presents the fiery serpents, not as types of sin, but as the means of divine punishment upon the people's sin! The same criticism might be made of most English sermons. Nitzsch wrote, back in 1848 in his *Praktische Theologie*: "The idea of a text requires that the sermon reproduce its distinctive characteristics."[18] And Steinmeyer insisted throughout his long career as teacher upon the same principle. It was inculcated upon the author of this text-book by his teachers, the brothers Johannes and Martin Deinzer, who had been pupils of Hofmann. Steinmeyer's theoretical development in his posthumous *Homiletik,* and the example of his sermons have only confirmed us the more in this position. Admirable, too, is Achelis' view, expressed in his *Praktische Theologie* (1911): "The force and dignity of the homiletic interpretation [by this he means what we have called the exposition of the text] consists on the one hand in comprehending the eternal thoughts of God, and on the other in the will to find these thoughts only where they are to be found; that is, it consists in chasteness, self-restraint, and the refusal to use in themselves useful and edifying thoughts, if they can be derived only by deviation, contrary to one's conviction, from the scientifically ascertained meaning of the text. Where this restraint, in the interest of exegetical truthfulness, is lacking the result is either a complete ignoring of scientific exegesis or a mischievous medley of science and caprice. The preacher may, e. g., interpret Heb. 12:2 to mean that the essence of faith was revealed and consummated *in Jesus,* and also at the same time that Jesus begins and completes *in us* the life of faith. By such a process the stigma of duplicity is attached to the Bible and the past period of the double sense of Scripture will rise from its grave. Whatever is lost in the treatment of this passage by a chaste self-restraint is gained ten times over in other passages; for the homiletical expositor will develop the ability to avoid generalities and use to the full the individual features of his text, in order to win from the inexhaustible veins of gold in Holy Scripture the unsearchable riches of Christ for the edification of his congregation."[19] Achelis also calls attention to Goethe's well known words,—"I am convinced that the Bible will become more beautiful the more it is understood, that is, the more one recognizes and perceives that every word which we understand in a general sense and apply specifically to ourselves had a peculiar, distinctive, and directly individual meaning, according to certain circumstances, and con-

---

[18]ii, 1 (2. ed., 1860), pp. 92, 97.—[19]Vol. ii, pp. 158 f.

ditions of time and place."²⁰ The ascertaining of this peculiar and individual meaning is the duty of the homilete in his exegetical study of the text; and the setting forth of this peculiar and individual meaning in terms of concrete life before his individual congregation, is the duty of the homilete in his application of the text. This is no easy task; it is "no mere assembling together of materials, long lying ready to hand and assembled together a hundred times before, but a delving, a drilling into the depths, a discovery."²¹ But while not easy, it is exceedingly profitable. It is profitable for the preacher; for it brings him joy, a firmer confidence in his message, spiritual and mental freshness, and a growing appreciation of the wondrous things in God's Word. It is profitable to the congregation; for it keeps its interest aroused, presents divine truth from ever new angles, and leads it to self-examination in directions hitherto unknown. In this respect it will be well for the preacher to study modern liberal exegesis, and the modern German sermon,—not indeed to follow their departure from Christ crucified and from the old Gospel of sin and grace, but to sharpen his sense for the natural and the unforced, and to learn to hate with perfect hatred whatever is forced and tortured.

The patent fact that there are many different kinds of text in no wise invalidates our rule that the application of a text dare be nothing other than the organic unfolding of its contents; at most it only slightly modifies this rule. For all texts may be reduced to two types: those that permit, or rather require, a *direct application* from past to present conditions, and those whose application can only be *indirect*. To the former class belong the majority of texts from the epistles, many from the gospels, especially the sayings of Jesus, and many Old Testament passages. Thus Lev. 19:2 ("Ye shall be holy; for I the Lord your God am holy") or John 3:16 or Romans 1:16 not only permits but requires a direct application to the present day. But besides these there is also a considerable number of passages, particularly in the Old Testament, but also in the New, and here especially in the gos-

---

²⁰*Sprueche in Prosa*, No. 467.—²¹Drews, *ibid.*, p. 45.

pels, which are not capable of direct application and can be brought to bear upon present conditions only by indirection.

In the case of Old Testament texts the indirect application will be *typical*. This typical application is based on the conviction that Old Testament revelation as a whole forms a type, that is, a prefiguration or prophetic similitude, of New Testament revelation. This may be, according to the particular passage, a prefiguration of Christ and His gifts, or of the relation of the Christian to God, the conduct of individual members of Christ's Kingdom, or the development of His Church as a whole and the fundamental principles governing this development. A text like Gen. 12:1-4 is to be treated typically: Abraham's faith is seen to mark his fundamental relation to God, and it is shown that faith is even today the one true correlative of divine grace. Israel's exodus from Egypt may be treated typically, since it is one of the principal prefigurations of the deliverance of the Church from all bondage. The journey through the wilderness, so long as we do not play with details, still less with names of places,[22] may be presented as prefiguring the pilgrimage of the New Testament Church and of its individual members. (Comp. 1 Cor. 10:1-13.) David's sufferings, in which he sings the Twenty-second Psalm, may be applied to the New Testament congregation, if we remember that they form a type of the sufferings of Christ and of His members. (P. 370.)

From what has been said, the applicability of Old Testament texts to the New Testament congregation should be sufficiently clear. A few additional notes on some outstanding Old Testament passages may, however, not be amiss. Ad Gen. 12:1-4: The call of Abraham is a type of our call to fellowship with God; for in our call, as in Abraham's, God reveals to us the riches of His grace in order to work faith in us; and when His call has wrought this faith, He demands of us, as He demanded of Abraham, that we separate ourselves from all that is not His. Ad Gen. 15:1-6: Like Abraham, the Christian

---

[22]Comp. above, p. 313.

is able to triumph over tribulation. The Christian, even though he has obeyed God's call and attained to fellowship with Him, must pass through tribulation; in this tribulation God's Word is his sure comfort; this comfort becomes his through faith alone; and this faith, clasping this comfort, experiences God's justification. Ad Gen. 17:1-9: The renewal of the covenant in Abraham's life is a figure of the renewal of the covenant in the life of the Christian. The text shows why this renewal is necessary; the conditions under which alone it can take place; its nature; and the obligation it imposes. Ad Gen. 18:16-23: The friendship between the believer and his God. (a) Its expression: God grants to the believer, as to a friend, an insight into His plan and purpose; and the believer speaks, in intercessory prayer, with God as with his friend. (b) Its foundation: not any merit on man's part, but solely God's free grace which chooses man to be His friend. (c) The condition of its permanence: profound humility toward God, and tender mercy toward the needs of the neighbor. Ad Gen. 19:15-26: Beware of obstacles to your Christian life that endanger the soul: of association with the ungodly; of doubt and delay when God interrupts these associations; of turning back to the old associations. Ad Gen. 22:1-18: The severest trial in Abraham's life and in ours. The homilete must make clear to his hearers the unique character of Abraham's trial; he must show how he was required not only to sacrifice his dearest possession, but while offering up his son, to believe in the blessed posterity promised him through that son. To this the Christian life offers no exact parallel. The lesson for our lives is this: we meet our trials in the spirit of Abraham, not by offering up our dearest possessions and then resigning ourselves dully to our fate, but by laying hold of the promise that all things work together for our good. When we are called upon, e. g., to give up our dear ones in death, we must hold fast the promise that we shall have them again in the glorious resurrection of the just. When we behold, with the eyes of faith, the angels of God guarding their dust and preserving and preparing it against the day of resurrection; when we realize that we are giving up our dear ones only to receive them back more glorious (1 Cor. 15), and when we trust that, despite all pain and apparent cruelty, our good Lord is only purifying and perfecting our faith—then we meet our trials in the spirit of Abraham. This is the only sense in which we can speak of a parallel between his experience and ours. There is in both cases the same apparent self-contradiction in God, which faith alone can solve. Ad

Ex. 14:13-31: Nothing but a miracle can save us; in many a temporal need, in every spiritual need, in our last and sorest need of all.

For the treatment of historical texts in general, Mosheim gave the following rules, which are still worth bearing in mind today: (1) The preacher should strive to impart to his hearers a connected conception of an event, and present it so clearly that the hearer will imagine himself actually present.[23] By this he means not merely a description of the external happenings, but a portrayal of their causes and their moral value. (2) The preacher should draw from his narrative its edifying and devotional application. (3) Above all, he should keep constantly before him the central thought from which alone this application can be safely made. As to the typical treatment of Old Testament texts he gives this necessary warning: "We must be especially on our guard against finding a type where there is no type, and ascribing to the Holy Spirit ideas which He never had. The law of Moses is indeed a shadow of things to come (Heb. 9:24), but we do not know if every part of this law was a type, and even if it were proved that it was, we should not always be sure what particular thing it typified. Hence it is the part of wisdom not to regard any passage as a type unless there is some reference to it in the New Testament."[24] But even such references need to be followed with caution. For his first readers Paul's discussions in Gal. 3:15 and 4:21 ff. were entirely in order, as illustrations—not as proofs[25]—of the truth with which he there dealt; for the congregation of today they have lost their illustrative value and are to be avoided.

The events narrated in Old Testament passages may, as the two last named of the above illustrations show, find their parallels not only in the life of the Christian or of the congregation as a whole, but in the life of Christ. Thus Gen. 32:22-31: Through conflict to victory, or striving with God and prevailing; so Jacob, Christ, we. Num. 21:4-9: The Lenten message of the brazen serpent: It tells of God's terrible punishment upon those that murmur against His leading and against His gifts; it points those in whom such punishment has wrought repentance to Christ lifted up by the cross to God's right hand. This is one of the passages most misused by careless homiletes.—The Old Testament text may be a portrayal of Israel's future in the messianic period, either in general terms or in

---

[23]Comp. what has been said above, pp. 340 f.—[24]*Anweisung, erbaulich zu predigen*, pp. 400 ff.—[25]So, too, Luther's allegorizings are not proofs but illustrations of the truth.

specific detail. So Num. 25:15-24: Final victory belongs to Christ: how hard this is at times to believe; how well authenticated it is; what follows from it by way of warning for us all. Isa. 42:1-8: The founding upon earth of the true Church; will it succeed? Success is assured by the nature of Him whose work it is; by the lowly and merciful manner in which He sets about this work; by the might and zeal of the Lord of hosts.[26]

The indirect application of New Testament texts may be either *tropological* or *symbolical*. In the former, what the text describes as having at one time happened is regarded as an expression of the unchanging τρόπος, the permanent and consistent nature, of God or of man.[27] Thus the narrative of the centurion of Capernaum reveals, when treated tropologically, the permanent tropos or character of faith, consisting in humility toward the Lord and unshakable confidence in His grace, as well as the permanent tropos of Christ, who is ready, now as then, to respond to the prayer of such faith. In the miracle narratives the tropological application is particularly indicated; likewise in the accounts of the pastoral work of Jesus. His conversation with the Samaritan woman, e. g., is intended to show the treatment He still employs in order to win souls: how He awakens a desire for higher things, a knowledge of sin, and true faith in Him as the only Saviour.

Other New Testament texts permit, beside the tropological, a symbolical application. The latter regards the external event as a symbol or image of a corresponding spiritual experience of the Church or the individual Christian. Thus the narrative of the healing of the deaf-mute directly invites this treatment. It may be transferred to present conditions by seeing in the physical cure an image of that inner experience by which a soul, deaf and dumb with respect to Christ's words and works, becomes, through the operation of Christ and His Spirit, able and eager to hear His word and to praise His

---

[26]For further illustrations see *Kirchl. Zeitschrift*, 1920.—[27]Achelis, ii, p. 172.

work. It would be fundamentally wrong, however, to make this the only or even the chief meaning of the miracles for us today. This would encourage the view that miracles belong to the realm of myth and fable, or that Christ cares only for our souls, not for our bodies. Miracles belong, on the contrary, to the sphere of historical reality; they actually happened, despite Huxley, and were intended to attract the attention of His contemporaries to Christ and to serve as object-lessons of the fulness of saving power residing in His person. They were thus important factors in His work as Saviour of men; and it is of the highest value to the Christian of today that he be shown by the miracles, or "signs" as John calls them, what a mighty and loving Saviour is his, for whom nothing is too difficult where the welfare of His own is concerned. The homilete dare, indeed, never treat the miracle as the most important factor in the ministry of Jesus, he must beware of arousing a mania for miracles among his members, and should make entirely clear to them that they cannot expect the Lord to work in this way today. For by His historical miracles He has once for all demonstrated what manner of Lord He is, and a true faith will never permit itself to dictate how and what and when He shall work. At the same time, he must bear witness that His arm has still its ancient power, and that there are no limits to the manner in which He can make all things work together for good to His beloved, far above all that they ask or think. We need to be reminded again and again of the omnipotence of our exalted Lord, to whom has been given all authority in heaven and in earth. (P. 373.)

Among modern homileticians Gottschick and Kleinert are ardent defenders of the symbolical application. Both of them, however, assign to it an undue scope. Kleinert writes: "In the foreground of the miracle-narratives is the profound symbolical trend that lifts these miracles (τέρατα) above the sphere of the extraordinary to the higher plane of signs (σημεία), to a sign-language, on the one hand, of the fulness of grace and glory in Him (John 2:11) and on the other hand, of the constant operation of the Spirit upon those who are His (Matt. 11:5). Considered merely as historical occurrences, they would prove only the omnipotence of God working through Christ, and the commissioning of the latter by the Almighty [?]. Even though this side may upon occasion [?] be dwelt on in the pulpit, especially when the text itself points the way (e. g. Matt. 9:6), nevertheless, the sermon would become wearisome and monotonous if it confined itself to this external side of the miracle and lost sight of the fact, proved by experience, that for the modern audience the evidences of religious truth must be drawn from the present realities of their own inner life, before they can recognize the manifestation of the divine in the past. But, considered as representation and exemplification of the merciful and redeeming, the **cleansing and vivifying love of the Healer** ('Ιησοῦς), and treated from the viewpoint that in the variety of the external ailments which He cured there is reflected the infinite depth of inner misery which He came to cure (Luke 5:31 f.), these healings of the sick and raisings up of the dead, the expressions of His mercy toward the hungry, broken-down, blind, deaf and lepers of earth, become a source of deep impressions of the nature of His saving work as well as of the most varied incentives to trust and self-examination. We are to 'draw living water from the ancient Scriptures' (Luther, *Erlangen ed.*, x, 367), and the pioneer and guide in this symbolic application of the scriptural word is none other than Jesus Himself."[28] Gottschick has this to say: "It is the practice of the preachers of all schools, following the lead of the Fourth Gospel, to use the narratives of Christ's external miracles as symbols of His spiritual miracle-working; especially to use the healings as symbols of deliverance from sin. This is fully justified. For it is a deeply rooted trait of the human mind, to make clear to itself the emotional value of spiritual events by means of externally perceptible images. Moreover, Christ's saving work concerns directly our deliverance from sin through the ethical power of God manifested in Him [?], and only indirectly our deliverance from evil, in the sense that our deliverance from sin brings with it, even now, our inner deliverance from evil, lifts us above pressure, and guarantees the future external deliverance. The symbolic use of the text is directly demanded whenever we find miracles of healing as proof of Jesus' messiahship, as in Matt. 11:4-6 and frequently in the Fourth Gospel. For the works of

---

[28] P. 54.

Jesus by which He produces spiritual life are the only accessible and truly adequate foundation of faith in Him today."[29]

Whether the text be applied typically, tropologically, or symbolically, the indirect application must in every case follow the same rule as the direct application—it must add nothing new to the text, but simply exhibit and set in operation the divine truth contained in it. It must, indeed, build a bridge from the past to the present; but this bridge must be straight and the road leading from it must be a direct continuation of the road leading up to it on the farther side. That this is true of the tropological application is self-evident. But no less true is it of the typical application, so long as it remains sane and sober, i. e., so long as it truly follows in the footsteps of the New Testament itself, in which the conception that Old Testament history as a whole is a prefiguration of the New Testament kingdom, its Head as well as its ordinances and principles, is explicitly set forth and copiously illustrated (cf. esp. John 6:22 ff. with 1-15, 5:39.; Luke 24:26 -27; Rom. 4; Gal. 3:6-9). The same holds true even of the symbolic application, so long as it keeps within proper bounds; for the miracles of Jesus, as σημεῖα, were intended to indicate His spiritual gifts and to represent them in their fulness.

The *allegorical* application is a different matter altogether. It is by no means identical with the symbolical application, although it is sometimes confused with it, even in textbooks on homiletics. In the symbolical application it is only the principal event in the text that is taken as the figure of a corresponding inner experience, while the allegorical application exploits all the details of the text. It is entirely justifiable to regard the ark as a symbol of the Church of Christ in which He saves believers; it is just as incorrect, and un-

---

[29] P. 48.

worthy of Holy Scripture, to follow in the footsteps of Origen and to discover a spiritual meaning for every detail of its structure and contents. Or take the parable of the Good Samaritan. We have every right and reason to apply this narrative directly to the present, or to apply it *tropologically*, in view of the preceding context. We should then set forth a truth somewhat like this: Do not wait to ask, who is my neighbor? but show mercy to everyone in need, wherever found. We may also treat this passage *symbolically* and develop the thought that Christ is the real Good Samaritan. Even this latter treatment would, however, overstep the bounds of the homiletically permissible if it forced into the background the principal thought or central purpose of the parable. The work of Christ as Good Samaritan may properly be set forth only as illustration or as motive of the duty we owe to our fellowman in the physical sphere. Altogether incorrect, and an undermining of all reverence for Holy Scripture, would be an *allegorical* treatment, in which every detail of the parable was applied. It need not go so far as the mediaeval interpretation (not extinct in the nineteenth century), which did not shrink from such an application as the following: Christ is the Good Samaritan, who finds man on the way from paradise (Jerusalem) to the world (Jericho) beaten and left half-dead by Satan (robbers), and who pours oil (extreme unction?) and wine (Lord's Supper) into his wounds, brings him to the inn (Church), hands the host (ministry) two pence (Old and New Testament) and bids him to take care of him until His return (Parousia). This is a mischievous abuse of Scripture; it destroys all historical understanding, exposes the congregation to the limitless caprice of the preacher, and profanes and makes a laughing-stock of sacred things. It is largely this allegorical treatment of biblical texts, especially of parables, that has opened wide the door to modern liberal theology, with its claim of going back of the Church's fanciful speculations to the simple and historical sense of Scripture. (P. 377.)

If it were not for ostentation in the pulpit and stupidity in the pew, allegory would long since have died a natural death. It is well known how Luther inveighed against it, though in practice he never completely rid himself of this relic of mediaevalism. Later it was especially Mosheim who raised his voice against it; his *Anweisung, erbaulich zu predigen* is noteworthy also in this respect. He says there: "Our fathers, in preaching on historical, prophetic or figurative passages, resorted to allegory and deduced from their texts truths of which there was not a thought in those texts. This practice they carried over from the papacy. Even in our day it is followed by many, who draw from their text inferences by way of allegory. But a truth deduced from a text by allegory is a non-sequitur. The ancients commonly preached analytical sermons, they explained their texts word by word and drew moral lessons from them. They wished to draw a lesson from every circumstance of a happening, but this was not possible without the aid of allegory. Thus they based most of their moral lessons upon allegory. An illustration will make this plain. We find in Matt. 8:1 ff., two historical facts—(1) Jesus descended from the mountain, and (2) much people followed Him. These two events in themselves contain no lesson for our life. But Catholics and Protestants alike resort to allegory. Instead of simply passing by these circumstances, they deduce from them the following truths: A Christian must humble himself, as Christ did when He came down from the mountain. We must descend, they say, from the mountain of worldly pride to the valley of humility. This is a perfectly correct moral truth, but it does not follow from the text. Simple hearers are not exacting; they do not reflect whether the lesson be rightly or wrongly drawn from the text. But more thoughtful persons, when they hear such rubbish, become disgusted and despise the preacher; their thoughts dwell not on the truth presented, but on the mistake of the preacher, and their devotion is consequently interrupted. When Jesus came down from the mountain, 'great multitudes followed Him.' From this no lesson can be drawn. But here is the application that is made: Men are in duty bound to follow Jesus. This sentence is true enough; but the text speaks of a natural following or going after one, not of a moral following. Verse 2: 'And, behold, there came a leper and worshiped Him, saying, Lord, if thou wilt, thou canst make me clean.' Neither the person nor his leprosy contains a lesson for faith or life. Nevertheless, they allegorize, make leprosy stand for sin and moralize thusly: Whoever will be freed from his sin must come to Christ. This truth is found in other places in Scripture, but not here. The petition in this verse contains these truths: 1. In asking God for temporal blessings we must humbly subject our petitions to His will and pray conditionally; 2. whoever prays must pray in faith and with confidence. The latter truth follows from the words, 'Lord, thou canst make me clean.' These truths may be deduced as general principles from the example of the leper, since Christ says nothing to the contrary. In verse 3, we are told: 'And Jesus put forth His hand.' From this nothing follows. From the words in verse 4 (cf. Mark 1:43-44), 'Go thy way, see thou tell no man,' some draw this conclusion: We must not publish abroad the blessings of God. But the reference here is only to one particular blessing. Christ commanded the man to show himself to the priests and to offer sacrifice. From this may [?] be drawn the general truth that we ought to obey all good and useful ordinances, out of respect to God and those in authority, even if we do not at once see the use of such ordinances. .... Care is necessary also in passages couched in exalted and figurative language. Here the mistake we are warning against is most frequently made. In Psalm 23:5 David said: 'Thou preparest a table before me in the presence of mine enemies: thou anointest my head with oil.' Many apply these words to the Lord's Supper, in which our Lord prepares a table before us. But David's meaning is: Although my enemies would rather see me starve, Thou sustainest my life and the lives of my dear ones. The lesson here is that the Lord will feed His people, even though their enemies begrudge it them. The words, 'Thou anointest my head with oil,' are based upon an oriental custom. The oriental anoints his head with oil, in order to refresh his physical powers, weakened by the heat. David therefore means to say: Thou alone givest me comfort and rest. But some find here the New Testament idea of the outpouring of the Holy Spirit upon believers, and draw false conclusions from these words. We ought not to deduce any truths from figurative texts until we understand the figure. The same thing is true of prophecies. Here great care is necessary, in order to prevent their wrong use and incorrect application. The words of Isaiah (1:5 ff.): 'The whole head is sick,' etc., are understood by some of human misery in general, whereas they refer to the Jewish people, to their king and priests. If a general moral lesson is to be drawn from them, it will be this: If the people who received from God such grace and so many advantages could sin so grievously against Him, we who have no such advantages should be all the more on our guard. By drawing from a text inferences and general moral lessons which are not contained in it, we may do much harm. The truth does not always suffer, but we make ourselves a laughing-stock. But oftentimes the truth does suffer, namely, when we generalize particular truths."

The fundamental rule, laid down above, governing the application of the text to present-day conditions, must be specially borne in mind in the treatment of *parables*. As it is the part of the exegete clearly to set forth the tertium comparationis,[30] so it is the part of the homilete to let this tertium comparationis govern his entire treatment of the parable. It must find expression in the theme or at least be clearly traceable through his whole development as its controlling idea. No rule has been broken so frequently and with such disastrous consequences for the Word of God. Preachers fear that by observing it they will not obtain sufficient material for their sermons. And it is true that its observance demands thought and labor; but it has this beneficial result, that the preacher will concentrate his thoughts upon a single truth, and that the congregation will have clearly presented to it in its sharpest formulation a truth that Jesus deemed important enough to be set forth in parabolic form. The hearer will realize something of the value of quiet concentration on Scripture, and will be driven to search aright the Scriptures for himself and learn to explain the individual passage in its connection. What lends to the homiletic application its truthfulness, force and dignity, is the very fact that the homilete, instead of reveling in ingenious trivialities, practices a chaste self-restraint and refrains from using what may be in themselves profitable and edifying elements, because they do not grow out of the text, which is his sole

---

[30]Which is, as Achelis correctly notes, only the scientific term for the immediate impression made upon their hearers by the first telling of the parables.

point of departure and guide. Here, too, self-restraint characterizes the master.

To what abuse has not the parable of the Ten Virgins been subjected, when the single truth it presents might be so impressively driven home, namely, that all depends on the endurance to the end of one's supply of spiritual life, which must therefore be constantly replenished by the divinely ordained means. Or the three parables in Luke 15—how much has not been read into them! One preacher actually preached and later published fifteen (15) sermons on the last of them! At bottom there is but a single truth in the three of them—a defence of Jesus' love for sinners, a defence that consists simply in showing how natural and self-evident this love is for one who is the Saviour of sinners. The preacher, who has realized this has laid hold of one of the most fertile homiletic thoughts, useful alike for reproof, exhortation and comfort; he sees into the very heart of Jesus and can never forget what he has there seen. He may treat it on the basis of the first of the three parables, which presents this self-evident love of Jesus for sinners under the figure of the natural anxiety of a shepherd seeking his lost sheep; or on the basis of the second parable, which throws light upon His Saviour-love by the self-evident solicitude of a house-wife turning her rooms upside down in order to find a coin lost out of her hard earned store; or he may treat the love of Jesus as something that, like true father-love, cannot be defeated by base ingratitude and shameful sin. This triad of parables shows also how the same thought may re-appear in different shades of meaning, which the careful homilete will not obliterate but scrupulously preserve, gaining thus variety and freshness in sermons on materials closely akin.

The tertium comparationis must, as we have said, control the whole application of the parable. This implies that no single detail—still less, all of them together—may assume independent importance in the application. It does not mean, however, that these details are always meaningless, the mere "drapery" of the parable, as they have been called. There are parables in which everything else but the central thought is indeed merely "drapery." Thus, the proposition which the unjust steward makes to his master's debtors has in its details no lessons for the present-day congregation; it serves merely as illustration of the single fact that the steward employed most shrewdly and to his own advantage the interval before he was dismissed. Not those individual items, but this central fact has value for the Christian today. Again, it would lead to an unchristian ethic if the dishonorable features in the conduct of the man who bought the field which he knew contained hidden treasure, were presented as an example to be followed. Even purely natural morality would designate such conduct as theft, or at least a defrauding of a fellowman.

In the case of other parables, however, certain details may and should find a rightful place in the application. Achelis refers to the parable of the Unmerciful Servant and queries: "The immeasurable debt, the impending judgment, the greatness of the mercy far above all asking and imagining; the tiny debt, the unmercifulness, the insistence upon one's own rights —are they there to no purpose?" We answer: True; but they must be so completely subordinated to the main thought that the latter will remain the unmistakable unit which holds together and governs all the rest. They serve but to emphasize and deepen the main thought,—viz., Let there be no limit to your mercy!— but they must never be allowed to overshadow it. A sense for the natural and a modicum of homiletic experience will help the preacher to determine, with increasing self-confidence, what is mere "drapery" and what is more. (P. 382.)

Luther said of sermons in which every detail of a parable is interpreted: "Such interpretations serve very well to pass the time, so long as one has nothing else to preach."³¹ In his *Clavis Scripturae* (1537), still a valuable hermeneutical treasury for the modern student, Flacius laid down the principle: "Nullae similitudines et parabolae per omnia conveniunt et explicandae sunt, sed tantum in principali scopa."³² Mosheim has a full and in the main correct discussion of the interpretation of parables, in his *Anweisung*.³³ He sums up his position in two rules: "(1) We must strive above all to find the main purpose of a parable and fit our interpretation to this purpose; other features which have no necessary relation to the main purpose should be regarded as embellishment and amplification of the parable. (2) We must carefully ascertain the point of comparison between things spiritual and things temporal, in order not to extend the scope of the parable farther than the Holy Spirit intends." In his explanation of the first of these rules Mosheim says: "Whoever compares two things, using one as similitude of the other, will necessarily say many things that do not belong to the main purpose but serve merely as amplification of the similitude. Thus, if one presents the Gospel under the similitude of sowing and reaping, one will naturally introduce a number of things that do not pertain to the main purpose, but that nevertheless have their place in the development of the parable. Hence we must distinguish two things in the parables: those that belong to the aim, and those that belong to the amplification, of the parable. The former alone are to be explained and their hidden meaning made clear; the latter may be passed by. We take as illustration the parable of the Ten Virgins in Matt. 25. The expounder of this parable must first of all determine carefully what was Christ's purpose in telling it. This will be seen to be: that Christians must watch always, for they know not when their Lord will come to judgment. From this viewpoint the whole parable must be examined. Whatever belongs to this main purpose must be set alongside it and the likeness between the two considered. The remainder must be treated as circumstances added by the Saviour in order to make the story hang together. When He mentions, for instance, how many virgins there were, no one should imagine a mystery behind this number. Again, while it is virgins to whom our Lord likens His kingdom, no one should look for a mystery in that. He naturally chose virgins because the parable is based upon the marriage customs of the Jews, according to which virgins went forth to meet the bridegroom. Hence, they are required by the decorum of the parable.

---

³¹*Erlangen ed.*, i, 2, p. 84.—³²Edition of Musaeus, Jena, 1674, ii, 53; cf. 152, 351, etc.—³³Pp. 430 ff.

The same is true of other circumstances. It is said that the bridegroom arrived at midnight. Here again we should scent no secret meaning; it was the custom among the Jews [?]. It is the same with all other parables. Many expositors err in this regard, especially the followers of Cocceius. It is their custom to take into account every circumstance of a parable and to draw from it special mysteries, and inferences respecting faith and life, These inferences are correct enough in themselves, but do not follow from the parable from which they are drawn, nor was the parable told for that purpose. Such expositions are to be avoided, because they furnish scoffers an opportunity for mockery. In the parable we have been considering, the wise virgins are represented as saying to the foolish, 'Go ye to them that sell, and buy for yourselves.' The question is, what did Jesus mean by this? Some say the merchants represent Antichrist, or the pope and his indulgence peddlers, to whom the foolish virgins are sent in order to adorn themselves with relics and works of the saints. If we ask these interpreters how they know this, they will be hard put to it for an answer."—In his strictures Mosheim is specially severe upon the Dutch theologian Cocceius (died 1669) and his school. Cocceius discovered in the parables the various epochs of church history, and adopted the following principle of interpretation, according to his sympathizer Teelman: "Verba omnia in parabolis Christi significantia sunt, adeoque et ipsorum anxia habenda est ratio et eorum adaptatio ad sensum spiritualem $\dot{\alpha}\kappa\rho\iota\beta\hat{\omega}s$ quaerenda." It seems hardly credible that, in the 1.st quarter of the nineteenth century, J. P. Lange could revive this principle and seriously defend it. No wonder that this dangerous trifling is not yet completely banished from our sermons. Juelicher's protest was, therefore, sorely needed, even though his own theory goes to the opposite extreme.

But did not Jesus Himself interpret some of His parables? This should point us to the right method. Compare, e. g., Matt. 13:36 ff., 49 f., 19 ff.; 21:42 ff., and the parallels. Jesus seems to interpret every detail and thus to reject the method we have adopted. But this is not actually the case. Heinrici gives the following explanation: "The purpose of the parable of the Fourfold Soil is to show how the same word is variously received and works differently according to the nature and circumstances of the one that receives it. In order to make this plain, 'the details of the parable are as essential to the exposition as eyes, nose, mouth are to a definite physiognomy' (Stockmeyer). The case is different with the Tares among the Wheat. It distinguishes between the present and the future. In the present the wise husbandman lets tares and wheat grow together; at harvest time the tares are burnt, the wheat is garnered. The interpretation confines itself to the latter feature alone. The same is true of the parable of the Dragnet. These interpretations bear the same relation to the parable as the application which is made of the parable of the Wicked Husbandmen. They show, and this corresponds to the purpose of the parable, that there is a limit to the longsuffering of God, but they refrain from expounding the specific features that illustrate this longsuffering. Does this do violence to the contents of the parable? Or is not rather the fact that before the end good and bad exist side by side, simply the necessary precondition for what the parable has to say of the final judgment? Hence, these interpretations appear to be, not distortions or a reading into the parable of something that is not there, but rather the setting forth of the religious truth for whose sake the parable was spoken. The determination of the details in the exposition is related to the res significata as the details in the parable are related to the res narrata. In the interpretation of composite parables, however, no detail may be interpreted by itself that does not subordinate and correlate itself to the truth, the principle, the fact, which is figuratively represented in the parable. The parable, as imaginative narrative, does not disdain to use pictorial elaboration. The latter is to the parable what arabesques are to a painting. But to find higher truths in these pictorial details, such as the three measures of meal in the parable of the Leaven, the petition, 'Lord, have patience with me,' etc., in Matt. 18:26, the various creditors in the parable of the Unjust Steward, would result in a rank growth of allegory and in religious monstrosities."[34]

After the homilete has found the scope and trend of his text and its general bearing upon present conditions, he will need, as was said above, to subject himself to his text. To the "Te totum applica ad textum" must come the "Rem totam applica ad te."[35] This will take the form of a *dialogue between preacher and text.* The preacher will ask himself what message the text has for his own life; what it contains for him of reproof, comfort or incentive; how his natural reason reacts to the text; what objections his old will advances; with

---

[34]PRE³, vi, 698 f.—[35]The motto, taken from J. A. Bengel, of Nestle's Greek New Testament.

what subterfuges it seeks to evade the force of the truth; what appeal the text makes to the new man in him—in short, what thoughts and emotions the text awakens in his own heart and mind. This is necessary not only because the homilete can preach with the requisite force and freshness only what he has himself felt, but because this is the surest way of finding what elements in the text will most appeal to and influence his hearers. Such quiet, sympathetic contemplation of and brooding over the text, in which one applies its truth to oneself, surrenders oneself to its influence, and brings to bear on it, by way of verification, one's experience in the Christian life, was in the minds of our older teachers when they declared "oratio, meditatio, tentatio," to be the prerequisites of an effective sermon.

The dialogue between preacher and text must be followed by a *dialogue between preacher and congregation.* Here the preacher will inquire how far the particular trend of the text answers to the specific need of his hearers, and how he may best bring it home to their hearts. Here the above mentioned intimate knowledge of the congregation, acquired by faithful pastoral care,[36] will stand the preacher in good stead. For, though the text itself frequently indicates whether the sermon is to address itself primarily to intellect, emotions or will, many texts are of so general a character that this can be decided only by a careful diagnosis of the particular needs of the congregation. From this point of view Steinmeyer's statement, that only one sermon can be preached from any one text, reveals its one-sidedness and exaggeration.

Since the liturgical life of the congregation is controlled by the Church Year, the question, What message has this text for my congregation? receives the further modification, What message has it for my congregation in this particular

---

[36]See chap. 8.

season? This should be carefully kept in mind, even though it applies only to the festival half of the year, and here in particular to the high festivals. Titus 2: 11 ff. treats originally of the appearance as such of the saving grace of God in Christ; but in a Christmas sermon the emphasis will fall altogether on the appearance of this grace in the birth of Christ. Similarly in the case of Titus 3: 4 ff. Isa. 61 or 40 receives a specific nuance when used as text for an Advent sermon. In Matt. 11: 28-30 certain features will be more prominent in a Reformation sermon than at other times. This is specially true of the text of occasional sermons, with their individual and personal application. Many a word of God reveals unsuspected beauties or a never experienced comfort and strength when used as confirmation, funeral or marriage text. Even here, however, the original meaning of the text dare never be distorted or wrested to the preacher's whim.

The preacher must not only ask, What message has this text for my congregation at this time? and study his text from this angle; he must ask further, How can I bring this truth home to my congregation without obscuring or impairing its force? This question involves a number of others: How can I best prepare my congregation, so that it will be able and eager to accept my main thought as having value for its life? What auxiliary thoughts and concepts must I use, in order to set my main thought before my hearers in concrete form? How shall I meet the objections of my hearers, overcome their recalcitrant will, and make them see the importance of the truth of my text for the Christian life as a whole? What illustrative materials should I employ? How can I make the connection between the new and the old and well-known, so as to further and not disturb the unity of the Christian view of life? How shall I formulate my conclusion, in order not to spoil or weaken what has already been said? In finding answers to these and similar questions the preacher will learn the value of the art of illustration; he will experience, especially in treating doctrinal passages, that the use of the personal element, i. e., the presentation of truth by means of concrete personalities, is of the utmost importance in lending to abstract teachings life and form; he will call to mind what has been said above of the use of the poetic element in preaching and of the characteristics of the sermon as an organic part of the service of the worshiping congregation.

When these questions have been answered, and the best method has been found of bringing the truth of the text to bear upon the individual congregation, there remains only the problem of the actual building of the sermon out of the homiletic materials thus assembled and prepared. Our last division will treat, therefore, of the structure or form of the sermon. (P. 389.)

The expressions, dialogue between preacher and text, and between preacher and congregation, come from Schleiermacher (*Praktische Theologie,* p. 248); the thing itself is as old as sound preaching. Theo. Grossgebauer wrote in 1661, in his *Waechterstimme*: "Sermons remain without fruit because after they are over so few preachers review them and ponder in their heart the question, What have we said in this hour on behalf of God, in order to save others and ourselves? We forget it, on the contrary, even before others, and are content with having toiled and perspired, and finished our work; whereas we should not rest until we found that what we preached to others had brought to our own hearts a special power of godliness, and made us still richer toward God in spiritual gifts, for the benefit of our congregation." If this is true, what shall be said of us preachers if we do not previously apply to our own hearts the Word of God which we are to present to our congregation? Achelis says: "The sermon which we preach to our congregation is worthless unless we have first preached it to ourselves. If we cannot always posit the effect of renewed repentance and faith on the part of the congregation, we must be able to posit it at least on the part of the preacher. The preacher who, while preaching to others, himself becomes a castaway, who demands repentance and faith of others and himself refuses them, who lets custom render holy things profane, and deals only in high-sounding words,—his sermons have lost their witness-bearing character. But the fact that the preacher himself is led, by each of his sermons, to walk more humbly before God, and increases in the knowledge of sin and the longing for salvation; that through each of his sermons his confidence in the sole and all-sufficient power of Jesus Christ to redeem and make perfect grows stronger or is at least stirred up anew, and that he decreases but Christ increases in him—this is for the preacher a criterion by which he may measure the worth of his sermons."[37]

In answering the question, What message has this text for my congregation? the preacher is not to follow the fivefold usus introduced, though not consistently followed, by Hyperius,—namely, to inquire, Is my text profitable for $\delta.\delta\alpha\sigma\kappa\alpha\lambda\iota\alpha$, $\H{\epsilon}\lambda\epsilon\gamma\chi o s$, $\epsilon\pi\alpha\nu\acute{o}\rho\theta\omega\sigma\iota s$, $\pi\alpha\iota\delta\epsilon\iota\alpha$, or $\pi\alpha\rho\acute{\alpha}\kappa\lambda\eta\sigma\iota s$? (cf. 2 Tim. 3:16; Rom. 15:4.) This should go without saying. He must be a stupid preacher, who after working through his text and having determined upon the application of its main thought, needs to ask: Must I now teach, admonish, rebuke, or comfort? He should preach the truth of his text to the whole man, though at different times the appeal will be more directly, now to the intellect, then to the emotions, again to the will. He dare never address the intellect alone, without stirring the emotions; he will not calm the emotions without satisfying the needs of the intellect, and he cannot move the will without influencing both the intellect and the emotions. Which appeal is to stand in the foreground, will be determined by the preacher's knowledge of his congregation. Kleinert's advice is well worth heeding, when he says: "First the quiet, consecrated contemplation of the correctly understood text, in order to become possessed of the central energy with which it projects itself into the preacher's own soul; then the contemplation of the congregation and the inquiry, in circumspect love, at which point it needs this energy of the text and at which point it can be brought home to it; and then the return to the text, to draw from this centre, out of its individual elements, the motives and quietives which are adapted to influence the congregational life by improving, soothing, strengthening and purifying it."[38]

---

[37]ii, 141.—[38]P. 88.

III

The Structure of the Sermon

§ 14. FUNDAMENTAL PRINCIPLES GOVERNING THE STRUCTURE OF THE SERMON

Fenelon, *Letter to the French Academy*, 1714. E. Porter, *Lectures on Homiletics and Preaching*, 1834. Chr. Palmer, *Ev. Homiletik*, 1842. Fr. Schleiermacher, *Praktische Theologie*, 1850. A. Vinet, *Homiletics*, Eng. tr. by Skinner, 1853, [2]1861. A. Phelps, *The Theory of Preaching*, 1881. A. Krauss, *Lehrbuch der Homiletik*, 1883. E. Chr. Achelis, *Lehrbuch der praktischen Theologie*, 1890, [3]1911. P. Drews, *Die Predigt im 19. Jahrhundert*, 1913. P. Kleinert, *Homiletik*, 1907. J. Gottschick, *Homiletik und Katechetik*, 1908. Herrick Johnson, *The Ideal Ministry*, 1908.

The subject-matter or material of the sermon is without question the chief thing. But if this material be presented in an inadequate form its inherent power cannot make itself felt, its edifying effect is impaired and may be completely neutralized. A proper regard for the material and the purpose of the sermon demands, therefore, that careful attention be given to its structure. The sermon, moreover, appears as public oration, and must, therefore, conform to the rules governing the oration as such. It cannot be permitted to degenerate into mere formless talk, but must possess an artistic—not an artificial—character expressing its peculiar nature and purpose. The sermon must be *a work of art,* as truly as the product of the sculptor or the painter. The artist, as distinguished from the artisan and from the dilettante, does not perform a series of mechanical manual acts and is not content with ineffectual and self-contradictory attempts, but gives to a unified, integral and ordered idea its corresponding outward form, able to impress itself upon others. Thus the preacher must assimilate the edifying materials of his text in such a way as to be able to mould them into a form which will bring these materials home to his hearers in a unified, coherent and ordered manner. In this sense we emphatically demand that the sermon shall be a work of art.

The first requirement of the sermon, with regard to its structure, is *unity*. A work of art may express a variety of ideas, but it cannot remain a work of art unless this variety is held together by the unity of a central idea. The sermon, too, may and should present a variety of thoughts, yet it dare not be a farrago of heterogeneous and arbitrarily assembled elements, but must form an organic unity. Whatever is merely accidental, occasional and out of alignment with the central thought, indeed whatever is not actually demanded by the central thought, must be ruthlessly excluded. It may stop a gap, but it disturbs the unity of the structure and effect of the sermon; instead of an harmonious, it becomes a discordant and destructive element. Here the preacher must practice stern self-discipline and mercilessly rule out every thought, be it ever so beautiful and valuable in itself, that disturbs the unity of the design and effect of his sermon. Not only the accidental is excluded by the demand of unity, but still more the contradictory and inconsistent, in which one sentence neutralizes another or one statement casts doubt upon another. The beginner is prone to this fault, but no less every poorly prepared preacher, who forgets at one moment what he has said at another, and the development of whose sermon does not grow out of a unified view of the subject. The unity of the sermon forbids also the dragging in of borrowed materials and of quotations that do not fit organically into the discourse. Even if the logical unity may not suffer hereby, the outer unity of design is disturbed and the laws of style are broken. Purple patches betray the poverty of the rest of the fabric. Finally, the unity of the sermon is marred by the unnatural excitement into which some preachers work themselves, and which is not warranted by the text nor the structure of the sermon and does not grow out of the preacher's own experience or world-view. It is palpably manufactured and "put on," and is, therefore, an inner insincerity.

A sermon without unity does not deserve the name, and cannot produce a permanent impression. For what is there to impress the hearer, when the preacher flits, without plan or purpose, from one thought to another, instead of so presenting his main thought from various angles that it will fix itself in the minds of his hearers and take possession of their life? Alas! it is true, as a glance into our sermonic literature will show, that this fundamental rule is transgressed times without number, many preachers appearing never even to have heard of it.

The second requirement is *completeness*. Not that every sermon is to be an epitome of the sum-total of Christianity, as demanded by German pietism and American Methodism. This would lead not only to continual repetition but to violation or mutilation of the text. It is necessary to make clear the connection between old and new truths, so that Christian truth may be seen as an organic whole; but the individual sermon need not present the whole of Christian truth, not even in outline. Completeness is rather to be understood in the sense that whatever portion of Christian truth a sermon treats should be presented completely and exhaustively. Neither the announcement of the subject nor the development of the subject-matter should awaken expectations that are not fulfilled. The hearer should not feel that essential features have been omitted, that more questions have been raised than answered, that the preacher has succeeded in drawing the attention of his audience to the problems but not in helping them to reach a satisfactory solution. By an exhaustive presentation of a truth we do not mean exhaustive in an absolute sense, but only so far as the particular text is concerned. Phases of a truth not touched on in the text, but essential to a complete treatment of that truth, may be discussed in the introduction or referred to in passing, in order to prevent misunderstanding.

The sermon, like other art products, must further possess *order*. It must be an organism composed of definite parts which are well articulated, mutually require each other and combine in their totality and interrelation to make up an ordered whole. Without such order there can be neither an oration in general nor a sermon in particular; without an orderly grouping of materials according to the laws of pedagogy and rhetoric the sermon can not make upon its hearers the impression which its contents warrant. Beside the laws of logic, which are binding upon the sermon as upon all other mental products, the laws of pedagogy and of rhetoric must be observed by the sermon, since its purpose is to produce a lasting effect upon the intellect, the feelings and the will. The following *pedagogic* principles come into play: (1) Accommodation to the apperception, the vocabulary and the ideas of the hearer. Without this it is impossible to reach his soul and to lead it farther. (2) Clear definitions of ideas and things. *Qui bene distinguit, bene docet.* A person who does not know how to connect what belongs together or to distinguish what differs, cannot but confuse. (3) A careful distinction between the essential and the non-essential, and a confining oneself to the former with a view to presenting it with greater clearness and driving it more forcibly home. (4) Progression from the simple to the complex, from the known to the unknown, from the near to the remote. The absolutely new and strange is instinctively rejected by the mind. If these pedagogic laws are binding on the teacher, they are no less binding on the preacher, for he, too, is a teacher. But he is also an orator; hence to the pedagogical come certain rhetorical rules which he should know and observe. As the former contemplate especially the effect to be produced upon the intellect, the latter contemplate the effect upon the feelings and the will. Especially four *rhetorical* principles are in question here. (1) A careful grouping of parts, both with respect to the sermon as a whole and to the various divisions, and the determination of the precise place in the whole at which the various parts will make their strongest appeal; for, according to Schiller's dictum, the art of oratory consists specifically in the proper distribution of lights (*Schlaglichter*). (2) A steady progression from point to point within these various parts, or the proper movement of the discourse. (3) A judicious variety in the development of the thought, whether this be achieved by the element of allocution, the formulation and refutation of objections, or by the summarizing of what has preceded, with the purpose of influencing the feelings and the will, introducing as it were a pause or rest in the flow of the discourse. (4) A climactic arrangement of thought-groups. This is especially in place when the appeal is to the will, so that each successive point will bear with stronger and ever stronger impact upon the will until the last crowns the whole. Augustine had this in mind when he put the genera of the sermon in the following order: *submisse docere, temperate monere, granditer movere.* This should be borne in mind especially by beginners, who commonly bring up their heaviest troops first, only to be left later on in the lurch; unless they husband their resources they will give out before reaching the conclusion, and their powers will be spent when they should be at their height.

Since the sermon is an oration in the service of the worshiping congregation, a further requirement must be noted. It dare never forget, in its structure and form, that it is delivered in the house of God and as an organic part of the service. This calls for *simplicity and chastity of form,* and rules out everything undignified, vulgar and low, as well as all rhetorical parade and "playing to the gallery." It excludes also the polemic element, and demands instead a lucid presentation of positive truth, by which the hearer is enabled to draw the negative conclusions on his own account, and is thus better armed against error than by listening to a dozen polemical sermons. When, by reason of special conditions, an apologetic treatment becomes necessary, it should never take the form of personal or worldly polemics, but be conducted in a serene spirit well grounded in the Christian world-view as a whole. It should always be the exception, never the rule; for "an habitual gladiatorial attitude belongs in the arena, not in the pulpit." The pulpit must be kept free from whatever does not minister to Christian contemplation, to the concentration of the soul upon God, and to the furtherance of the spiritual life of the congregation. These considerations will even help to determine the question as to the length of the sermon. A sermon becomes too long as soon as it ceases to hold the devout attention of its hearers. (P. 425.)

The *artistic character* of the sermon was emphasized by many of the Greek and Latin preachers of the ancient Church. The fact that they frequently crossed the line separating sacred from secular discourse does not invalidate the correctness of their position. Not a few of them produced sermons that are specimens of the artistic sermon at its best.[1] In the Middle Ages this side of the sermon received attention under the influence of scholasticism. While it led in most cases to artificiality, Bernard of Clairvaux and Berthold of Regensburg approached a purer type. The Reformation period, with its "loci" method, gave less attention to the art of the sermon. Luther's sermons, at their best, comply with the artistic canons of unity and order.[2] Siegfried Saccus, in his *Gospel Postil*,[3] has an introductory essay, "Unterricht von der Ordnung, so in Predigten kann gehalten werden," in which he says: "It is important that young preachers accustom themselves to good order and a definite manner of preaching. Some hold the vicious and pernicious opinion that order is not necessary in sermons; they babble on and on, anything that comes

---

[1] See for this and the following historical references, our forthcoming *History of Preaching.*—[2] Cf. his sermon on John 3:16 in the *Church Postil.*—[3] Magdeburg, 1589.

into their mouths, and despise languages and the liberal arts as unnecessary and unprofitable in the exposition of Scripture. They call an orderly sermon structure mere philosophy without spirit, and maintain that the Scriptures, too, are without order. I met one of this ilk at the beginning of my ministry. I had preached on the text, 'Call upon me in the day of trouble, etc.', and he said to me, *'Concio tua non placuit mihi,* I did not like your sermon.' When I asked him the reason he said, *'Quia erat methodica,* Because there was method in it,' and added, *'Aliud erat spiritus Lutheri,* Luther had a different spirit and observed no order in his sermons'. . . . . As though Luther deliberately preached confusedly, when the very opposite can easily be proved! Young preachers should know that God is a God of order and that there is in the Scriptures an exceedingly beautiful and glorious order, as can be shown by many illustrations from both Testaments. As God Himself appointed the holy angels, prophets and apostles in a wonderful order, so ought we to accustom ourselves to good order in our preaching. This is profitable for both preachers and hearers. For the former will thereby be enabled to memorize their sermons more readily and to deliver them with less exertion; the latter will be able more easily to understand and retain them." In more recent times it was especially Fenelon and Vinet among the French, and Mosheim, Schleiermacher, Palmer, Steinmeyer, Bassermann and Kleinert, among Germans, who claimed an artistic character for the sermon. Among English and Americans we may mention Dale, Watson, Garvie, Hervey and Brooks. Theoretically this side of the sermon, though not always called by this name, is generally recognized, though the practice still lags far in the rear.

In the first edition of his *Homiletik*[4] Palmer devoted a section to the sermon as a work of art, in which he said: "The text lies before us. How shall we deal with it? Our first main division gives the first answer: we are to expound it according to the manner there described. But that does not yet give us a sermon. For the sermon is a part of the cultus. And the cultus demands for all its component parts a beautiful form; it demands art. This can only be objected to, when no emphasis is laid upon the churchly, truly catholic principle, or when this principle is altogether excluded in the interest of a one-sided biblicism. We, however, are convinced that, just as we demand in the church-hymn not only a scriptural content but also a beautiful form, because that belongs to the cultus or worship, which

---

[4] 1842.

has the beautiful as its necessary attribute, so the churchly discourse should likewise be beautiful after its kind."—Bassermann, while admitting that to expect every sermon to be a work of art might seem a pretentious demand, nevertheless holds firmly to it. "I do not know," he adds, "what purpose can be served by writing a theory of preaching, if the sermon is to be less than this. It would then suffice to put together a few practical suggestions, or to show 'how it is done,' i. e., how it is the custom to do it, or it would be enough simply to impart a schema. . . . Whoever regards rhetoric as a scientific theory, eloquence as an art, an oration as an art-product, and the cultus as a representative act, must demand artistic form for an oration having its place in the cultus."[5] We agree entirely with this, although for us the cultus, and, therefore, also the sermon, is not only a representative but an effective act. We have already emphasized this point above, in connection with individual features of the sermon, such as style, etc. We now repeat this demand for the artistic character of the sermon, with respect to its entire design and structure. With Kleinert we say, "Not the form of the sermon as such is important;" but we also add with him, "Its importance consists in its relation to the content. No spiritual content can express itself completely and effectively without a corresponding form. The more closely, indeed, the form answers to the content, the more the content creates its own form, the more completely will the content be expressed and the more impressively will it affect the hearer. This is what lends to form its importance and makes it impossible that the sermon should be formless. Lack of form is a mark of awkwardness, that is, of weakness. In intercourse with men, it betrays one's lack of self-control; in the sermon it betrays the preacher's lack of control over his material or his expression, with the result that the force of his subject-matter is counteracted by his own powerlessness. Lack of form is, secondly, a mark of deficient reverence. Hence lack of form in sacred things is a mark of a lack of reverence for that which is sacred. The obligation to present a sacred subject-matter in its corresponding form constitutes the sermon a work of art."[6] Everything depends upon how this demand is understood. Palmer reduced the artistic side of the sermon to these three items: the unity of the sermon as a whole; the internal order of its parts; the conformity of each part to the whole, and the proper use of the means of expression in every part. Bassermann emphasized especially "the unity in variety, the inner harmony of the

---

[5]*Handbuch der geistl. Beredsamkeit*, p. 211.—[6]P. 139.

different parts assembled in a work of art, brought about by an idea ruling the whole and determining each part, the organic combination of a unified centre with a multiplicity of members, presenting itself to the hearer in such a way as to awaken pleasure and to compel him to estimate it as beautiful."[7] Kleinert, following G. Krause's *Vorlesungen ueber Aesthetik* (1882), sums up the matter in the demand for "Einheit, Selbheit, Ganzheit." We ourselves make a fourfold demand on the sermon in this connection. It must be (1) a unit, (2) complete in itself, (3) well ordered, and (4) possessing a chaste simplicity.

The sermon must be a *unit,* a single whole. We put this first because it is actually the fundamental requirement of a properly constructed sermon, and also because this unity is so often conspicuously lacking, whereby the sermon loses not only its artistic character but much of its effectiveness. Among the French, it was especially Fenelon and Vinet who enforced the demand for unity. The former says, in his *Letter to the French Academy,*[8] of the orator, including the preacher:

"He first lays down the principle which must serve to clear the subject he treats of. He sets this principle in the fullest light. He turns it every way to give his slowest hearers a clear view of it. He draws the remotest consequences from it by a concise and obvious train of reasoning. Every truth is set in its proper place with regard to the whole; it prepares, leads on, and supports another truth that needed its assistance. This just order prevents the trouble of needless repetitions, but it retrenches none of those useful ones, that serve to direct the hearer's attention frequently to that chief point on which the whole depends. The orator must often show him the conclusion that is contained in the principle, and *from this principle, as from the center, he must spread a due light over all the parts of the discourse; as a skillful painter places the light so in his picture, as from one single point to distribute a due proportion of it to every figure.* THE WHOLE DISCOURSE IS ONE; AND MAY BE REDUCED TO ONE SINGLE PROPOSITION, *set in the strongest light, by various views and explications of it.* This unity of design shows the whole performance at one view; as in public places of a city, one may see all the streets and gates of it, when the streets are straight, equal, and duly proportioned. THE DISCOURSE IS THE PROPOSITION UN-

---

[7] P. 212.—[8] We quote from the translation in Porter's *The Young Preacher's Manual* (1829), pp. 114 ff.

FOLDED, AND THE PROPOSITION IS AN ABSTRACT OF THE DISCOURSE.
Denique sit quodvis simplex duntaxat et unum (Horace, *De Arte Poet.*, 23).
He who perceives not the beauty and force of this unity and order, has never seen anything in its full light. He has only seen shadows in Plato's cavern. What should we say of an architect, who could see no difference between a stately palace, whose apartments are adjusted with the exactest proportion, so as to make one uniform structure, and a confused heap of little buildings, which do not compose one regular plan, though they be all placed together? What comparison is there between the Coliseum, and a confused multitude of irregular houses in a city? There can be no true unity in any composition, unless there can be nothing taken from it without spoiling it. It never has a right order, but when we cannot displace any part without weakening, obscuring, and disordering the whole. This is what Horace explains perfectly well:

—Cui lecta potenter erit res
Nec facundia deseret hunc, nec lucidus ordo.
Ordinis haec virtus erit, et Venus, aut ego fallor
Ut jam nunc dicat, jam nunc debentia dici,
Pleraque differat, et praesens in tempus omittat.—(*De Arte Poet.*)

An author who does not thus methodize his discourse is not fully master of his subject; he has but an imperfect taste, and a low genius. Order, indeed, is an excellence we seldom meet with in the productions of the mind. A discourse is perfect when it has at once method, propriety, strength, and vehemence. But in order to have this, the orator must have viewed, examined, and comprehended every point, that he may range each word in its proper place. This is what an ignorant declaimer, who is guided by his imagination, can never discern."

We have cited the entire passage, for though it covers a wider range than the unity of discourse, the latter is strongly emphasized, and is given classic expression in the sentence, "The discourse is the proposition unfolded, and the proposition is an abstract of the discourse." The sermon must, indeed, be reducible to a single sentence or proposition, because it should be nothing else than the organic unfolding of this sentence. Whatever be its wealth of thought, its variety of materials, all is justified only in so far as it flows from a single central idea and is the actual unfolding of this idea. Whatever is not directly connected with the one central idea and does not flow from it, whatever does not support, prove or illustrate it, and is not supported, proved or illustrated by it, has no place in that particular sermon.

Vinet returned to the position of Fenelon and further elaborated it. He begins with the proposition, "We advance the first rule or the first condition of pulpit discourse: its subject is one."[10] This he develops as follows: "The human mind inherently demands unity. Apart from unity, we can recognize neither truth, goodness, nor happiness. In morality, we want a principle to move and direct us; in life, a purpose; in institutions, harmony; in poetry, an idea; in history, a point of view; in the universe, one final cause of all effects. We are not pursuing identity under the name of unity. Where there is identity, the very idea of unity disappears; plurality is necessary to give unity a place; systems of identity spring from our impatience to find unity, and our repugnance to regard things as disconnected. Unity is essential to every work of art, art itself having as its chief aim to make one whole by combining scattered elements [*ars* from ἄρω, to adapt]. Every work of art is a work of subordination and of co-ordination. The first includes the second. All elements subordinated to one and the same principle, are thereby co-ordinated with one another. Unity in works of art, requires not only the exclusion from one and the same whole, one assemblage, of elements which are incompatible with one another; but the bringing of all the parts into relation to one and the same center, one and the same end. Oratorical discourse demands unity yet more imperatively. Not being read, but heard, it would very quickly weary our attention, if it were required to transfer itself successively from one side to another. Its duration being short, compared with that of other productions, it is less at liberty to entertain the hearer with a variety of subjects. *Having to act upon the will, it gains on this account by concentrating itself to a single thought. It is, when it does this, as different from discourse, which, however full, is incoherent, without definite aim, or confused, as an army is from a rabble.* The strongest thoughts, which are not interconnected, injure one another, and the more in proportion to their strength. Only very powerful minds can obtain profit from that which is without unity, or from that which is consistent with itself. Attacked by a crowd of mutually self-neutralizing impressions, we are made captive by none, and are fixed to nothing. Mark, when you have opportunity, the effect of such discourse on its seriously-minded hearers, taking them as you find them. Each hear-

---

[10]Eng. tr., p. 54.

er of this class, unconsciously to himself, will endeavor to give unity to a discourse to which the preacher has not given it; or will attach himself to one of the preacher's ideas, and adhere to that; or will perhaps force all these ideas to take the direction which pleases his own thought. The very solemnity of preaching requires unity. The solemnity would be less if the discourse, instead of being a procession, were a promenade. Evidently all this applies without abatement to the discourse of the pulpit, and we were right in saying that the first requisite in this discourse is to have one subject; for, when there are many subjects, there is none." At the close of this discussion Vinet adopts Fenelon's dictum, "The discourse is the proposition unfolded, and the proposition is an abstract of the discourse,"[11] and adds this important suggestion: "It is useful to subject each of your discourses to this test. Let it not be enough to be able to give them a title; endeavor to condense them into one proposition; and distrust your work when you cannot succeed."

But Vinet goes beyond Fenelon by emphasizing not only the unity of content but the *unity of aim or purpose*. This is implied in his statement, "On the whole I conclude that to have unity in a sermon, it must be reducible to an assertory proposition, which is readily transformable, and is in fact transformed, into an *imperative* proposition."[12] From the context of this statement it is clear that Vinet has in mind the thought that the sermon, as it must be reducible to a single proposition, must in its whole development have constantly before it a single goal, and must aim all along at a single impression upon the soul of the hearer. This point was taken up by A. Krauss of Strassburg, following in the steps of Fenelon and Vinet, but also of Schleiermacher.[13] He lays down the principle,—"The sermon possesses unity when its content is so complete in itself that the individual parts are not only related to one and the same subject, but contribute to produce one and the same total impression." Just as a single proposition must run like a thread of gold through the whole discourse, so the whole discourse itself must be so constructed as to contain nothing that could in any way disturb the unified impression of the proposition on intellect, feeling, or will. Every sentence of the discourse must be designed with a view to this effect; it must prepare for it, produce it, confirm it, or make it permanent. Drews takes up this thought when he writes in 1903: "It is not a mere art rule when we demand

---

[11] P. 67. — [12] Skinner's translation (p. 59) does not correctly reproduce Vinet's meaning.—[13] In his *Praktische Theologie*, pp. 222 ff.

unity of the sermon; it is a demand founded in the effect of the sermon. Only the art product that is complete in itself produces an effect. It is not otherwise with the sermon. If a sermon leads us, perhaps without even a plan, through a mass of thoughts that may indeed be subsumed under a theme, but that neither begins nor ends at a definite point, these thoughts lose much of their force. As a result of such general themes, the preacher treats not one, but two or three subjects, according to the number of divisions; the sermon falls in pieces; each division would fill a whole sermon, if thoroughly and convincingly handled. Let no one say that this lack of unity, this spreading out of rich materials under a theme as comprehensive as possible, is a harmless matter; that there is much truth in the familiar words in the prologue[14] to Goethe's 'Faust'—

Die Masse koennt ihr nur durch Masse zwingen.

We must not forget that Goethe puts these words in the mouth of the 'director,' who is avid of external success; not of the 'poet,' who seeks the success of the ideal. Whoever looks for the immediate superficial success of his sermon, whoever seeks to entertain, may, indeed, dispense with unity. But whoever would lead his hearers into the depths, induce them to accept a serious and important idea as their own personal possession, advance their religious understanding and educate them to a thorough examination of religious and moral subjects—most necessary task of all, it seems to us, today—will as a matter of course see that his sermon possesses unity."

But does this demand of German writers hold also for the American pulpit? Let us hear what American homileticians have to say on this point. Ebenezer Porter, the first American homiletician, from whom we have so often quoted, saw fit to devote an entire lecture[15] to this subject. He is concerned to show, first of all, that the unity of the sermon by no means spells sameness. "I do not mean by unity that sameness which excludes all interesting variety of thought and illustration in a sermon. If twenty pieces of coin, stamped with the same die, are spread before you, each is so perfectly like the rest, that though you turn them over and over, you see the same object still without variety. If you travel across an extended plain of arid sand, stretching around you, in a wide unchanging scene of barrenness, there, too, you have oneness, without variety. But how soon do you long for a hill, a rivulet, a cottage, a tree, or even a shrub, to relieve you from this intolerable unity of prospect. . . . There is a kind of

---

[14]He means the *Vorspiel.*—[15]viii.

unity in a sermon, which indeed is in no danger of distracting the attention of hearers, by the multiplicity of objects presented. It consists in a constant recurrence of the same thought, attenuated and repeated with undeviating uniformity. The hearers pass on with the preacher, not from one branch of the discourse to another, delighted with the richness of matter and variety of illustration; but from one topic, presented again, with some trifling changes of representation. The above sort of taste, indeed, does not always deign, in this last particular, to humor the caprice of hearers. It gives them over and over the same favorite thoughts, in the same favorite expressions; and often very consistently completes its claims to their attention, by a favorite monotony in delivery. Nor is this sameness limited to a single discourse of the preacher; it extends, perhaps, through the whole range of his instructions; so that whatever reason the hearers may have to expect a new *text,* they have the advantage of foreseeing, essentially, what the *sermon* will be, from Sabbath to Sabbath. Now, if this is the indispensable quality in sermons which we call unity, it is one, as all will agree, in which it is the province of dullness to excel. But to suppose that our hearers are benefited by such a sameness, in the pulpit, is to suppose that when they enter a place of worship they cease to be men." To the question, what is meant by the unity of the sermon, Porter replies: "It requires that the sermon should be one in subject, one in design, one in the adjustment of its parts to the principal end and to each other, and one in illustrations." He does not tarry long over the first of these items, which is for him self-evident; he pauses but to remark that unity is often obscured by too many preparatory matters, which scatter the interest, as well as by the mistaken attempt to present in every sermon a complete system of religion. More important for Porter is the second requirement, which is also more frequently overlooked. He says: "The wise preacher will propose to himself some chief *effect* which he hopes to produce by every discourse. . . . The good to be accomplished by a sermon, whatever is its subject, must depend very much on its adaptedness to leave on the hearers' minds some specific and predominant impression. Whether it bears upon insensibility, or error, or vice; whether it is designed to alarm the careless sinner, or to strengthen the wavering Christian, its bearing should be distinctly seen and felt. This requires not only that the sermon should *have* a definite subject and a definite design, but that these should be constantly *in the preacher's eye.* 'It is a favorite method with me,' said Cecil, 'to reduce the text to some point of doctrine. On that topic I enlarge, and then apply it.

I like to ask myself, 'What are you doing? What is your aim?'" Porter emphasizes more strongly the third item. "Here I lay it down as an elementary principle of great importance, *that a discourse should be adapted to produce an effect as a WHOLE.* It is not enough that there is a succession of good words, or of striking sentences, or of brilliant paragraphs, or even of weighty, detached thoughts. The choice and arrangement of matter should be such, as to produce a growing interest in the auditors, and to leave a strong impression of the *subject* on their minds. This supposes the preacher, before writing, to have examined well the materials of which the sermon is to consist, and to have settled with himself the *order* in which these are to be disposed, to the best advantage." There follow a number of illustrations from the realm of art, many of which are reminiscent of Fenelon, who was well known to Porter, and which recur in homiletic works down to 1900. "There is no work of art," Porter continues, "in which this principle of unity is not essential to perfection. The architect studies the *purpose,* for which a building is intended, while he adjusts its parts in his whole plan. Is it a church? It must have one chief apartment, so designed as to accommodate a whole assembly, in listening to one speaker, and uniting in the same acts of devotion, at the same time. Is it a senate house? Its dimensions, apartments, and proportions, must correspond with the particular *end* of its construction. Is it a private dwelling? Here again the main *purpose* must be kept in sight; and such a relation preserved between different stories, and different rooms, as the convenience of the occupants may require. Is it a country seat? The skilful architect will employ what is called the prophetic eye of taste. He will anticipate just what the principal edifice, and the subordinate buildings will be when finished. It is not a fine column, or window, or gateway, that makes a beautiful seat, but the combined effect of symmetry and fitness, which strikes the eye, in the structure and its appendages, when viewed as a whole. So with the landscape gardener. Give him a rude spot to transform into a beautiful garden; and he sees by anticipation, how each part of the grounds must be shaped, where each avenue must pass, and each tree and shrub must stand, when the plan is completed; and 'when he plants a seedling, he already sits under its shade.' So the historic painter, if he would represent a shipwreck, must not be satisfied to show you a broken mast or cable. Nor yet must he show you the mariners clinging to a tempest beaten ship, while other ships in the same prospect are becalmed. The heavens must frown with blackness, and the ocean swell in angry surges, and spread before you a *consistent* scene of terrific sublimity. So the portrait painter must not exhaust his skill on a single feature, but must exhibit the united expression of all features, in the human face divine.

> " 'Tis not a lip, or eye, we beauty call;
> But the joint force and full result of all.'

So the epic or dramatic poet, must not set before you an incongruous succession of characters or incidents, violating all probability and consistency. He must show you a *train* of things, growing in interest, and leading on to some common result. Shakespeare, though he has been called the stumbling block of critics, as often inelegant, obscure, and ungrammatical in style, and though he pays little regard often to what are called the unities of time and place, shows you men and things as they are. He not only pleases you with here and there a speech, but arrests your attention to the course of events, fills you with a restless eagerness to keep up with his incidents, and leaves you at last under some *strong impression,* that abides with you. Of this great dramatic poet Johnson says, 'He who tries to recommend him by select quotations, will succeed like the pedant in Hierocles, who, when he offered his house for sale, carried a brick in his pocket, as a specimen.' When you have read Julius Caesar, or Hamlet, you may be unable to repeat a single line, but you never can forget the *subject.* I have extended these illustrations, to show that preaching is not exempt from the common laws which apply to all other things, where good sense and taste are to be exercised. A sermon should have unity of plan. The matter, length, and order of its parts should be so adjusted, as to preclude anticipation, repetition, and collision. Good judgment will not so much inquire, whether a thought is *important,* as whether it belongs to the subject in hand, and in what *place* it may be introduced, so as most to increase the general effect. That is not useful preaching, which is a mere *collection of good remarks,* without the scope, connection and impression, which belong to a regular discourse. Nor is that a profitable sermon, which now and then startles the hearers, with a vivid flash of thought, or makes them remember a few eccentric phrases; *but that which fixes their eye on a SINGLE SUBJECT; which holds their attention steadily to THAT SUBJECT; which gives them as they go on, a clearer conception and a deeper feeling of THAT SUBJECT; and finally compels them to remember THAT SUBJECT, though they cannot repeat one expression uttered by the preacher."* With reference to unity of illustration, Porter has this to say: "Of a distinguished living preacher, it is remarked by a professed critic, that exuberant as are his resources, little or nothing is introduced by him without a distinct reference to his main design. Every additional figure or idea, illustrative of his chief topic, serves, for the most part, to convey it more distinctly to the mind, and though Pelion is sometimes heaped upon Ossa, in his gigantic sport, we do not view it as a useless exertion, when he appears himself to be reaching heaven by the process, and showing us a path to the same elevation.'"

Could any one dwell more strongly on the unity of the sermon than this? But Porter wrote almost a century ago; it may be that men have changed meanwhile and need a different sort of sermon. Let us listen to what Herrick Johnson has to say, after a long experience as professor of homiletics, in his book *The Ideal Ministry*.[16] "The necessity of unity is founded in the very nature of rational discourse. Discourse is one—not many. It is a flow. In unity, therefore, lies its very life. Its ideas, however varied, are vitally related. They are fused, and run like molten ore. They constitute, or are born of, one theme. A true discourse never has themes. Unity is demanded by the very nature of mind. It belongs to a poem and the drama. It is essential in painting, in architecture, even in landscape gardening. It is a deeper necessity in the sermon." He then mentions three items essential to the unity of the sermon: "(1) Singleness of theme. This lies at the foundation of all true unity. It is the first and broadest condition, one theme—and every thought, every illustration, *everything* in the sermon, subservient to it. (2) Singleness of object. All rational discourse has an object. It is an address. It has respect to others. It is mind to mind for some purpose. A single leading object must be fixed upon, and steadily pursued throughout, in order to unity. The true sermon will always have an end—a purpose outside of itself—to be accomplished. Just as this is single, specific and controlling, will the discourse have unity. Lines will all converge. Ideas will all bear one way. (3) Another demand of unity, and growing out of singleness of theme and object, is the *use only of that which will tend both to develop the theme and accomplish the object.* Nothing is to be admitted into the sermon that is not made rigidly subordinate and subservient to this two-fold work. The thoughts and illustrations are to be narrowed to the single theme and still further narrowed to the uses to which the theme is put in securing some single leading object. This demand of unity will be best

---

[16]Pub. 1908, pp. 334 ff.

secured by writing out both the subject and the object before proceeding to write the sermon; and then by challenging each thought that knocks for admittance to the sermon, and asking whether it consists with the chosen theme and end, and can in any way throw light on the one, or promote the other. If 'Nay'—then *no admittance on any terms whatever."* In conclusion he mentions the following three advantages of unity: "(1) It stimulates the *inventive* faculty of the preacher. Compelling not only a subject but an object, it gives the mind a spring and impulse in toil. For it is not in the nature of mind to put forth its best activities without aim. To think without a purpose is to think feebly. To wander at one's own sweet will, untrammeled by the demands of unity, may seem delightful and suggestive to the young writer, but it is the sure road to superficiality. No rich ores will betray their hiding-places to such thinking. Unity of aim reacts upon invention and arouses it, and so gives it command of materials that would otherwise never heed its call, or reveal themselves to its search. (2) Unity secures definiteness of impression. *Disconnected* thoughts are like a whirl of sparks. They may be brilliant and beautiful; but they come and go leaving no distinct impression. *Connected* thoughts—thoughts that are fused and made a living whole by one common animating purpose, are like a pointed tongue of flame. Disconnected thoughts are like dead words strung down the dictionary. Connected thoughts, born of one theme and convergent to one object, are like those same words put in a living sentence. The impression from the string of words is confused and vague. The impression from the living sentence is clear and definite. (3) Unity tends to cumulative force and effect. It leads to concentration, blow on blow, in one spot. Thus a wall is breached, an enemy's line broken, a cause carried. Thus is discourse made effective. It gathers momentum as it proceeds. Each succeeding thought promotes the impression of its predecessor—for they tend the same way, look for the same result, converge to one point. The blows all have one aim, and the truth goes home with ever cumulating power."

As recently as March 24, 1921, there appeared in *"The Continent"* a noteworthy editorial article, which we add here as a piece of contemporary testimony. "Sharpen your ideas to a point—if homiletic instruction in theological seminaries had to be condensed to a single sentence, this would be the one to retain. The very general complaint of church attendants about the lack of power in the pulpit is undoubtedly owing in the main to the almost universal fault in American sermons of failing to get to a plain point. This shortcoming is not a defect peculiar to the ministry. It is the reaction on the pulpit of a characteristic intellectual habit of the times. Americans in general do not think pointedly. ... To circle the universe in an airplane and never set foot for a minute on the ground of practical action is the favorite oratorical manner of the hour—favorite for both orators and hearers. The vogue of such vagueness may not be explained by the popularity of the moving picture, but it is at least a phenomenon that cannot be more accurately described than by saying that a moving-picture mind is the mind of these times in this country. The drama on the screen is certainly no school of logic—no training in continuity of thought or constructive linking of ideas. But people like it and go again and again to have their brains swept clear—as many frankly say —of all that induces thinking. And this is the way that most American preachers today have somehow and somewhere learned to preach. It is impossible that they could have adopted the fashion deliberately; they could easily foresee, if they had thought about it, *that the result would be to destroy the very purpose for which preaching was conceived*—the purpose to induce action. Yet any attentive hearer of much preaching must realize that the average sermon of the day is a sort of film-picture succession of sparkling phrases—not prepared with any aim of producing a cumulative effect on the hearer's will, but framed mostly on the idea of pleasing the ear momentarily with each polished sentence. Of course, as it is true of the picture reeled off so rapidly in the 'movies,' this swift, tumbling current of pleasant words carried on a pleasing voice appeals immensely to modern audiences. Hundreds of preachers have a fine repute for eloquence in their communities when in actual fact they have scarcely left their congregations one idea per sermon in years past. When, however, somebody comes by who knows that the fundamental test of a sermon is its efficiency in setting somebody to doing something, there naturally are heard certain bitter observations about the failure of the pulpit to accomplish its job. *The recovery of authority in the American pulpit—the reestablishment of the sense of force radiating from and through preaching—can only come with a radical revision of the terms in which most ministers think of their preaching duty.* The now prevailing conception is a sort of notion—itself hazy with typical modern fogginess—that the sermon is a spiritual refreshment offered to weary pilgrims along the road to heaven, spiced agreeably to the demands of their appetite and sufficient for the need of the case if those who have partaken of the feast feel cheerier and happier and more like going on at the end of the half hour than at the beginning. But the least study of the sermons of the past ought to tell the preacher that the pulpits which other generations of the church were agreed in calling great pulpits never earned their power with that sort of sermons. Spiced cake has never been the staple of any ministry that has won a name surviving in Christian history. And spiced cake won't make the American pulpit great today. Strong meat is the only commodity which preachers of Christianity in these urgent days have any right to be purveying. And the strong meat of Christian truth and Christian obligation can only be brought to the churches by men who wield a knife sharp enough mentally to cut straight along the severing lines between fiction and reality, trifles and essentials, poetic imaginations and harsh facts, literary niceties and dynamic arguments. All that calls for *thinking—determined and laborious thinking*. The true ideal of the sermon is identical with the ideal of a lawyer's plea before a jury—assuming an honest lawyer with a just case. The lawyer has a jury to convince. The preacher has a congregation to persuade. Neither can waste time with decorations. More particularly, neither can afford to think of the reputation he is going to make for himself. *Every thought must go into getting the men to believe what he believes—and then act on it.* Clearly enough, if there is going to be any success in such an aim, the preacher (forgetting the lawyer from now on) *must have precisely in mind, from the first moment that he opens his lips, what effect he means to get in the conscience of his audience. And every word he utters should be framed with studious care to carry him nearer the conviction he is pledged to produce.* He must needs use illustrations. But the illustrations must not be brought in to show off his own literary taste; they *must be employed wholly with a view to building up in the minds of hearers a mental preparation for the conclusion he is approaching.* He must frame epigrams. But not to adorn the path by which he saunters through his sermon period. The epigrams must all be *nails driven in a sure place* to hold the steps by which the congregation is led to the climax. *And at all events, when the sermon is ended, absolute assurance must have been achieved that everybody of ordinary intelligence in the whole body of hearers sees, understands, and is prepared to remember the one big thought which that sermon aimed at.* Every man and woman present—if it is really a good sermon—can answer at the close one central question: 'What is it exactly that he wants me to do?'"

These statements, though dwelling too narrowly on doing—Christianity consists to be sure in doing, but not exclusively nor chiefly—are undeniably correct. If a preacher wishes to flatter and cater to the taste of the present generation and to get himself praised, let him ramble about in his sermon at his sweet will, untrammeled by the demands of unity. But if he desires to educate his people, accomplish a lasting result, and truly edify his hearers, let him keep before him, while constructing his sermon, above all things its unity.

This matter is important enough to be illustrated by concrete examples. We select the pericope of the twelve-year-old Jesus (Luke 2:41-52). A sermon on this text by Theurer[17] has the theme: "Jesus, even as a Boy, Fairer than the Children of Men." This is developed as follows: (1) Fair in spirit, particularly in His humility. Joseph, Moses, David, praised for their physical beauty. Nothing said of Jesus' outward appearance. It is the beauty of His spirit that shines through His words and acts. This is the more glorious the more it is concealed by His deep humility. Rays of spiritual beauty are given forth by Jesus even in His childhood, not only in His remarkable utterance in the temple, but also in the steps by which He is led to this utterance. (2) Fair in His development, free from every hindrance to His progress, from childhood to His thirtieth year. This development, proceeding in an unbroken line, is contrasted with our development. Prayer: Lord, give us eyes to see Thy glory! (3) As Jesus submits to the laws of spiritual growth, so He submits to the ordinances of the Church with a fervent heart, fair even as a child. Prayer: Jesus, draw us after Thee! (4) As to the ordinances of the Church, so Jesus submits to human instruction with diligent zeal. Prayer: Make us anew to be Thy disciples. Let us keep Thy Word, that we may know the truth and be made free! (5) Especially fair is Jesus by reason of His filial obedience, combined with perfect trust. Prayer: Jesus, make parents worthy to be trusted, and children firm in obedience, fair as Thou wast, O Fairer than the children of men! (6) As in His obedience, so Jesus is glorious in His self-dependence in the service of His heavenly Father. Here v. 49 is expounded, closing with the prayer: O Lord, if Thou leadest us through the world to that sacred "I must," which so often runs counter to our will, grant us Thy free Spirit of obedience and understanding, that we may will nothing but to be about Thy Father's business! (7) Thus Jesus is precious and fair unto us, for He becomes to us an Easter gift full of light and life. It is Easter (Passover) as we behold Him sitting in the temple, representing even there the new

---

[17]Stoeckicht, *Die evang. Predigt,* i, 96 ff.

covenant, though eighteen years must pass by before this covenant is actually established by His death.—Conclusion: Is not He, even as a boy fairer than the children of men? Therefore, come let us seek Him; let us worship and bow down!

Gottschick and Krauss, both of whom adduce this sermon of Theurer's as a horrible example, criticize it correctly as follows. The sermon claims to have unity in so far as it has a theme under which its subject-matter is grouped. But this is only an external unity, for the divisions do not grow out of the theme; under the general head of fairness or beauty, there is thrown together a mass of thoughts suggested by the text. The sermon does not form an organic structure. Moreover, the concept of beauty is used in a double sense, now in an aesthetic, again in a moral sense. Again, the various divisions are not co-ordinated. Part 1 is nothing but the framework of parts 2 to 6, and part 7 no longer belongs under the theme. As the sermon possesses no unity of contents, neither does it possess unity of aim. Each division pursues a purpose of its own, so that the whole ends in the most general application: Let us seek Him. True, where there is not a single subject, the effect aimed at cannot achieve unity. But in this very fact lies a chief defect of this sermon outline. The hearer does not leave with a unified impression, acting as directive for his will; he will, indeed, be hard put to it to reproduce the sermon as a whole. Certain individual thoughts, valuable enough in themselves, he may carry with him; but he does not receive, as he ought, the final impression: This definite thing has been told me today from God's Word; this I will hold fast; in this I will rejoice and take comfort; in this particular there must be a change in my life; this will I do—according to what has been the subject of the sermon. Since this has not been the case, the sermon as a whole has been really in vain.

With Theurer's sermon Gottschick compares one by Thomasius on the same text, with the theme: "The Development in the Holy Life of the Child Jesus." Outline: (1) The earliest childhood: Hidden from the world, and removed from all rude contact, Jesus grows up in the home of His parents, whose spirit of piety assures Him the best training. A description of the opposite condition in the case of so many children closes with an admonition to parents to learn of Joseph and Mary. (2) The life of the Learner: In conformity with God's will, Jesus must be subject to human ordinances and to the law, in order in these to learn His lesson. In the house of God He finds Himself truly at home. General admonition: What a pattern for us all! In the temple He lets Himself be taught, and does not desire to teach or to shine. Contrast our youth, quick to judge and vainglorious. Follows an admonition to young folk. (3) The confession of His divine Sonship: Its importance is described. General admonition: Bow your knees before Him! (4) The voluntary filial obedience of the God-man: Jesus goes down with His parents to Nazareth. Admonition to young men and women to apply this to themselves. Here He remains until His thirtieth year. How this puts to shame so many, who hasten to thrust themselves forward! In this obedience He receives baptism and takes upon Him the cross. —Conclusion: It is our sacred duty to obey and serve Him and His Father, to follow Him in self-denial and simplicity of heart, to be enlightened and edified by the daily study of His words, to regard all good ordinances and relationships of man as a school, and when the church bells call us to service, to remember His saying, "I must be in my Father's house."

The sermons of Thomasius are extraordinarily rich in content, and are surpassed by few in the XIX century. The clear Lutheran note is nowhere lacking; their confessionalism is definite without being offensive. In structure, however, they are less exemplary. With respect to the sketch given above, we agree with Gottschick's criticism. In this sermon, as in Theurer's, there is an external unity, produced by the theme; there is also a certain internal unity, brought about by following step by step our Lord's development. But of unity of purpose there is even less than in the sermon by Theurer. Instead of a single aim, the preacher has pursued many. This produces a restless passing from one thing to another, so that the sermon loses its unified effect. The unity gained by following the various steps in our Lord's early life is destroyed by the heterogeneous subject-matter of the divisions. Hence the closing admonition, or final theme, not only becomes very lengthy, but cannot gather up the various admonitions scattered through the body of the sermon.

H. Schultz comes much nearer achieving the desired unity in his sermon on this text. His theme is: "The Christian must be in the things of his Father."[18] (1) The blessedness contained in this word: (a) For Jesus it means that He is at home in His Father's house; so the Christian should feel at home in the services of the Church. (b) For Jesus the word has a deeper meaning: it is His watchword in

---

[18]This is the rendering of Revised Version, margin, which corresponds exactly to Luther's German Bible.

life and death; in temptations and trials He holds to this "I must." Our life, too, should find its culmination in the sanctuary, should be lived before God's face, and devoted to Him. To be in the things of our Father means to live, in the midst of time, in an eternal world of the Spirit, i. e., of truth and love. Communion with God, this it is that makes us free and strong; this is blessedness. (2) The right way to this blessedness: (a) For Jesus this word is most natural; but we are able only now and then, in heaven-sent moments, to lift ourselves above the dust of the world. This is not yet to be in the house of God, but merely the brief sojourn of a stranger. (b) Hence the desire to live only for divine service and special divine works is only natural. But one takes the worldly heart with one into the monastic cell, and Jesus who must be in His Father's house went down with His parents to their house. (c) The right way to God's house is not an external way, but a way of faith. We must transform, by an act of faith, the world into the kingdom of God, which is to us a many-sided revelation of the Father. Daily there come new duties. The cross is the earnest of our final success.—Conclusion: We will, therefore, not approach this word of Jesus as men of little faith, but desire to learn to say it ever more confidently, until we shall break out, with the company of all those who have overcome, into the blessed confession of the Son of God, "I must be in the things of my Father."

It is possible to raise various objections to this sermon, such as that the idea of blessedness should have been more clearly and impressively elaborated in part 1; that in part 2 (c) there is a curious conception of the kingdom of God; that the answer given to the question as to the way is hardly correct, etc. But the sermon forms, nevertheless, a single unit as to contents and effect. The theme actually controls the whole development and re-appears at the close as final theme, offering the blessedness contained in the word of Jesus and the possibility of its attainment as a powerful motive to the soul of the hearer.

We add an outline to show how the whole passage in Luke 2:41-52 may be used and a living unity achieved. Introduction: **All ages** of man should be transformed into the image of Christ, so that His glory may shine through all.—Theme: When does the glory of Christ transfigure our children? (1) When, like the child Jesus, they have a desire for God's house, and feel nowhere more at home than in fellowship with their heavenly Father. (a) Thus it was with the child Jesus. (b) Thus it should be with our children. (c) What can we parents do to bring this to pass? (2) When, like the child Jesus, they show obedience toward their parents. (a) Thus it was with the child Jesus. (b) Thus it should be with our children. (c) How can we parents help to bring this about?—Conclusion: There is a Christ-head in every baptized child (allusion to Michael Angelo's well known saying). Our training should bring this out, feature by feature, in ever greater clearness, so that from a Christ-like childhood there may spring a young manhood over which may be written the word that characterized Jesus' growth from childhood to manhood, —"He increased in wisdom and stature, and in favor with God and man."

Here are no digressions. The text is correctly expounded. There is unity of subject-matter as well as of purpose. The whole sermon may be summed up in a single sentence, which though it appears as an assertory proposition, turns of itself at the close into an imperative proposition, into an admonition to the hearers. Since most of the latter are adults, the admonition is addressed to them, as they have been kept all along in mind, in subdivision (c) of each main part. Not that the sermon had nothing to say to the children, or that (a) and (b) contained nothing for the parents. The very fact that (a) and (b) draw so attractive a picture, in a purely objective manner, makes them appeal to young and old alike. That there is in the text a sufficient point of contact for (1) (c), need scarcely be proved, nor is it wanting for (2) (c), if we regard the festival journey of the Holy Family as an act of obedience to the law of God. The obedience of parents to God is the best means of instilling in their children obedience to both God and parents.

By characterizing, as we have done, the use of *borrowed material* as a disturbance of the unity of the sermon, we do not mean that the sermon should contain only original material. Who is really original, and to what extent? Emerson said that all literature since Plato was a quotation. Whatever material exists for the exposition and application of the text should be thankfully used, that is to say, diligently studied and made one's own inner possession. But in order to prevent the use of such existing material from gradually stifling his independent mental activity, the homilete, when expounding his text, should not turn to commentaries until he has made an independent exegetical study of the passage, and when applying his text and constructing his sermon, he should not turn to homiletical helps until he has fully determined, by independent meditation, what he intends to say. The study of sermonic literature in particular should form a regular and consistent course of reading, rather than a temporary makeshift resorted to in preparation for the individual sermon. It should be the rule to press into service whatever materials there are, making them aid us either positively or negatively, but to use nothing that has not first passed through the alembic of the preacher's personality. In this way the use of materials not original will not endanger the unity of the sermon.

If the sermon possesses unity of subject-matter and of purpose, it will necessarily be *complete in itself*. Not much need, therefore, be added here to what has been said under the subject of unity. The demand for completeness must be qualified, however, by the nature of the text; this follows from our conception of the relation between text and sermon. Within this limitation the demand must be rigorously enforced. If I take the theme—faulty, because too general—"What is our debt to the Protestant Reformation?" I may enumerate in my introduction all the blessings of the Reformation I can think of, but I must confine myself in the body of my sermon to the particular blessing mentioned in my text. I must, however, include everything that text and Reformation history have to offer in illustration of that particular blessing. Then my discourse will impress itself upon the hearers as a complete and exhaustive unit.

The *order* of a discourse was emphasized already by Quintilian. In his *Institutiones* he writes:[19] "Ut opera exstruentibus satis non est, saxa atque materiam et caetera aedificanti utilia congerere, nisi disponendis iis collocandisque artificium manus adhibeatur: sic in dicendo quamlibet abundans rerum copia cumulum tantum habeat atque congestum, nisi illas eadem dispositio in ordinem digestas atque inter se commissas devinxerit... Neque enim, quanquam fusis omnibus membris, statua sit, nisi collocetur; et si quam in corporibus nostris aliorumve animalium partem permutes atque transferas, licet habeat eadem omnia, prodigium sit tamen. Et artus etiam leviter loco moti perdunt, quo viguerunt, usum; et turbati exercitus sibi ipsi sunt impedimento. Nec mihi videntur errare, qui ipsam rerum naturam stare ordine putant, quo confuso peritura sint omnia. Sic oratio carens hac virtute tumultuetur **necesse est, et sine** rectore fluitet, nec cohaereat sibi, multa repetat, multa transeat, velut nocte in ignotis locis errans, nec initio, nec fine proposito casum potius quam consilium sequatur." We have seen above how Fénelon emphasized this. He says further: "It is an infallible proof of the want of just integrity in every writing, from the epopeia, or heroic poem, down to the familiar epistle,

---

[19]Ch. vii.

or slightest essay either in verse or prose, if every several part or portion fits not its proper place so exactly that the least transposition would be impracticable. If there be any passage in the middle, or end, which might have stood in the beginning; or any in the beginning, which might have stood as well in the middle, or end; there is properly in such a piece, neither beginning, middle nor end; it is a mere rhapsody, not a work, and the more it assumes the air or appearance of a real work, the more ridiculous it becomes." Another Frenchman, Buffon in his *Discours sur le style*, has the following comparison of a man going to work without a plan with a man who cannot begin without carefully planning his work: "For want of plan, from not having sufficiently reflected on his subject, an intelligent man finds himself embarrassed, and unable to begin writing; he perceives at once a great number of ideas, but as he has neither compared nor arranged them, nothing determines him to prefer some to others; he, therefore, remains in perplexity. But when he has formed a plan, when he has once collected and put in order all the thoughts which are essential to his subject, he perceives readily at once which should engage his pen, he is conscious of full preparation for intellectual effort, he is in haste to make it, he has only pleasure in writing, ideas follow each other readily, style is natural and easy; warmth, springing from this pleasure, diffuses itself everywhere, and gives life to each expression; all is more and more animated; the tone rises, the objects assume color, and sentiment, combined with light, increases it, extends it, transfers it from that which is said to that which is to be said, and style becomes interesting and lucid." Vinet expatiates on the importance of order: "A discourse has all the power of which it is susceptible, only when the parts proceeding from the same design, are intimately united, exactly adjusted, when they mutually aid and sustain one another like the stones of an arch. *Tantum series juncturaque pollet* (Horace, *Art of Poetry*, 242).... Oratorical discourse, and especially that of the pulpit, has a double purpose, to instruct and to persuade. In considering only the first of these objects, we see that order is all important. We are instructed only in so far as we comprehend and retain; but we comprehend and retain easily, surely, only in the proportion in which the matters on which our understanding is exercised are consecutive and connected. Teaching, in which order is wanting, hardly deserves the name of teaching; all that it can do, is to give more or less valuable information. And the inconvenience of disorder in this respect, is not merely negative; if it is unhappy not to understand, it is more so to have a wrong understanding. Now, to this danger does bad disposition expose our hearer; sometimes we teach him nothing; what is worse, we sometimes teach him error; for truth which is not regarded in its true light, in its proper place, is changed into error, and often in respect to the greater part of minds, to pernicious error. Thus as to instruction, or influence on the understanding. It is impossible that it should be otherwise as to persuasion, or influence on the will. A discourse badly ordered is obscure, and that which is obscure in weak. Decision cannot be conveyed to the soul of any one, by that which bears the tremulous impress of indecision. Conceive of a discourse, in which the chief laws of order are violated, in which an idea is abandoned before it has been thoroughly presented, unless it is reverted to afterwards, by cutting, perhaps, the thread of another idea; in which an accessory has as much place as a principal idea, perhaps more; in which the advance is not from the weaker to the stronger, but from the stronger to the weaker; in which nothing is grouped, nothing compacted; in which everything is scattered, wandering, incoherent; such discourse is contrary to the nature of human mind, to its just expectation to its wants; in the soul of the hearer, as in the discourse which is addressed to him, everything begins, nothing is finished; the elements, which by combination would have formed a solid mass (I mean analogous thoughts, homogeneous sentiments), are kept separate and at a distance; instead of a bright and burning flame, we have a whirl of sparks; lively impressions perhaps are produced, but transient and soon effaced and although none of the materials necessary to the composition of an excellent discourse may be wanting, no comparison can be made, as to the two-fold purpose of convincing and persuading, between the work of which we are speaking, and another in which, perhaps, there are fewer ideas, but in which order renders everything availing. In the first case we had, in intellectual order, the spectacle of a great fortune badly administered, of an unproductive consumption, of a dissipation."

Among modern writers, Professor Herrick Johnson says: "'Order is heaven's first law'. God is a God of order, and not of confusion. His works and ways are by method. Order is the handmaid of effectiveness. The human mind as by instinct demands order, and dreads chaos. The apostle says, 'Let all things be done decently and in order.' A mass of unsightly material, by an adjustment of order, is made a beautiful edifice. A rabble, under order's law, is changed into an army. The different parts of the body must have their true place, if the body is to have effectiveness and symmetry. Vinet goes so far as to say, 'There is no discourse without it.' Certainly the preacher who has no order in his sermon, is flinging to the wind the law of adaptation."[20] What are the demands of order? Johnson sums them up under three heads: "(1) Comprehensively, order in discourse demands of the preacher what Horace says it demands of the poet, 'that he just now say what ought just now to be said.' (2) Regard to the dependence of arguments on one another: Sometimes an argument presupposes another. Then it should always follow. Sometimes an argument explains another, prepares the way for it, throws light upon it, is vital to its best effect. Then it should always precede. Whether an argument goes before or follows after, may make just the difference between weakness and great weight, e. g., prove the antecedent probability of a thing, from the nature of the case, or on general principles, and the direct proofs will then come in with greatly increased and more conclusive force. Show cause why God should interpose with supernatural revelation, and then the internal evidence of the divine authenticity of the Scriptures will have tenfold weight. (3) Regard to the state of mind of the hearers: If they are filled with skepticism, a relatively weak argument at the outset would be a waste of breath. Let the best, the strongest blow, be struck first. To make the final impression strong in such a case, recapitulate, *reversing* the order, and thus get the power of climax. If the objection applies to a certain division of the discourse, it should be met on reaching that division. If the objection applies to the main statement, and is already known to the hearer, it should be met at the outset. Otherwise, the hearer, having the objection in mind, and not its refutation, would not be likely to listen to the argument without prejudice. This unanswered objection would constantly recur to him, and prevent the argument from having its full weight. If it be deemed best to defer the answer to objections, until the direct positive proof has been offered, reference should be made to the objections, and suspension of judgment asked, until they are fully considered. Order in pressing *motives* demands regard to antecedent knowledge and conviction on the part of the hearers. *These ground all motives and appeals.* Men must see clearly *what it is* that is pressed as a duty, and they must be convinced that it *is a duty*, before they are urged to its discharge. The most affecting exhortations are a waste of breath, where there is no sense of oughtness."[21] If one actually succeeded in moving for the time being the will of his hearers, without previously producing this conviction, he would experience ere long the truth of Mosheim's words,

[20] Pp. 337 ff.   [21] Pp. 264 ff.

—"To move the will blindly leads to no permanent result; it is a trick of jugglers and comedians." The advantages of order are also threefold according to Herrick Johnson. "They accrue to the preacher, to the sermon, to the hearer. (1) The preacher's mind grows *orderly*. Methodizing makes him methodical. Systematizing makes him systematic. He is cured of rambling. And digressions at last become an impossibility. His mind grows *fruitful*. Order enriches. It helps memory by the law of association. The suggestive faculty becomes fruitful in furnishing materials. Contemplating ideas in their proper connections is the sure way of commanding the reserved stores of memory. He will discover little, who knows not whither he is going or what he is in search of. (2) It makes the sermon *intelligible*. Perspicuity in style is not enough to give clearness to discourse. It must have proper arrangement. The successive remarks may be clear enough. Each idea may be readily grasped as presented. But if the succession is confusing, without natural order, with no regard to logical and oratorical method, the total impression will be that of an indistinct mass. We wonder sometimes that the pews take in so little of the sermons—hear so little understandingly. But when we think of the confusing, blinding sins of the pulpit against order, the wonder suffers an immense contraction. Order gives the sermon *power*. An arch of stones is stronger than a heap of stones. A built ship, buttressed and ribbed, beam to beam, is stronger than the loose timber. So ideas, arranged to the laws of association and logic, are much mightier than when thrown out in a disconnected, illogical way. Such ideas mutually aid and sustain one another. Part is adjusted to part for the best effect. But when lacking in orderly arrangement, they not only give each other no support, but often actually neutralize each other's power. They are not tied together by the living ligaments of a pervasive purpose. They are put forward without method. Ideas are deferred when they ought to be treated. They are anticipated and partially expanded before the way is prepared for them to have their full effect. They are dropped and then resumed. They are thrust into the midst of others, severing a close and needed connection. They are not grouped, marshalled, compacted. There is advance and recession —no coherence. Nothing weakens a discourse like these breaks, uncertainties, returns, digressions, partial presentations—these 'many almosts.' A sermon thus constructed may have power. So may a mob. But how a mob melts away before a little band, instinct with order, moving by method!—(3) As to the hearers, increased *pleasure* is one of the advantages of order. Order makes truth more beautiful.

Just as a collection of precious stones is made more beautiful, when, by the magic of good arrangement, it is changed into a rich mosaic. And the mind takes pleasure in beauty, rejoices in it. Confusion is distasteful. Chaos is repulsive. Order is pleasing. Another and great advantage to the hearer, is *facility of remebrance.* Try to remember fifty words with no connection—no natural succession. How difficult! Now wheel those same words into line by constructing out of them connected and living sentences, and how easily memory masters them. Mere contiguity is of little service in recollection. But one idea following another by some well defined law of association is greatly helpful. Let order reign in the sermon, let its various points have a natural and true succession, and the *sermon will stick.* Hence comes *increased profit.* Hearers are edified, other things being equal, just as the sermon sticks. No food so feeds the flock as that which is distinctly remembered; which the mind can carry away from the sanctuary for the heart to feed on afterwards. This sometimes makes just the difference, and all the difference, between failure and success in a pastorate. A sermon may not be profound or brilliant. But it may be, and should be, characterized invariably by order. And with order so important, it is an inexcusable sin and shame for any preacher to make sermons without it."

The difference between logical and rhetorical order is illustrated by Kleinert from the sermon on the mount. "If the sermon on the mount," says he, "began with its closing note, the parable of the house on the rock and the house on the sand, and if it went on to present its contents under these two points of view, if it showed, that is, in a logical development what it means to build on a rock and what to build on sand, how this works out in life, how it necessarily leads to opposite results, and that it is, therefore, right and necessary to build on the rock and to avoid building on the sand—the order would be irreproachable, logically correct and also pedagogically adequate. But how much more effective is the order as given in Matthew. . . . Beginning with the winsome invitation of the beatitudes, it continues with doctrine and direction, with impressive admonitions and warnings that compel to a decision, only to thrust at its close the parable, like a powerful lever, into the will, and thus to hold high the concentrated impression of all that has gone before."[22] The principal thing, as Kleinert makes clear, is the self-discipline of the preacher in the logical control and order of the thought groups in his discourse. "A

---

[22] Pp. 145 f.

whole," he says, "that does not stand clearly before me, with all its parts logically connected, I cannot even present correctly, to say nothing of rhetorical effect. Rhetorical order can proceed safely only on the basis of a survey in which the individual parts have been thought out and thought through to the end. It is necessary, therefore, to acquire and to perfect by practice the ability to arrange logically a given material, before the ability to arrange it rhetorically can be aspired to. The beginner in the art of preaching, like any other beginner, must possess the indispensable before he can attempt virtuosity. . . . The more logically thought out and arranged his sermons are during the first years of his ministry, the sooner may he hope to attain the higher goal of rhetorical proficiency. But to omit the preliminary steps, to neglect logical discipline and rigor at the beginning, will only lead one to imagine one possesses what one does not really possess, and to mistake a throwing of materials together for order."[23]

Among the rules governing rhetorical order, one deserves special attention—*movement,* the trend toward the goal, well named by the Germans "Zielstrebigkeit." Of this Herrick Johnson writes: "Movement is that quality by which the sermon bears the thought onward and the hearer with it." He dwells not only on continuity but progress of movement, as necessary prerequisites of a sermon. "Movement is the living energy of the living soul poured along the channels of speech for the attainment of some definite object. It is the quality that makes the difference between a river and a stagnant canal. Like the river, whose goal is the sea, the sermon will move with a steady constancy towards its end, turning aside to obviate an objection, to explain a difficulty, to summon a support, only to reach the goal the surer and the sooner." Horace already described the true oration as one that "semper ad eventum festinat." Before him Demosthenes practiced this principle, for he is never found making any step, in any direction, which does not advance his main object, and lead towards the conclusion to which he is striving to bring his hearers. "It is the steady, unceasing sweep of thought, gathering force as it proceeds, until it is a mighty torrent, that constitutes effective speech, that takes great audiences off their feet, melting their wills into one, and stirring them with a common feeling and purpose. The preacher must regard as a defect every thought, every word, that does not lead him nearer to his goal and must ruthlessly discard it. The thoughts and words that properly belong to his subject, he must formulate and combine in

---

[23] P. 146.

such a manner that they not only share in the goalward flow of his discourse, but actually strengthen and deepen it." Theremin well says: "As they first present themselves they are hard, brittle, separate particles; the mind must seize them—and by grinding them incessantly upon each other, crush them until the friction kindles the mass and they run like molten ore." And Johnson gives the preacher this counsel: "As soon as a thought is fully and fairly before the hearers, it is time for the preacher to leave it, and pass on. Every word after that is a sin against movement. It is continuing to explain what is already clear. It is pursuing details in description that add nothing to the effect. It is making men forget the object of an illustration in a too great expansion and elaboration of the illustration itself. The steady flow of discourse is retarded and checked by every needless repetition, by wire-drawn and tedious explanation, by hammering away at an idea after it is once fairly driven home. To avoid this, let description seize and present only the salient points, let narrative pass from incident to incident in a quick succession, let instruction add thought to thought, let argument confirm argument, each tending to deeper conviction, and let the preacher stop when he is done."[24]

In order to prevent the mental co-operation of the hearer from flagging, movement must be accompanied with *variety*. This may be introduced with good effect in the rhetorical pause mentioned above. In this way the objection may be met which Hervey raised against what he considered an undue emphasis on the unity and continuity of the sermon.[25] Herrick Johnson's words may fitly close this paragraph: "Unity, order, movement, these three; but the greatest of these is—well, it is impossible to say. They stand side by side—the three cardinal qualities of the sermon. They mutually help one another. Discourse without them is shorn of half its power. No one of them can be neglected without seriously impairing efficiency. Impression may be made without them, but by no means the highest and best. Good may be done, but not the most good. It will pay to toil for these qualities. And toil will be necessary. Unity and order and movement are not born. They are made. To have a single purpose dominate through the whole length of the sermon, from the first words of the introduction to the final appeal—to have order reign throughout every thought and illustration, every incident and argument marshalled to its place—and to have a constant flow, a steady onward progress in the sermon, bearing resistlessly to the goal—*hic labor, hoc*

---

[24] P. 344. [25] Pp. 343 f.

opus est. But power is the attribute crowning all a minister's accomplishments; and power, under God, lies only this way. Is it not worth while, therefore, to make every sermon with scrupulous regard to the demands of unity, order, and movement?"

Unity, order and movement cannot be attained without making, before the sermon is written out in full, a sketch or "skeleton," which should be filed and revised until it meets these three requirements. We mean a plan or sketch that shall, after the preacher has gathered his material by the exposition and application of his text, work everything up into one compact organism, set the parts together in climactic order, present a natural and orderly succession, exclude irrelevant material, and make the different lines of the discourse grow hot as they converge to one burning focus. This calls for work, faithful and unceasing labor. Sometimes the sermon outline as a whole will flash upon us, so that we need only hold it fast in writing. This will occur most frequently when we have been most faithful in our exposition and application of the text, or when we follow the analytical method. But it normally requires time and labor. One will often abandon one's work in despair, only to return to it later and find the thing fall of itself into shape. But no difficulties, however irksome, can absolve us from the duty of preparing a sketch or outline before working out the sermon in full.

Simplicity or chastity, the fourth of the items mentioned above, refers not only to the style, but also to the contents and structure of the sermon. This does not mean that the sermon may not include materials tending to correct errors in doctrine and life. Such teaching is as necessary today as it was in Paul's day; it is specially necessary in these days of wide-spread sentimentality and doctrinal and ethical indifference. The sharp edge of the Word of God dare not be blunted nor its point broken. The Word must ever remain what it is, a weapon sharper than any two-edged sword. But it must be wielded by love, the love of souls, and not by fleshly zeal or pride of scholarship, not even by personal predilection for the didactic. Moreover, every statement made by this love must be true, and just to the opponent. The preacher should have an accurate knowledge of the position he opposes and should set it forth with a scrupulous regard for truth. "It is not homiletic art," says Kleinert, "but an unworthy sophistic artifice, to caricature one's opponent and then slay him with platitudes. At best, it is not the faith but the darker passions of some hearers that will be satisfied thereby. But in no case is the opponent really refuted and won over; he is generally only the more embittered. Not only this, but the thoughtful friends of truth receive, instead of the desired edification, a painful shock to their sense of justice."[26] How grievously the Lutheran pulpit of our land has erred in this respect! A chaste simplicity will likewise exclude everything that tends to distract rather than concentrate the soul upon God. The American pulpit would do well to lay to heart the words of Kleinert, addressed to his German brethren; "Distraction is everything in the sermon that deflects the devotion of the hearer from the sacred and eternal, for whose sake the service exists. True, the sermon may and should take account of the temporal. It has its place in the world; its function is to discern the eternal in the temporal, and to prepare in the temporal a place for the eternal; in the fulfilment of this function it dare not shrink from illuminating marketplace and alley. But deliberately to hold the hearer fast in such places, and to profane the atmosphere of the sanctuary, this is a distraction. When Abraham a Santa Clara, to arouse the attention and even the laughter of his audience, portrays with untiring gusto and drastic touch the comic scenes of everyday life, this may be tolerated from a Romish pulpit; for there the sermon is a mere appendage to the service and may on occasion take the form of the satyric drama. The evangelical congregation, for whom the sermon marks the summit of the service, cannot but regard such distractions as unworthy. But even when serious problems of political and social life[27] are treated in the pulpit in such a way as to emphasize not the profound seriousness of their ethical aspect, but the narrowness of class and party interest that clings to them, when the poison-filled unrest of the strife raging without is dwelt on and the hearers are drawn into its passions,—this is no less a distraction; it clips the wings of devotion and prevents the tranquil and fruitful reception of the Word. Men do not go to church to be pursued even there by the streams of filth that rage outside, but to feel the peace of the divine presence and to carry it home with them."[28]

Hindrances to concentration are also all portions of the sermon which the preacher includes for his own sake rather than for the sake of the congregation, in order to shine before his hearers and to win their applause. Luther tells the preacher to put on the Word of God as his armor, but to beware of turning the armor into a mirror. And Kleinert adds: "The apostle's 'All things are yours' applies also to the preacher. His materials are illimitable; even what seems most remote may, if properly co-ordinated, contribute to the effect of his dis-

---

[26]P. 152.—[27]See above, pp. 51 ff.—[28]P. 153.

course. But when the preacher catches himself tarrying over the development of his material, not because it leads him to his goal, but because he imagines himself to be shining at that point or because it provides him a private satisfaction, he may be sure that this portion of his sermon has a distracting effect upon his hearers. As certainly as offences against good taste and the sense of the beautiful are homiletical faults, so the verdict that one has preached a beautiful sermon may in certain circumstances be a condemnation of the sermon; namely, when the sermon has left no other impression than this. The Roman moralist Musonius Rufus used to say, 'If you can stay to praise me, I have spoken in vain.' "[29]

---

[29] Pp. 153 f.

§ 15. THE STRUCTURE OF THE INDIVIDUAL SERMON

S. Goebel, *Methodologia homiletica*, 1672. J. L. v. Mosheim, *Anweisung, erbaulich zu predigen*, 1763. Th. Schott, *Theorie der Beredsamkeit*, 1815 and 1824. E. Porter, *Lectures on Homiletics and Preaching*, 1834. Chr. Palmer, *Evang. Homiletik*, 1842. K. I. Nitzsch, *Prakt. Theologie*, ii, 1848. F. Schleiermacher, *Prakt. Theologie*, 1850. A. Vinet, *Homiletics*, 1853. W. G. T. Shedd, *Homiletics and Pastoral Theology*, 1867. J. A. Broadus, *On the Preparation and Delivery of Sermons*, 1870. A. Krauss, *Homiletik*, 1883. J. G. Diegel, *Zur Entwicklung und Benennung der analytischen sowie der synthetischen Predigtform in der luth. Kirche Deutschlands* (in "Denkschrift des evang. Predigerseminars zu Friedberg"), 1886. G. v. Zezschwitz, *Homiletik oder Kunstlehre von der geistl. Beredsamkeit* (in Zoeckler's Handbuch der theol. Wissenschaften, iv), [3]1890. E. C. Achelis, *Lehrbuch der Prakt. Theologie*, 1889, [3]1911. T. H. Pattison, *The Making of the Sermon*, 1898. P. Kleinert, *Homiletik*, 1907. J. Gottschick, *Homiletik und Katechetik*, 1908. F. B. Meyer, *Expository Preaching; Plans and Methods*, 1910. D. J. Burrell, *The Sermon, Its Construction and Delivery*, 1913.

When its edifying materials have been lifted from the text and are now to be built up into the sermon, a double mode of procedure is possible. We may either take the main thought of the text as our theme and divide this thought into its constituent parts without regard to the divisions of the text, or we may let the divisions of the text determine the divisions of the sermon and by combining them into a unity arrive at our theme. The former is the *synthetic* or "topical," the latter the *analytic* or "textual" sermon-method.

In following either method it is important to remember that the subject-matter of the sermon must be none other than that given in the text; for what has been said in Part II concerning the relation of the sermon to the text must always be kept in mind. Hence the term "textual" as over against "topical," to denote the analytic sermon-method, is open to misconception. But while in both methods the materials of the text are used, in the *synthetic* method the text furnishes only the main thought or theme, which forms the source for the material of the sermon and from which its divisions are derived according to the rules of logic and rhetoric, independently of the text. The text is, indeed, drawn upon again and again in the development of the various divisions, but it does not determine the divisions themselves. In the *analytic* method, on the contrary, the text furnishes both the main thought and the material as such, and determines the divisions of the sermon. In the former method, the main thought is found first; in the latter, the main thought, combining into one the various divisions, is found last. In the former, we begin with the unity of the main thought of the text, and deduce from it the variety of materials contained therein; in the latter, we start with the variety of materials found in the text, and ascend to the unity of the main thought in which they are gathered together. In the former method, therefore, we proceed from a unity in which all is already gathered up (synthesis) to variety; in the latter, we proceed from a gathering up of the variety in the text (analysis) to unity.

For example, I follow the *synthetic* method when I take from the Christmas gospel (Luke 2:1-14) the theme: "The Saviour Is Come!" and logically develop from this the divisions: (1) This reminds us of the misery in which we hopelessly languish without Christ; (2) this proclaims to us the help and comfort that have come to us in Christ; (3) this summons us to let ourselves be saved and become partakers of this help and comfort in Christ. The same method is followed when I find in Luke 14:16-24 the theme: "Yet there is room," and deductively reach the following divisions: (1) This is a word of complaint, (2) a word of comfort, (3) a word of exhortation. But I proceed by the *analytic* method when I follow the divisions in John 20:1-18 and find there these two thoughts: (1) The Risen Christ makes the sorrowing rejoice, and (2) turns fearful souls into witnesses of His victory; combining both under the single theme: "The Risen One makes all things new." Similarly, when a study of the experience of Jesus in Matt. 4:1-11 shows me (1) how necessary it is that we should be tempted, (2) how serious and dangerous a thing this makes of our life, (3) how we may nevertheless prevail and gain the victory; by combining which I reach my theme: "The Christian's life is a passage through manifold temptations." Or, when I find in studying Matt. 7:15-23, that there are three distinct things spoken of in this passage: (1) We must beware of false prophets, (2) we should enter into personal relation with Christ, (3) from this flows the doing of the Father's will; and then gather up this threefold material under the single viewpoint: "How shall we be able to stand in the final judgment?"

Closely akin to the analytic sermon, yet presenting certain differences from it, is the artistically constructed *homily* (*Kunsthomilie*). In this, we not only follow the order of the text in assembling our materials, but draw upon each of its parts in turn in the construction of the sermon, gathering up, in our conclusion, the truths discussed into a unity which forms the climax and goal of the sermon, its so-called "final theme." Such a homily will result, if we pursue, step by step, the story of the Grateful Samaritan (Luke 17:11-19) and reach the following truths: (1) True gratitude always leads from the gift to the giver, (2) gratitude for temporal gifts opens the heart to higher, spiritual gifts, (3) the more the grateful person becomes aware of his unworthiness, the more receptive will he be to the grace of Christ. As goal and summary of this treatment will naturally come the exhortation: "Learn to be grateful, for gratitude is the way to greater salvation."[1] When properly worked out, the homily form has certain distinct advantages over the ordinary analytic sermon: it stimulates to keener intellectual co-operation, presents the several truths in a climax, and thus renders the hearer more ready to accept and apply to himself the conclusion. It presupposes, however, a **higher degree of spiritual maturity** in the congregation and of experience and ability in the preacher.

To the synthetic and analytic sermon English and American homileticians add what is called *the expository sermon*. This is not really a third genus, but a species of the analytic sermon, having for its specific purpose the expository treatment of longer passages or of entire books of the Bible. It must not, however, descend, as it is prone to do, to a formless discourse without unity, completeness or logical and rhetorical movement.

Which of the two methods, the synthetic or the analytic, is to be followed, cannot be determined by general rules. The decision will depend on the nature of the text and the individuality of the preacher. It may be said, however, that while the synthetic method excels in preserving the unity of the sermon, the analytic excels in promoting the understanding of the text. The careful homilete will use neither exclusively. Indeed, the one passes at times over into the other. The various divisions, namely, of the prefixed theme, while flowing logically from it, may at the same time agree fully with the divisions of the text. We have then a combination of both methods, the *synthetic-analytic*. This will be the case when we draw from Phil. 2:5-11 the theme: "Let us follow Christ along every station of His way!" and divide as follows: (1) In His humiliation, with the spirit of humility; (2) in His obedience unto death, by our willingness to suffer; (3) in

---

[1] G. v. Zezschwitz, p. 191.

His exaltation, by our confession of His Lordship. This division follows logically from the theme and also agrees with the divisions of the text. Similarly, when, emphasizing διό in v. 9 and bringing out more fully the peculiar force of 9-11, we take as theme: "Let this mind be in you, which was also in Christ Jesus," and divide: (1) Descend willingly into the valley of humiliation, (2) do not pause half way, (3) hold fast the hope of the glory to come. (P. 437.)

Though all accept the above mentioned sermon methods, there has been much discussion concerning the terminology. The distinction, in the ancient Church, between ὁμιλία and λόγος, or *homilia* and *sermo*, does not cover the same ground; the ancient Church knew nothing of a strictly synthetic sermon structure. In the second half of the Middle Ages, *homilia* denoted a sermon consisting largely of continuous exposition, and *sermo* one that treated, with or without a text, a special topic. Nevertheless, we do not find a strictly analytic, and still less an artistic synthetic sermon structure. The distinction begins to emerge in the Reformation period. Most of Luther's sermons were of the homily type, that is, analytic in the wider sense; there are among them, however, the beginnings of a synthetic structure. The sermon constructed on the "local" plan, i. e., treating a number of *loci*, or points, drawn from the text, without grouping them under a central theme, occupied a middle ground between the two. The XVII Century fell gradually into the use of the synthetic sermon, though with a curious scholastic structure controlled less by the logic of the theme than by an imported schematism. Seb. Goebel seems to have been the first to use our terms, analytic and synthetic, in his *Methodologia homiletica*, published in 1672. His definitions, too, are substantially correct: "Methodus analytica ad naturalem textus ordinem et cohaesionem est determinata, methodus synthetica est, qua unum alterumque thema eligitur et beneficiis textus tractatur et applicatur." Mosheim carried the subject farther.[2] He distinguished analytic, synthetic, and analytic-synthetic sermons. "When I preach *analytically*," he writes, "I divide my text according to the rules of hermeneutics and seek out its chief contents and take the divisions of the text as the divisions of my sermon. In Matt. 6:24-34, for example, Christ shows how foolish it is to be anxious about what we shall

---

[2]In his *Anweisung, erbaulich zu predigen*, pp. 258 ff.

eat and drink. This statement gives me the proposition of my sermon. I now give attention to the way in which Christ developed this subject, and not to the subject itself. I look, that is, for the main points in Christ's sermon, and these become also the main points in my sermon. I follow the order of the text and divide it into its parts. In v. 24, Jesus says, 'No man can serve two masters, etc.' He presents this statement (1) figuratively: 'No man can serve, etc.;' then (2) without the figure: 'Ye cannot serve God and Mammon.' From this He concludes, in v. 25, that temporal anxiety is useless and foolish. He employs many arguments. (1) He says, v. 26, that the soul is superior to the body, and concludes from this that, if God provides for the soul, He will provide for the body also. That is a conclusion *a majore ad minus.* He says (2) that God cares for birds; how much more for men! He says (3) in vv. 27-28, that men accomplish nothing by being anxious. (4) In v. 29, He points His hearers to divine providence, which extends even to the smallest matters. (5) In v. 32, He says that to distrust God is meet for heathen, but not for Christians. (6) In conclusion He teaches how Christians are to live, in order not to doubt or mistrust God's providence. If we take a survey of all this, Christ is seen to develop His sermon as follows: He lays down (1) a general proposition: It is foolish to be anxious for bodily food; (2) reasons by which this proposition is proved; (3) directions how the Christian is to live, if he would be free from this anxiety. These are the three parts of the text. The sermon adopts these same three parts. In an analytic sermon, the main thought of the text is the proposition of the sermon. The parts in which the main thought of the text is developed are the main parts into which the sermon is divided. I can, therefore take as my proposition and divisions: The folly of Christians who are anxious about temporal things, or the warning of our Saviour against anxiety about temporal things. We consider (1) the warning, or the folly against which our Saviour warns; (2) the reasons with which He demonstrates the folly of such anxiety; (3) the wise directions He gives to Christians who would be rid of such anxiety. In some such manner we may clothe the outline of the sermon. The form, however, may be changed. I may also present it thus: Beloved,—Jesus lays before you, in our gospel lesson, the proposition: Anxiety about temporal things is foolish. Consider here (1) the manner in which He presents this proposition, (2) the reasons with which He presents it, (3) the counsel of prudence which He gives to Christians.—When we preach *synthetically,* we must divide the matter about which we are to preach. We choose a doctrine from the text and develop this doctrine. Let us retain the gospel lesson which we used in the former illustration. In it Christ says, v. 34, 'Sufficient unto the day is the evil thereof.' Here we have the proposition: The life of man is wretched. Suppose I wish to speak of the wretchedness of human life. I need no longer regard the text in making my divisions; but I must rather regard the matter itself and divide as follows: The wretchedness of human life; (1) The causes of this wretchedness, (2) the wretchedness itself, (3) its consequences. —If we wish to preach a *mixed* sermon, we may proceed in a twofold manner. (a) We may divide the text and the matter. When the text contains the whole matter which we wish to develop, we may divide both text and matter. Suppose I am preaching on Luke 6:36. I may divide as follows: Mercy; (1) its nature, (2) its model. Here I have divided both text and matter. Suppose I am preaching on Rom. 12: 19-21. Here I find at once my proposition in the text. I see that Paul is speaking of the conduct of Christians toward their enemies. In a virtue or a vice two things are to be noted: its nature and its motive. Now I examine my text, and notice that in it (1) the duty is explained, and (2) motives are adduced. I, therefore, put together what belongs to the nature of the duty and what is presented in the text; then I do the same with the motives. From this I get the outline: The right conduct of Christians over against their enemies: (1) The duty itself. In this part I show how the text presents this duty, and assemble everything that bears on this; Paul, e. g., presents it both negatively and positively, he accompanies it with illustrations. From this I develop its nature and qualities. (2) The motives. The apostle has not put them together; the preacher must look them up, set them in the order he thinks most natural, explain when necessary the biblical expression, and develop the matter himself. Or (b) we may divide the sermon as the English and the French often do. The whole art consists in this: We first of all select from the text a certain proposition on which we desire to preach, and then declare that we wish (1) to explain the text, (2) ponder the doctrine itself or expound the matter, (3) apply this doctrine. Let us take as illustration Matt. 9: 1-8. Jesus said to the sick of the palsy: 'Son, be of good cheer; thy sins be forgiven thee.' Because of this the Pharisees accuse Him of blasphemy. Christ shows them that their judgment is a hasty one and deserves rebuke. The judgments of unbelievers on the doctrines and truths of faith are always too hasty. From this follows the proposition: The unconsidered and hasty judgments of unbelievers on the doctrines of faith; with these divisions:

(1) I desire to throw light on the judgment of the Pharisees and to show that it was unreasonable and hasty, (2) I shall consider the overhasty judgment of unbelievers on the truths of faith, and (3) I shall apply this consideration to our profit."

This long quotation from Mosheim contains much that is excellent, but also a number of fateful errors,—not so much in his discussion of the analytic sermon, though even this might lead to a superficial treatment of the text, but especially in what he says about the synthetic sermon. Here he altogether forgets that the thought to be taken from the text cannot be any arbitrarily selected thought, but must be the main thought of the text. What he says about the second type of the mixed sermon contains a truth that we, too, shall touch on later; but this cannot be considered a characteristic of the analytic-synthetic sermon as such. It is the merit of von Zezschwitz to have restored the correct usage of the terms, on the basis of a thorough investigation, in his *Katechetik*,[3] after the meaning of analytic and synthetic, in homiletic and catechetical usage, had been practically reversed. If we wish to retain the terminology, we should understand by an analytic sermon one that proceeds, in its development of the material found in the text, *a principiatis ad principia*, i. e., that from the variety of individual parts given in the text, advances to the unity of the theme. A synthetic sermon, on the other hand, is one that proceeds *a principiis ad principiata*, i. e., that from the unity of the main thought found in the text, advances solely by logical reasoning to the variety of materials contained in the main thought.[4] Zezschwitz went too far when he held that in the analytic sermon one must advance

---

[3] ii, 2, § 26.—[4] Hervey, too, employs the distinction between analytic and synthetic, but uses them in a diametrically opposite sense. He writes (pp. 313f.): "The former are such propositions as contain the proof within themselves, or the proof of which is derived from the very terms of the propositions; the latter are such as depend for proof on some fact or reason outside of themselves. By these two terms we also designate two methods of argumentation. When we adopt the first we begin by laying down the main proposition, and then resolve it into its elements; in other words, we place foremost the conclusion and then go back to the premises whence it is derived. When we adopt the second we gradually establish premise after premise, and then finally create our conclusion out of them; in other words, we reach our proposition by inducing our hearers to make a series of concessions which necessarily conduct us to it by way of inference." In Zezschwitz's book we may learn how a superficial consideration of the verbs ἀναλύειν and συντίθεσθαι led to this view and how utterly untenable it is.

from the variety of materials in the text to the unity of the theme, not only in making the divisions but also in developing the sermon; so that the analytic sermon would assume the form of the artistic homily as described above.[5] This is an exaggerated demand, which is excluded at once in the case of numerous texts which yet permit the use of the ordinary analytic method. Instead of being identical with it, the homily represents a species, the most highly developed species, of the analytic sermon.

English and American homiletics is in accord with most of what has been said here, although it employs often a different terminology and prefers to speak of textual or expository sermons rather than of analytical sermons, and of subject-sermons and topical or thematic sermons rather than of synthetic sermons. Porter, indeed, with his threefold division of textual, topical, and scholastic sermons, still labors under a misunderstanding of the terms.[6] Broadus, however, who distinguishes subject-sermons, text-sermons, and expository sermons, writes as follows: "Subject-sermons are those in which the divisions are derived from the subject, independently of the text; while in text-sermons, the divisions are taken from the text. In the latter case as well as in the former, there may be a definite subject, distinctly and even formally stated; but this subject is not divided according to its own nature, but only such divisions are made as are presented by the text. . . . . In subject-sermons we draw from the text a certain subject, usually stating it distinctly in the form of a proposition, and then the text, having furnished the thought, has no further part as a formative force in the plan of treatment pursued in the sermon, but the subject is divided and treated according to its own nature, just as it would be if not derived from a text." He knows also the mixed form: "Sometimes the two plans may coincide. Beginning with a subject, one may find so appropriate a text, that the logical divisions of the subject will all be contained in the text; or beginning with a text, he may state its subject in so felicitous a form of proposition, that the several divisions presented in the text will also constitute a complete logical division of the proposition. But they will not often thus coincide, and the fact that they sometimes do, will not make them less distinct in principle."[7] But since, on the one hand, a "text-sermon" may—and in the interest of unity should—have a subject or theme, and since, on the other hand, a "subject-sermon" must be also textual, it seems best to retain the older terminology.

---

[5]P. 427.—[6]Pp. 123 f.—[7]Pp. 307 f.

We referred above to the danger besetting expository preaching. This must be kept in mind in estimating whether the expository sermon covers the same ground as the analytic sermon, or whether it forms a subdivision of it rather than a distinct genus of its own.[8]

---

[8]Pattison distinguishes, in a merely external way, between topical, textual and expository sermons: "The topical sermon, in which the theme is especially prominent; the textual sermon, in which more regard is paid to the words of the text; and the expository sermon, in which, as a rule, a longer portion of the Bible is taken as the basis for the discourse"(p. 53). Several specimens taken from Dr. Burrell's *The Sermon* (pp. 64-68) may follow here, to illustrate the distinction that is made between the expository sermon in the narrower sense and the textual sermon.

    A. Text: John 3:16.
        First: Topical.
        The theme or topic is Justification by Faith.
            Any plan of treatment may be adopted without special reference to the text.
        Second: Textual.
        The theme is the same.
        Divisions: suggested by the text:
            1. God's love.
            2. Its measure.
            3. The purpose of it.
        Third: Expository.
        The theme is the same.
        Outline: following the precise order of the text:
            1. God.
            2. God is love.
            3. God loved the world.
            4. God so loved the world that He gave His only begotten Son to redeem it.
            5. The efficiency of this redeeming love is conditioned on faith.
            6. The outcome of faith is everlasting life.
    B. Text: Eph. 3:14-19.
        First: Topical.
        Theme: Spiritual Power.
            Any logical outline will do: e. g.,
            1. The importance of power.
            2. Our duty to be strong: weakness is a sin.
            3. How secured. By prayer, etc.
            4. Results; as to self, others and God.
        Second: Textual.
        The same theme.
             1. Its source: God the Father.
            2. Its agent: God the Spirit.
            3. Its condition: Faith in God the Son.

"Expository Preaching" and "Homilies" 435

As little does what is called "homily" form a class by itself; it is but a species of the analytic sermon. In its highest form it becomes what we have called the artistic homily. It is seen at its lowest and worst

---

        4. Its object: "That ye might be filled with all the fullness of God."
  Third: Expository.
  The same theme.
        Introduction: "I," e. g., Paul, "bow my knees unto God;" Paul is praying for the Ephesians, members of his former parish; praying for what?
        1. That they may "be strengthened."
        2. "In the inner man," i. e., spiritually.
        A Christian is morally bound to make the most of himself.
        3. By His Spirit. One of Moody's frequent sayings was, "Honor the 'Holy Ghost."
        4. To what end? First, that Christ may dwell in them. Second, that so they may be able to comprehend the divine will. Third, and be filled with all the fullness of God.
C. Text: Ps. 23.
  First: Topical.
  Theme: The Good Shepherd.
        Introduction: A favorite Psalm.
        1. Bring out the watch-care of God.
        2. He is helpful in all the vicissitudes of life.
        3. Also in death.
        4. And "forever."
  Second: Textual.
  The same theme.
        1. The Shepherd furnishes food.
        2. Correction on occasion.
        3. Guidance, even to the end.
  Third: Expository.
  The same theme.
        1. Faith. "The Lord is my Shepherd."
        2. Contentment. "I shall not want."
        3. Peace. "Green pastures and still waters."
        4. Restoration: hope for the backslider.
        5. Spiritual growth; "in paths of righteousness."
        6. Lifelong provision; "a table in the presence of mine enemies."
        7. Numberless and immeasurable mercies; the anointing oil and the full cup.
        8. A comfortable anticipation of death; no fear; his "rod and staff."
        9. Eternal felicity; "in the house of the Lord forever."

As models, these outlines can hardly be called a success. But they show the difference that is imagined to exist between textual and

when, after a rambling, disconnected talk about individual parts of his text, lacking the character of a true oration and anything resembling unity, a preacher seeks to excuse himself by saying he has only been delivering a homily!

---

expository sermons: the latter simply follow the text word for word and verse for verse. They also show how wide a scope is allowed to the topical sermon, so that what is an essential requirement of *every* sermon, namely, that it be born out of the text and explain and apply it to the hearers, is lost. No less do they show that with this conception of the expository sermon, it will only in exceptional cases attain to unity. Finally they show that the preacher cannot be sufficiently on his guard with respect to his models.

§ 16. THE THEME OF THE SERMON

Fenelon, *Letter to the French Academy*, 1714. R. Stier, *Grundriss einer biblischen Keryktik*, 1830. Chr. Palmer, *Evang. Homiletik*, 1842. A. Schweizer, *Homiletik*, 1848. K. I. Nitzsch, *Prakt. Theologie*, ii, 1848. F. Schleiermacher, *Prakt. Theologie*, 1850. A. Vinet, *Homiletics*, 1853. R. L. Dabney, *Sacred Rhetoric*, 1870. A. Phelps, *The Theory of Preaching*, 1881. A. Krauss, *Homiletik*, 1883. E. Chr. Achelis, *Prakt. Theologie*, 1889. J. Watson, *The Cure of Souls*, 1896. F. L. Steinmeyer, *Homiletik*, 1901. T. H. Pattison, *The Making of the Sermon*, 1902. P. Drews, *Die Predigt im 19. Jahrhundert*, 1903. H. Hering, *Die Lehre von der Predigt*, 1905. P. Kleinert, *Homiletik*, 1907. J. Gottschick, *Homiletik und Katechetik*, 1908. A. E. Garvie, *The Christian Preacher*, 1921.

When we have discovered the main thought of the text and with it the higher unity connecting its various parts, we have arrived at the theme of the sermon. Not necessarily, in the specific formulation in which it is to be announced in the completed sermon, but in the essential form in which it is to underlie and control the preparation of the sermon and which is to find final expression in the announced theme. Fundamentally, the theme is the formulated unity of the text. Hence only such a theme can be used as actually represents the main thought of the text. We say a theme is textual, when it expresses the main thought of a text, and not merely this or that secondary thought, however important it may be. The theme may express a secondary thought, only when one is compelled to preach repeatedly on fixed texts or when the prescribed pericope does not form a unity but includes disparate elements. It would be better, however, in the former case to choose another text, in which the theme appears as main thought; in the latter case, to read and use only that part of the pericope which is covered by the theme.

If the theme is the compendious expression of the main thought of the text, it follows that it must contain a proposition. The truth found in the text and used as theme can be expressed, like any other truth, only in the form of a proposition. This excludes the choice as theme of general concepts, such as "peace," "the righteousness of God," "brotherly love," "humility," etc. Such general concepts are not propositions. Nor do they as a rule express the unity of the text. Texts do not as a rule treat their main thoughts in this general way, but in a specific nuance. Instead of treating of peace in general, they treat rather of the necessity and preciousness of peace with God and one's neighbor, or of the way to obtain peace, or of the results of peace, or of its various manifestations. A sermon on so general a theme cannot treat it exhaustively, to say nothing of the danger it runs of becoming colorless and falling into the style of a treatise. The more sharply a truth has been defined in the exposition of the text, the more completely will the exegetical conscience of the preacher[1] be satisfied. And the more thoroughly this sharply defined truth controls the entire preparation of the sermon, the more fully will his homiletical conscience be satisfied. The result will be a unified sermon making straight for its goal, which is, as we have seen, the principal thing.

It follows further that the theme, as expression of the unity of the text and hence of the sermon, cannot contain two propositions. This would destroy the unity and divide the sermon into two independent parts, arbitrarily and externally connected. Witness Schleiermacher's theme in a sermon on John 1:23-27,—"The witness of John the Baptist, in which he terms himself the voice of one crying in the wilderness, and testifies of the Saviour as of one unknown." In the case of

---

[1] See above, p. 359.

very short texts, the text may serve as theme; as for example, "God is love;" "Little children, abide in Him."

The theme, which has underlain and controlled the preparation of the sermon, should appear formally in the sermon when preached. This is not absolutely necessary, but is advisable from practical considerations affecting both preacher and hearer. The preacher; for a stated theme will force upon him the question, whether he has grasped the main thought of his text and whether his sermon has before it a definite goal. The hearer; for a stated theme will present to him a fixed point to which his attention is to be held, round which the whole discourse is to turn, and from which he can readily reproduce what he has heard.

The theme stated at the beginning of the sermon must, like the preliminary theme underlying and accompanying its preparation, consist of a proposition or be readily reducible to a proposition. It may take the form of a declarative sentence (God is love; God's love for sinners cannot be thwarted; At the Holy Manger God opens to us His heart and lets us see His incomparable love; God answers the prayers of His children) or of an exclamation (Forward into battle; Come, for all things are now ready; See that ye walk circumspectly; Be ye doers of the Word) or of an interrogation (Is prayer answered? Why is man born to trouble? How may we become new creatures? How often should I forgive?) or of a prepositional phrase (The necessity of prayer; The preciousness of the pure heart; The supreme value of brotherly love; The blessedness of having Jesus as our Good Shepherd). It may take the form of the so-called "causal" or "logical" theme, indicating the *causa* or subject of which the sermon is to treat (The mighty power of faith) or the form of the "final" or "rhetorical" theme, indicating the *finis* or object which the sermon is to pursue (Let us forsake all and follow Jesus!). Which of these forms the theme is to take, will depend on the nature and purpose of the sermon, on the contents of the text, and on the circumstances of the hearers. Schleiermacher's dictum concerning the theme as such—"A sermon of which it can be said that it might have had a different theme, is a faulty sermon"—may be applied also to the formulation of the stated theme. It would be a mistake to expend one's best time and energy on giving to one's theme a striking formulation. Nevertheless, great care should be devoted to the formulation of the theme, not only because it is to occupy a prominent place in the sermon, but because it is to fix itself in the mind and conscience of the hearer. It should be brief and concise, clear and definite, easily comprehensible, and memorable. Here, if anywhere, every superfluous word should be omitted; although clearness dare never be sacrificed to brevity.

May the preacher do in the case of the formulated theme prefixed to his sermon what we were compelled to deny him the right to do in the case of the preliminary theme which underlies his preparation of the sermon? That is, may his formulated and announced theme consist of a general concept, or of a mere title or heading? If we are to judge by the actual practice and by the works of those homileticians who simply accommodate their rules to the prevailing practice, the answer will be affirmative. But if we are swayed by reasons only, there does not appear the slightest reason why an exception should be made here. If there is any point in prefixing and announcing the theme, it should certainly be as sharply defined and as specifically expressed as possible, in order by its very definiteness and specificness to control the discourse and stamp itself upon the hearer's mind. Whoever fears that the announcement of the theme might weaken the interest of the hearer in what is to come, either admits the inferiority of his theme, or confuses the question of prefixing the theme with the question of prefixing the whole disposition, or he is forced to the conclusion that the theme had better not be prefixed at all.

Themes consisting of bare concepts or resembling chapter-headings or book-titles should be avoided. Special care should be given to express in the theme the specific relation in which a concept occurs in the text and in which it is to be treated in the sermon. The more concisely and strikingly this specific relation is expressed in the theme, the better will the theme fulfil its purpose. In a sermon on 1 Cor. 13 a theme such as "Brotherly love" is to be avoided, while a theme such as "The supreme value of brotherly love" is to be commended. In a sermon on Luke 15:1-10, the theme "Jesus' love for sinners" would not express the specific meaning of the text, while the theme "The naturalness of Jesus' love for sinners" would. Themes resembling titles or headings are not altogether objectionable in sermons on longer historical passages. Preaching on Genesis 3, one may divide: The Fall; (1) The temptation; (2) the sin; (3) the results of sin. But even here such a theme would serve better as preliminary theme guiding the preacher in his preparation of the sermon, than as theme to be announced in the completed sermon. Little seems to be gained by announcing so general a theme and so general an outline; it would be better to omit them entirely and proceed at once to the treatment of the text. From this point of view many of the themes in German and especially in English homiletic literature must be judged as defective. We shall not go far astray if we maintain that most of the opposition to prefixed and announced themes is based on the general and indefinite character of the themes. When the preliminary theme that is to guide the preacher's preparation shares in this indefiniteness, the result cannot but be the impoverishment and deterioration of the sermon as such.

It cannot be too often repeated, that the theme must in every case express the unity of the sermon, govern every individual part, and be felt as controlling factor throughout the whole discourse. A theme, prefixed indeed, but not running like a thread of gold through the whole sermon, is of little use. Sometimes the theme will recur again and again in the sermon, like the refrain in poetry. The announcement of the theme at the close of the introduction should not occur merely by way of transition to the body of the sermon, but should be presented to the ear in as clearly discernible a manner as it would be, if the sermon were written out, to the eye. Its repetition in the body of the sermon should not occur invariably in the selfsame form, but with different shades of meaning, resembling the use of the refrain in the ballade. (P. 456.)

That the preacher, in order to turn the edifying materials of his text into a sermon, analytic or synthetic, needs a theme, from which to take his departure, which will hold his development together and focus the sermon upon the hearer's mind, requires no elaborate demonstration. If the sermon, as to its contents, is the presentation of the saving truth contained in a biblical text understood in its specific meaning, and if, as to its form, it should above all things possess unity both of contents and aim, it must necessarily be controlled not by many, but by a single thought; in other words, it must have a theme, which will gather up the variety into a unity or develop organically from the unity a variety. All we need do here is to apply to the individual sermon the conclusions arrived at above. If we assent to Fenelon's dictum, that every sermon must be reducible to a single proposition, it should be self-evident that every sermon must have a theme, not a general but a sharply defined, specific theme, which is nothing else than that single proposition to which the whole sermon must be reducible.

It will be well to set down several quotations from other homileticians, since this is a point that cannot be too strongly emphasized. First a more general counsel of Phelps's. "Preach," he says, "very little in general, and very much in detail. Preach little on truth, and much on truths. Preach rarely on religion, but constantly on the facts, the doctrines, the duties, the precepts, the privileges of religion. Divide, discriminate, define, sharpen, clarify, doctrine by doc-

trine, duty by duty, fact by fact, till the whole map of Christian faith
is outlined and clear. You thus gain the power of pointed preaching.
Thought will take the precedence of feeling, and intelligent action will
be the resultant of both. The final product which you accumulate
and build up will be not beliefs alone, not sensibilities alone, but character in those forms in which character is power. Your church will
become to the religious world what any other body of men of
character is to the secular world,—a consolidation of forces, and a
power of control."[2] Then several paragraphs from the admirable
homiletician Herrick Johnson, who writes under the heading, "The
ideal 'immediates' of the sermon" these pertinent words: "One
indispensable step in preparation is a clear, distinct conception of the
theme to be treated; or an answer to the question, What am I going to
talk about? Until the preacher gets this question definitely answered,
he should go no farther. He must have a theme and should know precisely what it is. And that he may know that he knows, he should
put it in words. If he can't put it in words, discussion is hopeless. If
his theme is in a haze, everything else will be: his introduction, his
arrangement, his proof, his object, his hearers, himself! It must be
vividly outlined in his thought, and given a precise verbal form. (a)
The theme should not simply *cover* or *include* what he is to say; it
should *exclude everything else*. Repentance, e. g., is not the theme of a
discourse which is designed to show the necessity of repentance, if
one would not perish. It does not fix a boundary to the subsequent
discussion. And a theme must do that if it is to tell the truth. (b) The
theme must be the very core of the text. . . (c) The theme should have
exact expression in words. The preacher should not be satisfied with
a general idea. Let him take time to be definite. It will often require time, and that, too, when the preacher may think he ought to be
dashing on to the construction of the sermon, which must be ready,
nolens volens, for the swiftly approaching Sabbath. Let the theme be
stripped of everything redundant. It is the epitome of the discourse—
the germ, out of which the whole structure is to grow. It should be
concise—explicit; phrased with painstaking care. One may be perfectly sure the thought is vague, so long as he cannot give it exact
expression. *Put it in words. Put it in words.* Time taken, no matter
under what pressure or call from other quarters—in getting a clear,
distinct conception of the subject, is time saved. In each preparation
for the pulpit, the first words written should invariably be *the exact*

---

[2] P. 289.

wording of the theme: or an answer to the question, What am I to talk about? A second indispensable step in immediate preparation is a clear, distinct conception of the object to be accomplished, or an answer to the question, Why am I going to talk about this theme? If I have a distinct end in view, what is it? There are only four possible, immediate, generic objects the preacher can have in view, viz., to instruct the understanding, to convince the judgment, to excite the sensibilities, to persuade the will. He may have any one of these before him, or more than one, or all. One may be chief and the rest subordinate. . . . Under these four generic objects there may be many specific objects. And some one of these more specific objects it may be the purpose of the preacher to secure. But in *every* preparation for the pulpit, a distinct conception should be had of some definite object to be accomplished. Of all the sinners from lack of purpose, a *purposeless pulpit* is the chief. *Without aim it is impossible to do one's best at any toil.* It is as true of brain-work as it is of handwork. It is not in human nature to get absorbed in vague, indefinite effort. Unity in aim is the very life of invention. Having no object in view, the mind has no spring—no stirring incentive. There is nothing to marshal its energies. This-one-thing-I-do inspiration is wanting. There is no focus-constraining convergence. The distinct conception of the object will go far to *shape the plan of treatment.* The preacher is now after a plan that will do a certain thing. He knows what he wants. Hence the greater likelihood of his getting it, and the greater facility in the process. Having determined on his object, much is at once decided that otherwise would be left in uncertainty. The kind of plan, the form it shall take, the amount of explication or proof or appeal it shall contain, will be largely determined by the object aimed at, and this will help immensely in the construction of the plan... To have a definite object is *essential to the truest unity.* Unity is the very life of discourse. Nothing can atone for the want of it. Everything must be subordinated and made subservient to this [cf. pp. 397 ff]. But singleness of subject will not give unity. Certainly not in its highest and best form. There must be an object also—a terminus *ad quem* as well as a terminus *a quo*, to which the mind shall be rigidly held, and which shall be steadily pursued throughout the discourse. It is here, perhaps more than anywhere else, that young sermon makers are apt to fail. But, alas, we know there are homiletic sinners who have grown old at this bad business. They take a subject. They are to make a sermon to cover twenty or thirty pages of manuscript. They give themselves to writing, with no clear, distinct, commanding object in view, that they are bent on accomplishing. The discourse will have truth in it, important truth—it may sparkle with brilliant flashes of genius—nevertheless, what is it after all but an accumulation of dead words, 'connected together by the lifeless rules of grammar,' if there is no single governing purpose running down through it, and dominating the entire discussion. The focal point to which all the lines of the sermon converge, is absolutely vital to the highest sermonic efficiency."[3] Phelps refers to Dr. Lyman Beecher, who "accomplished more for the evangelical faith in Boston by his bony sermons than by all other expedients of his pulpit. They were not graceful discourses; they were not literary discourses; they were not classically finished discourses (they would have been improved if they had been all these); but they were definite discourses. They reined up hearers to specific thinking. They made them see that the preacher was aiming at something. It was impossible to mistake what and where the target was. In this respect his sermons were in striking contrast with those of his opponents, whose antipathy to an angular theology expressed itself in smooth and rounded rhetoric, which presented to the popular conscience no protuberances of thought, no points of convergent force, and therefore no centers of burning power. The fruits of the two methods of preaching have entered into the history of New England, and are known and read of all men."

The question, whether and in what manner the theme should be announced, requires a fuller discussion. It has been claimed, wrongly, that there is no precedent in profane oratory for announced themes. Demosthenes, indeed, dispenses usually, but not invariably, which the *propositio;* in his First Philippic he announces his theme immediately after the exordium. Aristotle says proposition and proof are the indispensable parts of an oration. Quintilian counsels, in special cases alone, the announcement of the proposition.[4] The great majority of German homileticians demand it, though not as an absolute rule. We quote from a number of these. First from Palmer, who approaches the subject from the viewpoint of the sermon as work of art. "The condensation," he says, "of the contents of the sermon in a single proposition facilitates its retention by many. This, however, is not always borne out by experience, for many attentive hearers remember many other portions of the sermon more readily than the theme. Moreover, to accomplish this purpose it would be more appropriate and

---

[3] Pp. 313 ff.—Pattison quotes a saying of Archbishop Magee: "A good sermon should be like a wedge, all leading to a point" (p. 100).
[4] *Lib.* iv, c. iv, 2.

more natural to place the theme at the close as concluding proposition, gathering up the threads of the sermon and dismissing the congregation with this final impression. In our opinion, the prefixing of the theme rests upon the same basis as the whole artistic structure of the sermon, on the fact, namely, that the cultus requires a beautiful form. This beautiful form may, indeed, exist without a theme; theme and divisions may even mar and spoil it. But it is all the more certain that the sermon is seen more clearly as a work of art, that the beauty of the conception of a text, the eternal freshness and newness of all divine truths allied with the life of the human spirit is revealed in a stimulating and uplifting manner satisfying to the festival mood, when a good theme ushers in the sermon."[5] Schweizer has this to say: "Some announcement there must be, of the specific subject of the sermon as a whole or of its several parts; for this cannot always be indicated by the text. When it is indicated by the text, it will be natural to mention it. But the actual announcement of a formally correct theme cannot be demanded as an invariable rule. For no one can be prevented from presenting the subject in its various parts in order to arrive at its unity as goal. This procedure is to be preferred when the sermon has a 'final theme."[6] Krauss writes: "The preacher dare never under any circumstances shirk the labor of definitely fixing his theme before working out his sermon. The orator, above all, needs a formulated theme. Its formal and literal announcement may be dispensed with, in proportion as the sermon is built up consistently around its theme and his hearers are experienced in listening to oral discourse. Usually, however, such an announcement will materially facilitate and assist the comprehension and the effect of the sermon. For very few persons are able to listen with pleasure and profit for even a quarter of an hour to a lecture, unless its contents or purpose is previously stated in a brief and easily remembered formula. And since sermons are preached solely for the sake of their hearers, this consideration is of the utmost weight. But the formulated theme is altogether indispensable for the orator himself. Beginners in particular speak invariably at random whenever they permit themselves to discuss the various thoughts they wish to present, without having formulated in words their unifying thought."[7] G. v. Zezschwitz says: "The congregation needs pedagogic assistance in order properly to follow a sermon and to listen to it with understanding. To set up a definite proposition taken from a text has at least the

---

[5] P. 450. [6] P. 312. [7] P. 427.

advantage of fixing and concentrating their attention, and of fastening in their memory the principal contents of the discourse. *This is in accord with the highest interests of the care of souls.* Only, one should select thoughts of truly practical value and give to them a correspondingly striking expression. Such a proposition may form the permanent watchword for the whole mass of edifying material in a sermon. And if the disposition [this may be included here, though it belongs under the next head] is logically clear as to its order, the interrelation of its divisions, and its extent, and if the divisions themselves are lucidly expressed, then the prefixed announcement of the disposition not only furnishes a point of contact for the final impression: 'peroratum est,' but facilitates a survey of the development and the retention of its parts. Certainly, for a more refined taste, it will be a higher pleasure to watch the individual sentences which support the proposition emerge one by one and take their respective places, and it may appear more impressive when the proposition finds expression at the close. But how many hearers have this refined taste, and how many are attentive enough to follow the gradual development of the subject and to catch a glimpse of the proposition while its expression is being formed? But where these are lacking the hearer will have at the close a feeling of deplorable loss, in that he was unable, while listening to what has gone before, to relate each point to the proposition, and is now unable to compare it with what he hears at the close and recognizes only now as the goal of the whole discourse. It is, therefore, for the sake of the congregation, and in a pastoral spirit, that one will set one's self a lower goal artistically, and stoop to the comprehension of the average man."[8] And Kleinert writes: "Neither a strained endeavor to find out what the sermon is about, nor an indolent thoughtlessness that, without greatly caring what it is about, lets the sermon flow past it, corresponds to the spirit of worship. Over against both, the announcement of the theme of the sermon produces a clear inward calm of receptivity, facilitates the correct understanding of the sermon by relating the development of the subject to the theme as announced, and helps the hearer more easily to grasp and survey the sermon. It is, therefore, not accidental that the announcement of the theme has become customary in our services."[9] The French Vinet agrees with these German homileticians. He writes: "If the utility of the exordium is founded in the necessity

---

[8]Zoeckler's *Handbuch d. theol. Wissenschaften,* [3]1890, iv, 193.
[9]P. 168.

of preparing the mind and disposing it favorably toward the special subject before us, it is idle to prove that the subject ought to be announced in a precise manner, so that the mind may direct itself immediately and without hesitation to a determinate point."[10] Among American homileticians the pioneer Porter regards the announcement of the theme as self-evident. Instead of proving it, he proceeds at once to discuss how the theme should be formulated and announced.[11] About thirty-five years later Dabney wrote: "The propounding of the main subject of discourse at the outset of the main argument is demanded by this plain reason, that if you wish the people to understand what you say, you must inform them in advance about what you purpose to talk. Such an announcement is at once the necessary key to comprehension and the clue of connection for all that follows. The rule is, therefore, uniform and imperative."[12]

Phelps has entered into the fullest discussion of the subject. He writes: "The question is not whether a point to be proved is essential in every discourse; it is not whether the most scholastic form of statement is necessary to the proposition; it is not whether any single form of statement should be invariable in the proposition. The only point of inquiry on which difference of opinion can exist is this: Should the subject of a sermon invariably be so stated as to make hearers sensible at the moment that the subject is defined? The question of statement or no statement cannot be fairly dismissed as a question of form only. It is a question of the inner quality of preaching. Decide it in one way, and you decide in sympathy with shallow and effervescent preaching. Decide it otherwise, and you cultivate thoughtful, solid, elemental preaching." He then proceeds to the enumeration of nine reasons for the stated theme. We summarize the most important of them: "(1) The oratorical instinct of a good speaker demands that he shall have a proposition. Expressed or latent, the proposition must exist. We acknowledge this in the demand which we make upon every speaker, that he shall 'speak to the point.' What point? (2) The instinct of good hearing demands, on the same principle, that a speaker shall state his proposition. For what purpose does a speaker need to have a proposition for which the hearer does not also need the statement of the proposition? There is a hearing to the point, which is correlative to speaking to the point. The eye follows the arrow most easily if it sees the target. (3) It lies especially in the nature of a spoken address that it needs a statement of the theme. If an essay

---

[10] P. 308. [11] Pp. 105-106. [12] P. 164.

written might dispense with this, not so a speech delivered. In hearing, do we not instinctively, and soon after the commencement of an address, ask ourselves, What would the speaker be at? what is the aim? where is the target? If it seems to be concealed, are we not restless till it is discovered? This mental experience of a hearer is only the silent demand made upon the preacher that he shall not only have a proposition, but shall announce it. The instinct of hearing and the instinct of speech, in this respect, are of one mind. (4) The popular mind is peculiarly dependent on knowledge of the theme as an aid to unity of impression. Performers on the tight-rope steady their whole muscular system by fixing the eye intently on a point in the distance. Thus they cross a ravine where the wavering of the eye might be death. Not unlike this is the mental effort by which the common mind must often follow the mental operations of its superior. The knowledge of the subject at the outset will be to the power of attention what the fixed eye is to the muscles of the gymnast. (5) The subjects of the pulpit are in their nature liable to confusion in the popular conceptions of them. At this point the inquiry before us ceases to be a question of forms: it deepens into a question of things. The common mind is burdened with the sense of sameness in the discourses of the pulpit. No other criticism of the pulpit is so common as this, 'The preacher repeats himself. He is forever reiterating the old story.'. . The tendency to confusion of religious thought often increases with the excitement of religious emotions. . . One part of the mission of the pulpit, therefore, must be to divide and define and identify religious thought in the popular experience. . . Men need to be taught by the pulpit to know what they believe, and why they feel, what emotions are legitimate to one truth, and what to another, and why they differ. Truths need to be individualized. . . (7) The use of that class of expedients to which definite propositions belong, and of that kind of preaching to which they are a necessity, tends to form and consolidate the theological faith of a people. The question of the formal statement of the theme is a question of success. To achieve success, you must have constructive methods; for constructive methods, you must have a positive faith; and for a positive faith you must have centers of discussion which shall be visible. To make these centers visible, you must make them luminous; to make them luminous, you must have definite statements of them which shall penetrate the understanding, and remain in the memory. In no other way can you get possession of available forces with which to work upon the popular life. (8) The statement of the theme enables the common hearer to recognize clearly and unmistakably the point you want to make with your sermon. Some hearers will suppose you to be preaching on the omnipotence of God, when, in fact, you are discoursing upon his sovereignty. They will be thinking of the degree of depravity while you are describing its extent. You will preach upon Christ's work of intercession, and some of your hearers will advance no nearer to your thought than to imagine that they have heard a sermon on prayer. You will be praised or censured for sermons which you never preached. (9) The value of definite statements of themes is evidenced by the importance attached to them in other departments of oratory. Out of the pulpit public speaking is commonly a business. It has an object in real life. Men are in earnest in it. Speakers speak for a purpose; hearers hear for a purpose. What, then, is the testimony of the senate and the bar on the question of the necessity of propositions? Why is a lawyer expected to state his case to a jury? Why must a senator speak to a motion, upon a resolution, for or against a bill? Why is legislative business printed and circulated before it passes to a second reading? These expedients of legislative and forensic usage are among the equivalents of those helps to precision which a preacher seeks in choosing texts, and stating themes, and announcing divisions of sermons. . . Of Chief Justice Marshall a critic said, 'Marshall's force lay in three things: first, he understood his own purpose; secondly, he so stated it as to make a jury understand it; thirdly, he so stated it as to make them feel that neither they nor he had any concern with any thing else. For the time, the opposition was nowhere.' This criticism suggests an admirable model for the statements of themes of sermons."[13] Pattison is equally emphatic in advocating a definitely announced theme, and refers to Ruskin, who in *Sesame and Lilies* (p. 6) quotes with approval the opinion of men practiced in public address, that hearers "are never so much fatigued as by the endeavor to follow a speaker who gives them no clue to his purpose."[14]

For all these reasons we must decide in favor of the announced theme. For the same reasons we must insist upon a complete and precise announcement and reject abbreviated themes and such as are mere headings or titles. Kleinert is inclined to permit the abbreviation of a comprehensive theme with numerous modifying phrases or clauses, not easily grasped in its entirety nor readily fixed in the memory. He points to one of Schleiermacher's themes, which rolls

---

[13] Pp. 282 ff. [14] P. 100.

along thus: "How closely our Christmas joy is bound up with the fact that our faith that Jesus is the Son of God is the victory that overcometh the world."[15] And to another by the same: "What were the sufferings of the Saviour in relation to those who had power and authority over His people, with respect to His arrest."[16] The trouble with these themes is not that they are complete and precise, but that they are so awkwardly formulated. The former would gain if it were expressed somewhat after this fashion: "Rejoice, for our Christmas faith is the victory that overcomes the world!" (1) Wherein our Christmas faith consists; (2) what it is able to do; (3) how it is for this reason the basis of our joy. Or: "Rejoice today, for our faith in Jesus Christ, the Son of God, is the victory that overcomes the world." The latter theme might be put thus: "What was revealed in Jesus when He suffered Himself to be taken captive by the rulers of His people?" or: "What was the attitude of our Saviour toward the rulers of His people, when they came to arrest Him?" In this way both themes would set forth clearly and precisely as well as in an easily comprehensible and memorable form the subjects of their respective sermons. Schleiermacher takes as theme for another sermon the mere heading "Benevolence." But it would have been better to make this read: "What dangers must Benevolence avoid in order to be truly Christian?" Similarly, "There are good works which are harmful" is a better theme for a sermon on Luke 10:38-42, than the colorless heading, "Mary and Martha." Many sermons of otherwise admirable preachers would gain in effectiveness if they carried at their head a precise and definite theme. This applies, e. g., to many of the closely knit, thoughtful sermons of Bezzel and to most of the fresh, contemporary sermons of Benz. All that a psychologically oriented catechetic and pedagogic have to say about the announcement of the aim in catechization,[17] applies, *mutatis mutandis*, to the announcement of the theme in the sermon. The abbreviated theme is permissible when it appears in such forms as the following: The Christian and the world; Christianity and liberty; Faith and life; Christianity and labor. For these are only simplifications of the fuller themes: What is the relation of the Christian to the world? The inseparableness of faith and life, etc.

The announcement of the theme is not so necessary in the case of shorter sermons or addresses, especially at burials, baptisms, confirmation or public confession. The brief text on which they are

---

[15]*Predigten*, iii, 63 ff. [16]iii, 499 ff. [17]Reu, *Catechetics*, pp. 467 f.

usually based serves frequently as both theme and outline. But the text must actually pervade the entire address and gather it up into a unity. For example: "Commit thy way unto the Lord, trust also in him, and he will bring it to pass." "To me to live is Christ, and to die is gain." "The Lord is my Shepherd; I shall not want." Passiontide sermons, based on texts from the passion story, fall under this head. All of this shorter sermons must, however, have a definite theme and purpose; otherwise they will become mere harangues or fragmentary Bible studies.

The theme should be so announced as to appear as an independent entity, easily discernible not only by the eye of the writer, but by the ear of the hearer. Porter wrote on this point: "When you are prepared to state your subject, the form of expression employed should be such, as to give the hearers *a momentary premonition* that you are about to do it. For example: 'The doctrine which is taught in the text, and which I shall endeavor to establish in the following discourse, is this, that the only possibility of human salvation, consistent with the character and government of God, is suspended on the atonement of Christ.' Now, if language like this is employed, every intelligent hearer will perceive that you are about to announce your subject *before* you have done it; and accordingly that sentence of your sermon, which it is more important for him to remember than any other, he will be more likely to remember. But many preachers would reverse the order of members, in the example given above, and consequently the hearers, being told in the end of a complex sentence, that the subject of the sermon *was* stated at the beginning of it may recall the statement if they can." This is reiterated and amplified by Dabney.[18] "Some simple means should be used to arrest the attention of all the hearers when you are about to announce your proposition, and to advertise them that you are now proceeding to this cardinal step. This may be effected by a significant pause, by an emphatic repetition of the propounding sentence, or by a cautionary preface, following the end of the explication, in some such words as these: 'The following then appears to be the doctrine of the text,' or 'This explication of the text shows that it asserts the following proposition, viz.' In a word, the preacher upon pronouncing his proposition, should examine the countenances of his hearers, and be sure that he has their understanding as well as their eyes. If he perceives that a part of them are either inattentive or confused and doubtful of his real intent, he

---

[18] P. 185.

should not proceed until, by suitable repetitions, he has possessed every mind of his purposed object."[19] The refined Kleinert, foe to everything hackneyed, agrees with this. "The theme," he says, "should not only be woven, at the outset, into the flow of discourse, as is customary in secular oratory. It should be separated by its precise formulation and stand out, in the stream of discourse, as a proposition placed between the introduction and the body of the sermon. This mode of presentation will preclude the possibility of the hearer's attention failing to be caught by a rapid and merely passing reference. If the proposition is a happy one, sinking readily into the ear and pleasantly into the mind, and therefore gladly accepted, it will not only completely fulfil the function of an orientating aid to the apprehension of what is to follow, but will fix itself in the memory and materially assist the inner reproduction and the permanent retention of what has been heard."[20]

Thus we are brought to the question of the phraseology of the theme. Palmer demands brevity, color and euphony, understanding the second of these in the sense of preciseness of content. "The theme," he says, "must be brief, terse, precise; not an unnecessary word; no oratorical amplification; no long winded dependent clauses; better still, no dependent clauses at all; the possessive case and the adjective to be sparingly used." As examples he mentions the following: on Luke 2:25-32—"Ein schoener, alter Mann" (Rieger); on Luke 6:38-42—"Ein ganzer Christ" (Rieger); on 1 Cor. 12:1-10— "Von dem ewigen Halt fuer unsere Seele" (Hofacker).[21] With respect to euphony, Stier indeed says that "we should avoid, in the phraseology of the theme and the divisions, all artifice and calculation, running from a comparatively justifiable proverbial form or easily remembered assonance to a rhyme and rhythm which are out of place, at least in the pulpit. Not even the rhyme and rhythm of ideas will accomplish anything, but only and always a biblical-popular simplicity and content."[22] True enough, rhyme and rhythm accomplish nothing, but simplicity and content and a biblical and popular form are altogether compatible with beautiful, euphonious and ordered language. Though we reject, with Stier, the artificial, we by no means reject the truly artistic. Experience teaches us that the hearer seeking to be edified will delight in a beautiful and fresh theme and is put by it in a better mood for the sermon. "Euphony," Palmer continues, "may consist simply in the euphonious choice and position of

---

[19]P. 165. [20]P. 168. [21]P. 453. [22]*Keryktik*, p. 241.

words, in a more or less rhythmical symmetry, but also in unforced assonance and alliteration. For example: Wie heilig und hehr das Sterben des Heilands ist; Das Heilige und Herrliche des gemeinsamen Christenstandes; Irdische Lust, irdische Liebe, irdisches Leid, das sind die drei Maechte, welche die Menschen von Christo verscheuchen (Luke 9:57-62); Jesu Verklaerung in Pauli Bekehrung; Des Heilands Sterben, des Apostels Werben (2 Cor. 5:14-21)." But since the average man, clerical and lay, cannot distinguish between art and artifice, and since we cannot forget into what an unworthy playing with words German homiletical literature has often degenerated, it will be safer for the preacher to follow Stier rather than Palmer.

The question has been raised, whether figures of speech may be used in the formulation of the theme. Certainly: the Scriptures use them; but only such figures should be used as are suggested by the subject in question and as will be at once clear to the hearer. If we bear in mind the grotesque achievements in this field by the German pulpit of the XVIII century, and not a few curious things one has oneself heard in the XIX and even the XX century, it will not be out of place to utter a word of warning against this abuse. The same must be said of rhymed propositions, the father of which seems to have been Bernard of Clairvaux,[23] and which are affected by not a few poeticules in clerical garb. We may indeed, now and then, use a hymn verse or stanza as theme or division, provided it is well known to our hearers and actually expresses what we wish to say.[24] But to mount Pegasus every time he has to construct a theme, little becomes a mature preacher of the Gospel who feels deeply the seriousness and the sanctity of his calling. One of the least admirable traits of Ahlfeld's otherwise excellent sermons are his rhymed themes and outlines; the same is sometimes true even of the poetically gifted Gerok. That the phraseology of the theme deserves special care follows from the fact that it occupies so conspicuous a place in the sermon and is to serve as peg on which the whole discourse is to hang, as seed-grain from which it is to grow, as summary in which it is to gather itself up and fix itself in the memory. It should, therefore, be clear, euphonious, but also natural and unforced.

---

[23]Cruel, *Deutsche Predigt des Mittelalters*, pp. 292 f.—[24]A fine example of a sermon based on an entire hymn may be found in W. M. Clow's *The Cross in Christian Experience* (1908), sermon xxiv, "A Hymn of the Cross."

If, finally, the theme, with or without its outline, is an epitome of the sermon, expressing either its subject or its purpose, it must control and pervade the whole discourse. Pattison says truly: "We gauge the excellence of a sermon among other things by this: Is the theme evident throughout? Would a late-comer, arriving when the discourse was well under way, learn what were the text and theme before he had been listening five [?] minutes? Statement, argument, illustration, application, do they all bear closely upon the subject? If they do, the theme will remain as the final and ruling impression on the hearer's mind." This emergence of the theme throughout the sermon may degenerate, indeed, into a purely mechanical repetition, as is the case in many of Reinhard's sermons. Nevertheless, underneath his demand that the theme should be repeated at each transition to a new thought, there lies the correct principle that the theme incorporates in itself the essential unity of the sermon. This return to the theme dare of course never be awkwardly made. The preacher who is mastered by his subject and concerned for the unity of his sermon will be driven to make it by an inner necessity. When well made, such a repetition of the theme will not only impress upon the hearer from ever new angles the single divine truth to which the sermon for the day is devoted, but will assist and insure the single effect which this truth seeks to produce, so far as this effect depends on human art. Just as in Gothic architecture the cross motif is **all-controlling** and meets the eye at every turn, so the theme, if truly all-controlling, will of itself recur again and again.

§ 17. THE DIVISIONS OF THE SERMON

J. L. v. Mosheim, *Anweisung, erbaulich zu predigen,* 1763. E. Porter, *Lectures on Homiletics and Preaching,* 1834. A. Vinet, *Homiletics,* 1840 (1853). Chr. Palmer, *Evang. Homiletik,* 1842. C. I. Nitzsch, *Praktische Theologie,* ii, 2, 1848. A. Schweizer, *Homiletik,* 1848. F. Schleiermacher, *Praktische Theologie,* 1850. J. E. Ziegler, *Fundamentum dividendi,* 1851. D. P. Kidder, *A Treatise on Homiletics,* 1864. J. A. Broadus, *On the Preparation and Delivery of Sermons,* 1870 (rev. 1897). R. L. Dabney, *Sacred Rhetoric,* 1870 (^{8}1902). F. L. Steinmeyer, *Die Topik im Dienst der Predigt,* 1874. A. Phelps, *The Theory of Preaching,* 1881. A. Krauss, *Homiletik,* 1883. E. Chr. Achelis, *Praktische Theologie,* 1889 (ii^3, 1911). J. Gottschick, *Fundamentum dividendi* ("Halte was du hast," xxvi), 1903. T. H. Pattison, *The Making of the Sermon,* 1898. F. L. Steinmeyer, *Homiletik,* 1901. A. S. Hoyt, *The Work of Preaching,* 1905. H. Hering, *Die Lehre von der Predigt,* 1905. H. C. Graves, *Lectures on Homiletics,* 1906. P. Kleinert, *Homiletik,* 1907. J. Gottschick, *Homiletik und Katechetik,* 1908. D. R. Breed, *Preparing to Preach,* 1911. D. J. Burrell, *The Sermon, Its Construction and Delivery,* 1913. A. E. Garvie, *The Christian Preacher,* 1921.

From the theme the sermon falls into its component parts and thus arrives at its divisions, or its disposition. From the theme, not from the text; for a right theme contains in itself the main thought, or unity of the text, so that the divisions of the text are inherent in the theme. Hence the making of the divisions of the sermon is not a new and independent process, but consists merely in recalling to mind the reasons, and the divisions of the text, which prompted one to formulate the unity of the text in a particular theme. If the theme has been correctly formed, the only difficulty that should be encountered in making the divisions is that of giving them their proper formulation. This is seen most clearly in the analytic sermon, where, to find the divisions, we need simply to retrace the steps by which we reached our theme. If we

DERIVIATION OF THE DIVISIONS FROM THE THEME

reached our theme by gathering up into a unity the various elements of the text, we have now merely to go back from this unity to its various parts in order to arrive at the divisions of the sermon. It only remains to formulate these divisions in such a way that they may be seen to follow logically from the theme, and not to be externally and mechanically related to it. This is seen also in the synthetic sermon. Though the individual parts of this type of sermon are not determined by the progression of thought in the text, but are drawn by logical deduction from the theme, nevertheless, only that can be deduced from the theme which is actually contained in it and which prompted us in our preparation to decide upon this particular theme as expressing the main thought of the text.

We need enter, therefore, on no elaborate discussion as to the formation of the divisions of the sermon. It will not be amiss, however, to refer the student to the practical use that may be made of the logical categories, such as being and becoming, and of the topical or rhetorical categories, such as end and means, command and motive, necessity and possibility, need and satisfaction, privilege and responsibility. These are of value, however, in the disposition of the synthetic sermon alone; they can not be used in that of the analytic sermon, unless they are contained in the text and have been discovered in the exegetical study of the text (P. 460).

Suppose that in our exegetical study of Luke 17:7-10 we have found that there are two requirements that Jesus makes of His followers, viz.: they are to labor indefatigably in His vineyard, and they are not to be prompted by the hope of a reward. And suppose that we have found the point of unity for our sermon, which is to be analytic, in the thought: The requirements that Jesus makes of those who labor for 'Him. We may then formulate our theme in the question: What does Jesus require of His laborers? From this theme we reach the following divisions: (1) Labor on without pause or rest! (2) Regard your most diligent labor as merely the doing of what you are in duty bound to do! Or in our study of Matt. 7:7-11 we find that Jesus desires our prayer to be both fervent and confident

This will sum itself up, for an analytic sermon, in the unity: The true conditions of answered prayer, and our theme will be: When may my prayer be sure of an answer? From this theme follow the divisions: (1) When I always expect the best from God, (2) when my asking leads to seeking, and my seeking completes itself in knocking. Or, studying Matt. 6:5-8, I learn that this passage describes in a climax the manner in which we are to pray, viz.: not before men, but in secret, and with no vain repetition. If I take as my theme: How should we pray? the following divisions will naturally emerge: (1) We should not parade our prayers before men, (2) we should pray to our Father in secret, (3) we should put our whole heart into every prayer. Or I find in my exegesis of Jas. 1:2-4 the striking injunction that men should count their tribulation as joy, and for these three reasons: tribulation is a means of proving their faith; it leads to patient endurance; it issues in moral perfection. It is most natural to choose as my theme: Why may Christians rejoice in tribulation? and to divide: (1) Because tribulation is a test, which shows whether our faith is genuine; (2) because it works patient endurance, without which we cannot be true Christians; (3) because it leads to moral perfection, after which we should all strive. Or I take as my text Luke 12:35-48, which calls on us to be watchful and assigns the reasons for this. My theme will be: Watch against the Lord's coming! The divisions that flow from this will be: (1) Realize what this means! (2) Remember to what this should lead! Since this last disposition is drawn from the text and may also be deduced logically from the theme, we have here an analytic-synthetic sermon. From his exposition of Luke 13:18-19 the preacher has gathered the following truth: In His kingdom God brings great things out of small, and then recalls how this truth is verified in various departments of the kingdom. If he takes as his theme: God brings great things out of small, his divisions for a synthetic sermon may be: (1) This has been a law of the Church's life from its beginning, (2) this is a summons to the work of missions, (3) this is a comfort in all spiritual work.

In order to reach the disposition, in all these examples, we started with the theme and retraced the steps by which we had been brought to the theme. Then we put the materials already gathered in such form as to set them forth as the organic unfolding of the theme.

Logical and rhetorical categories are followed when we form divisions such as the following. On Luke 16:19 ff.: Rich and poor; (1) here, (2) hereafter. Or, on the same text: The poor rich man; (1) poor in life, (2) poor in death, (3) poor in all eternity. Luke

18:9-14: The right worshiper; (1) On the way to church, (2) in church, (3) on the way home. John 11:16: Let us go with Jesus, that we may die with Him; (1) What does this mean? (2) Do we mean this? 2 Cor. 12:7-9: How thorns turn to roses; (1) For ourselves, (2) for others. Gal. 3:26: We are the sons of God; (1) This is God's gift, and (2) our responsibility. 2 Cor. 5:19-20: Be ye reconciled to God! (1) You need reconciliation, (2) you find it in faith in Christ. Gal. 5:16-24: Many different trees grow out of the same soil; they differ (1) in their nature, (2) their fruit, (3) their end. Phil. 2:5-13: Follow Jesus! (1) In His humiliation, (2) in His exaltation. Ti. 2:11-14: The grace of God hath appeared, bringing salvation to all men; (1) The blessed fact, (2) the intended effect. 1 Pet. 1:3-9: Begotten again unto a lively hope; (1) The ground of this hope, (2) the road that leads to it, (3) the goal to which God desires to bring it. 1 John 1:4: The work of the Gospel ministry, a laboring to increase the brethren's joy; (1) The truth of this, (2) its consequences for the work of the Gospel minister. Ps. 46: A mighty fortress is our God; (1) This was Israel's consolation in dark days; (2) this was Luther's comfort in sore need; (3) this is today the Church's one support. Ez. 36:22-28: A new heart, the most precious gift of Pentecost; (1) Why a new heart? (2) whence a new heart? (3) to what end a new heart?

It was particularly Nitzsch who, in recent years, desired the general categories of thought to be pressed into the service of the sermon. "A disposition," he wrote, "that really and not only apparently follows the order of the text must consciously or unconsciously follow logical rules. The divine Word communicates itself by means of the human speech of prophets and apostles. The objective thought of Scripture contains in itself the same categorical relations the possession of which constitutes the logical consciousness of the apprehending subject. A talented person will without reflection find these categories which control the text, and as orator, will freely mobilize, apply and combine them. But in so far as reflection is required in order to produce the disposition, the homilete needs a deliberate knowledge of the fundamental categories. Theremin says correctly that the categories of possibility, necessity and reality, and the ethical fundamentals of duty, virtue and happiness furnish in most cases the *fundamentum dividendi*. But is the list of categories so meagre that we must needs be content with a single division into two fundamental parts? All theological and philosophical science is at the service of the oration in its divisions and logical order—logic, abstract and concrete, psychology, metaphysic, dogmatic, ascetic. Not to mention the division of the sentence into subject and predicate or subject and object, nor the fact that affirmation and negation; the generic, specific and individual; quantity, quality, duration; cause and effect; thesis and antithesis, offer their services to the disposition of the sermon, as do also the psychological and anthropological categories of intellect and will, intention and performance, reason and sensuality, external and internal—nothing can be more natural for the homiletic disposition than to use the ethical and dogmatic categories, the elements of the concept of religion itself, the analysis of the terms: Christ, salvation, righteousness and grace. For all truly valid ideal or abstract relations found by science may be pursued backwards and turned again into the concrete."[1]

There is only one mistake in this. The use of the logical categories is not to begin only with the framing of the disposition. This is done, indeed, in the synthetic sermon. But if it is invariably done, the effect will be that of dragging in an alien and formal element. If, on the contrary, these categories have been kept in mind already in the gathering of materials, and if the text has been studied from this point of view, their appearance in the disposition will not seem strange and adventitious, but only natural and advantageous. It was the merit of Steinmeyer to show, in his noteworthy work, *Die Topik im Dienst der Predigt,* that the supreme value of these categories of thought lies in their usefulness in the gathering of the materials of the text, on the basis of which they are to be employed in the development of the subject. He distinguishes three types of sermon: the didactic, which aims at the moral-religious understanding; the protreptic, which appeals to the will; and the mystic, which introduces to communion with God. To the first he assigns the categories of genus and species, *simile* and *dissimile, contrarium* and *repugnans;* to the second, those of *necessarium* and *debitum, utile* and μακάριον, *facile* and *difficile;* and to the third, the question of the hidden δοξα, σοφία and ζωή. We may not be able to follow Steinmeyer in his threefold division of the sermon nor in his distribution of the various categories; but we cannot deny that the matter itself is worthy of consideration both in the gathering of material and in the construction of the disposition.

All properly constructed dispositions follow one or another of the following three methods: the whole theme is

---

[1] P. 116.

simply divided into its several parts, or a part of the theme (subject, predicate, object, etc.) is used as principle of division, or the theme as a whole remains intact but the truth it expresses is treated from various aspects.

A.—The division of the *whole* theme into its several parts may be illustrated by the following dispositions. On 2 Thess. 2:14: The Holy Ghost has called me through the Gospel; (1) Who has called? (2) through what has He called? (3) whom has He called? Or on John 14:23-31: The Holy Spirit brings us true peace; (1) In what does true peace consist? (2) how does the Holy Spirit bring us this peace? A Christmas sermon on Heb. 1:1-3 may profitably be divided: On Christmas Day God spoke unto us in His Son; (1) God has spoken to us, (2) God has spoken to us in His Son, (3) this speaking in His Son is God's last word to us.

From this must be sharply distinguished, and unreservedly condemned, the practice of taking a portion of a text as theme and breaking it up in a mechanical manner to form the divisions of the sermon. In American manuals of preaching, for instance, one may find such "model" outlines as the following. From Matt. 21:28-32, the words, "Son, go work today in my vineyard," are chosen as theme, with these divisions: (1) The title given: Son; (2) the duty demanded: work; (3) the time designated: now; (4) the place appointed: my vineyard. Or, in a sermon on Luke 15:1-10, the words, "This man receiveth sinners, and eateth with them," form the theme, and the divisions are: (1) This man, (2) receiveth sinners, (3) eateth with them. To be sure, the sum of the parts equals the theme, in these examples; but no one will claim that the theme is organically unfolded or that the purpose of the text of the sermon is attained. The former example shows, moreover, how entirely unimportant elements are placed on a par with the principal parts; the word "son" denotes not at all our relationship as sons of God, but means in Hebrew usage little more than "thou."

B.—The use of a *part* of the text as principle of division may be illustrated by the following examples. The subject is used when with the theme, "God is love" (1 John 4:16), we divide: (1) He is love as our Creator, (2) as our Redeemer, (3) as our Sanctifier. The object is used when, on the basis of the theme, The Risen Christ brings us His Easter gift of peace (Luke 24:36 ff.), we outline: (1) Peace for the heart, (2) the home, (3) the church, (4) the world. The predicate is used when we divide the theme, Bethlehem, one of faith's holy places (Luke 2:1-14): (1) There we stand before the open gate of heaven, (2) at the cradle of a new humanity, (3) under the bow of an eternal covenant of grace. The adverb is used when we outline: To the eye of faith God is everywhere present; (1) in nature, (2) in history, (3) in our own life.

C.—The formation of the disposition by treating the text *from various aspects* may be illustrated by these examples. Preaching on John 12:24-25, we may choose the theme: Jesus' word concerning the corn of wheat, and divide: Let us set this word (1) over His death and resurrection—it will show us the source of all true mission work; (2) over the work of missions itself—it will show us the secret of its success; (3) over our own Christian life—it will show us the precondition of our fitness to take part in the work of missions. On Jas. 1:13-15 we may divide the theme: Every man is tempted when he is enticed by his own lust: (1) This fact accuses us of our guilt, (2) warns us against the deceitfulness of sin, (3) threatens us with the curse of death. On Luke 6:46 —"Why call ye me, Lord, Lord, and do not the things which I say?" (1) A King's rebuke of His subjects, (2) a Friend's rebuke of His friends.

The divisions, as the organic unfolding of the theme, must in their totality exhaust the theme, at least within the limits set by the text. Nor may they introduce anything not actually contained in the theme or suggested by the theme. In other words, they should contain neither less nor more than the theme. None of them should repeat the theme, unless it be stated negatively in the first and positively in the second part. No division should be subordinated to any other, but all should be co-ordinated. None should repeat, contradict or exclude any other.

The order and arrangement of the divisions must be determined by pedagogical and practical considerations. Such considerations will prevent an order as the following. On Luke 14: 15-24: "Yet there is room;" (1) A word of exhortation, (2) a word of comfort, (3) a word of complaint. They will suggest rather that the third of these divisions be given the first place, while the state of the congregation will determine whether the first or the second division had better be put last. Here, too, the law of progression is: from the easy to the difficult, from the simple to the complex, from the appeal to the intellect to the appeal to the emotions and the will.

The divisions should be easily recognizable by the hearer. This does not mean that they are to be artificially contrasted, one following on the other in an abrupt and disjointed fashion. That could not be done without violence, for the closing sentences of one division will usually lead up to and prepare for the next. But the divisions should be easily recognized in the sense that none should pass imperceptibly over into the other, but that the line of separation should be clearly marked. The hearer should be able readily to follow the progress from division to division, in order to advance from the comprehension of the several parts to the comprehension of the whole. Hence has arisen the custom of many preachers of announcing the divisions beforehand, along with the theme. This is not in itself necessary, and is not nearly so important as the announcement of the theme; but it is an aid to the hearer and gives him a synopsis of the subject to be treated and of the method of treatment, as well as a clue to its reproduction. If the disposition is correctly and clearly framed, its announcement contains in itself an element of convincingness, reassures the hearer, quickens his interest, and thus materially helps the sermon to attain its purpose. This it can do, however, only when it is skilfully and carefully formulated. The disposition, no less than the theme, must be lucid and logical, easily comprehensible and memorable; and this because it occupies, with the theme, so conspicuous a place, at the beginning of the body of the sermon. If carelessly and clumsily made, it will do more harm than good and will arouse a prejudice against the sermon as a whole.

Should the disposition, when announced, state the substance of each division or merely indicate its form? This question cannot be decided in advance for every case. The announcement of the substance of the divisions tells the hearer beforehand what is to be the actual content of each part and thus paves the way for its effect upon his mind. The merely formal announcement rouses his curiosity, and instead of answering his questions invites him to assist in seeking and finding the answers. The latter method is pursued in the following disposition on the theme: The Saviour has come (Luke 2:1-14); (1) Of what does this remind us? (2) what does this declare to us? (3) to what does this admonish us? Such a disposition is of little value; it would be better here to state the substance of the divisions. On the other hand, the merely formal announcement of the following divisions will prove of greater value: The Holy Spirit brings us true peace (John 14:23-31); (1) In what does this peace consist? (2) how does the Holy Spirit bring us this peace? The decision as to which of these methods of announcing the disposition is to be preferred will usually depend, like the decision whether or not to announce it at all, upon the standard of intelligence in the congregation, and upon the degree to which the preacher has trained his hearers in mental and spiritual co-operation.

It is self-evident that the main divisions should themselves be carefully subdivided. We need only refer once more to the figure of the general who musters his forces on the eve of battle and assigns to each regiment its strategic place. In like manner the proper distribution of the most effective parts of the sermon will result in the best disposition. The grouping of the divisions may follow such schemes as: exposition and application, past and present, negative and positive. There dare not, however, be a leaping back and forth from one member of the scheme to the other, a skipping from exposition to application and back again to exposition, etc. Nor should any one of these schemes become the preacher's invariable stock in trade; there are few surer methods of making his treatment stereotyped and monotonous, lulling rather than stimulating. It is absurd to demand that all divisions should have an equal number of subdivisions. It is no less absurd to demand that all divisions should be of the same length. Since they are co-ordinate in importance, none dare of course be permitted to become a mere appendage, but the exact length of each must be determined by the extent of its contents and by the needs of the congregation (P. 486).

After all that has been said concerning the importance of unity, order and movement in the sermon, a discussion of the necessity of a careful disposition might appear superfluous, for it is obvious that only a well divided sermon can possess unity, order and movement. But that such a discussion is not only not superfluous but highly necessary, is brought home to us by an experience of many years as teacher as well as by a study of the history of preaching, in which objections to the disposition crop out from time to time. It is important, however, to distinguish carefully between the questions, (1) whether or not there should be a disposition, and (2) whether or not the disposition should be formally announced. We shall treat these questions in their order. (1) Fenelon wrote in his second dialogue:

"I am far from approving divisions. For the most part, they give only a seeming order; while they really mangle and clog a discourse, by separating it into two or three parts; which must interrupt the orator's action, and the effect it ought to produce. There remains no true unity after such divisions; seeing they make two or three different discourses which are joined into one, only by an arbitrary connection. For three sermons preached at different times (if they be formed upon some regular concerted plan, as the sermons in Advent usually are) make one piece, or entire discourse, as much as the three points of any of these sermons make one whole by being joined, and delivered together. The harangues of Demosthenes and Tully are not divided as our sermons are. Nay, Isocrates did not follow our method of dividing. The fathers of the church knew nothing of it. Even St. Bernard, the last of them, only gives a hint of some divisions, and does not pursue them, nor divide his discourses in form. And for a long time after him, sermons were not divided: it is a modern invention, which we owe originally to the scholastic divines."[2] Almost a century later Robert Hall wrote in the same vein: "In the mode of conducting our public ministrations, we are, perhaps, too formal and mechanical in the distribution of the matter of our sermons, we indulge too little variety, and, exposing our plan in all its parts, abate the edge of curiosity by enabling the hearer to anticipate what we intend to advance. Why should that force which surprise gives to emotion derived from just and affecting sentiments, be banished from the pulpit, when it is found of such moment in every other kind of public address? I cannot but imagine the first preachers of the gospel appeared before their audience with a more free and unfettered air, than is consistent with the narrow trammels to which, in these later ages, discourses from the pulpit are confined. The sublime emotions with which they were fraught, would have rendered them impatient of such restrictions; nor could they suffer the impetuous stream of argument, expostulation, and pathos, to be weakened, by diverting it into the artificial reservoirs prepared in the heads and particulars of a modern sermon. . . Let the experiment be tried on some of the best specimens of ancient eloquence; let an oration of Cicero or Demosthenes be stretched upon a Procrustes' bed of this sort, and, if I am not greatly mistaken, the flame and enthusiasm which have excited admiration in all ages, will instantly evaporate; yet no one perceives the

---

[2] We use the translation in Porter's *The Young Preacher's Manual* (1829), pp. 68 ff.

want of method in these immortal compositions, nor can anything be conceived more remote from incoherent rhapsody."[3] Over half a century later Henry Ward Beecher said: "As it is, sermons are too often cast in one mold. Week after week, month after month, year after year, when the text is announced, every child in the congregation almost, as well as the minister himself, can tell that it will be divided into 'First,' 'Second,' and 'Third,' together with 'Then certain practical observations.' But what would be thought of one who should seek to enter every house upon a street or in a city with a single key, fitted to but one kind of lock? The minister is the 'strong man,' armed in a better sense than that of the parable, and it is his business to enter every house, to bind the man of sin, and to despoil him. But every door must be entered by a key that fits that door. . . The minister must seek entrance in every case, where God has put the door. In some men there is a broad and double open door, standing in the front and inviting entrance. The familiar path in other cases is seen to wind around to the side door. There be those industrious drudges who never live out of their kitchens, and if one would find them in ordinary hours, he must e'en go around to the back door. If one lives in the cellar, he must be sought through the cellar. It is this necessity of adaptation to the innumerable phases of human nature that reacts upon the sermon, and determines the form which it shall take. If it were possible, never have two plans alike. . . When you have finished your sermon, not a man of your congregation should be unable to tell you, distinctly, what you have done; but when you begin a sermon, no man in the congregation ought to be able to tell you what you are going to do. All these cast-iron frames, these stereotyped plans of sermons, are the devices of the Devil, and of those most mischievous devils of the pulpit, formality and stupidity."[4]

Summing up all the objections advanced against the disposition, we may enumerate: (1) It has no precedent in the great orations of antiquity, the preaching of the apostles and the sermons of the ancient and the early mediaeval Church. (2) It tends to excessive formalism in preaching. (3) It is unfavorable to the unity of discourse. (4) It impairs the freedom of direct appeals. (5) In argumentative sermons it gives needless prominence to weak arguments. In replying to these objections, we admit at the outset that there have been and still are sermons aplenty whose dispositions fall justly under the censure ex-

---

[3] *Works* (London, 1832), vol. i.—[4] *Yale Lectures on Preaching*, vol. i, pp. 220 ff.

pressed by Fenelon, 'Hall, Beecher, and others. Thus Caesar of Heisterbach (1180-1240), preaching on the words, *"Accepit Jesus panes, et cum gratias egisset, distribuit discumbentibus,"* discusses the fifteen different ways in which Christ and the saints are distributed on the fifteen chief festivals of the year. In the XVII century the preachers first expounded the text and then applied its truth, invariably, as exhortation, warning, recollection, consolation, etc. Or it was thought that all main divisions must have an equal number of sub-divisions which must follow an invariable schema (e. g., *respectu principii, modi, finis*) ; or that the exposition of the text must be followed by the proof of its truth, and this again by an externally connected application (comp. the familiar outline, especially popular in England and America: exordium, explication, proposition, argument, application, conclusion). Or the question is asked: What does this text teach? and given three or four answers that have no inner connection with one another. In all these and similar cases the most unsparing criticism is entirely in place. But this by no means says that all dispositions are to be rejected. Let us examine the arguments brought against them.

The first, the argument from history, is the weakest of all. With respect to the orations of classical antiquity, Porter has well said: "That the celebrated orators of old were less formal in this respect, than has been common in the modern sermon, is certain; and perhaps a sufficient reason for this appears in the object of their orations, and the character of those to whom they were addressed. But the most celebrated of these orations have method and some of them, method very distinctly expressed. Cicero, in his oration for the Manilian law, has three divisions: the nature of the Mithridatic war; the greatness of it, and the choice of a proper general. The first of these heads is discussed under four minor heads: the honor of the state; the safety of their allies; the public revenue, and the interests of private citizens. The third head, too, has four minor heads: Pompey is recommended as a consummate general, for his military skill; his courage; his authority, and his success. The same orator, in his seventh Philippic, dissuades the senate from making peace with Mark Anthony, by three heads of argument, showing the measure to be base, to be dangerous, and to be impracticable. In his oration for Muraena, the division has been allowed by some critics to be perfect. 'The whole accusation, O judges, may be reduced to three heads: one consists in objections against his life; the second relates to the dignity of his office; the third includes the corruption, with which he is charged.' His oration against Caecilius has two, and that for Publius Quinctius three general divisions. To mention no other examples, Quinctilian says, 'Divisions may be too many, but ought not, as some think, to be limited to three.' So much for an objection, drawn from antiquity, against that method in a discourse, which constituted so important a part of both theory and practice, in ancient eloquence."[5]

The reference to the preaching of the apostles is no happier. The abstracts of the sermons of Peter and Paul preserved in the New Testament reveal a careful plan; compare Peter's pentecostal sermon and Paul's address at Athens. How lucid and carefully developed is the argument in Paul's epistles, particularly Romans and Galatians, intended as they were to be read aloud in the congregational services. The unique influence of the Spirit operative in these productions did not prevent the speakers and writers from following in their presentation the laws of order. Nor is this to be wondered at, for is not God a God of order? Even in his reference to the sermons of the ancient and the early mediaeval Church, Fenelon goes too far. Most of these sermons have some sort of plan and divisions, even though they differ from the divisions as we know them today. What he says of Bernard is, to say the least, not adequate.

The other objections are no weightier. The most important of them refers to the unity of the sermon, which is said to be endangered by the disposition. If this objection were well founded, we should be obliged to give up the disposition, for the unity of the sermon must be preserved at all costs. It must be admitted that there are sermons that fall apart into as many independent discourses as they have divisions. This, however, is the fault not of the disposition as such but of a wrong method of division or of a fundamental lack of unity. The variety inherent in the unity of the theme is not properly developed or else the theme has no unity to begin with. A properly constructed disposition will develop the variety latent in the unity of the theme in such a way as to set this unity in the clearest light. So far from endangering the unity of the discourse, a right disposition will rather safeguard and promote it. The remaining objections need scarcely be noticed. For who will frame his disposition so awkwardly as to make the sermon stiff and formal? And what preacher will cling so slavishly to his disposition as to exclude a direct appeal to the hearers or the use of any new ideas that may occur to him in the inspiration of the moment? Beecher's thought, finally, that the heart of every hearer

---

[5] P. 117.

needs a different key is correct enough in itself, but it is an unwarranted conclusion from this that every sermon must have a different plan. What becomes of the other hearers, whose hearts the key chosen does not happen to fit?

We pass on to the consideration of the advantages of the disposition. "Among the advantages," says Porter, "I remark that *perspicuity* is promoted by it. The understanding is a faculty that delights in order. It contemplates with ease and pleasure things that are placed before it in the light of a just arrangement. Hence Horace properly calls such arrangement, 'lucidus ordo.' Hence again, *beauty* is promoted by order. Aside from those laws of mind, agreeably to which method facilitates our perception of relations among things; according to our principles of emotion, good taste is disgusted with confusion. A fine library, promiscuously jumbled together, without regard to connection of volumes, or distinct works, would offend the eye just in proportion to the intrinsic worth, or the elegant appearance of the several books. The same emotion of incongruity is excited by thoughts or expressions, however brilliant, which have no connection. *Brevity* is promoted by order. The poet above alluded to, says: 'This will be the excellence and beauty of method, that it will enable the writer just now to say, what now ought to be said, and to omit everything else.' He who classes his thoughts on a subject, will see what to use, and what to refuse, among the general mass of matter related to that subject. Besides, confusion of thoughts leads to repetition; and repetition leads to undue length. *Energy* is promoted by order; in two ways; the first is by concentration. The power of a discourse to impress the mind, depends not on the separate impulse of its parts, but on the combined effect of the whole. And often an argument derives all its strength from its standing in proper connection with other arguments. The united strength of five men might easily raise a weight which the separate efforts of the five would be unable to stir. The regular phalanx, disposed in order of battle, so that each individual may support the whole line, is irresistible in its onset. But the undisciplined rabble is harmless in its movements, if not contemptible."[6]

Phillips Brooks, after wavering at first, came out finally in favor of a careful disposition. He says: "In the desire to make a sermon seem free and spontaneous there is a prevalent dislike to giving it its necessary formal structure and organism. The statement of the subject, the division into heads, the recapitulation at the end, all the

---

[6]Pp. 118 ff.

scaffolding and anatomy of a sermon is out of favor, and there are many very good jests about it. I can only say that I have come to fear it less and less. The escape from it must not be negative but positive. The true way to get rid of the boniness of your sermon is not by leaving out the skeleton, but by clothing it with flesh. True liberty in writing comes by law, and the more thoroughly the outlines of your work are laid out the more freely your sermon will flow, like an unwasted stream between its well-built banks."[7]

The disposition found a specially vigorous and thorough defender in Austin Phelps. We quote the gist of his discussion. (1) "Divisions promote perspicuity of discussion. They aid a preacher in gaining perspicuity; clear mental action works instinctively by plan, and each assists the other. A preacher has a very critical work to do in attempting to bring down themes of high discourse within reach of the common mind, and to secure for them an intelligent and interested hearing. Science tells us that a drop of water contains a flash of lightning. Thus electric are the elements of the common stock of thought in pulpit discourse. Common are they as the raindrops; yet the forces of vivid conception and of intense impression are locked up in them. A preacher's work is to release and to develop those forces. To do this, we need every facility of expression which logic gives to vividness. Hence the divisions in a sermon. So far from their being a deformity, originating in the pedantry of the pulpit, they are one of the necessities to which the pulpit has been driven by the lofty nature of its subjects. How large a proportion of the common people, taken at random, could Ralph Waldo Emerson hold together by his cementless periods on Immortality? Yet the pulpit sets itself to the task of making immortality a living truth to men whose days are spent in shoe-shops and hay-fields, and to women who live over wash-tubs and cooking-stoves. The thing can not be done by the fluent and unscholarly method of the lyceum. (2) Divisions promote comprehensiveness of discussion. They assist a preacher in collecting and arranging the materials for such a discussion. Try the experiment on the materials of a half-digested sermon. Reduce such thoughts as you have to a plan. The effect will be to reveal to you at once what deficiency exists, and where it is. That is to say a deficiency, if it exists, is disclosed by classification. Is an argument missing? Is an objection unanswered? Is a fact wanting for illustration? Is one side of the subject a blank? Is an application of it impracticable, or far-

---

[7]*Lectures on Preaching* (1877), pp. 177 f.

fetched? Whatever be the gap in the fabric, classifying in a plan, in which statement shall be definite, and arrangement orderly, will discover the gap, and will set you at work to fill it. (3) Divisions promote unity of discussion. That preacher must habitually think in slipshod gait who can deliberately plan a vagrant discourse. The very effort to classify materials tends to unify them in the result. It is an excellence in divisions, that they thus stand guard over extemporaneous thinking, and shut out all that is not tributary to the result. (4) Divisions, further, promote progress in a discussion. Organization achieves in discourse that which it achieves in every thing else,—rapidity of execution. Sir Walter Scott lamented late in life that he had never habituated himself to compose his imaginative fiction by previously formed outline of materials. He advised young writers not to imitate his carelessness in that respect. He pronounced it intellectual recklessness to trust, as he did, to the excitement of composition for the evolution of his plots. That he could do it he attributed to the imaginative character of his work. (5) Divisions also promote conciseness of discussion. Skillful architects will tell you to the inch the shape and proportions of the building which shall most successfully economize space. So, in a sermon, good divisions help to compact structure. A perfect sermonizer will trust largely to them for crowding the greatest bulk of thought into the shortest time. (6) Divisions promote elegance of discussion. But are not divisions formal, hard, angular? I answer, Is there no beauty in a plan of thought, in logical order, in fitness, in proportion? Is transparency never beautiful? Are not the angles of a star beautiful? The truth is that there may be very great beauty in an outline of a sermon. Clearness of statement, finish of form, orderly succession, unity of aim, completeness as a whole, and growth in construction are all elements of graceful discourse. By having framed one such division, a preacher is unconsciously quickened. The hearer, too, feels the magnetism of it, though unconscious of its origin. (7) Divisions may be made to assist a preacher in meeting without loss of power the popular demand for brevity. This demand is a threatening evil. Audiences will not tolerate the old measurement of length of sermons. Preachers can not control the public taste. We have only to accept it, [?] and to make the best of it. How to do this is a very intricate problem. We can not do it by brevity of speech alone. Much as the popular mind craves brevity, it will not now, any more than it would a century ago, tolerate preaching which has no solid thought. The task of the preacher therefore, is to compress into the smallest possible amount of time in the delivery the greatest possible amount of solid yet interesting matter. To achieve this, well framed divisions are indispensable. With such divisions to emphasize the imperial points of a discourse, you can pack into it vastly more material than can by any ingenuity be put it into the same length of slipshod harangue. Take some of President Finney's sermons, for example. Although he carries division to an extreme, yet his sermons show illustriously the power of solid thought, when sharply stated, arranged in rigorous logical order, and enforced by a profound evangelical spirit. (8) Divisions promote interest in a discussion. The enthusiasm of the preacher is most vigorously sustained by a clear, unified, elegant, progressive plan of thought before him as a model. Observe the rhetorical structure which Coleridge has given to the essay which he has entitled 'The Friend.' He introduces several *excursus* from the main subject, which he terms 'landing-places.' They are chiefly a rhetorical device for relieving the tedium of prolonged and abstract discussion. John Locke would have sought the same effect by means of chapters and sections. Sermons find the same relief in the expedient of divisions. (9) Divisions promote permanence of impression. We may safely say, that, other things being equal, that is the best sermon which furnishes the most effective means of holding it in the memory. The most effective of such means commonly are the text, the proposition, and the divisions. These are the parts of a sermon which usually have the longest life. A preacher, above all other public speakers, aims at lasting impressions. He needs, therefore, as many expedients as are natural, to make truth penetrate the memory."[8]

This is assented to by T. H. Pattison, who devotes, in his fine book, *The Making of the Sermon,* an admirable section to the divisions of the sermon.[9] For his own part, he emphasizes the effect that a good division will have upon the easy, assured and well-balanced delivery of the sermon. He shows also how it will keep the preacher from committing the rhetorical blunder of writing an essay and calling it a sermon. He compares the preacher with the painter,—
" 'A painter,' says Mulready, who was himself an artist, 'cannot take a step without anatomy. The greatest masters of figure painting, such as Michael Angelo and Leonardo da Vinci, studied anatomy as diligently as though they had intended to become surgeons. Their figures were first drawn in the nude and then draped.' And so a sermon must be built up, the skeleton first, then flesh and the cloth-

---

[8] *The Theory of Preaching* (1881), pp. 365-376. [9] Pp. 155-174.

ing." Pattison also recalls this word of Archbishop Paley, who he says had no superior in the art of writing clear English: "A discourse which rejects the help of divisions to perspicuity will turn out a bewildered rhapsody, without aim or effect, order or conclusion." To which Pattison adds: "A sermon which fails under analysis cannot be a good sermon. By something akin to that providence, which is said to watch over intemperate persons and children, it may do good, but in itself it is not good."

Is it necessary to call any further witnesses for the value of the disposition? There are still Herrick Johnson, David James Burrell, C. Silvester Horne, Charles Louis Slattery, S. Parkes Cadman, Alfred Ernest Garvie and others. Just a word from each of them. Johnson: "With a subject and an object distinctly determined, the question that now faces the preacher is: How am I to treat this subject so as to accomplish this object? This means *plan*—plan of some kind—that shall work everything up into one compact organism, that shall set the parts together in climacteric order, that shall present a natural and orderly succession, exclude irrelevant material, and make the different lines of the discourse grow hot as they converge to one burning focus —this is without doubt essential to the most effective sermonizing. Just in proportion as the plan of treatment is clear, comprehensive and cumulative, will the sermon be impressive, and adapted to its end."[10] Burrell: "The preacher, as an architect, having informed himself as to the sort of structure required, proceeds, in the order of logical sequence, to construct the framework. This is as necessary to success in preaching as a lawyer's brief is to the effective presentation of his case."[11] Horne, speaking of the form of modern preaching: "In the first place I put in a plea for the careful arrangement of your material. It was my good fortune in my early ministry to have for a friend a very wise and acute deacon, who had been for a long lifetime an influential journalist. On one occasion our pulpit had been occupied by a stranger; and I tried to find out what impression had been produced upon my friend's mind by the sermon. He said: 'The sermon reminded me of the reply of a well-known dilettantist to a lady who asked him how she should arrange the furniture in her room. He said, "Don't arrange it at all; let it occur." I have seldom heard a more admirable criticism of a type of sermon which is by no means uncommon. All the things that are in it 'occur'; they are not there by virtue of any principle of arrangement; and what may have a pleas-

---

[10]P. 320. [11]P. 53.

ing effect in a drawing-room has a very confusing and tiresome effect in a sermon. I do not animadvert here on those gentry whose habit it is to select three anecdotes and a quotation from Browning, and then proceed to string them loosely together; and having fastened the ungainly resultant to some tag of Scripture, hasten to chastise therewith some defenseless and long-suffering congregation. You will, I should hope, in your student days be accumulating great stores of material drawn from your general reading. You will, as a matter of course, keep an every-day book, into which you will transcribe all such passages as seem to you specially striking and quotable. You will resist as a temptation of the Evil One—as I am convinced it is—the impulse to drag in hackneyed quotations and threadbare anecdotes simply as padding, or as rotten pegs on which to hang a string of platitudes. Illustrations which do not illustrate savour of the inconsequence which used to be the traditional privilege of the Sunday School address. As to the arrangement of your material, I personally believe, and strongly believe, in the practical utility of the old-fashioned habit of divisions."[12] Slattery: "The sermon of today must have sharp divisions."[13] Cadman: "You must articulate the bones in the body of your sermon, or its adverse fate is sealed. . . . The preacher who fully develops his outline and also clothes it skilfully should be your model."[14] Garvie: "As far as the writer has been able to gather from his intercourse with hearers, there is a general preference for a knowledge both of subject and divisions, as the pew likes to be taken into confidence by the pulpit, and not to be mystified by it; and further, there is no general objection to having the heads of the sermon distinctly indicated even in the formal *firstly, secondly, lastly,* and in as easily remembered words or phrases as possible."[15]

In our own opinion a careful division is demanded, more than by all else, by the nature and by the purpose of the sermon. According to its nature the sermon is the presentation of the Word of God contained in a text. Every text contains not only a main thought, pervading it as its unity, but also various subordinate thoughts or parts, which serve to develop the main thought. Even in very short texts these parts are contained at least implicitly. The sermon must be arranged in exactly the same manner, if it is to be a faithful presentation of the text. But the sermon has also a purpose; it is not

---

[12]*The Ministry of the Modern Church* (1907), pp. 144 f.—[13]*Present-Day Preaching* (1912), pp. 21-26.—[14]*Ambassadors of God* (1920), pp. 286 f.—[15]*The Christian Preacher* (1921), p. 424.

a pleasant means of passing the time, but seeks to accomplish something. This it can best do, humanly speaking, when it addresses itself, in a carefully arranged psychological and logical structure, to the spiritual faculties of its hearers and proceeds step by step to aim one truth after another at intellect, emotion and will in order to convince, to terrify or comfort, and to move to action.[16]

(2) Distinct from the question whether the sermon is to have a disposition, is the question whether the disposition is to be formally announced, either as a whole in connection with the theme or in its parts at the beginning of each division. Pattison gives the following answer to the latter question: "Should the divisions be made apparent throughout the sermon? Certainly they should. If you are treating your subject logically and progressively, it is surely right that any intelligent hearer should be told just where he is." And to the former: "Should the divisions be announced? Why not? The custom has the authority of long usage." Nevertheless, the matter is not so simple as that and the custom has been frequently challenged. Fenelon was one of its most energetic opponents. In his second dialogue he wrote: "Order is necessary, but not an order promised and discovered from the beginning of the discourse. Cicero tells us that

---

[16]Comp. with this what Fenelon says in his second dialogue about the structure of the sermon: "We ought at first to give a general view of our subject and endeavor to gain the favor of the audience by a modest introduction, a respectful address, and the genuine marks of candor and probity. Then we should establish those principles on which we design to argue; and in a clear, easy, sensible manner, propose the principal facts, of which we intend to make use afterwards. From these principles and facts we must draw just consequences; and argue in such a clear and well connected manner, that all our proofs may support each other, and so be the more remembered. Every step we advance, our discourse ought to grow stronger; so that the hearers may gradually perceive the force and evidence of the truth; and then we ought to display it in such lively images and movements as are proper to excite the passions. In order to this we must know their various springs, and the mutual dependence they have one upon another; which of them we can most easily move, and employ to raise the rest; and which of them in fine is able to produce the greatest effects, and must, therefore, be applied in the conclusion of our discourse. It is ofttimes proper, at the close, to make a short recapitulation, in which the orator ought to exert all his force and skill in giving the audience a full, clear, concise view of the chief topics he has enlarged on." (*The Preacher's Manual*, p. 70.) One wonders how such a structure can prevent and exclude the division of the sermon into distinct parts, as Fenelon holds.

the best method is generally to conceal the order we follow, till we lead the hearer to it without his being aware of it before. I remember, he says in express terms, that we ought to conceal even the number of our arguments, so that one shall not be able to count them though they be very distinct in themselves, and that we ought not plainly to point out the divisions of the discourse. But such is the undistinguishing taste of these latter ages, that an audience cannot perceive any order unless the speaker distinctly explain it at the beginning." Fenelon's reference to Cicero and other ancient rhetoricians was shown to be erroneous by Vinet, himself no ardent defender of the announced theme. Cicero says also the following: "In speaking the partition, rightly presented, makes the whole discourse luminous and clear. Its effect is, to enable the hearer, by keeping certain things in mind, to understand from what has been said that which remains to be said."[17] The counsel of Cicero mentioned by Fenelon should, therefore, be understood in its specific context and not be taken as a general rule. So, too, Quintilian would have the disposition concealed in an address before a judge, in order to take him by surprise. "The judge," he writes, "is sometimes to be led into pleasing deceptions, and amused by a variety of stratagems, to keep him from discovering our designs."[18] But he regards this as an exception from the rule; for he says further: "The partition, opportunely adopted, gives great light and beauty to a discourse. This it effects not only by adding more perspicuity to what is said, things by it being drawn out of their confusion, and placed conspicuous before the judges; but also by recreating the auditory by a view of each part circumscribed within its bounds; just so mile-stones ease in some measure the fatigue of travelers, it being a pleasure to know the extent of the labor they have undergone; and to know what remains encourages them to persevere, as nothing can seem necessarily long, when there is a certainty of coming to the end." The rare occurrence of divisions in the ancient orations that have come down to us is accounted for by Theremin as follows: "If we do not find this practice observed in the orations of the ancients, this may proceed from two reasons: First, the method to which they were obliged to accommodate themselves, was prescribed to them by the occasion on which they spoke, far more than is the case with the sacred orator; and since this method, especially in the instance of the orator before a court, was almost always one and the same it seemed unnecessary

---

[17]*De inventione*, lib. i, cap. 22.—[18]Lib. iv, cap. 5.

to announce it formally. Secondly, and this appears to me to be the chief reason, such a formal statement of the plan would have been evidence of study and previous preparation, the appearance of which they avoided as carefully as they sought to maintain that of extemporizing. For they had to deal with a suspicious public, who would have attributed such previous preparation only to the design to deceive."[19] To show that this is no argument either for or against the announcement of divisions in the sermon of today, Theremin continues: "But the case is different with the sacred orator, who may allow the diligence he has bestowed with an honest intention, to appear continually in his oration, since he can excite thereby in the hearer nothing but the expectation of a mass of information all the more fundamental for this." And before this he had said: "At the end of the introduction the orator may announce the two or three parts which contain the development proper; for why should he not carefully employ this, as well as every other opportunity, to aid the hearer's attention, and to facilitate his comprehension of the whole? If the hearer is compelled to stretch his power of attention too much, he either slackens it altogether, or else the effect of the orator is exerted on the cognitive powers alone, and not on the will, which for the orator's purposes, is tantamount to no effect at all." Nevertheless, he does not consider an announcement of divisions absolutely necessary, for he says in conclusion: "If, however, the sacred orator would, for any reason, omit the formal mention of the grounds of his oration, of the plan which he has sketched for himself, he is free to do so; for though, indeed, it is absolutely necessary that he endeavor to arrange his thoughts in the clearest and best manner, it is not absolutely necessary that he specify beforehand how he has arranged them."

Despite the opposition of Fenelon and Hall, and the lukewarm defence of Vinet, practically all French, German, Scandinavian, English and American preachers, and since 1850 the great majority of them, adhered to the announced disposition. The homileticians mentioned above as advocates of the necessity of the disposition favor also its announcement. Porter emphatically advocates it, because the sermon must take its cue not from the small number of cultured hearers who may not need this aid, but from the majority of its hearers who cannot do without it. He desires not only a single announcement, but a frequent repetition of the heads or divisions, for in this way alone they will be stamped on the memory and the sermon

---

[10]*Die Beredsamkeit eine Tugend* (Shedd's transl., pp. 60-61).

as a whole will be assured of its effect. "The reason," he says, "why familiar things are not forgotten is, that frequent recurrence stamps impression. . . . The importance of obvious method in a sermon is so unquestionable, that to affirm it is only saying in other words that the sermon of which the hearer remembers nothing is useless."[20] Phillips Brooks agrees with this and says: "I think that most congregations welcome, and are not offended by clear, precise statements of the course which a sermon is going to pursue, carefully marked division of its thoughts, and above all, full recapitulation of its argument at the close. A sermon is not like a picture which, once painted, stands altogether before the eye. Its parts elude the memory, and it is good before you close to gather all the parts together, and as briefly as you can set them as one completed whole before your hearer's mind. Leave to the ordinary Sunday-school address its unquestioned privilege of inconsequence and incoherence. But give your sermon an orderly consistent progress and do not hesitate to let your hearers see it distinctly, for it will help them first to understand and then to remember what you say."[21] A. Phelps discusses this subject, too, at length. What he says may be reduced to three fundamental considerations: a clearly stated division prepares the mind to follow the development of the sermon, holds the interest and attention of the hearers, and fixes the sermon in their memory. The fact that the hearer "must depend on the momentary perceptions of the ear, that he has no chance for review, for delay, for growth of thought, renders him specially dependent upon the facilities which logic suggests for an understanding of oral discourse. The whole argument for the statement of propositions bears with nearly equal force upon the necessity of stating divisions also." . . . Obvious divisions assist the hearer "in perceiving progress of discussion. Few things are so essential to impressive discourse as the sense of progress. Hearers crave the consciousness of achievement. Have you never listened to sermons in which this sense of achievement was so feeble, that hearing was labor? Very earnest and animated preachers may produce this effect. They remind you of a top at the height of its invisible revolutions, so tremendously busy are they spinning on their own axis; but you do not seem to get on with them. Why do hills, valleys, rivers, ravines, mile-stones, guide-boards make a traveler sensible of progress? Anything which diversifies the monotony of scenery creates the sense of advance." The use of firstlys and secondlys is said to have originated

[20]P. 121.   [21]P. 178.

in the Roman forum, where the speaker, from his position on the rostrum, emphasized the successive steps of his argument by pointing to the surrounding shops or *tabernae*, one by one, until he had completed the circuit. Thus the hearers' sense of progress was assisted...
"Even that class of hearers who are beguiled by false tastes and affectations can always be reined up to healthy thinking by a compact, racy statement of an elemental truth, like those which divisions should express. Plain sense pithily uttered will catch and hold a wandering mind. No sane man ever clears himself wholly from common sense. Let that speak in concentrated thought, and thought will spring to answer thought. On the contrary, that style of discourse which needs no divisions is not weighty enough to produce in the hearer any interest which demands relief... Why is it that the incidents often seem to make more impression than the doctrine of a sermon? An illustration, an anecdote, a pictorial passage, an antithetic sentence will be remembered and commented upon, when the drift of thought to which they were tributary will not seem to have been understood. The reason often is that the drift of thought has not been made palpable by land-marks. If you have ever read Carlyle's *History of the French Revolution*, you were doubtless sensible of the fact that it is unfit for a beginner in the study of French history. Familiarity with other histories of the same period is necessary to an understanding of Carlyle. Unity of aim exists in his work. Trained readers can perceive that unity. But to other readers it is a chaos of inconsequent remarks from which they get nothing but here and there a thought, a metaphor, an invective, which stands alone in a wilderness of incoherence. History to such readers the work is not. Very similar are those sermons which require trained thinkers to perceive the drift of them underlying their incidents."[22] 'H. C. Graves of Boston wrote in 1906: "Divisions in discourse are often hidden, hardly seen in the written sermon, rarely noticed in the preaching. This was the rhetorical habit of many noted preachers fifty years ago.[23] Masterly as many of their sermons are, they yet fail to fasten

---

[22] Pp. 365-377.—Comp. T. H. Pattison: "I commend to every preacher a little bit of noble English in which John Bright contrasts his oratory with that of W. E. Gladstone. 'Gladstone goes coasting along turning up every creek and exploring it to its source before he can proceed on his way; but I have no talent for detail. I hold my course from headland to headland through the great seas.' Divisions are the headlands by which the speaker holds his course through the great seas of thought." (P. 160.)—[23]See, e. g., the sermons of Bishop F. D. Huntington and Richard S. Storrs.

themselves on the minds of the hearers or readers because of this effort at concealment of the plan."[24] Slattery of New York, who emphasizes the modern requirements of the sermon, writes: "The sermon of today must have sharp divisions. If our age is restless, and so finds it hard to be attentive to careful sermons, it is essential that they be interesting. Nothing is more interesting than growth. The growth in a sermon must be so obvious to the listener that he can see the stages of growth. These stages of growth are the divisions of the sermon. The counsel to conceal the skeleton has often led to sermons, for which the owners would maintain that there were skeletons, but concerning which it would be rash to say which part held the skull and which the ankle-bones. The so-called skeleton is lost in the shapeless soft stuff which is thrown over it. It is wise now, I am sure, to say that skeletons ought to be in sermons and they ought to show. A gaunt and bony man is almost always attractive. The Bishop of London, though, perhaps, not a great preacher, is certainly an effective preacher, and the principal element in his effectiveness, after his striking personality, is the precision with which he marks the divisions of his sermons. You go away aware that he has made, let us say, four 'points'—and you know what they are. The master of blunt divisions, so far as we can tell from his sermons, as we now have them, was Frederick Robertson. He told at the start exactly by what stages he intended to mount to the climax of his subject. I suppose that there is no question that Robertson is read more today than the more recent and perhaps greater Brooks. Brooks always said vital and illuminating paragraphs all through his sermons; but there was not the angular structure of Robertson's sermons, which tells of strength and growth. The sermons that people will read are some indication of what sort of sermons will help people in our day. Beauty and smoothness are less helpful than the plain climbing, step by step, to a rounded answer. The amorphous thing called a sermon without divisions may arouse a certain flutter of passing emotion, as a bell that has been ringing for twenty minutes; but it is not likely to leave any important lesson behind. In planning a sermon, therefore, the preacher today *will dare to run the risk of allowing his divisions to be even ludicrously evident.* It is possible to be both elegant and clear; but if a union of clearness and elegance is beyond the preacher's art, he must ruthlessly sacrifice the elegance. The people must see the

---

[24] *Lectures on Homiletics*, p. 91.

divisions by which they are advancing to the best truth the preacher can give them.[25]

The chief reason why we plead for a clearly announced disposition is because it assists the sermon to attain its purpose and produce its designed effect. On this everything depends. Whatever contributes to this, we are bound to use. Sermons that aim merely to please, entertain or startle, or to influence their hearers only for the moment, may dispense with a definitely stated plan. But the real purpose of the sermon is permanently to enrich the understanding, to move the emotions, and to turn and propel the will toward God and all good things. And this purpose can best be served by a definitely announced plan or disposition. "The smooth ground-swell of discourse," says Phelps, "so often chosen in the pulpit by men who affect a literary style would find no favor among the leaders of the English or American bar." Why is this? Simply because they have a point to carry with the twelve plain men in the jury box, and are most mightily concerned with carrying their point. They are not above saying, "first," "secondly," "thirdly;" after they have clinched one point in the minds of the jurymen, they say, "I have now finished this part of my argument;" "I have now proved this or that;" they are not afraid to go on, "And now let me ask your attention to another point;" frequently they even enumerate, after a brief introduction, the various points which they intend to discuss. "Lyman Beecher used to tell an audience, in his uncouth way, at the close of a division which was vital to his argument, exactly what he wished them to remember. 'Hold that fast,' he would say; 'Nail that thought down;' 'Don't let this slip away;' 'Put a peg in there.' "[26] And the strange thing is, that men like Robert Hall and James Alexander, who were opposed in theory to divisions and their announcement,[27] often forgot their theory when they came to preach, and both divided their sermons and announced their divisions. This can be explained, since they were men of character not swayed by custom, only by the fact that practical considerations proved stronger than theoretical demands.

We conclude with Phelps: "The necessity of divisions and announcing them has been again and again, in certain intervals, underrated. The present drift of clerical taste underrates it. Secular literature ignores it. Wit, which has no claim either to piety or to

---

[25] *Present-Day Preaching* (1912), pp. 21 ff.—[26]Phelps, p. 376.—
[27] Alexander in his *Thoughts on Preaching,* at many places.

literature, makes a butt of it. Many preachers, therefore, are inclined to surrender it as an antiquated fixture of the pulpit, which should go with the sounding-board. Yet one thing is noticeable: that the depreciation of the use of divisions accompanies the depreciation of elaborate preaching. The less esteem a preacher has for them, the less he feels for the preaching which needs them. Argumentative sermons, doctrinal sermons, intellectual sermons are generally decried in the same breath which pronounces against divisions. Talks, exhortations, pious remarks take the place of sermons in the practice of such critics." And with Pattison: "The disposition to make everything subordinate to rhetoric will perhaps tempt you to resent a distinct and clearly announced partition of your subject. The temptation to indolence and insufficient preparation will possibly beguile you into making a talk and mistaking it—if your foolish mind be sufficiently darkened—for a sermon. But the sermon is no more a display of rhetorical skill than it is a string of disconnected platitudes. In contrast with these, it should be a careful and intelligent exposition and enforcement of the passage which you have chosen for your text." In proportion as the nature and purpose of the sermon are kept in mind, the necessity of the disposition and the importance of its announcement will need no defence. It is true, where the pulpit is occupied by a genius and the pews by an audience every member of which is a person of exceptional culture, both disposition and announcement may be dispensed with. But everyone knows how rarely this fortunate combination occurs. Likewise, in sermons on historical texts there is less need definitely to announce the divisions.

That sub-divisions should not be previously announced, need scarcely be said. That the formulation of each main division should be consistent with that of all the rest, will be equally self-evident for everyone with a sense for harmony. There follow a number of examples of the disposition.

Klaus Harms on 2 Cor. 11:3-4: The praise of simplicity; (1) It does not doubt when it may believe, (2) it does not hesitate when it should act, (3) it does not murmur when it must suffer, (4) it does not boast when it dare rejoice. Bezzel on Matt. 8:23-27: The miraculous presence of Jesus; (1) It leads us into storms, (2) it comforts us in the storm, (3) it calms every storm. The same on Luke 21:25-36: What is the Christian's attitude to the second coming of his Lord? (1) He waits for it, (2) he prays for it, (3) he prepares for it. The same on Mark 7:31-37: Jesus does all things well; (1) He lets the sorrowing come to Him, (2) He takes them aside from the multitude,

(3) He sends them forth in peace. Hauck on 2 Cor. 7:6-10: There is a godly sorrow; (1) What causes it, (2) in what it consists, (3) to what it leads, (4) what is its final end. Thomasius on Rom. 8:18-23: Who may rejoice in the glorious liberty of the children of God? (1) He that sympathizes with the present vanity and expectation of creation, (2) he that has experienced sin and death in his own nature, (3) he that has the first fruits of the Spirit and has become a child of God. Uhlhorn on Acts 10:34-41: Christ's resurrection, the seal of redemption; it assures us, (1) that He who was slain and hanged on a tree died for our salvation; (2) that in Him peace was made 'twixt man and God; (3) that this salvation is present in Him for all men. Robertson on Col. 2:16-17: The shadow and substance of the Sabbath; (1) The transient shadow of the Sabbath which has passed away, (2) the permanent substance which can not pass. Alexander Maclaren on Matt. 6:24-34: Anxious Care; (1) Anxious care is contrary to all the lessons of nature, which show it to be unnecessary; (2) contrary to all the lessons of revelation, which show it to be heathenish; (3) contrary to the whole scheme of Providence, which shows it to be futile.

It is not possible—and if it were possible it would be unwise—to lay down rules as to how the main divisions should be subdivided. Such rules would render the sermon stiff and mechanical, and crush all individuality and life both in the preacher and in his treatment of the text. All that can be said is that the divisions in their totality should so develop the theme and consequently the main thought of the text as to do full justice to the principles governing the exposition and application of texts. They should clearly present the situation portrayed in the text and exhibit its specific message. From this should be deduced truths universally valid. These universal truths should then be brought home to the individual congregation. Starting from the individual, the divisions of the sermon should pass to the general, in order to return to the individual. That is not to say that every division must invariably follow this threefold movement. It may often be done. I may, for instance, treat in each main division (a) the elements in the text that belong under that head, (b) deduce from them a general truth, (c) apply this specifically to my congregation. But this need not be the invariable method. Instead of serving as subdivisions, these three lines of thought may on occasion furnish the main divisions of the sermon. There are, in short, so many possibilities that it is unnecessary and undesirable to lay down rules governing the inner structure of the divisions. The study of well built sermons will bring us a great deal farther. Under "Practical Illustrations" we append, therefore, several fully worked out dispositions showing both main and subdivisions.[28]

---

[28]See below, pp. 605 ff.

§ 18. THE INTRODUCTION AND THE CONCLUSION

G. Menken, *Das elfte Kapitel des Briefes an die Hebraeer in Homilien ausgelegt*, 1821; cf. G. Menken, *Schriften;* vollstaendige Ausgabe, 1858 ff. Chr. Palmer, *Evangelische Homiletik*, 1842. A. Vinet, *Homiletics*, 1853. W. Taylor, *The Model Preacher*, 1859. J. A. Broadus, *A Treatise on the Preparation and Delivery of Sermons*, 1870. A. Phelps, *The Theory of Preaching*, 1881. J. M. Hoppin, *Homiletics*, 1883. T. H. Pattison, *The Making of the Sermon*, 1898. H. Hering, *Die Lehre von der Predigt*, 1905. P. Kleinert, *Homiletik*, 1907. Breed, *Preparing to Preach*, 1910.

"It belongs to the nature of discourse, especially of homiletical discourse, which is so nearly akin to the fraternal or pastoral address, not to burst abruptly on the hearer, but to introduce itself, and to familiarize him with the subject which is to be presented."[1] Hence the sermon must have an introduction, whose function it is to prepare the hearer for the subject as formulated in the theme. The make-up of the audience will determine whether this preparation will have to pursue a single or a double purpose. When the audience forms a homogeneous group, with understanding and interest for the truth to be presented, who have been prepared for the sermon by the preceding parts of the service and sit, in the spirit of Mary, at Jesus' feet to hear His Word, the introduction needs simply to form the transition from the reading of the text to the announcement of the theme. It may treat of the context and its bearing upon the text, the reasons why the text demands a certain theme, or the appropriateness of text and theme to the season of the Church year. If the theme presents a very familiar and frequently treated sub-

---

[1] Kleinert, p. 178.

ject, the introduction may show that the subject is one of those fundamental truths to which the soul needs to return again and again, as the body needs to be fed with daily bread; or it may show that it is always possible to discover new aspects and relations in old familiar truths. This will be necessary in order to forestall the idea that what is coming has been heard often before and does not call for special attention.

But more frequently the audience lacks this understanding, interest, inner preparation and readiness to submit to the truth to be presented. Or it does not form a homogeneous group, but includes persons only remotely connected or altogether unconnected with the congregation and consequently without any inner relation to the subject of the sermon. In such cases the introduction must pursue a double purpose. It must first of all arouse the hearer's interest, put him in a position to understand the truth and awaken a willingness to subject himself to it; it must prepare the soul for the reception of the truth and with it of the Holy Spirit. It must strive to perform the threefold function which Quintilian assigned to it,—*reddere auditores benevolos, attentos, dociles.*[2] With this the introduction must combine a second purpose; it must form, here as with the former group, the transition from the text to the theme. Frequently, however, this second purpose will hardly be distinguished from the first, the transition from text to theme being made in the course of the awakening of the hearer's interest, or disposed of in a single sentence at its close.

---

[2] "The reason for an exordium can be no other than to dispose the auditory to be favorable to us in the other parts of the discourse. This, as most authors agree, is accomplished by making them benevolent (*benevolos*), attentive and docile. Not but that a due regard should be paid to these three particulars during the whole of the action, but in the exordium they are of singular moment, as by it we so far gain an ascendancy over the mind of the judge as to be able to proceed farther."—Lib. iv, cap. 1.

The source of the contents of the introduction may be the text, the theme, the churchly season, or any department of human life or experience. The *text* is used, when we show its value for the Christian life in its relation to problems and phenomena of the present day, or when we refer to the historical situation in which it was written, or to the importance of the biblical book of which it forms a part. The presentation of its immediate context will be in order only when one is preaching before the former of the above-mentioned classes of hearers, for whom the individual text is sacred as a part of Holy Scripture and who are consequently interested in its connection with other parts of Scripture. Before the second class of hearers such a presentation will bore, rather than create interest; in any case it will accomplish no positive good. It will be better to take one's point of departure, if possible, in some striking or provocative word or phrase in the text.

The *theme* is used as source of the introduction, when we present its importance for Christian thought and life, illustrate its truth from sacred or profane history, or refute misconceptions or errors that might hinder its effect. The *churchly season* may be used as source for the introduction, provided the hearers have some knowledge of the Church year and provided the text actually fits into the season. In a heterogeneous audience one cannot presuppose a knowledge of sacred seasons except the chief festivals (Christmas and Easter; even Pentecost is little known), and here only in their most general bearing. The preacher's personal *life* and *experience* may be drawn on, when they actually contain eminent and universally valid elements. The preacher, however, who has had no striking experience, and whose modesty and humility forbid his parading his personal life before others, will make only a very sparing use of this source of materials. Happenings in the life of the Church and nation and in the life of the congregation are better adapted as points

General Rules for the Introduction

of departure for the introduction, as are also familiar sayings and proverbs, quotations from literature well known to preacher *and congregation,* or widely read and discussed books. Nothing human, indeed, need be foreign to the introduction, provided only that it is calculated to awaken interest, understanding and sympathy, and is in keeping with the sanctuary and with the edifying purpose of the sermon.

Of general rules governing the introduction, the following may be mentioned. Do not begin too far afield. Let your introduction contain few and only important thoughts; if possible, only one. Let it have an aim and make straight for it. It should prepare for the theme, not for any one of its divisions, not even the first. Do not pitch the introduction too high; keep something in reserve. (This applies to contents, form and voice!) Do not let the introduction become an end in itself, but keep it a means to an end. Make it attractive and winsome. Work it out with the greatest care. Do not forget that, as elsewhere so in public discourse, the first impression is often the decisive one. Augustine said: *Bona domus ex ipso vestibulo agnoscitur.* As to its extent, no fixed rule can be given. Sometimes it may be exceedingly brief; it would then be a crime to waste words. Where specific hindrances exist to the intelligent and willing reception of the subject, it must necessarily be longer. Even in such cases it should not exceed one eighth of the entire discourse. Though its actual contents can be determined only after theme and structure of the sermon have been decided on, it should be written in the same order in which it is to be delivered, that is, before the body of the sermon. Its delivery should follow immediately on the reading of the text (P. 502).

Does the sermon need an introduction? Hering argues: "In view of its character as testimony, the sermon must be free to begin at once by setting forth its contents; and in view of its dependence on a portion of Scripture, it must be equally free to present and develop the text without any intermediary thoughts. As a matter of fact, those preachers who were predominantly expounders of Scripture—such as Chrysostom and Augustine in the ancient Church, Luther and Calvin in the Reformation period, and Menken in modern times—often dispensed with the introduction. Usually those older preachers opened their sermons with a simple and sober reference, couched in certain formulas, to the Scripture lesson or the text. More recent preachers indicate by way of introduction, in a less unobjectionable manner, the thought round which their discussion of the text is to turn. That it is possible in this way to achieve a great and almost heroic witness-bearing exordium, is proved by the wonderful introduction to Menken's homily on Heb. 11."[3] But Hering not only admits that even this type of sermon permits an introduction—of which there are plenty of illustrations in Menken—but he also says in conclusion: "In a sermon with theme and divisions the absense of an introduction would be felt as a defect." The secular orations, ancient and modern, set out with some sort of introduction. Cicero and especially Quintilian laid down detailed rules for its construction. The Christian preachers of the ancient period employed it, unless their sermons were merely expository homilies. The scholastics were by no means the first to introduce it; they simply formalized and overburdened it. Vinet shows that even nature teaches us the art of preparation and gradation. In this he goes back to Cicero, who wrote in his *De oratore,* lib. ii, cap. 78: "There is no cause in the compass of nature which pours itself into effect all at once, and suddenly vanishes; in like manner, nature has disguised under gentle beginnings the progress of more violent commotions." Vinet also shows that even in accidental conversation no one begins *ex abrupto,* if he is free to do otherwise. But the chief reason lies for him in reverence for the subject to be discussed, and especially in the need of the hearer, in other words, in the intention of the speaker to win his hearer's interest in the subject.

When we adopt from the older rhetoric not only the *attentos et dociles reddere,* as the purpose of the introduction, but also the *benevolos reddere,* the latter is not to be understood in the sense of an empty *captatio benevolentiae,* often verging on the insincere and untruthful, but in the sense of winning the hearer's favor and good will toward one's subject, and this by such means only as are appropriate to the

---

[3] P. 541.

sanctuary in which the sermon is delivered and to the sacred office of preaching.[4]

William Taylor realized both the necessity and the difficulty of awakening the interest of one's hearers. In his *The Model Preacher* he devotes eighty pages to this subject. He begins by saying: "To preach the Gospel effectively, you must first arrest the attention of your hearers. The mind of every man, woman, or child you meet in the country or city is preoccupied, either revolving some theme, or, more likely, indulging a reverie. The same is true, also, of every person who comes to hear you preach. Every memory and imagination constitute the scene of a vast panoramic display of images and associations as wide as the world. If, like the prophet Ezekiel in the ancient temple of Israel, you could 'dig a hole through the wall,' and look into the secret chambers of the souls of your hearers, you would see, right there in the Lord's house, farms and farming implements, horses, dogs, and cattle; lumber yards and merchandise of every kind; railroads and canals; bank stocks, commercial contracts, deeds and bonds; houses of every kind of architecture, household furniture, and instruments of music; an association of old friends and new ones, engaged in public discussions and private confabs on all the exciting subjects of the times. In many minds you would see a train of gloomy associations—mistakes, forgets, mishaps, and wrongs unredressed. All these images, and a thousand more, preoccupy the minds of your hearers, and hold their preoccupancy, passing in and out in almost endless succession and variety. Now, sir, it avails nothing for you to arise before such an assembly and say, 'Please to give me your attention.' They can't do it. Not one in a thousand has sufficient mental discipline to give you undivided attention, till you arrest it by some power stronger than the sparkling reverie tide which bears him along so gently, as scarcely to awake his consciousness of the fact. Even high intellectual development and piety on the part of your hearers do not enable them to give you their attention unless you arrest it." He calls the power of sudden surprises the peculiar *lever* power of the orator. "A sudden surprise will always excite feeling—emotion pleasant or sorrowful, varying in degree and kind according to the nature of the surprise itself. The sudden flutter of a bird, the bound of the hare, the cracking of a falling limb in the

---

[4] When Paul began his speech on Mars Hill,—"Ye men of Athens, in all things I perceive that ye are very religious" (Acts 17:22), what was it but an attempt to render his hearers *benevolos?*

grove, the scream of a child in the wild-wood, anything, however insignificant in itself, producing a sudden surprise, must, in the same degree, excite feeling and arrest attention. The surprise power of sudden transition of the thought from the point anticipated by the hearer, to another point remote but apposite, is a lever by which the masses are often moved." Taylor realizes the abuse his rule may be put to, and adds, therefore, a whole chapter on "Surprises appropriate to the pulpit." As inappropriate he designates: (1) "All eccentric oddities in words or gestures not called for by the subject nor suited to the occasion; (2) all such oddities as are of a doubtful moral propriety, or likely to have a demoralizing effect; (3) I would set the contraband seal on whatever is silly or irrelevant; (4) all strategemical performances involving deception; (5) extravagant flights of fancy, and chimerical surprises; (6) all attempts at soaring above our capacity, 'grasping at the stars and sticking in the mud;' (7) 'flowery preaching' (pretty sayings, and fanciful figures, which represent no specific truths, and illustrate nothing but the want of ideas. . . they may tickle the ear, they are quite too light and ethereal to wake up the soul, having about the same effect on the conscience of a sinner as birdshot on the hide of a rhinoceros. Nearly akin to this, I will add, there is a highly-rhetorical style of preaching which arrests attention and excites admiration, but is too elaborate and abstract to impress the memory, and produce much lasting good)." The truly appropriate surprise power of the pulpit he finds in the divine truth itself, especially as expressed in striking passages of Scripture, and in the imitation of Jesus' use of parables and stories to arrest the wandering mind and turn it in a new direction.

Hoppin mentions as marks of a good introduction: simplicity, modesty, fitness, suggestiveness.[5] To these should be added directness. The main requirement is that it actually introduce, and prepare the hearer for the subject. It ought to attempt no more than this, and should not be overladen nor anticipate the contents of the sermon proper.[6] Broadus says: "The introduction must present some

---

[5] *Homiletics*, pp. 344 ff.

[6] Breed refers in his *Preparing to Preach* to a "plain worshipper who had been much upon the sea in the days of the old sailing vessels. He remarked with regard to the sermons of a certain minister that they were 'clipper-built.' Those who recall the special design of such vessels will understand his reference. The peculiar quality of the old clippers was in the formation of their prows, rather than in the general form of the vessel. The cut-water was sharp, clean,

thought closely related to the theme of discourse so as to lead to the theme with naturalness and ease, and yet a thought quite distinct from the discussion. Inexperienced preachers very frequently err by anticipating in the introduction something which belongs to the discourse; and the danger of doing this should receive their special attention. As a rule, the introduction should not aim to give instruction separate and apart from the lessons of the discourse. Its design is altogether preparatory. The preacher will often find himself tempted, especially in introductions drawn from the text or context, to remark in passing upon interesting matters which are somehow suggested, but are foreign to his purpose on that occasion. This temptation should be resisted, except in very peculiar cases. You have determined to carry the audience along a certain line of thought, hoping to arrive at a definite and important conclusion. Do not first wander about and stray a while into other paths, but lead on towards the route selected, and enter it. The introduction should generally contain a single thought; we do not want a porch to a porch." Here belongs also the habit of going back, in the introduction, to the creation of the world and the fall of man, picturing them in elaborate detail as something new and startling. "On the other hand," Broadus continues, "the introduction must not seem to promise too much, in its thought, style, and delivery. Let it be such as to excite interest and awaken expectation, provided the expectation can be fairly met by the body of the discourse. It should not be highly argumentative nor highly impassioned. As to the latter, it must be remembered that even if the preacher is greatly excited at the outset, the audience usually are not, and he had better restrain himself, so as not to get beyond the range of their sympathies. When Cicero broke out with his opening words against Catiline, the Senate was already much excited; and so with

---

and projected backward upon lines which offered the least possible resistance to the waves. Therefore, they were fast sailors, while at the same time capable of carrying considerable freight. And the introduction to the sermon is the 'cut-water;' it, too, should offer the least possible resistance. It should be no burden upon the attention of the congregation, but rather the reverse. A scow may carry more freight than a clipper, but its sailing qualities are so imperfect that it is capable of making but a single passage while the other vessel is making half a dozen. The clipper is the more effective, and there are some sermons weighted with an immense amount of learning, thought, and argument, which are not effective, only because they are not 'clipper-built.'" (Pp. 94 f.)

Massillon[7] when he at the funeral of Louis the Great, opened his speech with these words: 'My brethren, God only is great.' Such exceptional cases must be decided as they arise. Moreover, while earnestly seeking to make the introduction interesting and engaging we must shun the sensational and the pretentious. Whatever savors of display is exceedingly objectionable in a preacher, and particularly at the outset. And he should not merely begin with personal modesty, but also with official modesty, reserving for some later period of the sermon anything which it may be proper to state with the authority belonging to his office." With respect to the length of the introduction, Broadus tells these anecdotes: "An eminent preacher, much inclined to the fault of too lengthy introductions, was one day accosted by a plain old man as follows: 'Well, you kept us so long in the porch this morning that we hardly got into the house at all.' And it was said of John Howe by someone: 'Dear good man, he is so long in laying the cloth that I lose my appetite, and begin to think there will be no dinner.'"[8] And Shedd says that "where one sermon is faulty from being too abruptly introduced, one hundred are faulty from a long and tiresome preface."[9] It would, however, be a foolish mistake to attempt to keep the introduction within proper bounds by prescribing the number of sentences it should contain. No self-respecting preacher would submit to such dictation. While it should always strive to be brief, the preparation of the hearer for the theme will at times require an introduction of greater length. It is also important to "beware of set phrases and stereotyped forms of introduction; the people very soon begin to recognize them, and the effect is then anything else than to awaken interest and excite curiosity. Nowhere is it more important to have the stimulus and charm of variety." This applies particularly to the closing sentences of the introduction, which form the transition to and directly introduce the theme. The preacher should also avoid the invariable use of a *suspirium* ("with the gracious assistance of the Holy Spirit," etc.), often expanded into a prayer. It is taken for granted that the preacher has said a silent prayer in the pulpit before greeting his congregation and announcing his text, or offered after the reading of the text an audible petition for the divine blessing upon the sermon. Why then this suspirium in the announcement of the theme, especially since it is so often merely an empty form? It is a differ-

---

[7]Compare our forthcoming "History of Preaching."—[8]*Preparation and Delivery of Sermons*, pp. 272 ff.—[9]P. 182.

ent thing when it arises, now and then, from the preacher's heart by an inner necessity.

The custom of prefacing the reading of the text with a separate introduction, followed, after the text has been read, by a second introduction, usually briefer and leading up to the theme, is found in certain parts of Germany and has been transplanted to America. It was favored by Broadus for some sermons, but is not to be commended. Only in very exceptional cases will it prove effective. Palmer's verdict is correct: "In the case of every ten such pre-introductions, nine always appeared to us as either a waste of time and words, or as a discussion of something that might just as well have been discussed at some other time, or as an anticipation of following materials, before one was found that was really apropos."[10]

It would be instructive to offer illustrations of famous introductions from the various periods in the history of preaching. But our space will not permit this; we must refer the student to our forthcoming "History of Preaching." A few specimens, however, may be given. There is a fine climax in the introduction to the oration on the Feast of the Epiphany ascribed to Hippolytus. Treating of Christ's baptism, he begins with the perfection and beauty of all God's gifts, proceeds to the meaning and importance of water in the natural order of things, goes on to speak of the water of Jordan, in and with which Christ came, and then rises to the baptism of Jesus and Christian baptism. Into the midst of things, as suddenly as Cicero in his orations against Catiline, Chrysostom plunges in his discourse on Christians visiting the circus on Good Friday, beginning: "Is this to be tolerated? can this be borne?" Gregory Nazianzus works his way through the various Christian virtues until he comes to the one he wishes to discuss, in his sermon on charity and mercy toward the poor, with its characteristic address: "My brethren and fellow-poor." Bernard of Clairvaux, in his Christmas eve sermon with the theme: "Jesus Christ, God's Son, is born at Bethlehem in Judaea." lifts up in his introduction his hearers' heart without in the least anticipating the body of his sermon. Berthold of Regensburg, preaching on the three walls with which God has surrounded the field of His Church, sets out by picturing the boundless love of God for His Church, of which the theme gives a particularly illustrious instance. Not many steps bring Fenelon, in a sermon on the text: "Pray without ceasing," to his theme. The entire introduction follows: "Of all the

---

[10] P. 531.

duties enjoined by Christianity, none is more essential, and yet more neglected, than prayer. Most people consider this exercise a wearisome ceremony, which they are justified in abridging as much as possible. Even those whose profession or fears lead them to pray, do it with such languor and wanderings of mind, that their prayers, far from drawing down blessings, only increase their condemnation. I wish to demonstrate in this discourse, first, the general necessity of prayer; secondly, its peculiar duty; thirdly, the manner in which we ought to pray." Particularly happy is Adolph Monod's introduction to his sermon on the text: "God is love." "In a small town of Italy, which, eighteen hundred years since, an eruption of Mount Vesuvius buried beneath a flood of lava, some ancient manuscripts, so scorched as to resemble cinders more nearly than books, have been discovered, and, by an ingenious process, slowly and with difficulty unrolled. Let us imagine that one of these scrolls of Herculaneum contained a copy, and the only one in the world, of the epistle from which the text is taken; and that, having come to the fourth chapter and eighth verse, they had just deciphered these two words, 'God is,' and were as yet ignorant of what should follow. What suspense! That which philosophers have so ardently and vainly sought—that of which the wisest among them have abondoned the pursuit—a definition of God! Here it is, and given by the hand of God himself. 'God is'—What is he about to tell us? What is God who dwelleth in the light whereunto no man can approach, whom no man hath seen, nor can see—whom we feel after, if haply we may find Him, though He is not far from each of us—who constrains us to cry out with Job, 'Oh that I knew where I might find Him! If I go forward, He is not there; backward, but I cannot perceive Him; on the left hand, where He doth work, but I cannot behold Him; He hideth Himself on the right hand, that I cannot see Him?' What is He, that all-powerful God, whose word hath created, and whose word could annihilate every thing which exists,—'in whom we live, and move, and have our being'—who holds us each moment under His hand, and who can dispose as He will of our existence, our situation, our abode, our circle of friends, our body, and even our soul? What, in short, is this holy God, 'who is of purer eyes than to behold iniquity,' and whom our conscience accuses us of having offended; of whose displeasure nature has conveyed to us some vague impression, but of whose pardon neither conscience nor nature has given us any intimation—this just Judge, into whose hands we are about to fall—it may be tomorrow, it may be today—ignorant of the sentence which awaits us, and knowing only that we deserve the worst—What is He? Our repose, our salvation, our eternal destiny—all is at stake :—and methinks I see all the creatures of God bending over the sacred record in silent and solemn expectation, of what is about to be revealed concerning this question of questions.—At length the momentous word—love appears! Who could desire a better? What could be conceived comparable to it, by the boldest and loftiest imagination? This hidden God, this powerful God, this holy God—He is Love! What need we more? God loves us. Do I say, He loves us? Ah, in God is love. Love is His very essence. He who speaks of God speaks of love. God is love! O answer, surpassing all our hopes! O blessed revelation, putting an end to all our apprehensions! O glorious pledge of our happiness, present, future, eternal! Yes, if we can believe; for it is not enough that God be love, unless we can say with St. John that 'we have known and believed the love that God hath toward us.' The love of God can neither console, enlighten, sanctify, nor save us—the love of God, indeed, so far as we are concerned, is as if it had no existence, so long as it is not 'shed abroad in our hearts by the power of the Holy Ghost,' and 'mixed with us by faith.' As spiritual and responsible beings, we possess the glorious but fearful privilege of being able to accept [?] or refuse, and thereby to avail or deprive ourselves of this love of God—this is the thought with which I desire to impress you all. Oh, that I might send you away moved, possessed, penetrated with this thought—'God is love!' Lord, if it be true that Thou art love, make it known by directing my tongue by this love and by opening to the influence of this love the hearts of all these people!" A good illustration of the double introduction—the general introduction followed by the transition to the text—may be found in Robert Robinson's sermon of 1781 on John 14:15, whose first part is particularly well done:—"*'If* ye love Me!' *'If* ye love Me!' O cruel 'if', why is this? Is it possible that there can be a doubt? Love *Thee*, 'the brightness of the Father's glory, and the express image of His person!'—all my hope—all my joy; life of my life—soul of my soul. *If I love Thee!* Why it would be better for me to have my love to my wife, my children, my parents, my friends, my dearest enjoyments, doubtful, than to have this so; and is it possible Thou shouldst be in earnest, to preface such an expression as this with an 'if'? Ah, my brethren, however deplorable the case, let us tonight enter into our own hearts: let us do Jesus Christ justice, and let us acknowledge, that if on the one hand there be highest excellence in Him, which is the greatest reason of man's love to Him, on the other there is the deepest depravity in us; and it is matter of fact that though this should be the dearest of all things, it is, most of all things, with relation to man, that which may and ought to be doubted of. O this word 'if'! O that I could tear it out of my heart! O thou poison of all my pleasures! Thou cold, icy hand that touchest me so often and freezest me with the touch! 'If, if!' Would so God we might all tonight be desirous with the whole soul, and determined by grace to get rid of it! 'Hear your divine Master, Christians. He does not mean to put your souls to shame; He is the skillful Physician, telling you the worst of the case, but with the kind intention of restoring you to health. 'If you love Me'—if you would put your love to Me out of all doubt, 'keep My commandments.' May God write this word upon our hearts in all its sacred import!—Let us enter upon the subject. You know this was a part of Jesus Christ's final address to His apostles. There is something very affecting in this last discourse, and particularly in one word of it; no pencil can describe, the finest fancy can hardly imagine how Christ looked when He stood before the twelve and said, 'I have many things to say to you.' Who can doubt it? He was an ocean of knowledge, and He loved dearly to impart it; why did He not then? 'But ye can not bear them now.' Accordingly, therefore, as Jesus Christ's disciples could bear, when He came to die He opened His heart to them, and gave them the fullest display of His inward love the nearer He came to the verge of life; and thus, in some respects, all His servants imitate Him, for they each begin, if I may so speak, with a ray, and, to use an expression of Scripture, 'shine more and more to the perfect day,' and most of all, many of them upon their death-beds.—Christians, go home tonight and feast yourselves with this chapter. Think how happy the men were that asked and had, who could put up all their scruples to Christ, and who found in Christ a tender Master, not above answering the weakest of them. A great part of this chapter, particularly the verses just before the text, seem to be love; and without detaining you longer in the context, my text is a sort of conclusion from premises, and it contains the whole: 'If ye love Me, keep My commandments.' And, indeed, though I am not able to bear in this life all my Saviour could tell me—though I could not stand under the weight of that wisdom that He could impart to me—though my passions are not able to apply, and exercise, and work the ideas He could give me—though I have no penetration so deep, no love so high, no passion so strong that can carry on the great employ—yet surely here is one, and that is love. His love to me, and mine to Him. Here is one interwoven idea that I will even stretch my soul to come at, yea, I will turn out half the inhabitants of my soul to make it room. But in order to give our subject a sort of method, we will observe to you in the first place, that Jesus Christ merits the highest love of all His people; secondly, that there are in His disciples such things as render their love to Christ suspicious; thirdly, we point out to you the method proposed by the Lord Jesus to get rid of all that renders our love to Him suspicious."

The progression, in the introduction, from the natural to the spiritual is well illustrated in Spurgeon's sermon on Job 35:10, with the theme: "Songs in the night." After a few opening sentences referring to the context and the first half of the text and pinning the sermon down to the second half,—"Who giveth songs in the night,"— the preacher proceeds: "The world hath its night. It seemeth necessary that it should have one. The sun shineth by day, and men go forth to their labors, but they grow weary, and nightfall cometh on, like a sweet boon from heaven. The darkness draweth the curtains, and shutteth out the light, which might prevent our eyes from slumber, while the sweet, calm stillness of the night permits us to rest upon the lap of ease, and there forget awhile our cares, until the morning sun appeareth, and an angel puts his hand upon the curtain, and undraws it once again, touches our eyelids, and bids us rise, and proceed to the labors of the day. Night is one of the greatest blessings men enjoy, we have many reasons to thank God for it. Yet night is to many a gloomy season. There is 'the pestilence that walketh in darkness;' there is 'the terror by night;' there is the dread of robbers and of fell disease, with all those fears that the timorous know, when they have no light wherewith they can discern objects. It is then they fancy that spiritual creatures walk the earth; though, if they knew rightly, they would find it to be true, that 'Millions of spiritual creatures walk this earth, Unseen, both when we sleep and when we wake,' and that at all times they are round about us—not more by night than by day. Night is the season of terror and alarm to most men. Yet even night hath its songs. Have you never stood by the seaside at night and heard the pebbles sing, and the waves chant God's glory? Or have you never risen from your couch, and thrown up the window of your chamber, and listened there? Listened to what? Silence—save now and then a murmuring sound, which seems sweet music then. And have you not fancied that you heard the harp of God playing in heaven? Did you not conceive, that yon stars, that those eyes of God, looking down on you, were also mouths of song—

that every star was singing God's glory, singing, as it shone, its mighty Maker, and His lawful, well-deserved praise? Night hath its songs. We need not much poetry in our spirit, to catch the song of night, and hear the spheres as they chant the praises of the mighty God, who bears up the unpillared arch of heaven, and moves the stars in their courses.—Man, too, like the great world in which he lives, must have his night. For it is true that man is like the world around him; he is a little world; he resembles the world in almost everything; and if the world hath its night, so hath man. And many a night do we have—nights of sorrow, nights of persecution, nights of doubt, nights of bewilderment, nights of anxiety, nights of oppression, nights of ignorance—nights of all kinds, which press upon our spirits and terrify our souls. But, blessed be God, the Christian man can say, 'My God giveth me songs in the night.' It is not necessary, I take it, to prove to you that Christian men have nights; for if you are Christians, you will find that you have them, and you will not want any proof, for nights will come quite often enough. I will, therefore, proceed at once to the subject; and I will speak this evening upon songs in the night, *their source*—God giveth them; songs in the night, *their matter*—what do we sing about in the night? songs in the night, *their excellence*—they are hearty songs, and they are sweet ones; songs in the night, *their uses*—their benefits to ourselves and others."

Menken's above-mentioned homily on Heb. 11 illustrates how even this sermon-type will bear a well constructed introduction. The exordium to his homily on Heb. 11:1 follows in abridged form: "By faith alone man has father and mother. Without faith he is fatherless and motherless in the world. By faith alone he has brother and sister, and by faith alone he is fortunate enough to have a friend who is to him as his own soul. Incomparably the greater part of his knowledge of the things of this temporal, visible world, in which he yet uses his senses, is his through faith. Through faith alone there exist for him geography, the science of lands and peoples, history, chronology, the knowledge of foreign languages ancient and modern, etc. A thousand items, great and small, in his work and rest, his walk and conversation, his intercourse and activity with others, rest upon faith and take place through faith. He lives by faith, since he eats and drinks in faith, and is by faith lifted up above the thought of the possibility of being poisoned and above the reproach of acting in ignorance, for he knows nothing of the inner nature of food nor of the mystery of life nor how life can be imparted to him by means of such things. So many things are wrought by a human faith, that is, by a faith based upon human testimony. How much greater things will not a divine faith do for us, a faith depending on divine testimony, taught by the revelation of eternal wisdom, and resting on the promises of divine love! It will open to us a higher and eternal world. It will discover to us what we have sought, and sought in vain: the eternal and divine. It will turn our midnight into brightest day, by giving us the knowledge of God and bringing us to communion with Him. That which the world does not possess, that which neither eye has seen nor ear heard and which has not entered into man's mind, faith reveals, proclaims, imparts.—If faith can do this, how great, how deep, how strong, how blessed will be its effect upon the mind of man! How powerful its influence upon the whole aspect of things! On man's judgment, on his whole mental attitude! How it will give a totally new trend to all his willing, seeking and striving, and set a new goal to his whole life! It must, indeed, be recognized as a divine work in us, that transforms and begets us anew in God.—If faith gives all this and so greatly influences man's heart and life, what can equal it in worth and content? There never has been and never can be any controversy about this faith. It does not belong in the polemic theology of the schools. It is rather the inner life of whoever has it; and whoever has it not cannot but judge it as the blind judges color. With respect to it we must, therefore, forget all temporal concepts and judgments and all human opinions and decisions, and hold simply and solely to God's Word and testimony, from which it arises and without which it would not exist.—The chapter in Holy Writ that is, God willing, to be for a time the subject of our meditation is of high importance; we may say it belongs to the most important portions of the Scriptures, and this because it treats so directly, so definitely, so instructively, and from so many sides, of faith. It comprehends as it were the sum of all Old Testament Scriptures, the essential, the inner and profound character, the highest and holiest of Israel's religion and history. It gives us the sole and the highest viewpoint, so often almost universally neglected, from which Israel's religion and history must be regarded, estimated and judged, and from which no other truth and doctrine appears more deeply founded than this: 'Without faith it is impossible to please God; His eyes look upon faithfulness; the just shall live by faith.' The apostle tells us first what faith is, and then shows the imperishable value of faith, the mind and life that are peculiar to it, how it has manifested itself as divine power and divine comfort in the most different persons, in the most varied circumstances of life, in mighty works, in heroic deeds, in world-conquering suffering and invincible trust in God and truth."

As the introduction prepares the way for the sermon, the conclusion brings it to completion. Not merely to a close, but to actual completion. Its purpose is to gather up the various statements, appeals and motives of the sermon and bring them to bear in their united force upon the hearer, so that they may produce a permanent impression.

So long as this purpose is kept in view, the conclusion may assume various forms, according to the contents and structure of the sermon. If the sermon is causal,[11] exhibiting the *causa,* or subject in its various aspects, the conclusion may be a summary of all of these aspects; not, indeed, a dry, mechanical enumeration, but a strategically organized and forcibly expressed summation. If the subject has been a doctrinal one, the conclusion may apply its consequences to the practical life of the hearer and assume parenetic form. It will naturally take account of the varieties of spiritual life represented in the congregation, but it should not glibly employ the convenient classification of "saints and sinners." If the theme and the sermon are final,[12] the conclusion should not merely restate the purpose presented, but should fix it unforgettably in the conscience of the hearer, so that he will not be able to rest until this purpose has been realized in his life. This may be done by portraying a life in which this purpose has been achieved, or a life in which the inevitable consequences of its rejection are seen, or by means of an appropriate anecdote or parable. Frequently it may be simply a searching question addressed to the hearer's conscience, with or without Amen.

In distinction from other public orations, the sermon may also conclude with a prayer, either of supplication or adora-

---

[11]See above p. 440.—[12]See above p. 440.

tion. When an overwhelming sense of imperfection and need has been awakened by the sermon, it may conclude with a fervent prayer for divine help and comfort. Or when the greatness and wonder of divine grace have been borne in anew upon the heart, the conclusion may turn into adoring praise. When it is not artificially worked up, but arises spontaneously out of the subject itself and from the inner absorption of the preacher in his theme, such a conclusion may become intensely impressive. In accordance with the character of the individual sermon, the conclusion may recapitulate the subject-matter as a whole, or attach itself immediately to the last division, or simply coincide with its closing words (P. 508).

Broadus well says: "Preachers seldom neglect to prepare some introduction to a sermon, but very often neglect the conclusion; and yet the latter is even more important than the former. John Bright, who was one of the foremost political orators of the present age, stated that, however little preparation he may have made for the rest of a speech, he always carefully prepared the conclusion. Lord Brougham said that the conclusion of his celebrated speech before the House of Lords in defence of Queen Caroline was composed twenty times over, at least. The peroration of Burke's first speech at the trial of Warren Hastings was worked over sixteen times. The great orators of Greece and Rome paid much attention to their perorations, seeming to feel that this was the final struggle which must decide the conflict, and gathering up all their powers for one supreme effort. But how often we find it otherwise, especially on the part of preachers who extemporize. The beginning and earlier progress of the sermon show good preparation, and do well. But towards the close the preacher no longer knows the way; here he wanders with a bewildered look, there he struggles and flounders. Another, feeling excited at the close, launches into general exhortation, and proceeding till body and mind are exhausted, ends with what is scattering, feeble, flat. The conclusion ought to have moved like a river, growing in volume and power, but instead of that, the discourse loses itself in some great marsh, or ends like the emptying of a pitcher, with a few poor drops and dregs. Let us lay down the rule, then, that the conclusion should be carefully prepared. We ought in every case, to have ready, and well prepared, something that will make an appropriate and effective conclusion, even though leaving ourselves free, if the moment should so prompt, to strike in a different direction, or rise to a higher level."[13] Such preparation will also prevent repetition, when the conclusion consists of a recapitulation of the divisions. As Pattison says: "In recapitulation, the danger is that you fall into repetition. All that you should aim to do is to revive recollection. You are now in position to survey the field; and it is not necessary that you should fight your battle all over again. Vary your language, therefore; avoid the phrases which you have previously used; choose your words with great care; pack your sentences closely, and by compression gain cumulated force. 'In your introduction,' a homely Welsh preacher was wont to counsel young preachers, 'show the people where you are going, and in your application remind them where you have been.' So Phillips Brooks begins this part of one of his sermons with these words: 'Thus, then, I have passed through the ground which I proposed. See where our thought has led us.'"[14] Gregory Nazianzus and Basil the Great were masters of the massive conclusion, in the ancient Church; among moderns Spurgeon was often very happy in his conclusions. Breed well describes what a good conclusion should be like: "A sermon should be constructed somewhat like those great stockades that are built by game-drivers in Africa and elsewhere, extending perhaps over several miles of country, but converging as they proceed until they end in a death trap. Those who drive the game begin at a distance with much noise and other means whereby to alarm the game and drive it between the stockades, and so they are forced onward until they fall inevitably into the trap."[15] The preacher should not forget, however, two important matters: he cannot force the reason of his hearers and still less their will; and he must not imagine that it is his business, like a political orator, to drive his hearers by means of his sermon to any specific and immediate action.[16] On the other hand, the preacher should, as Phelps says, "never fall into the theatrical vein, never play upon the emotions as the end of discourse, never rest with working up a given heat of feeling, never pause with success in making tears flow." He should have ever before him the great goal of all preaching, namely, the edification of his hearers, the production or promotion of Christian character, on the basis of which the

---

[13]Pp. 298 f.—[14]Pp. 177 f.—[15]P. 113.—[16]See above pp. 203 f., 220 ff.

practice of Christian virtues, the performance of individual good works, will take place by an inner necessity.

The preacher who cannot conclude his conclusion, who cannot stop when he has finished, should lay to heart what Pattison says: "Learn to leave well alone, and to cease firing when your ammunition is gone. Congregations know blank cartridges, and they are not afraid of them. As you value your reputation for truthfulness and fair play do not announce that you mean to conclude and then fail to keep your promise. Do not say: 'Finally .... In conclusion ... One word more .... And, now before we part.' This is to recall Pope's ode, only in no seraphic mood: 'Trembling, hoping, lingering, flying; Oh, the pain, the bliss of dying!' "[17]

A few words must be said about the proper length of the sermon. In the ancient Church we find both long and short sermons, each running to an intolerable extreme. Augustine often preached scarcely more than ten minutes, although the average length of his sermons was nearer thirty minutes, that of his homilies still greater. Many of the sermons of the Greek preachers, especially the Cappadocians, ran over an hour. In the Carlovingian period the sermon was very short. Some of the fifteen sermons ascribed to Boniface could not have taken ten minutes. The folk-sermons of Berthold of Regensburg must have consumed an hour and a half, if they were delivered as they have come down to us. Toward the close of the Middle Ages indolent preachers killed time in the pulpit with long announcements of saint's-days, etc., leaving only a few minutes for the sermon itself. Several long sermons, however, have come down to us from this period. Luther counseled brevity. He said: "When you see your hearers most attentive, then conclude; for then they will come again more cheerfully the next time." But Luther's demand for brevity must be understood by way of contrast to the long drawn out sermons of Bugenhagen, and scarcely contemplated sermons of less than thirty minutes. He himself frequently preached longer than that. Many later preachers followed Bugenhagen's example and kept their hearers for an hour, an hour and a half, and still longer. Thus Balthasar Schuppius, and frequently Spener. Richard Baxter occasionally preached for two hours. Pattison tells us that "the delivery of one of his massive sermons occupied Charnock not less than three hours

---

[17] P. 184.

and a half. At the planting of the First Church, Woburn, Mass., the discourse lasted four or five hours."[18]

Today the demand is for short sermons. In Germany about thirty-five minutes is the average length, though some are shorter, while Walther of Rostock is able to hold the attention of his hearers for fifty minutes and longer. At a book-seller's shop in London John Henry Newman saw some sermons labeled: "Warranted orthodox, not preached before, and—20 minutes." "Twenty minutes with a leaning to mercy," was the pithy way in which an English judge answered our question. Abbe Mullois said: "The harangues of Napoleon lasted only a few minutes, yet they electrified whole armies. In fifteen weeks, with a sermon of seven minutes every Sunday, one might give a complete course of religious instruction, if the sermons were digested beforehand." To this Pattison replies justly: "So short a time as ten minutes would not suffice for the preacher who had not to harangue, as did Napoleon, nor simply to exhort or declaim, as is the practice of many Romish preachers; but rather to explain, instruct, and apply. A true sermon cannot be limited as a brief, impassioned harangue can. The length of the sermon must depend upon the character of the subject to be discussed, upon what measure the congregation has been accustomed to, upon the preacher himself, and even upon such minor considerations as the season of the year or the time of the day in which it is delivered." The warning today must be against unduly short rather than against unduly long sermons. The average hearer would rather listen to a sermon of twenty-five than to one of thirty-five or forty-five minutes. The spiritually minded hearer will judge differently. The question must not, however, be decided by the preference of the hearer, but by the nature and the purpose of the sermon. The preacher has to expound and to apply his text, and his text should not be invariably a short one; he must make his application vivid and graphic and bring it home to men's business and bosoms; he must really influence his hearers' intellectual, emotional and voluntary life. Though he dare never become prolix or verbose, yet all this requires entering into detail, meeting doubts and objections, and correcting current abuses; in short, it takes time. It is true, as Pascal says in his witty way, in his *Provincial Letters*, "I would have made it shorter if I could have kept at it longer." The more time I give to preparation for the pulpit,

---

[18] P. 187.—Stephen Charnock (1628-80) was an English Puritan theologian and preacher.

the shorter and more concise will my sermons be. But brevity and conciseness have their limits, beyond which the sermon may not go unless its effectiveness is to be sacrificed. If the majority of our hearers were people of advanced culture and intelligence, our sermons might well be shorter. One or two lines would suffice to portray a situation, a mere suggestion would point the moral. But where are there such congregations? Those who cry most loudly for short sermons are usually the persons who could not follow a merely suggestive sermon nor take to themselves a merely hinted moral lesson. The common people need—and when they are unspoiled, actually want—greater detail. Let us by all means strive after brevity, but let us not permit the limits of our sermon to be defined by a few intellectual clamorers for brevity, but first of all by the nature and purpose of the sermon, and then by the intellectutal ability and spiritual alertness of the congregation as a whole. Spurgeon considered, in general, forty minutes an adequate period in which to acquit himself of his task as preacher. Thirty minutes, although we may on occasion fall below or run beyond it, may be given as a fair average for the length of the sermon in the main service, if our congregations are to get from our sermons that which we as preachers owe them. For many the Sunday sermon supplies the only food for their inner man during a whole week.

It would be of little value to adduce illustrations of the conclusion; for, in contrast to the introduction, it is necessary to have the whole sermon before one in order to estimate the value of the conclusion. We must again refer to our "History of Preaching," in which many complete sermons will be provided.

§ 19. THE PREPARATION OF THE SERMON FOR DELIVERY AND THE DELIVERY OF THE SERMON

Chr. Palmer, *Evang. Homiletik,* 1842. A. Schweizer, *Homiletik,* 1848. F. Schleiermacher, *Praktische Theologie,* 1850. A. Vinet, *Homiletics,* 1853. D. P. Kidder, *Treatise on Homiletics,* 1864. J. A. Broadus, *On the Preparation and Delivery of Sermons,* 1870. G. W. Hervey, *System of Christian Rhetoric,* 1873. R. S. Storrs, *Conditions of Success in Preaching Without Notes,* 1875. Schuster, *Der gute Vortrag,* 1880. Palleske, *Die Kunst des Vortrags,* 1881. A. Phelps, *The Theory of Preaching,* 1881. J. M. Hoppin, *Homiletics,* 1881. Guttmann, *Die Gymnastik der Rede,* 1882. James Rush, *Philosophy of the Human Voice.* E. P. Hood, *Vocation of Preaching,* 1886. E. Chr. Achelis, *Praktische Theologie,* 1889, [3]1911. Hiram Corson, *The Aims of Literary Study,* 1894 (1901). J. Watson (Ian Maclaren), *The Cure of Souls,* 1896. Schuster, *Vorbereitung und Vortrag der Predigt,* 1897. Allihn, *Der muendliche Vortrag,* 1898. T. H. Pattison, *The Making of the Sermon,* 1898. S. S. Currie, *Vocal and Literary Interpretation of the Bible,* 1903 (1907). P. Kleinert, *Homiletik,* 1907. J. Gottschick, *Homiletik und Katechetik,* 1908. D. R. Breed, *Preparing to Preach,* 1911. O. M. Norlie, *Principles of Expressive Reading,* 1919. Sir Arthur Quiller-Couch, *On the Art of Reading,* 1920. A. E. Garvie, *The Christian Preacher,* 1921.

After the sermon has been fully sketched there follows its preparation for delivery. This should ordinarily consist not only in thinking through the contents of each part and mentally clothing the outline with flesh and blood, but in **writing out** in extenso the sermon in the form in which it is to be delivered. There are, indeed, exceptional preachers who are ready for the pulpit after a season of meditation on a fully worked out sketch, and still more exceptional ones who do not even find it necessary to work out a full sketch. But for the beginner, as well as for the majority of preachers, it should be an inflexible rule to write out the sermon in full.

This is made necessary by the demand for orderly arrangement of thought and expression discussed above.[1]

The writing of the sermon forms the best and most thorough preparation for its delivery. In the process of writing the preacher will often discover inconsistencies and obscurities in his interpretation or application of the text, and may find himself compelled to discard his outline and begin afresh. The writing of sermons promotes logical order, not only in the main divisions but in every part. It arms the preacher against the possible event of indisposition, mental or physical. It makes possible a choice of language appropriate to the subject and the hearer and characterized by convincing clearness, pleasing elegance, and moving power. It affords an opportunity to plan carefully in advance the whole process of delivery, making due allowance for the inspiration that may come in the pulpit, so that the sermon will not be merely reproduced but delivered as a fresh production. It guards against the pitfalls of improvisation—unwarranted and far-fetched statements, cant phrases, incoherent ranting, a slovenly style, and a halting, uncertain delivery; as well as against the pitfalls of extemporaneous speaking—vagueness of thought, diffuseness of language, and a lack of continuity. On the preacher of restless mind and wandering fancy it exerts a restraining influence, while to the preacher of heavy tongue and slow-moving mind it becomes a source of confidence and ease.

After the sermon is written, it should be *fixed in the memory*. This is advisable even when it is to be delivered from manuscript. Preaching from manuscript, if it is not to become intolerable and counteract the purpose of preaching, must be fluent, free, expressive, and direct; and this is possible only when the manuscript has been carefully read and pondered

---

[1] See pp. 173, 175 ff., 205.

over, certain words and phrases underscored, and the location of important passages fixed in the mind. Read sermons are, however, much less suited than spoken sermons to the character of the sermon as living witness. The history of preaching shows that in the ancient Church as well as in the Middle Ages spoken sermons were the rule and read sermons the exception, and that in the Reformation period read sermons became the rule only in a single country, and there under exceptional conditions. For the preacher who elects the method of free delivery the memorizing of his sermons becomes a necessity. The very act of writing will tend to fix the substance and much of the language in his memory, especially if he has put original and independent work on the gathering and arrangement of materials. Writing and memorizing may, indeed, coincide to such an extent that the latter need not become a separate factor in the preparation of the sermon for delivery. But this will be true only in exceptional cases. Ordinarily, the written sermon will have to be conned over carefully and repeatedly, and the outline as a whole, the development of the subject in main divisions as well as in sub-divisions, and last of all the phraseology, fixed in the mind. This should not be done in a wooden and slavish fashion, but so as to lead to a fresh and living reproduction. The preacher should so completely master the sermon as a whole and in its individual parts as to be able, in the act of preaching, to substitute one expression or one thought for another, whenever this becomes necessary. The sermon when delivered should not make the impression of mechanical reproduction, but rather of spontaneous production. A lifeless recitation of memorized materials is usually the result not of too careful memorizing, but of a failure to master the contents of the sermon. Here, too, practice will make perfect, and in time the preacher may dispense altogether with memorizing the language of his discourse, because long continued practice in writing and revising will have increased his word hoard. The introduction and the conclusion demand special attention and care. The memorizing of the sermon will present less difficulties the more closely it follows its writing. While the gathering of materials cannot begin too early in the week, the sermon should not be written too long before the time of its delivery. This is only another reason why the preaching of old sermons is not to be commended and cannot but be unsatisfactory.[2]

The sermon is prepared in order to be delivered before the congregation, with a view to its edification. A treatise on Homiletics cannot, therefore, omit to treat, however briefly, of the oral delivery of the sermon and its accompanying gestures. The *delivery* of the sermon falls under the rules of oratory. It must therefore be such an oral reproduction of the prepared sermon as will correspond to the peculiar character of its contents. This excludes not only a mechanical and lifeless recitation, but the abominable pulpit tone, which cannot but offend everyone of sound taste. While the former is characteristic especially of beginners, the latter is found not only among old practitioners but creeps in before one knows it and soon hardens into a habit. Men imagine that their speech in the pulpit must differ from the speech of ordinary life, and so they strive, as Kleinert puts it, "to achieve solemnity by means of a preternaturally deep or a high squeaking tone, a staccato utterance, a nasal sing-song, a thundering pathos, or an elegiac whine."[3] And as a result, our pulpits are filled, as Corson says, "with abominable drawlers, mouthers, mumblers, clutterers, squeakers, chanters, and mongers in monotony."[4] In this way the best sermons are spoiled, for such pulpit tones are the reverse of natural, and either offend or produce a comic effect. The preacher should

---

[2] See above p. 120.—[3] P. 224.—[4] P. 110.

above all be truly natural. Nor dare he, on the other hand, fall into the vulgarity of the street or the informality of familiar conversation. Pitch, tone and inflection should be determined by the contents of his discourse, so that the delivery will fit the subject as a well made garment fits the wearer, and express in every respect the preacher's personality and spirit.

In addition to this, the delivery of the sermon, as oration in the service of the worshiping congregation, dare never sin against decorum. It must exclude everything that smacks of passion, fury and noise, as well as of the flippant and vulgar, the theatrical and artificial. The preacher who has really mastered his subject, who has a sense of noble simplicity and true naturalness, and who is a Christian personality living and moving in the thought of his sermon, will find of his own accord the method of delivery best fitted to the subject and the sanctuary, and best adapted to impress the hearers. When the delivery of the sermon is upborne from beginning to end by a personality resting in God, seeking his brother in love, and sanctified by the divine Spirit, the discourse will be characterized by genuine and not spurious "unction." A particular warning is in place against such common pulpit abuses as loud shouting or shrieking, which frequently causes the voice to break or to give out entirely; the swallowing of final syllables, and the constant use of pet words ("you and I," "blessed," "don't you see," "and so on and so forth," etc.).

That the sermon should be delivered without accompanying *gestures* is unthinkable. As in ordinary conversation, gestures will naturally arise in the sermon whenever the speaker is deeply moved. The more the preacher lives and moves in his subject, so that his gestures become the spontaneous accompaniment of his words and an organic part of his utterance, the more natural and correct will they be. Specific rules governing gestures are, therefore, unnecessary. They should be above all natural and unforced, but also restrained, and hallowed by the Spirit of God.

In view of the unique importance of preaching in developing the spiritual life of the congregation, the faithful pastor will strive to improve and perfect his delivery of the sermon as to both voice and gestures. He will never allow himself to regard these as trivial matters. He will fully realize the great importance of this side of his pastoral activity, and as he approaches the preparation of his sermon in the spirit of prayer, so he will preface and conclude his delivery of it with the fervent petition that God may accept his preparation and bless it to his hearers. For his Lord alone, whose he is and whom he serves, is able to give the preacher strength and to turn the people's hearts as the watercourses.

On the important part played by the delivery of the sermon, Pattison writes: "No one will question that the way in which a sermon is delivered has very much to do with its effectiveness. Was not St. Francis de Sales right in saying, 'You may utter volumes, and if you do not utter them well it is lost labor. Speak but little and that well, and you may effect much'? John Foster was extremely fastidious in his choice of words and in the structure of his sentences; and no man of his generation was his superior in originality of thought. He insisted that the effect of the sermon should depend upon these things alone. Delivery he professed to despise. Consequently he failed as a preacher. Who can wonder, indeed, when we learn from William Jay that 'his delivery all through was in a low and equable voice with a kind of surly tone and frequent repetition of a word at the beginning of a sentence. He had a little fierceness occasionally in his eye, otherwise his face was set and his arms perfectly motionless.' The wit spoke not for one preacher but for many when he observed, on hearing that the sermons of a popular orator were to be published, 'They ought to print the preacher, for the principal merit of his sermons is his delivery.' Many a good sermon is wrecked on the reef of a poor delivery; and many a very ordinary sermon is saved by learning to avoid it. As the best laws are said to be those which are best administered, so we are tempted to think that the best sermons are those which are best delivered. With preaching (so Doctor Guthrie put it) it is as with firing a gun, the manner is the powder, the matter is the shot; and it is well-known that a tallow candle with a sufficient quantity of powder will go through a deal board that a leaden bullet would not pierce fired off with a feeble charge. And yet we should not convey the impression that the method of delivery employed is by any means the prime essential to successful preaching. No, the method is secondary to the matter, as both method and matter are secondary to the man. However he may preach, the true man, if he has a message from God, will make himself heard."[5] And surely, the "true man" will be deeply concerned to deliver his sermons as well as his physical and vocal powers permit and will strive constantly to improve these powers.

We may distinguish five methods of delivery,—improvisation, extemporisation, reciting, reading, and a composite method in which two or more of the foregoing are combined. By *improvisation* is meant the delivery of the sermon without previous preparation, either by way of outline or meditation. In *extemporisation* the structure and argument are prepared, and sometimes an outline is taken into the pulpit, but the language is left to the inspiration of the moment. *Recitation* and *reading* have in common the writing of the sermon in full; the difference between them is, that in the former the sermon is reproduced from memory, in the latter it is read from manuscript. The *composite mode*, to use Kidder's designation,[6] combines two or more of the foregoing methods. All of these methods of delivery are found in the history of preaching.[7] The great preachers of the ancient Church usually

---

[5] Pp. 291 f. [6] P. 314.

[7] Hervey has gathered the following material on the secular orators of Greece and Rome:—"The orators of Greece and Rome usually spoke from memory; and yet Isocrates undisguisedly wrote an oration and sent it to be read by another to Philip of Macedon. He and Demosthenes composed speeches for others. The latter seems habitually to have written his orations beforehand, and was not unwilling that it should be publicly known that he spoke only after preparation made to the utmost of his power (see speech against Midas, and cf. Plutarch's Lives). Aesion, a fellow-scholar of his, was of opinion that his speeches were less effective when heard than when read. In the course of his great speeches he often paused and bade the scribe read some decree, letter, oracle, or poem. Had the Greeks been so averse to reading as some modern critics fancy they were, Demosthenes would not have compelled his audiences to hear so many things read. The matter read during the oration on the Crown amounts to about one-eighth of the whole, to

wrote their sermons and delivered them freely. Occasionally they spoke extemporaneously or with the use of brief outlines; tradition assigns the latter method to Origen's later ministry. Now and then they approached the method of improvisation, which must have been employed by Augustine on those occasions when he did not choose the subject of his sermon until the *praelector* was reading the lesson; and by Chrysostom, when his choice of subject was suggested by an incident on his way to church or even during the service. There are also instances of read sermons. We do not mean by these the sermons Gregory the Great dictated on his sickbed and had another read to his congregation, nor the sermons of Ephraem the Syrian which were read in many churches in the East instead of original sermons.

---

say nothing of five additional documents (now lost) which were also read. Once a sophist being about to read a panegyric on Hercules, Antalcidas the Spartan said, 'Why, who has blamed Hercules?' (Plutarch, *Laconian Apophthegms*, Reiske, vol. vi, p. 217). This Spartan courtier did not, it seems, complain that the eulogy was to be *read;* and it is certain that Cicero read from manuscript to the Roman Senate the first speech he made after his return from exile (*Post Reditum in Senatu*). This we learn from his own words in the oration for Plancius (s. 30), where he says of it, 'which on account of the importance of the matter was pronounced from a written paper.' The younger Pliny (*Epist.* xvii, L. vii) apologizes to a friend for having read his speeches by saying that the reading of the orations was practiced both by the Romans and the Greeks—that he saw as much propriety in reading an oration as in publishing it. 'But,' says the objector, 'it is difficult to give satisfaction to an audience by the mere reading of an oration.' This objection, rejoins Pliny, may hold against the reading of some, but not against reading in general. Augustus, it is said (Suetonius, *Life of Augustine*, c. LXXXIV), did not want the talent of speaking ex tempore, but lest his memory should fail him, as well as to prevent the loss of time in committing his speeches, it was his general practice to read them. Tiberius, although he usually spoke best off-hand, read an oration at the funeral of this same Augustus. And Constantine spent much of his time in writing discourses which he delivered before his subjects; but he was, it would seem, so familiar with his manuscript that when new and important thoughts occurred to him in reading, then 'he immediately stood erect' and uttered them ex tempore (Life by Eusebius, L. iv, Chap. xxii). Even in the classical period of Rome the conspicuous use of notes was not forbidden to the orator, for Quintilian (Lib. xc, vii, sect. 131-132) recommends speaking ex tempore and from memory, but approves, nevertheless, 'short notes and small memorandum books which may be held in the hand, and on which the orator may occasionally glance.'" (Pp. 550 f.) All of which proves only that free delivery on the basis of careful memorizing of the written discourse was the rule, and reading an exception which needed to be justified.

We are thinking particularly of the sermon known as the Second Epistle of Clement, in which the author says expressly that he is reading an exhortation.[8] In the first half of the Middle Ages and undoubtedly later, the incompetence and indolence of preachers made the reading of sermons necessary. But original and faithful preachers, such as Bernard of Clairvaux, Berthold of Regensburg and Geiler of Kaiserswerth, delivered their sermons freely, many of them writing them in Latin and reproducing them in the vernacular. The numerous divisions and subdivisions in the scholastic sermon necessitated the taking of memorandum notes into the pulpit. Luther's delivery was free, based on careful meditation and, in his earlier period, on fully written sermons. He permitted, and indeed counseled, incompetent preachers to read the sermons of others to their people. Free delivery on the basis of a completely written sermon or a full outline was the rule in Continental Europe, and has remained the rule, with few exceptions, to this day. In England read sermons appear to have come in with the beginning of the Reformation, chiefly as a safeguard against the charge of unorthodox preaching.[9] With the publication, under Elizabeth, of the *Two Books of Homilies Appointed to Be Read in Churches,* this practice became the rule and applied also to the preacher's own sermons.[10] The purpose was twofold: to aid incompetent preachers, and to guarantee the orthodox character of all

---

[8] Sect. xix.—See our "History of Preaching."

[9] "Those who were licensed to preach being often accused for their sermons, and complaints being made to the King by hot men on both sides, they came generally to write and read their sermons, and thence the reading of sermons grew into a practice in this church; in which, if there was not that heat of fire which the friars had shown in their declamations, so that the passions of the hearers were not so much wrought on by it, yet it has produced the greatest treasure of weighty, grave, and solid sermons that ever the Church of God had [?]; which does in a great measure compensate that seeming flatness to vulgar ears, that is in the delivery of them"—Burnet, *History of the Reformation.* Calvin wrote in 1548 to Somerset, Lord Protector of England, insisting that lively preaching was much needed, and adding: "I say this, Sire, because it seems to me that there is little of preaching in the Kingdom, but that sermons are for the most part read."

[10] Charles II sought to abolish it and sent in 1674 a sharp letter to the Vice-chancellor of the University of Cambridge (printed in Broadus, pp. 435 f.); but the practice continued. In the eighteenth century, a curate was driven from a London pulpit, because he was accustomed to raise his eyes from his manuscript while preaching. (Neale, *Mediaeval Preaching,* p. 10.)

preaching. In Scotland the case was different. Here the example of Knox, who followed Calvin and always extemporised, and of Henderson, who seems to have written all his sermons but preached them from memory, so powerfully influenced the Scottish Church that objection was made to the ordination of one William Anderson, who had been licensed in 1820, because he read his sermons.[11] The practice of reading sermons was brought to America by the Puritans, though not without exception.[12] It prevailed in New England to such an extent that Whitefield's freely delivered sermons burst upon the colonists as a revelation and carried them away. To this day read sermons are by no means unheard of in the family of Reformed Churches in America, but they are no longer the general rule, not even in the Episcopal Church. What shall we say of those Lutheran preachers who still cling to this method, which before we learned to ape and borrow from others, was never the practice of our Church!

With respect to read sermons, Hervey mentions a number of eminent preachers who practiced this method, among them Chalmers and Edwards.[13] But Pattison says: "If the great name of Thomas Chalmers be appealed to in its defence, it is sufficient to answer that he who can read as Chalmers did—in tones of enthusiasm that made the rafters roar, hanging over his audience, menacing them with his shaking fist or standing erect, manacled and staring—can be suffered to do as he pleases.[14] And if reference be made to Jonathan Edwards,

---

[11] Comp. W. M. Taylor, *The Scottish Pulpit from the Reformation to the Present Day* (1887), pp. 54, 83, 248-49.

[12] John Cotton, e. g., who in two days could preach three sermons six hours long, said that "reading was not preaching." (John Brown, *The Pilgrim Fathers of New England,* p. 310.)

[13] P. 554.

[14] Broadus says of Chalmers: "Look at his style. He was extremely, in fact excessively fond of long sentences, formed of nicely balanced clauses, with the corresponding terms in each clause often indicated by alliteration, and he had an exceeding desire to achieve quaint felicities of phraseology. His images are frequently drawn on a grand and elaborate scale, and he was fastidious as to their color and finish. These well-known peculiarities go far to account for his persuasion that he could not extemporize. It would be almost as difficult to improvise a choral ode, as some of those elaborated passages in which he delighted. And, after all, Dr. Wayland states (*Ministry of the Gospel,* p. 126): 'A gentleman who was in the habit of hearing him, has assured me that his ex tempore discourses, delivered to operatives in the outskirts of Glasgow, were far more effective, and more truly eloquent, than the sermons which he delivered with so much applause in the Tron Church of that city.'"

it may further be affirmed that even when he was preaching his great sermons he did not always read, and that in his later years he abandoned the manuscript altogether. What is remarkable, preachers who have been in the habit of reading have not, as a rule, preferred the method; and treatises on Homiletics, written by those who in the pulpit are slaves to the paper, have rather commended extemporaneous preaching. 'Henceforth,' Chalmers wrote in his journal after hearing Andrew Fuller preach: 'Let me try to extemporize in the pulpit.'"[15] Pattison sums up the objections to read sermons as follows: "That the sermon should be read is philosophically objectionable. Between the speaker and hearer it interposes a paper which, except in very rare cases, such as that of Chalmers, produces two evils: (1) A sense of separation and distance. Mr. Blaine told a company of ministers at the Congregational Club in Boston, that when they put the nonconductor of a pile of manuscript between themselves and their hearers, they were not preaching the gospel, 'you are only reading it.' Dr. R. S. Storrs abandoned his written sermon when he had to address the throngs in the Academy of Music, Brooklyn, for the same reason. 'Inserting a manuscript between the audience and myself would have been like cutting the telegraph wires and putting a sheet of paper into the gap' (Storrs, *Preaching Without Notes,* p. 34). (2) A sense of unreality naturally follows this sense of separation and distance. The conviction that the message is with authority, which is absolutely necessary alike with preacher and hearers if the sermon is to do its best work, is very faint, and often, indeed, it is absent altogether unless the speaker is in close, conscious touch with his congregation. Rowland Hill had reason to gibe at the impotence of 'dried tongues.' Many will agree with Spurgeon when he says: 'The best reading I have ever heard has tasted of paper, and has stuck in my throat,' and the conclusion of Dr. Joseph Parker is still more worthy of being laid to heart by every preacher: 'Having tried both methods, the method of free speech and the method of reading, I can give an opinion founded upon experience, and I now give it as entirely favorable to free speech.' The pulpit will never take its proper place until the habit of reading sermons on ordinary occasions is entirely abandoned; it is official, pedantic, heartless, and ought to be put down. Let it, further, be remembered that the practice of reading in the pulpit has no rhetorical parallel. The lawyer in court, the political speaker on the platform, the actor on the stage, do not read. 'The

---

[15] Pp. 305 f.

practice of reading sermons,' Blair considered to be 'one of the greatest obstacles to eloquence.' 'Elocutionists may read,' a southern preacher says, 'but orators never.' Of what invaluable allies in effective speaking the habit of reading deprives a preacher. Gesture is crippled and contracted, and becomes tame and monotonous. The perfection of the art of gesture among the Italians and other nations which naturally possess it in fuller measure than do we, can make even 'their legs the emblem of their various thought.' To this extreme we may not wish to go, but still less can we hold with Dr. Samuel Johnson that 'action can have no effect upon reasonable minds,' and that 'in proportion as men are removed from brutes, action will have less influence on them.' Then again, the facial expression of the preacher who reads his sermons is almost wholly if not entirely lost. The lips, the pose of the head, the varied expression of the eye, can now do little. The eye is a most powerful auxiliary to the voice. Our Lord and his apostles used it for this purpose... This power of the eye has always been great in secular oratory; why shall it be less so in the case of those who occupy the throne of eloquence, the pulpit? By his opponents the glance of William Pitt was as much dreaded as was his voice. Robespierre, it has been truly said, could quell the French Assembly by his lion eye; while that of Daniel Webster was a gateway out of which marched conquest. Dr. Thomas Guthrie held that the objection to 'the paper lay deep in the feelings of our nature.' He said: 'It universally produces more or less of monotony, so much of it as to act like mesmerism on the audience. To keep an audience wide awake, their attention active and on stretch, all the natural varieties of tone and action are necessary—qualifications incompatible with the practice of reading.'"[16]

We admit that read sermons are often unjustly condemned because the critic has in mind a preacher who scarcely lifts his eyes from his manuscript or has never acquired the art of reading aloud, let alone mastered it. We admit likewise that read sermons become less objectionable in proportion as the preacher really is master of this difficult art. Nevertheless, it is our conviction and experience that this method lacks freshness and immediateness, and interposes a disturbing factor between the preacher and his audience. Nor does it accord sufficiently with the witness-bearing character of preaching.

Which of these methods should be adopted? Of improvisation little need be said. It can be justified only when God Himself has so

---

[16] Pp. 306 ff.

disposed events as to make preparation impossible. In such an event, that preacher will come through best who has been given most consistently to conscientious preparation for the pulpit. Extemporisation, in the sense defined above? Undoubtedly, all the objections made against reading fall here to the ground; naturalness, immediateness, the witness-bearing character of the sermon, the accompaniment of gestures, the aid furnished by the modulation of the voice and the expression of the face—all these are present. But does extemporisation retain also all the advantages of the read sermon,—order and logical progression of thought, clearness, elegance, and force of language? These are unquestionably lost when extemporisation has been the method followed from the beginning of the preacher's ministry. They will, on the other hand, characterize more or less the sermons of one who has been writing and freely delivering his sermons for a decade or longer. He has gained by this practice an orderly cast of mind, a mastery of language, and a freedom of delivery which will enable him to preach logically and elegantly even without writing out his sermons in full. And yet—why is it that mature preachers who, after writing for many years, have taken to extemporisation resort to writing and memoriter delivery on extraordinary occasions and when they have to face a specially critical audience? It would seem that what they consider the best method for such occasions ought to be their standing rule for all occasions. The souls of men are before them and God is present, Sunday after Sunday; and these surely deserve no less respect than festival occasions and critically minded audiences.

The objection that such memoriter preaching leads to monotonous and mechanical recitation has been met above. Even Garvie, no admirer of this style of preaching, admits that "if a man can after reading his MS only half a dozen times recall its contents without strain, and so can deliver it with freshness and force, the objection falls to the ground."[17] Our own long experience has convinced us that no other method leads to so completely free a delivery. We have always been least at our ease when we had not completely mastered our manuscript. In order, however, not to be helpless in special emergencies, when writing and memorizing are impossible, or when in later life memory is impaired, the preacher should seize every opportunity to make himself proficient in extempore speaking, in ad-

---

[17] P. 462

dresses before young people's societies and missionary or other organizations.

An important process in the preparation of the sermon for delivery is so charmingly described by Ian Maclaren in his *Cure of Souls* that the student will thank us for quoting it in full, before we pass on to the discussion of voice and gesture. "No photograph," he writes, "quite represents the face that was taken, or leaves the studio untouched. Certain lines have to be modified, certain blots to be removed. It will be a very gracious sermon that needs no retouching. Line by line the sermon has to be read over with the faces of his congregation before him, so that the minister may hear how it sounds in the living environment. Many things are incisive and telling, clever and sparkling on paper, which we feel will not do face to face. They are now too telling, too clever. A well-turned epigram, which cost much oil: but that white-haired saint will misunderstand it. Our St. John must not be grieved. So it must go. A very impressive word of the new scientific coinage: what can yon sempstress make of it? Rich people have many pleasures, she has only her church. Well, she shall have it without rebate: the big word is erased—half a line in mourning. A shrewd hit at a certain weakness: but that dear old mother, whose house is a refuge for orphans and all kinds of miserables, it is just possible she may be hurt. The minister had not thought of her till he said the words with Dorcas sitting in her corner. Another black line in the fair manuscript. This exposure of narrowness is at any rate justified: but the minister sees one face redden, and its owner is as true a man as God ever made. It is left out too. Somewhat strong that statement: an adjective shall be omitted: some people have a delicate sense of words. This quip may excite a laugh: better not—it may hinder the force of the next passage on Jesus. The sermon seems to be losing at every turn in harmony, vivacity, richness, ease; it is gaining in persuasiveness, understanding, sympathy, love: it is losing what is human and gaining what is divine; and after that sermon is delivered, and has passed into men's lives, the preacher will bless God for every word he removed."[18]

In the *delivery* of the sermon, all depends upon the natural tone of the voice, this antithesis of the abhorrent pulpit tone. In order to attain to this, the preacher will need, as Kleinert says, "to fix his attention especially upon two points: making himself understood, which de-

---

[18] Pp. 32-34.

pends on clearness of *articulation,* and bringing substance and utterance into harmony, which depends on *modulation.* A person reading something unfamiliar is apt to put the emphasis in the wrong place. Such an error would seem to be impossible when one is reading one's own composition. But it often occurs in elocution. This may be traced to embarrassment, the habitual use of a pulpit tone, or mechanical memorizing. In any case it prevents the hearer from understanding what is read, and shows that the essential prerequisite of a natural and finished delivery is lacking, namely, the certain mastery of the subject and of the voice. In order to overcome this defect and to acquire a proper modulation, we should note that modulation is determined by the co-operation of three equally important factors: the right emphasis upon the individual word, the right emphasis upon the sentence, and the right emphasis upon the thought group. In other words, word emphasis, sentence emphasis, and thought emphasis. Sentence emphasis takes precedence over word emphasis. For, though no word should be swallowed or slighted, but must be given its full emphasis, nevertheless to the chief word in the sentence all others sustain an enclitic or proclitic relation. Thought emphasis (rhetorical emphasis, in the narrower sense) takes precedence over sentence emphasis; because, first, the desire to secure for an idea its proper effect frequently requires the stress of the voice to fall on what is grammatically a minor part of the sentence, and second, because sentence emphasis must always remain within the compass of the tone of voice demanded by the connection in which the sentence as a whole is found. A proper modulation should be to the ear what punctuation is to the eye: it should make clear the divisions and connections of the discourse. Its neglect will result in monotony of delivery, the mark of lifeless discourse. Further directions for oral delivery are given by the principles of oratory. Since these determine utterance as such, they must be applied to the oral delivery of the sermon. Natural emphasis does not mean that the speaker's nature is to be left unrestrained to its own impulses. That which is to express itself is not undisciplined, but controlled, ethicized nature. It will conform to the principle of *unity,* by avoiding sudden changes of pitch, and by finding a middle ground that will control the inflection and harmoniously combine its contrasts. If inflection is to become neither uncouth nor theatrically affected, there must be a mean from which the voice may be raised or lowered, a dominant tone. Glaring contrasts overleaping these limits, abrupt changes from high to low pitch, from a whisper to a shriek, bellowing out the loud and swallowing the soft tones, disrupt the unity and disfigure the discourse. 'Luther,' said Alber, 'had a fine voice, both in singing and speaking; he was no shouter.' The *tempo* of speech is likewise governed by the principle of unity. The will of the hearer is not to be influenced by violence and clamor, but by persuasion. This excludes an undue rapidity of utterance. No less an evil, on the other hand, is the affected deliberateness of a would-be emotional delivery; as well as the lofty schoolmasterly tone, which so easily passes from the professor's desk into the pulpit and repels the hearer by its high and mighty manner. 'Promtum sit os, non praeceps; moderatum, non lentum,' counseled Quintilian. The principle of *variety*, applied to oral delivery, will suggest a gradation of tone, not indeed in the individual sentence, but in the various parts of the discourse. This will conform to the subject treated and make it easier for the hearers to grasp its meaning. Even when a sustained exaltation of sentiment pervades the whole oration, it is well to give the ear a rest by interrupting and setting off the weighty and elevated stretches of speech by uttering such portions as will permit it in a more conversational tone. The hearer will with difficulty endure a continuous elevation of emotion, even if this were permitted by the contents of the discourse. On the other hand, when the lighter tone dominates the discourse, it will be well to introduce a stronger emphasis now and then, in order to recall a lagging interest to the importance of the subject. It is necessary, however, to avoid an abrupt collision of violent contrasts, if the effect of the theatrical is to be prevented. *Climax* also has its place in delivery, provided it is not artificially worked up, but grows out of the subject itself. The voice is the reflection of the mood; the gathering intensity of feeling expresses itself involuntarily in the climax of oral delivery, which becomes for this very reason a suitable means of communicating one's own emotions to others. It follows that the preacher must be familiar with the resources of his voice, its range and power, in order to set out, at the beginning of his oration as a whole and of every individual part, with such a use of his voice as will permit a gradual ascent, without overstepping its possibilities. Beginning on too high or too low a note invariably leads to blemishes of speech,—a strained tone, the breaking or giving out of the voice, etc.—and results, when the limits of its power have been reached, in a huskiness that laboriously avoids complete exhaustion and leaves a painful impression. Both as to substance and utterance, the conclusion of the sermon should mark the summit of the preacher's power. Even the closing prayer should not appear as the product of spent, but of gathered and sustained power."[19]

Concerning *gestures,* Schleiermacher said: "The reasons why speech is accompanied by gestures are, that movement as such is the original means of representing a momentary state of mind as a whole; that wherever men do not as yet communicate by means of language, they invent a sign language consisting of gestures, by which to make themselves understood; and that even where spoken language is in use, this sign language comes to its aid whenever expression becomes animated." Kleinert calls attention to the fact that even in daily life a person of sprightly temperament will find himself accompanying with gestures the thoughts and emotions that he utters with animation, and the words that he wishes to make emphatic. Because this is so natural, Steinmeyer correctly said: "It is more natural and easy to preach with gestures than without gestures." What should be the nature of our gestures? They will naturally differ according to racial and personal peculiarities. The vivacious southerner is accustomed to more frequent and animated gestures than the composed northerner. What the former regards as permissible, the latter will frown on. The preacher of sanguine temperament will use more motions in the pulpit than his phlegmatic brother. Pericles stood motionless as a statue on the rostrum. Cleon gesticulated wildly. Schleiermacher made scarcely any gestures, depending almost solely on the force of his ideas. Many American preachers approximate the motions of the stage, to say nothing of the unworthy antics of a "Billy" Sunday. Over against such extravagances, one is sorely tempted to counsel a minimum of gestures. It must not be forgotten, however, that gestures suitable to its contents materially promote the effect of the sermon. "Especially," writes J. Mueller, "when the discourse seeks to influence the will, the hearer receives from the orator not only the definite sum of ideas which his words contain and the impression they are intended to make upon him; but by means of the tones of his voice and his gestures, the look of his eye and the expression of his face, the speaker's personality is stamped, along with the words, upon his soul. The effect of the words is thus capable of being enhanced; words which might otherwise find the heart closed to every influence will in many cases find, by means of this co-operating power of personality, an entrance to the heart. Not that something extraneous is added to the effect of

---

[19] Pp. 225 ff.

the ideas, but the whole material is absorbed into the personality of
the speaker and is given forth in a new form, so that the effect of
the material and the effect of the personality of the speaker upon
the personality of the hearer are woven into one."[20] Gestures should
not, of course, accompany every sentence, much less every word, for
the pantomimist is out of place in the pulpit. That they must adapt
themselves in a worthy manner to the harmonious effect of the service, is demanded by Kleinert, who indicates what they must on
this account avoid:—"This demand is even more in place in the
sphere of gestures than in that of oral delivery. For the eye is more
sensitive to disturbing influences than the ear. The preacher will do
well, in his activity in the service, to bear in mind that it is especially
the Pastoral epistles in the New Testament that most frequently hold
up to churchly practice the standard of the beautiful ($\kappa\alpha\lambda\acute{o}\nu$). Motions that are ugly, awkward and angular, restless and jerky, abrupt
and violent, must be barred. Gestures should be free, unembarrassed
and unforced, the unstudied expression of manly dignity, not interrupted by jerks betraying the constraint of uncontrolled nature. The
preacher should not give the impression of being overtaken by a
feeling of guilt by suddenly recalling that he has made no gestures
for a time and resuming them with precipitate haste. Nor the impression of absentmindedness, which is unavoidable when gestures
suitable to one train of thought are continued through a totally different train. Above all, he should avoid the impression of fright
produced by a convulsive clutching of the sides of the pulpit. So far,
finally, as the arms are concerned, gestures should not be one-sided,
only one arm being constantly in motion, the other never. Nor should
they be half-gestures, an incompleted beginning exhibiting at one and
the same time the natural faculty of motion and the inability to
carry out the motion. Nor should they be excessive, one or both
arms waving about the head like the arms of a windmill. As in oral
delivery, so in gesticulation, monotony must be overcome; the continual recurrence of the same motion should not cause the speaker
to be mistaken for a swimmer. As in oral delivery, schoolmasterly
mannerisms should be laid aside. The most common of these, the
outstretched right index finger, should not be transferred from the
lecture room to the pulpit. The dignity of the latter excludes also
the clenched fist and the spread fingers. The hand should follow the
movements of the arm, in a natural position, the fingers resting light-

---

[20] *Studien und Kritiken* (1856), p. 524.

ly one against another. The preacher will need to give attention also to his countenance; here, too, chiefly with the negative purpose not to fall into the habit of beginning or continuing his discourse with a set expression or even a grimace, whether it be a smile or a frown. The eye, controlling the face as expression of the soul, should not stray restlessly about mustering the congregation, nor rest abstractedly on this or that hearer; still less should it withdraw itself from sight behind closed or half-closed lids. Nor should the hearer seeking in the eye the mirror of the soul, be met with the annoying glitter of two eye-glasses reflecting the light from the windows. The glance should rather move about in the congregation in a free, unconstrained and easy manner, without lingering too intently on any particular part of the audience."[21]

Subject-matter, form, and gestures should be in keeping with one another, as well as with the purpose that the sermon pursues and the place where it is delivered. They should contribute, each in its turn, to the edification of the congregation. But the greatest of them is the subject-matter—the word coming from God, experienced by preacher and congregation, and witnessed in the sermon. This alone can truly edify the soul.

[21] Pp. 231 f.

PRACTICAL ILLUSTRATIONS

1. Illustrations of the Exegetical-Homiletical Treatment of the Text in the Gathering of Materials

OLD TESTAMENT PASSAGES

(1) Historical Texts

Gen. 18: 16-33.

Exposition.—Context: With Gen. 17 begins the third chapter in the life of Abraham. The second chapter closed with a certain relaxation of his faith. The continued barrenness of Sarah; the foolish attempt to hasten God's promise by his union with Hagar; the disappointing experience with Ishmael, the fruit of this union; the angelic prediction concerning Ishmael's future—all these had produced a weakening of Abraham's moral and religious life. Then, with the theophany in Gen. 18 a new chapter opens. As a result of this theophany with its reiteration of the promised seed, his languor disappears and his faith burns with a clearer, steadier flame. He is assured now that the covenant that God had made with him will soon be realized by His almighty power; of this he takes his new name as a pledge. God's relation to him is renewed, and with it Abraham's relation to God. He knows that God is his God and that he is God's servant, His chosen one. The second theophany, following soon after and described in the beginning of our chapter, though intended primarily to induce Sarah to believe, could not but increase Abraham's faith and strengthen the relation between him and his God, who sat down so intimately as guest at his table and supped with him as a friend with his friend. It is not surprising that this theophany is followed by a conversation between the two, which, more than anything else in Abraham's life, reveals the closeness of the relation between himself and God.

Vv. 16-19.—The visit of the three men has drawn to a close. Sarah has learned that nothing is too hard for the Lord and has been fortified by this thought against her lack of faith. The visitors set their faces toward Sodom. God's revelation of His grace and goodness is to be followed by a revelation of His holiness and righteousness. Abraham accompanies his guests, to speed them on their way. According to an old tradition, he went with them as far as the site of the later Caphar-Berucha, whence one looked down upon Sodom and its environs. While they go silently together, Yahveh arrives at an important decision in His mind, which betrays the full intimacy of His relation to Abraham. He says within Himself (for vv. 17-19 form a soliloquy): "Shall I hide from Abraham what I am about to do?" Two reasons are given why He should take His human companion into His confidence: (1) Abraham is destined to become the ancestor of a numerous and mighty people, and through him all nations of the earth are to be blessed; (2) God has known him, i. e., chosen him to teach his children and all his household the way of the Lord. According to biblical usage, *jada* denotes not simply to know, but to acknowledge, to choose (comp. Amos 3:2; Hos. 13:4; Gen. 4:1). The specific call of Abraham is, therefore, the reason why God will not conceal His intention from him. If Abraham had not been called for this high purpose, there would be no occasion for communicating to him the counsel of God. But since God has acknowledged him, i. e., called him out of a condition of remoteness to a relation of love and chosen him to become father of a nation, transmitter of divine blessing to all people, and teacher of his household and descendants, God feels Himself as it were obligated to reveal to him the doom that is so soon to fall upon five cities in his immediate neighborhood. As ancestor of a great people, Abraham cannot but be interested in the people with whom his descendants are to come into contact. As transmitter of blessing to all nations, he cannot be indifferent to the fact that five neighboring cities are to be destroyed without sharing in this blessing. As one who is to teach his household and descendants the way of the Lord, to do justice and judgment, which are the very conditions under which the promise given to him is to be fulfilled, it is of vital importance for Abraham to know why these five cities are to be destroyed. He is to see in their destruction a manifestation of God's justice, which is indeed longsuffering, but which punishes severely and finally, when unrighteousness is persisted in. Without divine instruction as to God's reasons for punishing these cities, Abraham might have regarded their destruction as a merely natural phenomenon caused by an outbreak of the volcanic forces that are still to be found in that region. But if he knew that it was a judicial act of divine justice, this would be for him a most effective means of instructing and warning his descendants. He could point them to Sodom's doom, in case they departed from the way of the Lord, and he could show them plainly how God deals with

1. THE EXEGETICAL-HOMILETICAL TREATMENT OF THE TEXT   529

those who refuse to do justice and judgment. This was the light in which Sodom's destruction was viewed by the prophets; comp. Deut. 29:23; Isa. 1:9-10; 13:19; Jer. 20:16; 23:14; 49:18; 50:40; Lament. 4:6; Ezek. 16:46.—At the beginning of v. 17 the Septuagint adds to "from Abraham" the words, "my servant," for which Philo has, "my friend." Whether or not this addition was found in the original Hebrew text, it is genuinely scriptural (Isa. 41:8; 2 Chron. 20:7; Gen. 26:24), and there is scarcely any other passage in which it would be more appropriate. Delitzsch says: "Abraham is God's friend, and from one's friend one keeps nothing secret." Since Abraham's call is described as the reason for this revelation of Yahveh to him, it is clear that the revelation has its ultimate cause in the grace of God, for it was this grace to which he owed his call. Hence Calvin comments on our passage: "Why does God constantly bestow upon us such innumerable blessings but that He has at one time embraced us in paternal love, and cannot now deny Himself? He thus honors in us as it were Himself and His own gifts. For to what does He refer here but to His gifts of grace? He draws, therefore, the matter for His mercy out of Himself, and not out of Abraham's merit; for the blessing upon Abraham proceeds from none other than a divine source."

Vv. 20-22a.—Yahveh has determined to reveal to Abraham what He has in mind to do. Hence He says to him: "The cry of Sodom and Gomorrah, verily it is great; and their sin, verily it is very grievous." The cry of Sodom is explained by Gen. 4:10 and Jas. 5:4. In the former passage it is the blood of murdered Abel that cries to heaven; in the latter it is the cries of the reapers whose hire has been withheld. According to Ezek. 16:49-50, this was the very sin of Sodom,— she did not "strengthen the hands of the poor and needy." But this recedes in the following chapter behind the grosser sin, the unnatural immorality, the peculiar vice of Sodom. As in Gen. 4:10 the innocent blood of Abel cried to heaven for vengeance, so the very bodies of the Sodomites, abused and tormented by lust, cry in God's ears. Hence the Lord will "go down," i. e., from the place where He now stands He will descend into the valley, "and see whether they all have done according to the cry that is come unto me." The emphasis lies upon "they all" (we read, with Buhl and Kautzsch, *kullam* instead of *kalah*[1]), which is placed at the end of the sentence. Yahveh, there-

---

[1]The masoretic reading hardly makes good sense. But if we read *kullam*, the language becomes clear; light falls upon the fact that *all* Sodomites took part in the assault on Lot's house, emphasized in

fore, determines to go down to see whether all Sodomites have been equally wicked. By His omniscience He knows beforehand what the result of this final visitation will be. He uses these words in order to show Abraham in a vivid way that He never punishes, least of all in this terrible manner, until guilt has been unmistakably established, and until he has carefully and personally examined whether there may not be some extenuating and restraining facts in the case. Only when a people in its totality has become a carcass, the eagles of judgment gather; only when the salt has lost its savor and cannot be salted, it is cast out and the end is at hand. This was an important truth for Abraham to learn as teacher of coming generations. He was, indeed, to teach them that God is a just God, but he was not to forget to present Him as patient and long-suffering, and His judgment as waiting until there is no longer any hope or possibility of repentance. Possibly the last words: "I will know it" are to be understood in the sense of "I will make experience of it," i. e., I will experience it in myself whether all the people of Sodom are as depraved as appears from the cry that has come to me. The language will bear this interpretation, which is supported by the account in Gen. 19, and finds a fine parallel in Matt. 21:37.—The Lord has confided His plan to Abraham, and the two men, who appear to have stood silently by His side, now turn and go toward Sodom. They are, therefore, appointed to make the final visitation. In and through them it is made by Yahveh Himself.

Vv. 22b-25.—Abraham's initiation into the divine counsel was a proof of the intimate relation with God to which by His grace he had been admitted. But it was also to be a test of his faith. He was to show whether he realized his call to be a bringer of blessing to all nations; whether he would regard with heartless indifference the destruction of his neighbors, or whether his calling and his love would prompt him to use his intimacy with God in order to procure, if possible, a blessing for them. Here, as in every step of his experience since he left his father's house, Abraham's faith is to be tested and trained. Never had God come so close to him as now. But every progress in the revelation of divine grace brings with it a corresponding demand upon faith, which is to prove its genuineness by laying hold of the new proffer of grace and making a venture upon it for itself or for others. Abraham emerges successfully from this test. After the two men had departed for Sodom, he "stood yet before the

---

Gen. 19:4; and Abraham's words follow naturally: "Peradventure there are fifty righteous within the city."

1. THE EXEGETICAL-HOMILETICAL TREATMENT OF THE TEXT 531

Lord." He drew, indeed, nearer to Him and began to intercede for the wicked cities. The Lord had not directly said that their doom was immediately at hand, but Abraham had gathered as much from His words concerning the final visitation. This doom pressed heavily upon his heart. There was in Abraham nothing of the spirit of Cain. And because Yahveh had said that He desired to know *all* the people of Sodom were in the same condemnation, and because Abraham's love for his neighbors cannot believe this possible, he ventures to make intercession for them, he ventures upon a prayer so hearty, persistent, childlike, bold, fervent, and unashamed, that it has, in Luther's opinion, no equal in Scripture. Says Luther: "Abraham prays a mighty and an aggressive prayer, with which he seeks to compel God to forgive. The words betray the depth of his feeling, in which the tears must have run down his cheeks and his heart have overflowed with groanings that could not be uttered." Expositors do not agree as to the contents of the prayer in vv. 23-25. But there is no insuperable difficulty, if we bear in mind the progression of thought. Abraham prays, first of all, that God will spare the *righteous* who may be found in the city (Sodom represents the five cities) and not consume them with the wicked. This would be unjust; for "this is the manner of tyrants, who burn houses, villages and cities, and care not whether righteous or wicked perish" (Luther). This is not God's way. As judge of all the earth, He must distinguish between righteous and wicked. To this first petition Abraham adds another: "Wilt Thou not rather spare *all the place* for the fifty righteous that are therein?" The latter petition he is most concerned with, and to this point his subsequent prayers are confined. In vv. 23-25 the first half of Abraham's prayer stands in the foreground, and for this reason the appeal to God's justice is found here only. In the following verses this appeal is omitted, and the emphasis falls on the second half of the prayer. With each repetition of the prayer Abraham's courage grows stronger.

Vv. 26-33.—The fervent intercession of His chosen, God cannot resist. Abraham's childlike confidence calls into play the fulness of His fatherly love. He does not enter into the first and less important half of Abraham's prayer, for it is self-evident that He will not consume the righteous with the wicked. He immediately grants Abraham's greater request, in which the smaller is included: He will spare all the place, if He can find fifty righteous in Sodom. Both Abraham and God speak of "righteous." That does not mean sinless and holy, but "upright men, who had kept themselves conscientiously and in the fear of God from the wickedness reigning in the cities" (Keil). And from the way in which both speak of a sparing of all because of these righteous, it is seen that the latter are regarded as restraining and preserving factors in the world. This is true in a preeminent degree of Abraham himself, who here leaps into the breach and restrains the arm of divine judgment. Luther well says: "There was a fine tale among the ancients, doubtless drawn from the preaching of the fathers, of a strong man, Atlas by name, who bore heaven upon his back and held it up. For there are always some saints on earth, who bear and hold back God's wrath, and for whose sake God spares the world. Thus Jerusalem might not be destroyed, because the apostles dwelt and taught therein. But when the time of its siege drew near, they were bidden to flee into the mountains and to depart into Galilee." It is God's mercy that permits Abraham's intercession to influence His world-government, and that will make one further attempt to see whether the little leaven of righteous may not leaven the whole corrupt lump. Seeing his prayer so readily granted, Abraham proceeds further to importune God, and reduces his fifty to five and forty, then to forty, to thirty, to twenty, and last to ten. The more God gives, the more he dares to ask. He haggles, chaffers, drives a bargain with God. Delitzsch: "This apparent haggling and begging is the essence of petitionary prayer, It is that sacred ἀναίδια of which our Lord speaks in Luke 11:8, the shameless persistence of faith that bridges the infinite distance between the creature and the Creator, unceasingly assaults the heart of God, and will not give over until He has capitulated. This would not be possible unless God, by reason of the mysterious interrelation of necessity and freedom in His nature and work, had granted to the prayer of faith a power by which He willingly suffers Himself to be overcome; unless, by reason of His absoluteness, which is far from being a blind necessity, He had entered into such a relation with men that He not only works upon them by grace, but lets them work upon Him by faith; unless He had woven the life of the creature into His own absolute life, and vouchsafed to created personality the right to affect His own personality through faith." But Abraham does not deal with God without the full consciousness of his unworthiness. Four times this consciousness breaks forth, as introduction and apology of his prayer. Twice he says that he has "taken upon him to speak unto the Lord;" once he adds, "which am but dust and ashes," i. e., dust as to his origin, ashes as to his end. Zezschwitz finely says: "It is true, Abraham stays the arm of the Judge Himself, and grasps God as

1. THE EXEGETICAL-HOMILETICAL TREATMENT OF THE TEXT

with arms of iron; but if we look closely, we see how his hands tremble. It is true, he casts himself in God's way, but in such a manner that he lies before Him in the dust." In this humility he also recognizes the limits of intercession. He does not reduce his figure below ten, although he might have been tempted to do so by the thought of Lot and his family. His prayer is not begging, but sacred bargaining with God. The consciousness of God's holiness compels him to pause. By his silence he gives glory to God's judgment and does not venture to ask more. When God, after answering his last petition, immediately departs, Abraham makes no attempt to detain Him. He recognizes the limit set by God, and returns slowly to his tent. He is comforted, and yet his heart is heavy. The Lord had promised to spare the cities for ten righteous. Abraham asks himself: "Are ten righteous to be found?" It must have been for him a restless and anxious night.

Application.—The text must be applied *indirectly* and by the *typical* method. The intimate relation between Abraham and God, —the main thought combining the two parts of the passage (vv. 16-22a and 22b-33) into unity,—is a type, a prefiguration of the intimate relation existing today between God and the believer.

In human friendships there is often a certain self-abnegation and sacrifice on the one part. Not so with Abraham. God chose him as friend, not because he had performed some mighty deed in the past, but because He Himself had called him in pure grace and desired to make him great in the future. So we Christians do not enter by our own work or worthiness into intimate relationship with God, but He calls us purely by grace and His free choice out of our lost and condemned condition into the relation of friends. The relation involved in justification is one of sonship, of friendship. It has the same two sides shown in our text. God becomes our Father, and adopts us as 'His children or friends; and we, as children and friends of God, have free access to Him and may talk with Him as a child with its father, as a friend with his friend.

Abraham's relation to God is so intimate that God deems it His duty to communicate to him His plans and purposes; that He regards it, indeed, as wrong to hide anything from him. That is not the manner of a master with his servant; he simply commands and expects instant obedience. It is not even the manner of a father with his child; though he loves it with all his heart, he does not confide to it all his plans and anxieties and duties. The child is not yet mature enough for this, and is not to be burdened with such matters.

But to one's friend one confides all, one tells one's troubles, one bares one's heart. With him one shares the joys and sorrows of life, to him one reveals one's secret purposes and ambitions. Such is the friendly relation of God to His chosen ones, even today, in proportion as they let themselves be drawn into ever greater intimacy with Him. We should, indeed, be servants of God, who do His will; we should be children of God, crying, "Abba, father"; but the highest and best is to be friends of God, who are in His confidence, to whom He vouchsafes an insight into His world-government, so that He does nothing without making it known to them, if not in all its details, yet in its underlying principles and its ultimate purpose. Jesus' word in John 15:15 applies to us,—"I have called you friends; for all things that I have heard of my Father I have made known unto you." The world gropes in darkness; but His friends know that He has made the world by the word of His power, and that He will destroy the world, when its sin, like Sodom's, cries to heaven, and when it refuses to submit to His spirit. The world dreams of a God resembling a weakly, sentimental parent, who cannot bear to punish; His friends know Him in the fulness of His revelation of love and grace, but they know also that He is a jealous God, a consuming fire, a living God, into whose hands it is terrible for impenitent sinners to fall. He has set us to be preachers of His righteousness in the midst of a wicked and perverse generation, to be teachers of generations to come. He has not revealed Himself to the world; but to His friends He has opened His heart. To us He has shown how we may be justified and saved; where we may find forgiveness for our sins and comfort in time of trouble; how even at the last, death need have no terrors for us, if we hold in faith to our heavenly Friend, whose friendship is stronger than death.

Abraham immediately asserts the right of the friendship granted him by God, and uses it in the interest of his neighbors who are threatened with divine judgment. Thus the justified Christian has the right of boldness of speech (παρρησία) with his heavenly Friend and may lay all his cares before Him. This is the blessed privilege of God's children and friends. Indeed, the Christian is not really God's friend, if he fails to make use of this privilege, if he hides his troubles from his Friend. But no less may and should the troubles of others be laid before Him. Here is a woman who has a husband living in sin, despising God's Word, and saddening her life by his coarse and vicious conduct. She has pleaded and remonstrated with him, but in vain. There is one thing left to her: she can

1. THE EXEGETICAL-HOMILETICAL TREATMENT OF THE TEXT 535

and should pray for him. She should place herself as a wall between God and him, so that the divine judgment may be delayed, and he may be granted a season of grace in which to repent. Here is a brother or sister or child; here is so many a member of the church. They are walking in the way of sin and will not turn back, the divine judgment is already gathering about them, one can almost see the lightning of divine wrath flash above their heads. In their behalf the Christian may and should seek to stay the arm of the Judge, cast himself in His way, and restrain Him with supplications and intercessions. Such prayers avail much. Many a pious man of God, by thus interceding for home or fatherland, has turned back the impending doom; for the friends of God are even today a preservative force in the world. Compare Augustine's mother, and Spener's confession that in his youth his father's prayers surrounded him like mountains, until he turned from his evil way. In such fervent intercession the intimate relation of the Christian to his God expresses itself most fully; by it he obtains victory upon victory. The peculiar conditions in the congregation and the immediate needs of the Church—not to forget foreign and inner missions, whose distinctive work is with those who are under divine judgment—will suggest to the preacher the specific objects of the intercession he is to practice and to persuade his hearers to practice. We cannot be God's friends unless we practice such intercession.

But Abraham's prayer would not have been granted, his friendship with God would not have endured, if it had not gone hand in hand with deep humility toward God and with hearty compassion for those exposed to judgment. This is true also of our friendship with God. The more highly He advances us in the ranks of His friends, the more prone we are to forget how great the peril in which we formerly lay and from which His grace has rescued us. True humility leads to true courage. Seasons of humiliation have always been seasons of victory. It was when the Syrophenician woman was content to be ranked among the dogs that Jesus raised her up to sit with the children. But humility must be accompanied with compassion, compassion that cannot bear to see a brother perishing by the way or rushing toward destruction. Christians must exercise the care of souls, and the soul of this care is deep compassion for those who are as sheep having no shepherd. Because this is lacking, so many efforts to save souls are in vain. Not to shut the heart to God, when He would open it; in faith to accept His grace; to walk humbly with God, to love the brethren, and to feel pity for all who are lost—this is to become God's friends, and to remain His friends until the day when He will openly acknowledge us as His friends, while the Sodom of this world sinks in the flames of judgment.

1 Kings 19: 1-18.

Exposition.—Context: Yahveh's power had been made manifest on Carmel, Baal unmasked as a dead idol, and Yahveh recognized as the living God. As prescribed in the law, the prophets of Baal had been slain; the heavens had been opened in answer to the prayer of Elijah and the parched land refreshed with a great rain. Ahab could not be admonished more plainly to repent and to alter his policies. Will he be mindful, give glory to God and resist the sanatic influence of Jezebel? Elijah was hopeful. Therefore, he had run before Ahab to the entrance of Jezreel, this very evening, in order to serve the king as spiritual guide and adviser; primarily, however, to aid a warning conscience over against Jezebel. The prophet could not but believe that the turning-point had now arrived. Verily, the turning-point had arrived, as our pericope indicates, but in a manner very different from that expected by Elijah.

Vv. 1-2.—Ahab told his wife everything that had happened on Mount Carmel, especially that the prophets of Baal had been slain. He may have done this in the terror inspired by the occurrences of the day, as is indicated by the fact that he afterwards granted audience to true prophets of Yahveh (1 Kings 20: 13, 22, 35-42). Jezebel, however, was impressed solely by what the king said of the tremendous blow dealt the laboriously established service of Baal by the despised Elijah. It roused her to fury, and Ahab proved too weak to offer resistance. He was induced to permit her to exile the much hated man, and in the event that the following day should still find him present, to threaten him with the penalty of death. In the latter case, he was to suffer the same fate as the prophets of Baal, whom he had slain but the day previous. In order to make sure that she would not revoke this threat, Jezebel bound herself with an oath, inviting the curse of the gods upon her, if she failed to carry it into effect. Because Jezebel has closed eyes and ears to all manifestations of Yahveh's might, answering merely with the threat to destroy His servant, and because Ahab proved too weak to oppose her, therefore the die is cast against Ahab and his entire dynasty. Henceforth, the king of Israel may expect only the execution of judgment from Yahveh. But what will the prophet of Yahveh do under such circumstances?

1. THE EXEGETICAL-HOMILETICAL TREATMENT OF THE TEXT

Vv. 3-4.—When Elijah realized the situation, he arose and departed. What else could he do, when the task that brought him to Jezreel was shown to be impossible? If God had required him to face the new situation, Elijah would doubtless have done this fearlessly, since but a short time before he had appeared before Ahab, knowing full well that Ahab would have done nothing rather than slay him. But there was no such indication on the part of God. Elijah, therefore, recognized it as His will to submit to exile. He departed "because of his soul" or "for his life," which certainly does not mean from fear of death. The prophet had received his life and his call from God. It would have been nothing less than sin against God to remain except by God's direct command, since to remain meant not only certain death, but death at the hand of impious Jezebel. What a triumph that would have been for Jezebel, and what a defeat for the cause of Yahveh and His worship. Had Elijah been entirely at liberty he would have preferred to stay. But he had learned to do nothing except at God's behest. Rather than disobey, he readily exposes himself to what seems like cowardice. Jezebel should not boast of having avenged the prophets of Baal with the blood of Elijah. He turned his steps toward Judah and came as far as Beersheba. Nor does he tarry here, but continues on into the wilderness. He desires to be alone and to meditate upon the wonderful ways of his God. The servant is, therefore, left behind in Beersheba. An entire day is spent restlessly roaming about in the Arabian desert. Even more restless is his spirit, vainly attempting to comprehend the ways of God. On mount Carmel he had firmly believed that the wonderful manifestation of God, prayerfully recognized by all the people, had won the king and would induce him to abolish the worship of Baal throughout the land; yet now he must experience how Jezebel is permitted to make all of none effect. As an exile, he, who alone dared to defend the God of the covenant, wanders aimlessly about in the wilderness. It was a complex problem difficult to comprehend. Night was falling, and still he had not found the solution. Then he sat down under a juniper tree desiring death. "O Lord, take away my life; for I am not better than my fathers" (i. e., I do not desire long life in distinction from my fathers), —thus spoke the prophet. Nothing could be more erroneous than the notion that these words signify disgust with life or, even worse, that they are the expression of a rebellious spirit. If that had been the case, Elijah would have been deserving of reproof and reprimand; yet the Lord sends, on the contrary, a heavenly messenger who strengthens and refreshes him, who speaks only cheering and encouraging words. The words of the prophet are rather to be understood in connection with his entire life-history, as well as with the various experiences he had just made. His entire life had no other aim but to lead Israel back to the service of Yahveh. Since this object had apparently been frustrated once for all, life had for him no further aim or object. To bring about the conversion of Israel, to guide and strengthen Ahab in the right way—for this he would have gladly lived and spent his strength, despite his age. In this sacred vocation nothing would have been too much or too difficult. But now that all was frustrated, life for him, who lived only for his vocation, was of no value; an extension of his life beyond the years of his fathers would be without purpose. Not only would it be torture for him to witness the progress and development of the worship of Baal, but under the circumstances he would be without position and calling. Menken correctly says that a sacred grief and sorrow took possession of him. His words bear testimony that his life and calling were one. He cannot even conceive of continued life without the possibility of exercising his calling.

Vv. 5-9.—With the request that he might die, the prophet fell asleep. The angel of Yahveh appeared to him, but did not take his life, nor command him to return, nor solve the problem that weighed so heavily upon him. He merely brought meat and drink, to refresh the prophet after his long journey and to strengthen him for further labors. When Elijah awoke the first time, but probably because of fatigue ate little and again fell asleep, the angel called him again to eat heartily in preparation for a long journey. Obeying the angel, Elijah ate and drank and in the strength of that meat proceeded to Mount Horeb. The fact that he journeyed forty days and nights until he arrived at the mount of God, seems strange, since this mount is but forty geographical miles distant from Beersheba and but an eleven day's journey from Kadesh (Deut. 1:2). This, however, merely indicates that Elijah originally did not think of going to Horeb, but roamed about in the wilderness without plan or purpose, until God Himself finally directed his footsteps thither. V. 7 is not opposed to this, since it is merely presupposed here that God well knew the aim of his wandering, though Elijah did not. Evidently, these forty days and nights were meant to serve the prophet as a time of sacred preparation for the revelations of God that he was to experience. The very fact that God, instead of granting his request, wonderfully prepares and strengthens him for continued life, must have shown him

1. THE EXEGETICAL-HOMILETICAL TREATMENT OF THE TEXT 539

that God had something else for him to do, that his work had not yet come to a close. Elijah finally brought himself to recognize this and was willing to serve the Lord further wherever he might be needed, since later, when he stands before the Lord, he does not repeat his former request. Fasting forty days and nights (cf. Ex. 24:18; 34:28; Deut. 9:9; 18:25; 10:10) was to be for his soul an opportunity to dwell upon God and the things of the heavenly world. The desert, where the history of the fathers of Israel everywhere revived, was a fitting place for this preparation. Here he could recall the wonderful ways of God; he could think of Moses,—how he despaired of the future of his people, so that he was inclined to resign his leadership, but how God, after having decimated the people through many judgments, nevertheless in the end granted them a season of grace and accepted them as His own. Thus prepared, Elijah is led to the mount of God, to the mount of revelation in the days of Moses. He spends the night in a cave. Since the Hebrew version prefixes the article, designating it as a cave well known, some expositors think it identical with that referred to in Ex. 33:22. Certainly, an acceptable idea.

Vv. 10-18.—Once more the cave serves as a place of revelation. The word of God comes to Elijah. When he is asked, "What doest thou here?" it is evident that these words are not to be taken as a reproach. If his actions deserved a reproach, or if it had been the intention of God to reprove him, that would have been done when the angel appeared to him under the juniper tree. The question is rather to be taken as an expression of tenderness. God intended to give Elijah an opportunity to speak out his heart, to bring his sorrow before his God. This is borne out by Elijah's answer. It is not an expression of natural passion, desirous of immediately calling down the revenge of the Almighty upon the worshipers of idols, nor is it an expression of discontent, but merely a simple, truthful statement of the situation in Israel which had induced him to journey into the wilderness. Four events had occured in Israel: The covenant made at Sinai had been broken; the altars dedicated to the service of Yahveh, still to be found here and there in the land of Israel, had been destroyed; all the prophets, except himself, had been slain; and even his own life was threatened. As emphasized by its place at the beginning of the sentence, all this had occurred despite his jealousy for the Lord. What is he to do among his people, when this zeal remains fruitless, when they even attempt to take his life? Under these circumstances he regarded the desert as the most proper place of refuge. As far as he could see, he had arrived at the conclusion of his work. His answer seemingly implies the reservation: "Or hast Thou still some work for me to do? Can I still serve Thee by serving my people, this being their condition? Serve Thee, who hast so wonderfully preserved me and even now hast led me to Horeb, the mount of revelation?" It is just this question to which the Lord replies in what follows, first by signs, then by words explaining the signs. By signs; for Yahveh passed perceptibly before him, yet in such manner that the strong wind, the earthquake and the fire went before Him. Then Yahveh Himself passed by in a sound of gentle stillness, much like the refreshing breeze after a storm. Elijah recognized that Yahveh was in the still small voice; therefore, he concealed his face and stood in the entrance of the cave. The real significance of the signs, however, remained hidden from him; therefore, the repetition of the Lord's inquiry drew forth the same answer. Then the Lord added the explanatory words to the signs (vv. 15-18). "Yes," was His reply, "I still have work for you, your life is not without aim or object, despite the deplorable backsliding of your people. Anoint Hazael to be king over Aram (=Syria), and Jehu to be king over Israel, and Elisha to be prophet in your stead. Just as I passed by you in the strong wind, the earthquake and the fire, so shall Hazael, Jehu and Elisha fall upon the kindred and kingdom of Ahab, and whosoever escapes Hazael shall be slain by Jehu, and whosoever escapes Jehu, him shall Elisha kill. Only after these three have served me as servants of judgment, will I reveal myself as I am to the seven thousand who have not bowed the knee before Baal, nor kissed the feet of the idol. Them will I refresh with my love and grace, as sweet breezes refresh the face of nature after the storm."

That this is the obvious sense of the entire transaction at Horeb, was clearly recognized by Koehler (*Lehrbuch der Biblischen Geschichte,* vol. 3) and again decisively emphasized by Koeberle (*Suende und Gnade im religioesen Leben Israels,* 1905). Its purpose was not to instruct Elijah concerning the nature of God, in order that he might realize the impropriety of his human zeal. The revelation of God's justice must stand in harmony with His love and grace. Elijah was not prompted by human zeal, nor did he doubt the grace of God. Much less was this occurrence to be of prophetic significance, so that in it the dispensations of the law and the Gospel, of the Old and the New Covenant are here contrasted. All these interpretations are excluded by the words of God addressed to the prophet. Only the interpretation suitable to what precedes as well as to what follows can be

1. THE EXEGETICAL-HOMILETICAL TREATMENT OF THE TEXT 541

correct. It may be clearly expressed that the nature of God consists of love and grace, yet emphasis is not placed upon that. It is placed rather upon this, that God cannot make His love and grace manifest where there is such stubborn resistance as appears in the kindred and kingdom of Ahab, unless His angels of judgment have preceded Him. Doomed to destruction, the house of Ahab must experience the earnest of God's judgment in an extreme form. When that is accomplished which the zeal of Elijah did not accomplish and the gracious exhibition of the power of God could not bring about, namely, the abolition of the worship of Baal, then He will reveal Himself to His people according to His true nature, according to 'His love and mercy. This is also in full accord with the following historical development. The house of Ahab fell prey to the judgment of God. In the reign of Jehu there was no worship of Baal in Israel. If they had renounced the service of idols and come to the upright service of Yahveh, then the grace of God would have been revealed even more abundantly after the judgment than really was the case. Henceforth Elijah should merely be a messenger of judgment; but God needed him even here, so that his future life was not to be without aim or purpose. Indeed, from now on, Elijah appears upon the scene only to announce and to prepare for the judgments of Yahveh (1 Kings 19: 19-21; 21: 17 ff.; 2 Kings 1: 3-16). Hazael and Jehu became God's servants of judgment upon Ahab and Jezebel. One recognizes that even Elisha was a prophet of judgment, when one considers that the miracles of assistance and blessing were always limited to the small circle of believers, or to a heathen like Naaman. For the people at large, he was a prophet of judgment primarily in the first period of his activity. Under him Hazael came to Israel and Jehu was made king. The first miracle he performed was an act of judgment. Thus we abide by our exposition.

Application.—Application to the present time must follow *indirectly*, and it is the *typical* application that is most fitting. The attitude of God toward Ahab and Jezebel is a type of His attitude towards individuals and nations even to this day. And the experience of Elijah is a type of the experience made by many a servant of God today.

The text must be taken as a whole and its significance set forth for the present time. Thus, we can not select a specific verse, for instance, the ninth, and with A. Rowland in the *Pulpit Commentary,* group everything about the question there contained: "A question from God for the consideration of man. I. The question came to a prophet in his hour of despair. This divine interposition taught him the following lessons: (1) That God was near; (2) that success was assured; (3) that work was waiting. II. This question came to a man in a false position. The question should pursue others who have fled to caves in which they would fain hide themselves from responsibility. (1) It comes to the impenitent in the cave of concealment; (2) it comes to the penitent in the cave of despondency; (3) it comes to the indolent in the cave of sloth; (4) it comes to the sorrowful in the cave of murmuring." Though the first part contains much that is correct, the second part is purely fantastic and is illustrative of how a text should *not* be applied. Was Elijah impenitent and slothful, did he murmur against God? Nor are we satisfied when the same author, on the basis of the twelfth verse, speaks of "The still, small voice," developing the thoughts: I. The spiritual weakness of what seems mighty: This is exemplified (1) By the experience of Elijah; (2) by the miracles of judgment; (3) by the penalties of the law; (4) by the events of providence. II. The spiritual strength of what seems feeble: The still small voice (1) follows on preparation; (2) it reminds of secret forces; (3) it typifies the influence of the Holy Spirit; (4) it whispers of the love of Christ. Thus v. 12 is torn from its connection and foreign thoughts are introduced as we have seen above in the case of Tholuck and Muellensiefen.[2] Such things must become ever more and more impossible to the preacher. Nor should we regard the fourth verse as central and speak of "The Causes of Despondency: (1) Reaction after exitement; (2) exhaustion of physical and nervous energy; (3) absence of sympathy; (4) influence of doubt; (5) invisibility of antagonists; (6) enforced inactivity." Nor can we limit ourselves to vv. 1-8, as J. A. MacDonald in the *Pulpit Commentary,* who treats: "Elijah's Prayer for Death: I. The occasion for this prayer: (1) Jezebel had threatened his life; (2) to save his life he fled; (3) alone with God he asks to die. II. The answers given to it: (1) They came in form of physical refreshment; (2) they came to him in spiritual blessings." We should thus have before us merely the beginning of God's dealings with Elijah. For this it would be even more appropriate to regard vv. 9-18 as central. The same J. A. MacDonald suggests, revealing in the main a sound understanding of the text, especially in the second part: "Elijah at Horeb: I. His intercession against Israel: (1) Observe the occasion; (2) the matter of the accusation. II. The answer of God unto Him: (1) This was first given in symbol; (2) it was afterward expounded in words (Elijah,

---

[2] P. 364.

1. THE EXEGETICAL-HOMILETICAL TREATMENT OF THE TEXT   543

the intercessor against Israel, and, therefore, the impersonation of anger against sin, was to return to Israel by way of Damascus, where he was to anoint Hazael as king over Syria. In Hazael we must look for the 'strong wind' that was to come up and make havoc upon the mountains and rocks of Israel (2 Kings 8:12, 13; 10:32, 33; 13:3), Jehu was the instrument of the 'earthquake' of revolution (2 Kings 9:1-3), Elijah was God's instrument of 'fire.' His words are to be swords of flame. So 'it shall come to pass that him that escapeth from the sword of Hazael shall Jehu slay, and him that escapeth from the sword of Jehu shall Elisha slay.' No sinner can escape the fire of God's word. But the 'still small voice' of the Gospel of mercy has its triumphs: 'Yet I have left me seven thousand in Israel.')"

If we treat, as is our duty, the text as a whole, which in reality it is, then its significance for the present time lies in the following two points: In the attitude of God toward His tempted prophet, and in the attitude of God toward His people.

The prophet is tempted because he does not accomplish in his calling what he would and should accomplish. Such temptations are experienced even today. Many a pastor stands in his pulpit Sunday after Sunday, year after year, proclaiming the good word of God, its seriousness and mercy, its law and Gospel, its judgment and grace, threatening and imploring. Yet they who need it do not hear it; and they who hear it pay no attention to it. With a heavy heart he complains: "My people turn from me; they are tired of the Gospel; though I preach to them, they do not follow." Many teachers and parents have similar experiences. They are brought into temptation; they imagine they are spending their energy in vain. Continued life and activity appear to be useless, because in their calling they do not accomplish that for which they exist. How does God deal with them? He does not reject them, as little as He rejected Elijah. He takes an interest in them. He assigns them new duties. As he did with Elijah, so He even permits them to see some of the fruits of their former labors. Thus he encourages them, so that they resume their tasks with renewed vigor. With these thoughts one may build up a fruitful sermon in accordance with the text.

But even so the heart of the text would not be touched. In its connection in the book of Kings, the object of our text is not to exhibit the attitude of God toward His tempted prophet. It is rather to show how God deals with His people and kingdom, whose only response to all His love and power is to persecute His prophet. From this viewpoint justice may be done to what is said in this chapter concerning the attitude of God toward His tempted prophet; but in the foreground will stand the school of discipline into which God has taken and will continue to take His people.

We realize from the context of our narrative, how God condescends to men in exceeding love and grace. How He condescended to Israel in love and mercy, from its unmerited selection (Deut. 7:7-8) to the times of David and Solomon. Nor did 'He cease even after the worship of idols had been introduced into the dual kingdom. How powerfully He worked through the instrumentality of Elijah in order to bring people to abandon the worship of Baal! So God deals with entire nations as well as with individuals, even to this day. With what wonderful condescension God favored Germany, making it the cradle of the Reformation and the teacher of nations. How many times in the past centuries did He not seek to guide them with love and mercy, granting them an awakening even in the dark days of rationalism. To what other purpose, than to train them as His people? What of our own country? Truly, here, too, there are not lacking many evidences of His love and favor. Through location, climate, fertility of soil and mineral riches, He has made it a land of almost unlimited possibilities. Through the importation of the vital elements of old-world culture, He has presented to it the experiences of all nations. Through liberation from the British yoke, He has given the possibility of independent development. Through the introduction of the Gospel and the examples of many truly Christian men and women, He has not left the way of life unknown. Through the implanting of the Lutheran Church He has added the necessary leaven to its Calvanistic church-life. All to the end that it might be trained in His school. So God also condescends to the individual Christians in love and mercy. Baptism, instruction, daily life. In trials and tribulations He destroys the idols in which they trusted, in order to reclaim their souls and reunite them with Him.

Because Israel refuses to be led to repentance by the goodness of God, He visits judgment upon them, one after another, if perchance He may yet succeed in His training of them. That was the purpose of the divine appearance at Horeb, saying to Elijah: "I have not given up my people. There is yet another means that I wish to apply before I reject Israel. The messengers of judgment must first come upon them, and then the judgments one upon another." So God deals even today. There are nations, even churches, congregations and individuals, upon whom all efforts of training by means of God's love

1. THE EXEGETICAL-HOMILETICAL TREATMENT OF THE TEXT 545

and mercy are thrown away. We have the history of Germany in mind. Did it not close itself to the seeking influences of divine law, serving self-made idols and stubbornly persisting in that service? Did God, therefore, forsake it utterly and cast it aside as hopeless? By no means. He came with His judgments one upon another. It is the wisdom of divine training that acts thus. What of our own people? Are conditions any better? Most certainly not. Everywhere one sees the ascending smoke of altars bearing sacrifices to their idols. Often they would like nothing better than to banish the messengers who speak the truth fearlessly and directly. Apparently they little regard the storm of judgment passing over the old world of culture. If this should continue, if the goodness of God does not lead us to repentance, then He must change His attitude toward us and take a new way—the way of judgment. He is abundantly able to let judgments follow one another, as in Israel, or even earlier in Egypt. No matter how often His arm of judgment may have descended with shattering effect, it is constantly extended ready to deal the next blow (Isa. 9:7-10:4). He will continue His chastisement until not a spot remains on the body politic, that has not been bruised or wounded. Even today, stormwind, earthquake and fire are at his disposal. We may conceive of these forces as literal or figurative. We may think of the stormwind in nature, or the stormwind of war; of the earthquake as it actually occurs, or of the dangerous forces of unrest within the nation, seething and seeking expression. We may think of the fire that reduces cities and villages to ashes, or of the fire of lies and hatred that burns brightly in boundless revolt. All must serve God as servants of judgment upon men, in order, if possible, to show them the folly and danger of their evil ways and turn them back to Him. Oh, that we would permit ourselves to be led by His goodness to repentance, that it may not become necessary to employ judgments as our task-masters. There are certain Christian congregations, left by pastors in utter despair, because any further efforts would apparently be fruitless. God is not ready, however, to abandon such a congregation immediately, but the means of training that He still possesses are His judgments, terrible and severe. If the individual will not permit himself to be led to repentance by the goodness of God, but rather grows satisfied and contented, proud and secure, if he refuses to listen to the truth by the mouth of man, God will deal with him in accordance with the principle: Whosoever will not permit himself to be led to repentance by God's goodness, upon him will God visit His judgments. Because judgment serves God merely as a means of training, therefore it is not final in His intention. It is meant to serve Him as a means for attaining something higher. It is emblematic of His innermost nature. When the judgments have accomplished their purpose on Israel, then He will reveal himself to the seven thousand who have been not only externally depressed, but spiritually crushed. He will reveal Himself as He is, and will refresh them with love and grace. Even today, judgment and punishment are not intended to be God's last word to us. When we will not permit ourselves to be led to repentance by God's goodness, there is no other means left but judgment. Our God can punish terribly, externally and internally. He can destroy our idols through the forces of nature and work upon our consciences through His law. In this He sometimes appears heartless and cruel. That, however, is not His true nature. As Luther expresses it, it is a "fremd Amt" of God. The love of God waits to be applied to develop freely. Let us, therefore, not resist, if He decrees to crush us by His judgment. His judgment, his crushing, is a means of training. After He has cast us down, He comes to us in the still small voice of His Gospel. He lets us see into His very heart, and we shall not be able to understand how it was possible for us to offer resistance so long. That is the beginning of a blessed time, a time of refreshment from the heart of God. That is God's object. If this object is not realized in us, we and we alone are responsible.

(2) Prophetic Texts
Isaiah 61:1-7.

Exposition.—Context: Our text is taken from the second part of the Book of Isaiah, subdivision three (ch. 58-66), section four. (The first section extends from 58:1 to 14; the second, from 59:1 to 21; the third, from 60:1 to 22; and the fourth, from 61:1 to 11). The entire second part of Isaiah is written from the point of view of the Babylonian exile. This is clearly seen in our passage. In it the prophet, who sees in spirit the people languishing in captivity, consoles them by pointing out the glorious future awaiting them after their return from exile. To the eyes of the prophet deliverance from Babylon, redemption through Christ, and final salvation appear as in one picture. Having described in ch. 60 the marvelous splendor of the Jerusalem of the future, Isaiah introduces the servant of Yaveh as speaker. Through him alone, through his mediation, will the future glory be established. Our pericope, taken from the fourth section, resolves itself into two parts: vv. 1-3a and vv. 3b-7.

1. THE EXEGETICAL-HOMILETICAL TREATMENT OF THE TEXT   547

Vv. 1-3a. "The Spirit of Adonai-Yahveh is upon me." Thus some one dramatically introduces himself as speaker. The speaker leaves it to the reader to guess at his name. Many have thought him to be the prophet himself. But this view cannot be maintained. For in the entire second part of the book the prophet seeks everywhere to conceal his own identity; why should he here make an exception and speak of himself, throughout seven, or rather nine or eleven verses, in so sublime a manner? Heretofore, only the servant of Yahveh has been credited with such wonderful works; not any servant of Yahveh, but the servant κατ' ἐξοχήν, whom God introduces in ch. 42, who himself speaks in ch. 49, and who forms the contents of ch. 52 and 53,—the promised Redeemer and Messiah. This servant of Yahveh is meant here. That this view is correct is further borne out by the fact that the speaker appropriates to himself the many little traits of character described in former verses and mentioned anew in this address. This interpretation also sheds new light upon Luke 4:18, in which passage Christ finds the fulfilment of this prophecy in Himself. We conclude, therefore, that the true servant of Yahveh here invites our attention, and speaks. What message has he for the captives in Babylon? When the Lord introduced him in ch. 42, He declared that He had put His Spirit upon him. Here the servant of Yahveh shows himself conscious of possessing this Spirit. He says: "The Spirit of Adonai-Yahveh is upon me;" i. e., rests upon me and abides with me. It will be the source of my strength and the standard of my conduct. The servant can even recall the time when this Spirit was put upon him; it is the time when he was anointed. He thus entertains no doubt as to having come into possession of the Spirit.

Why was he anointed? "To preach good tidings unto the meek;" i. e., those who are bowed down by vicissitudes and hardships, who are oppressed by the inner and outer circumstances of life, who are grieved over their burdensome lot, and who seek counsel and succor from God alone. In these few words the prophet sketches a picture of the faithful among the exiles. The glad tidings are for them, that they may again take courage and hope, put away their sorrow, and learn to rejoice. Six consecutive infinitives describe the contents of these glad tidings, introduced by the words: "(because Yahveh) hath sent me," which are a resumption of the thought: "because Yahveh hath anointed me." The servant is, first, to "bind up the broken-hearted." In Ps. 147:3 this work is ascribed to Yahveh, but here it is ascribed to His servant. Many faithful Israelites were broken-hearted over the destruction of the temple, the devastation of the land, and their deportation to Babylon. With Jeremiah they wept and lamented: "Oh, that my head were waters, and mine eyes a fountain of tears, that I might weep day and night for the slain of the daughter of my people" (Jer. 9:1). To these bleeding and broken hearts the servant is to dispense comfort and healing balm, that they may not bleed to death. His balm alone can cure, and his balm, as we learn from the context, is his word. Again, he is to "proclaim liberty to the captives." This work had already been assigned him by God (42:7); here he acknowledges it as his own. The captives in Babylon longed for liberty. He is to proclaim this liberty to them. Like the bird which has escaped from its cage and seeks the open sky; like the stream which has shaken off its burden of ice, and hastens into the free lands of the valley; like the slave whose prison door opens in the year of Jubilee, so shall Israel come forth from the land of captivity. The Hebrew word used here has these various shades of meaning; cf. Ps. 84:4; Prov. 26:2; Jer. 34:8; Lev. 25:10. It is the technical term used in proclaiming the year of Jubilee. The expression "and an opening to them that are bound" is more than a mere repetition of the foregoing. The Septuagint renders the expression τυφλοῖς ἀνάβλεψιν. The parallels in 4:27 and 35:5 favor this translation. The thought conveyed is not out of harmony with the idea of the year of Jubilee, when those who are in prison because of their debts are freed and those whose eyes have been blinded by the darkness of the prison cell see again the light of liberty. They will regard the world, and the world will regard them, in a different light. The servant is, thirdly, "to proclaim the acceptable year of Yahveh, and the day of vengeance of our God." The true year of Jubilee, of which the festival celebrated every fifty years was but a type, shall begin for Israel. God himself will appoint its time,—He before whom a thousand years are but as yesterday when it is past, and as a watch in the night. When this great day breaks, they shall return to their possesions as men were wont to return to their lands when the year of Jubilee approached (Lev. 25). The speaker declares that it will be "an acceptable year," when God will be pleased with His people, and will assemble them before Him in sabbatical rest and peace. No longer will He turn from them in anger, but will visit them with His love and mercy. But before this great year of grace and mercy can come, the enemies must be destroyed. For this reason the servant adds: "And the day of vengeance of our God." A short period of retribution will precede the long time of salvation.

1. THE EXEGETICAL-HOMILETICAL TREATMENT OF THE TEXT   549

The servant will, fourthly, "comfort all that mourn." When the prison doors are opened, and the day of salvation breaks, the sorrowing in Zion will be comforted. Their captivity is ended, and Yahveh's wrath is appeased. The fifth infinitive construction is incomplete. It must be explained in connection with the sixth construction: "to give them beauty for ashes, the oil of joy for mourning, the garment of praise for the spirit of heaviness." That memorable day will bring about wonderful changes. Those who, out of grief over the destruction of Zion and over their own guilt, have strewn ashes on their heads (Isa. 58:5; Ezek. 27:30; Job 2:8; Dan. 9:3) will then put on a wonderful headdress, a precious diadem, and will anoint their hair and face with the oil of joy (Deut. 28:4; 2 Sam. 14:2; Ps. 23:5; 45:8). Those whose spirits have been depressed and whose joy like a flickering candle, has burnt low will then dress themselves in a "garment of praise", i. e., they will be heard and seen ever praising God. In v. 1 the servant was said "to proclaim" and "to bind up;" here he is said "to appoint" and "to give." These latter expressions are significant. They distinguish the speaker from the ordinary prophets. He, the true prophet, can perform and give what he proclaims or promises. *Non praeco tantum, sed et dispensator,* remarks Vitringa. He can, as Luther says, fill all, move all, and give life to all, by reason of the Spirit which rests upon him.

Vv. 3b-7 describe the effect of the servant's work, and tell of the ultimate purpose of God in sending him. The people, weakened unto death, shall through his efforts regain new strength and vigor. Though they now appear like felled trees, devoid of life and growth, they shall become "terebinths of righteousness," i. e., they shall grow as strong, as stedfast, and as full of life as the terebinth with its massive trunk, its gorgeous green, its perennial foliage. They shall be called terebinths of "righteousness," because of their descent from the righteous stem of Jesse, and because of their fruits, accounted righteous by God. The entire nation shall become "a planting of God," a second Eden, and shall serve and glorify Him as its Creator (1 Pet. 2:9; Matt. 5:16). Luther says: "They shall appear like trees on whose every leaf are written the words: 'I thank Thee, Lord; I bless Thee.'" God intends that His servant shall restore the land to its former grandeur. Though thousands of years may have elapsed since it was desolated, it shall be rebuilt so that its outward appearance will harmonize with the inner glory of a new-born people. The very strangers who now hold the people in bondage shall then offer them their service and provide for their wants. They shall come before them, not as slaves, like the Gibeonites of yore (Joshua 9:21 ff.), not as a mongrel race of bondmen, but as freemen who, recognizing the special mission of Israel, are heartily glad to aid Israel in realizing its purpose in life. This thought leads on to the next: "ye shall be named the priests of Yahveh; ministers of our God ye shall be called." It was Israel's peculiar divine mission among the nations of the earth to act as teacher and priest, to be a kingdom of priests (Ex. 19). And the Gentiles, provided they accept the salvation offered them, and make Israel's God their God, are to constitute with Israel one large congregation. The priestly office, once held by Aaron and his descendants, is now to be held by Israel among the nations. With this may be connected the following thought: As the Levites possessed no property of their own, but received as their heritage the offerings of Yahveh, and were given the choicest parts of the sacrificial meals as their portion, so the new Jerusalem of Messianic times is to receive and "eat the wealth of the nations." Luther interprets this as meaning wealth, power, eloquence, etc.; Schmieder, as meaning whatever may be acquired through agriculture, commerce, art. and science. Compare the tithe, or tenth part, which Abraham gave to Melchizedek, priest-king of Salem. In "eating the wealth of the nations," Israel will "boast in their glory." The latter phrase conveys the same thought as the former, with a slightly different shade of meaning. V. 7 is difficult to understand. With Delitzsch and Orelli we render: "For your shame, double and for confusion they rejoice in their portion: therefore in their land they shall possess double and everlasting joy shall be unto them." In the present state of the text, this seems to be the only possible translation. The second half of the sentence explains the former more obscure half. The meaning would then be: To compensate them for their long exile, they will receive a double portion in the redivision of the land, and their joy over their possession will have no end. If we follow the revised text of Klostermann and Heyne, we shall have to translate: "Because their contumely was in double measure, and shame and spitting was their lot, therefore in their land," etc. The meaning will not be materially different.

Application.—The application will be indirect and typical. Israel's state during the Babylonian captivity, which the homilete should depict, is a picture of the state of the New Testament congregation at certain times. And the consolation given by Yahveh to Israel, as portrayed in our text, foreshadows the consolation of which the New Testament congregation of today may be sure. Indeed, the bearing of

1. THE EXEGETICAL-HOMILETICAL TREATMENT OF THE TEXT   551

our text on present conditions amounts to more than a mere application. Before the eyes of the prophet, the events of the future pass in review as making up one single picture. He sees the deliverance from Babylon, the deliverance from sin, death and the devil through Christ, the appropriation of this deliverance by the congregation of the present, and the perfection of the congregation through Christ's second coming, all in one grand vision. And the words of comfort recorded in our text apply also to the New Testament congregation of today, which marks an important stage of the prophecy's fulfilment. When the Spirit moved the prophet to write these words, He intended them to refer not only to the deliverance from Babylon and to the historical coming of Christ, but also, since He had in mind the Christians of today, to the congregation of the present. For this reason we feel justified in applying at least the first verses directly to the conditions of today. It is different with the second part of the text. Not that it has no message for the present, but because the pictures and figures used have been selected with special reference to Israel's return to Canaan and to its position among the nations of the world. This part of the text, moreover, will not reach its complete fulfilment until the new heaven and the new earth shall have come to pass. For these reasons the application of this part should be indirect. The homilete should beware, however, of giving both parts a merely spiritual interpretation. This would not do justice to the contents, since the various terms are used in their broadest meaning, like similar terms found in the New Testament, especially in the Sermon on the Mount, which contains ideas related to those of our text.

Israel, while in exile, longed for deliverance. Our life has much in common with that of exiled Israel, for are there not also among us many who are oppressed by the vicissitudes or the sins of life and who long for liberty? Are there not many whose hearts are broken, —broken by blasted hopes, misplaced trust, disobedient children, untimely deaths, and life's bitter sorrows; broken by bitter self-reproach, or remorse, by unforgiven sins, and by the reproving Word of God which, like a two-edged sword, pierces the soul? Do we not find men who live in vilest bondage, fettered body and soul to darkness and despair, who know of no deliverance, whose efforts to obtain freedom draw closer the bonds of slavery; men who are captives in the truest sense of the term, captives also in a spiritual sense, who have sold themselves under sin and are servants of vice; men who are in constant fear of death (Heb. 2: 15); men who are vassals of Satan? Do we not find men who are oppressed by the rod of tyrants, by godless neighbors and frivolous companions; men who are homeless and destitute, in whose breast still rankles grief over their lost heritage, who would gladly return home, yet have lost their way; prodigal sons and daughters who, amid the restlessness of this world, long for the land of peace and quiet where they may abide forever? Men who are profoundly depressed at the thought of their sinfulness, of God's wrath, of their base ingratitude toward His unbounded love, and whose hearts yearn for forgiveness?

How fortunate we are to know that in Jesus has appeared the servant of God, promised by the prophet; that in Him we have the proclaimer of salvation for all who will accept it. In order to prepare Him for His labors, God anointed Him at His baptism with the Spirit. In the synagogue at Nazareth, the servant publicly proclaims Himself. From the day He began His labors as prophet to the time of His ascension, He remained true to His mission,—to preach the Gospel and to proclaim salvation. Everywhere He spoke with authority. And this same Jesus is still among us, preaching the good tidings of deliverance. In the Scriptures and in the sermon He comes, in order to bear witness: "Captives may now be free. Wounds may now be healed. The brokenhearted may find a healing balm. Now there is a home for the homeless; there is comfort for the comfortless, strength for the weak, forgiveness, peace and joy for all sinners. The greater the want, the nearer the help and the more reassuring the message: Fear not; despair not; help is at hand!" Standing among us and viewing our misery, He invites: "Come, ye disconsolate, ye deluded, oppressed and wounded souls. Come, that I may prove to you that deliverance, redemption, salvation are for all." What comfort and peace this glorious message brings!

The servant can accomplish what he promises. His words are never idle or vain. Israel was delivered from exile and restored to its home land. The waste places were rebuilt and turned into a garden of God. So, too, Jesus' words are anything but empty words. They were followed by deeds. The lepers were cleansed, the deaf were made to hear and the dumb to speak, the dead were raised up, those possessed by Satan and his demons were set free, the crushed and down-trodden were raised up and given new life and hope. His little circle of disciples became a veritable new creation (Jas. 1:18, "a planting of God"). What they became, they became through Christ, the royal Creator of a new life and of a new world. And as Christ dealt with His disciples of old, so He will deal with us today. For us, too, He is more than a royal prophet, He is Creator and King of a

1. THE EXEGETICAL-HOMILETICAL TREATMENT OF THE TEXT 553

new world; for His Word is no empty sound, no mere message and testimony. It is His power to save. It is incorruptible seed able to beget salvation (Rom. 1:16; Jas. 1:18, 21; 1 Pet. 1:23; 2 Cor. 2:16; 3:6; Isa. 55:10). It carries within itself the gifts and blessings which it promises. And the Sacrament, through which we enter into union with Christ, through which we receive His body and blood, imparts heavenly life, and with it forgiveness and salvation. Wherever these heavenly powers, efficacious in Word and Sacrament, are transmitted to the heart of man, there a new life is born, there a "planting of God," a new creation (2 Cor. 5:7) springs into being. This we see especially in the field of home and foreign missions. How often new life is begotten in the desert of heathen lands, when entire tribes are transformed, both inwardly and outwardly, by nothing else than the creative power of God's Word. How many waste places have been rebuilt, how many lifeless and oppressed souls have been revived, how many bruised reeds have been strengthened until they grew into "terebinths of righteousness." It is true, man's earthly condition does not always change at once, neither does his eternal home assume form immediately, but time will bring both to pass. The redemption which we already enjoy, and the fact that God's Word has already brought forth new life in us are our surety that our physical being will also experience a new birth, a regeneration. Though time may not beget perfection, eternity will complete what time has left undone. Because suffering and lowliness have been our portion on earth, a double portion of rejoicing shall be our lot in eternity. Then we shall learn that, as St. Paul writes, "the sufferings of this present time are not worthy to be compared with the glory which shall be revealed in us."

In treating vv. 5 and 6, the homilete should not dwell on Israel's position among the nations, or on the relation of the nations to Israel, for it is doubtful, since Israel rejected the Messiah, whether the fulfilment of these words is still to be looked for. Things that are uncertain should not be made the theme of public discourse. They would satisfy idle curiosity rather than beget interest in salvation. One might, indeed, show from the history of the Church and of Missions how men, on becoming Christians, have placed their possessions at the service of the Church. This is, however, only one of the many thoughts in this rich passage.

The entire text is admirably suited for the beginning of Advent or for the Epiphany season.

Isaiah 53:1-7.

Exposition.—Context: If any scripture passage of the Old Testament may be called "sacred ground," it is the passage containing our text. It is the "golden passional" of the "Old Testament evangelist," written as it were under the very cross of Calvary. It shows an intimate and sympathetic knowledge of the mystery of the atonement that is unexcelled by any New Testament passage. Some scholars have sought to prove that the writer does not portray here the suffering of the Messiah, but rather that of the people of Israel, or of the faithful followers of Yahveh, or of the prophet Isaiah, or of some other prominent person such as Hezekiah or Zerubbabel. But their arguments are not conclusive. Undoubtedly, a definite person is meant. We learn from the context that this can be none other than "the servant of Yahveh" mentioned in chap. 42 and 49, and later in chap. 61. The ancient rabbis held this same view, so that R. Moscheho al Schech could write: "Basing their views upon tradition, our rabbis held that the Messiah-king was here meant." We can not enter here into a detailed discussion and must refer the reader to our work: "Die Alttestamentlichen Perikopen exegetisch-homiletisch ausgelegt" (2 vols., Guetersloh, 1901 and 1906), i, 382 ff. Luther says: "Few passages if any of the Old Testament treat the passion and the resurrection of Christ with greater clearness." In chap. 51 and 52:1-12 the prophet showed how the Church of God was to be delivered from the suffering and the shame of the Babylonian captivity, and rise from sorrow to glory. These thoughts prepare the way for 52:13-53:12. If Israel's way leads from the cross to the crown, so too will the way of the servant of Yahveh, in whom all God-fearing Israel is united, as in one body, and who in view of this fact is called "Israel" itself (49:3). Chap. 52:3-15, a kind of prelude to our text, sounds the theme: "From the greatest suffering to the *greatest glory*," with special emphasis on greatest glory. For, says the Lord, even the Gentiles shall be startled and kings shall kneel in silent worship when His servant, having completed his mission, shall stand before them. Chap. 53 introduces us to the time when the Gentiles will behold the majesty of Yahveh's servant.

Vv. 1-3. Who is the speaker in v. 1? **Some Gentile, mentioned** in the preceding chapter? No, for the Gentiles knew nothing of the servant, and could not confess, as in v. 8: "For the transgression of *my* people was he stricken." Is it the prophet? No; the plural constructions in v. 2 speak against this. Who then is the speaker? Whenever the prophet uses the plural form "we" and does not limit its

1. THE EXEGETICAL-HOMILETICAL TREATMENT OF THE TEXT 555

meaning, we may safely infer that he means Israel including himself (comp. 42:24; 64:5; 16:6; 24:16). Hence, Israel is here speaking. Reviewing its glorious past, it cannot but lament its own blindness. The Gentiles had accepted the servant of Yahveh as soon as God had exalted him and set him before them. But Israel, though it had received the message ages before and had witnessed his miracles, did not believe nor realize God's gracious purpose. Just at what period Israel is supposed to speak as recorded in the text,—whether in the time of the apostles, when the Gentiles believed on Christ and when, later on, individual Jews professed faith in him; or in the last days, when Israel, attracted by the blessings which God has heaped upon the Gentiles (Rom. 11), shall learn to believe,—is of little moment so far as our text is concerned. Of no more moment is it, whether we regard the speaker's words as a "prayer of penitence," or (which is more probable) as an expression of "self-accusation over against the Gentile nations." The simple fact is that a time will come when Israel will marvel at itself for not having recognized and come to faith in the servant of Yahveh. It will marvel because it had the message and beheld his wonderful birth, life, death, and resurrection, and did not believe. Such blindness is truly amazing! What can have been its cause? V. 2 gives the answer: Carnal-mindedness, which is impressed only by visible greatness. Had the Messiah appeared like a mighty, overshadowing tree, like a cedar of Lebanon, for example, Israel might have regarded him with favor. But he came like a twig or tender plant. It was a most insignificant beginning. Who would regard such a tender stem? How easily it might be crushed by a careless foot or broken by a thoughtless hand! As a "tender plant *before him*" he was to grow up,—solitary, unknown, passed over; not on the banks of some life-giving stream, but as a root out of dry ground, as a solitary shoot from a tree long since cut down. He appeared as a *homo novus*, a man without friends and connections, whose humble origin did not justify any high hopes for his future. "When he grew up," Israel continues self-accusingly, "he had no form or comeliness which might have appealed to us—no beauty that we should desire him." Sometimes a man born in obscurity will rise to fame and glory. Not so the servant of Yahveh. He showed neither kingly form nor royal glory. But now penitent Israel realizes why it was not impressed with his appearance. Its carnal eyes sought external splendor; for his inner beauty and nobility it had no appreciation. That was why Israel ignored him. It confesses: "We esteemed him not" (Deut. 33:9), i. e., we disregarded him; we "did not desire him," i. e., we were not attracted by him, for he had neither form nor comeliness of appearance. And what he did possess (v. 3) rather repelled than attracted. The natural man could not perceive his inner worth. "He was despised." This expression is characteristic of his whole life. He was despised of men. The unusual plural of "men" should be rendered as in Prov. 8:4 and Ps. 141:4,—men of note, of dignity and of office. In other instances such men might intercede for one of lowly birth, might enhance his reputation among his followmen, but the servant of Yahveh numbers no such men among his friends. His is the fate of Job (19:14),—to be a "man of sorrows," one who was never without pain and suffering, whose lot was to suffer. Israel was repelled by the sight of him. He was "acquainted with grief." This expression refers to illness which he often experienced, either in himself or in others. The Hebrew, however, is broader in scope and meaning than mere disease. It refers to any form of affliction which might distress and wound his soul. The climax of the description is reached in the words: "As one from whom we hid our faces." His misery is so profound that man can not endure the sight. More than this Israel can not say. It can only repeat and conclude its confession: "He was despised, and we esteemed him not." The Gentiles accepted him, but we esteemed him not.

Vv. 4-6. When Israel considers its past conduct in the light of its present experience, its sorrow knows no bounds. Vv. 4-6 show the thoroughness of Israel's awakening and the completeness of its former delusion with respect to the life and passion of Yahveh's servant. Now Israel knows: "He hath borne *our* griefs, and carried *our* sorrows." This passage refers to the effects of man's sins (cf. Matt. 8:17) and not to the sins themselves. He has taken upon himself all that man was to suffer in consequence of his sins. The verbs are significant. They denote a laborious lifting and bearing of a heavy burden. The heavy burden of man's guilt, resulting from his innumerable transgressions, the servant has taken upon himself. He has not, like some prophet, miraculously removed the burden. He has "shouldered" it, and now bears it for Israel, that same Israel which was once so arrogant and obstinate, but is now so humble and penitent. The idea of "substitution" appears here for the first time. Recognizing the servant in his true character, they now confess with bleeding hearts: "We did esteem him stricken, smitten of God, and afflicted." "Stricken;" i. e., we looked upon him as one punished by God with a shameful and malignant malady for his vices and wrong-doings. "Smitten;" i. e., we regarded him as one visited by God with many ills and sorrows, as

1. THE EXEGETICAL-HOMILETICAL TREATMENT OF THE TEXT 557

one smitten to earth by the lightnings of God's wrath and vengeance. Israel saw in him a second Job. But even now Israel's confession is not ended. It continues weeping (v. 5): "But he was pierced for our transgressions; he was bruised for our iniquities; the chastisement of our peace, it lay upon him, and with his stripes we have gained deliverance." The terms employed here are among the most emphatic in the Hebrew language. Without doubt, they have been purposely chosen, referring as they do to a violent and most painful form of death. He became the propitiation for Israel's and the world's sins; therefore, this violent form of suffering and death. Israel itself did not inflict the punishment. God it was who chastised him (Ps. 6:2), but their iniquities were the cause of his passion. The "chastisement of our peace" is an expression, like many found in this chapter, uncouth in form but fraught with deep meaning. The meaning seems to be: (He suffers) the chastisement which will lead us to peace. This expression also intimates the purpose of his passion. Through his agony Israel is to attain peace, inner and outer well-being, to be protected against everything that may cause strife and distress. The following clause conveys the same thought, but also calls attention to Israel's former state of illness (Isa. 1:5-6; Jer. 8:18 ff.). In the servant of Yahveh Israel has found the right physician. What cure does he bring the dying people? His stripes! Certainly, a remarkable figure of speech! Stripes usually wound; here they are said to heal. For the servant the stripes meant pain and anguish; for the people, balm and healing. This the people now know: Because of his wounds, they are healed. Here we have once more the idea of propitiation, or substitution. With the recognition of their guilt the confession of the people gains in earnestness and intensity. The more they contemplate the servant as a "man of sorrows," the more they comprehend the hideousness of their iniquities. V. 6 describes more fully their own and the servant's conduct, already mentioned in the preceding verses: "All we like sheep have gone astray." This short sentence characterizes their past conduct. As the sheep in search of new pastures ignores the voice of the shepherd, and consequently is lost in the desert, so Israel had repeatedly gone astray (in the desert; under the judges; during the time of the prophets; in exile). Israel had sought pastures of its own choosing, heaping guilt upon guilt. But while it was increasing its guilt and provoking God's wrath, what was Yahveh doing? He was preparing their deliverance; was quietly realizing His plan of mercy conceived before the foundation of the world. The people confess: "We insulted his holiness and provoked his vengeance, but—wonder of wonders!—boundless love and mercy have become our portion. His servant has become our substitute. He carries our iniquities and bears our griefs" (cf. 2 Cor. 5:21). As the blood of a murdered man accuses the murderer, and cries for vengeance, so Israel's iniquities should have come upon Israel and demanded chastisement. But God did not suffer them to fall upon Israel. He made them to fall upon His righteous servant. From him Yahveh's wrath exacted punishment. It is small wonder, then, that His servant possessed no beauty, that men hid their faces from him, and regarded him as smitten of God.

V. 7. This verse describes the conduct of Yahveh's servant when the iniquity of all was laid on him and Yahveh exacted punishment for Israel's guilt. "Oppressed" designates not only Egyptian bondage and kindred forms of oppression. It is a *terminus technicus* used of exaction of tribute or payment of unpaid debts (cf. Deut. 15:2-3; 2 Kings 23:35; Dan. 11:20). The servant willingly submitted to Yahveh's chastisement. Though he had not merited or deserved the guilt, he was willing to make restitution; though it was not just to exact payment of him, since he had not contracted the debt, he nevertheless accepted the debt as his own, and gladly made payment. He might have refused. He had a right to do so, for he was innocent; but he preferred to act as man's substitute and expiate man's crimes. Israel remembers him as the meekest among the meek,—as a lamb brought to the slaughter or a sheep brought to the shearers, that never opens its mouth. Now that Israel understands, it marvels at his meekness, and can only repeat: "Yea, he opened not his mouth."

Application.—This wonderful text, containing as it does a direct prophecy concerning Christ, should be applied directly, i. e., the homilete should show how things foretold in this text have found their fulfilment in Christ. He should also point out that it is Israel which here laments and confesses its guilt. His own faithfulness as an exegete, his knowledge that vv. 1-6 can not be fully explained in any other way, and his consideration of the tense forms employed throughout the entire chapter, will prompt him to do this. But he dare not tarry here, but should hasten on to the main theme: *"The Passion of Christ."*

Generally, we regard Jesus' passion as beginning with the agony in Gethsemane. This is correct if we take "passion" in its narrower sense as referring to that suffering in which all prophecies find their fulfilment. Isaiah, however, includes more. He thinks of the Lord's whole life as one continuous passion; for him Jesus' suffering began

1. THE EXEGETICAL-HOMILETICAL TREATMENT OF THE TEXT 559

at His birth in Bethlehem and found its consummation in Gethsemane and on Golgotha; in short, it extended from the cradle to the grave. "He shall grow up like a tender plant," he writes, "and as a root out of a dry ground." It is true, the Lord descended from the house of David, but this house, once the most powerful in Israel, had long lost its regal glory and been humbled to the dust. Like a massive tree it had once afforded shelter and happiness to Israel, but now it had been long cut down and its trunk appeared lifeless and barren. The fact that He, who was like unto God in essence, power, and glory, sprang, like a root out of a dry ground, from the despised tree of David was in itself no mean part of His passion. And as His birth, so were His childhood and youth. He grew up in dry ground; for Nazareth, the home of His youth, was held in contempt by all Galilee and Judea. Thus Nathanael could ask: "Can there any good thing come out of Nazareth?" He grew to manhood among an unbelieving people, ruled by heathens, blind to its true woe or weal. Even in His parents' home, He was lonesome. Not even Mary, His mother, comprehended the depths of His being, and His brothers, indifferent, unbelieving, once even scoffing, understood little of His true character. Thus His parents' home was not a temple of God, in which He could feel perfectly at home. Need we then marvel when the twelve year old boy says in accents both sorrowful and yearning: Luke 2:49? This was the passion of Jesus' youth.

And when, as a young man, He took up His prophetic labors, when He began His public ministry, His people found in Him neither form nor comeliness. Men listened to His sermons, more powerful than those of the scribes, and beheld His wonders, were even filled with enthusiasm by all they heard and saw; but when He called for disciples, few desired to follow Him. He was rejected of men. None of the leaders espoused His cause; they rather united to oppose Him, yes, to kill Him, so that the Israel of the last days must needs profess: "Who hath believed the report which came unto us? and to whom is the arm of the Lord revealed?" And when, as He was about to conclude His public ministry, He withdrew to Caesarea Philippi with His disciples and sought to sum up the result of His labors, when Peter alone, as spokesman of the other disciples, made a good confession, and it became clear that His labors among the people had been largely in vain,—then bitter pangs of sorrow and distress rent his soul because men spurned His love; then He was "a man of sorrow" who wept tears because the arm of the Lord was not revealed to His people. Thus, from the days of His birth, the Lamb of God was endowed with the sorrows and pains of death. He was acquainted with disease. Not that His own body was subject to illness, but His sensitive, sympathetic soul was moved by every woe and pain which pressed upon Him from the outer world and claimed attention. Even the sight of misery, begotten of sin, filled His tender being with sorrow, so that the Scriptures repeatedly state: "He was moved with compassion." The manifold sins of His people grieved and wounded His pure heart, and made His noble soul shudder long after the wicked deed had been done. Zeal for the honor of His Father filled His whole being and consumed His strength. How prophetic this zeal of the death which He would suffer! Thus we can also understand how, when He entered upon His greatest passion, His body was already afflicted, as it were, with death.

But the bitterest pains were still to be endured. When, in the garden of Gethsemane, He fell on His face and contended with God in prayer, He was a worm and no man, When He was sorrowful even unto death, and tasted death's agonies, He, the Prince of Life, was indeed a man of sorrows and of death. When the heavy burden of the sins of the world pressed upon His pure heart, He sank beneath the burden, and His sweat fell like great drops of blood to the ground. When His disciples forsook Him, Judas betrayed Him, Peter denied Him, the high priest's servants spat in His face and buffeted Him, then He was despised, and men esteemed Him not. When cruel whips scourged His holy shoulders; when the soldiers platted a crown of thorns and pressed it upon His brow until the blood flowed down His face; when they mocked Him and clothed Him with purple and made Him carnival-king, when the heathen judge led Him before the multitude and proclaimed: "Behold, the man!" and when the multitude cried out: "Crucify Him, crucify Him!"—then He was the most despised and rejected of men. And when, at last, in the hour of death, He hung on the cross, reviled by those about Him, suffering the pangs of thirst, forsaken by His God, humbly praying for deliverance, then He appeared as an outcast among His fellowmen, as one "stricken, smitten of God, and afflicted." Then, there was no beauty, neither form nor comeliness, which might have attracted His fellowmen; then He was so despised that they "hid their faces from Him." And when He bowed His head in death and yielded up the ghost; when His body was taken from the cross,—then His passion was complete and He had become the picture of sorrow and of death described by Isaiah through the power of the Holy Spirit.

1. THE EXEGETICAL-HOMILETICAL TREATMENT OF THE TEXT 561

"Now from Thy cheeks has vanished
Their color once so fair;
From Thy red lips is banished
The splendor that was there.
Pale Death with cruel rigor
Bereaveth Thee of life;
Thus losest Thou Thy vigor
And strength in this sad strife."

Behold, this is the servant of Yahveh in His passion. This is the extent and the depth of Jesus' sufferings.

But, "holy Jesus, how hast Thou offended,
That man to judge Thee hath in hate pretended?"

Why did Christ suffer thus? What is the real cause, the *mystery* of His passion? He had done no violence, neither was any deceit in His mouth. Was He not the only righteous among the children of men, whom no one could convict of sin? The Jews did not apprehend why He suffered. They looked upon Him as one who, because of His arrogance and self-deification, was stricken, smitten of God, and afflicted. Even His disciples did not comprehend the reason of His sufferings. They thought that He had at last fallen victim to the rulers' hatred, and become a martyr of the scribes and Pharisees whom His sermons had so often embarrassed. Not the least bitter drop in His cup was the knowledge that neither His beloved disciple John nor His mother Mary understood the secret of His sufferings. But do *we* understand the true reason of His anguish? Thank God that we, enlightened by the Holy Ghost, can say with the prophet: "Surely, He hath borne *our* griefs, and carried *our* sorrows..... He was bruised for *our* iniquities." Jesus suffered in order to achieve our redemption. He took upon Himself our sins. We all had wandered from the path of heaven; every one had turned to his own way. Sin upon sin, guilt upon guilt, separated us from God. *We* should have been chastised; *we,* who were in the power of death and the devil, had incurred God's wrath. For us there was no deliverance until Jesus became our surety and redeemer. We should have been punished, but now we are free. He took the load of our sins upon His holy, all-powerful shoulders. With our sins, He also suffered the wrath and curse of God, which, like a tempest, beat upon Him, wounded, pierced and crushed Him, pressed Him to the earth in Gethsemane, twined a crown of thorns about His head, laid the accursed tree on His shoulder, led Him out to Golgotha, drove the nails through His hands and feet, and fastened Him to the cross. Yet He suffered all of His own free will. Love urged Him on. To God's judgment He said yea and amen. The bitter potion of God's wrath and punishment He put to His lips and drained to the dregs. Though His heart trembled and though His soul was filled with fear and the terror of death, He did not set down the cup until He had tasted the last drop. Not the enmity of the Jews, not Satan's might and guile brought Him to the grave, but His fathomless love which sacrificed itself for our sins. How terrible our sins, that He, the Holy One, must endure such suffering in order to expiate them! "We have many fiery pictures of God's righteous wrath," says Cramer, "wherein, because of man's sins, God's thunders roar and His lightnings flash; such as those of the flood, of Sodom and Gomorrah, of Pharaoh and his host. But what are all these pictures compared to the one wherein we see God's wrath inflicting direst punishment upon His only-begotten Son,— punishment so heart-rending that the very stones might well grieve and the hard rocks burst in sorrow, as they did in the hour of His passion?" And how intense His love that it could make Him willing to endure all for us!

God laid on Him the iniquity of us all. Here is that mysterious *imputatio*, which is the heart and centre of the biblical doctrine of atonement, standing between and corresponding to the *imputatio peccati adamitici* on the one hand and the *imputatio justitiae Christi*, which constitutes the essence of justification, on the other. Our sins have been imputed to Christ. Brenz calls attention to the fact that the words "for us" occur twelve times in Isa. 53. The reason for this he finds, not in any attempt to add rhetorical embellishments to the text, but in the attempt to emphasize the great and all-important truth of substitution, in order that man may comprehend his great guilt, on the one hand, and receive consolation in times of doubt, on the other. The prophet also lays special stress on the words: "the iniquity of us all." He seeks thereby to convince us that *our* sins are among those borne by Jesus. Luther never tires of dwelling on the thought, "for us all." In his brief explanation of the fourth verse of this chapter, he says: "Here we have the article of justification, that we may believe that Christ died *for us,* as St. Paul writes Gal. 3:13. For it is not enough to know that Christ died, as we here find it expressed. We must believe that He bore our afflictions, that He suffered not for Himself but for us. He who comprehends this passage has found the essence of Christianity. This passage was the source from which St. Paul drew his many epistles, and his innumerable Scripture gems and Scripture consolations. If He suffered my pains and endured my afflictions, i. e., if He carried my sins and bore their

1. THE EXEGETICAL-HOMILETICAL TREATMENT OF THE TEXT 563

punishment, I am free, free from sin and guilt and punishment, and I have no reason to fear God's wrath."—"The chastisement of our peace was upon him, and with his stripes we are healed.". These are the blessed fruits of His patience and suffering (v. 7). He was born to bring peace; He died to establish peace, and 'He rose and ascended on high to dispense peace. "He is our peace" (Eph. 2:14). In Him we have atonement, reconciliation between God and man. No longer is God angry with us. He is our friend who wishes us well. A new relationship has been established. Instead of sin, God's righteousness stands between God and man.

> "To us no harm shall now come nigh,
> The strife at last is ended;
> God showeth His good will to men,
> And peace shall reign on earth again."

These are the blessed fruits of Jesus' passion.

B. NEW TESTAMENT TEXTS

(1) Gospel Texts Illustrating the Direct Application
Matt. 7:15-23.

Exposition.—Context: This text is taken from Christ's sermon on the mount, or to be more definite, from the closing verses of this sermon. The sermon itself was introduced in a most sweet and comforting strain. In contrast to this, the solemn tenor of the concluding verses is more clearly noticed, the nearer we approach the close. From the beginning of the seventh chapter, judgment is the most prominent thought; throughout the whole chapter, this theme is ever more clearly to be heard (7:2, 13, 19, 20-23); and in the powerful concluding verses it reigns supreme (vv. 24-27). The disciples of Christ are those who are addressed in the first place in this sermon. They are to take note that, unless their walk in life be that of true disciples, their way will only lead to judgment and damnation. In the verses immediately preceding our text, they received the admonition not to take offence at the narrow gate nor at the narrow way leading through this gate. Neither are they to take offence because they are practically alone and have but few companions on the narrow way. For only that way is broad and wide ($\dot{\eta}$ $\pi\acute{u}\lambda\eta$ in v. 13 does not belong to the genuine text) that leads to destruction; and only on this way are many traveling companions to be found. In contrast to this, the way upon which true disciples will find themselves in their Christian life is narrow, uncomfortable, and altogether irksome to the old Adam. But what if this be so, and their companions on this way but few?

This will but help to show them that they are on the right way. Since the preceding verses thus speak of the two ways, our text would seem to be very closely connected with them. For where there is more than one way that may be taken, there are usually enough guideposts to direct the traveler; and much, indeed at times everything, will depend upon the guide one follows. For if one permit the wrong guide to direct one, this will not help one to reach the goal; it will lead on the contrary away from it. In the case of believers, where there is but one way leading to the goal, following the wrong guide would lead nowhere else than to certain destruction, where judgment and damnation are the eternal lot of those who were once disciples.

In the first place, then, our text treats of false guides, whom disciples dare not follow (vv. 15-20). The disciples should beware of false prophets. Prophets who are truly sent by God are valuable guides, and true disciples of Jesus will always be ready and willing to journey on the way which they may direct. They are spokesmen of God, revealing His will to men in a trustworthy manner. Of false prophets disciples should, however, beware; for they are called false prophets for the very reason that they pretend to be divine messengers and guides who are directed by the Spirit of God to reveal His will, while in reality they are not sent by God, are only directed by their own ungodly spirit, and most certainly do not proclaim His will. In the relative clause that follows, Jesus characterizes the false prophets more fully. He describes them as persons able to make an outward pretence of being members of the congregation, while in their inmost hearts they are nothing less than the most dangerous enemies of the Christian congregation. That is the sense of the figurative description of false prophets here given. Jesus has a special reason for thus describing them. He does not picture them as appearing in sheep's clothing because sheep are innocent or meek or even useful animals; but this expression must be understood from the Old Testament. Here the congregation of God is commonly represented to us as a flock of sheep and God Himself as the shepherd (cf. Ps. 78:52; 80:2; 100:3; Ezek. 34:11 ff.). If, therefore, the false prophets appear in sheep's clothing, they do so in order to make it appear as though they belonged to the "sheep," the flock of God, or the congregation of Jesus' disciples. When, in view of their purpose and intention, Jesus designates them as "wolves," He does so in order the better to bring out the striking contrast between what they pretend to be and what they really are. For the wolf, the known enemy of the sheep (John 10:12), is also the enemy of the fold of Christ. As such He is familiar to us

1. THE EXEGETICAL-HOMILETICAL TREATMENT OF THE TEXT 565

from the Old Testament (Zeph. 3:3; Ezek. 22:27; compare also Matt. 10:16; Acts 20:29). If Holtzmann and Zahn are right in their view of this passage, the clause describing the false prophets as wolves in sheep's clothing would mean that they appear in the customary coarse garb of prophets, in order thereby to appear outwardly as prophets of God; for thus the prophets usually preferred to appear (Zech. 13:4; 2 Kings 1:8; Matt. 3:4). But, as Zahn himself admits, the stress does not lie on this. It is rather the deceptive contrast that is emphasized: they pretend to be members of the Christian congregation and laboring for its good, while the direct opposite is true. That they are not to be thought of as prophets who will appear in the world at large or even in Israel, but who will appear in future in the very midst of the Christian Church, needs hardly to be mentioned. The whole admonition, especially the relative clause in v. 15, rests on this supposition. That, however, is just what increases the danger. To be mindful of false prophets outside of the congregation and beware of them, should be self-evident to disciples. But that certain spirits should become active in her midst, who are false in their very nature and are only seeking the destruction of the congregation,—to be able to realize and know this, special enlightenment is necessary again and again. This was the experience of the Christian Church in her very infancy. For it was not so much the opponents and enemies from outside the Church with whom the Apostle Paul had the hardest battles to fight, but it was above all the false teachers of Jewish extraction who arose from her own midst. And to be able to recognize them with their destructive intentions, proved a far more difficult task for the Christian congregation than to recognize the enemies who approached from Jewish and heathen quarters. The very fact that they appeared in "sheep's clothing," that is, that they were baptized, that they confessed the name of Christ, that they by no means disregarded the cross and faith, and that they were enthusiastic in regard to moral perfection,—this made it especially difficult for the infant Church to recognize them in their true wolfish nature.

Since the Master knows this, He would prepare His disciples by giving them an unmistakable sign whereby they may know the false prophets in their true nature. "By their fruits" the disciples should be able to recognize false prophets, and distinguish them from prophets sent by God (v. 6). A tree will naturally produce fruit. Just so must certain fruits make their appearance both in the personal life of a prophet as well as in the life of those whom he may teach. In his own life godly words and deeds must make their appearance, while his disciples will acquire a true knowledge of God and will strive after a godly life. Both the teacher and the disciple must here be kept in mind, and this for the reason that it is a prophet or teacher whose nature is to be discerned. Prophets and teachers, however, are sent to instruct and influence others, and actual fruits must result from their labors (compare Jas. 3:13-18). Now, by these fruits one should be able to know whether they be false or true prophets. Clothes regulate the outward appearance, but as such they are only external. Fruits, on the other hand, must grow out of the inner nature, and they are bound to reveal the actual qualities of this nature. If the labors, therefore, of the prophets result in contrition and faith, humility of heart, and a sanctified life, if they bring peace instead of contention, overcome evil, and cause new life actually to spring up and grow from within, the prophets must be sent by God, and the Holy Spirit must be working through them. For those are results which no one but the Spirit of God can produce. If fruits could spring from a foreign source and merely be attached to a tree, they would certainly not reveal the nature of the tree. But because they are organically united with the tree itself, they are an unmistakable sign whereby the nature of the tree may be known. Each and every tree can only produce fruit after its kind. The fruits, therefore, produced by a prophet, both in his personal life and in that of his disciples, can only be of the essence and nature of his own heart and teaching, from which source they come forth. To look for grapes on a thorn hedge or figs on a thistle or briar bush would be folly; for it is contrary to their nature to produce such fruit. It would be just as foolish to expect false prophets to produce fruits pleasing to God. A good tree bringeth forth only good fruit; and a corrupt tree bringeth forth only evil fruit. Anything else would be unnatural. Therefore, knowing the fruits, one is able to draw a certain conclusion concerning the nature and condition of the tree. In regard to prophets, one may draw the same conclusion. If the results of their teaching and preaching are fruits pleasing to God, one may conclude that they are sent by God and that their preaching is Gospel truth. But if the results of their preaching and teaching, in spite of outward appearances, are not truly pleasing to God, one may conclude that they themselves are not pleasing to God. In certain instances it may not be possible to discern this so readily. But sooner or later fruits will make their appearance as an unmistakable sign. The Christian Church need but keep her eyes open, and there will be ample opportunity to know whether a prophet is divinely sent or whether he is a false

1. THE EXEGETICAL-HOMILETICAL TREATMENT OF THE TEXT 567

prophet whom one dare not follow. V. 19a only adds new force to the admonition to beware of false prophets. As surely as a tree that bringeth not forth good fruit will be cut down and cast into the fire, just so surely will the wrath and judgment of God come upon all false prophets. This is only another reason why the Christian congregation should beware of false prophets. For what have they to expect, who have given heed to the teaching of false prophets and have failed to bring forth the fruits required by God? Will the lot of the false prophets in judgment and damnation not be their lot also? There is indeed grave danger, for Jesus says plainly, "Every tree that bringeth not forth good fruit is hewn down and cast into the fire," and does not limit or modify this statement in any way. Therefore, O Church of Christ, beware of false prophets!

Vv. 21-23.—In addition to what has been said, v. 19a also serves as transition to the following. It prepares for the following in a twofold way. In the first place, judgment was referred to, and this is the thought that governs vv. 21-23. In the second place, the words "every tree" have widened the scope. The reference to judgment is no longer restricted to false prophets, but now includes every member of the Christian congregation. What follows likewise concerns the disciples of Jesus without exception, even though v. 22 shows us that the false prophets are by no means excluded. Here is something every one should bear in mind. Both now and in the future men will come to Christ calling upon His name. Some will pretend to confess Christ, others will pretend to petition Him. But as long as it is only pretence, nothing will be gained thereby. For even when the kingdom of God, which the prophets have foretold and which is now dawning, comes in its full glory, not everyone who says to Jesus, "Lord, Lord," will be able to enter. This is not to say that it is unnecessary to call upon Jesus and actually to confess Him as Lord. Jesus would have men both acknowledge and confess Him as Lord. He would have them approach Him and enter into intimate and personal relation to Him. But the same thing holds true of the words "Lord, Lord," as of sheep's clothing with which false prophets adorn themselves. Clothes are only external, and anyone can don them and pretend to belong to the flock, even though in his heart he be an enemy. So one can use the name of Christ, either confessing Him or seeking His help, and at the same time fail to enter into a personal union with Him, acknowledging Him as the only Teacher and Master and as Lord and King in truth. But when He is truly acknowledged as Lord, and one has actually entered into the personal relationship of a true disciple, obedience to the will of the heavenly Father must naturally follow as an inner necessity. This is just as true as it is that a good tree, because of its good nature, can bring forth only good fruit. The will of God does not, however, require merely outward acknowledgment of Christ, but contrition and faith, the sanctifying of life, which naturally follows (Lev. 19:2), and unrestricted submission to the divine will (1 Sam. 15:22; Ezek. 36:27; Jer. 31:33). Indeed, how would it be possible for anyone to enter into the kingdom of heaven without having done the will of Him who is in heaven? Since God who is in heaven is at the same time the Father of Jesus, the will of one does not differ from, much less does it contradict, the other, but they are in perfect harmony with each other. It is one and the same will. Now, if the disciples will bear in mind that Jesus came into the world in order to bring men to obedience of the will of God (Matt. 5:17), they cannot help drawing the conclusion: the truth of their discipleship and of their confession must reveal and prove itself by their doing the will of the eternal Father of Christ. Unless their "Lord, Lord" prove itself by their obedience, this very lack of obedience betrays the fact that their "Lord, Lord" is merely something external and not the expression of an actual inner relation to Christ. They who have not done the will of God, by which their inner relation to Jesus is revealed, will be in the end like unfruitful trees, and need not expect to enter into the kingdom of heaven, but have only to await judgment (v. 19). V. 19 has directed our thoughts to the final judgment. In v. 21 the scene does not change; for it is the final judgment that will decide who may enter into the kingdom of heaven and who may not. V. 22, therefore, transfers us directly to the day of judgment, and calls attention to one of its details. On that occasion there will be those present who have tried to maintain an outward connection with the congregation. They will know for certain that Christ and no one else is to execute judgment. They will approach Him, however, saying, "Lord, Lord," hoping and expecting that they may actually be permitted to enter into His kingdom of glory. And when the Lord will look upon them as though in doubt as to whether He can grant them this, they will make an attempt to prove their discipleship and their right to inherit the kingdom by calling attention to what they have done in His name; they have prophesied in His name, they have cast out demons, and have done many other wonderful and mighty works. It is as though they would say, "We have not only said, 'Lord, Lord!' again and again, but we have also used this name effectively and to good purpose." Those who

1. THE EXEGETICAL-HOMILETICAL TREATMENT OF THE TEXT 569

will speak thus belong to the aforementioned false prophets. But not all; there will be exceptions. The deeds which they here mention were not restricted to the prophets by calling, neither at the time of the apostles nor of Jesus Himself (1 Cor. 13:1-3; Mark 9:38-40; Luke 9:49 f.). But if they hope thus to influence the Lord and to gain for themselves a favorable sentence, they will be sadly mistaken. For the Lord, who sits in judgment, will also make a confession, namely, "I never knew you!" To this He will add, "Depart from me, ye that have worked lawlessness and iniquity!" That Jesus means by this that He has known nothing of their life and existence heretofore, is out of the question. Therefore, it is clear that we have here the verb "to know" in the sense in which it is so frequently used already in Old Testament. It means not simply "to have knowledge of" a person, but includes the thought of "acknowledging" or "adopting," and is thus synonymous with "electing" or "receiving into intimate communion or relationship" (Gen. 18:18; Amos 3:2; Hos. 13:4; Gal. 4:9; Rom. 8:29; 1 Cor. 8:3; 2 Tim. 2:19). Jesus chooses to speak in the past tense because those before His judgment seat have referred to deeds which they have done in the past. The sense of the whole verse will, therefore, be: even at the time that they were performing wonderful deeds in His name, they did not in reality belong among His true disciples, since they did not enter into that personal relation to Him which is a characteristic of true discipleship; it was only outwardly that they came into touch with Him, which also accounts for their failing to do the will of the Father. And since moral neutrality is an impossibility, they now appear before the Judge as what they truly are, workers of iniquity and lawlessness ($\dot{a}\nu o\mu la$). No wonder that the Judge, instead of opening the portals of heaven to them, will command, "Depart from me!" Everything depends, therefore, upon whether one has entered into that personal relation to the Lord, and has consequently become a doer of the divine will. Where this is not the case, there remains nothing but judgment and condemnation. By saying that prophetic utterance, the casting out of demons, and the doing of other wonderful works may exist where this inner relation to Him is lacking, Jesus shows His disciples that He did not have these works in mind when He spoke above of the "fruits" of the prophets. These fruits do not refer to external, visible deeds performed in His name, but to the ethical results of the prophets' labors in their own lives as well as in the lives of their hearers. Such fruits cannot exist apart from a proper state of heart or a true relation to Christ.

Application.—The warning here given applies to the Christian Church of today, directly and without modification. She, too, must beware of false prophets. Of false prophets outside her bounds. These are found aplenty in these days of materialism reaching down to our public schools. But especially must she beware of false prophets within her bounds, who are much the more dangerous. The prophets whose voices are raised outside of the Church have so completely severed their connection with everything specifically Christian that it is comparatively easy for a disciple of Christ to recognize them as being altogether hostile to Christ and, therefore, to reject their pernicious doctrines. But toward those voices heard within the Church they tend to be less suspicious and much more trustful. 'Is it likely that there should be a deceiver among the disciples of Jesus, even among those who within the Church occupy prominent positions?' they ask. They have forgotten that among the prophets of Israel were many false prophets, that among the apostles of Jesus there was a Judas Iscariot, that from the early days of the Church down to the present time such deceivers have been numerous, and that the pope with his many lies has arisen within the Church. These false prophets are the more dangerous because even today they come to Christ's people in sheep's clothing, but inwardly are ravening wolves. They even manage to be called to serve in Christian congregations, in theological schools, and other important positions, so that they may all the more easily give themselves the appearance of having been divinely sent. So they create the impression that what they say and teach is authoritative, and therefore, to be accepted, if one does not wish to run counter to God Himself. Let us not, however, think here only of the many deviations from Sacred Scripture and from the teachings of the Lutheran Church found among the various denominations and sects of our land. These are, indeed, serious enough, and no disciple of Jesus will underestimate their danger, but will constantly be on guard against them. But we should think rather of the many false prophets whose testimony no longer has the message of sin and grace as its heart and centre, no matter what church they belong to. They speak of all sorts of human works and performances, and laud them as instrumental in effecting one's salvation. They make much of fasting, mortification, prohibition, humanity, peace congresses, mission conferences, and indulge the opinion that one who identifies himself with these things is most surely the Lord's own and will be placed at His right hand in the day of judgment. But the message of Christ, who died for our sins and was raised again for our justification, that message

1. THE EXEGETICAL-HOMILETICAL TREATMENT OF THE TEXT 571

with its terrible appeal to guilty human consciences, which reveals the wrath of God as poured out on the children of unbelief and vividly portrays His punitive justice and holiness, yet at the same time discloses the very heart of God, makes known to the world His infinite love and grace as nothing else can, and is the only source of spiritual power and life,—that true message of Christ as Saviour, while not expressly rejected, is nevertheless relegated to the background by so many modern preachers and teachers. These are false prophets, exceedingly dangerous to the souls of Christians. The message of sin and grace rules out all legalism and asceticism as devised by the old man, to make room for the work of God in the form of forgiveness and let Christ take possession of the heart. The devil is never more depressed than when this message is proclaimed in all its truth and vigor, and he is never more elated than when men try to effect the salvation of souls by legalistic methods and human devices. For the message of sin and grace achieves results that mean the devil's dethronement, whereas the human devices by which men are told to work out their salvation tend to enthrone him, to give him power over the soul and enable him to effect its destruction.—"Ye shall know them by their fruits." This is true even today. In spite of all their outward display, these false prophets of our day have nothing to show that is truly born of God. With all their prating about prohibition and humanity, morality and social service, they have not been able to prevent a decline of all moral standards. The consciousness of sin grows fainter and fainter, sincerity of conscience rarer and rarer, conceit and self-righteousness more and more frequent; and the sermon of the past few years with its political coloring has even helped in a systematic way to deaden the sense of truthfulness. Many sincere souls no longer know what Christianity really is; and many truthful minds outside her bounds have lost to a greater or less extent their respect for the Church. But what else can be expected? "Do men gather grapes of thorns, or figs of thistles?" Only a good tree can bring forth good fruits. The results of the false prophets' labors may be likened to the ornaments on a Christmas tree. They are only attached to it outwardly, and have not been brought forth by the tree itself, even though they shine like marvelous deeds done in the name of Christ. Therefore, beware of false prophets! Only true preaching, appointed by God and offering the pure Word of God, is like a tree full of life and vigor, that bringeth forth its fruit in its season.

By such preaching, contrition and faith are wrought and personal communion with the Saviour is brought about. For in the testimony of true prophets and messengers of God we have not only the message of Christ and of His will, but in it Christ Himself is present; He truly approaches man and would draw him into blessed communion with Himself. And on this personal relation to Christ all depends. If He does not know us, draw us out of the world, elect us, and bring us into communion with Himself, all outward connection with the Christian congregation is of no value. Merely calling Him, "Lord, Lord," will gain us nothing. We must actually acknowledge Him as Lord and be received into blessed communion with Him. For He alone can make us righteous and blessed, and cause us to become good and fruitful trees. May we who go to service regularly and are members of the visible Church, never forget this important truth!

Obedience to the will of God is the all-important thing. Such obedience can proceed only from a personal relation to Christ, just as good fruit can grow only on a good tree. But from such a relation it cannot but proceed by an inner necessity. Luther expressed this thought in his own graphic way: "Believers are a new creature, a new tree. Hence it is improper to use terms that belong to the law and say that a believer *should* do good works. Just as it is wrong to say: the sun *should* shine, a good tree *should* bring forth good fruits, three and seven *should* make ten. It is not true that the sun *should* shine; it shines by its very nature, without being commanded, for it was created for this purpose. In the same manner, a good tree brings forth good fruit of itself; three and seven have always been ten and do not need to become this. Here we do not speak of what *should take place* or what *should be*, but of what *takes place* and *is*. We might, indeed, say: If it is a sun, it *should* shine; if you are a believer, you *must* do good. This would be proper in speaking of a counterfeit faith and a counterfeit sun; but to speak thus of genuine faith and an actual sun would be absurd." It is folly to require various works of obedience from one who is not regenerate and has not come into personal relation with Christ. Such works would be but empty form, without meaning or value. On the other hand, such works of obedience cannot but proceed from hearts that have come to faith in Christ and truly take Him as their Lord. How can anyone truthfully call Him Lord and not do His will? The one excludes the other. Because of disobedience, Adam and Eve were driven out of Paradise, thousands of the children of Israel perished in the wilderness, King Saul was rejected. Jesus, on the other hand, says in His missionary commission: "Teach them to observe all things whatsoever I commanded you." And Paul regards the

1. THE EXEGETICAL-HOMILETICAL TREATMENT OF THE TEXT   573

inculcation of the obedience of faith as his own duty and the duty of his co-workers. Even the blood of Jesus cannot release us from this obedience. On the contrary, Christ redeemed us to the end that we should be a people zealous unto good works. In the final judgment, not this or that individual act will be the decisive factor, but the question **whether or not, during** our life on earth, obedience to God's will sprang, as a natural and necessary fruit, from our personal relation to Christ. If not, then, however we may have shone in the Church upon earth, we shall be seen to belong to the class of those who have been working iniquity and lawlessness. What else can Christ do but command us to depart? Oh, that we may not deceive ourselves!

(2) Gospel Texts Illustrating the Indirect Application
Matthew 8: 5-13.

Exposition.—Context: The present section of the Gospel of Matthew relates the prophetic activity of Jesus in Galilee (4: 12-11: 2). After a general description (4: 12-25) the sermon on the mount is given as an example of how Jesus taught (5: 1-7: 29), followed by an account of how He healed and helped men (8: 1-17). The second item in this latter activity engages our attention. The sequence is characteristic, for it expresses the truth: Jesus not only speaks as never man spake, but His deeds bear out His words. He is able to cleanse lepers, He is able to heal the sick.

Over against the Jew, who on account of leprosy was unclean and had experienced the help of Jesus, Matthew places the Gentile, who pleads for help in behalf of his servant. The evangelist does not expressly state that the centurion was a Gentile; but since he was an officer in the service of Herod Antipas and since the Herodian troops consisted in the main of foreign mercenaries, this deduction is permissible. The parallel passage, Luke 7: 3-5, bears out this conclusion, and in our passage it forms the gist of the narrative (vv. 7-8, 10-12). Luke supplements the version of Matthew by characterizing the captain as one of the many Gentiles who were inclined toward Judaism, who had an active interest in the services of the synagogue, who were held in high esteem by the people and whose favor was sought even by the Jewish elders. This Gentile centurion makes, even today, a favorable impression upon the reader, for we hear that he is very much concerned over the recovery of his παῖς, which term hardly means a son, but rather, in accord with current usage, a servant, a personal servant, a valet. According to Luke, he first sent the elders to Jesus in behalf of his servant and later his friends; Matthew relates that he personally came to Jesus, the great worker of miracles. Obviously his servant is more to him than a mere chattel; he takes a personal interest in him, he does something for him, so much, indeed that, considering the social conditions of his day, one can understand it only from the fact that his servant was truly "dear (or precious) unto him" (Luke 7:2).

Like the Jewish leper, the Gentile centurion also addresses Jesus as "Lord." He does not acknowledge Him thereby as the promised Messiah nor consider him the equal of Yahve; this address is merely a courteous greeting of the famous teacher and miracle-worker. "My servant lieth at home sick of the palsy, grievously tormented:" with these words he lays his trouble before Jesus. By the expression βέβληται ἐν τῇ οἰκίᾳ he explains why he could not, as was customary with paralytics, have his servant brought to Jesus (Matt. 4:24; 9:2). The centurion does not in so many words ask Jesus to come to his house, lay His hands upon his servant and thus heal him, but that is what he expects. According to Matthew, at least, he does not realize what it means to expect Jesus, a Jew and a teacher of His people, to enter the home of a Gentile. He is a centurion, the highest official in Capernaum; he has performed many a good deed, to which the elders of the city bear witness. He is accustomed to command, and not to plead. How should his plea be rejected by Jesus, who is known to be glad and willing to help, merely because the man is asking an impropriety? In his heart he is convinced that his prayer will be answered. The more self-evident, however, it is to him that Jesus will do his bidding, the more imperative does it become for Jesus to make plain to the captain that he is not justified in making such a demand, that his petition implies something unusual and extraordinary, in short, that his request is a great imposition.

For that very reason Jesus in great surprise and with strong emphasis puts the question (for v. 7, ἐγὼ ἐλθὼν θεραπεύσω αὐτόν, must be taken as an interrogation and not as a declaration)[3]—"I, I should come into your house and heal your servant? Do you know what you

---

[3]After various Church Fathers had considered this passage as a question and Fritzsche later on revived this opinion, this interpretation was sponsored especially by Zahn. Johannes Weiss (*Die Schriften des Neuen Testaments neu uebersetzt und fuer die Gegenwart erklaert*, 1907, vol. i, p. 301), Bezzel (*Auf ewigem Grund*, Predigten, 1914, p. 133 sq.) and W. C. Allen (*The Gospel according to St. Matthew*, International Critical Commentary, 1913, p. 7.) have adopted this view.

1. THE EXEGETICAL-HOMILETICAL TREATMENT OF THE TEXT   575

are asking? I, a Jew, should enter your heathen home and for your sake ignore all the manners and customs of Israel and thus offer my adversaries a point of vantage against me? You do not know what you are asking!'

That was an emphatic refusal,—not so severe, indeed, as later in the case of the Syrophenician woman, yet a refusal, pointed and plain. But this refusal was to serve an educational purpose. It was to impress upon the captain that he had no claim on the miraculous help of Jesus; that on his part there was nothing whereby he deserved an answer to his prayer, and that on the part of Jesus there was no obligation whatever to help him. If Jesus helped him, it would be nothing but free grace, nothing but friendly and benevolent condescension to him, a Gentile and sinner. The centurion's answer proves that Jesus had won His point. Like a flash of lightning Jesus' reply enlightened his soul, and suddenly he realized the relation between himself and Jesus. He now recognized Jesus as the Chosen and Holy One, and himself as a sinner, and the more he beheld the radiance and holiness of Jesus, the more was he impressed with the darkness of his night and sin. Compared with other Gentile captains, he excelled, no doubt, in various ways; he refrained from many things in

---

Zahn writes (*Kommentar zu Matthaeus*, 1905, p. 333): "The customary traditional view that these words form a declarative sentence, in the first place, does not account for the strongly emphasized ἐγώ; for that none other than Jesus should help was plainly indicated by the fact that the present case was brought to Him, who was at that time healing so many diseases. What point would there be in Jesus saying: 'None other but myself will come and help; I personally will come and heal him'? Secondly, the increasing energy of faith displayed by the captain in his further petition for help, would be incomprehensible. If in v. 7 Jesus declares without any hesitation His willingness to go to the patient, what the captain says in vv. 8 f. is not an expression of admirable faith, but rather the expression of a practically unnecessary modesty. And we cannot help wondering why this modesty was not expressed in v. 6, and why the captain on the contrary plainly states his desire that Jesus is to come to his servant and thus into his house. In the third place, it is inconceivable why Jesus does not act according to His words, as they are generally understood, but lets the subsequent and irrelevant modesty of the captain move Him to an increased exhibition of His power beyond His former promise. These objections will be removed if Jesus in reply to the first petition reluctantly asks: 'Should I, a Jew, a teacher and physician of my people, who am accused already of disregarding the legal ordinances, —should I enter the house of a heathen?' Naturally, then, θεραπεύσω is not future indicative, but aorist subjunctive, as ἐκβάλω in Matt. 7:4 and the questions in Romans 6:1."

which they indulged. In comparison even with many a member of the chosen race of Israel, he fared well; and in the presence of the elders, as well, he need not be ashamed, particularly in view of his benevolence in building the school, of which everyone knew, to say nothing of his soldiers and slaves who highly respected him and no doubt loudly praised him as an excellent man. But as he stands before Jesus and hears His refusal, all his excellences vanish, and the good traits of his character as well as the benevolent deeds of his life appear to him as so many imperfections, failures and sins. As he beholds the Holy One he can only utter from the depths of his heart the words: "Lord, I am not worthy that Thou shouldest come under my roof." Instead of his self-sufficiency, which deemed it self-evident that Jesus would come to him, he is now filled with deep humility and knows that he has no claim whatever on Jesus and must depend entirely upon free grace. The continuation of the captain's answer proves, beyond a doubt, that the question of Jesus has accomplished still more. In face of the refusal of Jesus, which he acknowledged as justified, the captain's faith in the miraculous power of Jesus increased in an astonishing manner. There is awakened in him a sure confidence that it is unnecessary for Jesus to do what he had asked, that He is able to heal his servant without entering his home, and that He is able to do this by the power of His word, which is efficacious even from a distance. From his experience in the service in which he stood, in which he personally was on the one hand subordinate to his superior officers and was, on the other hand, the superior of his soldiers and master of his personal servants, he knows that it is not necessary for the commanding officer to be personally present when he desires something to be done. His own word of command is operative and effects, even afar off, what he desires, whether he commands one of his soldiers or a servant of his household. Thus Jesus need say but a word, which expresses His will, need command only that the servant be healed, and the result will be apparent. Zahn correctly remarks: "The elaborate comparison would be entirely meaningless if the man was not convinced that Jesus is, on the one hand, under God and has received from Him power and authority, and has on the other hand, servants and agents at His disposal, who bear His command invisibly through space and perform it at any given point. A Gentile who had lived for some time among the Jews, who was inclined toward the Jewish belief and worship, would conceive of these invisible servants under the command of the κύριος (as in v. 8 he addresses Jesus for the second time, and now

1. THE EXEGETICAL-HOMILETICAL TREATMENT OF THE TEXT

in a higher sense) as angels. He knew also that the Jews conceived of the angels as the mighty army of God, and at the same time, thinking in terms of his own military position, he regards Jesus as a commander upon whom the Most High has conferred the chief command over a part of his army."

Such faith was, indeed, surprising; it was an amazing and unshakable confidence, secure against all doubts, expecting nothing from itself and everything from Jesus. We need not, therefore, be surprised when Jesus, even before He assures the captain of His assistance, expresses His great wonder concerning this faith—as later in the case of the Syrophenician woman—and finds in it a promise of the future development of the kingdom of God. Beginning with ἀμήν, which on His lips is always significant, He expresses his amazement at the unprecedented faith of the captain: παρ' οὐδενὶ τοσαύτην πίστιν εὗρον, and is unable to complete the sentence without inserting ἐν τῷ 'Ισραήλ before εὗρον. It heightens and justifies His astonishment the more, and makes this case the more singular, that it is not a Jew but a Gentile in whom this faith is found. It is true, Jesus had observed various degrees of faith in Israel before this, but a faith which believes that He has an army of invisible servants at His command, who are able at His word to perform miracles at a distance, He has not found, no, not in Israel. And now, when He does find it, it is not a Jew who thus believes, but a Gentile.

Though it appears as a digression, when Jesus, on the strength of this case, looks into the future and prophetically adds vv. 11 and 12, in which He speaks of participation in the kingdom of heaven and its bliss, this presents no difficulties. Allen well says: "The gap between v. 10 and vv. 11 and 12 must be bridged by the thought that such faith as that exhibited by the Gentilic centurion would admit him into the kingdom, and he was only typical of a class. Many in all parts of the world would be found to have this faith." As in this case a Gentile is superior to the Jews in the matter of faith, so it will be also in the future. Many Gentiles will come to faith, be admitted to the kingdom of heaven and sit at table with Abraham, Isaac and Jacob, while the Jews, the children of the kingdom, for whom the tables were originally prepared, will not only sit at the foot of the table, but have no part in the joys of the kingdom, and be cast out into outer darkness, where one will hear nothing but weeping and gnashing of teeth, the signs of impotent rage. Jesus assuredly does not intend to imply that not a single Jew will come to faith nor have part in the ultimate kingdom of God, but rather that such will be the general course of history and that for the Jews the prospect is not bright. He also declares plainly that everything depends upon faith, upon a sincere faith that relies on Jesus alone. This can be properly inferred from the words which Jesus finally addressed to the captain, whom this peroration has doubtless filled with awe: "Go thy way; as thou hast believed, so be it done unto thee." And when he, arrived at home, found his servant healed, and healed in the selfsame hour in which Jesus had said these words, it served as a mighty confirmation of his faith, and his own experience taught him, to some extent at least, that everything is dependent upon faith, upon sure trust in the word of Jesus of Nazareth.

Application.—The application of this text must be made *indirectly* and by the *tropological* method. The character of Jesus, the nature of faith, the mode by which Jesus would lead to true faith, and the nature of faith itself, are the same today as they were then, although a difference exists between Jesus exalted at the right hand of God and Jesus who dwelt in humility here on earth, even as the centurion of Capernaum differs from men today. Christ still desires to offer His help, bodily as well as spiritual salvation, to man; but He will bestow it only upon those who believe in Him. And man, with all his needs, his own or those of others, his physical as well as spiritual wants, may even today come to Him. This help and salvation, however, he will experience only when he permits Christ to lead him to a twofold conviction: first, to the realization that he has absolutely no claim on the help of Jesus, and that if this help is accorded him, it is purely an act of free grace; and on the other hand, to a faith which depends on nothing except the word of God, which knows that Christ is able by means of this word alone to work miracles and to bring about salvation. Even today humility and faith are the sole means by which we can experience divine help, by means of which we may partake of temporal as well as spiritual salvation. They are very closely related to one another. Without true humility, which is in no way presumptuous and which realizes the one thing only: "I am not worthy, I am not worthy," true faith cannot exist for any length of time. Man never comes to true faith until every vestige of pride and conceit, of self-sufficiency and self-righteousness has been destroyed by God's holiness and majesty, and man has thus become so humble that he is willing to put all his trust in divine grace. How greatly was Paul, the self-righteous one, humiliated? So humble did he become that the things he at one time considered gain he later on counted as loss and refuse. In the cloister, Luther actually hated

1. THE EXEGETICAL-HOMILETICAL TREATMENT OF THE TEXT 579

God at times, because the divine eye was so keen as to discern sin even in the best of deeds. He found no rest for his soul until he had learned, under divine guidance and through God's rejoinder: "I, the holy and spotless One, before whose majesty seraphim cover their faces, I am to condescend to you a base sinner!" to relinquish all claims upon God and to say only "Not worthy, not worthy." But as this humility must always precede true Christian faith, so it must also accompany faith and be its constant companion throughout life. For in the development of the Christian life the old pride and self-sufficiency, though perhaps in a different form, ever and again assert themselves. Thus the Christian constantly compares himself with others and speedily becomes vain when he finds the least advantage on his side. Only as long as we daily remind ourselves of our sinfulness, daily consider ourselves as objects of aversion in the sight of God, and fail to comprehend why God, again and again, condescends to us sinners, will our faith be a living faith, which depends solely and entirely upon Jesus. And what else can such a faith, this ever justifying and sanctifying faith, be but trust and reliance upon the Word of God? To this word alone it will cling, and confide and abide in it. For when the Christian becomes aware of his sinfulness, when his conscience and Satan accuse him, the words: "Son, be of good cheer; thy sins are forgiven thee;" "Though your sins be as scarlet, they shall be white as snow;" "The blood of Jesus Christ, His son, cleanseth us from all sin,"—these words assure him of the forgiveness of sins and give him peace.

The same is true of his material wants. Though he may labor in storm and stress, if he trusts in the words: "When thou passest through the waters, I will be with thee; and through the rivers, they shall not overflow thee," he is on the way to beholding the salvation of God. Such faith, despairing of self and trusting in God's word instead of prescribing to God, will never be confounded.

Matt. 11:28-30.

Exposition—Context: In its wider connection the text occurs in that section of the gospel according to Matthew which describes how variously the ministry of Jesus in Galilee was received (11:2-14:12). This reception is illustrated by the account of the doubt of John the Baptist and Jesus' message to him, but especially by the description of the fickle and proud populace that undertook to prescribe to John as well as to Jesus what they should preach and how they should act, and by Jesus' upbraiding of the unrepentant cities, Chorazin, Bethsaida and Capernaum (11:12-19; 20-24). From this it might appear as if the labors of Jesus had been in vain; but the immediately following praise of God by Jesus, in vv. 25-27, prevents such a supposition. Though the self-complacent and conceited souls who dare to prescribe to Jesus the manner of His activity, have closed their hearts to Him and His revelation, there are the "babes," who are not intent on prescribing to anybody how he should act, but are conscious of being unlearned and simple. Their hearts He can open, to them He can impart His unique revelation concerning all things pertaining to their salvation, concerning His heavenly Father and His own unique relationship to Him. It may seem strange at first that Matthew immediately follows with the words of Jesus in our text, which are omitted by Luke, who has a parallel to Matt. 11:25-27 (in 10:21, 22) but not to 11:28-30. Matthew's reason for this probably was to teach us that Jesus will neglect no opportunity to call to Himself those that labor and are heavy laden. Nor can Jesus' invitation at this juncture seem strange, when we remember that the νήπιοι of whom he speaks in v. 25, and they that labor and are heavy laden, whom he addresses in vv. 28-30, while indeed not directly synonymous, do not exclude or contradict each other, and when we keep in mind that Jesus in v. 27 so strongly emphasized His unique position as mediator between God and man. Just because Jesus had claimed that all things were delivered unto Him of His Father, that no one really knows Him in His unique nature save the Father, and that no one can comprehend the true nature of the Father save he to whom the Son wills to reveal Him, He cannot close His discourse except with the tender invitation: "Come, therefore, to me." There is one thing that this close connection clearly indicates, and that is very important for a proper understanding of the text. It is this: The audience that surrounds Jesus in vv. 28-30 is the same that had heard the words in vv. 25-27, and had perhaps listened to Him ever since 11:2, at any rate since 11:7. Accordingly it consisted not of Jesus' disciples only, but of a greater or smaller number of people who had not as yet entered into closer fellowship with Him. Probably the greater part of them belonged to the σοφοί of whom He had spoken in v. 25, those haughty spirits who made bold to prescribe to John and to Jesus how they should act if they wanted to please them.

Though the latter may have formed the majority of the multitude listening to Jesus, it had not escaped His eye that looketh on the heart, that there were among them some that were toiling and bearing a heavy burden, so that they could not find the rest and comfort they longed for. These at once claimed His warmest solicitude,

1. THE EXEGETICAL-HOMILETICAL TREATMENT OF THE TEXT 581

so that He was ready to attend to them. But whom does He mean by the κοπιῶντες καὶ πεφορτισμένοι? Usually they are understood to be persons who are languishing under the burden of sin and who cannot find forgiveness. And surely there is no greater burden than sin, nor can the sinner find rest and refreshment unless by the forgiveness that Jesus grants. But neither the term κόπος or κοπιᾶν, nor the antithesis of which Jesus here speaks, viz., the yoke that He will lay upon them, seems to fit this interpretation. κοπιᾶν signifies to be weary or spent with labor, to exert one's self with all one's powers. This is the word that comes from Peter's lips (Luke 5:5) when he says that they exerted themselves all night long and labored wearily without attaining their purpose. Paul uses the word when he describes the tireless labor he has bestowed upon the churches in Galatia (Gal. 4:11); or when he tells the thief to steal no more, but to exert himself working with his hands (Eph. 4:28). Compare also Matt. 6:28; John 4:38; Acts 20:35; Rom. 16:6; 1 Cor. 4:12; 15:10; 16:16; Phil. 2:16; Col. 1:29; 1 Thess. 5:12; 1 Tim. 4:10; 2 Tim. 2:6; Rev. 2:3; 2 Cor. 6:5; 10:15; 1 Thess. 1:3; 3:5. So we are not to think here of the burden of the guilt of sin and of the wrath of God, which makes men weary and languid, but of some labor that they perform in order to attain a precious goal, some wearisome toil to gain a precious object or well merited reward. If the burden of sin that lay upon them and from which they would be freed were meant, how could Jesus designate what He gives them in its place as a yoke which He will lay upon them and which can give them rest? Whatever the yoke may mean (see below),—how can the yoke that Jesus lays upon them be the antithesis and opposite of sin? No; the opposite of sin and guilt can only be the removal of guilt, the remission of sin, forgiveness; but of this Jesus does not speak. We must seek another explanation. Others have understood the hardship of earthly labor imposed on man since Gen. 3:17-19. In that case κοπιᾶν is indeed rightly used, but it is difficult to see how the yoke of Christ can form an antithesis to the hardship of human labor, or how the acceptance of Christ's yoke can rid one of this labor and bring one the true ἀνάπαυσις to which Jesus would lead His hearers. Every exposition that fails to note that here persons are meant who are exerting themselves in wearisome labor, and that does not take into consideration that its antithesis is the acceptation of the yoke of Christ which leads to rest, must be rejected as incorrect. But both conceptions are safeguarded in another exposition put forth by such men as v. Holtzmann. A. Harnack, Zahn and Allen. These expositors call to mind that the audience of Jesus consisted of Jews, among whom there were certainly some earnest souls who took great pains to keep the Mosaic law, but did not succeed; who by their labor tried to merit the righteousness of God and thus to attain to rest, but could not in spite of all their efforts. This is exactly what κοπιᾶν expresses. And when we recall that the scribes who belonged to the σοφοί mentioned in v. 25, and who in 12:1-14 are represented as uncompromising guardians of the law, had made an unbearable burden of the Mosaic law by their additions and supplements, the term πεφορτισμένοι comes to its own as well. In Matt. 23:4 these additions are expressly called φορτία.

In order to realize the difficulty, the constraint and the unbearableness of these supplements and thus to visualize the situation of the times, we may mention a few of the scribal additions to the sabbath-commandment, in their opinion a chief commandment. Instead of being satisfied with the simple text, "In it thou shalt not do any work," they had ingeniously discovered 39 chief works prohibited on the sabbath day. It was forbidden to sow, to plow, to harvest, to bind sheaves, to thresh, to winnow, to cleanse fruit, to grind, to sift, to knead, to bake, to shear wool, as well as to wash, beat, dye, spin, and warp it, to tie two strains, to weave two threads, to undo them, to tie a knot, to unloose it, to sew two stitches, to tear anything in order to make two stitches, to catch a roe, to slaughter, skin, salt it, to prepare the hide, to scrape off the hair, to carve it, to write two characters, to erase anything in order to write two characters, to build, to tear down, to extinguish a fire, to build a fire, to flatten with a hammer, to carry anything from one place to another. Each of these general directions contained numerous specific commandments and prohibitions. For instance, since the tying of a knot on the sabbath day was considered work, and since women had to tie the ribbons of their hoods and men the laces of their sandals, exact regulations were made as to which knots were permitted to be made or undone and which were forbidden. Since the writing of two characters was looked upon as forbidden on the sabbath day, but since the two characters might be written on different materials and surfaces, it was exactly regulated what was forbidden and what permitted. A person writing on paper or wax, materials that held the script, was considered a transgressor of the law; a person writing in the sand, was not. If a person, wrapped in thought, wrote one character in the morning and another in the evening, he had broken the sabbath. A physician was allowed to attend a patient, but only if it was a case of life or death. If a person had merely a broken limb it was not permitted to set it on the sabbath

1. THE EXEGETICAL-HOMILETICAL TREATMENT OF THE TEXT 583

day. A sprain of the hand or foot was even forbidden to be dashed with cold water. Since the Scriptures said that no fire was to be built for the purpose of warming victuals, the scribes concluded that neither should a fire be extinguished, and rather than attempt to extinguish a conflagration in one's own or a neighbor's house it should be abandoned to the flames. In this way the law had been turned into a burden and a heavy yoke, under which the people groaned. Moreover, though the Scriptures had made a series of regulations regarding proper cleansings after contact with the sick and the dead, the scribes filled page upon page with further regulations which far surpassed the Mosaic law and were sometimes most ridiculous. They wrote long chapters on the vessels that might be used for purifications, what kind of water was permissible and what kind not, who was permitted to pour it and who not, how far the water was to cover the body or the hand. The latter regulations were to be followed before every meal. What a task it must have been for the sincere Jew to sit down with a good conscience to his meals; he might so easily have made a mistake while washing his hands! Even prayer, that inner sanctuary of the religious life, they had surrounded with legal regulations and had in this way strangled it. To say the daily prayers in the morning and evening was not enough; they had to be said at stated, but limited times, neither sooner nor later; and the phylactery had to be made and worn in a certain way, if the prayer was to be pleasing to God. The Mosaic law had prescribed that food and drink were not to be received without thanksgiving, but the scribes had added special prayers for every course and fixed the very text of each prayer. We smile at such prescriptions and do not deem them worth the paper they were written on, either then or now; to the Jew, however, that were no laughing matter; he had been taught from early youth to deem the traditions of the elders holy. He was convinced that to keep them was to attain to the way of righteousness, apart from which no man could please God. In this conviction he strove and labored to keep them all, but, faithful and sincere in his endeavors as he might be, he was bound to learn that he was carrying an intolerable burden. When he had succeeded in keeping one commandment, he found that he had transgressed others. He had no freedom of action whatever; he was hedged and hemmed in on every side. Regulations surrounded him like a vast net that threatened to strangle him. They became a heavy burden that must be carried through life. And whenever he made the repeated experience that it was impossible to follow these regulations, the result was sorrow and lamentation, bordering on despair.

Such κοπιῶντες καὶ πεφορτισμένοι Jesus recognized among His hearers. To them He calls: "Come unto me all ye that labor and are heavy laden; I will give you rest, I will refresh you. Take my yoke upon you and learn of me; for I am meek and lowly in heart; and ye shall find rest for your souls." Twice Jesus extended this invitation; the second is still more explicit than the first, and both offer the same reward to the laboring and heavy laden souls that accept His invitation. In each case the pronoun of the first person receives the emphasis, for Jesus places Himself and His yoke over against the Pharisees and their yoke. The word, "all" in v. 28 must indeed come into its own, but not so that the ἐγώ, the μου, the με, and the ἀπ' ἐμοῦ will lose any of the stress laid upon them. *He,* who just had said, "All things have been delivered unto me of my Father," who alone could reveal the will of His Father in a reliable way, and whose nature was so unique that He was known only of the Father, who is of the same nature, *He* it is to whom the toiling souls are to come, enter into a more intimate relation with Him, and run no more to the scribes. *His* yoke they are to take upon them, instead of being bowed under the yoke of the scribes. Of *Him* they are to learn, *His* disciples they are to become, instead of following the scribes. Though the scribes were strict and hard in their demands, had no feeling for the weakness of man and were proud, though they could bind heavy burdens on men's shoulders, yet they themselves did not lift a finger to help them (Matt. 23:4) but despised their victims as the multitude that knew not the law (John 7:49). *He,* however, is meek and lowly in heart. He is meek, friendly, gentle, appreciating the needs of the bruised reed and the smoking flax (Isa. 42), yea, all men's needs. He does not use brutal force, but treats them with care and gentleness, seeking only to help. He is lowly in heart, not only outwardly and seemingly, as was sometimes the case with the scribes, but in reality, one who will deal with men, lowly among the lowly, as though they were His equals. And His yoke and His burden are like Himself. His yoke is easy, it does not rub nor chafe; His burden is light, it does not crush to the ground. With Him, yea with Him alone, they will find what they long for,—relief instead of groaning; rest instead of incessant, yet fruitless labor; refreshment, comfort and satisfaction for their souls. (Comp. Eccles. 6:16; 51:31-36, esp. v. 35; Jer. 6:16.)

As soon as this antithesis, which runs through the entire text, has been clearly grasped, any further and detailed exposition is really un-

1. THE EXEGETICAL-HOMILETICAL TREATMENT OF THE TEXT 585

necessary. There is only one term left that needs to be examined, because many expositors, who otherwise correctly expound this text, have missed their footing and have mixed law into a saying of Jesus which is entirely gospel. We refer to the term "yoke". Usually it is understood as an image of guidance or leading, and the thought expressed would be, When the worn souls have freed themselves from the yoke of the scribes and have entered into fellowship with Christ, they must not expect to be unrestrained, free from all discipline and leadership, but rather placed under Christ's leadership and guidance. Such guidance is indeed different from the yoke of the scribes; it is directed by Him who is meek and lowly in heart and, therefore, it is a yoke that is easy, even salutary and agreeable, bracing and strengthening one's abilities, and a light burden. For a proof text Eccles. 51:31 ff. is referred to, where the yoke of wisdom is spoken of. Again, the usage of the Talmud is cited, where "to accept the yoke of the commandments" is an expression frequently used for submission to Jewish law. Attention is also called to the fact that in the New Testament a moral standard of life is not wanting, and that the Christian who lives up to it and truly loves God does not deem it a heavy yoke and burden, but gladly submits to it without finding it grievous (1 John 5:3). All this is true; but how do the following clauses agree with it: "And I will give you rest," and: "Ye shall find rest unto your souls"? Are we really to understand only that rest and satisfaction that goes with the performance of duty and obedience to Jesus' moral precepts? Does not the promise sound much fuller and richer? Does it not point chiefly to that rest which we have gained through Christ and the freedom from the law acquired through him, namely, the peace of the soul? If that is true, then the understanding of "yoke" as given above is impossible. An unbiblical thought would result: that by submitting to Jesus' moral precepts we can attain rest for our souls. It is well, therefore, to examine more carefully the Talmudic usage of "yoke." Here we meet the phrase: "to accept the yoke of the kingdom of heaven," beside the other: "to accept the yoke of the commandments." The former is understood to signify acceptance of faith in Israel's God as the only true God. Nothing is said of ethical duties or submission to law. Hence, "yoke" simply signifies doctrine, instruction, and this fits our passage very well. The souls who have grown weary under the yoke of the scribes are invited to come to Jesus and to accept His message, His doctrine; then they shall truly find rest. And the message or doctrine that is peculiar to Jesus is the *gospel*, the good news that salvation consists in faith in Him. To accept this message, to enter into personal communion with Him, leads to rest for the soul. This message cannot be called a yoke or a burden, if we take these terms in their present meaning; but it can, if we understand them according to the usage of Jesus' time, and if we remember that Jesus would hardly have used them if they had not been suggested by the antithesis. We repeat that the emphasis lies not so much upon "yoke" and "burden," as upon their personal pronouns.

Application: The application of our text to the present time can only be an *indirect* one. A sermon built on this text will dwell upon the truth that persons who endeavor to attain the righteousness of God by their own exertions must come to Jesus and accept His gospel, if they would find rest and peace. The people who listen to a Christian sermon are not under the Mosaic law, much less are they obligated to keep the requirements and additions of the scribes; if that were the case the application would indeed have to be a direct one. At times we cannot even escape the impression that many people regard the rest of the heart and their soul's salvation as a matter of slight importance, and that consequently little real and earnest thought, little real labor and exertion are spent upon them. But let us make no mistake. There are even today numerous souls who would fain attain rest and peace of heart, but who are following a wrong course similar to that of the Jews in Jesus' time. Their conscience being awakened, they realize that things cannot go on as in the past. Hence, they abstain now and then from the works of their former conversation, they practice this and that virtue; they begin to take part in various good works, they contribute liberally to collections, they go to church regularly, they introduce family worship, a custom long neglected, they support the cause of temperance and prohibition, they seriously engage in the various branches of social service, they attend all meetings in which the reconstruction of the nation is discussed. They honestly labor and exert themselves, and are convinced that they are accomplishing great things. For a while they make themselves believe that they have found rest and peace; but it does not last long. When they awake to the facts, they realize that their strength has been used up and all in vain, for they have not found true peace. In that case it is the office of the sermon to proclaim: "Away from your own devices and conceits! Come to Jesus, accept His gospel! It is the only way to find rest for your souls."

Luther, in a masterly way, performed this task for his generation, a generation that groaned under the innumerable precepts of the Church, but found no rest. (Our text is well adapted for a Reformation Day sermon). From him we, too, must learn it. We must invite men to a personal relation with Christ. To read the Bible at home and hear the sermon at church, to instruct one's children or have them instructed, to confess and to commune, to respect the ministry of reconciliation, is all very good and necessary, but it will only help us when it serves as a means to bring us into personal contact with Jesus. Jesus alone can save; He can refresh and He alone; He can give rest for our souls, and He alone. He must be our Saviour, in whom we trust; He must be the friend whom our soul loves; He must be the source, the sustaining power and the one aim of our lives; without Him we can do nothing. To take up His yoke is to believe His gospel, to trust that blessed message of His: "I have borne the yoke and the burden of the law, as well as the curse thereof; I have made you free from all bonds." The better we learn to know Him, the longer we commune with him, the more shall we experience that He is gentle, meek and lowly; that He does not demand, but give; that He demands, rather, only after He has freely given; that 'He has but one passionate desire, and that is to give us rest for our souls.

(3) Parabolic Texts

Matthew 25:1-13

Exposition.—Context: This text is taken from the last discourses of Jesus in Matthew, in which Jesus pointed to the future when Jerusalem should be destroyed and He Himself would return, hold the final judgment and bring about the consummation of all things (chap. 24-25). Because this coming of Christ is to be unexpected and will be a sifting of men like the Deluge, it is apparent that the disciples of Christ must be at all times ready (24:44). This duty of constant readiness for His coming Christ wishes to impress upon His disciples in the following three parables. With this aim in view He speaks (24:45-51) of the careless servant who says within himself, "my lord tarries," but who experiences how his lord will come unaware and surprise him and cut him asunder. With the same purpose in mind He speaks here of the ten virgins (25:1-13) and in the following verses (14-30) of the servant who did not use to advantage the talents entrusted to him and for that reason lost even what he had at his lord's return. The very setting of our text, therefore, characterizes it as an admonition to constant readiness for the Lord's coming.

"*Then*," says Christ,—viz., at that time when the Lord comes (24:50), which will be the decisive hour,—"then shall the Kingdom of

Heaven, as it shall then be and as it shall have found its expression in the church, the entire society of Christians on earth, be like unto ten virgins who had taken their lamps and had gone out to meet the bridegroom." What follows shows that the expression, "the Kingdom of Heaven shall be like unto" is inaccurate, which is often the case. For it is not really the Christians and the virgins who are compared with each other, but their attitude and their fate resulting from their attitude. The thought therefore is: The attitude and fate of all Christianity on earth will in the decisive hour of Christ's return be like the attitude and fate of ten virgins who had taken their lamps and had gone out to meet the bridegroom. In this instance the Master employs wedding customs to teach His disciples the preparedness which will not fail them when He returns. It is not likely that wedding customs were uniform throughout all Palestine in the time of Christ, just as they are not uniform today. According to Schneller's testimony (*Kennst du das Land?* 1892, p. 178), a wedding in the vicinity of Bethlehem takes place as follows: In the evening, when the sun has gone down and night is falling, a group of virgins, women who have never been married, go forth, holding lamps and torches in their hands. These are long poles whose tops are wrapped with rags soaked in olive oil. These flaming torches they carry in festal procession to the place of marriage, where they perform various dances and drills till their torches are burnt down. This festal joy, manifesting itself in various ways, lasts far into the night, for a whole week. In other sections of the land, according to Schneller's testimony (p. 177), we still find the following form of wedding: The marriage festivity proper does not begin until after sunset. First the bride is brought to the scene of festivity, amid loud shouts of joy, and with glowing lights which in the dark cast a weird light upon the houses. Congratulations and greetings sound through the night, and virgin friends lead the bride into her new home, where the bridegroom is awaited. At last he comes, surrounded by his friends and relatives. The virgins rush to meet him with flaming torches and glad greetings, and lead him to the bride. Whenever difficulties arise in the matter of money, his coming is sometimes deferred until midnight. This latter custom has much similarity with the customs in our parable, which Jesus presupposes are familiar to the disciples. In this case also, virgins had gone forth, either from the bride's new home or from their own homes, to meet the groom with their torches. In this case also, the groom tarries so long that the virgins become drowsy and soon are fast asleep. They are awakened only by loud

1. THE EXEGETICAL-HOMILETICAL TREATMENT OF THE TEXT 589

shouts, and at last some of them, at least, enter with the bridegroom into the bridal house. The fact that Jesus employs the number "ten" does not involve any hidden significance, any more than Jesus wished to say that at His return just one half of the Christian people would be saved, the other half lost. On the contrary ten seems to have been the usual number of virgins whose duty it was to meet the bridegroom, just as, according to other Jewish customs, ten men were necessary to constitute a synagogue congregation, and ten persons were thought necessary for a funeral procession.

Now there arises the question: Just what particular phase of these wedding customs is it in which these virgins reveal a likeness to the Christians at the last day? If interpreters, in their search for an answer to this question, had permitted themselves to be guided by the text alone, instead of by their fancy, they would have discovered that this likeness is to be found only in the second half of the narrative, that is, in what is recorded from v. 6 on. For if one does full justice to τότε in the first verse, then Jesus certainly does not say that the attitude and fate of Christians in general, in every respect and at any time, is like the attitude and fate of the ten virgins, but rather just at that particular time when He returns. For 25:1 and 24:50, 51 are inseparably connected. The element of Christ's or the bridegroom's coming is not introduced within the parable until we come to v. 6. What was previously recorded of the virgins in vv. 1b-5 was a necessary presupposition of what is recorded from v. 6 on. The first section of the parable may indeed contain many points of resemblance between the virgins and Christians, but the point of comparison intended by the Lord in this instance cannot possibly be found in this section, but only in that portion which treats of their attitude and fate after the announcement was made: "The bridegroom cometh!" All aorist tenses in vv. 1b-5 should therefore, be translated as pluperfects. For what they express belonged already to the past when that took place which is recorded from v. 6 on. Zahn referred to this fact (*Das Evangelium des Matthaeus*, ²1905, p. 669). Johannes Weiss was at least partly consistent in his translation (*Die Schriften des Neuen Testaments*, 1907, vol. i, p. 383). We go the full logical way and translate: ". . . ten virgins who had taken their lamps and had gone out to meet the bridegroom. But five of them were foolish and five were wise. For the foolish had taken no oil with them when they took their lamps, whereas the wise had taken oil in their vessels with their lamps. Now, while the bridegroom tarried, they had all become drowsy and fallen asleep." We meet with this use of the aorist instead of the pluperfect in Matt. 14:3. Comp. also Prof. A. T. Robertson's instructive discussion of this point in *A Grammar of the Greek New Testament* (²1915, pp. 840-41), where he discusses at some length the rather careless use of the Greek past tenses in narrative speech. From this point of view a great many interpretations are at the very outset proved erroneous. Jesus might just as well have placed vv. 3-5 after v. 7, if their insertion after v. 2 had not been required, to explain the statement, "five of them were foolish and five were wise." The foolishness of the five virgins, as far as their equipment was concerned, consisted in their want of forethought, in not taking an extra supply of oil in their special containers, over and above that which they had in their lamps; while the wisdom of the other five consisted in their forethought in taking, in addition to the oil in their lamps, a further supply of oil, so as to be prepared for any emergency. Both groups might have known that there might be a delay, for this was probably often the case. But only one group thought of this and prepared for it. And when the bridegroom actually was delayed for a long time and then suddenly appeared, it became apparent how poorly prepared were some of the virgins and how well prepared others.

When finally, at midnight, the bridegroom drew near, and the virgins were awakened (we are not told by whom, perhaps by people of the city who had heard him come), the latter without exception woke up and without exception trimmed their lamps. That does not necessarily mean that they now lighted their lamps. According to the custom, it is probable that they went out with burning lamps and left them burning while they waited. Otherwise one would have to accept what is very improbable, viz., that the five foolish virgins started without any oil whatever, even without oil in their lamps. No! All ten had set aside their lamps while waiting. We do not know whether these were really lamps or mere torches such as were described above. They were, in either case, burnt down during the long period of waiting. It was necessary either to trim the wicks or to rewrap the rags to insure a bright light. Above all, new oil had to be added, if the original supply was exhausted; or, if new rags were needed, they had to be soaked with oil. Here it became apparent how stupidly some, and how sensibly others had acted. Those who had brought an extra supply of oil were prepared and could meet the bridegroom with burning lamps. The others had nothing but extinguished lamps at the critical moment; when they should have had oil, they had none. What else could they do but say to their companions: "Give us of your oil; for our lamps are going out." But

1. THE EXEGETICAL-HOMILETICAL TREATMENT OF THE TEXT   591

we can also understand why the latter refused. There might well be another delay, and then they themselves would need whatever remained in their vessels. To divide with their foolish sisters might result in all the lamps going out at the critical moment and leaving the bridegroom with no light for his way. Thus they could only give them the advice: "Go ye rather to them that sell, and buy for yourselves." That was not irony. It might be difficult, but why should it be altogether impossible for them to waken an oil merchant and persuade him to arise from his bed and sell them some oil? V. 11 neither states that they arrived later with burning lamps, in which case they would have found an oil merchant and bought oil of him, nor does it exclude the possibility that they were unable to purchase oil, and sought to enter the bridal house in spite of that. The former view seems the more probable. The sole purpose of v. 11 is to emphasize that they came too late. They had gone forth with the others, they had proceeded with them to meet the bridegroom with burning lamps, they had slept neither sounder nor longer than the others; and yet, when the bridegroom came, the others were prepared and they were not. For the others had oil, while they had none, had none at the very moment when their participation in the marriage festivity depended entirely on their having oil and accompanying the bridegroom with lamps brightly burning. For only those who had burning lamps, at the bridegroom's coming, were permitted to accompany him, and only those who accompanied him were permitted to enter the house. For the others everything was in vain. Their subsequent knocking procured them no admittance; so that wedding joy reigned within while they had to remain without, and could only lament their stupidity and want of forethought.

The Master had probably often seen such a bridal procession, going out with lighted torches to meet the bridegroom. He had, no doubt, observed that many a bridesmaid was so foolish as to take only enough oil for her lamp, but no supply in her vessel. In His mind He can still see clearly in what a predicament she was when the bridegroom was delayed, and when, awakening, she found her oil exhausted. In His mind He still sees how, at the very moment when she needed it most, she found her oil wanting and in her excitement rushed off to the merchants to buy more. He still sees how she missed the wedding procession, found the door closed, and was refused admission by the bridegroom (This latter feature may also be based on actual conditions, otherwise Jesus could hardly have used it as He did). As He looks upon His disciples, the earthly becomes for Him a symbol of the heavenly. His disciples had also gone forth, had forsaken all, and were waiting for the marriage festival, the founding of His kingdom in glory. Oh, that their experience might not be like that of these virgins! Moreover, He Himself would soon be no longer visibly present with His disciples, and would later return to them from heaven, and take them into His eternal kingdom. Oh, that the fate of His disciples, the members of His kingdom on earth, the then living Christians, might not be like that of these foolish virgins! That they who once forsook the world and longed for His appearing might, when He came, not be unprepared! Otherwise, in spite of the fact that they had forsaken the world and given their love to Him and His coming, He would have to refuse them participation in His kingdom. That was the deep concern that filled His loving heart, when He delivered these last discourses and spoke of His final return. In order to save them from such a fate He spoke this parable, which differs from the preceding one in that the latter speaks of a careless servant who either gave the coming of his Lord no thought at all, or thought it still far in the future, while this parable deals with persons who had at one time really gone out from the world, been really added to His disciples, and actually awaited His coming. How sad it would be, if in the end even some of them would not be prepared when He came and would have to be excluded from the joys of His heavenly kingdom!

Application:—The application is a *direct* one, because the Christians of our day need the same warning which Jesus gave His disciples when He spoke this parable; they need it without change and modification. This warning is for them especially, because the return of Christ has come much nearer to them than it was to the disciples. The individual needs this warning, for if he should not live to see the day of Christ's coming in glory, Christ will come to him at least in the hour of his death, of which he does not know the time nor the circumstances, and will take him into His kingdom of joy, if He finds him prepared. In view of this latter consideration one may speak of an indirect application since the text does not speak of death, but of Christ's final coming to establish His eternal kingdom. But in either case, all attention is to be directed to the point of comparison proper. This point of comparison must be applied, and not this or that minor aspect, to say nothing of explaining allegorically each separate detail. In the latter case one ought to ask not only: Whom do the virgins represent, and whom the bridegroom? but also: Since the virgins represent the Christians of the last times, who is the bride? What is meant by the lamps, the vessels for the oil, the slumber of the

1. THE EXEGETICAL-HOMILETICAL TREATMENT OF THE TEXT

virgins? Who are they that announce the coming of the bridegroom? Who are the sellers of oil? and so on. If anyone thinks he can answer these and similar questions by giving his fancy free play, let him show where it is taught in Scripture that, after Christ has come and heavenly glory has begun, there will still be some standing at the door of heaven and craving admittance. This sort of thing leads only to trifling, against which the sound exegete and preacher, with a reverent regard for God's Word, cannot guard too carefully. Or it leads to downright absurdities and impossibilities. If, however, the application is limited to the point of comparison intended by Jesus, the central thought of our text is: Beware, Christian congregation, and individual Christian, lest when your Lord comes you be found unprepared! Or, positively: Watch and be ready always, in order that you may be prepared, however unexpectedly and suddenly your Lord may come!

There follows the question, in what this preparedness consists. In the parable the error lay in the fact that the five foolish virgins had no oil when they needed it most. That oil plays so important a part, lies in the nature of the parable; in another parable it might just as well have been something else. The careful expositor will therefore not simply ask: What does oil signify; of what is it a symbol in Scripture? and adopt a symbolical application,—oil, the symbol of the Holy Spirit and the life wrought by Him. He will rather ask: What does Scripture teach that Christianity and the individual Christian must have at Christ's coming, in order that they may enter with Him into glory? He will find that the only answer is: Faith, wrought by the Spirit of God. Only he who has faith when Christ comes will enter with Him into heaven. That the life of faith, or what is less doubtful, the Holy Spirit who effects this faith, is represented in Scripture under the symbol of oil, is an interesting and instructive coincidence, but can in no wise decide the question of the interpretation of our parable. The life of faith is, according to this parable, what constitutes preparedness, not because oil occurs elsewhere in the Scripture as a symbol of the Holy Spirit and the life wrought by Him, but solely because, in the relation of Christians to their coming Lord in general as well as in the hour of His return in particular, faith is as necessary and indispensable as oil was in the parable. The admonition of our text is therefore: See to it that you have faith when Christ comes, and since you do not know when He will come, see to it that you always have faith. Then, and only then, will you be prepared. 'Here the preacher will not be able to escape the question: How can a Christian always have faith? In answering this question he should call attention to the peculiar nature of faith, according to which it is not a fluid which one simply retains after it has once been infused into one, nor is it a capital which one possesses and cannot lose, after one has once acquired it; it is a divine gift which one has only so long as it is continually renewed in one day by day, and which is lost just as soon as it is not thus renewed by the Holy Spirit through the Word. This, then, is the specific admonition of our text: Watch always and see to it that your faith is daily renewed through the means of grace. For only then will you always be ready and well prepared, no matter when your Lord comes.

From this it becomes apparent that faith must have been wrought in me and that I must thereby have become Christ's disciple, if this parable is to have any message for me, just as the virgins in the parable, even those who were found foolish at the time of the bridegroom's arrival, must have gone out to meet the bridegroom before the question could arise. whether or not they would be admitted with him to the wedding. The reference here is to true disciples of Christ. The parable is not concerned with the visible church. For it is plain that among her members are many who never really forsook the world and joined the number of those who wait for the Lord. Jesus has in mind such as have truly become believers in Him and belong to the number of those who look and long for His appearing. The preacher cannot make this too plain nor drive it home too forcibly. If the condition of his hearers warrant it, he may devote the first part of his sermon to stimulating their consciences by asking: Have you really gone forth to meet the bridegroom? Has faith actually been wrought in you, and are you now living in this faith? But he must make it clear that such questions form merely the presupposition of the parable, whose specific message and purpose is to show those who have been brought to faith that they may nevertheless be found unprepared when their Lord comes, and that they will be prepared at all times only when their faith is renewed every day. How serious a text for every true disciple of Jesus! When He comes again, not even all of those who have once believed will be ready to receive Him. Will you be ready?

(4) Epistle Texts

Romans 3:21-28

Exposition:—After Paul has shown in part one of this epistle (1:18-3:20) that all mankind, Jews no less than Gentiles, are under

1. THE EXEGETICAL-HOMILETICAL TREATMENT OF THE TEXT

the wrath of God, he begins part two at 3:21, as with silent rejoicing: But now the righteousness of God without the mediation of the law has been revealed. Though Jews as well as Gentiles (1:18-3:8), and in one aspect of their nature, even Christians (cf. their previous state, 3:9-20) were under the wrath of God, the righteousness of God has been revealed entirely apart from the Mosaic or any other law and obedience to the same. Had it not been the righteousness of God that was revealed, there would be no cause for joy and exultation. The term, "righteousness of God," denotes the relation effected by God Himself through Christ, in which man conforms to the divine will and therefore enjoys God's favor. This, of course, is the opposite of a relation characterized by God's wrath. Who would not rejoice, therefore, to be able to say: That relation in which God's anger was directed against me has been removed and has been replaced by one in which the verdict of God, the absolute Judge, is in my favor? Ask him who is condemned to death how genuine this joy is. By what means the revelation of this righteousness prepared by God for man has been brought about, the epistle does not say. But we know it from other statements of Scripture. Its realization began with Jesus' own testimony (Matt. 20:28; John 10:12; Matt. 26:26 ff) and continued in the testimony of the apostles (e. g., Acts 10:34-43) and is still heard in the Gospel (hence the perfect tense, which denotes a past occurrence but one whose influence continues for all time). For this is the very heart and centre of all Gospel preaching, that God worked righteousness through Christ, that is, He has established a state in which God the Judge is for and not against us. The apostle cannot mention this blessed circumstance without characterizing God's righteousness somewhat more in detail. He does this in a threefold manner: (1) Already the law and the prophets, i. e., the entire old Testament, have witnessed it. Therefore he is not dealing with something opposed to the Old Testament, which the Jews must be wary of accepting. On the contrary, the righteousness now revealed is the identical righteousness to which the entire ceremonial law and its system of sacrifices, as well as the promises have pointed from the beginning (cf. especially Jer. 23:6). (2) This righteousness is appropriated not by any human effort, not by obedience to law, but solely through faith in Jesus Christ, which faith is itself a gift of the Holy Spirit (Gal. 3:23-25). (3) This righteousness of God is intended not for a few elect and favored ones, but for those who believe, whether Jews or Gentiles. Truly, the revelation of this righteousness is fraught with boundless blessing. No wonder that the

Gospel, through and in which this revelation is revealed (1:17) is the power of God unto salvation, a message concerning which Paul can have no misgivings, but which he cannot but be proud of and preach, confident of success, even in Rome the metropolis (1:15-16).

The following verses attach to the last of the three characteristics mentioned. Why is the righteousness of God available for all believers? Because there is no difference among them. (According to the context this assertion is made of believers, not of mankind in general). But how can one determine that there is no difference between all believers (whether formerly Jews or heathen)? (1) By the fact that all have sinned and, therefore, lack favorable recognition (δόξα, cf. 2:7, 9; John 5:44; 12:43) by God (1:18-3:20); (2) by the fact that they, though sinners, all become righteous in the same manner, namely gratuitously, i. e., not by way of reward for their efforts, but without such efforts, through the grace of God, by His favor and kindly disposition, by His not dealing with them according to their deserts but tempering justice with mercy by means of the redemption in Christ. That δικαιοῦσθαι as here used does not denote inner moral change, or *actus medicinalis,* as Rome would have it, becomes evident: (1) From the consideration that the conceptions "righteous" and "righteousness" as used in Scripture denote a relation. Therefore δικαιοῦν must denote the act of placing one into a new relation, in which God's judgment acquits and does not convict one, and cannot denote a metamorphosis into a new condition; (2) from the actual use of δικαιοῦν in profane Greek literature, as well as in the Bible where, with justum censere, it is correctly rendered, to regard as, or look upon as, or declare righteous (Deut. 25:1; Isa. 5:23; Luke 7:29, etc.); (3) from the circumstance that δικαιοῦν and δικαιοῦσθαι are used interchangeably with expressions denoting to reckon unto righteousness, not to impute one's sin to one, to forgive sin (Gen. 15:6; Ps. 32:2; Rom. 4:4, 5; Gal. 3:6ff.; Rom. 5:18, 19). In our context it must be so rendered because of the fact that those who experience the δικαιοῦσθαι are expressly characterized in v. 23 as sinners and those who lack favorable recognition by God. The question is, therefore, how sinners come into possession of the righteousness of God despite their sin; otherwise the exclusive particles here used (δωρεάν, τῇ χάριτι, διὰ ἀπολυτρώσεως) would have no meaning. A judicial verdict is involved, a pronouncing righteous, a becoming righteous, indeed, but in such a manner that the sinner is pronounced righteous by God and thereby placed in a state of righteousness.

1. THE EXEGETICAL-HOMILETICAL TREATMENT OF THE TEXT

What follows attaches to the third qualification, to the διὰ τῆς ἀπολυτρώσεως τῆς ἐν Χριστῷ 'Ιησοῦ. Through the redemption in Christ Jesus the believing sinner becomes righteous. This is the means, and it lies wholly outside man. As the χάρις of God the Father constitutes the inner cause, the *causa impulsiva interna,* so the redemption in Christ Jesus is the *causa impulsiva externa.* Vv. 25 and 26 specify how this deliverance, effected by God the Father and contained once for all in Christ Jesus, was brought about, and at the same time solve the mystery as to how sinful men (that is, believers), in spite of their sins, can be pronounced righteous by God, can be put into that state of righteousness in which God is for them and not against them. Redemption by Christ Jesus and justification of the sinner through the same could never have been actualized without that which vv. 25 and 26 describe. What is it that has occurred and that is of such importance that it constitutes the indispensable foundation of the believing sinner's justification? God the Father has set forth Christ, by means of the shedding of His blood upon the cross, before all the world as a means of propitiation, the effect of which is appropriated by faith (ἱλαστήριον like κριτήριον: the place of judgment, means of decision; ἁγνιστήριον: place of cleansing, means of cleansing; φυλακτήριον: place of the watchman, means of defence, amulet), i. e., as a means by which the sins of the world are covered over (1 John 2:2). Through His giving of Christ unto death upon the cross, God has wrought a means in His blood to cover the sins of the world, by which sin is actually atoned for, is covered. To what end did God the Father place 'His crucified Son before the world as sin-covering? For the showing (εἰς ἔνδειξιν) of His righteousness, a manifestation of the same before the world. This means two things: (1) The revelation of God's punitive justice, which revelation has become necessary because of the Old Testament times in which judgment was postponed (since the Deluge there has been no universal judgment). This postponement was possible only in view of the revelation of God's righteousness conceived from eternity and executed in the present. Had this revelation not come to pass, the frivolous would have concluded that God will not punish sin, and that whether or not we commit sin is a matter of indifference to 'Him. (2) The revelation of the righteousness which works salvation. God wished not merely to stand before the world as the Just One who punishes sin, but also as the One who pronounces righteous those who believe in Jesus. This twofold revelation was to redound to His own justification and also to the justification, the salvation of man. (1) By the death of Christ on the cross (He, the Innocent One, was unjustly accused and cruelly punished, a substitute for the guilty; upon Him was visited the whole anger and curse of God) was manifested the fact that God will not be mocked, that He is just and punishes relentlessly, that punitive justice was given its due and was satisfied; (2) by Christ's blood the sin of the world was covered, on the basis of which the sinner can be justified in the sight of God. Therefore, the work of expiatory propitiation is fundamental for justification. Were it conceivable that God could now punish the sinner who is in Christ through faith, He would be ignoring the fact that He had already punished this sin and expiated it, i. e., covered it over. Which is impossible.

Let us note the consequences of the important truth in vv. 24-26. If believers are actually justified despite their sins, and this out of pure grace by means of the redemption that is in Christ Jesus; if they are justified thanks to God's intervention and His achieving both a complete propitiation of His punitive justice and at the same time a covering of man's sin, how can there be room or reason for the justified believer to glory in himself? There can be none. All glorying in self is excluded by the very fact that God chose the way of salvation mentioned in vv. 25-26. When Paul adds, "By what law?" in v. 27, he presupposes that it came to pass through a law, a regulation of God ($νόμος$ is here plainly used in this wider sense), but he asks, By what kind of law? Not by a law or dispensation which requires works, but by one which asks only faith. For what works can be necessary on the part of the believer, when God has done all through Christ, in whose person the propitiation through which one becomes just is enacted? The manner in which God prepares salvation and now proclaims it in the Gospel admits of nothing save faith. Anything beside faith will not be considered by Him. Not he who does works, but he who believes shall receive righteousness, according to God's intention, i. e., he shall by a divine verdict be put into a state in which God is for him and not against him, and is secured for time and eternity. From the fact that God's plan of salvation is such as to admit of but one factor, namely faith, it follows (v. 28) that we Christians properly hold that a man is justified by faith apart from the works of the law.

Application.— Because of the remarkable wealth of *directly* applicable material in this text, the many features which lend themselves to practical treatment cannot even be mentioned. The following are a few of the leading thoughts. (1) We have sinned and lacked recognition by God. Instead of being favorably acknowledged by Him,

1. THE EXEGETICAL-HOMILETICAL TREATMENT OF THE TEXT 599

the Judge, His wrath and condemnation rest upon us. Here and now, the fact that His anger rests upon us is evident from all manner of ills and their culmination, death (1:18). In the last time His anger will be manifested with much greater intensity. Even Christians are subject in one respect to the judgment of God (3:9-20). Works of obedience to any law cannot rescue us from this predicament. As yet no one has been able by his own efforts to gain communion with God, or forgiveness of sins, or righteousness, i. e., that state in which God is favorably disposed toward one. The Jews, Paul, Luther, are witnesses to this truth. The Law was not given to overcome sin, but rather to manifest it, and to produce a cry of despair (3:19-20). (2) But God Himself has intervened and wrought righteousness without the mediation of the Law or any human agency, has established a relation according to which He is for and not against man, who is, therefore, truly saved for time and eternity. Through His Son He has brought about what the entire Old Testament had promised and typified. In Christ, release from God's anger and His curse exists, because Christ achieved on the cross of Calvary both the satisfaction of God's punitive justice and forgiveness of man's sin. God's holiness and justice received their due, but likewise His saving love. In the divine-human personality of Christ there is redemption for all. (3) What then is required of us? Works of one kind or another? Christ has done all. If redemption is in Him, why should you desire to earn it, you who previously attempted it in vain and incurred God's wrath the more by your efforts? When God has performed a work and in the Gospel assures you that it exists for you, you must either accept it in faith, or spurn it by reason of your unbelief. The wish to do works is either prompted by thoughtlessness or is equivalent to wilful rejection of God's work as insufficient. (4) The Gospel exists and is preached for this very purpose, that faith, the only correlative of the work of God proclaimed in the Word, may be creatively wrought in us. For this reason the remarkable revelation of the righteousness prepared by God occurs in and through the Word. (5) When the sinner believes and in faith appropriates this fully sufficient propitiation, atonement, redemption, then God justifies him through grace for Christ's sake, and puts him thereby in that blessed state in which He is for him and no longer against him. Then he may rejoice and thank God as Paul here does.

Let the homilete guard against a dry and one-sided doctrinal presentation of these fundamental thoughts; the joy which Paul experienced when writing this text should run through and inspire his whole discourse.

James 1:2-7

Exposition.—The first part of the epistle of James, of which our text forms the first subdivision, extends from 1:2 to 1:18, and describes the Christian's attitude to temptations or trials.

The very first verse of our text speaks of temptations, afflictions, trials. "Count it all joy, my brethren, when ye fall into manifold temptations." There are two kinds of temptation, those coming from without and those arising from within. That the latter class is not in the writer's mind is evident from the fact that he calls on his readers to regard their temptations as nothing but joy: temptations coming from within could never be the subject of rejoicing. Apparently, he thinks of such temptations as would be likely to shatter his readers' faith, afflictions to which they are exposed because of their Christian faith. James is not, however, thinking of an organized bloody persecution, but expressly states: many-colored, variegated, diversified temptations (ποικίλοι), that is, afflictions of every sort. However widely their temptations may vary according to locality and circumstances, none are to be excluded. To assume the correct attitude, to behave correctly in times of such temptation, is difficult. One grows easily disheartened, discouraged, gloomy, and despondent. These dangers were no less real for the readers of this epistle, the N. T. people of Israel (cf. v. 1), even though they could expect little else than temptations of many kinds, since they were strangers, sojourners in dispersion, no matter where they lived, strangers who had their real home in heaven and not on earth. To warn against wrong behavior in temptation and to teach them the right attitude, James writes: Regard it as nothing but joy if you encounter now this, now that temptation; if you are, as it were, entirely surrounded (περιπίπτω) by temptations. A strange attitude, indeed! Afflictions and temptations assail and distress, they harass and wound, they pierce the heart—how can one be expected to regard them as pure joy? James is well aware that this view of life and of suffering seems absurd to the natural man and is diametrically opposed to his world view. Probably for that very reason he places "all joy" in the most emphatic position in the sentence. If this seems harsh or severe, he does not forget to add the tender and compassionate "my brethren," lest his readers should be repelled by this admonition at first so incomprehensible.

But can temptations possibly be the subject of rejoicing? Verse

1. THE EXEGETICAL-HOMILETICAL TREATMENT OF THE TEXT 601

3 is the answer, giving the cause for the strange exhortation. The readers ought to regard temptation as pure joy "as those who know that the means of testing their faith produces stedfastness" (so δοκίμιον is to be rendered here; cf. Prov. 27:21). James presupposes that his readers know this as an axiomatic truth, else he would not command them to rejoice in their temptations. Temptation *per se* is no cause of joy, but rather of sorrow and pain; but considered in the light of the blessings that by God's gracious plan are to accrue therefrom, it is a fit subject of rejoicing. What is God's purpose and aim in permitting temptation to overtake us? James indicates the answer by joining two thoughts into one: (1) Temptation is a means of testing our faith, a criterion of faith; (2) as such it works stedfastness. This must be the author's opinion for otherwise it would be inexplicable why in v. 3 he goes on to speak of the testing of faith while v. 2 would lead one to expect some statement about temptation. Temptation is as efficient a means for demonstrating the quality of our faith as the furnace is for proving the genuineness of gold. Will anyone contend that temptations are no cause of joy, when they demonstrate the validity and genuineness of faith? In the Christian life everything depends on faith. What a calamity if we were to imagine our faith to be true and in the end to find that it had been mere illusion! Would our perdition not be due to self-deception? A true Christian, therefore, welcomes temptation as a touchstone of his faith; however much it may pain him, in view of its purpose he will gladly suffer it, he will even rejoice in it, knowing it to be salutary and propitious. Temptation, however, is more than a mere touchstone. Because it tests faith, it simultaneously results in those who permit themselves to be tested as to the genuineness of their faith and stand the test, in ὑπομονή, i. e., not only "patience," which is more or less passive, but corresponding to the root of the verb, something firm and lasting, endurance, constancy, perseverance, stedfastness, and since we are here dealing with moral values, not any kind of stedfastness, but moral stedfastness. If that is the aim and result of temptation—and the readers know it is—then the exhortation to rejoice may seem never so absurd and strange, in view of the blessed end they cannot but rejoice. Moral constancy is invaluable, indeed; it is the characteristic of maturity, the mark of the full-grown man (cf. Eph. 3:13, 14). If the readers possess this knowledge and nevertheless, instead of rejoicing, become despondent and bitter, then they betray thereby that they fail to appreciate the value of this glorious fruit of temptation, moral constancy and endurance.

"This constant stedfastness, moreover, shall have its perfect work, in order that you may be perfect and complete, remaining behind in nothing." So James continues, naming God's final salutary purpose in permitting temptations to harass Christians, viz., moral perfection. Note that in his eagerness he drops the construction, he does not finish the sentence as begun. The fresh idea of admonition moves him to complete the sentence in a more practical, effective manner He imagines a concrete case. Here is one of his readers, whose trials have begun to produce stedfastness, but who is about to yield to despair, who is at the point of surrender because in his estimation the trials are too wearisome and too difficult. His endurance is not so strong as it ought to be. Emphatically James exhorts him: Let stedfastness have its perfect work. The emphasis is on perfect: stedfastness is an act, an activity; it must fully and without reserve do what its name denotes, it must discharge its functions in all relationships. Though the particular affliction threatens to shatter their faith or undermine their faithfulness or make them indifferent or inconsiderate, they ought in every case to breast the tide and fight the waves; they must not submit but stand their ground; they must ward off all attacks in order that God's purpose may be attained: that they become perfect, reaching the aim (τέλειος from τέλος), completely and in every respect (ὁλόκληροι) realizing God's plan, and coming behind in nothing. Moral perfection—another glorious blessing of temptation! To be sure, absolute moral perfection, sinlessness, is unattainable here in this life; but even relative perfection is an invaluable quality, the perfection of the full grown man as compared with the weak beginnings of the novice. Very many things have ceased to constitute temptations for him, and when temptation afflicts him, he stands his ground. No matter, how prolonged and intense their temptation is, if only the readers will remember that it is a touchstone of their faith, if they will consider that this test gives stedfastness, and that stedfastness issues in moral perfection, then, indeed, temptation will be no stumblingblock, then they will attain to that point which James would have them reach: they will rejoice in their temptation.

The readers possessed the knowledge (γνῶσις, v. 3) necessary for understanding God's purpose; but its indispensable complement is wisdom (σοφία, v. 5), that faculty of practical judgment which points out correct behavior in times of adversity. Many a one has had all the elements of the former, yet lacking the latter he has fallen into new adversities and has aggravated the soreness of the trial. And while the original temptation came without his fault, purely in the course

1. THE EXEGETICAL-HOMILETICAL TREATMENT OF THE TEXT

of divine providence, this new temptation, in its aggravated state, is due to his own thoughtlessness and imprudence. There may be two men whose life of faith is equally vigorous and whose knowledge is equally sound, but who differ widely in wisdom. Lack of wisdom in itself is not considered by our apostle to be blameworthy. He simply exhorts: "If any lack wisdom, let him pray!" Instead of despairing because of its absence, let him ask God for it. May he be assured that God will answer his prayer? Most emphatically James says: "It shall be given him," it shall be given him at once (that is the force of the future $δοθήσεται$). James has three reasons for this unconditioned and unreserved promise: (1) God gives to all, He has no favorites whom He prefers, no stepchildren whom He neglects; He gives without partiality. (2) God gives $ἁπλῶς$, i. e., simply, in singlemindedness; there is no duplicity or cunning in His mind, neither self-glorifying ostentation nor self-seeking munificence, His sole aim is to help, to give. (3) He does not upbraid, He does not reproach the needy one for his lack of wisdom, contrary to our disagreeable human trait of heaping humiliating reproof upon those who ask gifts of us. If God thus gives, then indeed it is good to ask of Him, then He can be readily asked, much more readily than men. Therefore let everyone that lacks wisdom pray.

"It shall be given him." This was James' unreserved statement in v. 5. That compels him in vv. 6 and 7 to describe more closely the kind of prayer that alone is deserving of this unconditioned promise. Whoever asks for such practical wisdom and would have his prayer granted, "let him ask in faith, nothing doubting." The essential condition of correct prayer is stated positively and negatively, but the same thing is meant. Faith is the condition of right prayer. But faith is unwavering certainty, calm tranquillity. Its opposite, therefore, is doubt, which is fundamentally vacillation, incertitude, turbulence. The doubter is divided in his heart, at variance with himself, his thoughts are in turmoil and in uproar. He may still pray, as long as he is not quite certain that prayer is of no avail, but he does not pray with cheerful confidence, because again and again he gives way to the thought: Perhaps it is all in vain. No one who is so disposed can receive God's gift, not even the gift of practical wisdom. You cannot place a gift in a wavering hand; it must come to rest and be still. James uses the figure of the wave of the sea to explain the importance of calmness. Faith has a firm foundation, is not driven hither and thither by external influences; he who doubts is like the wave, restless and never still. The wind drives it, the storm whips it into restless fury. In exactly the same manner, the doubter who does not by faith rest in God is alarmed as soon as temptation approaches, and if it increases he falls into feverish frenzy. There the indispensable presupposition of effective prayer is wanting. "Certainly (γάρ) let not that man think that he shall receive anything from the Lord." So James concludes on a note of direct and impressive warning. Thus our text, consisting of two subdivisions, is an exposition on the subject of the correct attitude to temptations coming from without. The readers are admonished to regard them as pure joy, and in faith to pray for the necessary wisdom, whenever it is lacking.

Application.—The application in this case is *direct*. For, what James here writes to his readers applies equally to present day Christendom and to every individual Christian. Temptations coming from without are manifold. Afflictions assail the Christian on account of his faith and his confession; he is exposed to abuse and vituperation, to hostility and persecution if he frankly confesses his faith, if he lives accordingly, if he does not cheat or defraud, if he does not join a lodge, if he pleads the cause of the poor and needy. Besides this, there are many other afflictions in the wider sense, such as sickness, suffering, and sorrow. Many a Christian has commenced to run well, but such afflictions have caused him to stand still or to go back; many have become spiritual bankrupts because in times of adversity they did not have the correct attitude. They should have remembered that they are strangers and pilgrims in this world (Jas. 1:1; 1 Pet. 2:11), and that as such they must fall into many afflictions, as their Lord and Master did. But instead of this, they thought it strange (1 Pet. 4:12) that these trials appeared, and thus from the very beginning lost their inner composure. For that reason instruction concerning the right attitude to affliction ought to be welcome and valuable to every Christian. That afflictions are to be regarded as nothing but joy is indeed a hard lesson to learn even for the Christian who has expected them to come. He is human and therefore, sensitive; bodily suffering is painful; ridicule and scurrility hurt; he has a frail body and nerves that are affected by the stress and strain of temptation; and he thinks he has a right to live and be happy. The apostle has apparently very little sympathy for his condition, when he exhorts him to count temptation as pure joy. And yet, if he will not look at the 'old man after the flesh', but if the new man will look up to his God, whose heart he knows, if he will recall that God never intends anything but his salvation, if this Christian knowledge dominates all other thoughts, if in renewed faith he regards all the blessings that according to God's plan are to accrue to him from temptation—the test of his faith, stedfastness, moral perfection—then he will gradually progress from the point where he says: "I *must* suffer," to the higher plane where he will confess: "I *can* suffer," and "I *will* suffer," and will perhaps even reach that summit where he can exult: "I am permitted to suffer, I am accounted worthy of suffering!" He has begun to understand the apostle's strange command and begins step by step to follow it.

But that does not yet fully describe the Christian's behavior in temptation. He may recollect God's salutary purpose and still lack practical wisdom in a specific temptation. He has observed, perhaps certainly not in a cowardly or equivocating manner, but more thoughtlessness and carelessness and lack of self-control have aggravated and prolonged the temptation. He cannot but add to the prayer for forgiveness of his foolish and wrong behavior, the petition for the right wisdom, in order that in future he may act more circumspectly, certainly not in a cowardly or equivocating manner, but more thoughtfully and more moderately. God has rendered prayer easy for him, and he, the regenerated Christian, will certainly pray with the assurance of faith and with the cheerful confidence that God will answer his prayer. Whoever heeds this double counsel concerning the Christian's conduct in adversity, will not come to grief but will prevail and gain the victory.

2. Illustrations of the Arrangement of Materials in the Outline
Gen. 15:1-6

Introduction: St. Paul uses this passage several times as a proof for the doctrine of justification. With good reason. But it is more than this. It unfolds an important chapter in the spiritual history of Abraham. We notice these two things: that even after his call his life was full of severe temptations, and how he overcame them. As his call was a type of our own call into God's kingdom, so we find in this part of his biography laws of the inner life and truths which still hold good in the life of every one whom God has called by faith into His kingdom. Let us see:

Theme: How the Christian overcomes temptation.
Our text reminds us:
(1) *That the Christian, who has followed in faith the call of God into His kingdom, must still pass through temptations.*
   (a) So it was with Abraham.
   (b) So it is with us Christians. The Church of Jesus Christ is

the freeborn daughter of heaven. Yet she was the offscouring of the heathen world for nearly three centuries. She is a source of blessing for the whole world, but to this day she must submit to oppression and persecution. So it is with every one of her members. Christian and cross belong together. Even this specific form of temptation recurs frequently, when one's faith in God's faithfulness and truthfulness begins to waver, when God's promise and one's present condition do not harmonize, or when one incurs special danger because of a courageous venture in behalf of the cause of God's kingdom. But here, too, one must recognize the law of God's kingdom and must ask Him for wisdom lest the hidden blessing be cast away. Temptations come upon the Christian that he may see the loving purpose of God which is hidden in them, and that he may overcome the temptations.

Our text treats of temptation in order to present another thing more fully, namely, the comfort which the Christian finds in the midst of temptation. Let us, therefore, hear:

(2) *How the tempted Christan finds consolation in the Word of God.*

(a) So it was with Abraham. When he found it difficult to repress the doubts that assailed him the Lord appeared to him and consoled him with His gracious promise.

(b) So it is with the Christian. When he is in the midst of doubts and fears, his God comes to him in the Word and whispers: "Fear not; I am thy shield, and also thy reward," and opens his eyes, that he may see the great things which He has already given to him in spiritual blessings and bodily preservation. And then God admonishes him: "Let my grace be sufficient for thee. In the blessed hereafter thou shalt receive an hundredfold for all things."

But how can I appropriate this consolation, so that it may be really my own and that I may overcome temptation? This is the third thing shown in Abraham as a type. It is said of him, "he believed."

(3) *By faith alone the tempted Christian appropriates the consolation offered by God.*

(a) So it was with Abraham. To believe is to go out from one's self, to give up all hope in one's own knowledge and power, to cling solely to the almighty and gracious God, who offers Himself to us in the Word. This Abraham did, and by means of such faith he appropriated God's consolation and overcame the temptation.

(b) So it is with the Christian. Today, too, faith is the only means of appropriating divine confort in affliction and of overcoming temptation. You must first despair of your own strength, and in your helplessness stretch out your hand to God as your only Saviour. You must expect all aid from Him alone, and over against all doubt you must always rely upon 'His Word. Only thus will you overcome temptation. Comp. Heb. 13:5; Ps. 50:15; Ps. 90; 91; Isa. 1:18; 1 John 1:7. Then comfort will increase within your heart and rest will return to your soul.

(4) *While appropriating the comfort which God gives to him, the Christian will always have a new experience of justification on the part of God.*

(a) This is the final lesson in this part of Abraham's life.

(b) Wherever there is faith that knows of no salvation, no forgiveness and no future, except in fellowship with the God of salvation revealed to us in Christ, there is justification on the part of God, an ever renewed declaration of righteousness, out of grace for Christ's sake by faith and not through any work of the law. And where there is justification, there is peace and rest.

Conclusion: So you see that God has no intention of killing and destroying by means of temptation. On the contrary, He wants to lead us to higher levels of the inner life, to renewed joy in God, to closer nestling at the Father's heart. Then temptation has been really overcome, and we can joyfully exclaim: "If God is for me, who can be against me?" Only do not forget the only way that leads to such a victory. Its name is faith. Amen.

Isa. 61:1-7

Introduction: "Behold, thy King cometh unto thee"—this word sounds through the Old Testament, from Gen. 3:15 and especially Gen. 49:10 onward, like the leitmotif of a masterpiece of music, at first soft and low, almost fearful of being heard, then ever louder and clearer, until it swells into triumphant and all-dominating fulness in the prophecy of Isaiah. "Behold, thy King cometh unto thee"—this word is repeated in the period of fulfilment, every Adventtide. Advent, with its four Sundays, represents the 4000 years of Old Testament hope and expectation. Hence, this word forms its authentic message. The Old Testament saints looked longingly to the future for the coming of this King; we for whom His coming is a fact, look as longingly forward into the new church year, for a new and glorious manifestation of His coming. He is to us still the Coming One. We look for the same King, who was born at Bethlehem, who entered triumphantly into Jerusalem, who completed on Calvary His royal work of redemption,

—we look for His coming in Word and sacrament, in all His Saviour glory. Thus, at the threshold of a new year of grace, we take this old word and proclaim it to you anew:

Theme: Behold, thy King cometh unto thee! And in order that our hearts may greet Him aright, let us learn from our text that He comes (1) as royal preacher of redemption, (2) as royal creator of a new world.

(1) *He comes as a royal preacher of redemption.*

(a) You are in need of redemption, no less than Israel of old. Israel, according to our text, in captivity in Babylon; afflicted in body and soul; tyrannized over by heathen; recognizing its distress as God's righteous punishment for its sins; longing for freedom and return. Surely, in need of redemption of body and soul.—The life of men today resembles that of captive Israel. Distressed by results of sin and desiring to be set free; captive in vilest bondage to vice; under tyranny of godless neighbors or evil companions; longing for peace and rest; sighing under the exceeding sinfulness of sin, the thought of God's anger and their own ingratitude, and yearning for forgiveness. Surely you are, we are, in need of redemption.

(b) Rejoice, thou daughter of Zion: shout for joy, thou daughter of Jerusalem; for behold, thy King cometh unto thee! 'He comes as royal preacher of redemption. His coming foretold to Jews in Babylon. The Servant of the Lord is to come and preach good tidings: vv. 1-3. In Jesus this Servant appeared. (Luke 4:17-21). In this new church year He desires to come also to us, as preacher of our redemption. The greater our wants, the nearer will He come, the more cordial His greeting: "Come unto me, ye poor and distressed, ye broken-hearted and disappointed, ye captives and all that mourn. Here is the good tidings I bring: deliverance and salvation for all." What joy this message brings, what comfort and hope!

(2) Behold, thy King cometh unto thee, as *royal creator of a new world.* Blessed good tidings the King brings as preacher of redemption. But is He only a preacher? Has He nothing but words, gracious and glorious, indeed, still only words, no deeds? Is He only one of the long line of prophets, greater than Isaiah, indeed, but pointing to a future where alone help is to be found? No. Rejoice greatly, thou daughter of Zion, behold, thy King cometh bringing salvation. He comes as creator of a new world.

(a) Did God have only words for exiled Israel? When Christ came, fulfilling our prophecy, was He not more than a mere preacher of good news? He was the creator of a new world. By 'His word, renewing men inwardly and outwardly. Giving Himself a ransom for all. (2 Cor. 5:17; Jas. 1:18).

(b) *Rejoice; for in the new church year thy King cometh unto thee, not only as royal preacher of redemption, but as royal creator of a new world.* The divine Word, in and through which He comes, is no empty sound, no mere message and testimony; but power, the power of God unto salvation. (Rom. 1:16; Jas. 1:18-21; 1 Pet. 1:23; 2 Cor. 2:16; 2:6; Isa. 55:10.) It contains and conveys the gifts and blessings it proclaims. Where Word and sacrament reach men's hearts, there is a "planting of God," a new creation (2 Cor. 5:17) to the glory of God (v. 2b). This new life imperfect here below, but to go on from grace to grace and from glory to glory, including even the redemption of our body. The pledge and means of this is the renewed coming, this church year, of the royal creator of a new world.

Conclusion: Hence rejoice! Go forth to meet your King! Accept the message of redemption which He brings! Accept Him as the creator of a new world! Then this year will be for you an "acceptable year of the Lord." Amen.

Matt. 11:28-30

Introduction: The Church festivals are inspired by the mighty works of God. This is true today also. The burden of the Festival of the Reformation is the burden of our text: Jesus alone can give us rest. This shall be the burden also of our sermon.

Theme: Jesus alone can give us rest.

(1) Jesus alone can give us rest. *This was the message of Jesus to the Jews of His time.*

(a) They sorely needed this message. They sighed under the burden of the law, which gave them no rest. The law, a precious gift of God, turned through sin into a crushing fetter. God's anger heavy upon them. A worse captivity than that of Egypt or Babylon (Ps. 32; Ps. 6; Isa. 6). Especially after the exile, when legalism reached its height. No truth, no freedom; utter slavery, an intolerable yoke. Yet the heart desired rest and longed for peace.

(b) Then Jesus came, and cried: "Come unto me! Away from the teachers who burden you with laws! My yoke is easy, my burden light. I will give you rest." That meant: "I will bear for you the curse of the law, the wrath of God; I will find for you a way to God; I will lead you to freedom and inner peace." Ask the disciples if He kept His word; ask Paul if He was able to do this; ask all who came to Him if they did not find Him meek and lowly in heart,

His yoke easy, His burden light, rest for their souls. Truly, Jesus alone can give us rest.

(2) Jesus alone can give us rest. *This was the message God raised up Luther to reiterate in the Reformation period.*

(a) It was needed; for men had erected a new law, a new ceremonial law, a new priestly and church law. Priests and popes attempted to lord it even over men's thoughts. Thus there was produced a new burden, new Babylonian captivity, under which hearts groaned. They longed for rest, they sought it in many ways, they turned to Mary and a thousand other saints and helpers. But they found no rest. The spiritual history of the Middle Ages ends in weeping and lamentation, in anguish of heart and despair.

(b) Then God raised up Luther, to proclaim anew to all who labored and were heavy laden: "Come to Jesus; 'He alone can give you rest." Because he himself had groaned under the new captivity and had sunk under the burden of the new law, and because he had found peace through faith in Christ, he became Christ's true messenger. And what was the heart and centre of his message but the good news: "Not in the law nor in the works of the law, nor in the monastery with its system of merits, but in Jesus alone is rest to be found. Through faith alone in His divine-human person man is brought to peace with God." Then men experienced anew how meek and lowly in heart Jesus is, how easy His yoke and light His burden, how He alone can quiet the conscience and set the heart at rest.

(3) Jesus alone can give us rest. *This is our message for today.*

(a) This message is for all weary and sorrowing, for all who sigh under their load of sin and the wrath of God, for all especially who labor and strive to come to God and to peace by ways of their own devising. Are there none such today? Wherever they be, in or out of the Church, this message is for them: Jesus alone can give us rest. May it sound through all our hymns, our instruction, our preaching, our pastoral work! May it be witnessed by our life and conversation! Jesus alone can give us rest.

(b) You say you cannot be a herald of this message, because you have not yourself experienced its truth? Oh, then let this Word begin its work in you now! Let its law break your heart and make it contrite! Then you will grow eager to come to Jesus and to hear the Gospel. Then you will find in God's Word not merely commands, precepts of purity and self-denial, but the one great burden: "Come to Jesus; He alone can give rest." And then, if you do not close your heart, comfort, peace, rest will enter in, and all Christ's words will cease to be burdens, His commandments will not be grievous. You will experience that He is meek and lowly in heart; you will find His yoke easy and His burden light. You will become a witness and messenger, crying, "Jesus alone can give us rest."

Conclusion: It is the specific function of the Lutheran Church in America, and of every one of its members, in the midst of so many churches that lead the people in self-appointed ways and bring much labor and sorrow upon honest souls, to testify and cry incessantly: "Come to Jesus, who by His holy life and precious death has fulfilled the law, borne the curse, and turned God the stern Judge into our loving Father. He alone can give us rest." Amen.

Luke 2:1-14

Introduction: Christmas, the festival of world-wide joy. If only all knew the true source of this joy! What is this source?

Theme: Jesus the Saviour is come!

This is the content of our gospel lesson and the true source of Christmas joy. Let us meditate upon it.

(1) Jesus the Saviour is come! *This reminds us of our hopeless state without Christ.*

(a) The hopeless state of the heathen.

(b) The bitter need of Israel under the curse of the law, looking and longing for a Saviour.

(c) The desperate straits of the world today, without Christ, despite all progress in science and civilization.

(2) Jesus the Saviour is come! *This proclaims to us the help and comfort that have appeared in Christ.* In Him, despite His apparent lowliness and weakness, there is:

(a) Salvation from the curse and wrath of God;

(b) The surety of God's good will;

(c) An entrance into His Kingdom of peace here and hereafter;

(d) Help in every temporal need.

(3) Jesus the Saviour is come! *This summons us to let ourselves be saved by Him and to receive His help and comfort.*

(a) In spite of the appearance of the Saviour, there is so much unrelieved need—in the national life, in the life of the Church, in our own life—simply because men will not take Christ for their Saviour.

(b) Hence Christmas calls upon us: Since the Saviour is come, let yourself be saved by Him! Cast yourself unreservedly in His arms! Help Him to become the Saviour of all men!

Conclusion: The application of (3) (b) will form the best conclusion.

Heb. 8:7-13

Introduction: Pentecost, the festival of the outpouring of the Holy Spirit and consequently of the establishing of the Church.

Theme: The Church of Christ is established: do you belong to it? Let us not hastily and lightly answer this question, but learn from our text, how many serious and searching questions it involves.

(1) *The Church of Christ alone possesses the treasure of forgiveness: have you found this forgiveness?*

(a) The Church alone possesses the treasure of forgiveness. This constitutes its superiority to all other organizations, past and present.

(b) Have you found this forgiveness? Are you even now rejoicing in it? Only then do you truly belong to the Church of Christ.

(2) *The Church of Christ alone possesses the true knowledge of God: have you come to this knowledge?*

(a) The Church alone possesses the true knowledge of God. She does not only touch the hem of His garment, like the heathen; she does not only have certain aspects of His nature, like Israel; but she knows Him in His inmost person and being, on the basis of His self-revelation and self-communication to her.

(b) Have you come to this knowledge? Not a mere intellectual apprehension, but a personal experience of God. And does it make you happy? Only then do you truly belong to the Church of Christ.

(3) *In the Church of Christ alone God's will is done: are you doing this will?*

(a) In the Church of Christ alone God's will is not written only on tables of stone and visibly, but in mind and heart, so that there is not an external, compulsory, but an internal, willing, and therefore God-pleasing obedience.

(b) Are you leading such a life of obedience? Only then do you truly belong to the Church of Christ.

Conclusion: Thus, you see, the question of our theme involves three other intensely important questions. You see that you must become a different, a new man. This the Holy Spirit is waiting to do for you. Let Him have His way and will with you. For only when you daily appropriate the forgiveness of sins, experience God in truth, and obey His will, do you really belong to the Church of Jesus Christ.

James 1:2-7

Introduction: The Scriptures tell of various trials and temptations, those that affect the soul and those that affect the body. Our text treats of the latter sort, and shows us how men ought to bear them. We have all of us experienced such trials and should have an interest in the question:

Theme: *What should be our attitude when we fall into manifold temptations?*

(1) The apostle tells us: *We should count it all joy.*

(a) What a strange counsel, and how contrary to our natural feelings!

(b) But how well founded, if we keep in mind God's gracious purpose in sending trials upon us. They are intended

(a) To prove our faith;

(b) To work patience (stedfastness, endurance);

(c) To bring us to moral perfection.

(2) What should be our attitude when we fall into manifold temptations? *We should ask God for wisdom.*

(a) How sorely we need this wisdom. Even if we could perceive His loving purpose in sending trials upon us, we might so easily, by our wrong attitude toward them, defeat or hinder this purpose. Hence we need wisdom.

(b) How easy for us God has made this prayer for wisdom. He will give liberally and will not upbraid.

(c) How important it is that we ask in faith. The prayer of a doubting man receives nothing.

Conclusion: In proportion as we ask God for wisdom, we shall discover God's purpose in our temptations and even come to count them as joy. Thus we shall find the right and God-pleasing attitude toward them.

3. Illustration of Expansion of Outline Into the Completed Sermon.

A Whitsuntide Sermon on Heb. 8:7-13

We are celebrating today the Festival of Whitsunday or Pentecost, which calls to mind the wonderful work of God in sending His Holy Spirit upon the disciples of Jesus. This mighty work made an indelible impression upon these men and influenced them until the end of their lives. With the Holy Spirit a cleansing power came into their life, purging them from sin and arming them against temptation. A new will entered their hearts, prompting them to walk in the way of obedience and to ask at every turn of the road, "Lord, what wilt Thou have me to do?" A new knowledge flooded their minds revealing to them more and more clearly the person and will of God

The Spirit became to them a fountain of new life springing up within them and making them in turn fountains of living water to all their fellow-men. It is no wonder the disciples felt that this day made an epoch in their lives, that old things were passed away and all things were made new.

But this day meant for them more than this. The Spirit that came upon them was the gift of their departed Lord. After three precious years of fellowship with them, He had left the world and returned to His Father. At His ascension a cloud received Him from their sight and they saw Him no more. But in the Spirit, sent by Him according to His promise, they were conscious of His return to them and of His perpetual presence. They were not left orphans in the world, but were inwardly united to their glorious Lord. In the Spirit they had Him again, even more truly than before. More truly now than then, they were His flock, and He their Shepherd; they were citizens of His kingdom, and He their King; they were members of His body, and He their Head; they were His congregation or church, and He their Lord. They were this more truly than Israel in the days of the old covenant. They could appropriate, therefore, all God's promises to Israel under the old covenant and apply them to themselves and the new order of things now breaking upon them. What must have been their joy when they saw in the light of the Spirit that they were indeed the people of God, the congregation of the Exalted One, the holy Christian Church! Let the Jews put them out of their synagogues and drive them from the temple and banish them from the holy city. What did it matter? Were they not the flock of Jesus the great Shepherd and Bishop of souls; His Church, in the founding of which His life-work reached its culmination?

It is plain, then, that our festival commemorates not only the outpouring of the Holy Spirit, but also the founding of the Christian Church.

In this Christian Church, my beloved, you have become members. By the sacrament of baptism and by faith, the Holy Spirit joined you to the Church, to the flock of the Good Shepherd Jesus. That was your day of Pentecost, when, in the words of St. Paul, the Holy Ghost was shed on you abundantly through Jesus Christ your Saviour. But, dear friends, to have become at one time a member of the Church, and to belong at present to it, are two very different things. Suppose you no longer belonged to the Church of Jesus Christ! The Church, established on Pentecost, has His promise that the gates of hell shall not prevail against it. There is no such promise concerning your membership in it. Let us, therefore, keep this festival of the founding of the Church by facing this important question: *The Church of Christ is established: do you belong to it?*

Let no one answer this question in a hasty, superficial manner. Do not say: "Of course I belong to the Church. Do I not regularly attend its services? Is not my name enrolled on the membership list of St. John's Church here in this city?" We are not now asking whether you are a member of any particular congregation. What we are concerned with is to help you to discover whether you are truly a member of the Church of Christ, whether you really belong among the sheep of His pasture, whether He is indeed your Good Shepherd. A person may belong to St. John's congregation, and yet be one of those to whom Jesus will one day profess, "I never knew you." Let us, therefore, examine our text with particular care. It will point out to us our true state. It portrays the blessed time of the new covenant inaugurated by Christ and the Spirit, which is to take the place of the old covenant established on Mt. Sinai. Along with each of the blessings which belong to the Church of the new covenant, it gives us an unmistakable sign by which to judge whether or not we truly belong to this Church. The Church of Jesus Christ is established: do you belong to it? In accordance with the text, our theme presents itself first of all in this form: *The Church of Christ alone possesses the treasure of forgiveness: have you found this forgiveness?*

Under the old covenant there was no real forgiveness of sins. Forgiveness was not, at least, mediated by the law and its sacrifices. They were to remind the people of their sins, to testify of God's wrath and curse upon sin, to reveal the guilt of the sinner and the punishment demanded by a holy God. But they could not take away sin, they could not blot out its guilt nor break its power nor remove its penalty.

> "Not all the blood of beasts
> On Jewish altars slain
> Could give the guilty conscience peace
> Or wash away the stain."

The old order might, indeed, fill man's conscience with fear and trembling, so that he cried out: "Whither shall I go from Thy Spirit, or whither shall I flee from Thy presence?" But it could do no more. Therefore pious souls lamented their sins and sighed under the intolerable displeasure of God. Therefore they yearned for a new covenant and for a new heart. Therefore the prophets portrayed the Church that was to come as one possessing the treasure of forgiveness. Jeremiah, as quoted in our text, utters these significant words: "I will be merciful to their unrighteousness, saith the Lord, and their sins and their iniquities will I remember no more." This word the apostle quotes in order to show its fulfilment in Christ. The new covenant established by Him through shedding of His blood upon the cross, not only proclaims God's wrath but reveals His grace and mercy. It carries with it the inestimable treasure of the blood of Jesus Christ which cleanseth us from all sins.

The Church founded by Jesus on the day of Pentecost, by the sending of the Holy Spirit, is distinguished as a Church possessing forgiveness, having washed her garments, and washing them anew every day, in the blood of the Lamb. By the Holy Spirit she is united with her exalted Lord, who was crucified and raised from the dead, and with whom is plenteous redemption and remission for all who accept Him as their Saviour. To this Church of the new covenant is committed the glad tidings of God's love for sinners, the Gospel in which God constantly offers the cleansing power of Jesus' blood. She alone has Baptism, that precious means of grace by which even the smallest and the youngest are brought within reach of the divine love. She alone has the Absolution, that comfort and strength for all disturbed consciences. She alone knows of a Table at which God most personally dispenses His grace, imparting the body and blood of Jesus as the seal of His forgiveness, so that every one may become individually assured of His salvation and rejoice in such assurance. She alone has the Holy Spirit, who enters through these means of grace into the hearts and lives of her members, sealing to them God's pardoning love and restoring to them again and yet again the joy of His salvation.

Where in the wide world is there another institution with such a precious treasure? There are indeed societies and organizations, many with high sounding titles and ambitious programmes, associations political, social, religious, economic, beneficial. But which of them all has a saving word for the fallen brother, healing balm for the troubled conscience, the certainty of forgiveness for the sinful and penitent soul? Which of them can say to the man given up by all as hopeless and on the brink of despair, "Son, be of good cheer; thy sins are forgiven;" and say it over and over until its comfort lays hold of his heart and the joy of a pardoned soul beams out of his eyes? This is the prerogative of only one association on earth. The Church of Jesus Christ alone possesses this treasure of forgiveness, because it has Jesus Christ as its Saviour and is united to Him by the Holy Ghost.

Now, my friend, do you belong to this Church? That can mean only: Has this treasure become your own? Have you appropriated to yourself this forgiveness of sins, and are you daily appropriating it? How can you belong to the flock of the Good Shepherd unless you come to Him every day, with the wounds the old bitter foe has inflicted, and obtain from Him the healing balm of His pardon? How can you be numbered among God's people if you despise the cleansing power of Jesus' blood? Surely, you have not forgotten the parable of the wedding garment. You remember what the King bade His servants do to the man who refused to wear the festal robe, thinking himself fitly clad in his filthy rags. Those who sit, here below, at the table of the great King are, indeed, poor sinners and realize their unworthiness, but they are sinners who earnestly seek forgiveness, and whose nakedness Jesus covers with the garment of His salvation. Soft and low they chant the wedding hymn:

"Jesus, Thy Blood and Righteousness
My beauty are, my glorious dress."

Do you belong to this company? Oh, acknowledge your sinfulness, and let your soul thirst after forgiveness, as the hart pants after the water brooks. Take to yourself the forgiveness offered in God's Word and Sacrament. Let the Holy Spirit seal it to you by His witness in your heart. Then, dear friend, you will truly belong to the Church of Christ.

The Church of Christ is established: do you belong to it? This means, secondly, as our text informs us: *The Church alone possesses the true knowledge of God: have you come to this knowledge, and does it rejoice your heart?*

Even the heathen have a certain knowledge of God. We have this on the word of no less an authority than St. Paul. When they contemplate the beauty and harmony in nature, when they see the death of winter followed by the resurrection of spring, when they observe in the material world about them something like a mighty hand governing and ordering all, when they recognize in history the operations of a moral law according to which "righteousness exalteth a nation, but sin is a reproach to any people," when they hear the still small voice of conscience and give heed to its monitions and its warnings—then it is true that also among the Gentiles God has not left Himself without witnesses. But how far this is from the full knowledge, the saving revelation of God! It is but as the darkness of dawn compared with the perfect day. So far from reaching to the heart of God, such knowledge merely touches the fringe on the hem of the garment of His glory.

A more advanced knowledge of God is found in Israel. To them He made Himself known by mighty deeds and marvelous words. He revealed Himself to them, He told them His name, He showed them His face. He stood forth before them as the Eternal, the Almighty, the Holy and Righteous One, the Helper of His people in every need, the terrible Lord and King of men and nations. If we glance into the pages of the Old Testament, and listen to the words of Isaiah or Job, we must confess: "The Lord is a great God, and a great King above all gods." Surely, Israel possessed a knowledge of God vastly superior to that found among the Gentiles. And yet, neither did Israel's knowledge reach to the heart of God. Especially since the covenant of Mt. Sinai, with its curse upon all transgressors of the law, Israel's knowledge of God was a partial one. The thought of His majesty as Judge, of His wrath and anger burning down to hell, was so prominent that the thought of His love and grace was driven into the background. Only a few chosen ones, a few prophets and priests, saw behind the curtain and caught a glimpse of God's heart. That is why Jeremiah, in tracing his picture of the new covenant, emphasized this particular feature, that the true knowledge of God should then prevail and that men should know Him. "They shall teach no more," he writes, "every man his neighbor, and every man his brother, saying, Know the Lord; for they shall all know me, from the least of them to the greatest of them, saith the Lord."

The writer of our epistle shows that this prophecy was fulfilled in the Church founded by Christ through the sending of the Spirit. The Church possesses the full knowledge of God. To her Jesus unlocked the heart of God by His life and teaching, his work and death. To her He revealed the love of God our heavenly Father. To her He gave the Holy Spirit, who is to guide her into all the truth, to lead her, again and again, to Bethlehem and Golgotha, teaching her to see God with increasing clearness as the Father of Jesus Christ and in Him and through Him our Father. This is the second great prerogative of the Church. She alone has the true knowledge of God. All who are without her walls know God only as the blind know the sun. Glance into the rituals of unchristian and antichristian organizations; read the books and periodicals inspired by natural reason; listen to the deliverances of some of the men to whom have been entrusted the destinies of the nation; observe many of our "fashionable" churches in which the Spirit is all but stifled—everywhere you hear God mentioned, but it is a god created by the fancy of men, a god of human invention, not the God of the Scriptures, revealed in Jesus Christ. He is known only to the Church of Christ, the communion of those who in the anguish of sin and guilt have found in Christ their only Saviour, who have found in God their Father, and have been brought to fellowship with the Father and the Son through the Holy Ghost.

How can you belong to this Church unless you possess this knowledge of God? Do you know Him? I do not refer to the knowledge you gained in school. You may know your catechism ever so well and be able to recite glibly the Creed and Luther's beautiful explanation of the Lord's Prayer. You may have by heart all the Bible verses you learned and be able to frame a correct definition of God. And yet you may be, with it all, a child of this world and no true member of the Church. Anyone with a clear brain and a retentive memory can know God in a mere theological sense. But when I ask, Do you know God? I mean, Do you know Him in terms of actual personal experience? Do you know Him in the sense of intimate living communion with Him? The knowledge of a man by his friend differs widely from that by a stranger. Vital communion and personal intercourse alone lead to true knowledge. Why does the child know its parents so well, the wife her husband? Because they live together in intimate intercourse. Why are we so prone to misjudge our fellow-man? Because we are usually too hasty in forming our opinion of him, because we do not go to the trouble of understanding him by personal intercourse. Even so, you cannot know God unless you commune with Him and gain an ever deeper insight into His person and being by vital inner experience. When I still lived far inland in that little old-world village, the mighty ocean was to me but a name; of its magnitude, its might, its majesty, I had no conception. But the day came when I boarded a steamer and sailed across the ocean. Then I came actually to know it; I formed a definite idea of its magnitude, its marvelous power, its mysterious fascination. Have you thus come to know God? Have you walked and talked with Him, and listened to Him in precious silent hours? Have you followed Him with wondering eyes, when He passed by in 'His mighty works? Have you striven rightly to understand Him, entering into His very heart, and laying bare to Him your heart? If you have made only a beginning in this direction, God is not wholly a stranger to you.

And if you have communed with Him for years, He has become greater and better known to you, you have come to love Him better, and the more you loved Him the better you have learned to know Him. God is to you no longer a mere name, but life and reality, the highest Good, the source of all true blessedness. Have you, dear friend, begun thus to know God? You must have made at least a beginning, if you are to be numbered with the true members of the Church, of whom Jesus says: "I know mine own, and am known of mine."

The Church of Christ is established: do you belong to it? In the light of our text this means finally: *In the Church alone God's will is truly done: are you doing this will?*

Obedience to law, whether of the state or of conscience, is found also among heathen peoples. In a sense, there may be among them even obedience to the will of God. It is another question whether this is the obedience that God demands. In a much higher sense, this obedience was found among the people of Israel. They had God's will in the Ten Commandments, engraven in stone. There were among them those who strove earnestly to live their lives in accordance with this will. With most of them, however, these efforts were fragmentary and futile, the weary toil of slaves, because they served God chiefly from fear of His curse and judgment. While true obedience is like the stream leaping forth blithely from its source and flowing by its own impulse in the direction determined by its bed, the legal obedience of Israel was rather like jets of water laboriously pumped from a well, which cease to flow as soon as the external force is withdrawn. The old heart of sin was slow to respond to the divine will and command, and lacked the inward impulse to genuine obedience. No wonder that the prophets, describing the future Church, pictured her as composed of men who did the will of God eagerly, joyfully, from an inner impulse, without outward constraint and without reserve. As Jeremiah says: "After those days, saith the Lord, I will put my laws into their minds, and write them in their hearts." These words are quoted by the writer of our text in the certainty that they were fulfilled in the Church of Christ founded on the day of Pentecost. In this Church alone we find true obedience to the will of God. How could it be otherwise? Having the forgiveness of sins, she can no longer continue in sin but is moved by gratitude toward God to abandon the old life of sin and walk in the new life of the Spirit. Having the true knowledge of God and learning by constant communion with God to know Him ever better as the Holy One of Israel, she simply cannot banish Him again from her midst by wilfully transgressing His commandments. She would have to deny her own nature, she would have to destroy what is characteristic of her very life, if she did not become a fair garden bringing forth the flowers of obedience to the will of her God.

It is true, the world also speaks of its good works, often in a boastful vein. The world boasts of humanity, as if it alone possessed it; of mercy and neighborliness, as if they were its peculiar traits. But let us not be deceived. The good works of the world are like those Japanese plants that grow in the air. They lack the true soil, they have no roots, they have not grown out of God's will. Hence they can bear no fruit, they cannot stand in the judgment. Do men gather grapes from thorns, or figs from thistles? Whoever has not experienced, through the forgiveness of sins and the work of the Holy Spirit, an inner cleansing and been made a spiritually fruitful field, cannot fulfil the Lord's command, is not able to render true obedience.

Do you belong to the Church of Christ? That is to say: Are you living according to God's will? You cannot answer yes, if you merely force yourself now and then to put under the old Adam, from fear of God's anger; nor if you rouse yourself at times to a sense of shame on account of your lack of benevolence, your spiritual indifference and sloth, for fear of losing the respect of men; nor even if by heroic effort you perform an act that on the face of it merits approval. No, my friend: all these you may find also among the heathen, and perhaps more frequently than in your own life. They do not, therefore, imply membership in the true Church of Christ. The one criterion is this: the Spirit of God must have come into your heart, and filled it with a deep sense of gratitude and love toward God, and supplied therewith the one true motive for obedience to His will. If there is nothing of this in your heart, do not imagine for a moment that you really belong to the Church of Jesus Christ.

You see, our theme, which appeared at first so simple and so easy to answer, contains a number of serious and searching questions. So many things are involved in the simple query: Do you belong to the Church? The Church of Christ alone possesses the treasure of forgiveness: have you found this forgiveness? The Church alone has the true knowledge of God: have you come to this knowledge? In the Church alone God's will is truly done: are you doing this will?

Will you not ponder well these questions until you have found the answer they demand? Whatever these answers may be, one thing is certain. You will not be able to rise from your self-examination without the cry, "Lord, have mercy upon me!" nor without the prayer,

"O Holy Spirit, enter in,
Within this heart Thy work begin,
Thy temple deign to make me!"—Amen.

INDEX OF SUBJECTS

Ability, the linguistic, of the preacher 233, 235 ff.
Acts of Apostles, source of sermon-material 256, 277, 280, 286.
Adjectives, use of 186 f., 204, 207.
Advent texts 303.
Allegorical application 373 ff., 375 ff.
Allegorical explanation 275 f., 281, 369.
Allegory (figure of speech) 193.
Alliteration 186.
Allocution 173.
Allusions, see illustrations.
Analogies 204, 213, see illustrations.
Anecdotes in sermon 226.
Antithesis 186, 193, 204, 208.
Apocrypha of the Old Testament 253.
Apologetic, the, element in the sermon 139, 180.
Apostrophe 193, 204, 212.
Application of the text, in general 361-382, to the preacher himself 382 f.; to the individual congregation 383-386; varied by the church year 383; compare text, its relation to the sermon.
Arrangement, strategic, of paragraphs, sentences and words 204; see order.
Art and sermon 17 f., 170-172.
Ascension Day, texts for 306.
Asyndeton 204, 208.
Attention of the hearer, how to arrest it 122 ff.
Authorized version and rhythm 191.

Baptismal address, its nature and its texts 310.
Beautiful, the, in the sermon 182 ff., 193 f., 202.
Bible, the language of the, 197, 205, 207, 208, 209, 229 ff.
Book of Prayer, the, its lectionary 336.
Books of Homilies, the Two, 336.
Brevity of the sermon 215.

Cacophony 188.
Canonical books, canon according to which they may supply texts for the sermon 254 f.
Catechism, the, 225, 229.
Categories, logical, topical, or rhetorical, a help to find the division of the theme 457, 458, 459 f.
Chastity of form of the sermon 393 f., 422 f.
Choice of texts, see texts, selection of.
Choice of words for the sermon 135 f., 182, 185.
Christmas texts 302 f.

Church Hymns 225, 229.
Church Year, the, governing the selection of the text 302-308, 326; its development 326; its value 327 f.
Clearness, convincing 173 ff.
Climax 193, 204, 208.
Colloquialism 185.
Combat, the sermon a, 179, 204.
Comes Hieronymi 329.
Communion address, its nature and texts 310.
Completeness of the sermon 391 f., 414.
Composite method of delivery, see delivery.
Conciseness of style 215.
Conclusion, the, of the sermon 502-505; its purpose 502; its different forms 502 f.; its preparation 503 f.
Concrete, the, element in language 183, 193-203, 204, 205 f.
Confessional address, its nature and texts 310.
Confessions of the Church and the sermon 68 ff., 85 ff., 251.
Confirmation address, its nature and texts 310.
Conscience, exegetical 349 ff.
Consciousness of preacher, no source for the sermon material 247, 248 ff.
Consciousness of the Church, no source for the sermon material 247, 251.
Consecration address, its nature and texts 312.
Consonants and vowels, their choice 182, 188.

Delivery, the, of the sermon 511-513, 521-524; gestures 513, 524-527; pulpit tone 511 f.; must observe decorum 512; improvisation, extemporisation, recitation, reading, composite method of delivery 514; history of these methods 514 ff.; reading 517; best method 519 ff.
Dialectic, the, element of the sermon 173, 178 f., 180, 213.
Dialogue between preacher and congregation 383 f.
Dialogue between preacher and text 382 f.
Dialogue form of the sermon 180, 181 f.
Direct application 366.
Directness of style 239 f.
Disposition of the sermon 456-485.
Dividing, the proper, of Law and Gospel 140 ff.
Division, the, of the sermon 456-485; its necessity 465; objections against division 466-469; advantages of division 470 ff.; how to find and form the divisions 456 ff.; divide the whole theme 461, or a part of the theme 462, or treat the whole theme from various aspects 462; qualities of the divisions 463; should be recognizable 463 f.; is it to be formally announced 476 ff.; in what form 464 f.; frequent repetition of the division 478 f.; subdivision of the main division 465, 484 f.; subdivisions not to be announced 483.
Doctrinal, the, element in every sermon 147.
Doctrinal, the, element of the sermon 130 f., 148-156; its dangers 151 ff.; its necessity 148 f.; examples 154 ff.
Dramatization 204, 210, 212, 213; see dialogue.

Easter texts 304 f.
Edification, the purpose of the sermon 98-168; what it means 98-103; what it involves 103-119; 119-128; what it presupposes on the part of the preacher 128-145; what makes it possible 119-121; impossible without the doctrinal element 146-148; edification is the purpose whether you preach a doctrinal sermon 148-156, or a pastoral sermon 157-163, or a hortatory sermon 163-167.
Efficacy of the Word of God preached 167 f.
Elegance, pleasing, of the sermon, and means to procure it 182-203.
Emotions, to be influenced by the sermon 119-127, 182 ff.
Energy of the sermon, see force.
Epiphany texts 303.
Epistles of the New Testament, source of sermon material 255, 265-267.
Epithets, ornamental 186 f., 193, 207.
Ethical sermons 267.
Ethical teachings of Jesus, source of sermon material 260 f.
Euphony 182, 187 ff.
Evangeliarium of Cuthbert 330.
Examples in the sermon 204, 213, see illustrations.
Exclamation 204, 209, 212.
Experience, the spiritual, and the preacher 74-93; not the source of his sermon material but the necessary prerequisite of every sermon necessitated by its witness character 75-83, not including reference to specific experiences in the life of the preacher 82 f.; the extent of the spiritual experience of the beginner in the ministry 83-85, 88-92; distinction between spiritual experience and intellectual assent to the contents of Scripture and confessions of the Church 85-88; duty of the minister who lacks spiritual experience 84, 88 ff.; who comes to doubt some point in the creed of his Church 87 f.; the spiritual growth of the preacher 90-92.
Exposition of the text 317-361, see text, its relation to the sermon.
Expository preaching 319, 320 ff., 323 f.
Expository sermon 428.
Extemporisation 512, 521, see delivery.

Faith, how to preach it aright 110-112.
Fear of punishment, how to preach it 161.
Feelings, see emotions.
Figures of speech 193, 205, 207.
Force of the sermon 203-224; wrong conception of 203 f., 220 ff.
Fundamentum dividendi 460.
Funeral sermon, its nature and texts 311.

Gestures 512, 524-526.
Gospel, dividing Law and Gospel 140 ff.
Gospel preaching, what it is 142 f.
Gospel, source of sermon material 255, 256-265.
Gospels, the, contents of sermon 57-65, 104, 106-110.

Harvest festival, its nature and its texts 307.

Homiletics, origin of the term 6 ff.; treats of congregational sermon 9 ff.; its justification 15-28; Homiletics and the Holy Spirit 16, 22; and rhetoric 15, and nature 16, and art 17 f.; training in Homiletics 19, 24 ff.; its relation to the other theological disciplines 27; its division 29-33.
Homiliaria 77.
Homiliarium of Charlemagne 330 ff.; of Bede 330.
Homilies, Book of, 8, 336.
Homily, artistic 427, 433, 435.
Homily, origin and history of the term 6 ff., 292, 430.
Hortatory or awakening sermon 131, 163-167; Law and Gospel its means 164; aims at the conscience, not at the nerves 164.
Hymns, the, of the Church 225, 229.
Hyperbole 208.

Illustration 204, 213 ff., 226 ff.
Imagination, its role in the sermon 183, 193-196; its dangers 196-202.
Improvisation, see delivery.
Indirect application 366 f.
Individualisation 206.
Individuality, the, of the preacher 92, 132.
Installation address, texts for the 312.
Intellect, to be influenced by the sermon 119 ff., 173-182.
Interest, what it is 124; how to awaken it 121-126.
Interrogation 204, 209, 212.
Introduction, the, of the sermon 486-502; its necessity 486, 489 f.; its purpose 486 f., 490-402; its source 488 f., 492 f.; general rules governing it 489, 492-494; illustrations of introduction 495-502.
Introductory address, its texts 312.

Jesus, how to preach Him 57-65, 116 f., 264 f., 256-265.

Knowledge, the preacher's, of his age 132; of his congregation 128 f., 132-145; of its social life 134; its intellectual life 135; of the realm of its sensations, perceptions and concepts 136; of its cultural standards 138; its reading material 139; its spiritual life 140; its young people 143.
Kunsthomilie 427, 433, 435.

Language, the, of the sermon 135, 137; its conciseness 215; its concreteness 183, 208; its perspicuity 173; its beauty 182 ff.; its poetical element 183, 193-203; its force 203 ff.; its popularity 224 ff.; common language 219; colloquialism 185; market language 219; slang 185; vulgar language 219; scientific and theological language in the sermon 219; means to improve language and style 233, 237-243; no improvement without study 233, 235 ff.; see choice, euphony, variety, rhythm.
Law, what it is 142 f.; the contents of the sermon 104; who is in need of it 142 f.; how to preach it aright 142 f, 158-161, 164; dividing Law and Gospel 140 ff., 142 f, 158-161, 164.
Lectio continua 4, 328; selecta 4, 329.
Length, the, of the sermon 505 f., 509.
Lenten texts 304.
Liber comicus 330.

Life, the spiritual, how to preach it aright 111, 113 f., 151 ff.
Literary taste, the, of the preacher 239.
Literature, the study of, a means of improving style 239.
Local method or arrangement of the sermon material 394, 429.
Loci method, see local.

Market language 219, see vulgar, slang.
Marriage address, its nature and texts 311.
Metaphor 193, 205, 207.
Miracle stories, source of sermon material 257-260; how to preach them 371 ff.
Missionary, the, element in the sermon 118 f.
Mission festival, its nature and texts 308.
Morality, how to preach it aright 113 f.; see life spiritual, Law and Gospel
Movement, the, of the sermon 420 f.

Nature, the, of the congregational service 39 ff.

Old Testament, source of sermon material 271-288; see sermon, source of the.
Onomatopoeia 207.
Oration, the sermon as 169-244; the peculiarity of the oratorical discourse 170-173; the qualities of the sermon as oration 173-244; convincing clearness 173-182; pleasing elegance 182-202; moving force 203-224; popularity 224-232; the corresponding duties of the preacher 233-243.
Order, the logical, of the sermon 173, 175 ff., 205.
Order, the, of the sermon, a necessary quality 392 f., 414-422; demanded for the oration by Quintilian 414; for the sermon by Fenelon 414 f.; Vinet 415 f.; Johnson 416; pedagogic rules of order 392; rhetorical rules of order 393, 419 f.; movement 420; variety 421.
Ordination address, its texts 312.
Outsiders, how to influence them by the congregational sermon 117 f.

Painting by means of speech 183, 193-196.
Parable 193, 204.
Parables, source of sermon material 262; how to treat them 377-382.
Paragraph, its arrangement 218; see order.
Parallel passages 343, 356.
Particularization, 206.
Pastoral sermon 130, 157-163; its didactic element 157; its centre is the Gospel, not the Law 157,-158.
Patience, necessary for the preacher 167 f.
Pauline theology in the sermon 266 f.
Pericopes 146, 166; their justification 300 ff., 308 f.; their history 328-331; defects of the old pericopes 331-337; Luther and the pericopes 334; new pericopes 337.
Personification 193, 204, 212.
Perspicuity of the sermon 173-175.
Phrases, meaningless, should be avoided by the preacher 125
Poetical, the, element of the sermon 183, 193-203; its dangers 196-202
Polemical, the, element in the sermon 73 f., 139, 394.

Political, the, element in the sermon 50 f.
Polysyndeton 204, 208.
Popularity, the, of the sermon 224-232.
Preacher, a sower of seed 167; a witness 76 ff; must divide the Word of Truth 129, 140 ff., 147; must have a logical mind 234; an ability to speak 234, 236; a sense of the beautiful 235, see beauty, elegance, language; must know his congregation 132-143; must study the Bible 230 ff., 235, 241; must practice in writing and speaking 240, see preparation; spiritual qualification of the preacher 75-83, 88 ff.; of the beginner 83 f.; his intellectual assent to the confessions of the Church 85 ff.; the preacher and doubt 87 f.; the preacher's spiritual growth 90 f.
Preacher's, the, assurance about the efficacy of the Word 167.
Preaching, the term 8, 10; its importance 19 ff.; its nature 43-93; see nature of sermon; its purpose 98-167, see edification; what it presupposes on the part of the preacher 128, 133-146, see knowledge and spiritual qualification; history of preaching 19, 29, 33, 239; Pietism and Methodism and preaching 80 f.; preaching and truthfulness 80 f.; congregational preaching and outsiders 117 f.; preaching and psychology 119-127, 173, 182, 203.
Preparation, careful, preacher's duty 19, 22-24, 235-237.
Preparation of the sermon for delivery 508-511 f.; its five different methods 514-521; how they were applied in the history of preaching 514-517; by the Greek and Roman orators 514 f.; the reading of the sermon 517 ff.; the best method 519 f.; Ian Maclaren on preparation 521.
Prose, rhymed, and prose rhythm 189.
Psychology and preaching 119-127, 173, 182, 203.
Pulpit tone 511 f., 521 ff.
Reading of the sermon 517 ff.
Recitation of the sermon 509 f., 519 ff.; see delivery and preparation.
Reconciliation, the biblical use of this term 351 ff.
Reformation festival, texts for the 307 f.
Repetition 204.
Revelation of St. John, source of sermon material 256, 268 ff.
Reward, hope of, how to preach it 161.
Rhetoric, in its relation to the sermon 15 f., 169 ff.
Rhythm 182, 189-193.

Selection of texts, see texts, selection of.
Sentences, the structure of, 217.
Sermon, its nature as a part of the congregational service 39-93; in its relation to the Word of God 44-65 (the sermon is the proclamation of the Word, not discussion of political or social problems 44-57; proclamation of Christ, not merely as teacher, prophet or exemplar, but as God-man and redeemer by means of His life, death and resurrection 57-65); in its relation to the congregation and the Church 65-74 (the sermon is the proclamation of the Word as experienced by the Church 65-68, and confessed in her confessions 68-74); in its relation to the preacher 74-93 (see experience, the spiritual).
Sermon, the term 7 f., 292, 430.

INDEX OF SUBJECTS 629

Sermon a work of art 389 f.; 394-397; not a work of "pure" art 170.
Sermon, its purpose as a part of the congregational service 94-168; edification the purpose of the congregational service and the sermon 94-100; what edification means 98-103; what it involves 103-119; 119-128; what it presupposes on the part of the preacher (knowledge of his age 132; of his congregation 133; of its social 134; its intellectual life 135, of the realm of its sensations, perceptions and concepts 136; its cultural standards 138; its reading material 139; its spiritual life 140, its young people); what makes edification possible 119-121; impossible without the doctrinal element 146-148; to meet the requirements of the individual congregations the sermon must be a doctrinal sermon 148-156, or a pastoral sermon 157-163 or a hortatory sermon 163-167.
Sermon, the, as oration, see oration.
Sermon, the source of its subject-matter is not the preacher's consciousness 247, 248 ff.; nor the consciousness of the Church 247, 251; nor theological science 248, 251 f.; but Scripture 248, 252 f.; qualification of this statement 253 ff.; Gospels 255, 256-265, (narratives of the works of Jesus 256; miracle stories 257; words of Jesus 260; ethical teaching of Jesus 260; parables 262; the self-witness of Jesus 262; intercourse with His disciples 264); Epistles 255, 266 (Pauline theology in sermon 266; not to be confined to the ethical portions of the epistles 267; helpful literature 268 f.); Acts 256, 258; Revelation 256, 268 f. (history of religions does not change this 269 ff.); Old Testament 271-288 (what is source of sermon-material and what not 271-273; what two facts a preacher on Old Testament has to keep in mind 274; short history of the homiletical use of the Old Testament 274-287, Luther 276 ff.; literary criticism of the Old Testament and historical study of religions and the preacher on Old Testament texts 287 f.; helpful literature 288).
Sermon, the structure of the, fundamental principles governing it 389-424; of the individual sermon 425-436; synthetic (topical) sermon method 425 f.; analytic or textual method 425, 429-436; which one to select 428; synthetic-analytic 428 f.
Sermon, how it reaches the soul 119-128; its psychology 119-128, 169-232.
Sermon, doctrinal 148-156, see doctrinal; expository 428, 433 ff.; hortatory 131, 163-167; interesting 123; pastoral 157-163; polemical 73 f., 139, 394; political 50 f.; social 51 f., 116, 134.
Sermon a combat 179.
Sermon, the congregational, in relation to the outsiders 13 f.; 117 f.
Sermon-Bible, the 267.
Service, the congregational, its nature 39-42; its purpose 94-97.
Service, the, of the Jewish synagogue 3 ff.; of the early Christendom 2; 5 ff.
Simile 193, 204, 207.
Simplicity, the, of form of the sermon 393 f., 422 f.
Sin, how to preach it aright 159.
Skeleton, sermon sketch 422.

Slang in the sermon 185.
Speculum Ecclesiae 292.
Style 169-244; see language, directness, conciseness, perspicuity, beauty, elegance, force, popularity; literature on style 243 f.
Subject-sermon 433.
Sunday and worship 5 f.
Symbolical, the, application of texts 370 ff.
Terms, technical, in the sermon 136, 219.
Text, its relation to the sermon in general 317-318; the **exposition** of the text 338-386; how to derive the sermon material from the text 338-361, from the original text 320, 345 ff.; to ascertain its literal meaning 339, 349 in view of the context 349 ff., and of the biblical use of words and phrases 351-354; to picture the situation 340 f., 354; to find the scope 342, 355 f.; to view the single text in the light of the sum total of Scripture 344 f., 356 f.; advisability of correcting a received Bible translation 357 ff; exegetical conscience 359; how much of the exegetical labor should appear in the finished sermon 359 f.; helpful exegetical literature 355 f.—The **application** of the text 361-386; the duty of application 361; the right of application 361; the all important canon of application 361-366; keep the individual coloring of the text 363 f.; direct application 366; indirect application 366; typical application of Old Testament texts 367 ff.; indirect application of New Testament texts is tropological 370, or symbolical 370, 371 ff.; never allegorical 373 ff.; how to apply parables 377-382; application to the preacher 382 f.; to the individual congregation 383-386; varied by the Church Year 383 f.
Texts from Scripture, necessary for individual sermon 289-299; double texts 298; must be properly bounded 299; preaching on entire biblical books 300; selection of texts 299-317.
Texts, selection of 299-337; preaching on entire books 299-301, 318-326; homiletical literature on entire books 277-280, 320; on selected texts 323-326; text must be properly bounded 299 f.; what texts ought to be selected 301 f.; according to the Church Year 302-308; old pericopes 308; new pericopes 309; texts for occasional sermons 310-312; necessary qualities of a text 312-317.
Text-sermon 434.
Textual is more than scriptural 364.
Textual method 426 ff.
Thematic sermon 434.
Theme, the, of the sermon 437-455; what it is 437 f.; it ought to be stated 439; in what form 439 f.; causal theme 439; final or rhetorical theme 439; its announcement 440 f., 445, 451; it must be specific 362 f., 441, 442 f.; should run through the whole sermon 442, 455; qualities of the theme 442 ff.; the announced theme must be easily discernible 452; phraseology of the announced theme 454 f.
Topical sermon, method 425 ff.
Topics, their use for the preacher 251.
Translations, is the preacher to refer to their inaccuracies 348 f.
Tropes 193.

Tropical application 370.
Typical application 367 ff.

Understanding, the, to be influenced, see intellect.
Unity of the sermon 390 f., 397-414; demanded by Fenelon 397; by Vinet 399 ff.; by Porter 401; by Herrick Johnson 405 f.; by a writer in "The Continent" 406 ff.; unity and the want of unity illustrated 409-413; unity excludes borrowing of material 413; unity of aim and purpose 400; unity of effect 402.
Usus, the fivefold, of the sermon 146, 386.

Variety 182, 185-187, 421.
Virtues, how to preach them aright 114 f.
Visibility of speech 123, 193 ff.; see language and concrete.
Vulgar language 219.

Whitsunday texts 306.
Will, the, to be influenced by the sermon 119 ff., 203-224.
Works, good, how to preach them aright 111, 113 ff.
Worship, the, of the Jewish synagogue 3 ff.; willed by Jesus 5; of the Christian congregation in the Early Church 2 f. 5 ff.

Young People, their psychology 143 f.; how to preach to them 144 ff.

INDEX OF NAMES

Abraham a Santa Clara 127, 226, 423.
Achelis, E. Chr. 14, 102, 292, 365, 370, 377, 379, 383.
Adams, President John Quincy 236 f.
Addison, Jos. 187, 239.
Aeschbacher, R. 117.
Agassiz, L. J. R. 237.
Ahlfeld, F. 126, 162, 202, 226, 363, 455.
Alanus ab insulis 292.
Alexander, James W. 32, 92, 148, 153, 320 ff., 324, 482.
Allen, W. C. 574, 577, 581.
Ambrose 114, 291.
Anderson, Wm. 517.
Andreae, Jac. 202.
Apuleius 189.
Aristotle 189, 190, 214, 295, 446.
Arnold, Matthew 187, 240.
Augustine 7, 30, 83, 110, 126, 133, 162, 180, 183, 186, 189, 209, 210, 223, 275 f., 393, 489, 490, 515.
Augustus, the Emperor 515.

Bacon, Lord 27, 139, 191, 197, 239, 240.
Bacon, Roger 293.
Barrow, Isaac 216, 239.
Basil, the Great 114, 223, 291, 504.
Bassermann, H. 42, 78, 94, 107, 395, 396 f.
Bates, Wm. 219.
Baumgarten, M. 297.
Baumgarten, O. 56, 80, 90, 122, 266.
Baur, G. 31, 33, 106.
Baxter, Rich. 82, 90, 92, 165, 208. 223, 238.
Beaumont, Francis 190.
Beecher, H. W. 33, 126, 182, 202, 214, 223, 226, 467, 469.

Beecher, Lyman 32, 445.
Bengel, J. 382.
Bente, F. 141.
Bentham, Jer. 139.
Benz, G. 117, 267, 452.
Bernard of Clairvaux 162, 394, 454, 466, 469, 495, 516.
Berthold of Regensburg 137, 165, 202, 212, 223, 292, 394, 493, 505, 516.
Beyschlag, W. 180.
Bezzel, H. 138, 162, 223, 239, 451, 483, 575.
Bitzius, A., 117.
Blaine, J. S. 518.
Blair, Hugh 519.
Boardman, Geo. D 319, 320.
Boniface 292, 505.
Bossuet, J. B. 209, 210, 238.
Bourdaloue, L. 181, 223.
Braun, Th. 78.
Breed, D. R. 492, 504.
Brenz, J. 562.
Brewster, W. T. 242.
Bright, John 480, 503.
Broadus, J. A. 20, 32, 148, 151, 153, 174, 175, 184, 185, 186, 187, 188, 207, 216, 236, 237, 238, 316, 318, 320, 491, 493 f., 495, 503 f., 516, 517.
Brooks, Phillips 10, 33, 126, 150, 172, 198, 202, 395, 470 f., 479, 481, 504.
Brougham, Lord 503.
Brown, J. 517.
Brown, Sir Thomas 239.
Buechsel, K. 119.
Buffon, G. L. L. 236, 415.
Bugenhagen, J. 505.
Buhl, Fr. 287.
Bullinger, H. 336.
Bunyan, John 165, 239.
Burgess, D. 219

Index of Names

Burke, Edm. 51, 187, 213, 219, 239, 503.
Burnet, 517.
Burrell, D. J. 20, 33, 54, 56, 150, 173, 325, 434, 474.
Burton, N. J. 33.
Bushnell, Horace 52.

Cadman, Parkes 475.
Caesarius of Arles 137, 138.
Caesarius of Heisterbach 468.
Calvin, J. 279 f., 336, 490, 516, 517.
Campbell, Geo., 205, 215, 217, 285, 359.
Carlyle, Thomas 125, 239, 480.
Carpenter, W. B. 33, 150, 152.
Caspari, H. 126, 137, 191, 239, 287.
Cecil, J. 402.
Chalmers, Thomas 23, 181, 216, 239, 517 f.
Chamberlin, Jas. 24.
Charlemagne 77, 330.
Charles II of England 516.
Charnock, St. 535 f.
Chatham 219.
Cheyne 550.
Christlieb, Th. 78.
Chrysostom, John 7, 68, 138, 162, 191, 202, 210, 223, 239, 291, 329, 490, 493, 495, 515.
Cicero 30, 171, 176, 183, 184, 188, 189, 190, 216, 219, 223, 238, 241, 466, 468, 476 f., 490, 493, 515.
Claudius, M. 240.
Clement of Rome, 6, 291, 329, 516.
Cleon 524.
Clow, W. L. 239, 454.
Cocceius, J. 381.
Coleridge, S. T. 473.
Constantine, the Roman Emperor 515.
Continent, a writer in The, 406 ff.
Corson 511.
Cotton, J. 517.
Cowper, W. 187.
Cranmer, Th. 18.
Crashaw, R. 188.
Cremer, H. 78.
Cruel, R. 454.
Crusoe, Robinson 187.
Cunningham 53.

Dabney, R. L. 24, 27, 49 f., 55, 140, 149 f., 189 f., 199 ff., 206, 214, 320, 324, 448, 452.
Dale, R. W. 33, 150, 395.
Damasus, Bishop of Rome 329.
Dannhauer, J. K. 336.
Deichert, G. C. 285.
Deinzer, J. and M. 365.
Delitzsch, Franz 284, 532, 550.
Demosthenes 23, 207, 210, 216, 420, 445, 466, 514.
DeQuincey, Thomas 185, 216, 239.
Dickens, Charles 191.
Dietrich, Veit 162.
Dionysius of Halicarnassus 188.
Dobschuetz, E. v. 119, 270.
Donne, John 202, 208.
Drews, P. 363, 366, 400 f.
Dungersheim, Hieronymus of, 30, 61.

Eckhart, Master, 292.
Edwards, Jon. 165, 223, 517 f.
Ehrenfeuchter, F. 94.
Elizabeth, Queen of E. 8, 516.
Eliot, Geo. 241.
Emerson, R. W. 240, 413, 471.
Ephraem, the Syrian 165, 202, 215, 223, 515.
Erasmus of Rotterdam 77.
Ewald, P. 358.

Falke, R. 180.
Fenelon, Archbishop 171, 194, 197, 395, 397 f., 403, 414 f., 442, 465 f., 469, 476 f., 478, 495.
Fichte, Joh. 175.
Ficker, Chr. D., 31, 33.
Finney, Charles, 148, 181, 473.
Fisk, Fr. W. 215.
FitzGerald, Edw. 240.
Flacius, M. 380.
Foster, John 241, 513.
Frank, Fr. H. R. 141.
Frenssen, G. 137.
Fritzsche, Th. 575.
Frommel, E. 122, 126, 162, 226.
Frommel, M. 162, 202.
Fuller, Andr., 518.
Fuller, R. 238.

Garvie, A. E. 395, 475, 520.
Geiler, Joh., of Kaisersb. 137, 223. 292, 516.

Index of Names

Gerhard, J., 240, 348.
Gerok, K. 166, 187, 202, 454.
Gibbon, Edw. 186.
Gladstone, W. E. 216, 480.
Goebel, Seb. 429.
Goethe, W. 239, 257, 365, 401.
Goldsmith, Oliver 187, 236, 239.
Golladay, R. E. 157.
Gossner, Joh. 145.
Gottschick, Joh. 13, 41, 88, 298, 371, 372, 410.
Graebner, Th. 192, 193, 218.
Graves, H. C. 9, 480.
Gray 187.
Gregory 51.
Gregory the Great 329, 330, 516.
Gregory of Nazianzus 189, 292, 495, 504.
Gregory of Nyssa 291.
Grimm, Jacob and Wilhelm, 240.
Gros, E. 137.
Grossgebauer, Th. 385.
Guthrie, Thom. 514, 519.
Habermann, J. 333.
Hall, Newman 192 f.
Hall, Robt. 191 f., 209 f., 239, 466 f., 478, 482.
Hanne, J. R. 297.
Hare, Jul. 152.
Harless, A. 141.
Harms, Cl. 22, 78, 269 292, 481.
Harms, L. 137, 223.
Harnack, A. 581.
Harnack, Th. 32, 33, 76, 78, 97, 106, 229.
Hastings 267.
Hauck, A. 484.
Hazlitt, W. 240.
Heinrici, G. 381.
Henderson, Alex 517.
Hengstenberg, E. W. 284.
Henke, E. L. Th. 81, 87 f.
Henry, Patrick 219.
Herder, J. Gottfr. 8.
Hering, H. 26, 81, 85, 88, 121, 127, 221, 489 f.
Herrmann, J. 287.
Hervey, G. W. 32, 181, 186, 187 f., 189, 190, 196, 206, 395, 420, 432, 514, 517.
Hesselbacher, K. 134 137, 138, 202.

Heubner, L. 251.
Hieronymus of Dungersheim 30, 61.
Hieronymus, see Jerome.
Hill, Rowland 518.
Hippolytus 292, 495.
Hofacker, L. 165, 223.
Hoffmann, H. 162.
Hofmann, J. Chr. K. 281, 284, 300, 316, 355, 358, 365.
Hollen, G. 226.
Holtzmann, H. J. 565, 581.
Homer 197.
Honorius Scholasticus 292.
Hoppin, J. M. 9, 11, 492.
Horace 76, 398, 415, 420, 470.
Horne, C. Silv. 474.
Horton, R. F. 33.
Howerton, 52.
Hoyt, A. S. 23 f., 33, 91.
Huc, M. 174.
Hudson, W. H. 240.
Hunnius, Aegidius 151.
Hunzinger, A. W. 259.
Huxley, Th. H. 24, 237, 258, 371.
Hyperius, Andr. 30.
Ihmels, L. 161, 162, 180.
Ingersoll, R. 114.
James, Henry 183, 239.
Jay, Wm. 316, 322 f., 513.
Jefferson, C. E. 52.
Jerome 329, 330.
Johnson, Herrick 53, 56, 64, 65, 114, 405 f., 416 f., 418, 420, 421 f., 443 ff., 474.
Johnson, Sam. 23, 219, 519.
Jowett, J. H. 54.
Juelicher, A. 381.
Justin Martyr 3, 6, 329.
Kant, Imm. 16.
Keil, J. C. 532.
Kessler, J. 151.
Keyser, L. S. 151.
Kidder, D. P. 9, 32, 197, 201, 214, 220, 514.
Kleinert, P. 81, 82, 112, 118, 252, 266, 285 ff., 288, 346 f., 357, 371 f., 386, 395, 396, 397, 410 ff., 422, 423 f., 447, 450, 453, 486, 511, 521 ff., 524, 525.
Kliefoth, Th. 87.

Index of Names

Klostermann. A 550.
Knox, John 223, 319, 517.
Koeberle, Justus 274, 287, 540.
Koegel, R. 186, 285, 298, 364.
Koehler, A. 540.
Koenig, Ed. 287.
Krause, G. 397.
Krauss, Alfr. 22, 32, 33, 73 f., 81, 178, 229, 254, 400, 410, 446.
Krummacher, F. W. 90, 126.
Krummacher, G. D. 313.
Kuehl, E. 356.

Lactantius 10.
Laible, W. 47 f., 79, 109.
Lamb, Charles 187, 247.
Lange, J. P. 381.
Langsdorff, W. 285.
Latimer, Hugh 219.
Leighton, Archbishop 320.
Leland, John 203.
Lenski, R. C. H. 155, 337.
Leonardo da Vinci 473.
Leyser, W. 8.
Liddon, H. P. 285.
Livy 174.
Locke, John 473.
Loehe, W. 94, 135, 162, 239, 336.
Longinus 194, 216, 361.
Loofs, Fr. 133.
Lotz, W. 287.
Louis XIV, his preachers, 198.
Lowell, Amy 189.
Lowell, J. R. 239.
Loy, M. 151.
Lucian 186.
Luther, Martin 8, 13, 40 f., 46 f., 48, 60, 61 f., 63, 66 f., 71, 83, 94 ff., 100, 110, 115, 116, 137, 138, 140, 145, 148, 159, 160, 162, 165, 191, 202, 219, 223, 229, 239, 253, 266, 276 ff., 280, 292 f., 308, 325, 330, 331, 334 f., 345 f., 347 f., 369, 372, 375, 379, 394, 423, 429, 490, 505, 516, 531, 532, 554, 562 f., 572.

Macarius (?) 162.
Macaulay, Th. B. 63, 242.
MacDonald, J. A. 543.
Machen, J. G. 346.
Maclaren, Alex. 54, 126, 162, 185, 239, 267, 285, 319, 484.

Maclaren, Ian 33, 395, 521, (J. Watson).
Magee, Archbishop 445.
Mahling, F. 161.
Marshall, Chief Justice 450.
Martensen-Larsen 145.
Mason, J. M. 238.
Massillon, J. B. 181, 212, 223, 494.
Mathesius, J. 137.
Mathews, Shailer 51.
Melanchthon, Ph. 111, 295.
Melvill, H. 240.
Menander 6.
Menken, Gottfr. 8, 163, 166, 180. 280 f., 319, 490, 500 f., 538.
Meredith, Geo. 239.
Meyer, F. B. 285, 320.
Meyer, H. A. W. 355.
Michael, Angelo 473.
Migne, J. P. 331.
Miller, Hugh 236.
Milton, John 189, 239, 297.
Monod, A. 239, 496 f.
Morgan, J. Campbell 320.
Mosheim, Lor. von 30, 369, 375 ff., 380, 395, 417 f., 429-432.
Muellensiefen, J. 364, 542.
Mueller, H. 126, 137, 202.
Mueller, J., 524 f.
Muenkel, K. K. 162.
Mullois, Abbe, 506.
Mulready, Wm. 473.
Munz, 30, 88.
Musaeus, S. 137, 162, 202.

Naumann, Fr. 117, 202, 239.
Neale, J. M. 516.
Newman, John Henry, 24, 193, 239, 506.
Niebergall, F. 88 f.
Nietzsche, F. 185, 239.
Nitzsch, C. Imm. 31, 293, 309, 337, 365, 459.
Norden, E. 190.

Oosterzee, J. J. van 19.
Orelli, C. von 550.
Origen 7, 275, 291, 374, 515.

Paley, Archbishop 475.
Palmer, Chr. 85 f., 94, 106, 269, 293 f., 295, 395 f., 445 f., 453 f., 495.

Index of Names

Park, E. A. 65, 180, 181.
Parker, Jos. 319, 320, 518.
Pascal, B., 506.
Pater, Walter 239.
Pattison, T. H. 10 33, 297, 434,
    450, 455, 473, 476 480, 483, 504,
    505, 506, 513, 517.
Paul, the Apostle 137, 145, 209.
Paulist fathers 199.
Paulus Diaconus 8, 330.
Pepin, the Short 330.
Pericles 525.
Petri, Ad. 162.
Pfatteicher 138.
Pfeiffer, A. 285.
Phelps, A. 10, 33, 297, 326, 442,
    448 ff., 471 ff., 479, 482 f., 504.
Phidias 173.
Philippi, A. 254.
Philo 4.
Photius 7.
Pieper, Fr. 160.
Pitt, Wm. 519.
Plato 198, 398, 413.
Pliny 5, 516.
Porter, Ebenezer 9, 20, 23, 32,
    294 f., 348 f., 357 f. 359., 360,
    401 ff., 433, 448, 452, 468, 470,
    478.
Prescott, W. 'H. 186.
Procksch, O. 287.
Proudfoot J. J. A. 9.
Quiller-Couch, Sir Arthur 202 f
Quincey, Thomas De 185, 216, 239.
Quintilian 16, 174, 175, 190, 194,
    208, 361, 414, 445, 469, 477, 487,
    490, 515, 523.
Raabe, W. 239.
Rambach, J. J. 30, 146, 152.
Randolph, A. M. 150.
Ranke, E. 337.
Reinhard, F. V. 455.
Renan, E. 236
Reu, M. 285, 337, 554.
Rhodes, W. 9.
Ricard, Olfert 145.
Rieger, Geo. C. 126, 154 f., 165 f.,
    223.
Rietschel, Geo. 327.
Ritschl, Albr. 59.
Rittelmeyer, F. 117.

Robertson, A. T. 590.
Robertson, F. W. 126, 138, 162,
    222, 285, 320, 481, 484.
Robespierre, M. M. I. 519.
Robinson, Rob. 497.
Rossetti, D. G. 77.
Rothstein, J. 287.
Rowland, A. 541.
Ruehling, J. 351.
Rufus, Musonius 424.
Ruskin, John 191, 239, 450.
Saccus, Simon 333, 394 f.
Sachsse, E. 32.
Saintsbury, Geo. 191.
Sales, St. Francis de 513.
Saurin, J. 126, 180, 181, 212 f., 215.
Schiller, Fr. 393.
Schlatter, A. 356.
Schleiermacher, Fr. 12, 31 f., 42,
    78, 94, 104, 106, 282 ff., 363, 385,
    395, 400, 440, 450 f., 524.
Schmitthenner, Ad. 203, 239.
Schneller, L. 588 f.
Schoeberlein, L. 94.
Schuerer, E. 3.
Schultz, H. 411 f.
Schultz, K. W. 363.
Schultze, Vict. 68.
Schuppius, Balth. 137, 223, 505.
Schweizer, A. 14, 31, 33, 94, 102,
    106, 446.
Scott, Walter 472.
Scriver, Chr. 126, 137, 202.
Seeberg, R. 27.
Shakespeare, Wm. 191, 203, 215.
Shedd, W. G. T. 32.
Sheldon, Chr. M. 117.
Sickel, G. A. F. 12.
Siedel, E. 145, 154, 226.
Simeon, Ch. 181.
Simpson, M. 30.
Skoofgaard-Petersen 145.
Slattery, Ch. L. 474, 481.
Slattery, C. P. 240.
Smith, L. P. 202.
Smith, S. A. 285.
Souchon, A. F. 223.
South, R. 198.
Spaeth, H. D. 218.
Spalding, J. J. 252.
Spencer, H. 139.

Index of Names

Spener Ph. 100, 505.
Spurgeon, Ch. H. 22, 79, 90, 126, 165, 203, 210, 212, 217, 223, 226, 239, 285, 325, 499 f., 507.
Steinmeyer, Fr. 32, 182, 217, 248 ff., 251, 252, 254, 255, 395, 460, 524.
Stevenson, R. L. 24, 183, 185, 191, 239.
Stier, R. 11, 294, 453.
Stoecker, A. 138.
Stockmeyer, Imm. 381.
Storrs, R. S. 518.
Sunday, Wm. A. (Billy) 127, 524.
Surgant, Ulrich 30, 292.

Tatian 7.
Taube, E. 285.
Tauler, J. 292.
Taylor, Jeremy 186, 187, 202, 239.
Taylor, Wm. 196 f., 492.
Taylor, Wm. H. 517.
Taylor, W. M. 320.
Teelman 321.
Tennyson, A. 241, 297.
Theremin, Fr. 127, 219 f., 229 f., 421, 459, 477 f.
Theurer, K. 409 ff.
Tholuck, Aug. 78, 126, 165, 166, 213, 223, 293, 364, 542.
Thomasius, Gottfr. 126, 162, 309, 337, 410 f., 484.
Thucydides 23.
Tiberius, Roman Emperor 515.
Tillotson, J. 198.
Trajan, Roman Emperor 5.
Trench, R. Ch. 239.
Tupper, Kerr B. 63, 65.
Tyndall, John 237.

Uhlhorn, Gerh. 155 f., 484.

Vaughan, C. J. 320.
Vieyra, Antonio 206.
Vinet, Alex. 18, 32, 172, 174 f., 176 f., 179, 181, 198, 209, 210, 223, 228, 230, 242, 295 ff., 395, 300 f., 415, 416, 447, 477, 478, 490.
Virgil 194 f., 197, 242.
Vitringa, 549.

Walther, C. F. W. 141, 147 f., 156, 158.
Walther, W. 141, 155, 162 f., 506.
Ward 220.
Watson, John 395, see Maclaren, Ian.
Watson, R. 181.
Watson, Thomas 181.
Watson, W. 77.
Wayland, Dr. 517.
Webster, Dan. 219, 519.
Weiss, H. 297.
Weiss, J. 574, 590.
Weitbrecht, Th. 145.
Wesley, John 90, 165.
Wessel, L. 138, 156.
Westphal, J. 336.
Whately, R. 206, 207.
Whitefield, Geo. 165, 219, 223, 517.
Wiegand, F. 331 f.
Wilkins 24, 32.
Wilkinson H. C. 238.
Wilson, Woodrow 139.
Winstedt 241.
Wolf, F. A. 363.
Wolf, W. 80.
Wolff 328.
Wordsworth, Wm. 77.

Zahn, Theo. 300, 347 355, 358, 565, 574, 575, 581, 590.
Zastrow 263.
Zezschwitz, Gerh. von 14, 94, 136, 432, 446 f., 532 f.
Ziethe, W. 364.
Zinzendorf, Count 13.
Zwingli, Ulr. 94, 279 f., 336.

INDEX OF SCRIPTURE PASSAGES

Old Testament

Genesis 3:1 ff. 441
Genesis 12:1-4 367
Genesis 15:1 354
Genesis 15:1-6 ......367 f., 606 ff.
Genesis 17:1-9 368
Genesis 18:16-33 ......368, 528 ff.
Genesis 19:15-26 368
Genesis 22:1-18 368
Genesis 33:22-31 369
Exodus 14:13-31 369
Numbers 21:4-9 ....364, 369
Numbers 25:15-24 370
1 Kings 19:10-18 ......364, 536 ff.
Psalm 23:5 376
Psalm 23 435
Psalm 46 459
Psalm 95 106
Psalm 114:3 162
Psalm 119:66-67 363
Eccles. 1:8-9 363
Isaiah 1:5 376
Isaiah 40:1 ff. 384
Isaiah 42:1 ff. 370, 384
Isaiah 53:1-7 .... 554 ff.
Isaiah 61:1-7 ......546 ff., 607 ff.
Habak. 2:4 ....341, 344

New Testament

Matthew 4:1-11 427
Matthew 6:5-8 458
Matthew 6:24-32 ......429 f., 484
Matthew 7:7-11 457
Matthew 7:15-23 ......427, 563 ff.
Matthew 7:24-27 350
Matthew 8:1-13 156
Matthew 8:5-13 .... 573 ff.
Matthew 8:1 ff. 375
Matthew 8:23-27 483
Matthew 9:1-8 431
Matthew 9:2 355
Matthew 9:6 372
Matthew 10:19 16
Matthew 11:1 ff. 355
Matthew 11:4-6 372
Matthew 11:28 ....358, 384
Matthew 11:28 ff. ....
   ....162, 579 ff., 609 ff.
Matthew 13:1 ff 381
Matthew 13:24 381
Matthew 13:31-32 382
Matthew 13:44 379
Matthew 13:47 f. 382
Matthew 18:26 382
Matthew 18:23-35 379
Matthew 20:1-16 156
Matthew 21:1-9 165
Matthew 21:33 ff. 382
Matthew 21:28-32 461
Matthew 25:1-13 ....
   ....360, 378, 280 f., 587 ff.
Mark 6:17-29 163
Mark 6:45-51 162
Mark 7:31-37 ....156, 483
Mark 16:1-8 154
Mark 16:14-20 166
Luke 2:1-14 ....462, 464, 613
Luke 2:23-40 156
Luke 2:25-32 453
Luke 2:33-40 155
Luke 2:41-52 ....409 ff.
Luke 3:1-14 426
Luke 6:36 431
Luke 6:38-42 453
Luke 6:46 462
Luke 9:57 62 454
Luke 10:38-42 451
Luke 12:35-48 458
Luke 13:18-19 458
Luke 14:1-11 156
Luke 14:15-24 463
Luke 14:16-24 ....166, 486
Luke 15:1-10 ....441, 461
Luke 15:1-32 ....358, 378
Luke 15:25-32 163
Luke 15:34-37 363

Index of Scripture Passages

Luke 16:1-9	379	2 Cor. 6:2	343
Luke 16:19 ff.	458	2 Cor. 6:1-10	364
Luke 17:7-10	457	2 Cor. 7:6-10	484
Luke 17:11-19	423	2 Cor. 11:3-4	483
Luke 18:9-14	458	2 Cor. 12:7-9	459
Luke 19:1-9	163	2 Cor. 12:7-10	155
Luke 21:25-36	166, 483	2 Cor. 12:9	342
Luke 24:36 ff.	462	Gal. 3:1-15	299 f.
John 1:23-27	438	Gal. 3:24	347
John 1:45-50	155	Gal. 3:26	459
John 3:3-8	156	Gal. 5:16-24	459
John 3:16	434	Eph. 1:13-14	163
John 4:30-36	363	Eph. 2:4-10	155
John 11:16	459	Eph. 2:19-22	99
John 12:24-25	462	Eph. 3:14-19	434
John 14:2-6	163	Phil. 1:3-11	358
John 14:23 31	461, 464	Phil. 2:5-11	428 f., 459
John 15:9, 14-15	363	Phil. 3:17-21	358
John 16:5-15	156	Col. 2:16-17	484
John 16:11-23	156	2 Thess. 2:14	461
John 18:37-38	163	Titus 2:11-14	343, 384, 459
John 20:1-18	427	Titus 3:3-8	155
John 20:24-29	155	Titus 3:4 ff.	384
John 21:15-17	347	Heb. 1:1-3	461
Acts 10:34-41	484	Heb. 1:1-14	155
Acts 10:42-48	156	Heb. 8:7-13	154, 611, 614 ff.
Romans 1:16-17	166, 341	Heb. 9:11-15	156
Romans 3:21-28	595 ff.	Heb. 11:6-7	166
Romans 5:1-6	154	Heb. 12:2	365
Romans 8:18-23	484	James 1:2-4	458
Romans 12:19-21	431	James 1:2-7	600 ff., 612 f.
Romans 13:11-12	343	James 1:8	349 f.
Romans 13:11-14	364	James 1:13-15	462
Romans 15:4-13	358	James 1:13-18	154, 316
1 Cor. 2:4, 15	16	James 1:13-27	316, 350
1 Cor. 12:1-10	453	James 1:19-20	349 f.
1 Cor. 12:31-13:1	363	James 2:14	350
1 Cor. 13:1-13	442	James 4:13-16	363
1 Cor. 15:33	6 f.	1 Peter 1:3-9	459
2 Cor. 2:14	347	1 Peter 3:15	363
2 Cor. 3:3	163	1 Peter 5:5	348
2 Cor. 4:5-7	248	2 Peter 1:19	316
2 Cor. 5:14-21	454	1 John 1:4	459
2 Cor. 5:17-21	154, 351 f.	1 John 4:16	462
2 Cor. 5:19-21	163, 460	1 John 4:19	155
2 Cor. 6:1	351	Rev. 5:1	347

BOOKS BY THE SAME AUTHOR

Quellen zur Geschichte des kirchlichen Unterrichts im evangelischen Deutschland zwischen 1530 und 1600. Guetersloh, 1904-1934, 9 Vols. A standard publication subsidized by the former German Emperor and by the Government and Church of Germany.

Thirty-five Years of Luther Research. Chicago, 1917.

Luthers Kleiner Katechismus. Die Geschichte seiner Entstehung, seiner Verbreitung und seines Gebrauchs. Muenchen, 1929.

Luther's Small Catechism. A History of its Origin, Distribution, and Use. Chicago, 1929.

The Augsburg Confession. A Collection of Sources with an Historical Introduction. Chicago, 1930.

The Life of Dr. Martin Luther. Chicago, 1917.

Katechetik oder die Lehre vom kirchlichen Unterricht. Chicago, 1918.

Catechetics or Theory and Practise of Religious Education. Chicago, 1927.

Luther's Small Catechism, explained in thetical form. Chicago, 1904.

Luther's Small Catechism, explained in questions and answers. Chicago, 1918.

Wartburg Lesson Helps for Lutheran Sunday Schools. 11 vols. Chicago, 1914-1929.

How I Tell the Bible Stories to My Sunday School. 2 vols. Chicago, 1928.

Sunday School Teachers Training Course. Columbus, 1933-34.

www.ingramcontent.com/pod-product-compliance
Lightning Source LLC
Chambersburg PA
CBHW052108010526
44111CB00036B/1565